Military History of
Late Rome AD 518–565

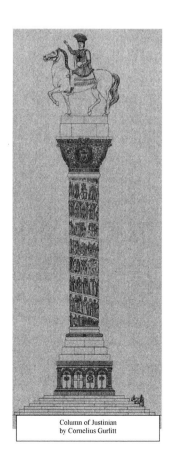

Column of Justinian
by Cornelius Gurlitt

For my wife Sini, and children Ari and Nanna for their patience; and Robert Graves and Lord Mahon for having raised my interest in this era

The Military History of Late Rome AD 518–565

Dr. Ilkka Syvänne

'Nothing is more shameful than to fall in with the plans of the enemy.'
Belisarius to his soldiers according to Procopius, Wars *6.23.33, tr. by Dewing, p. 75.*

Equestrian statue of Justinian in Augusteon.
Public domain drawing from the period when it still existed.

Pen & Sword
MILITARY

First published in Great Britain in 2021 by
Pen & Sword Military
An imprint of
Pen & Sword Books Ltd
Yorkshire – Philadelphia

ISBN 978 1 47389 528 7

A CIP catalogue record for this book is
available from the British Library.

Printed and bound in the UK by CPI Group (UK) Ltd,
Croydon, CR0 4YY.

Pen & Sword Books Limited incorporates the imprints of Atlas, Archaeology,
Aviation, Discovery, Family History, Fiction, History, Maritime, Military,
Military Classics, Politics, Select, Transport, True Crime, Air World,
Frontline Publishing, Leo Cooper, Remember When, Seaforth Publishing,
The Praetorian Press, Wharncliffe Local History, Wharncliffe Transport,
Wharncliffe True Crime and White Owl.

For a complete list of Pen & Sword titles please contact

PEN & SWORD BOOKS LIMITED
47 Church Street, Barnsley, South Yorkshire, S70 2AS, England
E-mail: enquiries@pen-and-sword.co.uk
Website: www.pen-and-sword.co.uk

Or

PEN AND SWORD BOOKS
1950 Lawrence Rd, Havertown, PA 19083, USA
E-mail: Uspen-and-sword@casematepublishers.com
Website: www.penandswordbooks.com

Contents

Acknowledgements

First of all, I would like to thank the Commissioning Editor Philip Sidnell for accepting the book proposal, and Professor Geoffrey Greatrex for having recommended me. Special thanks are also due to Matt Jones, Tara Moran, Barnaby Blacker and other staff at Pen & Sword for their stellar work and for the outstanding support they give the author. I would also like to thank many of my friends and family for their support and patience. If there are any mistakes left, those are the sole responsibility of the author.

I owe special thanks for the Björkvist Rahasto (Brjörkvist Fund), Kangasala, Finland, for the research grant that made the writing of the book possible. Such funding is always needed by historians, authors and writers. I am also grateful for the ASMEA, Washington DC, for the grants that it has given over the years towards research of subjects related to this book because those have also proved helpful in this project. And I am grateful to the University of Haifa for the support it has given.

List of Plates

Coins of Justin/Iustinus I. Source: Warwick Wroth, British Museum.

Coins of Justinus/Justin I and Justinianus/Justinian I. Source: Warwick Wroth, British Museum.

Coins of Justinianus/Justinian I. Source: Warwick Wroth, British Museum

Bust of an empress claimed to represent Theodora. Source: Joseph Wilpert.

Gold medallion depicting Justinian, British Museum. Photo by author.

Mosaic in S. Apollinaire Nuovo variously claimed to represent Justinian or Theoderic the Great. Source: Public domain.

Justinian (or Anastasius) depicted in a diptych. Source: Public domain.

Mosaic in San Vitale, Ravenna, depicting Justinian with his court. Source: Public domain.

Mosaic in San Vitale, Ravenna, depicting Theodora with her court. Source: Public domain.

Mosaics in San Maggiore, Ravenna, ca. 500. Public domain.

Belisarius and his horse Phalios/Balan. Author's painting.

Two more mosaics from San Maggiore, Ravenna, ca. 500. Public domain.

Still another mosaic from San Maggiore, Ravenna, ca. 500. Public domain.

A mosaic depicting Roman cavalry in San Maggiore, Ravenna, ca. 500. Public domain.

A Gothic/Ostrogothic cataphract. Author's drawing.

Roman multipurpose horseman. Author's drawing.

Lightly-equipped Hun. Author's drawing.

Cabades/Cavades, Persian prince in Roman service. Author's drawing.

Re-enactors in the process of forming the foulkon and wearing typical gear of the period. © Jérémie Immormino

Roman officer gesturing with his hand. © Jérémie Immormino

The Roman soldiers at rest. © Jérémie Immormino

A sixth century Roman heavy-armed footman and other members of the military in the background. © Jérémie Immormino

A dashing Roman officer enjoying a moment of rest. © Jérémie Immormino

Typical sixth century Roman heavy infantry. © Jérémie Immormino

A dashing Roman officer in in fancy gear. © Jérémie Immormino

List of Maps

Introduction

The intention of this book, the sixth in a series of seven, is to present an overview of all of the principal aspects of Roman military history during the years 518–565. It was then that the East Roman Empire began its reconquest of the west under the leadership of the emperor Justinian I. The structure of the book follows the reigns of the emperors in chronological order, and the events and wars are also usually presented in chronological order. However, for the sake of ease of reading some events that took place in one particular sector of the empire are grouped together. The uneven survival of evidence means that there are huge gaps in our knowledge and some of my conclusions are only my best educated guesses.

The text follows the same principles as the previous books and includes direct references to sources only when necessary, for example when my conclusions can be considered controversial or new. I have also not included descriptions or analyses of the sources used and their problems, because there exists expert literature devoted to this subject. When I refer to some chronicle, for example by Isidore of Seville, Jordanes (*Romana*), Paulus Diaconus etc, the exact point of reference can be found in the annalistic dating even when I do not always state this in the narrative. These sources are conveniently collected in the MGH series, available online for example from Internet Archive.

In this study when I refer to Spain I mean the whole of the Iberian Peninsula including Lusitania (modern Portugal). When I refer either to North Africa or Libya, I mean the entire section of North Africa west of Egypt just as Procopius did. I have also usually incorporated the discussion of events that took place in the Balkans into the chapters dealing either with the Persian wars or with the wars in the west (Italy, Spain, Balkans). I follow in this the approach adopted by Procopius who also grouped the events in the Balkans into other books. As far as language, transliteration, and titles are concerned I have usually adopted the easiest solutions. I have used the transliterations most commonly used except in the case of Greek military terms where I have generally used the original F instead of using PH. I have also adopted the practice of the Oxford UP and used capital letters for all offices which could be held by only one person at a time. I have also used capital letters for all specific types of troops and military units. However, when I have referred to several office holders simultaneously (e.g. *comites*/counts, *duces*/dukes) I have used small letters. Since this is a military history of Rome I have purposefully adopted Roman names for the Persian rulers.

All illustrations, drawings, maps and diagrams etc. have been drawn and prepared by the author unless stated otherwise. I have used the *Barrington Atlas* as the principal source for the maps.

Abbreviations

Cav.	Cavalry
Inf.	Infantry
LI	Light infantry
Mag. Eq.	Magister Equitum (Master of Horse)
Mag. Ped.	Magister Peditum (Master of Foot)
Mag. Eq. et Ped.	Magister Equitum et Peditum (Master of Horse and Foot)
MGH	Monumenta Historia Germaniae
MGH AA	Monumenta Historia Germaniae Auctores Antiquitissimonum
MVM	Magister Utriusque Militiae (Master of All Arms of Service)
MVM Praes.	Magister Utriusque Militae Praesentales (Praesental MVM)
Mag. Mil.	Magister Militum (Master of Soldiers)
Mag. Off.	Magister Officiorum (Master of Office)
Marc. Com. or Marc.	Marcellinus Comes
Or.	Orations
PLRE1	See Bibliography
PLRE2	See Bibliography
PLRE3	See Bibliography
PP	Praefectus Praetorio (Praetorian Prefect)
PPI	Praefectus Praetorio Italiae et Africae (PP of Italy and Africa)
PPIL	Praefectus Praetorio Illyrici
PPG	Praefectus Praetorio Galliarum
PPO	Praefectus Praetorio Orientis
PSC	Praepositus Sacri Cubiculi (Leader of Sacred Bedroom)
PVC	Praefectus Urbis Constantiopolitanae (Urban Prefect of Constantinople)
PVR	Praefectus Urbis Romae
QSP	Quaestor Sacri Palatii (Questor of the Sacred Palace)
REF1	See Bibliography
REF2	See Bibliography

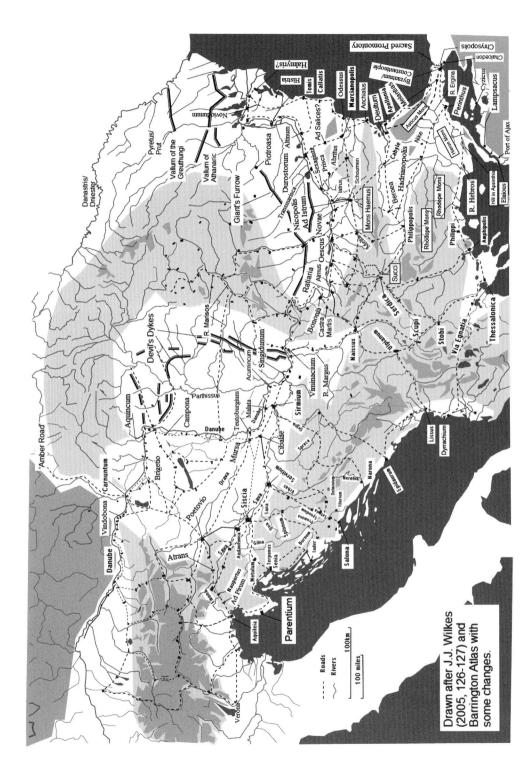

Drawn after J.J. Wilkes (2005, 126-127) and Barrington Atlas with some changes.

- - - - Roads

〜〜〜 Rivers

|———————|———————|
0   100km
|———————|———————|
0   100 miles

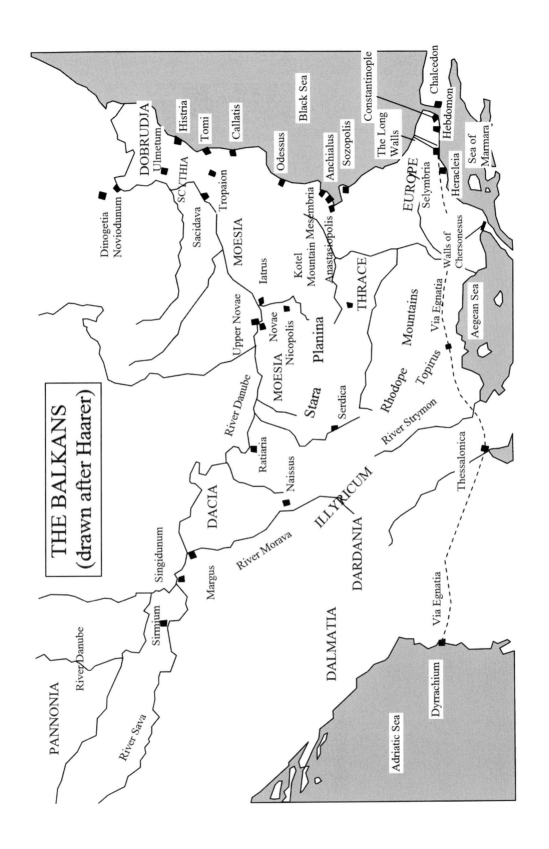

THE BALKANS (drawn after Haarer)

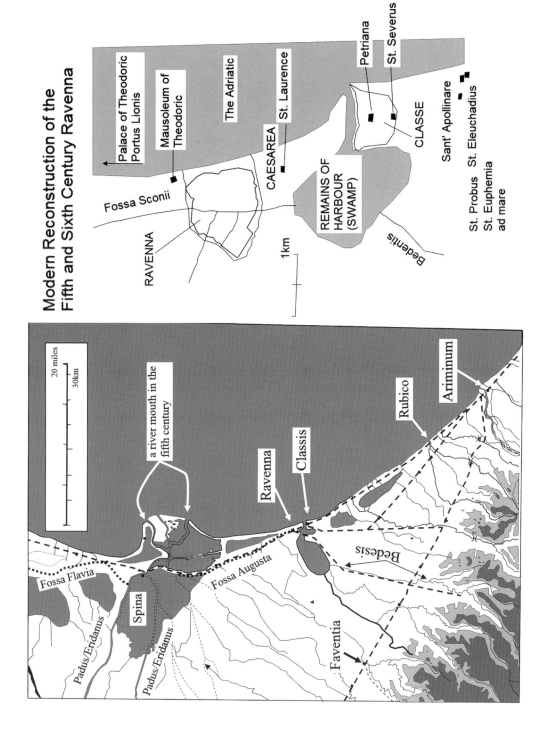

Modern Reconstruction of the Fifth and Sixth Century Ravenna

Palace of Theodoric Portus Lionis

Mausoleum of Theodoric

The Adriatic

Fossa Sconii

RAVENNA

CAESAREA

St. Laurence

REMAINS OF HARBOUR (SWAMP)

Bedentis

Petriana

St. Severus

CLASSE

Sant' Apollinare

St. Probus   St. Eleuchadius

St. Euphemia ad mare

1km

Fossa Flavia

Padus/Eridanus

Spina

Padus/Eridanus

a river mouth in the fifth century

Ravenna

Classis

Fossa Augusta

Bedesis

Faventia

Rubico

Ariminum

20 miles

30km

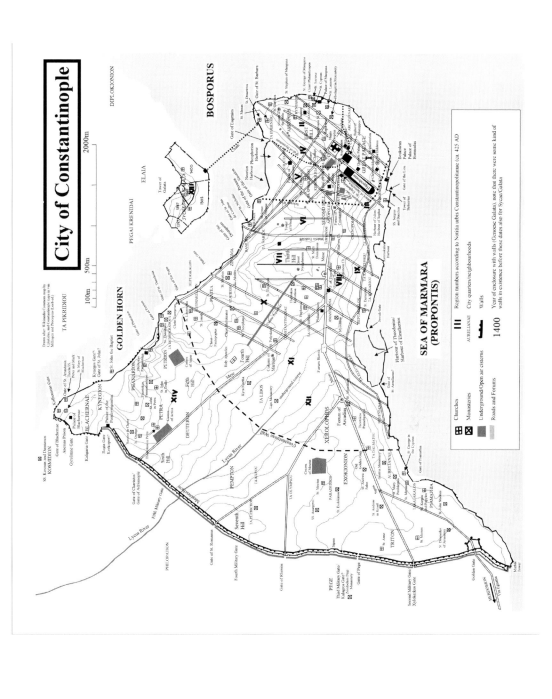

City of Constantinople

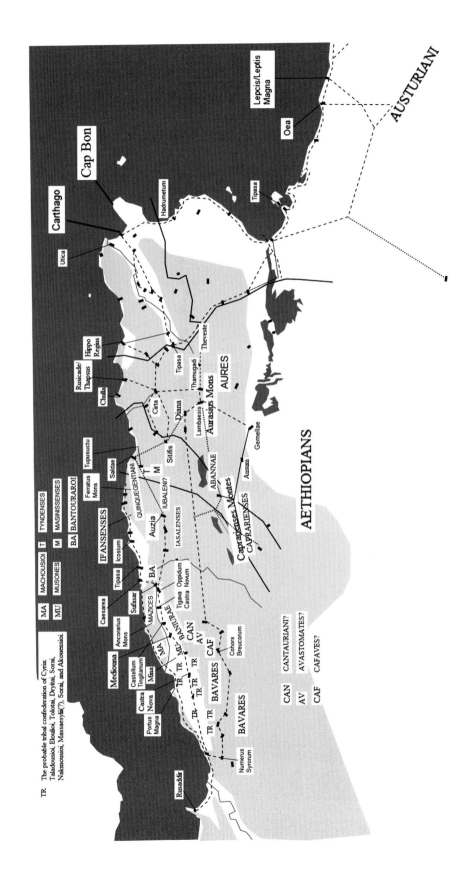

TR   The probable tribal confederation of Cyria:
Talaedousioi, Eloulioi, Tolotai, Drytai, Sorai,
Nakmousioi, Massaesyloi(?), Sorai, and Akouerusioi.

MA	MACHOUSIOI	T	TYNDENSES
MU	MUSONES	M	MASINISSENSES
		BA	BANTOURAROI

IFANSENSES

QUINQUEGENTIANI

IUBALENI?

IASALENSES

BANTURAE

MAZICES

CAN   CANTAURIANI?
AV   AVASTOMATES?
CAF   CAFAVES?

AETHIOPIANS

AUSTURIANI

Lepcis/Leptis
Magna

Oea

Tipasa

Carthago

Cap Bon

Hadrumetum

Utica

Hippo
Regius

Rusicade/
Thapsus

Chulla

Cirta

Diana

Theveste

Tipasa

Thamugadi

Lambaesis

AURES

'Aurasips Mons

Gemellae

Ausum

ABANNAE

Capraçinses Montes

CAPRARIENSES

Sitifis

M

Tupusuctu

Saldae

Ferratus
Mons

Auzia

Icosium

Tipasa

Caesarea

Ancorarius
Mons

Sufascar

MA

Mediouna

Castellum
Tingitanum

Mina

Castra
Nova

Portus
Magna

MU

TR

TR

TR

TR

TR

TR

TR

TR

TR

TR

BA

Tigava
Oppidum
Castra Nouum

CAN

AV

CAF

BAVARES

BAVARES

Cohors
Breucorum

Numerus
Syrorum

Rusaddir

PROVINCES IN THE NOTITIA DIGNITATUM

1. Narbonensis II
2. Alpes Graiae et Poeninae
3. Alpes Maritimae
4. Alpes Cottiae

Britannia II
Flavia Caesariensis
Maxima Caesariensis
Valentia
Britannia I

Germania II
Belgica II
Lugdunensis II
Lugdunensis Senonia
Lugdunensis III
Belgica I
Germania I
Maxima Sequanorum
Raetia I
Raetia II
Aemilia
Venetia et Histria
Liguria
Alpes Cottiae
Viennensis
Aquitania II
Aquitania I
Narbonensis I
Novem Populi
Tarraconensis
Gallaecia
Lusitania
Carthaginiensis
Baetica
Tingitania

Mauritania Caesariensis
Mauritania Sitifensis
Numidia
Africa
Byzacena
Tripolitania

Valeria
Pannonia I
Pannonia II
Savia
Dalmatia
Noricum Ripense
Noricum Mediterraneum

Tuscia et Umbria
Picenum Suburbicarium
Corsica
Roma
Valeria
Samnium
Sardinia
Sirmium
Campania
Sicilia
Apulia et Calabria
Lucania et Brutii
Flaminia et Picenum
Balearcs

Dacia Ripensis
Moesia I
Dacia Mediterranea
Dardania
Praevalitana
Macedonia
Epirus Nova
Epirus Vetus
Thessalia
Achaea
Creta

Moesia II
Scythia
Europa
Haemimontus
Thracia
Rhodope
Insulae

Pontus Polemoniacus
Helleno Pontus
Paphlagonia
Armenia I
Armenia II
Honorias
Galatia
Bithynia
Galatia Salutaris
Phrygia II
Phrygia I
Cappadocia
Pisidia
Isauria
Pamphylia
Lycaonia
Lydia
Asia
Caria
Cilicia I
Cilicia II
Lycia
Cyprus

Mesopotamia
Osrhoene
Euphratensis
Syria Salutaris
Phoenice Libanensis
Arabia
Syria
Phoenice
Palaestina II
Palaestina I
Palaestina Salutaris
Augustamnica
Aegyptus
Arcadia
Thebais
Libya Inferior
Libya Superior

1000 km
500
0

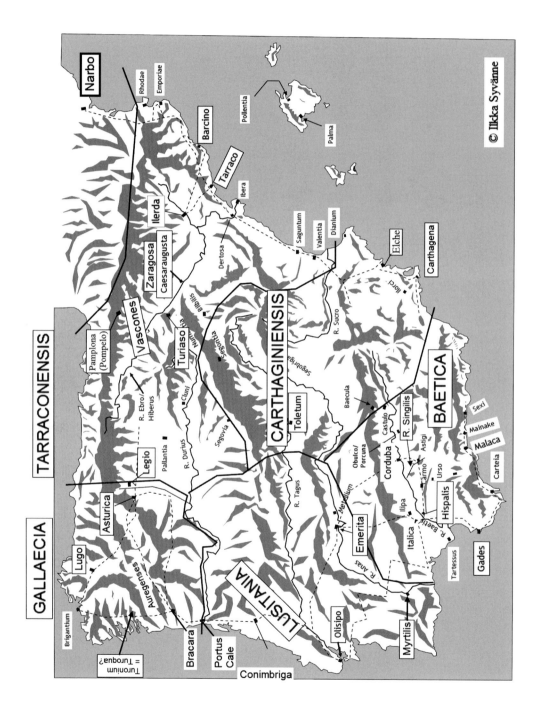

GALLAECIA

TARRACONENSIS

Narbo

Rhodae
Emporiae

Barcino

Tarraco

Ibera

Ilerda

Saguntum
Valentia
Dianium

Zaragosa
Caesaraugusta

Elche

Carthagena

Dertosa

Vascones

Pamplona
(Pompelo)

R. Ebro/
Hiberus

Cluni

Turiaso

Pollentia

Palma

R. Sucro

Iucar

Segontia

Segovia

Ilorci

CARTHAGINIENSIS

Segóbriga

Toletum

Baecula

Castulo

R. Singilis

BAETICA

Sexi

Mainake

Malaca

Carteia

Legio

Pallantia

R. Durius

Corduba

Astigi

Carmo

Urso

Asturica

Lugo

R. Tagus

Obulco/
Porcuna

Ilipa

Hispalis

Italica

Tartessus

Gades

Brigantium

Auregenses

Metellium

Emerita

R. Anas

R. Baetis

Turonium
= Turoqua?

Bracara

LUSITANIA

Portus
Cale

Olisipo

Myrtilis

Conimbriga

© Ilkka Syvänne

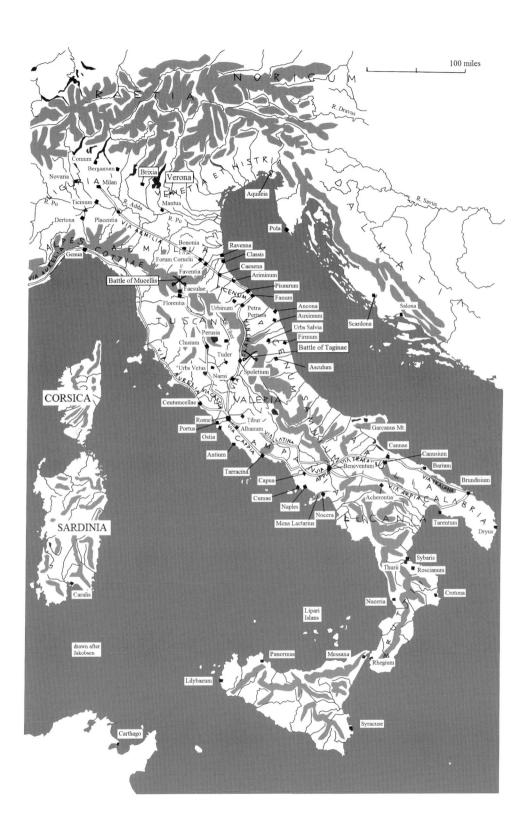

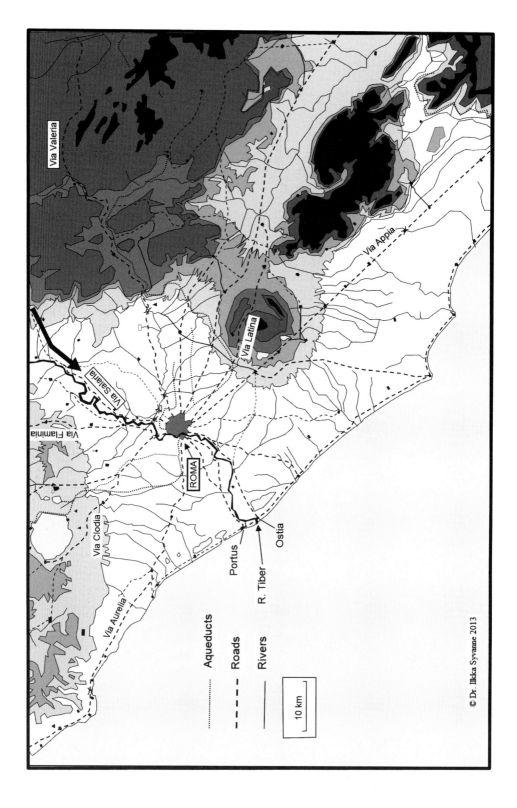

Via Valeria

Via Salaria

Via Flaminia

Via Latina

Via Appia

Via Clodia

Via Aurelia

ROMA

Portus

R. Tiber

Ostia

Aqueducts
Roads
Rivers

10 km

© Dr. Ilkka Syvänne 2013

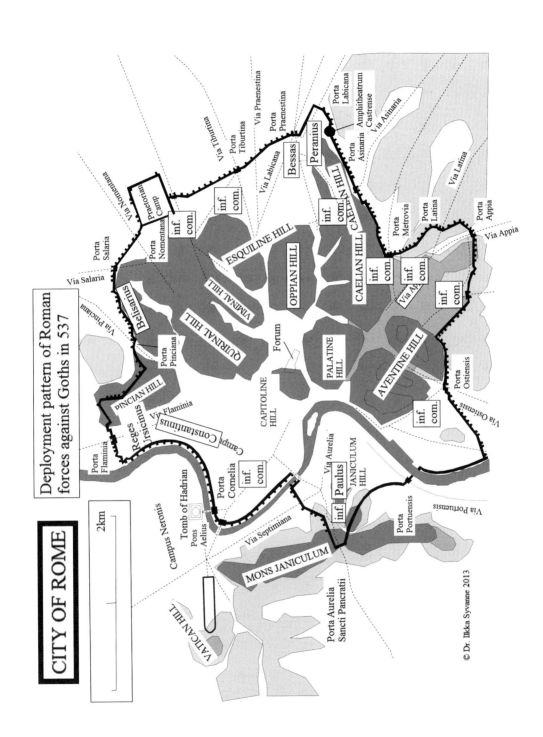

CITY OF ROME

Deployment pattern of Roman forces against Goths in 537

2km

© Dr. Ilkka Syvänne 2013

Labels on map:

VATICAN HILL

MONS JANICULUM

Porta Aurelia Sancti Pancratii

Via Portuensis

Porta Portuensis

JANICULUM HILL

Via Aurelia

Paulus

inf.

Via Septimiana

Pons Aelius

Tomb of Hadrian

Campus Neronis

Porta Cornelia

inf. com.

Campus Constantinus

Reges Ursicinus

Via Flaminia

PINCIAN HILL

Porta Flaminia

Via Pinciana

Belisarius

Porta Pinciana

QUIRINAL HILL

VIMINAL HILL

ESQUILINE HILL

CAPITOLINE HILL

Forum

PALATINE HILL

AVENTINE HILL

inf. com.

Porta Ostiensis

Via Ostiensis

inf. com.

Via Ap

inf. com.

inf. com.

CAELIAN HILL

Porta Metrovia

Porta Latina

Via Latina

Porta Appia

Via Appia

Porta Asinaria

Asinaria Amphitheatrum Castrense

Via Asinaria

Porta Labicana

Peranius

Bessas

Via Labicana

Via Praenestina

Porta Praenestina

Via Tiburtina

Porta Tiburtina

inf. com.

inf. com.

OPPIAN HILL

Porta Nomentana

Via Nomentana

Praetorian Camp

Porta Salaria

Via Salaria

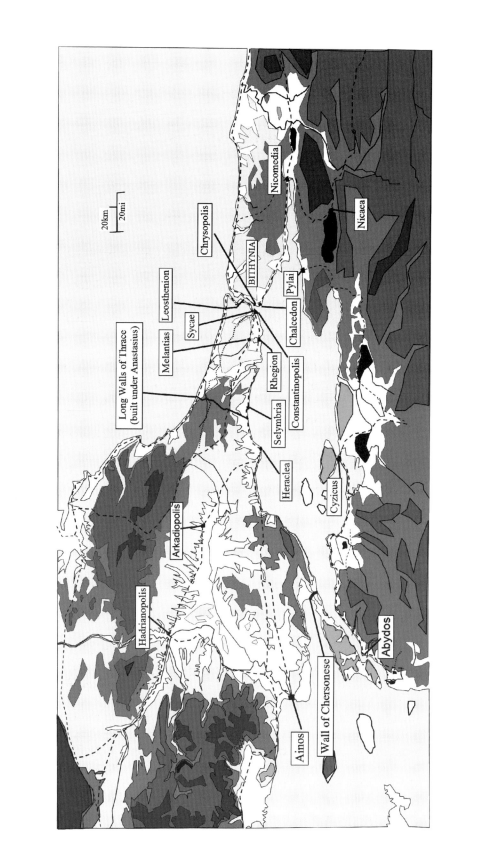

20km
20mi

Chrysopolis

Leosthenion

BITHYNIA

Sycae

Pylai

Melantias

Chalcedon

Long Walls of Thrace
(built under Anastasius)

Rhegion

Constantinopolis

Selymbria

Heraclea

Arkadiopolis

Hadrianopolis

Nicomedia

Nicaea

Cyzicus

Abydos

Aïnos

Wall of Chersonese

Chapter One

The Roman Empire in 518

The General Situation

Anastasius left his successor Justin I a mixed heritage. He deserves full credit for having ended the Isaurian problem for good. Similarly, he had reinstated Roman naval supremacy on the Red Sea so that commerce between Rome, Africa and India flourished under him and brought a windfall of customs duties to the state coffers. The victory over the Persians in the war that lasted from 502 until 506 and the building of the fortress of Dara/Daras opposite the Persians at Nisibis secured the eastern border until 527, so it is clear that Anastasius's policies in the east can be considered to have been a great success. He was ready to listen to his military commanders when they recommended the fortifcation of Dara. The Persians realized how well placed this fortress was and it was because of this that it became their prime objective to destroy and/or capture it, as we shall see.

Reforms in the fields of administration, taxation and coinage made under Anastasius meant that the imperial administration probably worked better then than at any time during the late Empire because corruption was kept to a minimum so that the taxpayers were protected from the abuse of the rich. Under Anastasius the civil service consisted of men who were known for their learning, ability and experience, so it is not a surprise that the civilian administration worked well to support the state apparatus and its military forces. The end result was that the state coffers were full. Anastasius left his successor 320,000 lbs of gold. However, Anastasius's nominations to high military posts were not quite so successful and sometimes even disastrous, for example the appointments of his relatives Hypatius, Pompeius, and Aristus, and that of Vitalianus as *Comes Foederatum*. But this would not have mattered had Anastasius not made serious mistakes in his religious policy.

In retrospect it is clear Anastasius's greatest mistake was the support he gave to the Monophysite/Miaphysite interpretation of the *Henoticon* of Zeno and the exiling of the Patriarch Macedonius, because these were used by his enemies against him. The making of these mistakes resulted from Anastasius' own personal religious beliefs. He made the situation worse by denying *annona* to the *foederati* in the Balkans and by keeping the *coemptio* (produce sold at fixed prices for the army) also in effect in the Balkans. The *Comes Foederatum* Vitalianus used these three grievances to raise a revolt in the Balkans which united the *foederati*, the *comitatenses*, *limitanei* and peasants in the Balkans under his rebel flag. The naval defeat suffered by Vitalianus in front of Constantinople meant that after 515 Vitalianus no longer posed a serious threat to the capital, but at the time of the enthroning of Justin I much of the Balkans was still in his hands. At that stage it was also clear that the Roman imperial authorities could not defeat him militarily.

The principal reason for this was that the Romans had lost most of their remaining regular native infantry forces in disastrous campaigns conducted under the leadership of Anastasius's incompetent relatives against Vitalianus. In 518 the Romans simply did not possess enough combat-ready forces to defeat the rebel. The solution to the problem had to be a negotiated settlement, and this was realized by Justin I, and surprisingly easily accomplished.

The period from ca. 395 until 518 had seen a rise in the numbers of combatants involved in wars and battles so that the development to employ ever larger numbers of men saw its height at the battle of the Catalaunian Fields in 451. However, it did not end then. The Romans continued to use large armies until the reign of Anastasius, but by then the general quality of these was quite low so that during the reign of Anastasius the cavalry was clearly the queen of the battlefield. The employment of cavalry forces meant that the numbers of men in battles became lower because the maintaining of cavalry was more costly than that of infantry and because it was also more difficult to assemble cavalry forces than it was infantry. The massive culling of Roman armies during the last years of Anastasius's reign meant that his successor Justin I had fewer men available for combat when he took the reins of power in 518. Thanks to the massive hoard of gold in the state coffers Justin I could have raised more men, but this did not happen, for reasons unknown. Justin I and Justinian I clearly relied more on the *bucellarii, foederati* and foreign mercenaries than any of their predecessors. Perhaps they just did not believe that it would be possible to recreate an effective regular army out of native recruits.

Roman Society, Administration and Military in 518[1]

At the apex of Roman society stood the emperor with the title of *Augustus*. Actual power, however, could be in the hands of some other important person like a general or administrator or family member, the best examples of which are the roles of Justinian under Justin I and Theodora under Justinian I. There still existed senates in Rome and Constantinople, but the former was now in Gothic hands. The Senate could be included in the decision-making process when the emperor (or the power behind the throne) wanted to court the goodwill of the moneyed senators. However, it could also be bypassed when the emperor so desired. Late Roman imperial administration was divided into three sections: 1) Military; 2) Palatine; 3) Imperial and Fiscal Administration.

Roman Armed Forces in 518[2]

Sixth century Roman armed forces consisted of the imperial bodyguards (*excubitores, scholae, domestici*),[3] praesental forces (central field armies), *comitatenses* (field armies), *limitanei* (frontier forces), *bucellarii* (private retainers), *foederati* (federates) and other mercenaries, and temporary allies, in addition to which came the civilian paramilitary forces.

Most regular soldiers were volunteers, but conscription was also used when necessary to fill up the ranks. The *foederati* and *bucellarii* were all volunteers. Because of this their quality was usually higher than the regulars. During this era the effectiveness of the regulars suffered badly from arrears of payment and from the corruption of officers. It

Augustus Caesar

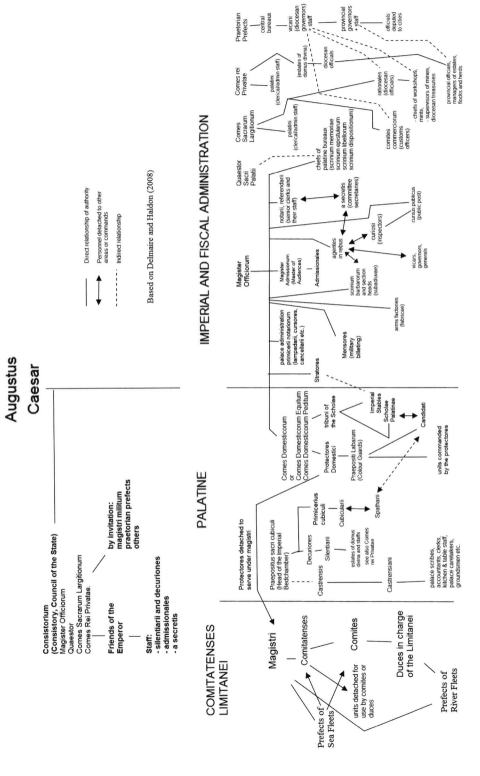

Consistorium
(Consistory, Council of the State)
Magister Officiorum
Quaestor
Comes Sacrarum Largitionum
Comes Rei Privatae.

Friends of the Emperor

by invitation:
magistri militum
praetorian prefects
others

Staff:
- silentiarii and decuriones
- admissionales
- a secrets

Direct relationship of authority

Personnel detached to other areas or commands

Indirect relationship

Based on Delmaire and Haldon (2008)

IMPERIAL AND FISCAL ADMINISTRATION

Praetorian Prefects — central bureaux — vicarii (diocesan governors) + staff — provincial governors + staff — officials deputed to cities

Comes rei Privatae — palatini (clerical/admin staff) — (estates of domus divina) — diocesan officials — rationales (diocesan officials) — provincial officials, managers of estates, flocks and herds

Comes Sacrarum Largitionum — palatini (clerical/admin staff) — comites commerciorum (customs officers) — chiefs of workshops, mints, - supervisors of mines, diocesan treasuries

Quaestor Sacri Palatii — chiefs of palatine bureaux (scrinium memoriae scrinium epistularum scrinium libellorum scrinium dispositionum)

Magister Officiorum
- Magister Admissionum (Master of Audiences)
- Admissionales
- notarii, referendarii (senior notarii and their staff)
- a secretis (committee secretaries)
- agentes in rebus
- curiosi (inspectors)
- cursus publicus (public post)
- vicars, governors, generals
- scrinium barbarorum and section heads (subadiuvae)
- arms factories (fabricae)
- Mensores (military billeting)
- palace administration primicerii notariorum (lampadarii, cursores, cancellarii etc.)
- Stratores

PALATINE

Comes Domesticorum or Comes Domesticorum Equitum Comes Domesticorum Peditum
- tribuni of the Scholae
- Protectores Domestici
- Praepositi Labarum (Colour Guards)
- Imperial Stables Scholae Palatinae
- Candidati
- units commanded by the protectores
- Spatharii

Protectores detached to serve under magistri

Praepositus sacri cubiculi (Head of the Imperial Bedchamber)
- Primicerius cubiculi
- Castrensis
- Decuriones
- Silentiarii
- Cubicularii
- estates of domus divina and staffs see also Comes rei Privatae
- Castrensiani
- palace scribes, accountants, clerks, kitchen & table staff, palace caretakers, groundsmen etc.

COMITATENSES LIMITANEI

Magistri
Comitatenses
Comites
Duces in charge of the Limitanei
Prefects of River Fleets
Prefects of Sea Fleets
units detached for use by comites or duces

was largely because of this that the *bucellarii* formed the main striking forces. The two principal reasons for this are: 1) most of them were recruited on the basis of their ability; 2) they usually received their salaries in time.

The Roman field army consisted of two groups: 1) The two praesental armies stationed in and around the capital as central reserve; 2) the regional field armies (Army of the East, Thrace and Illyricum). Justinian changed the structure to create a new regional field army for Armenia within a year of his accession and after the reconquest also for Spain, Africa, and Italy, one each. The bulk of the new Armenian Field Army consisted of the retinues of the Armenian nobles. Field armies were usually commanded by the *magistri militum*.

The *limitanei* posted along the frontier zones were regular soldiers commanded by *duces* (dukes) or at times by *comites rei militaris* (military counts) or *magistri militum* (masters of soldiers). Justinian created new units of *limitanei* for the reconquered areas in Africa and Italy, and presumably also for Spain.

The *foederati* originally meant treaty-bound barbarians, but by this time these were usually fully incorporated into military structures so that their overall commander held the title of *Comes Foederatum* (Count of Federates). The exact difference between the *foederati* and *symmachoi* (allies) is not entirely clear, because there seems to have been quite a bit of a grey area in this respect and for example the Arabs could be considered either *foederati* or *symmachoi*. However, there is one basic distinction that can be observed which is that the *foederati* were considered permanently treaty-bound while the *symmachoi* retained more freedom to negotiate their position so they could also consist of temporary allies.

The *bucellarii* were basically private retinues consisting of persons with known combat abilities that any wealthy person could employ, but in practice the emperor exercised full control over these troops. The best *bucellarii* forces obviously served under those who had an eye for talent and enough money to hire it. Belisarius was clearly the best in this respect. The *bucellarii* not only had an important role in combat, but also in keeping discipline. A large force of them enabled their commander to impose his will on the other officers in situations in which their loyalty was suspect. Belisarius had 7,000 men at the height of his career. The military hierarchy of the greater households consisted of: 1) the overall commander (*efestōs tē oikia*, majordomo), 2) a treasurer (*optio*); 3) officers (*doruforoi/doryforoi*); 4) privates/soldiers (*hypaspistai*). The flag-bearer of the bodyguards (*bandoforos, bandifer*) may have been the second-in command, but this is not known with certainty. The commanders and officers of the *bucellarii* were also often used as commanders of regular armies and divisions.

Basic tactics and military equipment remained much the same as before. Infantry tactics were based on variations of the phalanx with a clear preference for the use of the lateral phalanx or hollow square/oblong array, while cavalry tactics were based on variations of formation with two lines. Phalanxes consisted of rank and file formations of heavy infantry in which there were typically 4, 8, 16 or at most 32 ranks of heavy infantry footmen. Light infantry was placed behind the heavy infantry, between the files, or on the flanks as required and could also be used for harassment and pursuit of the enemy. The phalanxes consisted of smaller units the most important of which were the *mere* – divisions (sing. *meros*) consisting of at most about 7,000 men, about 2,000–3,000 men *moirai* (sing. *moira*) and about 200–400 men *tagmata* (sing. *tagma*). If the army consisted of less than 24,000 footmen it was deployed as three phalanxes (*mere*) and if it had more than 24,000 it was deployed in four phalanxes (*mere*). The standard way to use these was to deploy the phalanxes side-by-side either as a single line or as a double phalanx (heavy infantry units divided into two lines of four ranks, or two lines of eight ranks). The cavalry was typically posted on the flanks and the reserves for both infantry and cavalry were posted behind the front line where required. The phalanxes could then be manoeuvred to form hollow square/oblong, oblique arrays, rearward-angled half-square (*epikampios opisthia*), forward-angled half-square (*epikampios emprosthia*), wedge (*embolos/cuneus*) and hollow wedge (*koilembolos*), convex (*kyrte*) and crescent (*menoeides*). The *Peri Stragias/Strategikes* (34) suggests that it was also possible to deploy one, two or several lines of phalanxes in depth. The smaller units could also manoeuvre on their own to open up the formation for enemy cavalry/elephants to pass through, or to form a wedge or to form a hollow wedge, or double-front (which in practice usually faced all directions), etc.

The general fighting quality of infantry of the period, however, was very low at the time Justin I took the reins of power so that its ability to manoeuvre and form the arrays mentioned above was very restricted in practice. The infantry consisted mostly of men with no combat experience and its morale was very low because it had been repeatedly defeated. It was therefore prone to flee at the first sight of any setback suffered by the cavalry, so that its ability to protect the cavalry was very limited. Because of this Urbicius had recommended the use of protective devices around the infantry hollow square already protected by wagons and ballistae-carriages during the reign of Anastasius. The infantry of the early sixth century required extra protective measures against enemy cavalries. Neighbours could not provide infantry recruits that could readily be converted into Roman infantry forces. The Romans had to train the men to fight as heavy infantry formations. The Romans did employ the Slavs and Moors as footmen and their combat performance was usually very good, but these consisted of light infantry which was not well-suited to serve in heavy infantry roles. The Isaurians inside the Roman Empire were also recruited into the Roman infantry, but once again they were more useful as light infantry in difficult terrain or during sieges than as line infantry, as the following discussion makes abundantly clear. This means that there was no alternative available for the Romans than to train natives to fight in the heavy infantry phalanxes if they wanted to possess infantry able to influence the course of the war.

The Roman heavy infantry consisted of several basic categories. Firstly the heavy infantry in its standard gear wearing armour (mail, scale, lamellar, muscle) and helmets (various types including ridge, segmented, one piece), shields and sometimes also shin guards. Shields were typically round or oval, but works of art from the turn of the sixth century suggest that rectangular shields could also be used. The size of the shield varied from ca. 80–90 cm in width to the extra large shields mentioned in the *Peri Strategias/Strategikes* (16). This treatise states that the shields were to be no less than seven *spithamai* in diameter which would usually mean about 1.5 m. It is clear that this figure cannot refer to width but height.[4] The *Peri Strategias* also required that front-rankers had spikes in their bosses and there is evidence for this too. When equipped in their standard gear the heavy-armed footmen (the '*skoutatoi*', shield-bearers) were armed with *spatha* (medium to long two-edged swords), *semi-spatha/machaira* (short swords), darts (*plumbatae* placed inside shield), and cavalry *kontarion*-spear (ca. 3.74 m in length).[5] Large numbers of heavy infantry were also required to use bows which were also carried. In fact, the sixth century *Strategikon* demanded that half the footmen were to consist of archers if there were over 24,000 footmen. All were also trained to use slings and throw stones. Darts, stones and bows were used in field combat to support the main line in the most effective manner. The so-called heavy infantry *skoutatoi* could also be equipped lightly for use in difficult terrain so they did not wear armour or helmets and had only a small shield with javelins and swords. The Slavs, Moors and Isaurians formed excellent recruits for use as javeliners in difficult terrain, but they were not that good in the traditional role as line infantry.

The light infantry consisted of archers, slingers and javeliners so that an infantry phalanx with a depth of 16 ranks would have had at least 8 ranks of light infantry accompanying it. In combat the light infantry was typically placed behind the heavy infantry phanlax, but it could also be placed between its files, in front and on the flanks as required. The light infantry was at its best in the harassment of the enemy, in pursuits, and in difficult terrain.

The third category of foot soldiers consisted of dismounted cavalry, which were required to be able to fight on foot as well. These forces were obviously equipped in standard cavalry gear, so those units that did not possess shields were less effective on foot than those that had shields. However, at this time most of the Roman cavalry possessed shields even if they were smaller than their infantry variants. Cavalry was equally well-adapted to fighting at long and short distances so that it combined both the heavy infantry variant equipped with bows and that of light infantry.

Unit formations were the open array used in marching, irregular array *droungos/drungus*, close order (shields rim-to-rim), and *foulkon/fulcum/testudo*. The *foulkon* had two variants at this time. The first of these was the offensive *foulkon* in which the men placed their shields rim-to-boss in width and depth, which was typically used when the men did not have armour. The second was the *foulkon* used against cavalry in which the shields were placed almost rim-to-rim in width to allow spears to protrude outside the array while the shields of the first three ranks were deployed rim-to-boss in depth with the front rankers kneeling, second rank crouching and third standing upright.

In phalanx formation the spears were used in three different ways. Firstly it was possible to form a spear-wall against the enemy by having four ranks point spears forward while others behind them supported the attack with missiles. This was used against both infantry and cavalry. Secondly, it was possible for the first row/rank to throw the extra-long spear even when fighting against enemy infantry and use sword while those behind supported the front-rankers with their spears and those behind them with missiles. Thirdly, it was possible that the heavy infantry used bows against enemy cavalry. In this case the first three ranks placed their spears on the ground after which the two front ranks aimed their arrows directly at the horses, while those behind shot their arrows at higher angle. When the enemy cavalry came close, the men picked up their spears and prepared to receive them with a wall of spears. When the footmen were equipped with javelins it was obviously more typical for these to be thrown in combat, but the javelin-armed men could also be used in other ways as well as is well demonstrated by the earlier *pilum*-armed armies.

the standard infantry battle formations of the fifth and sixth centuries

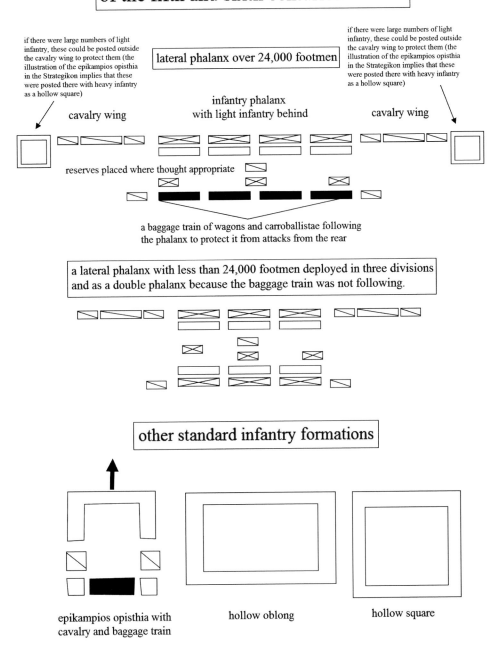

if there were large numbers of light infantry, these could be posted outside the cavalry wing to protect them (the illustration of the epikampios opisthia in the Strategikon implies that these were posted there with heavy infantry as a hollow square)

lateral phalanx over 24,000 footmen

if there were large numbers of light infantry, these could be posted outside the cavalry wing to protect them (the illustration of the epikampios opisthia in the Strategikon implies that these were posted there with heavy infantry as a hollow square)

infantry phalanx with light infantry behind

cavalry wing

cavalry wing

reserves placed where thought appropriate

a baggage train of wagons and carroballistae following the phalanx to protect it from attacks from the rear

a lateral phalanx with less than 24,000 footmen deployed in three divisions and as a double phalanx because the baggage train was not following.

other standard infantry formations

epikampios opisthia with cavalry and baggage train

hollow oblong

hollow square

The cavalry forces of the period did not suffer from the same problems as the infantry. The Roman cavalry had proven itself in combat many times and it included large numbers of men who were combat veterans. In addition, it is clear that the availability of recruits across the borders from the 'barbarian lands' made it possible for the Romans to fill its ranks with combat-ready soldiers without time-consuming training, which was always necessary for infantry. The cavalry was similarly divided into units of *mere* of 6,000–7,000 horsemen, 2,000–3,000 *moirai* and about 200–400 *tagmata*/*banda*.

Cavalry was equipped with bows, spears and swords. Typically the horsemen also wore armour (muscle, mail, scale, lamellar, ersatz), helmets (ridge, segmented, single piece etc.) and shields (smaller than the infantry variants), but there were also units that could be without these. The best example of this is the Heruls who were typically unarmoured, but their squires did not even have shields before they had proved themselves in combat. In practice the type of equipment used depended on the nationality of the unit, on the individual soldier and booty the soldier had taken. In the case of the *bucellarii* the type of equipment obviously depended on the soldier's personal wealth, the presents and salary given by the employer and on the booty gathered. The types of cavalry therefore consisted of lightly equipped horsemen all the way up to the heavily equipped and armoured cataphracts. The cataphracted horsemen consisted of two basic variants: 1) horse with frontal armour and head piece; 2) horse with full armour and head piece. The amount of armour and types of armour and helmets worn by the cataphracts also varied. Some wore mail or scale from the neck and shoulders to the ankles and wrists with possible additional pieces (e.g. muscle or lamellar armour protection for the torso, and shin pieces), while others wore less armour and/or combined different elements of these. The type of helmet worn by the cataphract depended on the nationality of the horseman, his wealth and booty gathered.

The standard cavalry formations were: 1) large army of 10,000/12,000/15,000 or more horsemen which had three divisions with outflankers and flank guards in the first line, four divisions with units between them in the second line, and a third line with two units on the flanks; 2) medium sized force of 5,000/6,000/10,000/12,000/15,000 horsemen which had three divisions, outflankers and flank guards in the first line and two divisions with a unit between them in the second line; 3) small forces with less than 5,000/6,000 horsemen that had three divisions with outflankers and flank guards in the first line and one division in the second line. In addition, the Romans could have separate units of ambushers on both sides, or elsewhere. If the Romans outnumbered the enemy, they would outflank the enemy on both sides; if the Romans had roughly equal numbers, the enemy would be outflanked on the right; if the Romans had fewer men, the middle division in the front attacked first.

The cavalry used three different unit orders: 1) open order for marching; 2) *droungos* irregular order usable in difficult terrain and whenever there was need for speed, e.g. in skirmishing or pursuit; 3) close order used in pitched battles. In combat the cavalry was divided into units of *koursores* (skirmishers) that used the *droungos* while those assigned as *defensores* used the close order because of its psychological advantage over the irregular array (the closeness of the men and horses gave confidence and made flight more difficult). In combat the *koursores* were usually used for skirmishing and pursuits so that the *defensores* protected them. The typical Roman cavalry attack had three variants:

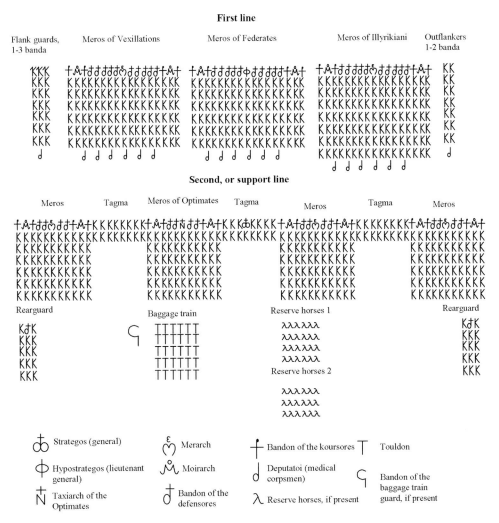

First line

| Flank guards, 1-3 banda | Meros of Vexillations | Meros of Federates | Meros of Illyrikiani | Outflankers 1-2 banda |

Second, or support line

| Meros | Tagma | Meros of Optimates | Tagma | Meros | Tagma | Meros |

Rearguard

Baggage train

Reserve horses 1

Reserve horses 2

Rearguard

Strategos (general)	Merarch
Hypostrategos (lieutenant general)	Moirarch
Taxiarch of the Optimates	Bandon of the defensores
Bandon of the koursores	Touldon
Deputatoi (medical corpsmen)	Bandon of the baggage train guard, if present
Reserve horses, if present	

Large cavalry army (over 12,000/15,000 horsemen).

1) the battle began with the *koursores* skirmishing in the *droungos* array and then when the enemy attacked them, they retreated back to the close-order *defensores* and then faced the pursuers together; 2) the entire first line, consisting of both *koursores* and *defensores*, maintained close order and attacked together at the canter/trot. 3) the entire first line attacked at a gallop so that the array became irregular by the time it reached the enemy, which was often done during this period. If the enemy retreated, then the *koursores* pursued them in irregular order. If the enemy managed to defeat the first line, it sought safety from the second line, and if everything failed then all sought protection from the third line (this was possible only in the largest variant).

The Romans had a permanent professional navy, with fleets with permanent bases all over the Empire (Constantinople, Antioch/Seleucia, Alexandria, frontier fleets along the Danube). In addition to this they posted detachments and patrols wherever needed. The

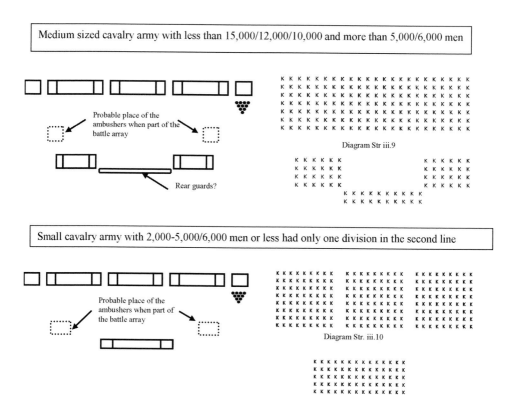

Medium sized cavalry army with less than 15,000/12,000/10,000 and more than 5,000/6,000 men

Probable place of the ambushers when part of the battle array

Rear guards?

Diagram Str iii.9

Small cavalry army with 2,000-5,000/6,000 men or less had only one division in the second line

Probable place of the ambushers when part of the battle array

Diagram Str. iii.10

Romans possessed a clear advantage over most of their enemies in naval warfare owing to the high quality of their seamen, rowers and marines together with better ship designs, but after the Vandals gained possession of the Roman fleet in Carthage the advantage was not so pronounced. Here lay the glitch. The East Romans had superiority over the Vandals only when their forces were led by competent commanders. The Romans typically used their navy in support of land armies in whatever way was needed e.g. by carrying troops and supplies or by clearing the waters of enemy vessels. However, the fleets naturally performed normal policing missions as well.

The standard workhorse of the Roman navy was the fast *dromon*, which was typically a single-banked smaller variant at this time. Naval combat formations were single line abreast with reserves, the double line/phalanx with reserves, convex to break through the enemy centre, crescent to outflank, and circle for defence. In advance of these two or three ships acted as scouting ships, which could also be used to break up the cohesion of the enemy array by leaving them exposed in front. The transport ships were usually placed behind the combat ships.

In the field of siege warfare the Persians were the only equals of the Romans, but then the rest were plain incompetent. The Romans continued to employ all the devices and measures they always had done and readers are referred to previous volumes and this text for further details and examples of equipment and tactics used.

For the equipment worn at this time, see the Plates and the images of soldiers in the text. The attached drawings by Mai of the images included in the *Ilias Ambrosiana* (fifth

Two images from *Ilias Ambrosiana* depicting combat. Drawing by Mai, 1819.

Military saints in sixth century Roman military gear depicted in a weight located in the British Museum.

Mounted archer depicted in a textile. Egyptian sixth century. Source: Diehl.

century or turn of the sixth century) give a good overall picture of types of equipment used, but the Romans used many other types of gear, many of which are included in the Plates.

It is not recognized often enough that the late Romans could wear truly fancy equipment and the officers even more so. In his *Iohannis* or *De Bellis Libycis* Flavius Cresconius Corippus has preserved for us a good description of what kinds of equipment the Roman officer cadre and *bucellarii/armigeri* wore, but I limit myself to the list he gives for Geiserith because his was probably among the fanciest. This Geiserith wore shining steel armour that covered his whole body. It was a glittering sight in which the scales were adorned with gold. His golden helmet was dazzling with steel and it had an apex and crest adorned with a horse's mane. The belt was bejewelled and his sword had an ivory sheath. He wore greaves which were bound with Parthian hide and golden fittings to his legs. These he had wrapped in bright purple and decorated once again with gems. He was armed at least with a sword and bow.[6]

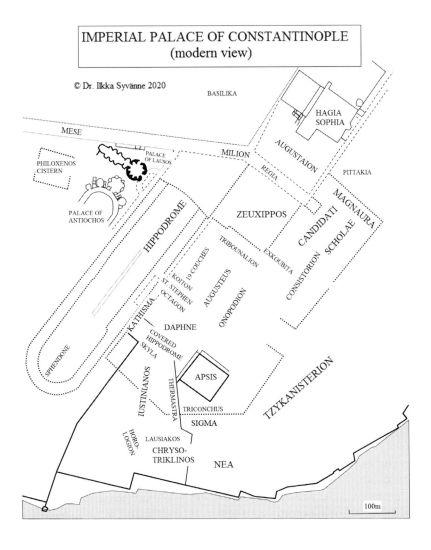

Chapter Two

Enemies and Allies

The principal enemies of the Romans at this time were the Germanic peoples (Vandals, Goths, Visigoths, Gepids, Heruls, Lombards, Franks), Slavic peoples (Sclavenoi, Antae), Huns (Utrigurs, Kutrigurs, Sabiri), Avars and Persians with their allies and subjects.

The Slavs and Antae[1]

The Antae and the Slavs (*Sklavenoi*) make their first appearance as enemies at the beginning of the sixth century. The later *Strategikon* classifies both as a specific type of enemy. The early history of the Slavs (*Antae, Sklavenoi, Venethi*) is much disputed, but certain general conclusions can be drawn. The Slavs, who lived in the eastern part of Europe, formed an ethnically diverse group united by their language. The only Slavic groups which concern us here are the abovementioned *Antae* and *Sklavenoi*. At the beginning of the sixth century the *Sklavenoi* (henceforth Slavs) inhabited roughly the area between Lake Neusiedler (near Vienna) and the Novae, in other words the Moesia/Pannonia, in which area there was a power vacuum in the wake of the Gothic movement to Italy. The Antae on the other hand seem to have been situated somewhere at the curve of the Black Sea between the Dniester and the Dniepr rivers.

As noted in volume 5, Anastasius had refortified much of the Balkans and this policy was continued by Justin I and Justinian I. These were sorely needed against the Slavs. The *Strategikon* categorized the Slavs and Antae as enemies that could always be engaged in pitched battles thanks to their weak organization and poor equipment, which meant that the Romans needed a field army in the region for this to be possible. The fortifications could not stop the mobile Slavs who could simply pass them by abandoning the main highways and could use their *monoxyles* (ranged in size from canoes/boats to Viking-size longboats) to cross rivers. The occasional use of wagons to transport loot decreased this possibility, which enabled the Romans to catch the invaders if forces were available. However, for much of the sixth century the Romans lacked sufficient field forces to engage the Slavs in the field because of their continuous wars elsewhere.

The Slavs and Antae lived in small groups based on family or groups of families. They lived in pitiful hovels in nearly impenetrable forests, rivers, lakes and marshes. They did not possess a unified social or political structure, and it was because of this that their raids across the border usually consisted of independently-operating war bands each under its own chieftain. The richer chieftains might have their own retinues. It was only on special occasions that they united their tribal groupings for some specific purpose like a massive invasion under some recognized leader who could be called a king. The fact that they lacked established peacetime leaders made it difficult for the Romans to negotiate with them. However, if invaded by the Romans, they could join together to oppose the invaders. It was because of this that the *Strategikon* recommended the bribing of some of the kings/chieftains to their side, a practice which was also followed by Justinian before this.

To defend themselves against the Romans the Slavs needed to cooperate. Because of this they started to unite their forces so that they could field armies that consisted of over 100,000 men.[2] The Romans needed a large army, which they seldom had available in this area, to defeat a force of this size. Indeed, as we shall see, armies with as few as 3,000 men could achieve remarkable results against numerically superior but poorly led Romans. Army size was not everything.[3]

The later *Strategikon* is the only source which gives us details of how Roman operations against the Slavs and Antae were conducted; we do not possess any period evidence. However, we can make the educated guess that these practices were already followed during the early sixth century because we possess information of the exploits of *MVM per Thracias* Chilbudius (Procop. *Wars* 7.14.1–6) who conducted successful operations against the Slavs for three years in succession until he was killed north of the Danube by the Slavs in about 533. It is likely that his operations followed the principles described by the *Strategikon* (11.4). For example, when operating along the rivers, attacking from two directions simultaneously was an old method.[4]

The *Strategikon* (11.4) recommended dividing the enemy with alliances and the use of surprise attacks so that the Slavs would be unable to unite and hide in the woods. The general was instructed to leave superfluous baggage and a *moira* of cavalry behind. This acted both as a guard and as a threat against the Slavs so that they would be unable to unite. Troops were also equipped lightly with materials for building bridges, and the navy was to be used where needed. It was also recommended to make the invasion simultaneously from two directions if possible, so that the Slavs would be unable to flee and unite (Tactic 1). The *hypostrategos* was to advance 22–30 km through unsettled land behind the Slavic settlements, after which he was to start pillaging while the *strategos* advanced from the other direction. This confused the Slavs. The soldiers were not to take prisoners if the Slavs put up resistance so that they could advance forward quickly. This instruction fits well what we know of Chilbudius. He was known for his lack of avarice and refusal to enrich himself and for operating along the Danube.

If there was only one suitable road, the army was still divided (Tactic 2). In this case the *hypostrategos* would take half or more of the army while the *strategos* followed. As the *hypostrategos* advanced, he would detach one to two *banda* per Slavic settlement and continue his march as long as there were enough *tagmata* in his command (not further than 22–30 km). He was to retain three to four *banda* (1,000–2,000 men) for emergencies. After this, the *hypostrategos* was to turn back and gather up the pillagers along the route of his march while the *strategos* did the same from the other direction. The methods promoted by the *Strategikon* were logical. It was easier to destroy the enemy in the scattered settlements where they lived rather than chase around the small raiding parties when they were invading. The general was instructed to pay particular attention to security measures when encamping his army. He was to avoid wooded terrain in summer as much as possible and operate only in open areas. It was recommended to invade during the winter when trees were bare.

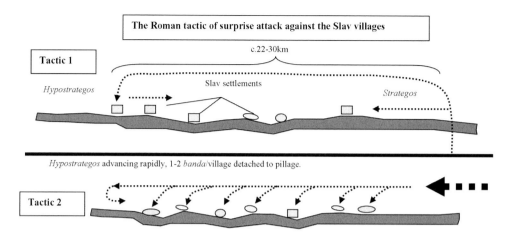

The Roman tactic of surprise attack against the Slav villages

c.22-30km

Tactic 1

Hypostrategos

Slav settlements

Strategos

Hypostrategos advancing rapidly, 1-2 *banda*/village detached to pillage.

Tactic 2

Syvänne, 2004:

'The majority of the Slavic soldiers were unarmoured light infantry carrying large oblong shields or small shields, knives, and two to three short javelins. The Croats also used axes. In addition, some carried wooden bows and arrows smeared in poison. The Slavic armies/hordes apparently consisted of separate groupings of archers, slingers, and javeliners. Consequently, the *Strategikon* instructed the soldiers to prepare themselves for combat by taking an antidote. The wooden bows were obviously weaker than the composite bows used by the Romans. However, some Slavs had also adopted the use of the reflex bow. According to a later Muslim source, the Slavs used their own peculiar archery draw, which sacrificed power to the speed of delivery. Some of the men were evidently cavalry, perhaps formed of wealthier Slavs and of the remnants of Germans and Huns. These were probably later called Druzhinas, i.e. military retinues of the voivodes (clan chieftains) and zupans (subordinates of the voivodes). The elite also used better equipment. In fact, the smaller armies and raiding bands could consist of these elite horsemen that could also be dismounted if needed.

The military methods of the Slavs and Antes were similar. Their way of fighting arose from the type of terrain they inhabited (forests, rivers, lakes, and marshes) and from their fiercely independent nature. The Slavs specialized in the use of ambushes, sudden attacks, and raids. They were very adept at crossing the rivers. Their raids across the borders were often long and brutal in nature and quite often the Roman armies were unable to stop their ravages. Besides this, their armies were able to conquer a large number of cities and fortresses through a variety of methods. The Slavic armies consisted principally of light infantry, but as noted, they also possessed small numbers of cavalry. As light infantry, the Slavs generally avoided open and level ground except when marching with wagons loaded with loot. The wagons were used as a fort when needed. They were not ready to fight a close order battle on open and level ground. Effective use of javelins required probably even more space than was offered by the rim-to-rim order. The Slavs had their own peculiar way of fighting. In battle they first shouted all together (possibly howled like wolves) and moved forward a short distance to see if their opponents would lose their nerve. If this happened, they would attack violently. If not, they themselves turned around and ran for the woods. See below. As light infantry, they were very adept at fighting in such difficult terrain. In fact, the Slavs were the foremost experts of fighting in difficult terrain. They could also use feigned flight to induce the enemy to come into their chosen terrain. The Slavic leaders and kings also appear to have fought in the forefront of the battle.'

The Slavic tactics in the open consisted of posting a horde or a disorderly line in the woods or edge of the woods and then charging forward. They probably used ranks and files but the lack of regular drill ensured that the formations were disorderly. The place of the cavalry in the battle array is conjectural. The sources do not mention their place or role. They may also have been dismounted.

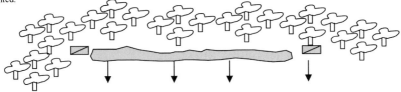

The combined Roman cavalry and infantry armies obviously had a clear tactical advantage over the Slavs and Antae in open terrain because the latter's armies consisted primarily of light infantry. Thus the *Strategikon* instructed the Roman general to seek a battle in open and unobstructed ground. The Slavs and Antae were vulnerable to the combination of archery, sudden outflanking manoeuvres, hand-to-hand fighting and fights in open and unobstructed ground. If the Slavs occupied a strong position, which secured their rear, the general was instructed to feign flight to draw them out. The only adaptations that were required from the Romans was to equip the footmen more lightly than usual and to use large numbers of javelin-equipped light infantry and to have dromons to support river crossings. The battle line was also modified by making it shallower because as light infantry the Slavs lacked 'punching power'. This means that the Romans had tactical superiority when battle was joined in open and level terrain, but in wooded terrain it was a different matter. The flower of the Roman armies, their cavalry, was practically useless in the forests and mountains unless they dismounted or the enemy could be lured out as noted above. The long spears of the heavy infantry were only a hindrance among the woods. Their helmets also hindered their all-important field of vision when fighting in looser formation. The solution was to employ looser and shallower formations and lighter equipment. Marching in wooded terrain meant adapting equipment, marching formation and combat formation to the circumstances.

Fighting in difficult terrain[5]

Fighting in wooded, rough or otherwise difficult terrain differed significantly from pitched battle in open terrain. It consisted of fighting while in marching formation (see the diagrams). During this era this was principally used against the Slavs/Antae and their light infantry. Compact deep phalanx formations with wide frontages simply could not be used when the terrain prevented it. In wooded areas, rough terrain, narrow passes, and against the Slavs and Antes, the army had to be lightly equipped and without many horsemen. The nature of the terrain also dictated that they were to march without wagons, and were to carry only the most essential supplies and equipment. For ease of movement and speed, soldiers were not to have heavy armament such as helmets, long spears, and mail coats with them.[6]

The lightly equipped heavy infantry force was not deployed in flat and open country but, depending on the size of the force, into two, three or four phalanxes (mere), each two, three, or four ranks deep. The phalanxes were placed about a stone's throw apart from each other and were to maintain march-in-column formation unless the situation called for a line. If the Romans reached open terrain that allowed the use of the normal phalanx, the columns could, by making a quarter turn, form the lateral phalanx formation. The columns of lightly-equipped heavy infantry/skoutatoi (carrying shields, swords and javelins) were therefore still used like ordinary heavy infantry in tight phalanxes. If the army included cavalry and/or baggage trains (consisting of mules and horses), these were posted so that the trains were behind the mere and the cavalry behind the train. The extreme rear of the formation was protected by a rearguard consisting of a detachment of heavy and light infantry. The protective screen, consisting of light infantry and lightly equipped heavy infantry, and/or of a small unit of cavalry, proceeded about a mile ahead of the main body. The rest of the lightly-equipped infantry, with possible small cavalry detachments, were posted in irregular groups on the flanks for their protection. Most of the archers were kept with the phalanxes since they were useful in rough, steep, narrow, and open terrain, whereas the javelin throwers were particularly useful in the thickly wooded areas.

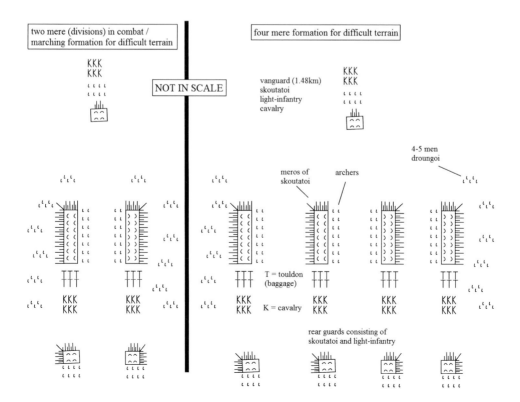

The main striking force of this array consisted of lightly-equipped soldiers that were placed outside and around the phalanx structure. These consisted of irregularly deployed four to five man throngs (*droungoi*) in which three or four men were armed with javelins and shields and one with a bow. The archer was to provide covering fire for the rest. These little groups were not to advance any further from the main body than where they could still hear its trumpets and bugles, because otherwise they risked being cut off from their support; these throngs were deployed one after the other so that they could protect each other's back. If the leading group encountered resistance, the groups behind them were to move up to higher ground unobserved and attack the enemy's rear. The main objective of the light infantry was always to seize higher ground and get above the enemy. The *droungoi* consisted of very disciplined and well-trained infantry. Their autonomy demanded mutual trust. The deployment pattern of the *skoutatoi* columns with the archers depended on the situation and terrain. In open terrain the columns deployed into two to four phalanxes with archers posted behind and light infantry *droungoi* and cavalry forming the wings. Where this was not possible the *skoutatoi* used deep files with wide intervals (= open order) and marched forward as columns until they could deploy in close order phalanxes. Where the terrain did not allow even this, the columns/phalanxes halted and the light infantry with a few *skoutatoi* and cavalry to support them would move forward against the enemy. If these were hard pressed, they were to retreat to the protection of the main body.

The Nomads: The Huns, Bulgars, Turks and Avars[7]

The Romans had been familiar with the fighting habits of the steppe nomads from the first century onwards and with the fighting methods of the so-called 'Hunnic peoples' (henceforth Huns) from the fourth century onwards so the Romans knew exactly how to defeat them. The main problem for the Romans was not how to face them in combat but that they often lacked adequate numbers of soldiers when they faced fighting on other fronts. For additional details, see the previous volumes in this series and Syvänne (2004, Chapter 10.2). Most of the following analysis is a summary of those.

The most powerful and threatening of the nomadic confederacies facing the Romans had been the one assembled by Attila. But after his death, the Hun Empire fell to pieces and its fragments never again mounted a serious threat to the Romans. The sixth century Romans faced a conglomeration of various Hunnic and Turkish groups that either fought against them or served as their mercenaries or allies. In the Balkans these tribes included the Bulgars, Kutrigurs and Utigurs. In the Caucasus appeared the Sabirs, probably a Turkic group, who were employed as mercenaries by both the Romans and the Sasanians. Unlike the other nomadic groups, the Sabirs also served as infantry (probably dismounted horsemen) in sieges. Towards the end of the period under discussion the nomadic Avars made their appearance initially as allies only to emerge as among the most dangerous enemies in the latter half of the century. The former overlords of the Avars, the Turks, maintained mostly friendly relations during this period. Unsurprisingly the best analysis of nomadic combat methods is to be found in the military manual *Strategikon* (11.2). According to this treatise, the nomads preferred to prevail over their enemies not so much by force as by deceit, surprise attacks, and cutting off supplies.

The sizes of the nomadic forces varied greatly from one tribe and confederation to another, but none attained the massive numbers wielded by Attila. The typical nomadic raiding force probably consisted of about 20,000–40,000 men, but these could be divided into roving hordes of raiders. The Avars who emerged on the scene towards the end of our period could wield field armies of 60,000 to 100,000 horsemen plus the forces provided by their allies or subjects, but the Romans did not have to face these during this period. How the Romans later coped with them is discussed in detail in volume 7.

The tactical unit of all of the steppe peoples was a *tümän/tümen* or a 10,000 man unit, but in practice its strength varied greatly. The *tümen* was apparently divided into 1,000-man units. The nomadic territories were divided into districts called 'arrows' (Old Turkic oq, pl. ogdz, later – ġuz, Hunnic pl. oġur, later – ġur) that supplied one *tümän*. This means that the steppe tribes were expected to send about 10,000 horsemen to war when they were part of a confederacy of several tribes. The whole nomadic way of life was based on the horse and on their ability to control the herds, which in its turn was based on castration. The Huns and other nomads rode to war on geldings, more docile than stallions or even mares and more easily handled. Geldings lacked the herd instinct which could have been useful in making the horses charge madly, but their obedience suited nomad tactics better. Unlike other horses the steppe ponies could survive merely by grazing.

The equipment of the wealthy nomadic elite consisted of the composite bow, lance (c.3–4 metres), sword, lasso, wicker shield or small shield (*pelte/parma*), segmented helmet (had a nasal which demanded the so-called straight or intermediate archery position even on horseback, which did not allow the archer to draw the bowstring as far back as would have been the case when the archer faced the enemy sideways) and chain mail or scale armour, but the vast majority of the Huns were less heavily armoured. The horses of the tribal nobility wore frontal armour of felt or iron. The better-equipped men among the nomads were placed in the front ranks followed by members of their tribal followers or members of their kin or clan whom they led during the war.

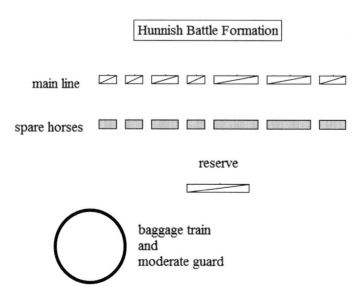

Hunnish Battle Formation

main line

spare horses

reserve

baggage train
and
moderate guard

The standard combat formation of the nomads consisted of a single line of irregular sized units which were further divided into smaller irregular units of about 40 to 50 horsemen. They posted a separate reserve behind, which could be used to ambush the enemy or as support troops to the first line. Spare horses were placed close behind the main line and their baggage train with a guard on the right or left two to three miles behind the array. See the diagram above. The standard tactic appears to have been to array the units in ranks and files just like the Romans, Alans and Mongols did; armoured troops were placed in front to protect the lightly equipped. The attack would then begin with a charge while shooting arrows. If the enemy showed signs of disorder, the attack was immediately pressed home, but if the enemy withstood the volleys of arrows and the frightening sight of the madly shouting nomads, the nomadic units retreated in irregular *droungos* (wedge) arrays. If this happened and the enemy pursued, the nomads could attempt to ambush them or outflank them. Otherwise the charge was repeated again and again until either arrows ran out, enemy resistance collapsed or the enemy pursued carelessly. The Huns, Bulgars, Turks and Avars were particularly fearsome warriors because they did not only fight with bows and arrows but also with spears and swords at close quarters, and they could do this even without the preparatory archery stage. When their enemies protected themselves against spear thrusts or sword cuts, other nomads threw lassoes and entangled their limbs, whether they were on foot or on horseback. The other standard tactical variation consisted of the so-called Scythian drill, described in the attached diagram.

According to the Scythian Drill of the *Strategikon* (6.1), the Scythian units were all formed in the same manner (no *koursores* or *defensores*) in one line so that it was divided into two *moirai* (instead of three). In combat these units were used so that the two flanks advanced as if to encircle and then moved towards each other so that they continued in a circle so that the right wing was on the outside and the left on the inside until they reached the opposite part of the line previously occupied by the other left. Contrary to my previous interpretation, I have interpreted this so that the left wing galloped in front of the enemy line to the right while the right wing galloped around the enemy to the left. This interpretation has been inspired by Roy Boss' recent analysis of Hun tactics. This makes more sense than placing the left wing inside a circle where they would not have been able to shoot towards their enemy on the right.

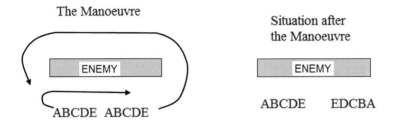

The Manoeuvre

Situation after
the Manoeuvre

When the Romans used cavalry on its own or as a vanguard, the best tactic was to charge the Hun battle formation before it could spread out or manoeuvre, but not to follow too far if they fled because the Huns often placed an ambush behind their line. As we have already seen from previous volumes, Hun/Bulgar cavalry could not really make any impact on Roman infantry as long as there were enough footmen who maintained their order – this was obviously not the case during Vitalian's revolt. The infantry on its own without cavalry support was also quite helpless because it could not catch the mobile Huns unless there was some obstacle (ditch, valley, mountain, river, lake, sea etc.) behind the Hun lines. If Roman infantry fought Hun armies in the open terrain, the side that had more supplies to outlast the enemy won, but the Romans did not face any really serious difficulties in dealing with the Huns before or after the reign of Attila. See vols. 2–5.

With the exception of Sabirs, the nomads proper were inept both as besiegers and when besieged. Their own native siege skills consisted solely of surprise attacks, betrayals, blockade or ravaging of the countryside to obtain payments. This meant that in normal circumstances the Romans could weather an invasion even when they did not possess enough men to engage the nomadic invaders or when the emperor ordered them not engage as Justinian sometimes did. However, if the nomads could obtain into their service Roman turncoats or allies (e.g. the Slavs/Antae) or other sedentary populations, then the situation changed because these gave the nomads an ability to conquer even heavily defended fortifications, as the exploits of Attila attest. This, however, was not usually the case during this period and it was because of this that the Romans could allow the nomads to roam freely in the Balkans and still survive those invasions. The situation changed during the late sixth century, but that topic will be dealt with in volume 7.

The Germanic Peoples[8]

1) The Ostrogoths and their subtribes
The enemy the Romans faced when they began their reconquest of Italy was no longer the enemy they had faced when Theoderic the Great had led the Gothic nation. Gone were the veteran leader and the veteran forces, which we have seen in action in volume five. These had been replaced by relatively incompetent military leadership and by cavalry forces whose fighting tactics had lost their versatility. Even though the principal tactic of the Gothic cavalry was the lancer charge also under Theoderic, most of his cavalry forces could still use the bow while mounted and fight at long distance if necessary. This had now been replaced by a simpler tactical system, which consisted of the use of the cavalry as cataphracted lancers for the breaking up of the enemy formation behind which were posted Gothic footmen as a defensive bulwark for the cavalry if they needed to retreat. The cavalry no longer used bows while mounted – only the footmen used these. This presumably reflected three things, even if this is nowhere stated in the sources. The great successes achieved by Theoderic the Great with lancer charges conducted frontally straight at the enemy had undoubtedly led to the false conclusion that the Gothic lancer charge was irresistible and that the Goths did not need any other tactical system. The fact that the Goths were no longer required to fight alongside the Romans meant that there no longer existed a training system which required the Goths to train mounted archery tactics. The possession of Italy with its arms factories made it possible for the Goths to equip practically all of their horsemen and horses with armour, which created the illusion that the cavalry charge would now be even stronger than before. Subsequent accounts make it clear that Belisarius knew how to exploit this weakness.

Theoderic had also built a large navy, but his successors had allowed it to decay through neglect. On top of this, even though the Goths knew how to build siege towers, they were inept users of them and other siege techniques so it was easy for the Romans to exploit these weaknesses.

There was one thing, though, that made the Goths more fearsome than they had been before, which was that the conquest of Italy had given them permanent abodes and livelihood which in its turn had increased the size of the Gothic population so that they now possessed 200,000 well-equipped men in arms of which they were able to assemble a field army of 150,000 men.[9] This was a fearsome foe for any enemy to face, but once again Belisarius knew how to counter it.

2) The Vandals

The Vandals the Romans faced in Libya were a shadow of their former selves in the fifth century. Easy living had made them the weakest of the successor states the forces of Justinian faced. It is probable that their population had grown since the days of their arrival in Africa when their total male population consisted of 80 chiliarchies (80,000 men). At that time their able-bodied men probably numbered about 63,000 of whom those below the age of 50 were about 56,000. Even if their population grew, the number of combat-ready forces probably fell to about 30,000–40,000 men at most. Easy living had also resulted in the abandonment of mounted archery training, and the infantry appears to have been completely useless. The Vandals had also torn down important sections of the walls in all of their cities except Carthage, which made the conquest of cities easy for the Romans. Not even their navy was its former self, even if the Romans believed it to be so. For a fuller discussion of the Vandal capabilities, see later in the text.

3) The Franks[10]

'The Franks are not nomads…, but their system of government, administration and laws are modelled more or less on the Roman pattern… They are in fact all Christians and adhere to the strictest orthodoxy. They also have magistrates in their cities and priests …, and for a barbarian people strike me as extremely well-bred and civilized and as practically the same as ourselves except for their uncouth style of dress and peculiar language.' Agathias 1.2.3–4, tr. by Frendo p.10.

This is a good summary. The Frankish kingdom and its army were well organized and followed a mix of Roman and Germanic models. The armed forces were based on the king's personal following, war bands of the Frankish chieftains, armed followers of the magnates, descendants of the Roman soldiers which included actual Roman units, and Rome's former barbarian allies. The infantry formed the flower of the Frankish army, but the Franks also possessed effective cavalry forces. The principal tactic employed by the Franks consisted of the use of either barbed javelins or of the *francisca* throwing axe to prepare an attack with swords or axes. The aim was either to kill or wound the enemy and to throw it into disorder with a missile attack. Javelins and axes rendered shields useless, as did the barbed *angon* which was used like the *pilum* before. Very few native Frankish warriors wore any armour or helmets because their warrior culture frowned on it. However, some of the wealthier elite warriors and their retinues wore armour and helmets as did the former Roman units in their service. Their combat tactics were based on the use of phalanx formations and close quarters combat even if the Franks also possessed both foot and horse archers. An attack was typically impetuous and fast. The sizes of the invading Frankish armies could be huge, with 75,000 up to 100,000 men reported. We have no reason to suspect these figures because even one medium-sized city in Gaul was able to put to the field an army of 20,000 men – the reason for this being that Frankish armies mainly consisted of footmen, cheaper to upkeep than cavalry. The major weaknesses of the Frankish forces were their relatively poorly organized system of provisioning and poor skills as besiegers. The Franks also possessed fleets, but these were posted in the Channel and North Sea because the Mediterranean Sea was in Gothic hands at the beginning of the sixth century, so the Romans did not have to face any naval threat from this direction.

The Romans had tactical superiority over the Franks because of their better organization, better command structures, and more varied and better-trained army, but the Franks were still formidable enemies who could and did cause any poorly led Roman army considerable trouble.

4) The Visigoths of Spain

We know next to nothing about the military practices of period Visigoths outside their few law codes and some scattered short references in the narrative sources. However, events prove that as a military power the Visigoths were not strong. They were too few in number and suffered from continuous internal disorder, which the Romans and others were able to exploit. After the death of Amalric in AD 531, the throne passed from one usurper to another. The law codes prove that their military organization was based on the combination of Germanic inheritance with Roman titles and practices. Their kings had their own cavalry retinues (*fideles, gardingi*) possibly commanded by *comes spathariorum* and their nobles were likewise required to possess readily available forces of cavalry retinues of their own. The commander-in-chief was called the *dux exercitus Hispaniae* and his generals the *preapositus hostis* or *comes* or *dux exercitus*.

Most of the common Visigoths and local population fought in units called the *thiufa* led by a *thiufadus* whose subordinate officers were the *quingentarius, centenarius* and *decanus*. This system implies a decimal unit structure of 1,000-man units with subdivisions of 500, 100 and 10, which probably in practice varied considerably. The system was based on territorial principle rather than on any tribal practice. It is therefore possible that the Visigoths maintained standing armies. Most of the levies probably consisted of infantry (spearmen, slingers, archers, club-men) of variable quality, but this is not known with certainty. Their armies appear to have been usually disorderly, undisciplined, poorly equipped, and often unwilling to serve, and their battlefield effectiveness was questionable. It is therefore not surprising that the Romans did not face as many troubles with the Visigoths as they had with the Goths or Franks.

5) The Lombards, Gepids and Heruls

During the sixth century, the Lombards at first served as allies of Rome. It was only after 565/6 that the situation changed so it is only in Volume 7 that I give a fuller description of their combat methods. The Lombards were the archetypical Germanic foe. The freemen class formed the backbone of the Lombard army and the entire population was required to fight when required. Their strength lay in their horsemen. The typical equipment worn by the Lombard horseman consisted of the *contus*-lance, shorter spear or javelin, sword and short sword. It was also typical for them to use armour and helmets, but not necessarily shields. Their tactics were based on the single cavalry line with possible reserve which was used for the making of impetuous cavalry charges at the gallop; it was hoped that this would break enemy morale.

The other Germanic peoples, the Heruls and Gepids, exhibited the same general military characteristics. The Romans used both as allies and mercenaries while they also faced both as enemies depending on the political situation. Both nations were primarily horsemen who specialized in wild cavalry charges and mêlée. Both nations, especially the Heruls, valued warrior qualities above all else. Heruls did not wear helmets or metal armour, while their squires went even without shields until they had proved themselves in combat. As far as the evidence allows the making of speculations (see Vol. 5), the Gepids appear to have used shorter spears than the Goths and as a result were usually not as effective in frontal combat as the Goths, but this is only a partial picture of the state of affairs because the sources prove that both the Gepids and Heruls were able to achieve great things through their personal bravery, demonstrated in mad charges against their enemies with nothing but sword in hand.

6) The Moors/Berbers[11]

The Moors that the East Romans faced in North Africa consisted of several different tribes which were sometimes united as one confederate force. According to Procopius the Moors of his day did not wear armour, had small shields, carried two javelins and used terrain or palisaded camps as bases of attack. This is a good general description of their fighting methods; for additional details, see the narrative. As lightly-equipped forces the Moors did not pose any serious threat on the battlefields except when they possessed a significant numerical advantage or managed to ambush the Romans. Their only advantage over the Romans was that they could use mountains and deserts as their places of refuge. But the Romans could isolate them in these areas until they wanted either a decisive battle or a treaty. For a fuller discussion, see the text.

7) Sasanian Persia[12]

The most formidable of the enemies facing the Romans were the Sasanians. They possessed a well organized administrative system which collected resources for the armed forces, and the society was well organized to support the war effort. Its greatest weaknesses were that it faced strong enemies in Central Asia and India and that it was economically weaker than East Rome. Its society was also considered so restrictive by its neighbours and its treatment of religious minorities like Christians was so bad that even its allies soon grew tired of Sasanian rule, as we shall see.

Cavalry formed the flower of the Persian armed forces. Their elite units consisted of the royal bodyguards, but the personal retinues of the magnates and those of the Persarmenians could be equally effective in the right circumstances. It was during this era that the supreme commander of the Persian armies was abolished and replaced by four generals so that the resulting hierarchy still resembled the earlier division but with the absence of the supreme commander. This change appears to have taken place under Kavadh/Cobades. The aim was to weaken the hold of the noble houses on power. Chosroes followed the same policy and thus improved the position of the minor nobility, the dehkans, in relation to the nobles, the *asvaran/savaran*, so that from his reign onwards the flower of the army consisted of both the savarans and dehkans who formed the elite heavy cavalry component of the army. He also increased the importance of the infantry in Persian armies, not least because they were needed in sieges.

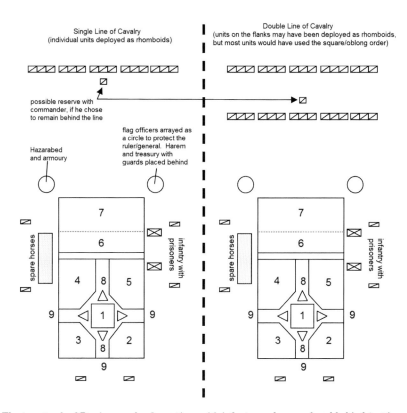

The two standard Persian cavalry formations with infantry and camp placed behind (not in scale)

- the probable structure of a Persian marching camp based on the supposition that later Muslim practices mirrored those of old Persia: 1) King or general, his entourage, guards, war chest etc. 2-5) Officers, officials, doctors, elephant keeper, entourages, guards, servants etc. 6) Cavalry. 7) Infantry. 8) Roads. 9) Gates. The Persians also posted a strong guard unit on one side of the camp to act as ambushing and guarding forces against any army trying to surprise them in their camp.
- the rear half with the ruler's entourage (1-5, 8-9) was the camp proper, and the front half (7) with infantry and wagons, hospital (could also include a trench and caltrops) was the portion facing the enemy (with no gates) that served as bulwark against attackers. The cavalry advanced from the camp proper and from (6) against the enemy to form the cavalry battle array. When the camp was built behind the battle line to protect the army in battle, it could include separate cavalry detachments to protect the flanks and rear, which I have added to the illustration on the basis of the later practices. The reason for this reconstruction is that the Tafrij, which includes these detachments, includes several borrowings from the earlier Persian treatises as a result of which it is possible that these were also used by the Sasanians.

After Chosroes, the Sasanian armed forces consisted of the following elements: the bodyguard units (the most important being the 10,000 Immortals), old heavy cavalry (*asvaran/savaran*), new heavy cavalry dehkans, light cavalry provided by mercenaries and tribal forces, elephants of the royal house, foot soldiers (*paygan*), the navy, and the logistical services, all of which had their own role to play in the overall strategy. The Sasanians posed a major threat to the Romans for four reasons: 1) they could stay in the field for long periods because of their well-organized logistical system; 2) they had greater numbers of high quality cavalry than the Romans; 3) they were the equals of the Romans in siege warfare; 4) the Sasanians were often able to field greater numbers of men than the Romans, with armies of 50,000 men or even 130,000 (sometimes including infantry but at other times infantry and servants should be added to these figures). The allied and mercenary forces fielded by the Persians could form a formidable threat on their own right. These included for example the Daylami infantry and Saracen cavalry of the Lakhmids.

The Persian navy posed no threat to the Romans because it did not operate in the Mediterranean and also because it consisted of weakly constructed dhows which were no match against the Roman nailed war galleys (*dromones*). The Romans feared that the Persians would become a naval threat if they gained full control of Lazica, but in my opinion they did not need to as the dhows would never have posed a threat. The Persians would have needed access to Roman shipbuilders as they later had in the seventh century. The results that the Muslims achieved with the ships of Syria and Egypt against the East Romans prove this nicely.

Some Sasanian infantry formations (there were also other variants). The defensive circle was usually formed by infantry and dismounted cavalry. A fuller discussion of this will appear in Volume 7.

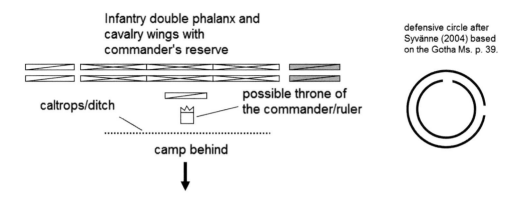

Infantry double phalanx and cavalry wings with commander's reserve

defensive circle after Syvänne (2004) based on the Gotha Ms. p. 39.

caltrops/ditch

possible throne of the commander/ruler

camp behind

Persian tactics remained the same. They showered the enemy with a devastating barrage of arrows after which they charged into hand-to-hand combat. In emergencies the Persians retreated to higher ground or formed circle array. The cavalry array usually had two variants that could have infantry and marching camp behind: the single line and the double line. These formations could be used for double outflanking or outflanking one side depending on the relative lengths of the opposing. If the enemy had longer combat lines, the Persians refused the wings while their centre attacked.

As noted above, it was during this era the Persians started to use increasing numbers of infantry. This gave them an advantage over those Roman armies that possessed only cavalry because the combined arms approach negated all the advantages that the Roman cavalry possessed in cavalry combat. The Persian infantry ensured that the Romans were unable to defeat the Persians as long as their morale held and the numerically superior Persian cavalry forces ensured that the Romans could not harass the Persian army effectively with guerrilla war that would prevent the Persians from obtaining supplies.

Chapter Three

Justin I (9 July 518–1 August 527)

Left: Justin. **Centre:** Justin. **Right:** Justin and Justinian. Source: Wroth
These coins demonstrate quite well how the period coins cannot be used to determine the outward
appearance of the period emperors. Contrary to the common politically correct view I do not hesitate to
state the obvious: The artistic standard had fallen considerably in the course of the past two centuries.
However, the coins still retain their value as evidence of the period clothing, equipment and propaganda.

The Internal Policies of Justin and Justinian 518–27

Justin and Justinian secure their position in 518[1]
Justin/Iustinus I became emperor on 9 July 518. How he achieved this was described in
Military History of Late Rome Volume 5 (457–518). The role of his nephew Justinian/
Iustinianus was pivotal in this and he was to play a similarly pivotal role in the
determination of Justin's policies throughout his reign. The sources make it clear that he
was involved in the running of the Empire from the start. This is not surprising in light
of the fact that Justin was an elderly uneducated man who had risen through the ranks
to become emperor. His origins were very humble. He had been born to a peasant family
and started his career as a herdsman. In fact, according to Procopius (*Anek.* 6.11), he
was the first illiterate emperor. This has been contested by some modern historians but I
see no reason to do so. It was largely because of this that Justinian, who had received an
excellent education, was able to dominate his uncle.

  The circumstances of the rise created immediate problems for the pair, Justin and
Justinian.[2] Both had openly declared themselves supporters of Chalcedon against the
Monophysites, which made for them both supporters and enemies. The supporters
included most of the members of the upper class who were staunchly Chalcedonian and
usually supporters of the Blue Circus Faction/Blue Faction/Blues. Justinian at this time
was a staunch supporter of the Blue Faction and used it to gather support for the regime
of his uncle; it was widely known that the Blue Faction was one of the powerbrokers
behind the rise of Justin.

The opposition to Justin and Justinian was led by the *cubicularius* Amantius who had previously given money to Justin so he would ensure the nomination of Amantius's own *domesticus* Theocritus on the throne. As noted in the previous volume, Justin and Justinian had used this money to bribe their way to the power. The conspirators against the new rulers included Amantius, Theocritus, Marinus (*PPO* and hero of the year 515), *cubicularius* Misahel/Misael, *cubicularius* Ardaburius and *cubicularius* Andreas Lausiacus. All of these men were Monophysites and therefore also opposed to the Chalcedonian religious policies of the new pair in power. The plotters entered the church of St. Sophia on 16 July 518 with the idea of denouncing the rulers while gathering support for and from the Monophysites. The plan failed and the men were shouted out of the church. Justinian did not hesitate. The men were arrested. Amantius, Theocritus and Andreas were executed on 18 July 518. The property of senator Patricius was confiscated. Misael and Ardaburius were exiled, but strangely enough Marinus escaped punishment altogether. In fact he was promoted, to *PPO* in 519. I would therefore suggest that he had exposed the other plotters after which he had readily converted to the Chalcedonian faith. However, Procopius (*Anek.* 6.26) and some other sources state that there was no real conspiracy at all, but that Justinian had the men killed for no good reason. These sources claim that Amantius was executed only because he had spoken some hasty words against the Patriarch John. It is impossible to be certain which of the versions is correct. It is not impossible that there was a real conspiracy to overthrow the new rulers with the help of the populace, but it is equally possible that Amantius and other Monophysites just wanted to protect their faith with a riot. It is easy to see why even the latter would have been seen as a plot to overthrow Justin.[3] However, in my opinion the fact that Marinus escaped punishment suggests that there was a conspiracy and that he betrayed his fellow conspirators.

In his *Secret History* (*Anek.* 24.15ff.) Procopius mentions that when Justin became the emperor his nephew Justinian opened the positions in the *Scholarii* to those who paid him money, and when there were no longer any open positions left, he added 2,000 new recruits to the force which were then called supernumeraries. He dismissed them when he became the sole emperor. These measures were probably an attempt to weaken the *Scholae* who had opposed the rise of Justin I by recruiting men loyal to Justinian. However, since the exact date for the creation of the 2,000 supernumeraries is not known, it is still possible that the reason for their creation was merely the greed for which Justinian became famous.

The recall of exiles and reconciliation with Vitalian[4]

One of the first measures of the new rulers was the recall of exiles. The idea was that these men would form a group indebted to the new rulers. This also secured Justin and Justinian the support of those who were the friends of the exiles. They included Apion/Appion from the powerful Apion family of Egypt and the senators Diogenianus and Philoxenus. Apion was appointed as the *PPO*, the position of which he held in 518/19 until Marinus became *PPO* in 519. Diogenianus was appointed *MVM per Orientem* and Philoxenus *MVM per Thracias*. Many of the bishops that Anastasius had deposed were similarly allowed to return as was only natural in a situation in which the religious policies were changed.

The most important person to return to Constantinople was the rebel Vitalian. Previous events had proved it was impossible to defeat him so the only option available to the new rulers was to find a way to reconciliation. The rulers also feared the power of Vitalian so they had to find a way to solve the problem. The change to pro-Chalcedonian stance had removed the religious stumbling block, but the new rulers still had to find a way to convince Vitalian to trust them in a situation in which Anastasius and his officers had repeatedly betrayed their oaths to Vitalian. When the invitation to return reached Vitalian, he made it a precondition that Justin and Justinian would make their assurances of good faith with solemn religious formalities together at a meeting in Chalcedon in the Church of St. Ephemia, the place where the Council of Chalcedon had been convened in 451. There Justin, Justinian and Vitalian swore oaths and took the holy sacraments, after which all entered Constantinople together. Vitalian was also appointed *comes et magister utriusque militiae praesentalis*. The most immediate result of this was that the Balkans was now pacified. It also eased the relationship with the Goths of Theoderic the Great. The Pope Hormisdas called Vitalian 'our most glorious brother' in his correspondence with him. This was a great victory for the Chalcedonians. However, Vitalian's branch of the Chalcedonian faith was too strict even for the new rulers, on top of which he was too popular among the soldiers and populace. Because of this it was only a matter of time before the rulers would attempt to kill him. The opportunity came in 520. Vitalian and his closest friends were assassinated in the Palace. The oaths of the emperors had meant nothing. They had planned to kill Vitalian through subterfuge from the start. This was a wise decision worthy of Justinian's fame as a devious plotter, and according to the sources it was Justinian who was behind the plot to kill Vitalian and not his uncle. The elderly and infirm Justin just followed the directions given by his gifted nephew. Justinian was duly appointed as Vitalian's successor in the office of *MVM praesentalis*. Details of the murder are given later in the context of the Persian war.

The circus factions under Justin I and Justinian[5]

Justin and Justinian were supported from the start by both the nobility and the Blue Circus Faction. The Blue Faction was pro-Chalcedonian while the Greens had supported the *Henoticon* of Zeno possibly because Zeno had been so pro-Green. Anastasius, however, had been supporter of the Red Faction even if he promoted a Monophysite interpretation of the *Henoticon*. This means that the Greens were still closer to the views of Anastasius than they were with the views of the new rulers. Both the Reds and Greens were therefore on the losing side. The Blues were naturally overjoyed by the fact that they had played a role in the appointment of Justin. According to John of Nikiu (90.16), Justinian incited them to riots and disorders all over the Empire and in particular in Antioch and Constantinople during the years 519 and 520.

It is not entirely clear what was the purpose of these riots, but in my opinion one may make the educated guess that Justinian got rid of some of his rivals by means of these faction riots. Another possible explanation is that Justinian would have incited men of high position into these criminal actions so that he could then confiscate their property. This could be one of the explanations for Procopius's claim (*Anek.* 6.18ff.) that Justinian confiscated the property of countless thousands by having them murdered. Still another possible explanation could be that the Blues were the ones committing the murders and thefts on behalf of Justinian. Procopius (*Anek.* 11.3ff.) also states that Justinian plundered the homes of the affluent because he spent lavishly on useless buildings and because he gave large gifts to the barbarian rulers. This policy was followed from the start of Justin's reign (e.g. the Church of the Holy Apostles at Constantinople was built by Justinian by June 519) and it was continued under Justinian's sole rule so that it did not take long for the massive war chest left by Anastasius to evaporate into thin air so that Justinian had to come up with new sources of income to be able to maintain his spendthrift habits. As we shall see, it was because of this that Justinian found himself unable to finance his wars. He certainly left beautiful buildings for us later generations to gaze at, but he did this at the expense of his own citizens and at the expense of all those who suffered from his simultaneous imperialistic policies all over the Mediterranean. It is also probable that the persecution of the Monophysites and other heretics was motivated at least partially by financial needs.[6]

When these riots had served their purpose, whatever it was, in 523 the rulers duly put a stop to them by appointing the former *Comes Orientis* Thedototus the Pumpkin as Urban Prefect with the duty of punishing the guilty rioters regardless of their colour. Despite being the Urban Prefect of Constantinople, the position also gave him police chief authority elsewhere. Theodotus acted as instructed. However, he overstepped his mission by being too impartial. He executed Ztikkas, an *illustris* who had supported the Blues, without consulting Justin. This was too much because the man held a high position in society. Consequently Theodotus was sacked and exiled. Once in exile Theodotus hid himself in fear of his life. However, it is also reported that the real reason for his dismissal was that he wanted to investigate Justinian. In my opinion it is very likely that this was the real reason for his dismissal and not the execution of Ztikkas. Theodotus's investigation had now come too close to Justinian, the real power behind the throne and the riots of the Blues. Theodotus's replacement was Theodotus the Fryer (i.e. he who fries/cooks). However, the harsh measures of Thedototus the Pumpkin ended the troubles caused by the Blues so he had still fulfilled the wishes of the rulers. The Blues were not allowed to grow too powerful.

Regardless, all such measures to pacify the factions in the sixth century were doomed to be short-lived in their success. There were other circus faction riots later during the century and Justinian was forced to send orders to all cities to punish severely all rioters regardless of their colour in 527, and this was not to be the last or even the most serious of the troubles that he faced. The rulers Justin and Justinian were forced to forbid Olympian Games in Antioch and other spectacles in other eastern cities and all dancers were exiled to calm the rioting. The only exception to this was Alexandria where the dancers and other entertainers were allowed to continue to practice their trades – in this case these amusements actually kept the populace happy.

Justin's collaborators and councillors[7]

The principal collaborator of Justin was obviously Justinian, the real power behind the throne, but Justin and Justinian had other important collaborators too. At the beginning of their rule the most important of these was Vitalian, but this situation had been forced on them so they got rid of him at the first opportunity in July 520.

The most influential person after Justinian was Proclus, the *Quaestor Sacri Palatii*. He was known as honest, courageous, just and an incorruptible expert on legal matters. Both Procopius and John Lydus (*De Mag.* 3.20) praise him. As we shall see he was the man who subsequently advised against the adoption of Chosroes as son of Justin I in 525. In my opinion this was detrimental to the Empire, as will be made clear later, but there is no doubt that he was incorruptible and just in his actions and stated his mind openly. It is clear that he had an important role in the administration.

Euphraemius (Ephraim) of Amida was another important administrator. He was appointed to the positions of Prefect of Constantinople, *Comes Sacrarum Largitionum* and then *Comes Orientis* in 522 and was in this office at least until 524/5. He administered the east at the time of its greatest natural disasters, the most important of which was the massive earthquake which hit Antioch (his seat) in May 525 in which 300,000 lost their lives. The Patriarch of Antioch lost his life in this disaster and Ephraim was appointed as his successor by the local clergy which was approved by the rulers. He combined in this office his experience as civilian administrator while he provided them religious guidance. This combination was very important for the upkeep of public morale at this time just as was the combination of military experience with the office of bishop or patriarch when this was needed in the chaotic situation. Ephraim was a staunch Chalcedonian whose Patriarchate lasted from 525 until 545 so he was able to persecute Monophysites with great harshness for a long time. Downey called him a warrior bishop while Bury called him a grand inquisitor. It is clear that he implemented the policies of Justin and Justinian with great effectiveness. This also gave the rulers money they sorely needed and it is quite possible that Ephraim was appointed Patriarch for this reason. Ephraim knew who had money and who could be convicted as a Monophysite.

Theodorus Philoxenus Sotericus was another whose career prospered under Justin. According to Vasiliev, on his arrival from exile Philoxenus was appointed *MVM per Thracias*, in 520 he was appointed *Comes Domesticorum*, and in 525 attained the honour of being nominated *consul ordinarius*. This order of appointments is contested by the PLRE3 but due to the problems with the sources and their interpretation the question is open. However, in light of Philoxenus's appointment as consul in 525, it would seem most likely that he held some high posts before that under Justin, so Vasiliev's views find support from this.[8]

Demosthenes was the *PPO* in about 520/21 before which he had been Prefect of Constantinople. He was therefore an important figure in the administration, but his contemporaries criticised him, possibly unfairly, because he refused to grant any privileges without the prior written approval of the emperor. He was later appointed by Justinian in 531 to construct storehouses for the army to support the war effort, so he was certainly considered to be an able administrator at least by Justinian. However, after his death on 10 January 532 Justinian and Theodora repaid this with ingratitude, as was their habit. They forged his will and took his property.[9]

Archelaus served as *PP Orientis* during the last years of Justin's reign in about 524–7, and before this *PP Illyrici*. He appears to have served well because he was subsequently appointed *PP Vacans* to accompany Belisarius during his Vandal campaign in 553–4 after which he was appointed *PP Africae*. This suggests an ability to organize the delivery of supplies to the army and also to collect taxes.[10]

As noted above, Diogenius was one of those allowed to return from exile, after which he was appointed *MVM per Orientem*. He served as a general during the Isaurian revolt, but this unfortunately is all that we know of him. He was evidently no longer in office when the Persian war started so his tenure in office was probably 518–20. His replacement by Hypatius proved a mistake.

Apion, the exile from Egypt, was also an important figure under Justin. He readily abandoned his Monophysite views and adopted Chalcedonian faith to regain his old office, *PP Orientis*. The Empire needed such flexible career men, but he was by then old so his term was short. He was dead by 533.

As noted above, Marinus was one of the able career administrators of the Empire who survived the plot at the beginning of Justin's reign. In my opinion the reason for this was that it was he who betrayed the conspiracy. Marinus also converted into the Chalcedonian faith and was duly rewarded with his old office of *PPO* in 519, but soon after that he was dismissed by Justin. He was an able administrator. He kept a lamp burning together with a pen-and-ink stand by his bedside so that he could write down any ideas that came to him. However, it is still clear that Justin and Justinian saw him as too unreliable.

The other important figures in the court of Justin were the nephews of Anastasius: Probus, Pompeius and Hypatius. They apparently did not possess personal ambitions to become emperors so the emperors trusted them to such an extent that Hypatius served as *MVM per Orientem* in 520–25 and then again in 527–29. However, as noted in the previous volume, he was utterly incompetent as commander. Pompeius was similarly incompetent but we do not know whether he held any military posts under Justin. However, he was *MVM* under Justinian in 528. Their brother Probus held the position of *stratelates* (probably *MVM*) in 526 when he was dispatched to obtain Huns for use in Iberia against the Persians. He was given great sums of money for this. However, he spent most of his time in efforts to convert the Huns when he found out there were Christian missionaries present. The mission was a failure. The nephews must have been convincing speakers to obtain their positions repeatedly even after horrible failures. None of them proved successful in their endeavours.

Justin I and the West[11]

The adoption of Chalcedonian faith and the reconciliation with Vitalian created opportune circumstances for the warming of relations with Theoderic the Great and Pope. Justin exploited the opportunity to the hilt by making a conciliatory gesture towards Theoderic at the very beginning of his reign, appointing Eutharic, husband of Theoderic's daughter Amalasuitha, as his co-consul for 519. This was an unprecedented move. Theoderic's Italy had recognized Constantinople officially as its overlord. All nominations of consuls were made in the East during this period. The Romans had never appointed Goths as consuls so this was a great move by Justin and Justinian. It resulted in a thaw in relations so that the Balkans was secure from threats from the west at the time the Antae made their first major incursion into the Balkans in 520. Justin made a further gesture of goodwill in 522 by allowing Theoderic to nominate both consuls, which was unheard of.

However, from 523 onwards the relationship started to worsen because Justin and Justinian persecuted Arians in the East, and because of the change of rulers in Vandal North Africa. There was a clear contradiction between the treatment of different groups of Christians in Italy and the East. In Italy there was religious tolerance but in the East the co-religionists of the Goths were persecuted alongside the Jews, Manicheans (this term also meant the Monophysites), pagans and other heretics. Theoderic started to entertain probably quite well-founded suspicions concerning the loyalties of his Roman Senate, populace and the Chalcedonian Church. Because of this he arrested Boethius and Symmachus and put them on trial at the Senate. Both were convicted and executed for treason. Procopius called this the only act of injustice committed by Theoderic and most historians have agreed with him, but in the light of subsequent events I would not completely preclude the possibility that there were good reasons to suspect these two individuals because it is clear that Justinian appears to have started to prepare the ground for the reconquest of Italy already during the reign of Justin I. Theoderic sent Pope John to Constantinople in 526 with the mission of asking the Romans to stop the persecution of Arians. He was successful, but when he returned Theoderic received him coldly because John had received a very warm welcome in Constantinople so that his motives were suspect. John died a few days later on 18 May 526, and I would suggest that he was murdered by Theoderic.

The last blow to the relationship between Rome and Constantinople came from the Vandal Kingdom of North Africa. Thrasamund, the Vandal king who had married Theoderic's sister Amalafrida, died on 6 May 523. The widow Amalafrida was accused of conspiring against the new king with the result that she fled to the Moors of Byzacium, but she was captured and imprisoned. The 1,000 Goths that served as bodyguards of Amalafrida were all massacred. Amalafrida was dead by 526/7 and the Goths believed she had been murdered. The new king Hildericus stopped the persecution of Catholics to improve relations with Constantinople. It was now Constantinople and Carthage that formed a new alliance; Hilderic even minted coins bearing the head of Justin I. This alliance formed a grave threat to the Gothic kingdom, because the Goths possessed nothing to oppose the joint naval forces of the Vandals and Romans. On the basis of Theoderic's actions in 526 it seems probable that it was only then that Carthage and Constantinople formed their alliance officially with the purpose of invading Italy in late 525 or early 526. I would suggest that it was because of this that Pope John was held in such suspicion and probably murdered and that it was then because of this that we find Theoderic the Great ordering the building of the 1,000 *dromones* for use against Greeks (Romans) and Africans (Vandals). The fleet was to be assembled in Ravenna on 13 June 526. His Praetorian Prefect Abundantius achieved the impossible by having the fleet ready by the date specified. This was a huge accomplishment and it was also a massive effort by the state. Not only were the ships built, but the fleet was manned with 110,000 mariners, marines and rowers. However, Theoderic died on 15 August 526 so his plan came to naught. It was reported that just four days before he died he had ordered the confiscation of Catholic churches for the Arians on 30 August. This has been suspected by modern historians, but I would not consider it impossible. Theoderic was clearly disillusioned with the Italians, Catholics and Romans by then and the war preparations could have made him confident that he would prevail in the struggle. As we shall see, the Gothic army was also formidable. It consisted of 200,000 men so that it could put to the field about 150,000 horsemen most of whom were fully equipped as cataphracts. Theoderic had good reasons for his confidence.

Theoderic's successor was his grandson Athalaric who was still a minor so his mother Amalasuntha/Amalasuitha held the reins of power. Her position was insecure and as a woman she could not lead armies in person. Therefore she sought peace with the East. She dispatched a letter and envoy to Justin I with offers of peace, which Justin readily accepted. Justin and Justinian had their hands full with the situation in the East and were similarly eager for peace. However, it is clear that Justinian had already formed a plan for the reconquest of Italy by then. It was only postponed to the future; the plan was to attack Italy in conjunction with the Vandal King Hilderic.

The Antae and Slavs make their first appearance in the sources as a major threat to the Roman Balkans during the reign of Justin I. We possess very few details of this beyond the Spartan comment by Procopius (*Wars* 7.40.5–6) that Germanus inflicted so crushing a defeat on the Antae who had crossed the Danube during the reign of Justin that it secured him everlasting fame among both the Roman soldiers and among the Antae and Slavs. We also know that Justin appointed Germanus as *MVM per Thracias*, but it is not known when so we can only state that he achieved his victory some time between 518 and 527. My own suggestion is that it is likelier that it took place early in the reign rather than late because the Balkans would still have been in a state of chaos in the immediate aftermath of the ending of the revolt of Vitalian. We also know that there were both Slavs and Antae in this region and that they were recruited into the Roman armies as they appear in the Roman armies during the campaigns of Belisarius, for which see the text below.

The Persian War by proxy in 518–527[12]

The Proxy War during the Armistice in 518–25
There was no official peace between the Roman and Persian empires, because the war of 502–6 between the emperor Anastasius and Persian *Shahanshah* Cabades/Kavadh had ended only in an armistice. However, the war had been so costly that neither side was willing to renew it anytime soon. The Persians had demanded that the new ruler, Justin I, would continue to pay the upkeep of the Persian garrison at the Caspian Gate, which Justin refused to do. As a result Cabades attempted to put pressure on Justin to resume payments by fighting by proxy, so he unleashed the Lakhmids against the Romans in about 519/20. This changed nothing. On top of this, Cabades suffered a significant loss of prestige. Much akin to the previous agreement concerning Armenia when it was still an independent kingdom, the Romans and Persians had some sort of official agreement concerning the status of Lazica/Colchis. The area was a Roman protectorate, but at this time its rulers were appointed by the Persian *Shahanshah* possibly because the 'feudal lord' of the king of Lazica was the king of Iberia and the latter was a Persian protectorate at this time. Ztathios, who was to succeed his recently deceased father as king of Lazica, did not want to adopt the Zoroastrian faith in order to be crowned by Cabades so he sought to be crowned by Justin I. Justin was happy to comply and Ztathios travelled to Constantinople where he was baptized and crowned. It is possible that Ztathios was already a Christian like most Lazicans and Iberians were at this time, but this gesture

was still important because it connected him with the Roman emperor. Cabades faced Mazdakite revolt and was therefore unable to do anything else but complain.[13]

When Cabades had launched the abovementioned Lakhmid raid Justin was by no means in the mood to fight a full-scale war against the Persians. It was in 520 that he was finally in a position to kill Vitalian. The *magister militum praesentalis* Vitalian had been made consul for this year and according to the preserved Slavic version of Malalas he was then killed after having presided over a race in the hippodrome when he had returned to the palace. His treasurer or bodyguard (depends on reading) Celerianus was killed with him. Vasiliev suggests that it is possible that it was the support Vitalian got from both the Greens and Blues that made it compulsory for Justin and Justinian to have him killed as soon as possible after the races. This is possible, but it is equally possible that the murder had nothing to do with the races but had been planned all along. According to the version preserved by Zachariah (8.2), Vitalian was bathing in the city when Justin and Justinian commanded him to come to a banquet. When he and Paul the Notary, and Celer his domestic (bodyguard), went as commanded they were ambushed and killed, presumably in the palace. In my opinion this is probably the way the murder was committed.[14] We do not know why it took so long for Justin to get rid of Vitalian, but my educated guess is that it took that long for Justin and Justinian to lull Vitalian into a false sense of security so that he was not accompanied by large numbers of bodyguards. The appointment as consul must have been the key thing that fooled Vitalian.

The murder of Vitalian at this time must have had repercussions which are not mentioned by the sources. His friends in the military must have been angry over his betrayal and assassination. This in turn would have made it unwise for Justin to fight a full-scale war against Persia, and it is in light of this that we should see his attempts to conclude a true peace with Persia. The Persians in their turn were not seeking peace, but rather a war. The ruler of Persia needed money and the only source of extra income was Rome, but the Romans were too proud to pay even the modest sums the Persians demanded.

The fact that Cabades lacked the resources to punish the Romans for the Lazica incident meant that he sought allies from the Huns. His plan was clearly to conduct a two-pronged invasion of Roman territory in about 520/21. The Lakhmids would invade Roman territory again to draw resources away from the main invasion conducted by Cabades and his allies the Huns. Cabades managed to bribe a king called Zilgibi with 20,000 horsemen to join him. This Zilbigi had previously been paid to join the Romans and when Justin learnt of this from his spies he was exceedingly angry. It is possible that this was one of the instances in which Justinian had bribed the Huns with money as he was wont to do also under Justin. Consequently he devised a stratagem which took care of both the threat of war and the treachery at the same time. He sent an envoy to Cabades proposing peace while also incidentally informing Cabades that Zilgibi had taken money from the Romans to betray the Persians in the middle of a battle. Cabades asked Zilgibi if he had received money from the Romans to fight against the Persians. Zilgibi confessed, so Cabades believed that Justin's message was real. He put Zilgibi to death and destroyed many of the Huns with a night attack. The rest of the Huns fled back to their country. Cabades was now convinced that Justin's suggestion of peace had been made in good faith and informed Justin of this through the envoy Labroios so that the negotiations regarding the terms could now start.[15]

The negotiations appear to have brought results because the sources suggest that Rome and Persia concluded another truce in 520 which included the Lakhmids who released two captured Roman generals as part of the treaty, but this was to be only a temporary solution because the Romans did not continue to pay the money for the upkeep of the garrison in the Caucasus which the Persians thought of as their right.[16]

However, the events took a new turn in about 524/5. Cabades wanted to secure the position of his chosen successor and son Chosroes against Chosroes' elder brother. He attempted to achieve this by proposing an alliance with the Romans in the same manner as had taken place between Arcadius and Yazdgerd I. It was then that Yazgerd I had adopted Arcadius's son Theodosius II as his son so he had sent his own representatives to Constantinople to coordinate the affairs on both sides. Arcadius's idea had been to use the threat of Persian invasion to keep the Roman generals from usurping power and it worked because Yazdgerd was a man true to his word – when Arcadius died Yazdgerd threatened the Romans with war if they overthrew the underage Theodosius. For this see *Military History of Late Rome Volume 3* (395–425). Consequently Cabades proposed that Justin adopt Chosroes. Justin and Justinian were initially enthusiastic about the prospect of *détente*, but unfortunately in the atmosphere of mutual mistrust the legalistic approach taken by *quaestor* Proclus/Proculus won the day. Proclus warned that the adoption would make Chosroes the legal successor of Justin. Therefore, Proclus suggested that they would resort to the use of the so-called adoption 'by arms' that the Romans had used with barbarian kings. Justin and Justinian agreed. It is quite easy to understand that Justinian, a man who thought in legalistic manner, saw the proposed adoption as a threat because he too was only an adopted son of Justin.[17]

Justin dispatched the *MVM per Orientem patricius* Hypatius and *patricius* Rufinus to meet the Persian envoys *Adrastadaran Salanes* (*Arteshtaran-salar*) Seoses and *Magister Offiorum* (*Hazarpet*) Mebodes on the border while Chosroes waited at a distance of two days' travel on the other side of the Tigris in readiness to travel to Constantinople for the adoption ceremony. But then things unravelled. Seoses brought up the claim that the Romans had overtaken Lazica, which from time immemorial had belonged to Persia. This the Romans found insulting and without any basis in truth. Then the Romans proposed 'barbarian adoption' by arms, which the Persians considered insulting, so the negotiations broke down. When Chosroes learnt of this he vowed to punish the Romans for their insult. The fact that the Mebodes and other Persians then accused Seosos of having caused the failure with his referral to Lazica suggests strongly that the Persians were earnestly seeking to accomplish the same kind of agreement as had existed between Arcadius and Yazdgerd and that the legalistic approach of the Romans had destroyed a once-in-a-lifetime opportunity for peace. Cabades convened the Royal Council to judge Seoses. The result was clear from the start because Seoses had angered most of the members through his arrogant and incorruptible behaviour, so he was condemned to death despite the fact that Cabades owed his life and throne to this man. According to Procopius, he was the last man to hold the office of *Adrastadaran Salanes*, which suggests that it was actually Cabades who was also responsible for the abolition of the office of *Iran-Spahbed* and the division of the Persian Empire under four regional *spahbeds*, which reform is usually credited to his son Chosroes. However, there are possible ways to reconcile the different versions which are that the office was merely left unfilled at this time and the actual reform took place later under Chosroes, or that Chosroes was responsible for the reform during the lifetime of his father, or that the offices of *Arteshtaran-salar* and *Iran-Spahbed* were abolished at different times.[18]

The only result of this attempt at alliance was therefore the sowing of further seeds of distrust between the rulers. This was particularly important because Chosroes succeeded his father on the throne. It is clear that the legal training that most members of the Roman upper class had received made them blind to the demands of *realpolitik* – and this concerns in particular Justinian because he was clearly the man who thought in terms of legal practice in this case. It is not a coincidence that he was the man who became famous as a codifier of Roman laws, the results of which were published only a few years later as *Codex Iustinianus*. Justinian and all those who thought in legalistic terms failed to understand that in international politics the maintaining of agreements and laws was (and is) meaningless unless it is in the interest of the state. The Romans were under no compulsion to follow the agreement even after the signing and were under no compulsion to accept Chosroes as their ruler even if he had an equal legal right to do so. The Persians would have needed to defeat the Roman armies first and the legal claim was not sufficient as a propaganda tool in a situation in which everyone understood Chosroes as Persian. The end result of this was not the alliance between the empires as envisaged by Cabades and Chosroes but a situation in which the Romans were forced to seek to improve their relative position vis-à-vis Persia for the now inevitable conflict. Had the Romans accepted the proposal, they could have improved their relationship with the Persians without any compulsion to fulfil their part of the agreement at some point in the future. This would have given them far longer to improve their defences in the east than was the case now.

Roman defences along the eastern border were in a state of disarray. The long peace and the clauses in peace and armistice agreements had prevented the building of fortifications during the fifth century and then again after 506 with the result that the Romans now needed to rebuild their fortifications fast before the Persians invaded. The aim of these treaties had been to make both empires mutually vulnerable to invasion, but the Anastasian war in 502–6 had demonstrated the importance of fortifications for defence. The idea behind the open borders without fortifications was similar to the modern concept of mutually assured destruction (MAD). Anastasius realized after the Persian invasion that this was not really wise from the Roman point of view and built Dara as a forward defensive and offensive base and started the refortification project, which was still unfinished at the time of the negotiations.[19]

The proxy war intensifies in 525–7: The flames of war are kindled

The Romans apparently interpreted the suggested alliance as a sign of weakness so they started a proxy war either during the negotiations to put pressure on the Persians or immediately after the negotiations had broken down.

At the turn of the sixth century Himyar (Yemen) was a client kingdom of Aksum (Ethiopia). This situation persisted until Ma'dīkarib Ya'fur died in about June 521/June 522 and was succeeded by Joseph (also known as Yūsuf As'ar Yath'ar/Masrūq/Zur'a dhū Nuwās/Dhu Nuwas/Dounaas). He was a Jew by religion and it did not take long for him to rebel against his Christian overlord, the Aksumite king Ella Asheba (also known as Hellesthaeus/Maʿdikarib Yaʿfur/Kālēb Ella Aṣbəḥa). After massacring the Ethiopian garrison, Joseph launched a massive persecution of Christians in 522–3. The Alexandrian Church authorities duly informed Justin of what had happened. Justin decided to act but left the actual conduct of the war in Ethiopian hands. In about 525 he dispatched forty-two ships to support the Christian Ethiopian ruler Ella Asheba against the Himyarite/Yemenite king Joseph. Joseph in his turn had allied himself with the Persians and Lakhmids (Saracen allies of Persia). The joint campaign proved to be a success and Himyar once again became a client kingdom of Aksum. The Jews were systemically slaughtered in revenge for their previous activities. Asheba installed a new ruler called Esimiphaeus (Sumūuyafaʿ Ashwaʿ) on the throne, left a garrison of Ethiopian soldiers and then returned to Ethiopia. The Romans used their allies the Kindite Saracens for the same purpose as they had used the Ethiopians. They sent them against the Lakhmids, the allies of Persia, and conquered their capital Hira also in 525.[20]

The Roman response to all troubles in 526–7 was hampered by natural disasters. The most destructive of these was the Antioch earthquake of 525 which levelled much of the city and killed 300,000. The aftershock continued for eighteen months during which Seleukeia (the harbour of Antioch) and Daphne suffered serious damage. Justin sent help to the afflicted cities immediately and Justinian and Theodora did the same next year once Justinian had been appointed co-ruler. The damage done was undoubtedly considerable as Seleukeia and Antioch were important logistical bases for the Roman armies in the east.[21]

The Persian response was to wage war also by proxy. They allowed their client Lakhmid king Alamoundaros (al-Mundhir) to launch a series of raids into Roman Arzanene and areas close to Nisibis in late 525 and/or 526. It is clear that the Romans had gauged correctly that the position of Cabades and Chosroes was not strong, but following events prove that they had made the serious miscalculation of underestimating Persian resolve and military power. It is probable that the very successful defence of Roman territory during the Anastasian War contributed to this.[22]

By this time Cabades's early foolish support of the Mazdakites as a counter-force against the nobility and magi had become its mirror image. Now Cabades tried to secure his position against the Mazdakites by following a strict Zoroastrian religious policy. This brought him the support of the Persian and Parthian nobility, but it alienated the Christian Persarmenians, Iberians and Lazi. The Nestorian Church of Persia was an exception to this, but they did not possess adequate support in those areas or in the areas controlled by the Romans. It is therefore not surprising that the example of the Lazi was followed by the Iberian king Gourgenes in 525/6.[23] At about the same time, the Romans secured their land communications with Lazica and Iberia by conquering the restless Tzanica/Tzania. Its lightly-equipped small forces were no match for the determined Romans. Justin promised to help Gourgenes, but he was not yet ready to do this openly because he wanted to avoid full scale war. So Justin sought to protect Iberia by recruiting enough Huns for this. He dispatched the nephew of Anastasius Probus to Bosporus in 526, but he failed in his mission. After this, Justin dispatched Peter with those Huns that had offered their services to Iberia in about 526/7. It is probable that this is also one of the instances in which Justinian had bought the services of the Huns. This was practically an open declaration of war and Cabades' response was to dispatch a large army under Boes to Iberia also in about 526/7.[24]

Justin I the Emperor

Justin I died of natural causes on 1 August 527 and was succeeded by Justinian I, who had been made co-ruler on 1 April 527. The Persian war had already started and the details are therefore provided in Chapter Five. Procopius's judgment of the reign of Justin (*Anek.* 6.18ff.) is that he did not do his subjects any harm but he did not do any good for them either. However, he levelled against Justin one important accusation which was that he allowed his avaricious nephew Justinian to rule in his name and cause a plethora of trouble and problems. Procopius claims that Justinian was already murdering people under Justin with the slightest of excuses to get their money. This seems an unjust assessment because at the time of Justin's death Justinian had not yet launched his most disastrous campaigns of money hoarding. It would be fairer to say that Justin was not a good emperor but neither was he bad. He does have some very important achievements to his record. He pacified the empire at the beginning of his reign by concluding peace with Vitalian and then secured the situation further by having him murdered with the help of Justinian. Justin also managed to create the right circumstances for the beginning of the reconquests of the west under Justinian. It is of course difficult to know what Justin's input in these was because Justinian was the de facto ruler during his lifetime – in my opinion there is no reason to challenge this view because it is so clearly stated, for example by Procopius. One thing which is certain: Justin deserves full credit for having named Justinian as his successor during his lifetime; it is actually this that Procopius criticizes because he disliked Justinian intensely.

Chapter Four

Justinian and Theodora:
The Years of Triumph 527–40

Medallion of Justinian
source: Diehl

The Policies of Justinian and His Collaborators[1]

After the death of Justin, Justinian set out to reform all imperial policies in a manner that he had not yet been able to do while Justin was still alive. These reforms were a reflection of Justinian's own personality, but those around him, his collaborators, heavily influenced the outcome. Jones (270) has aptly stated that Justinian had two major passions which overrode all other considerations. He was a Roman to the core who boasted that Latin was his native language. He was well versed in Roman history and an admirer of Roman law, reviving antique titles like *praetor* and *quaestor* and codifying the law. His second passion was Chalcedonian Christianity and he sought to crush all forms of heresy and paganism. Justinian thought he would gain the favour of God for his wars and endeavours if he could secure the orthodoxy of his subjects. It has also been claimed that Justinian intended to reconquer the West and because of this he continually sought to find a way to end the Persian war that started in 527. This is probable, but it is also possible that he formulated this plan only after he realized that there was an opportunity after events that took place in the Vandal realm.

Justinian and Theodora[2]

Justinian's nature often bordered on the ascetic workaholic. He was deeply religious and dutiful, and was deeply in love with his wife Theodora who was de facto his co-ruler. Procopius calls Justinian a hypocrite who feigned ideas and emotions, and a man who was disloyal to his friends and hated his enemies without restraint. As noted by Tate, there is no evidence that Justinian was any more hypocritical than any of his predecessors. Hypocritical lying is part of the repertoire that all leaders have always used to further their goals. Justinian rewarded men for their ability except when they had not respected his orders or when their loyalty was suspected for some reason. He was also not cruel towards those who had acted against him, as the cases of John the Cappadocian, Belisarius, and Artabanes the Arsacid show.

Justinian sought to strengthen his powers by multiple means but did this apparently under the impression that this was beneficial to his subjects. One part of this was the aggrandizement of his position through titles and ceremonies. He was the first emperor to adopt the title *nomos empsychos* (a living law) to stress that his word was the law and his right to rule was divine. He was the first emperor to adopt the title *Philochristos* (friend of Christ). He called himself *Restitutor* (restorer) because he considered himself the restorer of the Roman Empire. This was not a new title, and in fact its use was justified. The idea was to propagate his own special position among the emperors. Justinian required that everyone call him *Kurios/Dominus* (Master). This title was also not new but the obligation to include it in an address was. Ceremonial changes in the presence of the emperor and empress were also meant to stress their superior position vis-à-vis the commoners and foreign envoys who approached them. That Theodora also received ceremony appropriate to an emperor was one of the innovations which reflected Justinian's love for his wife and her exalted position within the Empire. Justinian harnessed imperial propaganda in an unprecedented manner. He distributed his own image throughout the Empire. He had his name inscribed everywhere in official statements, and in churches in the capital and provinces. The image of Justinian in coins, frescoes, monuments, and gates of the cities was made to look like that of Christ. Liturgical church chants made allusions to him and to his position in Christian cosmology. For example in one of the church chants the entry of Justinian to Constantinople was likened to the entry of Christ into Jerusalem, and he was the first after Adam to get entry into heaven at the day of redemption.[3] Justinian had risen to power from a humble background and the adoption of these grandiose titles and ceremonies can be seen as a reflection of this.

Senators were forced to bow their heads to the ground in Theodora's presence and show the same humility to her as they did the emperor. To Procopius this was demeaning. In contrast to all precedents, she was not only the power behind the throne but a co-ruler in practice and did not hesitate to use her powers even against senators. She had her own servants, soldiers and even her own cells in the palace for those she decided to imprison. It is clear that Theodora was behind many of the decisions and laws that Justinian adopted during his reign. It was Theodora who intervened on behalf of prostitutes, women and Monophysites. It was the last-mentioned which was the most important. The couple, Justinian the upholder of the Chalcedon faith and Theodora the Monophysite, maintained at least a modicum of peace between these two Christian groupings as long as the latter was alive. And it is well known that Justinian owed his life and throne to Theodora after the famous Nika revolt in 532. She was a formidable person.

The collaborators of Justinian and Theodora[4]

Justinian was lucky to have a series of able administrators, lawyers and soldiers to advise him and to implement his policies. This was not only luck: it is clear that Justinian had promoted the careers of these men. This in turn means that he had an eye for talent. Most came from humble origins, which proves that the role of Justinian in the promotion of their careers was pivotal. Most remained loyal to their employer for this reason, but there were some notable exceptions as we shall see.

The most important of Justinian's collaborators was Germanus, his cousin. Germanus had strengthened his position by marrying Passara who belonged to the ancient House of the Anicii. The Anicii were one of the most powerful families in the Mediterranean and Germanus was immensely rich. He had already served as *magister militum per Thracias* between 518 and 527 in the course of which he had gained great fame as a general (see above). In 536 he was *magister militum praesentalis* with Patrician rank. It is unfortunate that we do not know what Germanus's position was in the years 527–536. In my opinion it is probable that Justinian had not given Germanus any important military commands in 527–532 because he and Theodora both had feared his fame and military talents, so Germanus's rise to *magister militum praesentalis* would have taken place only after the Nika revolt in 532 which would have demonstrated Germanus's loyalty to Justinian. Had he been given important military commands during that period we would surely have heard of it. This exalted position proves that Germanus was one of the trusted men of Justinian despite the fact that Theodora detested him. Theodora saw Germanus and his children Justin (Iustinus) and Justinian (Iustinianus) as possible successors of Justinian and therefore as potential threats to her. The third child of Germanus, his daughter Justina, might also marry a man of influence. These factors meant that Justinian was reluctant to give Germanus important military commands outside the capital before the death of Theodora in 548. After her death he was considered the most influential of Justinian's relatives.

The codification of laws, which was one of the pet projects of Justinian, owed a lot to Tribonian (Tribonianus). He was a legal expert famous for his learning, and contributed to all of the codification projects of Justinian's reign. According to Procopius, he had one major vice: avarice.

The second of the major characters of Justinian's reign was John the Cappadocian. He lacked a proper education, but possessed great skill in finding sources of revenue. It was this that caught the attention of Justinian while John served as *scriniarius* in the staff of Justinian himself when he had served as *magister militum*. Justinian duly promoted John's career, enrolled him among the senators and then nominated him as Praetorian Prefect of the East in February 531. His skill at collecting revenue for Justinian together with his avarice earned him, and Tribonian too, the hatred of the upper classes and provincials. This manifested itself during the Nika revolt so that he and Tribonian were both sacked from office on 14 January 532. John however was immediately reinstated. John was also detested by Theodora, but thanks to his financial talents Justinian relied on him.

There were many other loyal and skilled administrators besides those already mentioned. Hermogenes was originally from Scythia and secretary of Vitalian, but this did not hinder his career because Justinian recognized his talents and nominated him *Mag. Off.* twice in 529–533 and then again in 535 when he was nominated Patrician before his death on 15 April 535. He was to play a very important role in the Persian war. Patrician Basilides served in many posts. He was *PPO* in 528 and a member of the commission compiling the law. He was *PPI* from 529 until 531, then deputy *Mag.Off.* in 531/2, *Quaestor* in 534/5 and *Mag. Off.* from 536 until 539. The other important administrators of Justinian during his early reign were the Count of the Largesse Constantinus (528–33) and Strategius (533–37) and *Comes rei Privatae* Florus (531–36).

The most important generals of the early part of Justinian's reign were Hypatius, Belisarius and Sittas. The first-mentioned was the incompetent nephew of Anastasius who was soon enough replaced by the latter talented commanders. Belisarius and Sittas both began their careers in the private bodyguard of Justinian who recognized their talent early on and promoted their careers. Sittas secured his position further by marrying Komito, Theodora's elder sister, while Belisarius secured his by marrying Antonina, Theodora's closest friend and confidant. In the case of Belisarius, however, this was not mere political calculation because he was truly in love with Antonina, sometimes to his own detriment as we shall see. Antonina was also to play an important role on her own right in the wars both as wife of Belisarius and as a henchwoman of the empress Theodora. Other important commanders of the early reign included the barbarian Mundus and the Armenian eunuchs Solomon and Narses. Mundus had originally served as a mercenary leader under the Goths, but he changed allegiance in 529. Solomon was promoted to high command from the household of Belisarius while Narses was promoted to military commands from the imperial bedchamber thanks to the talent he had shown for military matters. He was a confidant of the emperor. All showed great military talent like many other commanders not mentioned here. Justinian had an eye for talent and did not hesitate to promote any talented person who caught his eye.

The codification of laws[5]

Justinian set up a ten-man commission headed by former *Quaestor* John to produce a new law code on 14 February 528. The commission went through the previous three collections (Gregorian, Hermogenian and Theodosian codes) and the so-called novels produced since the *Theodosian Code* and systematized and simplified them. The work was done with great efficiency so that the result of their labours was published as the *Codex Iustinianus* on 7 April 529. After this Justinian set up a new commission comprising sixteen legal experts headed by Tribonian to codify and shorten the works of the Roman jurists on 15 December 530. They went through 2,000 books to produce an end result known as the *Digest*, published on 16 December 533. In addition, Justinian had commissioned Tribonian to produce, together with the leading academic lawyers of Constantinople and Beirut, a short textbook for the use of law students. The aim was to produce civil servants for the needs of the administration. The end result was published as the *Institutes* on 21 November 533. It was the final, definitive form of Roman law, which undoubtedly helped to keep the populace at large satisfied and less prone to oppose the imperial authorities, so it can be claimed to have had positive consequences also for the security of the Empire.

Justinian did not stop his legal work at this point but continued to produce new novels/legislation some of which simplified and updated the already published *Codex* with the result that a new second edition of the *Codex Iustinianus* was published on 16 November 534, which is the one we possess today. However, since legislative work is always a never ending process, Justinian continued to issue new novels, either to alter or clarify the existing law while also issuing novels on issues that he wanted to reform or change. The man who advised him in all of these matters was Tribonian, *Quaestor* from 529 until 532, temporarily removed from office as a result of the Nika revolt, appointed *Magister Officiorum* in 533 and reappointed *Quaestor* in 535 in which position he remained until his death in 542. He is reputed to have been a pagan and atheist, but as noted in the PLRE3 it is unlikely that he could have been so too openly because his predecessor Thomas had been sacked for being a pagan.

The guiding principle behind the legislative work of Justinian was his concept of what a dutiful Christian ruler should do. However, one can detect three broad areas on which he paid particular attention. Firstly, he thought that the Roman Empire could prosper only if proper Orthodox forms of Christianity were followed by all and that the Orthodox clergy and monks would perform the correct religious rites. Secondly, he also sought to make the administration of the provinces more efficient and less corrupt with a series of novels which he issued whenever he thought necessary. Thirdly, he changed the organization of the provinces, creating new ones and amalgamating civilian and military powers in some. All of these questions are dealt in their proper places and are not discussed here. A fourth area of interest was the rights of women in which Theodora's influence was apparently paramount. Justinian banned brothels from the capital while Theodora transformed a palace on the Asian shore into a convent for former prostitutes, some of them against their will. She also bought freedom for a number of girls who had been forced into prostitution. This concern is not surprising in light of her past as a prostitute, and in light of the fact that the brothels could house girls less than 10 years old. Justinian also legislated about marriage, under which circumstances couples could divorce, and about the status of concubines. It is impossible to say whether any of this was important for the security of the Empire, but at least it made the conservative elements within Christian community happier with their rulers.

Gaining God's Favour[6]

Justinian sought to gain God's favour by three means: 1) He built churches and monasteries on a massive scale; 2) He legislated against pagans and heretics; 3) He persecuted and legislated against male homosexuals.

The first mentioned was obviously very costly and one may question the sanity of Justinian in a situation in which he with the help of John the Cappadocian economized on the upkeep of the armed forces and intelligence services; but then again Justinian thought he could not win wars unless God was on his side.

Justinian began to act against the pagans and heretics immediately after he became emperor in April 527 and he and his co-ruler Justin I launched a persecution of Manicheans. This was also a safety measure because the Manicheans were considered to be fifth-columnists in Persian service.[7] When the Montanists of Phrygia faced persecution a little bit later they chose to commit mass suicide. Justinian issued a law against the Samaritans some time between 527 and 529 which ordered their synagogues destroyed. This resulted in the uprising of the Samaritans in the summer of 529. See later. He also legislated against the Jews, but not with the same severity as against the Samaritans and pagans. He only made their position worse. However, when North Africa was conquered, Justinian ordered the synagogues of Africa to be converted into churches, with the result that the Jews of Italy sided with the Goths. Justinian launched a great persecution of the pagans/Hellenes in 529, forbidding them from holding state office. All pagans were ordered to be baptised or be exiled. He also purged the Constantinopolitan aristocracy and several important persons were executed. Other heretics had a grace of three months to embrace the Orthodox faith. The persecution of the pagans and atheists had the consequence that a number of philosophers fled to Persia when they heard that Chosroes had become ruler in 531. However, they came soon to regret their hasty decision and were allowed to return home in 532 when peace was concluded.

Justinian adopted an entirely new approach on the southern border region of Egypt some time in 530–7 or 541–2. The *PLRE3* suggests 535 as the likeliest year. The Christian rulers before him had accepted that the Blemmyes and Nobades (Nubians) would be allowed to maintain a pagan temple for Isis on the island of Philae together with permission to take the image of Isis in a boat for a journey to the land of the Blemmyes. Justinian ordered the local *Dux Thebaidis* Narses, brother of Aratius, to put an end to this, which he duly did. Because of this the conversion of the Blemmyes and Nobadae became part of imperial policy, which in fact succeeded in this case. Eventually this conversion secured these areas even better than the previous arrangement so that not all instances of persecution can be considered a waste of resources.

The Monophysites were a special case because Theodora was a Monophysite. Justinian took no action against the Monophysite Patriarch of Antioch Timothy IV. Instead he tried to find common ground between the Chalcedonians and moderate Monophysites of the school of Severus of Antioch. He organized a discussion of six Chalcedonians and six Severans in 532. They found a compromise formula next year which Pope John II approved in 534. In 535 Timothy IV died and was succeeded by Theodosius who was a Severan Monophysite. He was then thrown out by extremists with the result that Narses was sent with 6,000 men to reinstate him. It was then that the Patriarch of Constantinople, Epiphanius, died and was succeeded by Anthimus who had been one of the six Chalcedonians behind the compromise formula. At this point things appeared to go in the right direction, but then in 536 the new Pope, Agapetus, arrived as envoy of Theodahad. Agapetus was one of those fanatic churchmen who made compromise impossible. He rallied the Chalcedonians and convinced Justinian to depose Anthimus and replace him with Menas. Theodora gave Anthimus and other Monophysites a place of refuge inside her palace. Agapetus died a few weeks later. My personal view is that his death is suspicious. It was certainly very convenient for Theodora as we shall see. Menas went on to hold a council in May 536 which anathematised Severus of Antioch and his doctrine. The Monophysites were now subjected to persecution in Syria, which Justinian extended to the capital.

The defeat of the Monophysite cause was not welcome to Theodora who apparently formed a plot of her own without the approval of her husband. She wanted to make *nuncio* Vigilius successor of the deceased Agapetus, and Vigilius in his turn promised to

Theodora to repudiate the Council of Chalcedon. Theodora gave him 200 lbs of gold and letters to Belisarius and Antonina. However, by the time Vigilius reached Italy it was already too late because the Gothic king Thodahad had already contributed to the nomination of Silverius as new Pope in June 536. Theodora sent a letter to Silverius in which he demanded the restoration of Anthimus. When this request was denied, Theodora decided to get rid of Silverius and sent a letter to Antonina with instructions to remove him from office and replace him with Vigilius. Antonina duly fabricated a treasonous letter or used a perfectly innocent letter of Silverius to the Gothic king as proof of treason. Belisarius then arrested Silverius and exiled him to Lycia, and Vigilius was ordained as the new Pope on 29 March 537. Subsequently, Justinian appears to have given his permission for the return of Silverius to Italy, which only led to his death when Belisarius and Antonina handed him over to Pope Vigilius. Vigilius, it turned out, had lied to Theodora and did nothing he had promised, but his representative silver-tongued *nuncio* Pelagius managed to pacify both Theodora and Justinian.

Justinian ordered Theodosius, the Patriarch of Alexandria, to accept the Chalcedonian faith, but when he refused to do so, Justinian replaced him with Paul in 538. Paul was given full powers to use the military in his persecution of the Monophysites, but his actions were so brutal that Justinian replaced him with another Chalcedonian, Zoilus, in 542. In the opinion of a firm Chalcedonian bigot all of the above was justifiable, but in my opinion this was a misuse of military force when military forces could have been used against real enemies. The above makes it clear that one should not overestimate the influence of Theodora on Justinian. It is clear that Justinian's religious views overrode his love of his wife in this case.

Justinian was also merciless towards male homosexuals, summoning to Constantinople bishops who were accused of being homosexuals in 528. Victor the City Prefect punished them. Isaiah was tortured and exiled and Alexander was castrated and paraded around the city on a litter as a warning. Justinian ordered that after this all homosexuals were to be castrated, and many were arrested and castrated. The *Institutes* (4.18.4) legislated against homosexuality and the novel (77.1) published in 535 stated the reason why Justinian acted with such brutality against gays. According to this novel, the *Scriptures* stated that homosexuals brought the wrath of God to cities where they lived bringing famine, earthquakes and disease. Thenceforth male homosexuals were to be executed; the laws had nothing to say about lesbians.

Expenses and Taxation[8]

When a series of terrible earthquakes in 527–9 caused widespread damage in the Oriens, Justinian was prepared to help them in every way he could. The affected cities included Antioch in 527, Pompeiopolis in Moesia 1 in 528, Antioch again on 29 November 528, Laodicea in Syria on 2 January 529, Amasea, Myra, and a number of other places. This required money.

Justinian's massive building projects detailed by Procopius also required money. They included the building of churches, monasteries and fortifications. From the point of view of defence the building, rebuilding and restoration of fortifications in the Balkans and East were the most important projects. They also benefited the populace and can be considered money well spent. However, as a deeply religious person Justinian thought the building and repairing of churches and monasteries just as important for the defence of the Empire. This can be criticised, because at the same time Justinian failed to provide salaries for the soldiers, as we shall see.

The wars that Justinian waged and then the wars of reconquest also required money and lots of it, and Justinian needed to reform the finances and the way in which money was gathered. The man who did this for Justinian was John the Cappadocian. John began fleecing the populace in 531 while the Persian war continued which, as mentioned above, was one of the reasons for the Nika revolt in January 532. After his dismissal from office he was reinstated, and proceeded to launch another series of measures to collect money by whatever means possible while making massive cuts in spending on the armed forces, intelligence gathering and administration to the detriment of Roman defensive capability in the east, as we shall see.

Chapter Five

The Persian War Nobody Wanted under Justinian in 527–32

Important Places of the Persian War 527-532
drawn after Katarzyna Maksymiuk with some changes based on Barrington Atlas and Lillington-Martin (paper presented in 2015 available online at academia.edu)

100km

Satala

Pharangium

Bolum

Theodosiopolis

Armenia

Citharizon

Persarmenia

Sophene

Martyropolis

Arzanene

Samosata

Amida

Attachas

Dara

Cilicia

Edessa

Cyrrhestica

Minduos

Nisibis

Hierapolis

Oshroene

Thebetha?

Thannuris

Litarbe

Antioch

Callinicum

Singara

Gabbulon

Thebetha?

Chalcis

Soura

Mesopotamia

Apamea

Euphratesia

Circesium

Emesa

Euphrates

Tigris

The beginning of the Persian War in 527

The Persian war started under Justin I in early 527, but since Justinian was in practice already a co-ruler, it is clear that he bears the greatest responsibility for this. The Romans tried to protect Iberia and therefore sent Peter with his Huns to Lazica to help Gurgenes against the Persians. The services of the Huns had probably been bought by Justinian. The Romans also dispatched Belisarius and Sittas (*bucellarii* of the general Justinian) to make raids into Persarmenia before 1 April 527, the date when Justinian was officially made co-ruler. The naming of Justinian signalled to Romans and Persians that negotiations were over and Justinian would be the only adopted son. The first raid conducted by Belisarius and Sittas was a great success, but the second ended in defeat. Two Persarmenian generals managed to intercept the Roman raiders and defeated them in battle. The diversionary operation therefore failed with the result that Gourgenes, Peter and the Romans were forced to flee to Lazica. There the combined Roman, Iberian and Lazi forces proved strong enough to defend the Lazican border against the pursuing Persians. The two superpowers were now in open conflict. The Persian attack against Lazica frightened both Justin and Justinian because there now existed the possibility that the Persians could gain control of the Lazican coast and conduct naval operations in the Black Sea against Constantinople.[1]

In 527 war preparations were in full swing. Soon after his appointment on 1 April 527, the new emperor Justinian appointed a new *Comes Orientis*, Patrikios, with instructions to rebuild Palmyra to serve as a protective bulwark for Jerusalem. He stationed there a *numerus* of soldiers (the *comitatenses*) with the *limitanei* (frontier forces) and ordered the *Dux* of Emesa to protect Roman territories and Jerusalem.[2]

Despite the above, Justin and Justinian had not yet given up hope of a peace settlement, and they continued his attempts to find a peaceful solution from April until June 527. It was only when this had failed that they launched new diversionary and pre-emptive invasions of Persian territory with forces posted near the border. The chosen strategy was to build two fortresses along the border with the help of a diversionary invasion led by *Magister Militum per Orientem* Libelarius. Libelarius advanced first against Nisibis but was unable to take it. After this, he continued his march against Thebetha, but was once again unsuccessful. The sieges were half-hearted because Libelarius's real intention was just to divert Persian attention. Therefore he withdrew his army to Dara. The retreat was costly because he lost many footmen to the oppressive summer heat. Libelarius was clearly incompetent – this should never have happened. Justinian therefore dismissed Libelarius and appointed the experienced Hypatius as his successor with the mission of stopping the Arab raids. The Roman plan failed. The Arabs and Kadishaye in Persian service prevented the Romans building fortifications at Thannuris while the Persian commander of Arzanene prevented similar fort-building attempts at Melabasa. These setbacks however did not put an end to the fort-building project. It remained a priority throughout the reign of Justinian.[3]

After Peter had failed to protect Iberia he was recalled to Constantinople either by Justin or by both emperors (the date is uncertain) and according to Greatrex's reconstruction, the emperor(s) then sent three *magistri militum*, Iranaeus, Cerycus and Gilderich, to retake Iberia. Justin died on 1 August 527 so Justinian became sole emperor. Unsurprisingly, the divided command structure of three *magistri* resulted in confusion, and the invading Roman army suffered heavy losses in 528 with the result that Justinian dispatched Peter back to the Caucasus to take command of operations. Peter decided to muster all of his available forces in one place, withdrawing all forces from Iberia, and then inflicted a crushing defeat on the Persians. Peter exploited the victory by garrisoning the two strategic border forts with Roman forces. Roman strategy was clearly built around the holding of strategic forts. However, the two forts proved too difficult to supply so the Romans withdrew the garrisons in about 529, the Persians then occupying them.

The successful defence of Lazica, however, required alliances and Justinian was a master in this field. In 527 he managed to conclude an alliance with Boa, queen of the 100,000 Sabiri Huns. This paid great dividends in 527/8. Boa destroyed 20,000 other Huns who were on their way to join the Persians. Thanks to this Peter did not have to face these Huns in Lazica. Justinian received Grepes, King of the Heruls, in Constantinople and baptized him in about 527/8. In return for this and for service as *foederati*, Justinian gave him the city of Singidunum together with some other cities in Dacia.[4] This freed forces for use elsewhere. Similarly, in about 527/8 Justinian managed to conclude an alliance with the Hunnic king of Bosporus who arrived in Constantinople where he was baptized and given a garrison of Romans to protect him.[5]

Once sole emperor Justinian continued the refortification project all along the eastern frontier and reorganized defences where necessary. Justinian created a new Armenian field army in 528, which he put under Sittas. The Armenian feudal lords who now lost their autonomy were enrolled into this new field army and reinforcements were sent from the Balkans to the *Magister Militum per Orientem* (Ayvazyan e.g. 46–7; Greatrex, e.g. 154). Justinian also strengthened the fortifications of Citharizon and Theodosiopolis and maybe others, and rebuilt those of Martyropolis. According to Procopius (*De Aed./Buildings* 2.1.11ff.), one of the refortification projects of Justinian was Dara, because it had been hastily built under Anastasius. Procopius states that besides the need to restore or rebuild many fortifications in the east, there was another thing that the Romans needed to take into account: the elephants used by the Persians. Justinian is claimed to have realized that the Persians would never allow the existence of such a bulwark as Dara close to their border and that they would assault the city with all their might using all the tools available. These tools included great numbers of war elephants with wooden towers on top. The main danger of elephants was their mobility. The Persians could move them about as needed to give covering fire for those who assaulted the walls. This description suggests that both the Romans and Persians considered the pachyderms useful as sort of siege towers.

In the southern sector, Justinian refortified Palmyra and transferred reinforcements there in late 527. However, then a catastrophe struck. The Kindite Phylarch Arethas (al-Harith) and local *dux* quarrelled. Arethas withdrew to the desert. This was exploited by Alamoundaros who managed to kill Arethas. Justinian responded by ordering the *duces* of Phoenicia, Arabia and Mesopotamia, together with the other Arab phylarchs, to avenge the death. The Roman *duces* failed to catch Alamoundaros but they pillaged his camp and captured four Persian forts in the area before returning to Roman territory in April 528.

The troubled year 528 and the Battle of Thannuris/Minduos[6]

In the central section of the eastern frontier Justinian ordered the newly appointed *Dux* of Mesopotamia Belisarius to construct a fort at Minduos right on the border next to Nisibis. The fort has now been convincingly identified by Christopher Lillington-Martin (2015), for which see the accompanying map. Justinian's strategy was clearly defensive. The Persians considered all border forts, even the smallest ones like the one at Minduos, as threats. The Persians threatened the Romans that they would invade if the work was not stopped. Justinian's response was to reinforce Belisarius's force with the *duces* of Phoenicia Coutzes (according to Malalas *ex-dux* of Damascus) and his brother Boutzes, Sebastian, some Isaurians, the *Dux* of Phoenicia Proclianus (according to Malalas), Vincent, *comes* Basil, and the phylarch Atafar/Tapharas. This was a sizable force because even if one presumes that the commanders took only half of the forces available to them this would have amounted to a minimum of about 7,000 infantry and 15,000 cavalry plus the Arabs and *bucellarii*. However, it is clear that the figure was greater because the building of the forts so close to the enemy required footmen to protect and assist the builders and the subsequent description of the battle notes the presence of infantry. Therefore one can make the educated guess that the infantry contingent was at least 10,000 strong with the Isaurians. It is equally clear that the vast majority of the relief forces brought to the scene must have consisted of cavalry and that probably most of the forces near the theatre of operations were mustered for combat. In short it is probable that the size of the cavalry contingent was considerably larger. I would therefore suggest that there were at least 25,000 regular *Limitanei* horsemen plus the *bucellarii* and Arabs so that the overall total would have been about 30,000 horsemen. This is supported by the fact that the Romans were ready to march against the Persians, which suggests that the Romans outnumbered the Persians significantly. However, there was one major weakness in the Roman command structure. Belisarius was only a *dux* and this seriously weakened his authority over the other *duces* and the *comes* Basil with dire consequences.

When the Persian army advanced against the Romans to put a stop to the building of the fort, they found out to their horror that the Romans outnumbered them. The Persians had managed to assemble only 30,000 men under Peroz Mihran and Xerxes, son of Cabades. Malalas gives us the reason for this: the Persians were simultaneously operating a large army in Lazica. However, they had one major advantage over the Romans: Mihran was unquestionably the overall commander.

On the basis of Zachariah Rhetor (9.2) we know that the battle took place close to Thannuris. This means that Mihran resorted to a double stratagem. He first led the Persian army near Mindous to provoke the Romans into action, after which he feigned fear and retreated to Thannuris where he had prepared a trap for the Romans. The Romans followed confidently because they had a numerical advantage. Once he reached the area near Thannuris, Mihran resorted to the same stratagem that the Hepthaelites had used to defeat the Persian *Shahanshah* Peroz in 485. The Persians had dug several concealed ditches among their trenches leaving several openings through which their troops could retreat. When Belisarius and the Roman army arrived, the Persians duly deployed their cavalry in front of the ditches, after which they feigned flight. Two rash young brothers, Coutzes and Boutzes, swallowed the bait and charged after them. Their example was followed by the rest of the cavalry. The Roman cavalry line galloped with abandon straight into the trenches at full speed and fell into the pits. The attached diagram presents my best educated guess of the likeliest deployment pattern of the armies, which is based on the information provided by the *Strategikon* (12.3) of the Roman combat formation which was used when there was fewer infantry than cavalry present.

The Persians wounded and captured the rash Coutzes. Tapharas and Proclianus were killed on the spot. Sebastian and Basil (both in charge of the infantry?) were captured. The remnants of Roman cavalry, which must have consisted primarily of the second line, together with Belisarius fled to Dara, but the infantry was left to be butchered or taken captive. The morale of the footmen was not strong enough for them to make a fighting retreat in a hollow square/oblong formation to Dara; this means that the Persian cavalry had a clear numerical advantage over the Roman infantry. And there were also other problems. The Isaurian combat equipment was ill-suited for fighting against cavalry (although this would not have been decisive had the infantry possessed the will to fight, as is so well proven by the good combat performance of earlier Roman infantries armed only with *pila*-javelins against cavalry forces). It is clear that the battle was an utter disaster for the Romans. It destroyed their morale completely, and they had now lost most of their regular army of the east. The results of this disastrous defeat were still visible two years later at the battles of Dara and Satala. On the basis of the fact that Belisarius was

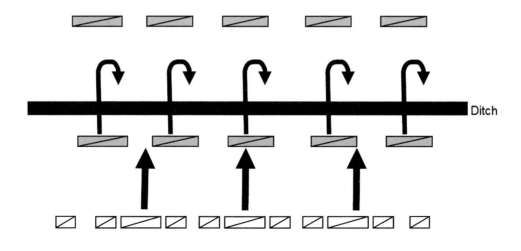

Belisarius

Infantry

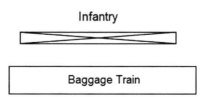

promoted to *Magister Militum per Orientem* after this in 529 (see below), it is clear that the catastrophe had not been his fault. As *dux* Belisarius had not had enough authority over the other *duces* so he needed a grander title. He was not the man who had ordered the rash cavalry charge, and it is also probable that he had opposed the pursuit of the Persians from Minduous to Thannuris but had had it forced on him by his subordinates.

The defeat at Thannuris not only meant the abandonment of the project to build Minduous, but it also opened up the east for enemy invasion. The emperor was forced to resort to emergency measures. Justinian dispatched several senators with their *bucellarii* and regular units from the Balkans to guard the cities. These forces were placed under Pompeius, the brother of Hypatius and nephew of Anastasius. The Romans were lucky. The arrival of an exceptionally severe winter put a stop to all hostilities. This was doubly lucky because several cities were struck by earthquakes which weakened their walls.

Typically troubles accumulated. As noted above, in 527/8 the king of the Crimean Huns had become Christian so had become an ally. The king's subjects, however, were not happy. They were pagans and opposed the conversion and killed the king together with the Roman garrison that had been posted at Bosphorus. This took place probably in the summer 528. Justinian had to react. He dispatched a large force of Gothic Federates under John (now appointed first *Comes* of the Pontic Straits) together with the *Magister Militum per Thracias* Godilas and *Magister Militum/Dux* of Scythia Badourios in late 528. The Huns fled and the Crimea was now permanently secured for the Romans. This ensured better availability of information from the steppes and thereby better chances of affecting the alliances the nomads could conclude with the Persians. And, as we shall see, it also gave the Romans the ability to use Utigurs against the Kutrigurs. However, the transfer of troops to the east and temporary garrisoning of the Crimea created a power vacuum. These left Lower Moesia and Scythia open for invasion by the Bulgarians. They inflicted a defeat on the Roman commanders Badourios (who had by then returned from the Crimea) and Justin, and then penetrated as far as Thrace. This meant that the Romans could no longer spare any troops for the eastern frontier. Justinian was now forced to negotiate with the warlord/chieftain Mundus, who with his mercenaries was duly appointed *Magister Militum per Illyricum* in about 529/30. At about the same time, Justinian made Childbudius *Magister Militum per Thracias*. Mundus severely defeated first the Goths (see Chapter 8) and then the Huns, consisting of various barbaric tribes (Bulgars in Marcellinus), and captured their booty and one of their kings. According to Marcellinus, 500 Bulgars were killed, but it is possible that this figure leaves out the casualties suffered by the other tribes. These two new *magistri* managed to restore the situation in the Balkans in 530.[7]

Alamoundaros's revenge for the Roman sack of his camp was terrible. In early 529 he made a lighting attack and advanced from the south via Emesa and Apamea all the way to the gates of Antioch and then returned before the Romans were able to collect their army against the raider. Justinian's response to this consisted of three parts. Firstly, he sent reinforcements to the east to avenge this raid, but we do not know what they achieved if anything. All that we know comes from Malalas, and he only states that Justinian dispatched a considerable force of infantry, known as the *Lykokranitai* from Phrygia,[8] and that they were sent against Saracen and Persian territory. Justinian also sacked *Magister Militum per Orientem* Hypatius for his failure to stop Alamoundaros and appointed Belisarius as his successor – the incompetence of Hypatius comes as no surprise to those who have read my analysis of his capabilities in *MHLR* Vol.5. The raid proved that the southern section of the frontier was too weakly defended, so Justinian appointed the Ghassanid sheik Arethas as phylarch of the Arabs. This unification of the Arab tribes under a single leader created a counterbalance against the Persian Saracens.[9]

In these circumstances it is not surprising that Justinian decided to seek peace. He dispatched the trusted *Magister Officiorum* Hermogenes as his ambassador to the Persians. The resulting negotiations, however, failed because it was then that the persecuted Samaritans finally revolted. Furthermore, Cabades had also by then in about 528/9 destroyed the last Mazdakite resistance to his rule so that Cabades's negotiating position was now very strong. Because of this Cabades demanded that the Romans either demolish the walls of Dara or paid him gold for the upkeep of the garrison at the Caspian

Gates. Justinian's response was to play for time: he agreed to a truce that would last a year from July 529. His goal was to improve his negotiating position, and he used the intervening period well by crushing the Samaritan revolt.[10]

According to Malalas, the revolt had resulted from the Roman response to the rioting of the Samaritans, Jews and Christians, in the process of which many parts of Scythopolis were torched by the Samaritans. This angered Justinian so that he sacked and beheaded the governor Bassus for his failure to curb the riots. This frightened the Samaritans with the result that they revolted in earnest and crowned a bandit chief called Julian as emperor, after which they proceeded to kill Christians and burn estates and churches. When Julian then entered Neapolis during chariot races, he presided over them as if he were an emperor. The winner, however, was a Christian charioteer. Julian's response to this was the beheading of the winner in the hippodrome after which he proceeded to kill the local bishop. It was only then that the governors of Palestine and the *dux* Theodoros the Snub-nosed responded to the crisis. The *dux* collected a large force which included the forces of the Arab phylarch of Palestine and marched with these against the rebel. When Julian heard of this, he retreated from Neapolis with the *dux* hot on his heels. Theodorus caught up with the fugitive and forced him to fight a battle. The Samaritans were decisively defeated. They lost 20,000 men, Julian was captured and the Saracen phylarch took 20,000 Samaritan girls and boys as slaves. Theodorus beheaded the rebel and sent his diadem to Justinian, but the latter was far from happy because in his opinion the *dux* had acted too slowly. Furthermore, some of the Samaritans had managed to flee to the Garizim Mountain and others to Trachon, also known as Iron Mountain. Theodorus was therefore relieved of duty and placed under arrest, and Eirenaios the Antiochene was sent as his successor. Eirenaos advanced against the Samaritans on the mountains immediately and killed masses of them in revenge for their actions. The Samaritans tried to obtain help from the Persians, but their envoys were captured, interrogated and then killed when they were returning from Persia in late 530.[11]

In 529, while Hermogenes was negotiating with Cabades, Justinian made several important decisions and faced some internal troubles. Several cities and villages in Asia Minor were ravaged by earthquakes and the emperor was forced to send help. There was also a serious riot in the theatre at Antioch. We do not know why this riot took place, but we know that it was after this that Justinian forbade theatrical performances at Antioch. It is quite easy to see why he did this because Antioch was important for the defence of the east and there existed a danger that the Arabs or Persians could take the city as a result of some disturbance – the advance of Alamoundaros up to its suburbs was just the latest demonstration of this danger. It was also during this same year that Justinian took from Antioch the cities of Laodikeia, Gabala and Paltos, and from Apameia the city of Balaneia, and created a new province, Theodorias, and gave metropolitan status to Laodikeia. Malalas places this decision before the riot, so perhaps it was the cause of it.

The year saw other important actions undertaken by Justinian. The Law Codex was finally ready and distributed to the cities. This certainly improved the morale of the population in cases where legal action was needed.

The great persecution of Hellenes was launched. They were forbidden to hold any public offices. Their property was confiscated and many important Hellenes were executed. These included Makedonios, Asklepiototos, Phokas son of Krateros, and

Thomas the *Quaestor*. Priscus, an ex-consul and former imperial secretary, was among those whom Justinian punished at this time. His property was confiscated and he was made a deacon of Cyzicus. We do not know what it was that caused this, but since he was a former imperial secretary it is possible that his punishment was related to matters of espionage and plotting. In this way the emperor purged the imperial household and the central administration from the pagans and others whom he did not trust. Justinian also ordered that all of the other heresies were to be purged from the Roman state – they had three months to embrace the Orthodox faith or face the consequences. The idea was clearly to unite all Romans under the same belief and the same law.[12] As we shall see, the result of this was demonstrations.

In June 530 Justinian still thought that they had one month to negotiate with the Persians, but Cabades had other thoughts. His intention was to surprise the Romans by making a surprise attack before the truce ended. With this in mind he had posted one force in Persarmenia in readiness to invade and cut off Lazica from Roman support, while another force had been assembled at Nisibis in readiness to attack Dara.[13] This shows nicely the legalistic thinking process of Justinian: he trusted Cabades to honour the truce, while Cabades sought to exploit this.

The battle of Dara in June 530[14]

Cabades' plan was to invade before the truce ended in July, and had assembled two large armies in readiness to invade Roman territory in June, one in Persarmenia, the other at Nisibis. This was not a great surprise: the Romans were also making preparations for war despite the truce still being in effect. According to Procopius, Justinian appointed Belisarius as *Magister Militum per Orientem* with the mission of conducting an expedition against the Persians. He collected an army of 25,000, which Procopius calls a large army, and marched it to Dara evidently to attack or at least threaten Nisibis. According to Malalas the army was encamped outside the city. *Magister Officiorum* Hermogenes was sent to assist Belisarius. The presence of *Magister Officiorum* was of utmost importance because it compelled the other commanders to obey Belisarius, which they had refused to do during the previous campaign. The emperor also sent Rufinus to act as his ambassador, but with orders to stay at Hierapolis until further notice. The army under Belisarius may have been considered large but it is probable that it included large numbers of inexperienced soldiers because the Romans had lost large numbers of soldiers (especially footmen) at Thannuris and because Procopius' text refers to this (*Wars* 1.14.15–17). Furthermore, previous encounters had proved that Roman commanders were prone to attack without being ordered to; it was indeed because of this that Hermogenes was there. My educated guess is that the Romans had about 7,500 cavalry and 17,500 footmen. It was when the Romans had reached Dara that they suddenly learnt that the Persians were expected to invade Roman territory shortly. They had arrived in the nick of time.

Belisarius and Hermogenes started to make hasty preparations for the battle, building field fortifications to withstand the Persian attack. According to Procopius, they built a short ditch in the middle with cross trenches connecting it to the two longer parallel ditches left and right of it. The trench had passages to enable the men to move across it.

The unfortunate thing about this is that it leaves open whether the short ditch protruded from the formation or was placed inwards. I consider the former likelier because it was the standard way for the building of marching camps. Furthermore, the separation of the two forces of Huns in the middle would imply that there was some space between them. However, I have included both versions in the accompanying maps (see pages 60–2) depicting the initial deployment of the armies.

Belisarius posted Bouzes with a large force of cavalry at the left extremity of the trench so that it extended as far as the hill. This means that the cavalry forces were posted outside the trench. Bouzes' forces included 300 Heruls under Pharas so I have estimated the size of his force to have been roughly about 2,300 horsemen. To the right of these outside the trench at the angle, Belisarius posted the Massagetae Huns Sunicas and Aigan with 600 horsemen with orders to attack the Persians in the flank if they forced Bouzes to retreat. I would suggest that the orders for Bouzes were to feign flight from the start. The deployment pattern on the right was the same so that there was a large force of horsemen commanded by John son of Nicetas, and by Cyril and Marcellus; and with them were also Germanus and Dorotheus. I estimate the size of this force to have been about 2,000 horsemen. The right flank did not have any hills to protect it. At the right angle of the trench were 600 Massagetae Huns under Simmas and Ascan with orders to attack the Persians in the flank if the right wing cavalry retreated. Procopius then states that it was thus that along the trench stood the *katalogoi* of cavalry and the infantry, and that behind these in the middle stood the forces of Belisarius and Hermogenes. I estimate the size of this force to have been 2,000 horsemen because it is unlikely that Belisarius could have possessed so many *doruforoi* and *hypaspistai* at this stage as he did later. Indeed, contrary to his usual practice Procopius appears to have included the *bucellarii* of the officers in his figure of 25,000 men because he states that all of the above consisted of this number of men. Belisarius clearly did not trust that his infantry was combat ready and because of this placed it behind the ditch to protect it against the Persians. Their morale was not high after the defeats and it is also probable that the footmen included many recent recruits. It is also very likely that Belisarius deployed his infantry in a deep formation to bolster its morale, so the heavy infantry phalanx was deployed sixteen deep and the light infantry eight deep so that the total depth of the formation was twenty-four ranks. This would mean that the width of the infantry phalanx was about 850 metres. If deployed seven deep, the corresponding width of the cavalry wings would have been about 700 metres so that the total width of the Roman battle formation would have been 1,550 metres or more. It is possible that the length of the array was slightly longer because some of the cavalry units were elite and military doctrine would have allowed them to deploy only five deep.

According to Procopius the Romans built the trench about a stone's throw from the *pulê* facing the city of Nisibis. This has resulted in two different interpretations. The vast majority of historians have followed Dewing's translation and interpreted '*pulê*' as gate so that the battle would have been fought right in front of the city of Dara, but Christopher Lillington-Martin (2007; 2013, 599–611) has suggested that *pulê* should be translated as the geographical gap which was located just east of Ambar at a distance of 2–3 km south of Dara. This is supported by the statement of Malalas who wrote that the Romans encamped outside Dara. This is not conclusive; both interpretations are plausible. The arrowhead finds at the gap are not conclusive because this area saw several battles, sieges and skirmishes while the fortress city existed and many fortified camps with field fortifications were built there by both sides. The fact that Procopius states (*Wars* 1.13.25–28, 1.13.15–16) that the left wing of the Roman cavalry retreated up to the wall (*teichos*) is also not conclusive because it could refer either to the city wall or to any fortification including the fortified marching camp located outside the city walls. However, the following quote from Procopius (*Wars* 1.13.32, tr. by Dewing, 111) suggests strongly that the battle took place close to the city: 'Then Andreas with a small knife slew him like a sacrificial animal as he lay on his back, and a mighty shout was raised both from the city wall (*peribolos*) and from the Roman army (*stratopedon*).' This and another reference in Procopius (*Wars* 1.13.38) separate those on the wall from those of the army with the implication that those on the wall were inhabitants of Dara. However, the subsequent statement that the Roman army withdrew inside this *peribolos* (Procop. *Wars* 1.13.38) makes it quite possible that the *peribolos* still meant the marching camp so that those who cheered would have been the servants. Regardless, the combination of *pulé*, *teichos* and *peribolos* makes it likelier that the battle was fought right next to the city itself, but not conclusively so. I will therefore give both versions in the attached larger map (p.60), but analyse the battle itself in other maps (pp.61–2) in greater detail without the inclusion of the specific location. All that we know for certain is that the Roman battle formation was at least about 1,550 metres wide, that the Romans used field fortifications, and that there was a hill on the left.

The commander of the Persian army of 40,000 men posted at Nisibis was Perozes Mihranes (i.e. Peroz Mihran). His mission was to conquer Dara and with this in mind he led the army to Ammodius, 7.7 km south of Dara. The location was well-chosen because Ammodius was well supplied with water, so necessary for the Persian horses. The first day of the battle began with the Persians against the Roman field fortifications. The Persians were deployed in a deep and tight battle formation. The idea was presumably to make their army seem smaller than it was to induce the Romans to attack. This was one of the standard ploys employed by ancient commanders when their army outnumbered the enemy. When this did not happen they were at a loss what to do and stood still for a long time.

Then the Persians dispatched a *moira* (2,000–3,000 horsemen or detachment of unspecified size) of cavalry against the Roman left wing which duly feigned flight up to the wall. The Persians didn't follow because they quite rightly feared that this was a ruse. When Bouzes and Pharas noticed this they turned and charged with the result that the Persians returned to their phalanx. After this both returned to their stations in formation. If the Persian plan had been to lure the Romans into breaking their formation, this had failed. The Persians lost seven men in this skirmish. Then a young Persian challenged the Romans to a duel. This challenge was answered by Bouzes' bath attendant Andreas, who was an expert wrestler and a trainer of youths in a wrestling school in Constantinople. Andreas did this without permission, suddenly charging forward with his horse and hitting the Persian with his spear in the right breast knocking him to the ground. Andreas jumped off his horse and then killed the man with a *machaira* (a short sword, dagger or knife) as if he had killed a sacrificial animal. The Persians then sent forth another more experienced duellist who had signs of grey hair. Now Hermogenes issued an order that none of the Romans were to accept the challenge, but this was disobeyed, once again by Andreas. He and the Persian charged madly against each other. Their spear thrusts were deflected by armour and their horses collided, head hitting head. Both men flew in the air but survived. Andreas was faster on his feet thanks to his training while the Persian was slower because of his massive size. Andreas hit the Persian first so that he fell again to the ground and Andreas killed him. The Romans on the wall and in the battle array raised another mighty shout, and the disillusioned Persians withdrew to Ammodios while the Romans raised the paean and retreated inside the fortifications (*peribolos*). Peroz Mihran understandbly hesitated to commit his men against the well-ordered Roman line that was protected by field fortifications especially after the disappointment of the duels.

There was no action the next day, but the Persians were reinforced by 10,000 additional men from Nisibis, who must be the famous Immortals. During this lull the two sides exchanged messages. Belisarius and Hermogenes were the first to send a letter to Mihran. They urged Mihran to refrain from hostilities because the Roman envoy was already present in the neighbourhood (meaning Rufinus at Hierapolis). Mihran responded that he did not trust the Roman oaths and told them to prepare for war. Belisarius and his generals answered with another letter stating that the Romans had acted honestly and that Rufinus was really waiting to begin the negotiations, but then stated that since the Persians were breaking the peace the Romans would fasten the letters of both sides on their banners to show their case just. This was a brilliant piece of propaganda. The Romans could show their cause just and thereby uplift the fighting spirit of the soldiers. Mihran's response was that the Romans should prepare a bath and lunch in readiness at Dara where he would arrive the following day.

Procopius gives us important pieces of evidence regarding the relative strengths of the armies in the speeches that he has placed in the mouths of the two commanders. According to him (*Wars* 1.14.13ff.), Mihran stated that the Romans typically advanced into combat in complete confusion and disorder, but now awaited the advancing Persians with a kind of order that was not characteristic of them. This refers to the Roman officers' habit of attacking in a disorderly fashion without being ordered to do so. He encouraged the men by stating that the Romans had not become better warriors, or more valorous. On the contrary, the facts that the Romans had not had the courage to face the Persians without a trench and not had the courage to advance against the Persians proved the opposite. This was partially true. Belisarius definitely did not trust that his infantry would be able to withstand the Persians without the trench. Mihran also noted that the Romans had immediately withdrawn to the wall instead of facing them. He promised that when the Persians fought at close quarters the Romans would be seized by fear so that their inexperienced force would be disordered. Mihran ended the speech by stating that the King of Kings would punish them if they were not valorous in the combat. It is uncertain how close to the actual exhortation this was but it is clear that Procopius thought that the Persians would refer to the known weaknesses of the Roman forces of the time. The reference to punishments appears to have been the standard way the Persian rulers acted when their forces suffered a defeat. This was foolish because it ensured that the Persian commanders were unable to learn from their mistakes because they were always replaced if they suffered a setback.

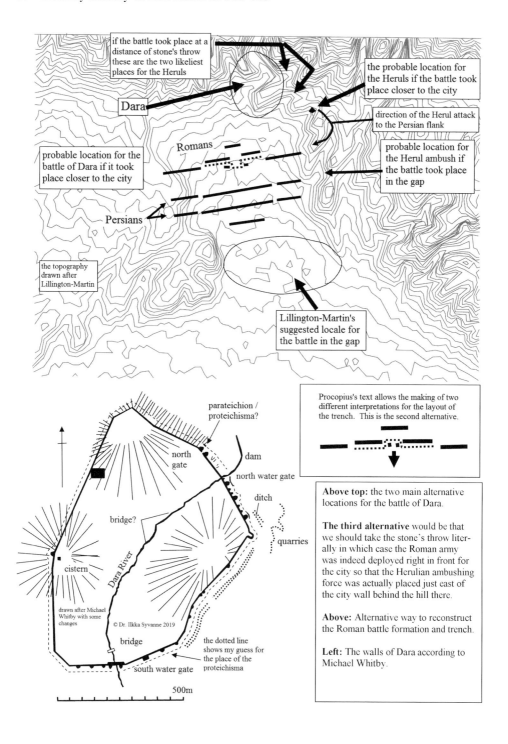

if the battle took place at a distance of stone's throw these are the two likeliest places for the Heruls

the probable location for the Heruls if the battle took place closer to the city

Dara

direction of the Herul attack to the Persian flank

probable location for the battle of Dara if it took place closer to the city

Romans

probable location for the Herul ambush if the battle took place in the gap

Persians

the topography drawn after Lillington-Martin

Lillington-Martin's suggested locale for the battle in the gap

parateichion / proteichisma?

north gate

dam

north water gate

ditch

bridge?

quarries

Dara River

cistern

drawn after Michael Whitby with some changes

© Dr. Ilkka Syvänne 2019

bridge

south water gate

the dotted line shows my guess for the place of the proteichisma

500m

Procopius's text allows the making of two different interpretations for the layout of the trench. This is the second alternative.

Above top: the two main alternative locations for the battle of Dara.

The third alternative would be that we should take the stone's throw literally in which case the Roman army was indeed deployed right in front for the city so that the Herulian ambushing force was actually placed just east of the city wall behind the hill there.

Above: Alternative way to reconstruct the Roman battle formation and trench.

Left: The walls of Dara according to Michael Whitby.

Belisarius and Hermogenes also encouraged their men and the speech that Procopius (*Wars* 1.14.20ff.) puts into their mouth contains similarly important pieces of evidence. They encouraged their men by stating that in the past the Romans had been defeated only because the Romans had not obeyed their officers and not because they were less brave or strong. They noted that the only hope that the Persians had of winning lay in this disorder and when this did not take place the Persians would be powerless as the previous encounter demonstrated. They also told the soldiers not to be frightened by the enemy numbers because the Persian infantry consisted of pitiable peasants that had come to the battle only to be used in sieges or as servants of the horsemen. It was because of this that the Persian infantry hid behind their enormous shields. These comments were by and large true. Most of the Persian infantry consisted of poor quality forces and the Persians had won the previous battles largely thanks to the poor discipline of the Roman soldiers. The presence of Hermogenes in the army removed these weaknesses.

Day 2 Phase 1:
Persian right wing attacks and is crushed by the flank attacks of the Heruls and Huns.

As promised, on the third day of the battle the Persians attacked with full force. Peroz Mihran deployed the army in two lines with cavalry wings, while Mihran himself stood behind with the Immortals. The commander of the Persian right wing was Pityaxes (means probably *Vitaxa*/Viceroy) and the commander of the left was the one-eyed

Baresmanas (probably *Marzban*, warden of the march). At the suggestion of Pharas the Romans altered their previous dispositions so that Pharas took his Heruls behind the hill on their left flank. The Persians waited until midday to exploit the fact that the Romans ate their meal at that time, before they moved into action. The Persians followed their military doctrine to the letter so that the battle began with a prolonged archery duel. The Persians rotated the troops between front and rear to maintain steady and rapid fire against the Romans, but the contrary wind checked the impact of Persian archery. Still, many men fell on both sides. When both sides had exhausted their missiles, Mihran sent his men into the attack with spears. This stage of the battle appears to have consisted of different units advancing and retreating until the Persian right wing, which included the Cadiseni, charged against the Roman left wing in strength under their commander *Vitaxa*. The Romans answered by feigned retreat to lure the enemy after them, which the Persians swallowed. The Heruls and Huns exploited this by charging against the Persian flanks. The Romans were able to surround the Persian right wing from all sides, killing at least 3,000 of them. The rest managed to flee back to the safety of their phalanx with great difficulty. The Romans did not pursue them but assumed their previous positions.

It is probable that the abovementioned Persian cavalry attack followed the standard Persian cavalry tactic in which the first cavalry line consisted of lightly equipped mounted archers and the second line of the heavily armoured cavalry. When the Persians then decided to charge, they typically united these two lines so that the heavily equipped men formed the front ranks of a single line.

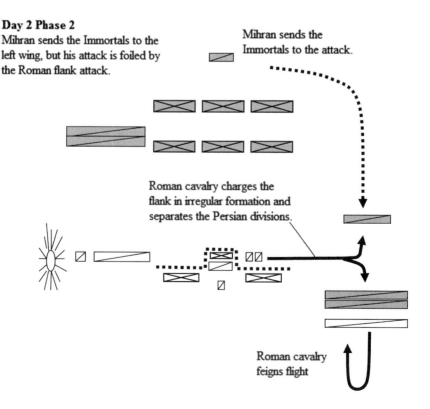

Day 2 Phase 2
Mihran sends the Immortals to the left wing, but his attack is foiled by the Roman flank attack.

Mihran sends the Immortals to the attack.

Roman cavalry charges the flank in irregular formation and separates the Persian divisions.

Roman cavalry feigns flight

Mihran's next move was to transfer the Immortals to the left wing with the purpose of crushing the Roman right wing because its flank was not protected by any terrain feature. Belisarius and Hermogenes noticed this and ordered Sunicas and Aigan to take their positions on the right angle with Simmas and Ascan, and placed behind them many of Belisarius' men. When the Persians under Baresmanas then attacked the Roman right wing the Romans performed the feigned flight and drew the Persians in hot pursuit. The Huns and Belisarius' reserves exploited this and charged in irregular order against the Persian left wing dividing it in two so that the bulk of the enemy forces were on their right and only Baresmanas with the Immortals were on their left. It is probable that the Huns engaged those on the left (the Immortals) while Belisarius' men engaged those on the right. The reason for this conclusion is that Procopius tells us that it was Sunicas who charged and killed Baresmanas' standard bearer with a spear after which a *lochos* of Immortals (1,000 men?) and Barasmanas charged against Sunicas. Sunicas responded with a counter-charge and killed Baresmanes with his own hand. The death of Baresmanes demoralized and panicked the Immortals who all fled in total disarray. Meanwhile Belisarius' reserves had wheeled right and attacked the Persian left wing from behind so that the pursuing Persians were completely surrounded when the Roman right wing turned around. The encircled Persian left wing was routed losing 5,000 killed.

The destruction and rout of the Persian left and right wings panicked the Persian infantry and the remnants of their cavalry with the result that the entire Roman army attacked. The pursuing Roman cavalry was able to kill the fleeing Persians at their will, but the ever-cautious Belisarius and Hermogenes halted the pursuit so that the Persians, who still possessed superior numbers, would not regroup in desperation and turn their defeat into victory. It is clear that in this battle the Roman cavalry showed great discipline and obeyed their officers and that it was largely because of this that the Romans won the battle. It is also clear that Belisarius' plan for the battle was masterful. It took into account the relative strengths and weaknesses of each side so that the Romans had all the advantages on their side. However, it is unlikely that even this would have sufficed without Hermogenes – it was his presence on the battlefield that forced the other officers to follow the plan of battle that Belisarius had devised for them. According to Procopius, the Persians lost more than half their men in this battle and no longer wished to engage the Romans in pitched battle. However, this left the Persians still with ca. 25,000 men which was enough to prevent the Romans from attempting to take Nisibis. Therefore, the rest of the year 530 in this sector of the frontier was spent in skirmishing warfare in which the Romans usually came off as winners.

Battle of Satala June 530[15]

Meanwhile the Persians had assembled another army in Persarmenia. The Persian strategic object for the invasion was probably aimed at cutting off the Lazi and Tzani from the Romans, and also gaining the support of potential Armenian deserters. The Roman commanders in Armenia were the *magister militum praesentalis* Sittas (overall commander) and the *Magister Militum per Armeniam* Dorotheus. The Roman commanders took the initiative and disrupted the Persian war preparations by making a surprise attack against the Persian camp, but the Persians still managed to assemble a force of 30,000 horsemen under Mermeroes (Mihr-Mihroe). This army consisted entirely of allies, which included 3,000 Sabiri Huns. However, most of this 'Persian army' consisted of the feudal contingents most of which would have been provided by the Armenian Siwnik. In the fourth century they had been required to contribute a contingent of 19,400 cataphracts for their own king and it is likely that the requirement had remained the same. Therefore there is every reason to say that at the battle of Satala two Armenian cavalry armies fought against each other.

Mermeroes aimed to exploit his numerical advantage and sought a decisive battle while the Roman commanders resorted to guerrilla warfare until both armies reached the vicinity of Satala. It was then that Sittas selected 1,000 men and posted them in ambush behind one of the hills, while Dorotheus stayed inside the walls of Satala. It is probable that Satala was still the HQ of the *Legio XV Apollinaris* or its successor and therefore possessed footmen to protect its walls. When the Persians reached the site they spread around the city to invest it. Sittas had been expecting this and now charged downhill. The clouds of dust created by the 1,000 galloping horsemen created an illusion of great numbers and caused panic among the Persians. Mermeroes recalled his forces and attempted to form a battle line. Sittas prevented this by dividing his ambushers in two groups so that he managed encircle one section of the retreating enemy force. At that moment Dorotheus opened the gates and led his cavalry out of the city. Despite the double surprise, the Persians were able to regroup the remnants of their forces thanks to their superior numbers. Both sides now formed a regular battle line opposite each other. According to Procopius, the resulting battle was a fiercely fought encounter in which both sides quickly advanced and retreated, as was typical for cavalry battles. Then the Thracian Florentius and his '*katalogos*' of horsemen charged against the enemy's centre. Florentius was killed, but not before he threw Mermeroes' standard to the ground. This panicked the Persians, and so the battle was decided by the heroism of a single individual. This attack also shows the very high quality of the Thracian *katalogoi*. Therefore the battle between two Armenian armies was decided by the heroism of the Thracians. The demoralized Persians fled on the double back to their camp and retreated the next day.

The Persian defeat caused the desertion of two Armenian border forts (Pharangium and Bolum) and three Armenian lords to the Roman side. The loss of Pharangium was a particularly hard blow to the Persians. It was their principal source of gold, and this affected their ability to continue the war.

Peace negotiations begin anew

Cabades now initiated peace negotiations, summoning the Roman ambassador Rufinus to his court. Cabades, however, simply stated his previous demands, and the Roman ambassadors returned to Constantinople for further instructions. Justinian was now ready to conclude a peace. He had already set his eyes on the reconquest of the West, so he dispatched the ambassadors back with instructions to make the agreement. But when they reached the frontier at the turn of the year 530/31, they found out that Cabades had had a change of heart. The Romans had not exploited their victories so the Persians had been able to regroup. In my opinion it is entirely possible or even probable that Cabades had planned to do this from the start. In other words, he initiated the peace negotiations

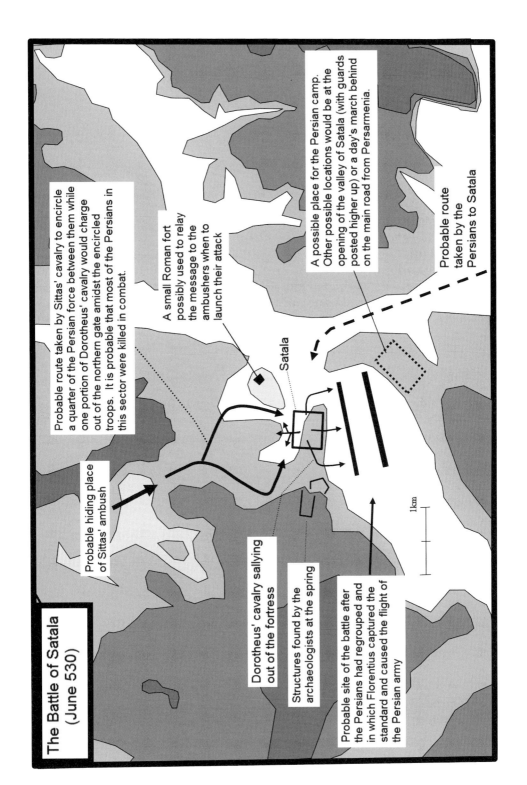

The Battle of Satala
(June 530)

Probable route taken by Sittas' cavalry to encircle a quarter of the Persian force between them while one portion of Dorotheus' cavalry would charge out of the northern gate amidst the encircled troops. It is probable that most of the Persians in this sector were killed in combat.

Probable hiding place of Sittas' ambush

A small Roman fort possibly used to relay the message to the ambushers when to launch their attack

A possible place for the Persian camp. Other possible locations would be at the opening of the valley of Satala (with guards posted higher up) or a day's march behind on the main road from Persarmenia.

Probable route taken by the Persians to Satala

Satala

Dorotheus' cavalry sallying out of the fortress

Structures found by the archaeologists at the spring

Probable site of the battle after the Persians had regrouped and in which Florentius captured the standard and caused the flight of the Persian army

1km

only to buy time to regroup his forces. It is clear that Cabades also wanted to improve his relative position in the future negotiations by renewing the attack. The defection of the Armenian forts and lords showed that the Persian position was precarious and Cabades knew that he needed victories.

Justinian's plans for the Ethiopians and Yemenites in 531

In about 530/1 Justinian came up with the idea of using the Aksumites and Himyarites against the Persians. He dispatched an embassy to Yemen and Ethiopia in about April–September 531. The ambassadors asked the Aksumites to take over the Indian trade from the Persians and asked the Himyarites to attack against the Ma'add in Central Arabia because these had revolted against the Kindites and overthrown their phylarch Caisus. After this, the two were to unite their forces and advance against the Persians. Both rulers promised to help, but the project ultimately failed because the Himyarite king Esimiphaeus was unwilling to fight on behalf of Caisus because he had killed a relative of his, and the Ethiopians were unable to buy their wares directly from the Indians as decades of neglect had given the Persian traders advantage in India – the Aksumites were forced to buy their ware from the Persians. The changing of the situation would have required a significant Roman naval intervention in the Indian Ocean and Persian Gulf. We do not know why the Romans did not do this at this moment, but one may speculate that the potential threat posed by the vaunted Vandal navy kept the Alexandrian navy at its stations, or that the Romans simply lacked the will or resources. On the other hand, it is also possible that they did mount an intervention and that we don't know anything about; the sources provide us details of the activities that took place in this area only sparingly, as the following discussion makes clear.[16]

The Himyarite king Esimiphaeus, who had caused so much trouble for the Romans by failing to act, was soon overthrown by Abraha who was the commander of the Ethiopian army in Yemen and Arabia. According to Procopius, Abraha was a Christian and originally a slave of a Roman who was engaged in shipping in the city of Adulis in Ethiopia, and that he was elevated to king by the Ethiopian garrison with the help of certain others. We do not know the exact date for this, but it took place soon after 531. The exact length of his reign is also unknown. The Arabic sources preserve a lot of material, but nonetheless the details remain murky so we are forced to rely on four extant inscriptions. These and other sources suggest that Abraha ruled Yemen for about thirty years between 535 and 565, and that he was definitely dead by the 570s. Ethiopia and Yemen remained in a state of war until Kaleb died. After this, Abraha recognized the Aksumites as his overlords and paid them tribute. According to the interpretation of Robin concerning the Arab-Islamic tradition, the Romans also intervened in the affairs of Western Arabia during the first half of the sixth century, helping the Qusayy and his Qurayshite clans to gain control of Mecca, and a few decades after this the Romans appointed a king for Mecca. This tradition connects these events with the reign of Abraha in Yemen.[17] When this and the following are taken into account, it raises interesting prospects for the reconstruction of events that took place during the period from 531 until about the 550s.

According to Procopius, Kaleb's response to the revolt of Abraha was to send 3,000 men under his relative against the rebel, but the men deserted to Abraha. After this,

Kaleb sent yet another army against Abraha which was also severely defeated and Kaleb gave up. He also states that at a later time when he had secured his position Abraha promised Justinian he would fight against the Persians but failed to do anything but begin a campaign which was immediately abandoned.[18]

The above, indeed, is not the whole story because we know that the Romans still had a defensive alliance with Ethiopia in 539–40 and that Himyar (Yemen) together with the Red Sea and the so-called Palm Groves of the Arabian Peninsula (located inland) were considered parts of the Roman Empire in 539–40.[19] Unfortunately Procopius fails to tell us how this was achieved. This leaves open many possibilities, but my educated guess is that the abovementioned overthrow of the Himyarite King Esimiphaeus by Abraha was orchestrated by the Romans so that Himyar (Yemen) was annexed at this time. The principal sources of evidence for this are: firstly, Procopius states that there were certain others besides the Ethiopian army who raised Abraha to the throne. These others are likely to have been the Romans. This would suggest that the Romans may have sent a fleet and expeditionary force into the area at this time, possibly disguised as merchants and their guards. Secondly, after he had secured his position this Abraha promised to campaign against the Persians and even began his campaign, which is in contrast to his predecessor who had failed to act as he had promised. I would connect Abraha's readiness to begin the campaign with the death of Kaleb possibly in about 543–547.[20] It is possible that the halting of the campaign should therefore be connected with the conclusion of the truce between Rome and Persia in 545. I would also connect the Roman activities in Western Arabia mentioned above with the possession of the Red Sea which may mean that the Romans conducted a campaign in this area at the same time as they helped Abraha to gain the throne. Obviously all of this is speculation, but at least it is learned and reconciles the sources. Whatever the timing and circumstance, it is clear that the possession of the Red Sea and Yemen and the alliance with Ethiopia gave the Romans the chance of bypassing the Persian traders as long as they could buy their wares directly from the Indians, which they could theoretically do thanks to the fact that their coinage was based on gold while the Persians relied on silver. But since Procopius specifically states that this part of the plan failed it is safest to assume that the Persian traders retained their hold on the India trade and that the Romans did not conduct 'show of flag' operations in the Indian Ocean to convince the Persian traders to remain in their home waters – this is not surprising because the Romans still needed naval assets against the Goths and then a reserve force in Constantinople as long as there existed the threat of Persians building a fleet at Lazica/Colchis (see later).

The battle of Callinicum 19 April 531[21]

The defeats had proved to the Persians that the Romans now possessed large enough forces in Mesopotamia and Armenia to protect the newly fortified cities. Therefore Cabades decided to attempt something else, eagerly adopting the advice offered by the phylarch Alamoundaros. Cabades appointed Azarethes (probably *Hazaraft/Hazarabed/Chiliarch*) commander of the 15,000-strong Persian contingent. This means that the Persians probably had about 20,000 horsemen altogether when one adds the Saracens of Alamoundaros. Alamoundaros acted as a scout for the army because he knew the route.

The unexpected direction of the attack took the Romans by surprise, but the ever resourceful Belisarius acted quickly and moved south to face the enemy. He left most of his army behind at Dara taking with him only 3,000 horsemen and 5,000 Saracens so that he could move quickly. This precaution served him well, because the Persians under the command of some member of the Mihran family besieged Dara after Belisarius had left (Greatrex, p.197, n.12) and failed. In these circumstances Belisarius's only goal was just to prevent the Persians from inflicting serious harm and force them away from Roman territory without taking any unnecessary risks. This cautious approach was to become the mark of this great commander. With this in mind, Belisarius sent orders to his commanders not to attack the Persians before he had assembled his army. However, the *dux* Sunicas showed personal initiative and disobeyed Belisarius's direct order, but with great results because he surprised and defeated the Persians in their fortified camp with a mere 4,000 men. It is not entirely clear which angered Belisarius more, the disobedience or the success. The quarrel between the two officers was significant enough to need the personal attention of *Magister Officiorum* Hermogenes. He possessed the necessary authority to force the two men to cooperate. The arrival of Hermogenes means that at that point in time the Roman army had finally been assembled. As far as strategy was concerned, Belisarius and Hermogenes agreed. They intended only to goad the Persians away from Roman territory and not fight battles. Belisarius was well aware that his army, which consisted of about 20,000 men of infantry and cavalry, was not well suited to facing the Persians. His forces also included forces that he considered to be of inferior quality like the Lycaonian infantry. If Procopius's views of the Arabs as soldiers reflect those of his superior, it is probable that Belisarius had very little faith in the fighting quality of his Arabs.

The Romans followed Belisarius's chosen tactic until the retreating Persians reached Callinicum. This was the last place where the Romans could engage the enemy, and the Roman officers and soldiers were eager to fight thanks to the previous victories. Belisarius and Hermogenes tried their best to oppose this, but they were in the end forced to lead the men to combat or they would have faced mutiny. Belisarius and Hermogenes now had even more reason for their cautious approach, because by this time the soldiers were exhausted from their long march, and the Easter fasting did not help either. On top of this a part of their infantry forces had not even reached the site but were still behind marching. The officers and soldiers had one argument in their favour which was: Roman military doctrine expected the Romans to engage the retreating invading enemy force when it was exhausted and close to the border. It is therefore not surprising that Belisarius and Hermogenes could not change their minds.

Belisarius adopted a single line formation to make the Roman line equal to the length of the Persian. This array was called the mixed formation in Roman military parlance and was meant for situations in which the enemy force consisted of cavalry. The regular infantry forces under Peter were posted on the left against the river Euphrates. The cavalry centre between the infantry followed the standard tripartite structure so that the left wing of the centre consisted of the *koursores* (the Huns of Sunicas and Simmas), with the *defensores* of Belisarius forming the centre of the centre, while the right wing of the centre consisted of the *koursores* (the Huns of Ascan). Next to them towards the right were the Lycaonian infantry recruits under Longinus and Stephanacius. They were posted there because they were supposedly better suited to the rougher terrain. The 5,000 Saracens under their phylarch Arethas guarded the right flank. When the Persians observed this, they arrayed their army opposite the Romans so that on the right were the Persians under the *Hazaraft* and on the left the Saracen allies under Alamoundaros.

The situation was opportune for the Persians because the adoption of the mixed battle formation by the Romans left the initiative to the enemy. It was defensive. The Roman cavalry could not charge far out of the infantry array without endangering the cohesion of the whole battle formation. Thanks to this the Persians could pepper the static Roman formation with arrows at their will. This means that the Persians probably divided their array into two lines that could be rotated to shoot at the enemy.

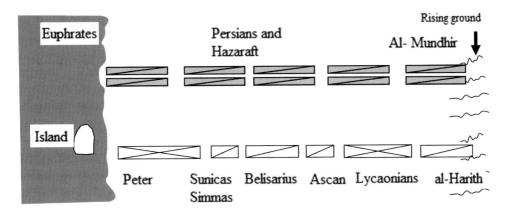

The battle began with a prolonged arrow duel. The Romans had stiffer bows and stronger men together with foot archers that enabled them to shoot more powerful shots, but this did not give them a decisive edge because the Persians had a favourable wind and a faster shooting rate. The archery contest proved inconclusive. By now the Romans must have been utterly exhausted from the fasting, marching, and fighting, and they had not eaten a meal at midday.

The next move of the Persians was an attempt to lure Sunicas and Simmas to charge out of the formation. They made a feigned attack against them, but this didn't bring the desired outcome. Then the *Hazaraft* decided to outflank the Romans by sending the elite Persians to the left against the Saracens of Arethas. In my opinion this means that the *Hazaraft* divided his elite Persian cavalry in two so that the files of heavier cataphracts were transferred to the left to outflank Arethas. Since there were no reserves, Ascan attempted to prevent this by attacking the Persians.

Unfortunately we do not know exactly what happened next due to the fog of war. Procopius states that Arethas did not wait for the oncoming enemy but fled immediately. This gave the Persians the chance to attack the rear of the Roman formation with the result that the Lycaonians were routed and most killed. Procopius claims that Ascan put up a good fight and fought until he and 800 of his men fell. Belisarius was then forced to retreat and dismount his men to join the remaining regular infantry on the left.

The account of Malalas however is entirely different, but it has the advantage of being based on the official report made afterwards. He claims that the Saracens of Arethas fought bravely, and that the rout of the right wing was actually caused by the death of Ascan who had charged into the middle of the Persians. It was the death of Ascan that caused the flight of the Lycaonians with the result that the Saracens also fled except those around Arethas. Malalas also notes that some (i.e. Belisarius, Procopius and their friends) said that the flight of the Arabs was caused by the treachery of the phylarchs. The friction of war naturally makes it impossible to know which of the versions is correct, but it is possible to reconcile the accounts if one assumes that the Arabs were already starting to flee at the moment Ascan made his desperate charge at the enemy to stop the flight and that his death was the final straw that caused the rout of both the Arabs and Lycaonians as claimed by Malalas.[22]

The Persians pursued the fugitives for a short distance and then returned to attack the infantry phalanx, which consisted of Belisarius's dismounted cavalry and regular infantry. Those who blamed Belisarius for the defeat claimed that he fled on the boat almost immediately, but Procopius states that he stayed with his men. The phalanx had massed together to form a barricade of protruding spears. The tightness of the phalanx formation, the effective archery by men on foot, the clashing of the shields and the wall of spears were more than enough to break up the frontal Persian cavalry charge. The Persians however did not give up. They repeated their charges and attacked again and again until late in the day when they finally gave up in frustration after having lost many men. The Persian withdrawal gave the Romans the chance to retreat to the nearby island from where they retreated to Callinicum on freight boats the following day.

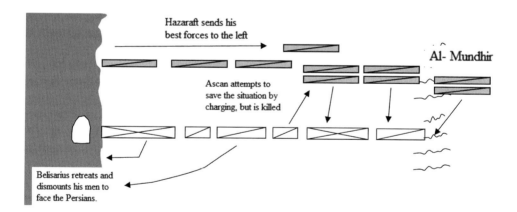

Neither of the rulers was happy with the results of this battle. Cabades sacked the *Hazaraft* because his army had suffered too many casualties for its achievements. The only spoils the army had managed to take consisted of the booty taken from the small and insignificant town of Gabbulon. When Hermogenes reported the results of the battle to Justinian, he ordered the *magister militum praesentalis* Sittas, who resided in Armenia with the *Magister Militum per Armeniam* Dorortheus, to go to the assistance for the eastern armies. Sittas showed initiative once again by making a diversionary invasion into Persian domains where he captured a number of places and then crossed the Armenian mountains into Samosata. Justinian also dispatched Constantiolus to the east to make an official inquiry into the conduct of Belisarius during the battle.[23]

The siege of Abergesaton and the sacking of Belisarius in 531[24]

The above setbacks did not deter Cabades in the least. He wanted to retain the initiative and ordered the Persians to besiege Abgersaton in Oshroene which had been built in the past by toparch Abgar.[25] The city had an old brick wall, which made it vulnerable. The garrison, however, fought bravely. They killed 1,000 Persians with their arrows, and when they ran out of arrows they killed more by using stones. Bouzes advanced from Amida to relieve the city, but in vain. The Persians had in the meantime used a variety of siege engines with which they had breached the brick wall. However, when the Persians rushed into the opening, the defenders responded by descending from the wall and cut down with their swords all those who entered the city. When the Persians realized this, they sent some of their men with ladders against the wall during the night while the Romans concentrated their attention on the breach and thereby managed to force their way in. Once inside, they killed everyone except a few who managed to escape.

Belisarius and his men had stood idle because the emperor had sent Constantiolus to investigate his behaviour during the battle of Callinicum. As a result of this investigation Belisarius was sacked, which means that Constantiolus found the account of his enemies more believable. This, however, does not mean his analysis was correct. As we have seen there were two divergent views. Furthermore, it is possible that the results of the investigation reflected a need to flatter the Arabs so that they would stay loyal to the Romans – and the Romans certainly needed their help. Moundos was appointed the new *Magister Militum per Orientem* and *magister militum praesentalis* Sittas was ordered to take command of the defence of the east while Demosthenes was sent to organize the supplying of cities and forts, which means that the latter organized the logistics for the defensive operations and campaigns.[26]

Malalas's text shows that the religious intolerance of Justinian resulted in some minor troubles at Antioch at this time and one may assume that similar demonstrations against Justinian's policies took place on a smaller scale also elsewhere in the east. According to Malalas, in 531 Justinian repeated his demand that all were required to take communion in the holy churches and that those who refused were to be exiled. This resulted in a riot at Antioch and the mob burst into the bishop's residence. The men who were inside the residence and the men of the *Comes Orientis* defended the building with force and killed many with missiles and stones. When this was reported to Justinian, he ordered many punishments. This shows that the religious intolerance of Justinian was alienating the population in the midst of the Persian war, which begs the question was this really the wisest course of action to take in the circumstances? This instance and all the succeeding ones show that it was impossible to force the Monophysites and others to obey orders to convert. The emperors were fighting against windmills and were only causing troubles for themselves and the empire by alienating a significant section of the Christian community. Still, it didn't cause any serious problems at this time – only police action was required.[27]

The battle of River Nymphius in 531[28]

The objective of the next Persian invasion by 6,000 Persian horsemen under Gadar the Kadisene appears to have been Martyropolis, but this was forestalled by the Romans under *dux* Bessas. He marched out of Martyropolis with 500 horsemen and attacked the

Persians when they had encamped in the area of Amida by the River Nymphius, but the attack failed. After this, Bessas feigned flight. The foolish Persians pursued in disorder. The Romans turned around and cut down 2,000 of them. The pursuit of the defeated was continued up to the River Nymphius, where most of the remaining Persians appear to have been drowned in the currents. The Romans captured some of the Persian generals and standards. The men captured included the nephew of the Vitaxa of Arzanene. Bessas exploited his victory by pillaging the personal possessions of the Persian *Shahanshah* in Arzanene. This was a great personal insult to Cabades, which had to be punished. At about the same time, the *Magister Militum per Armeniam* Dorotheus exploited the momentum gained by the battle of Satala and invaded Persarmenia and captured several fortresses.

The siege of Martyropolis in about July-November 531[29]

After the above had taken place Alamoundaros realized that the Romans had the upper hand and tried to conclude a separate peace with the Romans in June 531, but Justinian refused and instead tried to conclude peace directly with the Persians through his ambassador Rufinus, but to no avail, because Cabades had decided to launch still another invasion to exact vengeance against Bessas. The Persians collected another larger army led by Chanaranges, Aspebedes and Mermeroes to besiege Martyropolis, which was garrisoned and under Bouzes and Bessas, but the defences of the city were incomplete and therefore assailable. The walls had been built only recently, there were inadequate provisions, and the defenders did not have engines of war in their arsenal.

During the siege the Persians attempted to undermine the wall of Martyropolis with many mines, tried to storm the place by using scaling ladders, used a mule (= onager?), and finally constructed a tall wooden tower, but to no avail. Amongst the defenders, there was a clever engineer who worked out countermeasures. The Romans built a taller tower inside the walls and used a machine to drop columns/stones that smashed the Persian siege equipment. The Romans mustered a relief army under Sittas, which included the phylarch Bar Gabala, *Magister Officiorum* Hermogenes and a new bishop for the city of Martyropolis to replace the one who had passed away. They reached Amida in October or November 531. One of the professional Persian spies changed sides and disclosed all the Persian state secrets to Justinian. Most importantly he provided the Romans with information of the impending invasion of the Sabir Huns as allies of Persia. Justinian sent this spy back to the Persian army to announce that the Huns would shortly arrive to assist the Romans. This was a masterful ploy. On top of everything, the Persians soon learned that Sittas with the ambassador Hermogenes was approaching to help the defenders (only 20km away at Attachas). It is unlikely to be a coincidence that we read about the Roman and Persian professional spies and of the Persian double agent working for the Romans when *Magister Officiorum* Hermogenes was present near the border. The *Magister Officiorum* was not only the 'prime minister' and 'foreign minister', but also the spymaster and we should certainly count Hermogenes among the best spymasters the Romans ever had.

When Cabades learnt of the setbacks the Persians had suffered he undergone a paralysis of the right side of his body on 8 September 531. He proclaimed his second son Chosroes emperor by placing a crown on his head. Cabades's closest confidant the *Hazarbed* Mebodes asked Cabades to write a document to this effect. Cabades died five days later on 13 September at the ripe old age of 82. According to Malalas, he had ruled for 43 years and two months. The eldest of the sons of Cabades, Caoses, assumed that he would be the ruler and made a claim to the throne after the burial, but Mebodes opposed this. The matter was put to a vote of the magnates, which confirmed the nomination of Chosroes thanks to the document Cabades had written. After this, Chosroes dispatched a message to the Roman ambassadors to advance immediately on Persian territory to make a peace treaty. When the news of the death of Cabades arrived, the Persians besieging Martyropolis withdrew to their own territory. Chosroes was a new ruler and wanted peace to secure his throne. Hermogenes refused to do so without the permission of the emperor, which he received soon afterwards.

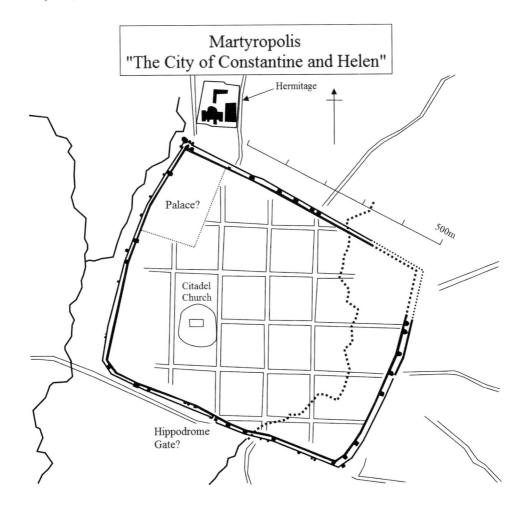

It was only after this that the Huns arrived to assist the Persians, but their invasion turned out to be a failure, contrary to what Zachariah and Malalas state. It is quite clear that they have exaggerated the success of the Huns. They note that the Huns plundered the Armenias and then crossed the Euphrates and spread out, some raiding as far as Euphratesia, Second Cilicia, Kyrrhestike and even reaching the suburbs of Antioch. These two sources claim that only the *dux* of Martyropolis (Bessas), the *dux* of Citharizon, and Dorotheus fought back and recovered part of the booty captured by the Huns. Procopius's disparagement of the importance of the Hunnish invasion is certainly closer to the truth in this case. The details make it clear that the defence against the Huns was performed in textbook manner following military doctrine to the letter. The Romans were well aware of the imminent arrival of the Huns which even happened during the winter. This means that they had adequate time to place most of the populace and their possessions inside the cities for safety so that the raiders found the countryside empty. It is obvious that the Roman strategy of shadowing/guerilla warfare that was based on the use of fortifications and ambushes was very successful in this case and that the Roman commanders were able to engage the retreating Huns at their leisure when the latter were exhausted by their mostly fruitless campaign – only those civilians who had failed to obey the command to seek safety from inside the cities and forts for some reason would have been outside the fortifications.

Meanwhile the Romans were facing trouble further south. Two Arab phylarchs quarrelled, but the newly appointed *Dux Palestinae* Summus (first term in office 531 to before 534) managed to reconcile the two men by scolding them. Some nomadic barbarians also raided Roman territory in Palestine, captured booty and then withdrew to a stronghold located on a hill. Summus assembled his forces and defeated them. Shahid considers it unlikely that the Bedouins in this case would have been in Persian service because they withdrew to a craggy hill, and suggests that they were some independent group located in this area. After this Summus was forced to march south to the Egyptian border where some raiders (Arabs or Blemmyes?) had enslaved pro-Roman nomads. Summus defeated the enemy and released the captives. According to *Laudatio Summi*, the cities under his jurisdiction were freed from the fear of attack and enjoyed peace. He was put in charge of reassessing the taxes of Arabia and according to the praise he received his assessment was fair. This suggests that he was still in charge of Palaestina after the hostilities with Persia stopped.[30]

Legal Practice and the Morale of the Populace Improved in the Cities[31]

In the midst of the war Justinian did not forget civilian matters either but sent to all the cities laws concerning the expenses involved in obtaining legal judgments. He also decreed that nobody was to take more than the amount he prescribed for the payment of *sportulae*. Even if it is clear that there was a need for these laws purely from the legal point of view, it is equally clear that these decisions also had military significance because they were likely to make the citizens less likely to desert to the enemy when they approached.

The 'Eternal Peace' in the spring of 532[32]

After a long period of negotiations Chosroes/Khusro I, the new *Shahanshah* of Persia, and Justinian concluded a peace which was ratified in the spring of 532. The two parties agreed to exchange forts that they had conquered from each other. The Romans handed over to the Persians Pharangium and the fortress of Bolum while the Persians returned the fortresses they had conquered in Lazica. The former were very important concessions from the Romans because these areas produced gold. Both sides also agreed to hand over the prisoners they had taken. This exchange returned to the Romans Dagaris, who, according to Procopius, in later times defeated the Huns several times in battle and drove them out when they had invaded Roman territory. In addition to this, the Romans agreed to pay one lump sum of gold (11,000 lbs) and move the HQ of Master of the East away from Dara to Constantia in return for 'eternal/endless peace'. This was acceptable to the Romans. The Romans could pay the sum easily, being only half the annual tax yield of Egypt. Most importantly, the peace enabled Justinian to begin the reconquest of the West by punishing Gelimer for the overthrow of his friend and ally Hilderic.

Nika Revolt in January 532[33]

Early January 532
In the meantime, before the conclusion of the so-called Eternal Peace, there had taken place one of the most serious civil uprisings in the annals of Roman history – the Nika revolt. It began as a factional rioting against the authorities, but ended as a revolt and usurpation attempt. Before becoming emperor Justinian had been an avid supporter of the Blue Faction, but once he had become emperor he changed his views. He no longer needed the support of the Blues in a power struggle. It was now more important to act impartially for the benefit of all subjects. So he sent an order to all cities to punish impartially those guilty of faction riots. A number of people had been arrested in Constantinople by the men of the Urban Prefect because of rioting that had resulted in deaths. The Prefect Eudaemon found seven of them guilty of murder, ordered four to be beheaded and three hanged. The hangman botched his job, two falling to the ground. The monks of St. Conon intervened and offered these two men a place of asylum in the Church of St. Laurentius across the Golden Horn. The Prefect sent his men after them and besieged the church.

Tuesday, 13 January 532
On the ides of January there were horse races held in the Hippodrome with the emperor present in person. The Blues and Greens exploited the situation and pleaded mercy on the two men. The emperor did not answer. At the 22nd race the spectators heard the shout 'Long live the humane Greens and Blues!' which had clearly been agreed beforehand by the factional leaders. This signalled to all that the two factions had now united against the authorities. They now agreed publicly to unite their forces as the *prasino-venetoi* (the Green-Blues) and use as their watchword *nika* (conquer). The united rioters assembled at the Praetorium in the evening and demanded that the Prefect of the City release those besieged. When they received no answer, the rioters broke into the prison, killed the guards, released the prisoners and set the building on fire partially burning it. After this they ran to the Augusteum/Augusteon and set fire to the Chalke, the entrance of the Imperial Palace. The fire spread northwards and burned the Senate-house and the Church of Hagia Sophia.

Wednesday, 14 January 532
On the following morning the emperor ordered the races to be renewed in the Hippodrome. The Green-Blues continued their rioting and torched several buildings just north of the Hippodrome so that the baths of Zeuxippus and the portico of the Augusteum were burned. Their demands had grown by now. They demanded the sacking of Eudaemon, the Urban Prefect, Tribonian the *Quaestor*, and John of Cappadocia, the Praetorian Prefect. Justinian, attempting to calm the rioters, agreed and Tryphon now became the new Prefect of the City, Basilides the *Quaestor* and Phocas the Praetorian Prefect. This did not calm the rioters. Bury is probably correct in stating that this resulted at least partly from the presence of country folk among the audience who were particularly animated against John the Cappadocian, the emperor and the administration in general so it was possible for those among the senatorial block who wanted to see a regime change to incite them to further rioting. Their plan was to exploit this riot, overthrow Justinian and to replace him with one of the nephews of Anastasius. Since the more prestigious Pompeius and Hypatius (like many other senators) were in the Palace with Justinian, the rioters tried to proclaim Probus as emperor and with this in mind they rushed into his house. Probus had fled the city because he feared that something like this could happen; the frustrated rioters torched his house. This proves that the senatorial plot to overthrow Justinian was already known at this stage. Why else would Probus have been so afraid?

Wednesday, 14 and/or Thursday 15 January – Saturday, 17 January 532
Justinian needed to restore order quickly or he would lose his crown, but he faced a serious problem. The *excubitores* and *scholarii* were unwilling to intervene on the side of their unpopular emperor and rather wanted to wait for the outcome of the riot. The same was also true of the other regulars present in the capital or nearby. Fortunately for Justinian there were still some loyal soldiers left in the capital. They consisted of the sizable force of *hypaspistai* and *doryforoi* of Belisarius, most of whom were Goths, and of the Heruls serving under Mundus/Moundos. The former had come to the capital for the purpose of taking over the campaign against the Vandals once the war against Persia was over, and the latter was in the capital to meet the emperor. The important point here is that Justinian could rely only on the foreigners.

These forces were now sent against the rioters, possibly on Thursday 15 January, and a battle was fought probably in the Augusteum. It was hard fought and many men fell on both sides, but there were too few soldiers present to crush the popular uprising. The soldiers continued to try to put a stop to the revolt and there was continuous street fighting during the next two days, and further torching. On Friday 16 January, the rioters set the Praetorium on fire again because the previous fire had damaged it only partially. The baths of Alexander were also torched and the northerly wind also burned the hospices of Eubulus and Sampson and the Church of St. Irene. On Saturday 17 January the soldiers engaged the rioters on the street which led north from Middle Street to the Basilica and the quarter of Chalkoprateia. The rioters occupied the Octagon, which was close to the Basilica. It was now the turn of the soldiers to use fire. They set the Octagon on fire to smoke out its defenders. The northerly breeze spread this fire southwards to the Church of St. Theodore Sphoracius and the Palace of Lausus, destroying in the process the colonnades and the Church of St. Aquilina. It was at this point that Justinian made a fateful mistake. He did not have any trust in the loyalty of the *excubitores* and *scholarii* and feared that Hypatius and Pompeius could exploit this. Therefore he ordered both out of the Palace despite their protests. Now the rioters finally gained access to the men who they wanted to proclaim emperors.

Sunday, 18 January

The emperor once again held races at the Hippodrome in an effort to pacify the populace. He had in his hand the Gospels and swore that he would grant amnesty to all the rioters. This move had clearly been copied from Anastasius who had similarly made a personal appearance to calm down the rioters. However, Justinian was not Anastasius and he was not trusted. The audience was hostile and reminded Justinian of his betrayal of the oath he had given to Vitalian. Some of the men were also shouting 'Long live Hypatius' because they had by then learnt that he was no longer in the Palace. It is in fact possible that the rioters had already raised him as their emperor before these shouts. The people flocked to the house of Hypatius and took him away despite the best efforts of Hypatius's wife Maria. All she could do was shout that they were taking him to his death. Hypatius was taken to the Forum of Constantine where he was crowned.

After this the senators and Hypatius held a council in which it was discussed whether they should attack the Palace immediately or whether they should adopt a more cautious course. The bolder course won the day and Hypatius and the rioters went to the Hippodrome, next to the Palace. Hypatius took his place at the Kathisma. Justinian and those loyal to him held another council. Everyone else, Belisarius included, favoured flight, but Theodora would have none of that. She made a speech in which she favoured bold action and stated that royalty was a good burial shroud. She was braver than all the men in the room. The others were ashamed and decided to take action as Theodora had urged.

In the meantime, the mob that had gathered at the Hippodrome believed that Justinian had already fled. This was confirmed by Hypatius's messenger. Hypatius, who apparently did not want to become emperor, had sent Ephraem to the Palace with the message to Justinian that he should order his soldiers to attack the mob in the Hippodrome where he had assembled them. Ephraem had brought this message to Thomas, an imperial secretary, who had told him that Justinian had already fled. It is impossible to know for certain whether this was a ploy to lull the enemy into a false sense of security or whether Thomas really thought it was true. The emperor was now putting into action the final plans for the crushing of the revolt. Narses the Eunuch had been dispatched to the Blues with orders to bribe them. This appears to have been at least partially successful. Belisarius and Mundus were tasked with the actual crushing of the revolt. Mundus was sent to the gate called the snail while Belisarius intended to advance directly from the Palace to the Kathisma to capture Hypatius. When Belisarius then attempted this, he was prevented by the soldiers posted to guard the entrance because they did not want to appear to support either. Belisarius was therefore forced to return to Justinian and declare that their cause was lost because the guardsmen had rebelled against Justinian. Justinian however ordered Belisarius to go to the Bronze Gate and propylaea. The exact location of these is not known, except that they were in the northern part of the Palace close to the part which had been torched. Belisarius was forced to make his way through the ruins of the Chalke with great difficulty into the Augusteum and from there to the western entrance of the Hippodrome to the Blue Colonnade, which was located next to the Kathisma on its right northern side. This suggests that Narses had managed to bribe some of the Blues to assist Belisarius and that Justinian had ordered Belisarius to exploit this. Now Belisarius faced a problem. To gain access to the Kathisma he would have needed to go through still another small gate, but if he had done that he would have exposed his men to attack from the side and rear. So Belisarius made the only tactically sound choice. He needed to kill the rioters first before attempting to reach the Kathisma. He drew his sword and ordered his men to do the same. After this they advanced at a run while making a war-cry against the mob which stood in front of them. The mob panicked and started to flee. When Mundus saw this, he ran to the Gate of Death and charged against the mob from the opposite direction. The location of this gate is unknown; it has been speculated that it was on the south-eastern or the south-western side of the Hippodrome. When these two groups of Germanic soldiers advanced from the opposite directions against a panicking mob the end result was butchery. More than 30,000 people met their end in this massacre while two cousins of Justinian, Boraides and Justus, made their way to the Kathisma without meeting resistance from the guards who now knew who the winner would be. They captured Hypatius and Pompeius and others who were with them. Hypatius and Pompeius were executed on the following day, Monday 19 January, their corpses were thrown into the sea, and their property confiscated. Justinian also confiscated the property of at least eighteen senators and exiled them. However, true to his nature, Justinian later forgave the senators and returned to them all their property except that which he had given to his friends. He acted similarly with the children of Hypatius and Pompeius.

The end result of the revolt was the crushing of all opposition to Justinian and the diminishing of the importance of the factions for a while. The torching of Hagia Sophia proved to be a blessing in disguise. Justinian decided to rebuild it in much grander scale and gave this task to the master architect Anthemius of Tralles who had as his assistant Isidore of Miletus who was a masterful architect in his own right. The end result is the wonderful and amazing Hagia Sophia we can still seen in the city now named Istanbul (*eis ten polis*).

The reward of the Eternal Peace: The economising policies of Justinian and John the Cappadocian[34]

Justinian and John the Cappadocian exploited the 'Eternal Peace' by depriving the *limitanei* of their salaries for four to five years saying that the peace made their services unnecessary. This proved to be a dangerous precedent because, according to Procopius, Justinian repeated this economising in salaries every time he made peace with the Persians. In fact Procopius goes on to claim that Justinian took the regular troops (*strateia*) away from the frontiers for no good reason leaving them without guards and the soldiers were forced to beg subsistence from the church. He had already put a stop to the practice of paying five gold staters as a donative to each soldier every four years so these reductions made the profession of soldiering unattractive. It is clear that the economising in the salaries after 532 was the most important reason for the very poor performance of the Roman army in 540, and this at a time when Justinian possessed enough money to construct new churches and monasteries.

As if this was not enough, Justinian also severely reduced the money spent on *cursus publicus* and on the professional spies maintained on the eastern front. This reduced the amount of intelligence available of Persian activities and lowered the speed with which messages of enemy invasions could be sent from more remote areas. Justinian was foolish enough to believe that the 'Eternal Peace' was eternal and that he would no longer need to maintain the same readiness on the eastern front as before so he basically destroyed the defensive system just before the Persian invasion of 540.

Justinian's blind trust in the treaty also led him to abolish the camel corps that the Romans had maintained for logistical reasons so that campaigning in the desert conditions became even more difficult. The results of this became obvious soon enough. The Romans were ever more reliant on their Arab allies.

Justinian also disbanded the four units of *scholae* that Justin I (or rather Justinian) had raised without returning the payments the men had made for the position. On the basis of Procopius's disparaging comments this has usually been seen as meaningless: Procopius describes the *scholarii* as 'expensive parade ground soldiers'. In my opinion this was only partially accurate because as we shall see in the events of 559, the *scholarii* could still be used for military duties and their combat performance was actually not that bad. The cashiering of the four units of *scholae* lowered the reserves available in the capital. However, since it was known that the *scholarii* served in their units mainly for the salary and prestige, this was exploited by Justinian. On several occasions he threatened to send the *scholae* and *protectores domestici* to the front with the idea that they would give up their salaries in return for permission to stay at home. The units did this every time Justinian used this ploy. So the *scholae* and *domestici* were indeed parade ground units, but this should not blind us to the fact that they were still relatively useful, as they showed in 559.

Justinian and John the Cappadocian sent out *discussores* (*logothetai*) from among the *scriniarii* to audit the accounts of the military units and cities. The idea was to make certain that public funds were not misspent, but the *logothetai* misused their position to the detriment of all. According to Procopius, there was a *logothete* called Alexander Snips who made so many accusations against the soldiers in the east that he became the chief reason why the soldiers were few and poor and unwilling to fight. Justinian's aim was undoubtedly good, namely the removal of the abuse of public funds, so absentees, the aged and those unfit for service were removed from the military registers, but the end result was severe dissatisfaction in the ranks and among the officers as stated by Procopius. Alexander was able to gather a massive amount of money for Justinian by these means while he also enriched himself through his corrupt practice of snipping the edges of the gold coins for himself. Therefore this policy added a third reason for the poor state of the defences in the east before the fateful year 540.

In short, the blind trust that Justinian put into the Eternal Peace resulted in the destruction of the defensive system in the east. Justinian trusted that the Persians would respect the treaty. This was sheer stupidity based on a worldview in which the peoples and nations would abide by the treaties that they had concluded, and this in a situation in which Justinian failed to abide by his treaties.

John the Cappadocian's reorganization of Dioceses and Provinces[35]

John the Cappadocian initiated a complicated series of changes in the provincial organization of the dioceses in Asiana, Pontica and Oriens in 535–6 after which he reorganized the administrative structures also in Egypt possibly in 539. The dioceses in all these areas were abolished so that the governors were now directly under the *PPO* – the diocese of Thrace had already been abolished before this. The *PPO* supervised the governors directly through his *tractatores* so that there was no longer any need for vicars. The combining of civilian and military duties in these areas were meant to make it easier for the governors to control brigandage in their areas. However, this change concerned only those areas which did not face serious external threats. The division of civilian and military duties continued in the frontier provinces presumably because in these areas there were more soldiers, which made their commanders potential usurpers if they could combine their military duties with the ability to collect taxes and revenues. All the governors who now received military duties and other governors too were given pay raises when these changes were made. The probable reason for this was that the *PPO* wanted to keep these men happy in a situation in which their duties were increased so that they would not be enticed to corruption or usurpation. The simultaneous economising (abolishment of vicars and uniting of provinces) meant that the increased salaries cost nothing extra for the exchequer.

In short, the Vicariates of Asiana were abolished and the provincial governors of Phrygia Pacatiana and Galatia Prima were given both civilian and military duties with the title of *comes* and higher salary. Honorias and Paphlagonia were united and their governors became praetors and moderators with military duties. Helenopontus and Pontus Polemiacus were also united and governors obtained the same titles and duties. The posts of the military *comes* and civil governor were combined in the provinces of Pisidia and Lycaonia. In Cappadocia I the offices of *comes domorum* and governor were united with military duties. In Armenia there was a complete overhaul of the provinces and duties, for which see the events of 539. Oriens faced fewer changes. The office of *Comes Orientis* was abolished and his title was given to the governor of Syria I. The posts of *comes* and civil governor were once again united in Isauria. The civilian governors of Arabia and Phoenice Libanensis received the title moderator together with a pay raise. The governor of Palaestina I was raised to the rank of proconsul. The changes suggest that these areas faced banditry and that there was a need for the combination of civilian and military duties for this reason.[36] In short, the abolition of the dioceses was meant to place the governors directly under the *PPO* John the Cappadocian.

There is also evidence of banditry at least for the area of Palaestina I in a panegyric of Choricius addressed to *Dux Palaestinae* Aratius the Persarmenian, the brother of Narses and Isaac, and governor Stephanus. As noted above the latter governorship was raised to the rank of *proconsul Palestinae Primae* on 1 July 536 which dates the panegyric to the period before this (ca. 535/6). The panegyric includes several scattered references to the problems in this area in the interwar period. There was a revolt of religious dissidents in *Palaestina*, which Aratius ended without having to use force. Similarly, after several failed attempts Aratius captured some unknown fortress considered impregnable from the Saracens/Arabs. This fortress must have been located *extra limitem*, somewhere in

Hijaz. It is likely to have been of importance because of gold mines. Thanks to the threat posed by Saracens there was an impassable pass which needed to be cleared up to open up a route. Aratius achieved this with threats combined with a small force of less than twenty men and there was no need for fighting. There is no way of knowing whether this route was inside or outside the borders, but Shahid notes that if it was located inside it must have been near Gaza or Caesarea. As if this was not enough, some groups of Arabs lived on the island of Iotabe/Jotabe and had a fortress on the mainland. The island of Jotabe was important because some of the cargoes from India came from there and the imperial tax collectors collected taxes on ships that put in there. This group of Arabs attacked the island, destroyed the local church and captured the taxes meant for the emperor. Aratius responded by assaulting and capturing the fortress together with its defenders and the island after which he left the fortress in the hands of trustworthy men and thereby returned the taxes to the emperor. Shahid has speculated that the Ghassanids may have participated in Aratius's campaign because the area lay under their jurisdiction. The other possibility is of course that the rebels were Ghassanids themselves.[37]

There was another serious incident on the Arabian frontier in 536. The Saracens/ Arabs in Persian territory were in trouble because drought had destroyed their pasture lands. Because of this about 15,000 Arabs migrated under their phylarchs Chabus and Hezibus to the territory held by Alamoundaros/Alamundarus, but he forced them to continue their journey to the Roman province of Euphratesia where the local *dux* Batzas managed to pacify them with flattery and other peaceful means so that they became Roman allies.[38] It was therefore the troubles with the various Arabic groupings that were behind the administrative changes in this area.

In Egypt John the Cappadocian abolished the authority of the *praefectus Augustalis* over the entire diocese in about 539. The *Dux Aegypti* became his superior, controlling both civilian and military matters in the two provinces of Aegyptus with the *praefectus* controlling Aegyptus II on his behalf. *Dux Thebaidis* was similarly given dual function over both civilian and military matters as *dux et Augustalis*, but in such a manner that he had two subordinate civilian governors. Libya also had a *dux* under whom there was a civilian governor and there is every reason to believe that the provinces of Augustamnina I and II, Arcadia and Pentapolis had similar arrangements. This once again suggests that the *duces* of these areas faced internal and/or external threats which required better control of the financial situation so that the salaries of the soldiers could be paid and supplies bought for them.

Chapter Six

The Campaign Against the Vandals in 533–34

The background[1]

In 530 Justinian received the news that Gelimer had usurped power in North Africa and had imprisoned his guest-friend Hilderic/Hildericus/Ilderic who was the grandson of Geiseric and on very friendly terms with the Romans. This destroyed Justinian's dreams of using the Vandals for the reconquest of Italy from the Goths. The reason for the overthrow of Hilderic was the humiliating defeats suffered at the hands of Moors. Justinian's first reaction was to write to Gelimer and demand the restoration of Hilderic on the throne because he was the legitimate ruler and therefore the man who was party to the peace agreement made earlier by Zeno and Geiseric. There was little else he could do because the Romans were in the middle of the Persian war. Gelimer sent the envoys back empty-handed, blinded Hilderic's brother Hoamer and kept both Hilderic and Euagees (another brother) in close confinement. Justinian sent another letter in which he demanded that Gelimer send the prisoners to Constantinople with the threat that he would otherwise exact vengeance on behalf of Geiseric. Gelimer did not fall into this trap. He did not send the prisoners. Procopius claims that it was only after the second mission had failed that Justinian decided to conclude peace with Persia and punish the Vandals, but in my opinion it is likelier that Justinian had already formulated his plan when he demanded the release of the prisoners because they could have been used to divide the enemy during the campaign to retake North Africa.

The preparations[2]

Justinian convened his consistory to discuss how to invade North Africa. According to Procopius, the Praetorian Prefect John the Cappadocian and every one of the *strategoi* (generals) and soldiers[3] were frightened about the prospect of having to fight the Vandals. However, he also noted that there were others who wished to. These included the Roman merchants and clergy and all those who had lost land and property when the Vandals had conquered North Africa. The only one of those present to dare voice his opposition to Justinian's plans was John the Cappadocian. Justinian was on the point of giving up his plans, but then one bishop from the East noted that it was the duty of the emperor to protect the Christians of Libya from the tyrants. The words of the bishop convinced Justinian who immediately began to collect army, ships, and supplies of weapons and food for the campaign, and ordered Belisarius to be in readiness to lead the offensive.

Procopius presents subsequent events as if they were a local initiative, but it is clear that the locals who revolted against the Vandals did so after they had been instigated to do so by the special operatives sent by Justinian. In my opinion, the principal reason for

Procopius's silence about these matters is that he was himself a member of this ultra-secret spy organization (*kastaskopoi*) and it is not a coincidence that he performed an intelligence gathering mission during this campaign. Consequently Procopius claims that Pudentius, a native of Tripolis, revolted on his own and then sent an envoy to the emperor begging him to send an army to his assistance. Justinian sent Tattimuth with a small army. Pudentius united it into his own forces and liberated the province of Tripolis. Gelimer wanted to punish him immediately, but the revolt of Godas, by birth a Goth, in Sardinia prevented this. Godas also asked Justinian to send him an army. Justinian duly sent Eulogius to negotiate with him. He promised to send soldiers and a general, but Godas stated that he did not need a general, only soldiers. In the meantime Justinian had assembled an invasion force for the North African campaign and a separate force of 400 men under Cyril to assist Godas. It is unlikely to be a coincidence that Pudentius and Godas both revolted at the right time. It is evident that the Roman spy network had incited them to do so. The following discussion will show that these spies operated throughout the Mediterranean disguised as merchants. The fact that Tripolis was far away from Carthage and that the Roman army under Tattimuth had already reached the scene caused Gelimer to abandon the idea of attempting to march there. Instead he sent his brother Tzazon and 5,000 Vandals on 150 ships to Sardinia to reconquer it before the Romans could send reinforcements.

The campaign force that Justinian assembled was a very significant effort and consisted of the following components. Procopius lists first Cyril (*Kurillos/Cyrillus*) with 400 soldiers designated to sail to Sardinia, after which he lists 10,000 footmen and 5,000 horsemen, the latter of which were collected from the regulars (*stratiotai*) and *foederati* (*foideratoi*). Procopius specifies that these were originally barbarians enlisted for service on the basis of treaties (*foedera*), but during his time the *foederati* included anyone who had entered service as *foederatus*. In other words, the *foederati* were basically mercenaries who served under contract as long as the terms of their treaty stated.

The commanders (*archontes*) of the *foederati* were Dorotheus ('*ho tôn en Armeniois katalogôn stratêgos*') and eunuch Solomon, the *domesticus* of Belisarius. Under them served Cyprian (Kuprianos/Cyprianus), Valerianus (Valerianos), Martinus (Martinos), Althias, John (Ioannês/Iohannes), Marcellus (Markellos) and the Cyril destined for Sardinia. If each of the subordinates and commanders had about the same number of men as Cyril, then the *foederati* consisted of 3,200 men altogether plus the 400 men of Cyril. The commanders of the regular cavalry were Rufinus and Aigan from the house of Belisarius, and Barbatus and Pappus. To make the numbers match the figure of 5,000 horsemen I have estimated that each of these commanded about 450 men so that the regular cavalry consisted of 1,600 men altogether. In combat the regulars would presumably have been deployed in a shallower formation (e.g. five deep while the *foederati* would have been deployed ten deep) to make the width equal to the twice as large as the numbers of *foederati*.

The overall commander of the 10,000-strong infantry force was John of Dyrrachium/Epidamnus. Under him served Theodorus Cteanus, Terentius, Zaidus, Marcian, and Sarapis. This would imply that each of the subordinates commanded about 2,000 men.

The army also included true allies, which Procopius calls *symmachoi*. These consisted of 400 Heruls under Pharas and about 600 Massagetae Huns under Sinnion and Balas, the latter of which were all mounted archers.

The fleet consisted of 500 ships which carried 30,000 sailors mostly from Egypt and Ionia, and also from Cilicia. *Archegos* (prefect of Alexandrian Fleet?) Calonymus of Alexandria (Kalonymos) was placed in command of all the ships. In addition, there were ninety-two fast warships called *dromones* (runners), presumably also under Calonymus. These were *monoremes* (single-banked) with decks to protect the rowers. In these there were 2,000 men of Byzantium who were all rowers and fighters simultaneously. This number is far too small to include all of the rowers for these 92 war galleys. It is probable that the *dromones* in question were so-called fifties (25 oars per side), but we do not know if the oars had two rowers per oar or just one. The former is likelier, but I include here both alternatives. If there were two rowers per oar, then the Fleet of Byzantium (i.e. the Imperial Fleet in Constantinople) had detached 20 *dromones* for this campaign and if there was just one rower per oar then the Imperial Fleet had detached 40 dromones to the campaign with the implication that the rest of the ships, 72 or 52 *dromones*, came from the other fleets. If we assume that these ships came from the same places as the sailors, then these *dromones* would have been detached from the Alexandrian Fleet (Egyptians) and from the fleets of Ionia and Cilicia. The Cilicians would probably mean the old *Classis Syriaca*, but Ionia is more problematic because no known fleet is close to that site. However, we know from later sources that in the latter half of the seventh century there was a fleet called *Karabisianoi* based at Samos just south of Ionia, and we also know that in the fourth century the cities of Asia Minor contributed ships for war. It is therefore possible or probable that there existed a separate fleet for Ionia and/or for the Aegean islands at this time which was the precursor of the *Karabisianoi*, the marines of which were possibly known as the *Lykokranitai* at this time.[4]

The overall commander of the campaign was Belisarius with the title *strategos autokrator* (*dux/magister imperator*). Justinian gave him written instructions which showed others that Belisarius had the power to act as if the emperor (*Basileos*) was present in person. Belisarius was assisted by the Praetorian Prefect Archelaus (Archelaos) who acted as Prefect of the Campaign Forces for its duration to ensure they would get all necessary supplies. Belisarius was also accompanied by his *bucellarii*, which Procopius called *doryforoi* (spearmen = officers) and *hypaspistai* (shield-bearers = rank-and-file). Large households such as that of Belisarius also had a commander in chief, the majordomo (*efestôs tê oikia*) and paymaster (*optio*).[5] Procopius does not provide us with any figures for the size of this component, but at a later date he states that Belisarius had 7,000 bodyguards. So one is forced to make an educated guess. The private army of Belisarius was probably smaller than later, even if one cannot rule out that it was already 7,000 strong, but it is still clear that it was large enough to form the centre division of the cavalry array at the battle of Tricamarum, in addition to which there were still enough men to serve as reserves and also to be detached for other uses. This means that there had to be at least 3,000 men, but the figure of 5,000 men is actually the more likely (see later).

The Enemy 1: The Vandals[6]

At the time of their arrival in Africa, the total male population of the Vandals consisted of 80 chiliarchies (80,000 men). The able-bodied men numbered perhaps about 63,000 of whom those below the age of 50 were about 56,000. When the Romans began their reconquest, the Vandal population would have increased, but on the basis of Procopius the size of the field army was not much larger, perhaps 30,000–40,000 men at most, presumably because of the easy living conditions. On top of that, the Vandals had torn down the important sections of the walls in all of their cities except at Carthage to make it more difficult for the natives to revolt. This worked to the advantage of the invaders, which in this case were the Romans, because they did not have to stop to besiege any cities or forts. Pringle has suggested that the vast majority of the population was indifferent in its attitude to the Romans and that only those who thought they would gain from them sided with them. However, the fact that the Vandals had torn down the walls suggests that a significant number of the natives were either friendly or potentially friendly towards the Roman invaders. Furthermore, Procopius (*Wars* 3.5.12ff.) specifically noted that the Vandals had not only confiscated property but also overtaxed the locals. Because of this it was important for the invaders to treat the locals with respect. The Vandals were therefore quite vulnerable as far as their numbers and defensive structures were concerned. The principal threat for the Romans was the Vandal navy, but even that was not as effective as it had been because it had not conducted the vast piratical raids in the manner it had under Geiseric. Regardless, the fame that it had achieved as a result of the 468 war was such that the Romans did not take any risks but diverted it to a secondary target when they finally disembarked their troops in Africa.

According to Procopius, the Vandals had grown so soft in peace that even the 'naked Moors' had defeated them several times over. However, before the campaign the Romans were unaware of this. Their knowledge of the Vandal way of fighting was based on their last encounters which had taken place decades ago. On land the main strength of the Vandal kingdom lay in their cavalry, which was usually deployed with reserves posted behind. The cavalry was equipped in the typical Germanic manner with spears, swords, and shields. The Vandals also employed mounted archers and javeliners, but their importance was not great; Procopius (*Wars* 3.8.27) specifically states that the Vandals were not good with the javelin or bow. I take this to mean that the Vandals placed their mounted archers and javeliners in the rear ranks just as they are in the sixth century *Strategikon* and that their tactic of attack was therefore considered a charge with lancers just as the *Strategikon* (Book 11) called the Roman cavalry charge with this array a 'lancer attack'. This means the Vandals were at grave disadvantage when facing the Romans or the Moors who could also fight at distance with javelins and arrows. Furthermore, they did not dismount their cavalry, which made them vulnerable to infantry formations and to the Moorish camps consisting of camels and other defensive features. The most telling weakness however, was their lack of fighting spirit resulting from years of peace and easy living followed by the defeats they had suffered when fighting against the Moors.

The Enemy 2: The Moors/Berbers[7]

Unlike with the Vandals, the East Romans' knowledge of the fighting methods employed by the Moors was up to date because they faced them in Cyrenaica. Procopius states that the Moors of his day did not wear armour, had small shields, carried two javelins and used terrain or palisaded camps as bases of attack. This is a very good generalized description of their fighting methods. Corippus elaborates further by noting the differences in fighting methods from one tribe to another. For example, according to Corippus: the Frexes employed both infantry and cavalry; the Austur specialized in the use of the camp and camels; the Ifuraces were noted for their shields and powerful swordplay while their charge was characterized by leaping up and down for dramatic effect; and the Aurasitians (Austuriani) employed only cavalry armed with a two-ended lance and shield. Previous research has suggested that we should identify several of the tribes which are sometimes named separately, such as the Austurians, Llaguas/Laguatan, Marmaridae and sometimes also the Garamantes, to belong to the same tribal confederacy which is usually called either the Austuriani or Laguatan depending on the period of time. At the beginning of the invasion of North Africa, the Moors were not the principal enemy but only a potential enemy on their own or as Vandal allies if the situation was mishandled. When the Romans then occupied the area, the Moors became the principal problem, and when this happened the potential troublemakers came to include even some Moorish ploughmen who had simply joined for the sake of plunder.

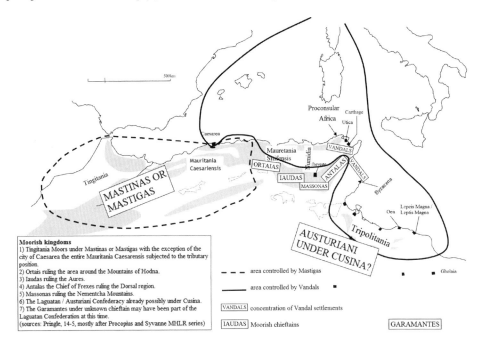

The Moors usually sought to avoid hand-to-hand combat in open terrain with the Romans, because they employed only light forces, but this does not mean that they would not have occasionally been forced to do so. It was more typical for them either to raid and retreat before the Romans could mount a counter-strike, or to use difficult terrain and fortified camps as defensive barriers or as places from which to launch ambushes possibly with the use of feigned retreats. Moorish cavalry tactics with their horse javelin throwers resembled the African Drill used by the Roman cavalry for training in which each group or groups of horsemen attacked in turn while the other groups waited. One of their standard combat methods was to lure the Romans into the desert by fleeing before them and let the thirst and heat do the rest until the Romans were ready to be defeated.

The Roman counter-tactic was not to follow them too far but merely to cut off access to the rich farmlands of the north with the idea of forcing the enemy to return north so that they would be forced to fight a decisive pitched battle. Regardless, when well-led and supplied, the Romans could expect to win their encounters with the Moors even in difficult terrain. On top of that they were quite ignorant of siege craft so the Romans possessed an absolute superiority in both defensive and offensive sieges.

The Moors of North Africa the Romans faced in the sixth century were no longer the weak enemies they had faced in the fourth century thanks to the fact that weakness of the Vandals had allowed them to form larger and more powerful confederacies. At the time the Romans arrived there were six Berber chieftains with significant numbers of men to oppose the Romans. The most powerful of these had 30,000 to 50,000 men, but when several of these united they could mass together armies of 100,000.

However, although numbers do matter in warfare, quality also matters. In this the Romans excelled. They possessed all arms of service and could exploit their combined arms concept and higher quality equipment and soldiers to win wars with significantly fewer men. On top of this, the Romans were now blessed with some very skilled commanders. The main problem for the Romans was how to retain the loyalty of their own men who were prone to revolt when things didn't progress as they wished. Roman soldiers of the time were greedy men whose primary source of motivation for fighting was the prospect of booty, and this spelled trouble. In these situations when the Romans fought against other Romans the Moors provided untrustworthy allies for either side.

The fleet sails[8]

Justinian launched his long-planned campaign at about the spring equinox in 533. Epiphanius, the Bishop of Constantinople, prayed for success. After this the commander of the expedition, Belisarius, and his wife Antonina raised anchor and set sail from in front of the Palace.

The fleet stopped at Perinthus/Heraclea to embark horses from the royal horse pastures of Thrace after which it continued its journey to Abydus. There two drunken Huns killed one of their comrades. Belisarius had the two impaled as a warning, because the keeping of discipline during this campaign was of utmost importance. The Romans were reconquering territories lost and it was vital to treat the local populace well to gain their goodwill which would have been impossible if the soldiers lacked discipline. The impaling, however, caused anger among the Huns, in particular among the relatives of the killed. Consequently, Belisarius had to upbraid the Huns and other soldiers with a speech which stressed the importance of military discipline. Notably, Belisarius considered the intoxicated state of the Huns to have been sufficient grounds for punishment, not to mention the murder. Belisarius invoked God and justice in his speech. His claim was that success would only come to those who had both on their side. At this stage of the journey, Belisarius also decided that the best way for him to keep his fleet in order was that he and the three ships which carried his following were to advance in front of all the rest. To make these ships more visible he had the sails painted red from the upper corner and erected upright poles on the prows with lights hanging from them. In addition, trumpets were used to signal the time when the fleet was to set out from a harbour.

1) Constantinople: Belisarius, Antonina, Procopius and most of the forces set sail and the Bishop of Constantinople Epiphanius prays for success.

2) Perinthus/Heraclea: Fleet stays for 5 days and horses from the royal pastures of Thrace are embarked on the ships.

3) Abydus: 4 days waiting for favourable winds; Two Massagetae kill their comrade while intoxicated; Belisarius impaled these and gave a speech to stress the importance of discipline during this campaign. The three leading ships under Belisarius have their upper corners painted red and poles in the prow carry lights to enable all ships to follow the commander's three ships.

4) Sigeum/Sigeion: Strong winds carried the fleet from Abydu there.

5) Malea: Calm weather allows the fleet to stay together and the sailors showed their skill by keeping the ships apart with poles when the ships were anchored.

6) Taenarum / Caenopolis.

7) Methone: Valerian (Valerianus) and Martinus with their men joined the campaign force. The fleet anchored because the winds were not favourable and Belisarius assembled the army, puts the commanders in place of their units and drills the soldiers. The *bucellatum*-hardtack became spoiled thanks to the corrupt practices of the Praetorian Prefect John of Antioch with the result that 500 men die. Justinian fails to punish John.

8) Zakynthus: Enough water taken for the crossing of the Adriatic Sea.

9) Deserted location near Mt. Aetna. Belisarius fears possible ambush and sends Procopius on a ship to obtain information of the enemy activities from the city of Syracuse. Officially Procopius was buying supplies from the Ostrogoths as had been agreed in advance by the rulers. While doing so Procopius meets a childhood friend who was engaged in shipping business. It is probable that this merchant is actually a spy even if Procopius does not state so. He informs Procopius that the best Vandal soldiers had sailed against Godas and that Gelimer was staying in Hermione at a distance of four days from the coast so the Romans could land wherever they pleased at their own leisure. Cyril is dispatched to Sardinia.

10) Caucana / Kaukanai (Punta Secca); Dorotheus dies and Procopius meets his employer and gives the good news.

11) Islands of Gaulus (Gozo) and Melita (Malta).

12) Belisarius makes a landing at Caput Vada at a distance 5 days' march from Carthage. A War Council held. Belisarius decides to march on land while the fleet sails along the coast. The forces are disembarked, and a fortified camp built. An abundance of water is found on the locale. The fleet is anchored and the warships form a circle around them. On the following day some soldiers took fruits from the field. Belisarius punishes them, because it was important to treat the locals as Romans to obtain their goodwill.

13. The Romans and Vandals encounter each other at Ad Decimum on 13 September 533 while the fleet sails to the Cape Bon. Belisarius wins.

14. Belisarius advances to the city of Carthage.

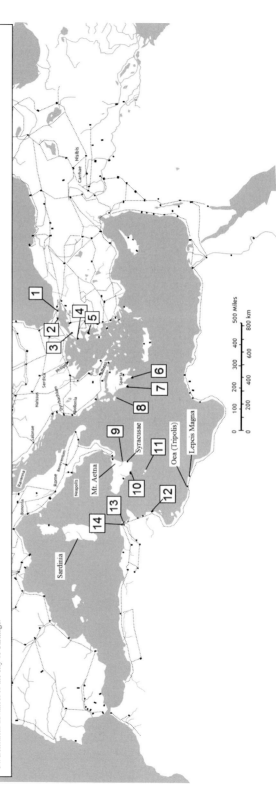

The next stops mentioned by Procopius are Sigeum/Sigeion, Males, Taenarum/Caenopolis, and Methone, where the forces of Valerianus and Martinus joined the rest of the army. When adverse winds kept the Romans at anchor, Belisarius exploited the situation by assembling his army for review and drilling. He distributed the units to their commanders and then drilled the soldiers. Then a disaster struck. The Romans typically carried *bucellatum*/hard-tack on campaigns, but this time the hard-tack had become spoiled because the Praetorian Prefect John the Cappadocian had attempted to economise. It was supposed to be put into the oven twice, but he had put it in only once. Five hundred men died before Belisarius realized what was happening. Belisarius reported the fact to Justinian, but Justinian did not punish John, presumably because of his ability to bring money into the state coffers. The journey continued to Zakynthus where the fleet collected enough water for the crossing of the Adriatic Sea.

The Fleet anchored at a deserted location near Mt. Aetna. The ever-cautious Belisarius feared that the Vandal fleet could lie somewhere in ambush and so he sent Procopius on a ship to obtain information of enemy activities from Syracuse. His instructions were for Procopius to meet him and the fleet at Caucana/Kaukanai (Punta Secca). Procopius' cover was that he was buying supplies from the Ostrogoths as had been agreed in advance by the rulers. The Romans also bought horses from the Goths at this time (Procop. *Wars* 5.3.22), which means that they did not have enough with them. This incident is valuable because it shows us one of the means by which the Romans gathered intelligence. It is clear that Procopius was a member of the secretive organization called by the generic name of *kataskopoi* (spies). He had officially been appointed legal adviser and personal secretary of Belisarius in 527, but the task given now makes it is clear that Procopius was indeed a spy with the double duty of spying on his superior while also helping him with other intelligence matters. Procopius claims that when he sailed to Syracuse it was just a lucky accident that he met a childhood friend who had been living for a long time in Syracuse, who was engaged in the shipping business, and who just happened to know that the best Vandal soldiers had sailed against Godas and that Gelimer was staying in Hermione four days from the coast so the Romans could land wherever they pleased at their leisure. The domestic of the merchant had also just arrived from Carthage on the same day and could confirm that the Vandals had not placed any ambush for the Romans. Obviously the trader could not know these things unless he had actively sought out this information on behalf of the Roman invaders. Procopius claims that the Vandals (Proc., *Wars* 3.20.5ff.) directed their vengeance against the Roman merchants because Gelimer suspected the merchants of having influenced the emperor to begin the war, but it is also clear that Gelimer understood that some of the merchants were spies like the friend of Procopius. Procopius immediately walked to Arethousa harbour with the domestic and boarded the ship. When he reached Belisarius at Caucana, he was able to deliver the good news for his delighted commander. The only thing that marred the joy was the death of Dorotheus, but this did not influence the outcome of the campaign. Belisarius ordered the sails to be raised and the Roman fleet sailed via the islands of Gaulus (Gozo) and Melite (Malta) and anchored in front of Caput Vada, which was at a distance of five days' unencumbered march from Carthage.

Belisarius assembled his war council on his ship. The Praetorian Prefect Archelaus recommended they should sail straight to Carthage, but Belisarius vetoed this on the grounds that his soldiers feared to fight on the sea so it was safer to march on land while the fleet sailed along the coast. So the army disembarked and built a fortified camp. When doing so, they found an abundance of water, which was naturally interpreted as a lucky omen. The fleet was then anchored and the warships formed a protective circle around them.

The march begins[9]

On the following day some soldiers took fruit from a field. Belisarius punished them because it was important to treat the locals as Romans to obtain their goodwill. When Belisarius learnt that there was a town called Sullectus/Sullectum one day's march away which had improvised walls built against the Moors, he sent Boriades with a detachment of bodyguards to capture it with orders not to harm the inhabitants. Bordiades hid his forces for a night in a nearby ravine and then entered the town with a convoy of wagons without encountering any resistance. The local priest and notables handed over the city. At the same time the local overseer of the public post deserted to the Romans and as a result the Romans were able to capture couriers called *veredarii*. Belisarius attempted to use the overseer for propaganda purposes by giving him the letter from Justinian to be delivered to the Vandals which stated that the Romans had come as liberators and were there to dethrone the tyrant Gelimer. The letter, however, did not serve its intended purpose because the overseer was too frightened to deliver it. He showed it only to his friends, and this was not enough to affect the situation.

It was then that Belisarius began his march to Carthage. He posted 300 of his bodyguards under his *optio* (paymaster of the *bucellarii*) John as vanguard at a distance of at least 20 stades (c. 3.7 km) in front of the army. The right flank was guarded by the coast and fleet. On the left flank he posted 600 Huns at a distance of at least 20 stades away from the main force. The best of the cavalry under Belisarius formed the rearguard against Gelimer with the implication that infantry and some of the cavalry marched in the middle of the array presumably as a hollow square/oblong.

When the Romans reached Sullectum, the locals provided a market for them. After this, the Romans continued their march, marching about 80 stades each day stopping for a night either in a city or marching camp. The marching route was Sullectum, Thapsus, Leptis Minus, Hadrumentum, Horrea Caelia, Uppenna, and Pupput. When the Romans reached Grassa, their scouts had a skirmish with the scouts of Gelimer whose forces were following behind the Romans. At this point, Belisarius was forced to divide his forces, continuing his march along the most direct route to Carthage while his fleet was sent around Cape Bon with orders not to approach Carthage closer than 200 stades (37 km) before Belisarius gave the order.

Some time during his march Gelimer formed a plan to attack the Romans at the narrows of Ad Decimum from two directions. With this in mind, he sent orders for his brother Ammatas to kill the imprisoned royal family and all their local supporters, and to collect the Vandals in the city after which he was to march to Ad Decimum to attack the Romans from the front while he Gelimer attacked from behind. Gelimer also thought it necessary to send reinforcements to Ammatas. He appears to have turned left when the Romans continued straight towards Carthage with the purpose of sending Gibamundus with 2,000 men around the Salt Lake Sebkrat es-Sedjoumi with orders to join forces with Ammatas.

The Campaign to take Carthage

1) Belisarius disembarks his army at Caput Vada, builds a fortified camp, and anchors his ships as a circle.

2) Boriades sent to capture the city of Sullectus / Sullectum, which he accomplishes with a combination of surprise and promise.

3) Belisarius arrayed his forces for march to Carthage: 300 men under John formed the vanguard; 600 Huns protected the left; infantry formed the centre; the best of the cavalry under Belisarius formed the rear guard against Gelimer; Navy protected the right flank.

4) Belisarius reached Sullectum. The locals provide a market.

5) The Romans continue the march by marching about 80 stades (14.8 km) each day stopping for a night either in a city or marching camp. The marching route was Sullectum, Thapsus, Leptis Minus, Hadrumentum, Horrea Caelia, Uppenna, and Pupput.

6) When Belisarius reached Grassa, his scouts had a skirmish with the scouts of Gelimer who was behind the Romans. At this point, Belisarius was forced to divide his forces so that he continued his march along the most direct route to Carthage while his fleet was sent around the Cape Bon with orders not to approach Carthage before Belisarius would order them to do so.

7) When the Romans were approaching Ad Decimum, Gelimer sent Gibamundus with 2,000 men around the Salt Lake with orders to join his forces with Ammatas so that Ammatas and Gibamundus would attack the Romans from the front at Ad Decimum while he himself would attack them from behind.

8) Gelimer's plan failed because the Roman vanguard under John surprised and killed Ammatas and pursued the fugitives up to Carthage and because the Huns defeated Gibamundus at Pedion Halon.

9) When Belisarius was at a distance of 35 stades (6475m) away from Ad Decimum, he built a fortified marching camp for his infantry and decided to skirmish with his cavalry forces in order to learn the strengths and weaknesses of the enemy before committing his infantry to the battle.

10) Belisarius sends his *foederati* forward and follows with the rest of his cavalry.

11) *Foederati* find the corpses at Ad Decimum and after that see the army of Gelimer which was advancing along the centre road that had hills on both sides hiding it from Belisarius while also making sure that the Vandals did not see the Romans. The foederati ask Belisarius to send help.

12) Gelimer attacks the foederati and routs them. The 800 men sent by Belisarius join the fugitives, but Gelimer does not press his advantage but is grief stricken with the sight of his dead brother Ammatas.

13) Belisarius attacks with all of his cavalry and routs the disordered Vandals.

14) The Vandals flee towards the Plain of Bulla and the route is opened up to Carthage.

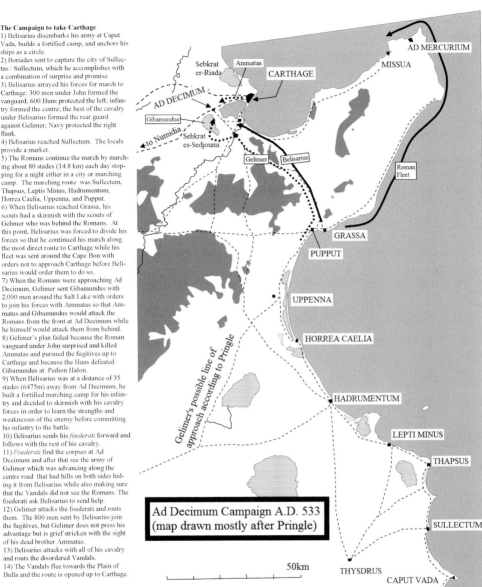

Ad Decimum Campaign A.D. 533
(map drawn mostly after Pringle)

50km

The battle of Ad Decimum on 13 September 533[10]

Gelimer's plan failed for two reasons.

The first was that Ammatas came to Ad Decimum about midday well ahead of the appointed time. On top of this, he left his forces behind with orders only to follow him so that he arrived at the meeting place accompanied by very few followers while the rest of his forces followed in scattered disorderly groups of 20 or 30 men. It was then that Ammatas came face-to-face with the forces of John. Ammatas fought bravely and killed twelve front rank fighters from John's forces, but was then killed himself. When this happened, the remaining Vandals panicked and fled, and their panic infected all the following small groups of Vandals. The Romans went in hot pursuit and killed the fugitives all the way to the gates of Carthage.

The second of the reasons was the poor fighting skills and morale of the men under Gibamundus. These forces came face-to-face with the Massagetae Huns at a place called Pedion Halon (the Salt Marsh) which was about 40 stades from Ad Decimum. The Massagetae Huns had a custom according to which battles could be started only by members of certain families. Because of this one Hun approached the Vandals who halted and did not even shoot missiles at the Hun. When the Hun saw this he returned to his lines and said to his compatriots that God had delivered these strangers to them as a ready feast. After this the Huns charged. The Vandals panicked and fled, and according to Procopius they were all killed. So the Romans had now destroyed by lucky coincidence the entire Vandal force posted in front of them.

Belisarius knew nothing of the above when he reached a place suitable for the building of a marching camp 35 stades from Ad Decimum. He halted the march and built the camp where he placed his infantry and wife. His purpose was to test the Vandals with cavalry skirmishes before committing his whole army to the battle. Belisarius was unaware of the whereabouts of the Vandals, and vice versa Gelimer was unaware of the Huns and the Romans thanks to the hills that hid the armies from each other. It was then that Belisarius sent his *foederati* cavalry forward to reconnoitre the narrows close to Ad Decimum while he followed with the rest of the cavalry.

When the *foederati* reached Ad Decimum, they found the twelve killed members of Belisarius' *bucellarii* together with the corpse of Ammatas. The locals told them what had happened. Then some of the *foederati* who were on the hill saw Gelimer approaching from the south along the central road and sent an urgent plea for Belisarius to send help. After this the commanders of the *foederati* quarrelled amongst themselves whether it was wiser to attack or retreat because the Vandals outnumbered them. Then the Vandals charged.

The *foederati* and the Vandals started to fight over the possession of the highest hill in the area. The Vandals, who also had a numerical advantage, reached the hill first. The *foederati* fled towards Belisarius, who had sent Uliaris with 800 of his *bucellarii* to their assistance. They met their helpers at a place 7 stades from Ad Decimum, but instead of stabilizing the situation, the assistance joined the fugitives in flight. Procopius suspects that the Romans would have lost the war then and there had Gelimer pressed his advantage, but instead of doing this he halted his forces and descended from the hill at a walk and when he reached level ground and saw the corpse of his brother Ammatas, he turned to lamentations and did nothing. This gave Belisarius the chance to regroup. This was also very fortunate for the forces of John because they had scattered to loot the corpses after their pursuit and it would have been easy for any organized force to butcher all of them. The *foederati* and forces under Uliaris were then arrayed again in combat order presumably as a second line for the cavalry of Belisarius, and Belisarius reprimanded them for their cowardly behaviour. When Belisarius learnt what had happened and what type of terrain he faced, he ordered his cavalry to attack at full speed. The Vandals were then in complete disorder and paid the price. They fled and it was only the night that put

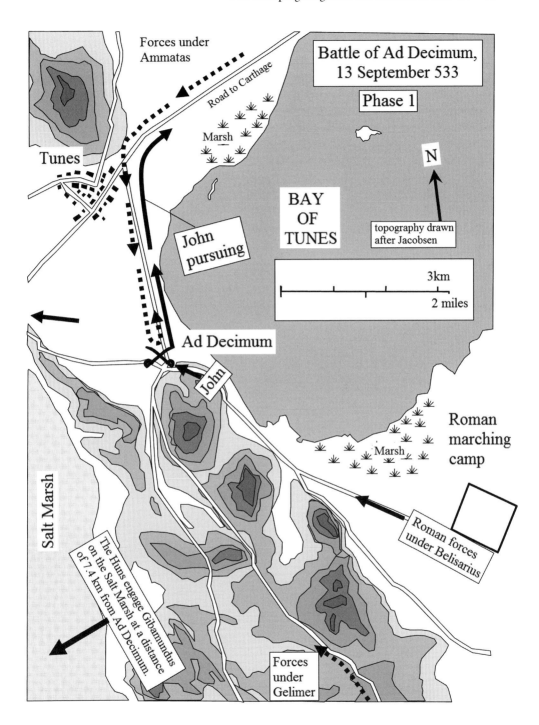

Battle of Ad Decimum, 13 September 533

Phase 1

Forces under Ammatas

Road to Carthage

Marsh

Tunes

John pursuing

BAY OF TUNES

N

topography drawn after Jacobsen

3km

2 miles

Ad Decimum

John

Salt Marsh

The Huns engage Gibamundus on the Salt Marsh at a distance of 7.4 km from Ad Decimum.

Roman marching camp

Marsh

Roman forces under Belisarius

Forces under Gelimer

a stop to the killing. The Roman attack had also forced the Vandals to flee from Carthage towards the Plain of Boulla/Bulla so the route to the city was now open. The forces of John and the Huns returned to the main army at about dusk.

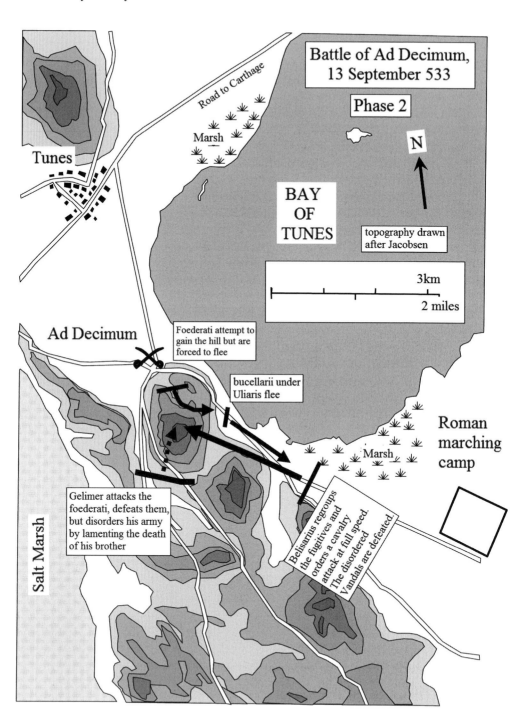

Battle of Ad Decimum,
13 September 533

Phase 2

N

Road to Carthage

Marsh

Tunes

BAY
OF
TUNES

topography drawn
after Jacobsen

3km

2 miles

Ad Decimum

Foederati attempt to
gain the hill but are
forced to flee

bucellarii under
Uliaris flee

Roman
marching
camp

Marsh

Gelimer attacks the
foederati, defeats them,
but disorders his army
by lamenting the death
of his brother

Belisarius regroups
the fugitives and
orders a cavalry
attack at full speed.
The disordered
Vandals are defeated.

Salt Marsh

Carthage[11]

The Roman cavalry spent the night at the hills south of Ad Decimum and at Ad Decimum presumably because they did not want to endanger the possession of the strategic narrows. The infantry with the wife of Belisarius arrived on the following day and the entire Roman force advanced to Carthage which they reached in the late evening. The Romans did not enter the city but passed the night in the open. The Carthaginians opened the gates and burned lights through the night, but Belisarius did not enter because he feared that there could be an ambush inside the city. He also feared that his men might start looting if they entered during the night. On the same day the Roman fleet had already reached the headland so its ships were visible to the Carthaginians who reacted to it by removing the iron chains of the harbour called Mandracium. The prison in the palace called Ancon held many of the eastern merchants that had been imprisoned because Gelimer suspected them of having urged Justinian to begin the war. As noted above, I would suggest that these merchants included spies working for the Romans. Gelimer had ordered all to be executed on the same day the battle of Ad Decimum was fought, so they were lucky to be alive. When the guard in charge of the prison heard the result of the battle of Ad Decimum and saw the Roman ships at the horizon, he decided to save himself. He promised the prisoners their freedom if they would do their utmost to save his skin. This they did.

Meanwhile the men on the ships had not heard anything about the battle of Ad Decimum, so they send some of their ships to the town of Mercurium. There they learnt that the Romans had been victorious, and joyfully continued their 150-stade (28km) sail from Carthage. Archelaus and the soldiers (*stratiotai*: note that there were also soldiers onboard) asked the sailors to anchor the fleet there because they remembered the orders of Belisarius, but the sailors refused because in their opinion the place lacked a suitable harbour and the indications were that a well-known storm which the locals called Cypriana was about to arise. This shows that the sailors included men who were familiar with the local waters and weather signs. The commanders then held a council. They did not think it would be wise to try to reach Mandracium because Belisarius had forbidden it, because they feared that access to it would be prevented by the iron chain, and because it was possibly too small to hold the entire fleet. The sailors suggested that they sail to Stagnum, 40 stades from Carthage, because it was large enough to hold the entire fleet and there were no obstacles. So they sailed to Stagnum which they reached at about dusk, but Calonymus and some of the sailors disregarded Belisarius' orders and the entreaties of others and continued to Mandracium where he and his men looted the property of both foreign and Carthaginian merchants. The Vandals had now lost access to their shipyards and fleet.

The next day Belisarius sent orders for the fleet to disembark, after which he put his army in combat formation and marched to Carthage. He still feared that the enemy had posted an ambush inside the city, and he reminded his men of the importance of keeping order and discipline. When Belisarius entered the city he realized that there were no enemy in sight so he was able to march directly to the palace where he met a crowd of merchants and other Carthaginians who complained about the behaviour of Calonymus and his sailors. Calonymus promised on oath to return all of the plunder, but failed to do so. In contrast to the navy, the army retained its discipline and was billeted in orderly manner inside the city as if it had been any city within the empire. According to Procopius, there was not a single incident of unruly behaviour on the part of the soldiers so the clerks assigned the soldiers to their lodgings in an orderly manner while they also bought their food at market prices. The Vandals of the city had fled to the sanctuaries, surrendering when Belisarius promised not to harm them. The walls of the city were in need of repairs because a section had collapsed due to lack of maintenance. This was one of the reasons why Gelimer had chosen not to attempt to hold the city, but the Romans did not see it that way. Belisarius put the local artisans and workmen to work. First he had a trench dug around the wall and had stakes set up to form an excellent stockade around the fortifications. He then had the collapsed sections of the wall rebuilt. The churches were also purged of Arian priests and taken over by the Orthodox.

While this was going on Gelimer had not been idle. He had distributed a lot of money to the Libyan farmers, securing their loyalty. They were ordered to kill any Romans they met in return for a fixed sum per man killed. Thanks to this many slaves and servants that the Roman soldiers sent to the villages were killed.

Belisarius was also eager to learn what his enemy was up to. He dispatched his *doryforos* Diogenes with twenty-two *hypaspistai* to reconnoitre. When they reached a local village at a distance of two days from Carthage and occupied a second floor of a house to spend the night there, the local villagers informed Gelimer. Gelimer dispatched 300 Vandal horsemen to capture the scouts. The Vandals arrived there at early dawn and made a phalanx in a circle around the house and blocked the doors. One of the Roman soldiers, however, was roused from sleep and heard the Vandals assuming their positions. He woke up his comrades and all put on their clothes and took up their weapons silently. They went downstairs, put bridles on their horses, leaped upon them, formed up in the courtyard, and then charged through the entrace. The Vandals converged upon them, but the Romans, who covered themselves with their shields (*aspis* = a round hoplite style shield) and used spears (*doration* = a small spear), were able to break through by riding their horses hard. The Romans lost only two men. Diogenes, however, received three blows to the face and neck and came close to dying. He also received a blow to his left hand as a result of which he was unable to move his little finger.

In the meantime, Tzazon, brother of Gelimer, had also reached the harbour of Caranalis (Cagliari) where he had disembarked his men. He won the resulting encounter at the first onset, captured the city and killed the tyrant Godas. Soon after this he learnt about the Roman landing at Caput Vada so he dispatched a ship with a letter to Gelimer. This ship and the letter were duly captured by the Romans when the ship entered the harbour of Carthage, but Belisarius did no harm to the envoys. Gelimer had also sent envoys to Spain just before Belisarius reached Libya to propose an alliance against the Romans. These envoys tarried on their journey so that they reached Spain only after its ruler Theudis had learnt of the Vandal defeat. Consequently, Theudis sent the envoys back empty-handed. However, since they had not learnt of the loss of Carthage, they sailed straight into the Roman trap. Belisarius kept them imprisoned but did not harm them. In the meantime, Cyril, who had been sent to help Godas, also sailed to Carthage because some sailors he met close to Sardinia informed him of the fate of Godas. At about the same time Belisarius also dispatched Solomon to inform Justinian of the success achieved. My own educated guess is that one of the reasons for the sending of Solomon was that he had not been able to keep the *foederati* under his command at the battle of Ad Decimum.

When Gelimer reached the plain of Boulla four days' march from Carthage, he began to assemble the remnants of his army and those Moors who were friendly. But not many Moors joined him and those who did were insubordinate. Most of the rulers of Moors in Mauretania and Byzacium sent envoys to the victor of the previous battle and asked that the emperor would confirm them in their office as had been the ancient custom. Belisarius sent them the symbols of their office together with money as bribes. In practice however, the Moors did not join the Romans but stayed neutral in the sidelines and waited to see who would win. Gelimer dispatched an envoy to Sardinia with orders for Tzazon to return with his men. What is notable about the letter that Procopius claims Gelimer sent is that it called the Roman army small. This was indeed the case. Tzazon duly sailed to the boundary of Mauritania and Numidia and joined his brother on the plain of Boulla. After this, Gelimer led his army against Carthage. They tore down a portion of the aqueduct but did not attempt to storm the city. They encamped before the city for a while, but then withdrew when no Romans came out. This is not surprising because Belisarius was a cautious leader. The Vandals then placed guards on the roads leading into the city thinking that by doing this they were besieging the city, as Procopius states with sarcasm. This was quite meaningless because Carthage was a coastal city. The Vandals hoped that they would be able to capture the city through treason on the part of the Carthagians or with the help of Roman soldiers who were followers of Arius (meaning the Germanic *foederati*). They also dispatched envoys to the leaders of the Huns with great promises if they would desert to their side. The Huns indeed were ready to betray the Romans, which proves that the Vandals must have had some prior knowledge of this from spies located inside the city. According to Procopius, the Huns were not happy that they had been transferred to North Africa contrary to the sworn oath given by the *strategos* Peter (Petros). So the Huns promised to betray the Romans. According to Procopius, Belisarius had a suspicion that this was the case because enemy deserters had informed him of it. Belisarius was also reluctant to attack the enemy because the repairs of the circuit wall were not yet finished. He also learned from his spies that one of the Carthaginians, called Laurus, was collaborating with the Vandals. This Laurus was duly impaled as a warning to those who contemplated treason. One wonders whether Procopius and his spies had any role in this. Now since Belisarius was also aware of the planned treason of the Huns, he attempted to win them over with gifts and banquets and with flattering. With these measures he was ultimately able to learn what the Huns had promised to Gelimer and what Gelimer had promised to the Huns. He also learned what were the grievances that the Huns held against the Romans. They feared that if the Romans won they would not send them back to their native lands but would keep them in Libya. They also feared that the Romans would take the booty away from them. In answer Belisarius promised that he would send them back to their homes with their booty if they would defeat the Vandals decisively. The Huns took oaths and promised to fight loyally, but in truth they just decided to stay outside the fight and wait for the outcome.

Tricamarum mid-December 533[12]

After Belisarius had refortified Carthage satisfactorily, he sent out John the Armenian in the vanguard with all the cavalry except the 500 horsemen that he kept with him. The next day he followed in John's footsteps with his infantry and 500 horsemen. The Vandal camp in Tricamarum consisted of a stockade behind which they safeguarded their possessions and families. Morale in the Roman army was high. The only exceptions to this were the Huns who resented being far from their homes. They were unwilling to fight against the Vandals. The Vandals still had superiority in numbers, but not in quality or morale. In general one can safely say that the Vandals had grown weak in the luxury of the African province. In addition, their fighting method of using spears and swords was quite unsuitable for facing the Roman horse archers as those were led by Belisarius. John the Armenian pitched a marching camp opposite the Vandals and awaited the arrival of Belisarius. At mid-day on the following day, the Vandals formed their battle lines just when the Roman cavalry was eating its midday meal, a practice that was widely known.[13]

The Vandal cavalry formed themselves behind a small stream or brook. The use of the protective barrier shows how badly shaken their morale was. The flanks of the Vandal army were commanded by chiliarchs each with a *lochos* of horsemen (1,000?). In the middle, the Vandals posted their best troops, the 5,000 men of Tzazon, and behind him were the Moors. Gelimer, with his bodyguards, was behind the cavalry encouraging his men. Gelimer apparently ordered that the Vandals were not to cross the river under any circumstance and ordered them to use only swords.[14] The strength of the Vandals was perhaps about 15,000–20,000 horsemen plus the Moors. Procopius puts into the mouth of Gelimer the claim that the Vandals possessed more than ten times the number the Romans had. If true, this figure must have included the Moors and the men left behind in the camp which did not take part in the actual fighting. It is clear on the basis of the composition of the forces (Tzazon and his men forming the centre) that the actual numbers that mattered, the numbers of Vandals posted in the line of battle, cannot have exceeded 15,000–20,000 men.

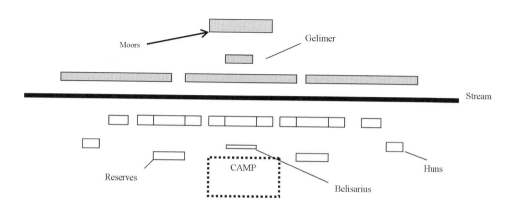

In response, the Romans hastily deployed their forces on the other bank of the small river. On the left were the Federates under Martinus, Valerianus, John, Cyprian, Althias, Marcellus, and others. The other commanders probably included at least Cyril. On the centre were posted the bodyguards of Belisarius under John the Armenian. The other commanders with John the Armenian were Uliaris, Boriades, Diogenes, and others. On the right were the regular horsemen under Pappus, Barbatus, Aïgan, and others. Among the others, one probably should include at least Rufinus. Belisarius also arrived in time and took his position behind the centre. He had left the infantry a march behind. The Huns took separate positions outside the formation, as was their usual practice. They intended to await the outcome of the battle before committing themselves.[15] The existence of the second line in this battle is obvious. Firstly, it is known that Belisarius was behind the first line with his men. Consequently, Belisarius assumed his place as *strategos* behind the centre while John the Armenian acted as *hypostrategos*. Secondly, Procopius states that there were other commanders besides the ones he mentions. It is probable that he only mentions those who were posted in the front line. When one takes into account these others, one has enough men left for the reserves. The reserves would have then consisted of the men of Solomon (sent to Constantinople), men of Dorotheus (though he himself was dead), Cyril, and Rufinus.[16] Since the size of the cavalry probably was about 8,000–11,000 men, the reserve probably consisted of two divisions, one on one side of the camp and the other on the other. That there was an opening in the middle of the second line is shown by the fact that the centre of the first line could retreat to their camp while performing a feigned flight. This solution resembles the use of pits or caltrops between the lines in the *Strategikon* (4.3.35ff.). For a diagram of the battle array see the attached diagrams. The Huns, presumably with the Heruls, served as 'ambushers' behind the first line. The first line was undoubtedly divided into the *koursores*, *defensores*, flank guards, and outflankers. We just do not know who were designated into these roles or who were in overall charge of the wings.[17]

After both sides had arrayed their forces on the opposite banks nothing happened for a long time until, on the advice of Belisarius, John the Armenian chose a few men with whom he crossed the river and attacked the centre. This probably means that John sent the so-called *koursores* (one wing?) to skirmish and to lure the Vandals to pursue across the river. Tzazon's men crowded upon the Romans, forced them back and gave chase as far as the river, whereas John's men retreated as far as the camp. After this, John led even more of Belisarius' bodyguards across the river, but again Tzazon's Vandals repulsed them and John's men retreated back to their camp. These men probably consisted of both wings of the *koursores*. After this, John with almost all of Belisarius' *doryphoroi* and *hypaspistai* made a third attempt carrying Belisarius' standard forward as a sign of charge across the river, during which his men shouted wildly.[18] This attack was then done with the whole centre division, which consisted of Belisarius' bodyguards sans the reserves with Belisarius. The fighting in the centre became fierce when both sides were locked in close combat. Tzazon and many other nobles died in the centre before the Roman wings also set in motion. The attack followed the standard method of engaging the longer enemy line.[19] The use of cries in combat contradicts the instructions of the *Strategikon* for keeping silence and is probably representative of earlier practice. The Vandal front collapsed starting from the centre and the Huns joined the pursuit. The pursuit was stopped in front of the Vandal camp, as called for by the 'regulations'. By this time the Vandals had lost about 800 men and the Romans less than 50, so the battle can be said to have been quite one sided. The bodyguards of Belisarius were the true elite soldiers and the Vandal elite were no match for them.

PHASE 1: One wing of the *koursores* feigns flight

PHASE 2: The *koursores* feign flight

PHASE 3:
The centre attacks. The wings wait until the Vandal centre begins to collapse and the Vandal wings try to engage the centre. As this happened the wings attacked the Vandal wings in flank.

After the infantry, which was needed for the taking of the camp, had arrived in the late afternoon, Gelimer was the first to flee and caused the flight of the rest of his army. After this, Belisarius lost control of his army who began to plunder until the next day when he finally managed to restore some semblance of order. This he did by climbing on a certain hill near the road at daybreak where he was visible to all. The amount of booty was so extraordinarily rich and the soldiers so poor that Belisarius was able to assemble only those who were near the hill and most of these consisted of Belisarius' own *bucellarii* and even these did not obey Belisarius immediately but sent money and slaves to Carthage with their own tentmates and messmates before returning to Belisarius to hear his commands. The reference to the tentmates (*homoskênoi*) and messmates (*homostrapezoi*) is important because it shows how comradeship was exploited in the Roman army. The tent-group (*contubernium*) was the basic building block, above which was the group which ate together at the table, presumably meaning the *hekatontarchia/centuria* and/ or *bandon/tagma*. Consequently, he was forced to resort to the sending of 200 men under John the Armenian to pursue Gelimer. At the same time, he also sent orders to his subordinates in Carthage to take into the city all those Vandals who had sought safety from the sanctuaries around the city. They were told to promise the Vandals safety in return for their weapons. The disobedience of the soldiers had made it impossible to capture any other Vandal fugitives but those who had sought safety from the sanctuaries. It was important to disarm all of them immediately so that they would not become a threat. Meanwhile Belisarius himself went about everywhere and gathered his men while giving pledges to all the Vandals that it was safe to surrender. With these measures, he was finally able to assemble his army and to organize the sending of the booty and disarmed Vandals under guard to Carthage. After this, Belisarius with the greater part of his army started his own pursuit of Gelimer.

The aftermath[20]

John the Armenian had pursued Gelimer for five days and nights and was very close to catching the fugitive, but then a disaster struck. The group of pursuers included a *doryforos* (an officer/aide) of Belisarius called Uliaris who was a man known for his buffoonery and drunken revelry. On the sixth day of the pursuit, this Uliaris, while intoxicated, saw a bird sitting on a tree. He took his bow, drew the cord and shot an arrow at the bird, but missed it. Instead, his arrow hit John, who was behind the bird, in the neck. The wound was fatal and John died shortly afterwards. The men were beside themselves in sorrow, and leaderless. When Uliaris realized what he had done, he fled to a nearby village and sought safety from the local sanctuary. The soldiers cared for John as long as he lived and then buried him. They informed Belisarius of what had happened, and then waited for him to arrive. When Belisarius learnt of the accident, he was grief-stricken but did not punish Uliaris because John had asked that Uliaris should not be punished for the accident.

Belisarius continued the pursuit of Gelimer, but when he reached the vicinity of Hippo Regius he learnt that Gelimer and his most immediate followers and relatives had reached a mountain called Papua controlled by Moors loyal to the Vandals which could be climbed only with great difficulty. Because of this and because of the winter season Belisarius decided to put the Vandals and their Moorish allies under siege rather than attempt to capture the place. He chose a suitable number of soldiers (*stratiôtai*) for this task, putting them under Pharas. The use of *stratiôtai* in this context suggests that Pharas was also given command of a detachment of regular soldiers besides his own 400 Heruls. Procopius' view about Pharas and Heruls in general is interesting. He called them the basest of all barbarians who mated with males and asses and did many other things that he considered horrific, to which he adds at this place drunkenness and treacherous behaviour.[21] Because of this Procopius stated that it was so great an achievement for Pharas and his followers to be disciplined and upright unlike their brethren.

Then Belisarius learnt that there were also Vandals in the sanctuaries of Hippo Regius and that they included members of the Vandal nobility. They were once again granted security in return for surrender after which they were dispatched under guard to Carthage. The greatest catch, however, was the treasure ship which contained the royal treasure. Gelimer had put a loyal Libyan called Boniface (Bonifatius) in charge of the ship and treasure with orders to sail to Spain with the money to buy the support of Theudis if things did not turn out well. When Boniface learnt of the defeat at Tricamarum, he had attempted to sail out of the harbour, but the strong wind had forced him to return. When Belisarius then entered the city, Boniface sent some men to meet the Romans. These men were instructed to ask for freedom and the right to keep what was Boniface's own in return for telling Belisarius where the treasure was. Belisarius swore an oath and got most of the treasure, but Boniface was a crafty fellow and claimed part of it as his own. On the basis of Procopius' text it is clear that Belisarius knew what was happening but considered it better to retain a reputation for honesty to obtain the surrender of men more easily.

After this Belisarius returned to Carthage to finish the conquest of Vandal territory and to start the process of incorporating the Vandal kingdom into the Roman Empire together with the reorganization of its defensive structures to follow the Roman system. He sent Cyril with a great force and Tzazon's severed head to Sardinia to annex it to the Roman Empire with orders to send a portion of his force to Corsica so that it too could be added to the Empire. John (of Dyrrachium?) was sent to take Caesarea in Mauretania with the infantry *lochos* (2,000 men?) that he usually commanded. John, one of Belisarius' *bucellarii*, was dispatched to take control of the Straits of Gibraltar and the fort of Septem Fratres. Belisarius dispatched Apollinaris with a fleet to take control of the islands of Ebusa, Majorica and Minorica (the Baleares). This Apollinaris was a native of Libya who had fled to Constantinople when Gelimer had usurped power. He had urged Justinian to begin the war and had fought with distinction at Tricamarum. This suggests the probability that Apollinaris and other locals like him had worked in the background as part of the underground network that undermined the position of the Vandals in North Africa and which had also contributed to the rising of Tripolis against the Vandals. It is also clear that these men and the Roman spies posing as merchants provided information of enemy activities and terrain during the course of the campaign. Sometime later Belisarius dispatched another force to Tripolis to assist Pudentius and Tattimuth against the Moors who were harassing them. The only place where Belisarius faced opposition was Sicily. The fortress of Lilybaeum had been given by Theoderic the Great as a dowry to his sister Amalafrida when she married the Vandal king Thrasamund and had as a result of this become part of the Vandal Kingdom. Now that Belisarius sent some men to take control of this fortress, the local Goths resisted. This resulted in an exchange of letters in which Belisarius threatened war, but in the end he accepted the suggestion made by the other side that the emperor Justinian should arbitrate in the matter with Queen Amalasountha.

Meanwhile Pharas had become tired of the siege under winter conditions and decided to attack. He armed all of his followers and started the ascent, but was repulsed with heavy casualties. 110 men were killed and the rest thrown back down the slope. After this he settled on guarding the area closely. When the winter was coming to an end after a siege of three months, the Vandals had had enough. They had become so used to luxurious living, with sexual pleasures, good food and wine, and silk clothes that they just could not put up with the hardships that living among the Moors meant. Consequently, they were ready to surrender in return for pardon and the position of senator for Gelimer in Constantinople. When Pharas informed Belisarius of this, Belisarius dispatched Cyprian, an archon of the *foederati*, and others, to promise all this with oaths. Gelimer and his relatives and followers surrendered and were duly led as captives to Carthage. Belisarius reported to Justinian and asked for permission to bring Gelimer, Vandals and booty to Constantinople.

In the summary of the campaign, Procopius (*Wars* 4.7.20–21) states that the Vandals had been defeated in a very short time by a mere 5,000 men, which was the number of horsemen who followed Belisarius and who carried through the whole war against the

Vandals. I would suggest that Procopius is here purposely vague with the use of the *efepô* (to follow) and 5,000 men. The reference to the 5,000 horsemen could be taken to mean the 5,000 *foederati* and *stratiôtai* horsemen sent by the emperor, which would give the credit for the victory to the emperor, but the use of the horsemen who followed Belisarius could be taken to mean the *bucellarii* of Belisarius. In my opinion, the latter is meant. The Vandals had indeed been defeated by the household troops of Belisarius at the battle of Tricamarum, and their role had also been decisive at the battle of Ad Decimum. These men were clearly the best soldiers of the era and Belisarius certainly deserves full credit for having hired such skilled fighters into his private army.

The reorganization of North Africa/Libya in the spring of 534

The reconquest of North Africa/Libya also entailed the re-establishment of Roman administrative and military organization in the area. The Praetorian Prefect Archelaus received a law from Justinian on 13 April 534 which reorganized the newly recovered territories. Archelaus was himself appointed *Praefecto Praetorio Africae* and under him were placed seven provincial governors. These consisted of the consulars of Proconsularis, Byzacena and Tripolitania and of the praesides of Numidia, Mauretania Sitifensis, Caesarensis and Sardinia. The armed forces of this territory were placed under *Magister Militum per Africam* under who served five *duces* of Tripolitania, Byzacena, Numidia, Mauretania Caesarensis and Sardinia. Since all territory west of Caesarea was in Moorish hands, Justinian instructed the *duces* of Africa to make Lepcis Magna, Capsa, Thelepte, Cirta and Caesarea their headquarters. In addition to this the *dux* of Mauretania maintained a garrison at Septem (Ceuta), the only surviving area remaining of Mauretania Tingitana. Justinian ordered the *duces* to recover the lost territory and to re-establish the old limes with its *limitanei*. The idea was to form self-sufficient frontier forces which would be supported by local taxes so that Justinian could withdraw most of the expeditionary forces from Africa. This proved wishful thinking. It took a further fifteen years of hard fighting for the Romans to pacify the territory.

Belisarius recalled in the summer of 534

The success, however, had its downside. Procopius states that some of the subordinates of Belisarius plotted against him and sent two letters in two ships to Justinian in which they accused Belisarius of plans of enthroning himself as King of North Africa. He adds that this accusation had no basis in truth whatsoever. One of the ships reached Justinian with the result that Justinian dispatched Solomon back to Belisarius with instructions for Belisarius to decide for himself whether he wanted to come to Constantinople with Gelimer and Vandals or whether he wanted to send the prisoners to him and remain in Carthage. Even though this is not stated by Procopius, it would seem very probable that the messengers had the order to assassinate Belisarius if he chose the latter option. Belisarius was aware that he had been slandered because the second of the ships had been captured and searched. Consequently he chose to leave and all ships were prepared for the journey and the bodyguards were put on board, some time in the summer of 534. Procopius (*Wars* 4.8.24, 4.12.17) states as a sort of afterthought after he tells his readers that Belisarius left most of his bodyguards for Solomon when he left, that Justinian had also sent another army to Solomon under the *Comes Excubitorum* Theodorus the Cappadocian and Ildiger. It is very likely that this army had arrived with Solomon and that the *Comes Excubitorum* Theodorus was the man charged with the task of killing Belisarius if the accusations against Belisarius were found true. It is also probable that Tryphon and Eustratius, who were tasked to make a census so that the tax records could be put in order, arrived with Solomon. The Libyans were not happy about the taxes that these two men imposed on them.

Then came the unwelcome news that the Moors had revolted. According to Procopius, there were two reasons for this revolt. The first was that the female oracles stated that the Romans would achieve success against the Moors only under an unbearded leader (Belisarius and his commanders had beards), and the second was the imminent departure of Belisarius with his bodyguards in a situation in which the rest of the soldiers were spread out so that their numbers were few in each area and their defences were not ready. The latter of the reasons prove that Belisarius had immediately started to reorganize the defensive structures of the area previously held by the Vandals to follow the standard Roman system with *comitatenses* field army and *limitanei* frontier armies all posted inside some fortified places. Their numbers were clearly still too few and the rebuilding and building of fortifications to house in particular the *limitanei* was not completed. Therefore the situation was opportune for the Moors. Since the preparations for the journey had already been completed and Belisarius knew of the plotting against him, he wisely decided that it was now too late for him to crush the revolt in person. Consequently, as noted, he placed the beardless eunuch Solomon in charge of the defence and gave him most of his *doryforoi* and *hypaspistai*. After this, he took the booty to Constantinople. It is probable that the appointment of Solomon as leader of the Roman forces exploited the superstitions of the Moors.

The great triumph of Belisarius[22]

When Belisarius reached Byzantium/Constantinople, Justinian granted him an extraordinary favour which no general had enjoyed after Augustus for about 550 years (Procopius has about 600 years). The form, however, did not follow the ancient practice because Belisarius walked on foot from his own house to the hippodrome and then from the barriers (the starting point of the chariots at the open end) to the place before the throne, the imperial box in the middle of the course. The entire massive booty taken from the Vandals had been piled up there. It included all the treasures the Vandals had taken from the Imperial Palace at Rome and all the rest of the booty they had captured from the Romans. It also included the treasures of the Jews taken by Titus. According to Procopius, when one of the Jews present saw these, he approached one of those who knew the emperor and stated that it was not a good idea to carry these treasures to the Palace because the proper place for them was the Temple of Solomon and for all others these treasures had brought misfortune as could be seen what had happened to the Romans and Vandals. When Justinian heard this, he sent the treasures to the Christian sanctuaries located at Jerusalem. The triumph included Gelimer and other slaves. When they were brought before the imperial box, they fell prone on the ground just like Belisarius to show their obedience. Justinian and Theodora gave money to the children of Hilderic and to all those who were offspring of the family of the emperor Valentian, and gave Gelimer and his family lands in Galatia. However, Gelimer was not enrolled into the Senate because he refused to convert from the faith of Arius.

Not long after this Belisarius was nominated consul for the year 535, which was a very high honour. Procopius calls this a triumph, but in fact it was merely a ceremony. On 1 January 535 the captives carried Belisarius in a curule chair while he distributed spoils of the Vandal war among the populace. Belisarius fully deserved these honours. He had accomplished what the previous commanders and emperors (Bonifatius/Bonifatius, Aspar, Aetius, Majorian, and Leo I) could not – he had defeated the Vandals and that with very few men. It is therefore not surprising that he was also made patrician (*patricius*) at about this time probably as a reward for his conquest of North Africa because he is recorded to have possessed this title in 536. He fully deserved this honour too. According to Cedrenus and some other later sources, the recovery of Africa by Belisarius was celebrated on the imperial coinage, but modern research has shown this to be a misunderstanding of genuine medallions, which are no longer extant.

Chapter Seven

Victories of Solomon in Libya in 534–535

The Moorish revolt in 534[1]

Justinian had appointed Solomon as *Magister Militum per Africam* and *Praefectus Praetorio Africae* to combine the military and civilian functions to make it easier for him to accomplish the rest of the goals set up by Justinian for the newly acquired territory. The news reaching Solomon and the Romans at Carthage was troubling. Reports claimed that the Moors had destroyed the Roman soldiers in Byzacium and Numidia. The most troubling of these was the news that Aigan the Massagetae, the *doryforos* of Belisarius, and Rufinus the Thracian, the *bandoforos* (*bandifer*) of Belisarius, together with their 500 men had been killed. These two commanders had stayed in a narrow pass where the enemy could not outflank them and observed from there that the Moors were taking Libyans as captives. Consequently, they had charged out of the pass and released the captives. The Moors then reported this to their leaders Cusina (Coutzinas), Esdilas, Iourphountes and Medisinissas, who had then led their entire army against the Romans in the late afternoon. The Romans were now shut inside the narrow pass with thousands of Moors advancing against them from both ends. This proves how dangerous the practice of posting horsemen in a narrow pass was, but it still appears to have been the standard tactics that the Roman cavalry adopted at that time when they intended to stay in hiding. According to the harangue of Solomon (Procopius *Wars* 4.11.23), the Moors had 50,000 warriors, but it is possible that this was just meant as an excuse for the previous defeat suffered by Aigan and Rufinus. Rufinus, Aigan and their men ran to the top of a rock and kept the enemy at bay with their bows as long as they could, but when the arrows ran out the Moors attacked at close quarters. The Romans fought with swords but were overrun with superior numbers. Aigan was hacked to pieces and Rufinus taken prisoner. Medisinissas had the head of Rufinus cut off as a trophy which he took home to show his wives. Procopius does not call the above incident an ambush prepared by the Moors for Aigan and Rufinus, but it is possible that the Moors used the Libyan captives as bait.

According to Procopius, despite the above Solomon asked first why the Moors had revolted and offered the Moors lenient terms of surrender presumably because he feared the numbers the enemy possessed. The Moors responded that Belisarius had fooled them with great promises which had not been kept, and it was because of this that they had revolted. In light of Belisarius' initial reaction to the Moorish envoys this is indeed quite probable. Belisarius had probably promised all sorts of things, which he had no intention of delivering once the Vandals had been defeated. The contents of the letter sent by the Moors left Solomon no alternative but to prepare his men for war.

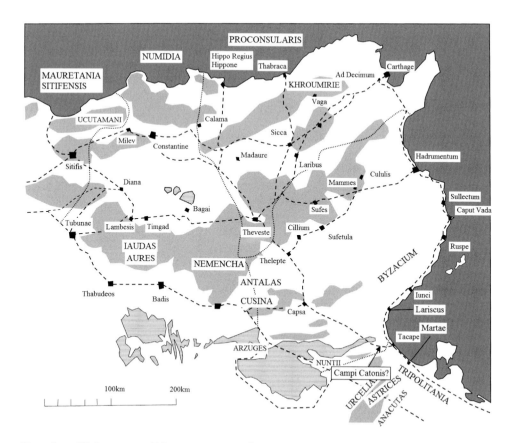

Battle of Mamma (Mammes) 534[2]

According to Procopius, Solomon arranged matters at Carthage as best he could and then led all his troops to Byzacium. This, however, should not be taken literally. It is clear that he left a strong garrison inside Carthage. Cusina, Esdilas, Iourphountes and Medisinissas had assembled their forces at Mamma (place uncertain). The Moorish leaders had encamped their army on level terrain at the foothills of lofty mountains inside a circle of camels. The camels were tied together twelve deep to form a barricade. The families were placed inside the stockade and footmen between the camels. Each of the Moorish footmen had a small shield, sword and two short spears. Some of the Moorish horsemen were posted behind in the mountains to act as ambushers. The speech of Solomon (Procopius *Wars* 4.11.27ff.) shows that the principal weakness of the Moorish infantry forces and tactics was that if their enemy withstood the attack by two thrown spears, the Moors were prepared to flee.

Procopius does not mention the exact composition of the Roman force nor the battle array, but since Solomon had both infantry and cavalry in his army and Procopius describes only cavalry action it is possible that the infantry was left behind at Carthage or at the marching camp. The Roman attack was directed against only one side of the Moorish camp to avoid the danger of being attacked in the rear by the horsemen left in the mountains. The Roman cavalry attack faltered before the camels because the horses were unfamiliar with the sight and noises the camels made. The Roman horses reared and threw off their riders and most of the Roman cavalry fled in disarray enabling the Moors to make sorties out of their encampment. This enabled the Moors to hit the Romans while they were defenceless and unable to remain in position. The ever resourceful Solomon knew what to do. He leaped from his horse, dismounted his cavalry, ordered them to retain their position and to form a wall of shields for their protection while he himself led less than 500 men against another portion of the circle, which would obviously be the flank or rear. Procopius does not tell us why the Moorish horsemen that had been left in the mountains failed to attack. The likeliest reason for this failure is that the speed of the Roman attack took them by surprise or that the attack was directed to the side which was not clearly visible from the mountains. The men under Solomon killed the camels with their swords and opened the route for the attack, and then advanced at a run to the middle of the camp where the women were and caused the Moors to flee in panic towards the mountains. The pursuing Romans were able to kill 10,000 Moors and capture all of the women and children who were all duly enslaved. The slaves and the camels which had not been killed were taken to Carthage.

The above account provides us with two very important details. Firstly, the Roman cavalry could be used very effectively as infantry. Secondly, the cavalry shield used by the *bucellarii*, *foederati* and *stratiotai* was large enough for the formation of shield walls on foot.

The battle of Mount Bourgaon 534[3]

In 534, after defeating the Moors at Mammas in Byzacium, Solomon returned to Carthage, but was forced to return immediately because the Moors had reassembled and were once again ravaging Byzacium mercilessly. The Moors had encamped on Mount Bourgaon (unknown location). It was accessible from the west, but its eastern side was extremely difficult to climb. It had two peaks on the eastern side with a steep and narrow vale in between. The Moors had built their camp on the western side at the middle of the ascent and had left the peaks on the eastern side unoccupied because they thought it inaccessible. The Moors had myriads of men. This time Solomon brought with him a combined force of cavalry and infantry, which suggests the likelihood that he had previously used only cavalry at Mammas and that he had now learnt his lesson so that he also took infantry with him. Solomon was unwilling to besiege the Moors because the mountain was located in deserted terrain. At first he tried in vain to lure the Moors away from the mountain, but then he noticed that they had left the peak of the mountain unoccupied. He sent Theodorus, the *Comes Excubitorum*, with 1,000 infantry to scale the east face of the mountain with instructions to remain hidden from view until the next sunrise. Solomon gave them some of the standards to make them more visible to both the enemy and his own forces so that everyone would think that there were more than 1,000 footmen threatening the Moors from behind. Their mission was to occupy one of the peaks behind the Moors from which they were then able to shoot directly into the Moorish camp. The plan was also hidden from possible traitors amongst the Romans by claiming that the 1,000 men acted as a vanguard for the rest. The plan worked like a dream. The footmen climbed the eastern face of the mountain during the night and were ready to begin the slaughter of the Moors in the morning. When the Roman main force then started its ascent they and the enemy suddenly saw one of the peaks occupied so that the Moors now faced showers of arrows both from their front and rear. The Moors panicked. Some of them fled to the other peak while others fled to the vale between the peaks. The Moors trampled on each other and many fell to their deaths in the vale. When the vale was filled with corpses of men and horses, the rest were able to flee over their bodies.

According to Procopius, the surviving Moors said later to the Romans that 50,000 Moors had succumbed in this slaughter. However, all of the Moorish leaders with the exception of Esdiasas, who surrendered, were able to flee. The survivors continued their flight to Numidia where they surrendered themselves to the Moorish ruler of Aurasium called Iaudas. The only Moors who remained in Byzacium were those under Antalas who had not revolted against the Romans. The victory resulted in the taking of a huge amount of booty in the form of slaves so that the price of a sheep and boy slave were equal.

From the point of view of analysis of Roman infantry tactics, the above includes one important point which is that Procopius did not claim that the footmen sent to occupy the peak would have been light infantry archers with the implication that the men in question were regular footmen who were able to fight both at long distance with bows and at short distance with spears and swords. This is in agreement with the details given by the *Peri Strategikes / Strategias* (36) and similar information can also be found in Vegetius (1.15, 3.14) who included archers among the so-called heavy-armed. The former implies that almost all of the Roman infantrymen were equipped with bows and close quarters weapons, and this may indeed have been the case because even the *Strategikon* (12.2.8–12) implies this when it states that the commander was to vary the number of his archers according to the size of his infantry contingent with the implication that many of those who were assigned to serve among the heavy infantry could also use bows when required. Periodic combat training clearly made both the footmen and horsemen very versatile forces.

Battle of Mt. Aurasium 1, 535[4]

The above mentioned Iaudas, the ruler of Mount Aurasium, was one of the Moorish leaders who had revolted. With the addition of the survivors of the battle of Mt. Bourgaon, he had over 30,000 warriors in his field army with which he plundered Numidia and led Libyans away in chains. This situation was obviously intolerable.

Procopius mentions an incident that took place during this time and which deservedly became famous. While Iaudas was doing all of the above, Althias, the *Comes Foederatum* who was in charge of the forts in Centuriae, wanted to do something and not stay idle inside fortifications. Consequently, he took almost seventy Huns with him and went outside. He knew that seventy men would not be able to fight the enemy on equal terms so he initially planned to occupy some narrow pass from which he would then have charged out to release prisoners, but since there were no such passes in the area[5] he decided to go to the nearby city of Tigisis, which at the time was still unwalled but which had a great spring at a place which was closely shut in. He knew that the enemy would be compelled to go there because there were no other water sources nearby. His plan seemed insane to all, but he adopted it anyway. When the Moors arrived thirsty and wearied by the heat of the summer weather, he posted his men in front of the spring. The Moors halted. Their leader Iaudas considered his men too tired to fight and promised Althias a third of their booty in return for being allowed to drink. Althias refused and challenged Iaudas to a duel, which the latter accepted because Althias was short and lean. The Moors would give up their booty if Althias won and the Romans would let the Moors drink if Iaudas won. Both men were mounted. Iaudas hurled his spear (*doration*) first, but Althias, who was ambidextrous, caught it with his right hand, while he drew his bow from its holster and killed the horse of Iaudas with an arrow. The Moors brought a horse to their commander, which Iaudas mounted and fled with his army following after him in complete disorder. The prisoners and booty were left behind so the Romans took possession of all. This is what legends are made of. Althias the superhero had defeated the enemy army of thousands.

After a short stay at Carthage, Solomon led his forces out again, this time to Mt. Aurasium, the official reason being that Iaudas had pillaged Numidia while the Roman army was in Byzacium. The personal enemies of Iaudas, the Moorish chieftains Massonas and Ortaias, were also urging Solomon to take action. The Romans and their Moorish allies built a camp on the river Abigas which flowed along by Aurasium with the idea of engaging Iaudas, but the latter chose to stay at Aurasium. The meeting of Althias had undoubtedly taught him a lesson. The Romans possessed superior fighting skills.

When Solomon realized that he would have to lead the forces up into the mountain, he bribed the Moors with great sums of money and exhorted them. After this, the Romans and their allies began the ascent of Mt. Aurasium in battle formation. The Romans were under the false impression that the Moors would fight them. Consequently they took only their battle rations with them, just enough to feed them and their horses for a few days. They advanced about 50 stades (c. 9 km) in very rough ground and bivouacked. The army marched for seven days and arrived near an ancient fortress called Shield Mountain (*Aspis, Scutum*) where their Moorish scouts claimed that they would meet the enemy. There were no Moors to be seen. The Romans encamped on the spot and stayed there for three days. Now when the supplies were running out and the enemy was nowhere to be seen Solomon and the Romans started to entertain well-founded suspicions regarding the intentions of their allies. The fact that Iaudas and Ortaias cooperated very soon after this makes it very likely that the traitor was Ortaias.[6] So the Romans withdrew from there with all speed to level ground where they built a fortified camp and from there back to their base camp. After this Solomon left a part of his army behind to act as a guard against the Moors of Iaudas while he returned to Carthage. This episode demonstrates that the Roman infantry and cavalry had at least 8 to 16 days worth of supplies with them when they advanced to fight the enemy, and also the untrustworthiness of the allied Moors.

When Solomon reached Carthage he began preparations for another campaign against Aurasium, but this time without the Moors as allies. At the same time, he prepared generals and another army and fleet for an expedition against the Moors of Sardinia who were called Barbaricini. These 3,000 Moors were former allies of the Vandals who now occupied the mountains near Caranalis from which they made raids against the Romans. While these things were taking place in North Africa, Belisarius was dispatched against the Goths in Sicily. Even though Procopius fails to mention any of the following, it is clear that once Belisarius arrived in Sicily Solomon and Belisarius coordinated their efforts so that the sending of the soldiers to Sardinia against the Barbaricini should be seen as part of the same effort to secure the islands around Italy.

Chapter Eight

West: The Balkans and Northern Theatre of War under Justinian from 527 until 540

Description of the Balkans under Justinian

After the de facto abandonment of Pannonia in the fifth century, the different regions of the Balkans were united under the Praetorian Prefect of Illyricum. The dioceses of Thrace and Macedonia were Greek speaking, but the dioceses of Dacia and Dalmatia were Latin speaking. Most of the population favoured the Chalcedonian doctrine, but the church organization of Illyricum was divided so that most of its bishops followed the wishes of the Pope rather than the Patriarch of Constantinople. Justinian approached the Pope before he began the conquest of Italy to find a mutually acceptable compromise to this situation, and it is possible that this formed a part of his plans of reconquest. In 535 Justinian limited the influence of the Pope by making a new division of the bishoprics in the Balkans. In 545 Justinian followed with a new measure to strengthen imperial control, but in practice the bishops still continued to turn to the Pope if they faced problems. This was obviously problematic, but as long as the Romans controlled the reconquered city of Rome, this did not become too serious.

Just as in the rest of the provinces, the principal source of revenue was agriculture. But the Balkans was also important for another reason. It produced metals: gold, silver, copper, lead and iron. At this time the most important mines were located in Macedonia and Thrace. Illyricum as a whole was not rich in comparison with Syria or Egypt, and it was also sparsely populated in comparison as a result of the devastation suffered in the fifth century. All of this made Illyricum a sort of periphery in imperial policies. However, the facts that Justinian was a native of the Balkans from Dardania and that the Balkans formed the defensive zone of the capital Constantinople meant that this region was not entirely neglected either. The principal problems were that the Danube with its fortifications was not an adequate obstacle for the invaders and neither were the mountain ranges with their fortified valleys. Because of this the Romans had adopted a defensive system which consisted of several tiers: 1) the linear defence along the borders; 2) the fortification of the interior, which included the fortifications in the passes and the fortified cities; 3) the long walls of Anastasius; 4) the Theodosian Walls which formed the last line of defence for Constantinople; 5) the Walls of Chersonese; 6) the Walls of Thermopylae; 7) the Walls of Corinth. The fortifications therefore blocked all the main arteries of movement, but, as we shall see, without the backing of sizable field armies, these were only a hindrance to mobile enemies like the Antae, Slavs, Huns and Bulgars. Often it was only the Theodosian Walls that stood between the Romans and their enemies. These walls were then, however, more than adequate to put at rest any dreams of conquest that foreign enemies could have entertained. They were breached for the first time by the Crusaders in 1204.

The early years of the sole rule of Justinian

The nomadic threat raised its head again during the reign of Justinian I against the background of the ongoing Persian conflict. For the context and additional details, see the chapter on the Persian war. In both cases Justinian had actively sought friendship with the Hunnic rulers located in the north of the Black Sea and in both cases his diplomacy paid off. It was only after this that the other tribes located in the Balkans started to exploit the situation, namely the transferral of forces to fight against the Persians and then after that the transferral of forces to North Africa and Italy.

In about 527 Justinian received Grepes, the King of the Heruls, in Constantinople and baptized him. In return for this and for service as *foederati*, Justinian gave him the city of Singidunum together with some other cities in Dacia.[1]

The Sabiri Huns, who were located north of the Caucasus Range, could serve as allies of both Rome and Persia, so it was a real coup for Justinian to convince Boa, the Queen of the Sabir Huns, to side with Rome. She had under her an army of 100,000 men (horsemen who could also fight dismounted) and she used these forces with great skill in 528 defeating and capturing two Hunnic kings who were attempting to go through her territory to assist Cabades, who had managed to convince them to join his forces. In about 527, the Hunnic king of Bosporus called Grod visited Justinian in Constantinople and was baptized as a sign of his alliance with the Christian world. Justinian gave him a *numerus* of Roman or Italian troops known as Spaniards under the command of a tribune, which was stationed in the city of Bosporus. The pagan priests of the Huns, however, were upset, with the result that they killed the king and *numerus* and then installed Grod's brother Mougel as their king. This did not sit well with Justinian, who duly organized a military expedition against Mougel. Justinian's response was the appointment of John the *Comes* of the Straits of the Pontic Sea (*Comes Angustiatum Pontici Maris*)[2] with headquarters at Hieron with the duty of leading a joint and combined force against Mougel. Hieron was a customs post, one of the pair Abydos and Hieron, which implies that John was to use the income obtained from the customs to finance the expedition that he was ordered to lead against the Bosporan Huns. The land army consisting mainly of the Goths of Thrace was put under Baduarius and Godilas, while another army together with an exarch was embarked on ships and sent by sea to Bosporus. The land army marched through the lands occupied by the Antae and Bulgars, and when the Huns heard of the approach of this massive force they fled so that the Romans were able to occupy the territory and place it under the rule of the exarch.[3] It is possible or even probable that the march of the Roman land forces, consisting mainly of the Gothic cavalry, soured the relationship between the Romans and Bulgars, because we find the latter invading the Roman Balkans after this.

The Bulgars invaded Scythia and Moesia in the same year after Baduarius and Godilas had withdrawn from the north, which may mean that they had actually pursued these when they were marching back to Scythia. According to Malalas, the two *magistri militum* on the scene were the abovementioned Baduarius (*Magister Militum et Dux Scythiae?*) and (*magister militum vacans et dux Moesiae Secundae* or *Magister Militum per Moesiam*) Iustinus (Justin). These two marched against the invading Bulgars and when they engaged them in battle Justin was killed in combat. Malalas unfortunately fails to state what the outcome of the battle was. However, the fact that we find the Bulgars in Thrace after this suggests the probability of defeat, but is not conclusive because this could also have easily resulted from the confusion of Roman leadership after the death of Justin. If the battle had ended in defeat, then it is easy to see that the root cause of that could have been a divided command structure. However, if it did not result in defeat, then the reason why the Bulgars were still able to continue to Thrace could have been the withdrawal of Baduarius to his own territory in Scythia for its protection, while the forces previously under Justin failed to act decisively in the absence of their commander. Whatever the reason for the ability of the Bulgars to advance to Thrace, the situation changed when Constantiolus was appointed as Justin's successor. Constantiolus, Godilas, and the *Magister Militum per Illyricum* Ascum/Askoum the Hun advanced against the invaders, surrounded them in combat, captured all of their booty and killed two of their kings. However, when they were returning from combat they encountered another band of Huns and in the ensuing battle the Romans were utterly defeated, being exhausted from previous fighting. The Romans were scattered in flight, but the Bulgars managed to lasso all three commanders. Godilas drew his sword and cut the cord, but the two other commanders were captured. The Romans ransomed Constantiolus with 10,000 *nomismata/solidi*, but the Bulgars refused to surrender Ascum the Hun. After this the Huns retreated to their own territory with the prisoners they had taken, which were numerous. The above sequence suggests that the Roman commanders engaged first the main encampment of the Huns and then came face to face with one of the raiding forces that had previously been dispatched from there, which defeated them. The war appears to have been equally costly for both, because Malalas then claims that after this the region of Thrace was at peace with the implication that the Bulgars had suffered at least the same number of casualties as the Romans, possibly even more as the Romans had encircled and annihilated the forces of two kings with the implication that the Bulgars suffered at least 20,000 killed. This would have been the reason why the Bulgars withdrew on this occasion. However, they repeated their ravages again two years later.[4]

In 529 Justinian received the very welcome news that the mercenary commander Mundos had left Rome and when he had reached the Danube he had sent envoys to Justinian with the message that he was ready to desert to his side. Justinian appointed Mundus *Magister Militum per Illyricum*. According to the version preserved by Marcellinus Comes, when Mundus reached Illyricum in about 530, the *Getae* who had previously ravaged Illyricum attacked him on arrival, but Mundus put all of them to flight. The *Getae* are often interpreted to have been the Slavs, but Broke (Marcellinus p.43) is surely correct to translate the term as the Goths (Marcellinus usually uses the term *Getae* in this sense) because that would surely not have been the only incident in which the Goths invaded Roman territory in the Balkans. Procopius (*Wars* 5.2.17) refers to one such incident in which the Roman envoys complained in 534 that Goths had pillaged Gratiana while they were fighting against the Gepids. It is possible that the envoys complained about the same incident in which Mundus engaged the Getae, or of a similar incident that had taken place in 533. The latter is likelier. According to Marcellinus, after Mundus had defeated the Getae in Illyricum, he continued his journey to Thrace where he engaged and defeated the Bulgars and killed 500 of them in battle. According to the version preserved by Malalas, when Mundus reached Illyricum, the

Huns together with a large army of various barbarians attacked him. However, Mundus attacked these and destroyed them all, and then sent the booty and one captured king presumably to Constantinople. The various barbarians are likely to have included at least the Slavs and Antae. If one tries to reconcile these two accounts, then it is probable that Mundus first engaged Goths who had crossed into Roman territory in Illyricum (as a deserter from the Goths, Mundus could have been the intended object from the start) after which he continued his march to Thrace where he defeated the various different tribal forces, ravaging the area and defeating the Bulgar contingent led by their king separately from the others, killing 500 Bulgars in this encounter and capturing their king all in the same year 530.[5] The Bulgars and the other tribes had clearly exploited the transferral of the troops to the east to fight against the Persians.

The Balkans 530–40

Justinian continued his previous policy of appointing members of his own household to high positions by naming Chilbudius *Magister Militum per Thracias* in 530. This was a happy decision because Chilbudius was one of the best commanders of the era. He was famous for his lack of avarice and ability as commander. So there were now three members of Justinian's household holding important commands: Sittas, Belisarius and Chilbudius. Justinian had an eye for talent. Chilbudius exploited the success achieved by Mundus by taking the war to enemy territory. He crossed the Danube on three consecutive years in 530–33 and defeated the Bulgars, Slavs and Antae in offensive warfare until he was finally killed in action by the Slavs in 533.[6] Mundus was sent to replace Belisarius as *Magister Militum per Orientem* in 531, but we do not know who his successor was as *Magister Militum per Illyricum*, but we know that he was back in this position by 532 and that he was at Constantinople at the time of the Nika revolt in January 532 en route back to Illyricum. Mundus held this position until his death in 536, but we do not know anything about his exploits between 532 and 535; if the abovementioned sacking of Gratiana took place in 533, it is possible that he had been unable to prevent it, for example because of some unknown invasion or that he drove the Goths out after the incident had already taken place, but this is all speculation on my part. For his very important role as commander during the early part of the Gothic war in 535–6, see the relevant chapter.

The Bulgars had clearly recovered enough from their previous defeats by 535 because they are recorded as having invaded Moesia II then. It is probable that the Bulgars were exploiting the absence of Roman forces from the eastern half of the Balkans because it is more or less likely that Justinian had transferred forces from there into the armies of Belisarius and Mundus who were beginning the reconquest of Italy at that time. The Bulgars however made a terrible miscalculation because they came face to face with one of the best Roman commanders of the era. Sittas engaged and defeated them at Iatrus in Moesia. The location suggests that the Romans had prior intelligence of enemy activities so that the *magister militum praesentalis* Sittas had been able to march his forces to the theatre with the result that he was able to engage the enemy immediately after they had crossed the Danube. In fact, it is very likely that Sittas had been able to force the invaders against either the Danube or Iatrus River running beside the Iatrus city. This was first-rate generalship.

In about 536 the Heruls who had been settled as *foederati* in Singidunum and other towns by Justinian killed their king, Ochos, with the explanation that they did not want a king. However, they repented their action immediately after it had been committed and decided to seek a new ruler from the royal family living on the island of Thule (this probably means modern Sweden). They dispatched envoys to find them a suitable king and found one, but when they reached the land of the Dani, the king fell sick and died. They tried again. This time their choice fell on a man called Datius. His brother Aordus and 200 Herul youths joined the envoys and began their journey. However, in the meantime the Heruls who had stayed behind changed their minds once again and asked Justinian to give them a ruler. Justinian did so gladly and chose Suartuas, who lived in Constantinople. The Heruls in Singidunum welcomed him, but then a messenger arrived who told them that the new king from Thule would arrive shortly. Suartuas decided to lead his men against Datius, but when the armies were at a distance of one day's journey from each other the followers of Suartuas abandoned him during the night so Suartuas had to flee to Constantinople. This resulted in the further division of the Herul nation. The followers of Datius numbering 3,000 men revolted and fled to the Gepids while others remained loyal to the Romans. These consisted of multiple different federate forces serving in different places so that only about 1,500 loyal Heruls remained in Singidunum and the area around it. The revolt of the Heruls took place before 538 because it was then that we find the loyal Heruls in Italy.[7]

The troubles reappeared in 539. However, there is another possible explanation for the 'peaceful state' or at least for the lack of references to invasions of Roman territory by the Huns. According to Procopius (*Wars* 1.22.19), Dagaris defeated the Huns (i.e. Bulgars) several times in battle and drove them out when they had invaded Roman territory at some unknown time after the year 532. In my opinion the likeliest period for these victories would be 535–8, and this would also explain the silence of the sources, but I will also suggest other alterative dates in the subsequent discussion.

If one places the exploits of Dagaris to this period, it is possible to connect his victories with the administrative changes that Justinian made in the Balkans in 535–6. In 535 Justinian joined together the military and civil vicariates of the Long Wall as Praetorship of Thrace. The idea was to improve the defence and administration of the Long Walls. It is possible that this was a precautionary step in a situation in which Justinian had dispatched armies from the Balkans to the west. This suggests that at this time Justinian was engaged in matters concerning the defence of the capital and Balkans. The next reform was the creation of the *questura/quaestura exercitus* in 536 to improve the supply of the troops of the Thracian frontier along Moesia II and Scythia. The *Quaestor Exercitus* became a sort of junior praetorian prefect with five provinces being detached from the office of the Praetorian Prefect of the East. These and the Province of the Islands (Cyclades together with the islands between Lesbos and Rhodes), Caria, and Cyprus were used to support the troops posted in Moesia II and Scythia.[8] I would suggest that the reason for this reform had been the first of the successful defensive campaigns of Dagaris and that Dagaris had made a request for the improvement of the supply situation. I would also suggest that the reform was a success and helped Dagaris to achieve the subsequent victories over the invaders. If my learned speculations are correct, then it is unfortunate that we do not know what happened to Dagaris after 538 – all that we know of it is that he was successful to the end of his career, which must have come at that year.

It is probable that at least some of the fortification projects of Justinian in the Balkans were carried out during these years. Procopius lists 430 such sites for Illyricum, but Tate suggests that the total for the Balkans could have been as many as 600. The fortification project included fortifications both along the Danube and in the interior. The latter consisted of cities that received repairs and improvements and also of the fortification of strategic locations such as the Gates of Iron, the Plain of Adrianople, Thermopylae, and the Isthmus of Corinth. Fortifications and the armed forces were not the only means that Justinian employed in the defence of the Balkans. His diplomacy was at least as important and in this field Justinian was to achieve some of his greatest successes later.[9]

Justinian reformed the structures of the internal security apparatus of Constantinople. This suggests that he and his staff saw a need for this in the 530s. In 535 Justinian replaced *Praefectus Vigilum* with a new better paid official called Praetor of the Demes. The aim was presumably to control the factions better. In 539 Justinian created a new office called *Quaesitor* with the duty of checking temporary visitors to the capitol. He had the double duty of keeping an eye on the visitors during their stay and making certain they returned to their homes once their business had been conducted. The *Quaesitor* was also put in charge of deporting the unemployed from the city and of putting to work those who remained. The idea was clearly to prevent the forming of idle urban mobs that could revolt as had happened in the Nika revolt. There was a real danger that this could happen in a situation in which the Balkans was ravaged by enemies.[10]

The peaceful years for the Balkans were over by 539. This year saw two major invasions: one in the west by the Gepids and the other by the Bulgars which ended just before the Persian invasion in spring 540 (with the implication that we should date the latter invasion to the turn of the year 539/540). The likely reason for both invasions was the troop transferrals from the Balkans to Italy, North Africa and Armenia (for the last, see Chapter 11). Justinian had sent Narses together with other commanders to Italy in 538 (5,000 soldiers and 2,000 Heruls) and in 539 he gave Solomon a large army when he reappointed him commander of North Africa. It is clear that at least some of these forces had been transferred from the Balkans because they included Heruls. If most of the men dispatched west consisted of the army of Illyricum – at least those who had previously advanced to Venetia would have consisted of these – then further transferral of them in 538–9 together with the transferral of Heruls and the surrender of the Goths would have created a power vacuum in Illyricum, which the Gepids then exploited. The opportunity was just too good to dismiss because the Goths and Gepids had been fighting over the region for a long time. The *magister militum* Calluc advanced against them and, considering what happened later in the year, it is likely that he took with him reinforcements from the armed forces posted in Thrace. Calluc defeated the Gepids at first in an epic battle, but was defeated and killed in the next with the result that the Gepids were able to take possession of Sirmium.[11]

The second of the major invasions was a massive Hunnic (presumably the Bulgars) invasion of the western Balkans described by Procopius in some detail. This would have been the result of the troop transferrals to Italy, North Africa and then by Calluc to Pannonia. The invasion took place just before the spring offensive of the Persians in 540 so it can be dated to the turn of the year 539/40 with the implication that the defeat of Calluc in Pannonia contributed to its success. According to Procopius, the Huns caused never-before-seen damage to the Balkans. They crossed the Danube and plundered the entire area from the Adriatic to the suburbs of Constantinople. They captured thirty-two fortresses in Illyricum and stormed Cassandria (Potidaea) – they had never captured walled cities before. This implies that the Bulgars had been considered inept besiegers up to that time. Had they received help from some Roman turncoats as happened during Attila's time? One of the Bulgar divisions attacked the wall of the Chersonesus and bypassed the fortifications by using the surf of the sea so that they were able to scale the walls from the Black Gulf, kill some inhabitants and put the rest in chains. Then they advanced against Sestus and Abydus where they crossed the straits and plundered Asiatic country after which they returned to Chersonesus. It is probable that this force was the one that had advanced against the suburbs of Constantinople. Another force had advanced against Illyricum and Thessaly. This force was brought to a halt by the wall and garrison posted at Thermopylae, but like so many other enemies before, the Bulgars found the path which enabled them to bypass this. Consequently they pillaged almost all of Greece except Peloponnesus. This means that the walls and defenders of the Corinthian Isthmus were able to stop their advance. The Bulgars took 120,000 captives and other loot and returned without having faced any other opposition except where they had attacked fortresses. According to Procopius, at later times the Huns did the same and brought great calamity to the Romans.[12] It is possible that Procopius meant these later instances in his *Anekdota* (8.5–6, 11.5, esp. 21.26ff.) when he stated Justinian was in the habit of forbidding his generals of Thrace and Illyria from attacking the Huns so that they could be used as allies against the Goths or other enemies. However, it is clear that this was not the case in 539/40: it is difficult to imagine that Justinian would have allowed the taking of 120,000 captives. In short, it is likely that the *Anekdota* meant the invasions that took place after 540. It is likely that we do not know all of the invasions of Roman territory. It is also possible that Justinian gave his permission on other occasions if the exploits of Dagaris took place after 540 – it is impossible to date these when Procopius (*Wars* 1.22.19) merely states that Dagaris defeated the Huns several times in battles after 532 and drove them out.

Chapter Nine

West: Reconquest of Italy by Belisarius in 535–40

Left: Theodohad
Right: Vitigis

Source: Diehl

Rome and Ostrogoths from 526 until 535[1]

Theoderic the Great, the founder of the Ostrogothic Kingdom of Italy, died in 526. He had ruled well and was loved by Goths and Italians alike. He was succeeded by Athalaric, the 8-year-old son of Theoderic's daughter Amalasuntha, who acted as a regent for the underage son because her husband had already died. She respected the rights of the Italian/Roman populace and prevented her Gothic subjects from abusing their position, but this did not sit well with the Goths. Amalasuntha controlled Athalaric with an iron hand and taught him Roman customs. Athalaric resented this and sought help from the Gothic nobles with the claim that his mother had attempted to kill him. The nobles eagerly grasped this opportunity to weaken Amalasuntha's grip on her son and stated that Athalaric should be educated like a Goth among young men of his age and not by old weaklings. They stated that Theoderic had not allowed the Goths to send their children to school because if they started to fear the strap they could not be taught to face sword and spear. Furthermore, Theoderic had conquered a large kingdom for himself without a school education. Amalasuntha was forced to do as they wished, so Athalaric became a depraved womanizer who drank too much and did not follow his mother's advice. By then several Gothic nobles were opposing her quite openly and plotting her downfall and this was done with Athalaric's full acceptance.

Amalasuntha decided to get rid of the three principal plotters by dispatching them separately to different parts of Italy, officially with the mission to guard these areas against enemies. She also sent an envoy to Justinian in which she asked for a place of asylum, which was granted. She sent her possessions in a ship to Epidamnus (Dyrrachium) with orders to stay in the harbour and wait for further orders. Her plan was to kill all three plotters, and if even one of them survived she planned to flee to Epidamnus and from there to Constantinople. When the assassination attempts succeeded, she recalled the ship. However, she faced other troubles.

Theodahadus, son of Amalafrida the sister of Theoderic, had built for himself a powerbase in Tuscany. He was a well-educated, unwarlike and greedy man. He had accumulated his wealth through illicit means and it was because of this that he promised to deliver Tuscany to Justinian if he would protect him. At about the same time as he came up with this plan, two envoys, Hypatius (priest/bishop of Ephesus) and Demetrius (priest/bishop of Philippi in Macedonia), arrived in Rome to discuss Christian doctrine with the Pope. Theodatus met these two envoys secretly and disclosed to them his wishes.

As if this was not enough, Athalaric had succumbed to drunken revelry and had caught what Procopius calls a wasting disease, which the physicians stated would lead to his death. Now Amalasuntha knew her days were numbered, so she decided to deliver her kingdom to Justinian. Just then envoys arrived from Justinian at Ravenna, senators Alexander and Demetrius and Hypatius. Their official task was deliberate on the issue of Lilybaeum in Sicily as had previously been decided between Belisarius and Goths, to ask the return of ten Huns who had deserted their colours in Libya and who received a place of refuge among the Goths, and to complain about the sack of the Roman city of Gratiana by the Goths when they had fought against the Gepids near Sirmium. Their secret mission was to ask why Amalasuntha had failed to join the ship she had sent in advance to Epidamnus. When this Alexander then had arrived in Rome, he had left the abovementioned priests there and had himself continued his journey to Ravenna. There the two dealt with the official business publicly, so Amalasuntha gave a stern reply to the demands[2] while secretly confiding to him her plan to hand over the kingdom. When Justinian then learnt of the wishes of Theodahadus and Amalasuntha he was overjoyed.

In the meantime, the Tuscans denounced Theodahadus to Amalasuntha with the result that he was called to the court to be investigated. At about this time, Athalaric finally died, so Amalasuntha came up with an emergency plan which was to marry Theodahadus if he swore that Amalasuntha could retain her powers. He did this and was duly nominated as king, but he had no intention of keeping his word and imprisoned Amalasuntha on the island of Marta in Lake Vulsina (Bolsena) in Tuscany, and then sent Roman senators Liberius and Opilio with others as envoys to Justinian with orders to hide the fact that Amalasuntha had been harshly treated by him. However, before any of this had happened Justinian had sent Peter to Italy without anyone's knowledge, with the secret task of arranging the handing of Tuscany from Theodahadus to Justinian and then after that the handing of all of Italy from Amalasuntha to Justinian. His official mission was to continue to discuss the previously mentioned topics. However, en route Peter met the envoys that Theodahadus had sent to Justinian. He learnt from them that Theodahadus had become king. After this, Peter accompanied the envoys up to the city of Aulon and learnt from them everything that had happened. It was then because of this that Justinian learnt all of the above from Peter before the envoys arrived. Justinian decided to exploit this knowledge to throw the Gothic realm into confusion with a plot. He wrote a letter to Amalasuntha in which he promised to back her cause, which he then instructed Peter to make public. Consequently, when the envoys from Rome arrived and Liberius spoke openly while Opilio continued to lie, Justinian was already aware of their mission.

However, Justinian's plot did not work as he had planned because when Peter arrived in Italy, Amalasuntha had already been killed by her enemies who had forced Theodahadus to concede to their wishes. Peter threatened war and Theodahadus attempted to excuse himself by accusing the actual murderers of the deed. This did not work. Justinian formulated a skilful strategy to overthrow the Goths. According to Zachariah of Mitylene (9.18), Justinian was assisted by Dominic/Demonicus. This man had been one of the chief men of Italy. He had quarrelled with the ruler so he had been forced to seek a place of refuge in Constantinople. Dominic was apparently privy to state secrets and was therefore a great asset in the formulation of policies and strategies concerning Italy.

The strategy of reconquest: The return of the Romans to Italy in 535[3]

Justinian's plan consisted of three elements: Mundus, the *Magister Militum per Illyricum*, was ordered to conquer Salona in Dalmatia which was in Gothic hands at this time; Belisarius was dispatched to Sicily to take it with a surprise attack; the third element was the forming of an alliance with the Franks against the Ostrogoths. This was achieved by dispatching a letter and envoys to the Franks. The Franks answered in the affirmative and promised to dispatch an army to Italy.

We do not know the size or composition of Mundus's force but it is probable that it consisted for the most part of cavalry and that it had at least 5,000–10,000 men for it to be effective. We are on safer ground with the force of Belisarius sent by sea because Procopius gives us a list of the units serving under him. He had 4,000 *katalogoi* and *foederati*, and about 3,000 Isaurians. The *katalogoi* of cavalry (in this case this includes the *foederati*) were commanded by Valentinus, Magnus and Innocentius. The infantry were commanded by Herodian, Paulus, Demetrius and Ursicinus, and the Isaurians by Ennes. My educated guess is that each of the cavalry commanders had about 400 horsemen so that there would have been about 1,200 horsemen, and that each of the infantry commanders had about 700 footmen for a total of 2,800 infantry. There were also 200 'xymmachoi' (= *symmachoi* = allies) Huns, and 300 Moors (presumably also cavalry). In addition to this, Belisarius was accompanied by Photius, the son of his wife Antonina from his previous marriage, and by his bodyguards, the *bucellarii*, which appear to have numbered at this stage about 7,000 horsemen. This means that Belisarius had about 8,700 horsemen and 5,800 infantry, but we should add to this figure the sailors who seconded as marines and the engineers, squires, servants and other support units. Belisarius was instructed to act as if he had been dispatched to Carthage via Sicily and once he reached Sicily he was to disembark his men with some excuse and then conquer the island if this was possible and if it was not he was to continue his journey to Carthage without betraying his intention. This means that the military campaign against the Goths was intended to begin with the surprise attack of Sicily by Belisarius. Justinian and his staff were clearly masters at this game of international chess.

Justinian's masterplan progressed like clockwork. Mundus duly advanced into Dalmatia, engaged the Goths and defeated them in battle after which he took possession of Salona. It is possible that this part of the campaign took place before Belisarius disembarked his men in Sicily because the Romans must have coordinated their efforts. However, I would still suggest that it is probable that Mundus's attack was timed to take

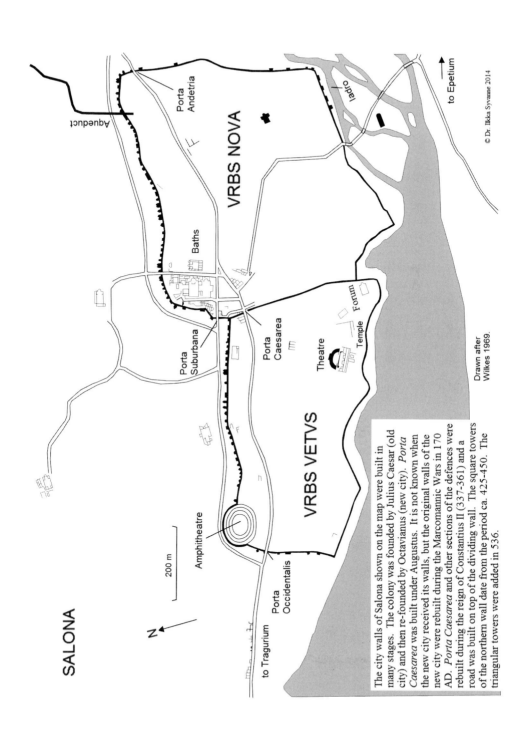

SALONA

N

200 m

to Tragurium

Porta
Occidentalis

Amphitheatre

Aqueduct

Porta
Andetria

Porta
Suburbana

Baths

VRBS NOVA

Porta
Caesarea

VRBS VETVS

Theatre

Temple

Forum

Iadro

to Epetium

© Dr. Ilkka Syvänne 2014

Drawn after
Wilkes 1969.

The city walls of Salona shown on the map were built in
many stages. The colony was founded by Julius Caesar (old
city) and then re-founded by Octavianus (new city). *Porta
Caesarea* was built under Augustus. It is not known when
the new city received its walls, but the original walls of the
new city were rebuilt during the Marcomannic Wars in 170
AD. *Porta Caesarea* and other sections of the defences were
rebuilt during the reign of Constantius II (337-361) and a
road was built on top of the dividing wall. The square towers
of the northern wall date from the period ca. 425-450. The
triangular towers were added in 536.

place just after the disembarkation of Belisarius's forces. The best way to coordinate the campaigns would have been for Mundus and Belisarius to meet each other somewhere close to Epidamnus/Dyrrachium after which both would have gone their separate ways. It is probable that Mundus was ordered to wait for the news that Belisarius had invaded Sicily because it would not have taken many days for the news to reach him by ship. This would have preserved the advantage of surprise.

Belisarius achieved complete surprise. He disembarked his forces and then took Catana, which he made his base of operations. Then he captured Syracuse and the other cities without trouble through surrender with the exception of Panormus (Palermo) where the local Gothic garrison resisted because they trusted its defences. Indeed Belisarius considered it impossible to capture the city from the landward side so he dispatched his fleet to the harbour which extended right up to the wall. When the fleet was then anchored there the sailors observed that the masts were higher than the walls. This enabled them to hoist small boats to the tops of the masts filled with archers who were then able to shoot at the enemy from above. This frightened the Goths who then duly surrendered the city. The attached images from Athanaios and Heron of Byzantium show how the Roman military treatises depicted similar use of ships in sieges.[4] The use of ships' masts against enemy walls was a standard means of attacking coastal cities. After the taking of Panormus, Belisarius marched back to Syracuse which he entered on 31 December 535, the last day of his consulship. Because of this he threw gold coins around when he entered the city in the midst of cheering soldiers and Sicilians. The Sicilians preferred to be under Roman rule and what better way of rewarding them than this. As noted above, it is also probable that Solomon in Carthage coordinated his actions with Belisarius at this time when he dispatched a fleet to Sardinia because it clearly took place at about the same time Belisarius attacked Sicily, so that there was also a fourth element to the plan of reconquest.

When the Roman envoy Peter learnt of the conquest of Sicily, he put additional pressure on the weak Theodahadus. Theodahadus agreed to the surrender of Sicily, the payment of 300 litrae of gold every year, the sending of 3,000 Gothic warriors on request, and to recognize Justinian as the emperor in Italy. However, ever the coward, Theodahadus later recalled Peter when he reached Albani (Albano) on the Appian Way. He was fearful of what Justinian's reaction would be if the above concessions did not suffice. Peter advised that in that case Theodahadus was to resign from the kingship in favour of Justinian. Theodahadus made Peter swear that he would present the first agreed concessions and only after that the second if Justinian had not agreed to the first. Peter swore and officially presented these as Theodahadus had wanted, but of course as Justinian's envoy he told Justinian everything so Justinian's refusal to the first concessions and acceptance of the second is not surprising. Justinian's reply was that Theodahadus was to organize the details of the surrender with Athanasius brother of Alexander, and Peter, and that Belisarius was to visit him to complete the arrangements as agreed.

However, in the meantime there had been a new development which changed the equation. The Goths had assembled a great army under Asinarius and Gripas and others which advanced to Dalmatia against Mundus. When this army reached the neighbourhood of Salona, Mundus dispatched his son Mauricius to reconnoitre. He encountered the Goths, killed their leading members, but the Romans lost almost all of their men including *strategos* Mauricius. Mundus was grief-stricken and furious at the same time. He led out his forces without delay or order and attacked the enemy head-on. The battle was hard fought and proved to be a Cadmean/Pyrrhic victory for the Romans. Most of the enemy fell on combat and they were decisively routed, but Mundus was killed during his furious pursuit of the fugitives. This put a stop to the pursuit and the two armies separated. The disheartened and leaderless Romans did not return to Salona but went back home, while the Goths who were now also leaderless retreated to nearby forts but did not attempt to retake Salona because they did not consider its defences sufficient and because the local Romans were hostile to them. When the vacillating coward Theodahadus heard of this, he became puffed up with newly found false pride and refused to pay attention to the envoys that Justinian had sent him. Theodahadus taunted the ambassadors and threatened to kill them, but in the end he settled on just keeping them under guard.

The problems related to Belisarius's family life surfaced for the first time when he had conquered Sicily. He was married to Antonina, whose grandfather and father were charioteers and whose mother was a prostitute. She had adopted the lifestyle of her mother so she was mother to several children at the time she married Belisarius, and despite being already well past her prime she continued in the same lifestyle during her marriage with Belisarius. Antonina was a close confidante and friend of the empress Theodora and it was primarily because of this that she was careful to conceal her escapades. Despite the fact that marriage with Antonina was a politically savvy move thanks to her friendship with Theodora, the marriage was still a love marriage on Belisarius's part. He was madly and blindly in love with Antonina. However, she was not in love with him, on top of which she was a manipulative adulteress. Belisarius had adopted Antonina's son Photius and an unnamed daughter, and Antonina may have had other children as well. Antonina and Belisarius had only one child, Ioannina, probably largely due to the advanced age of Antonina which made it impossible to have more. It was presumably because of this that Antonina and Belisarius adopted still another child whose name was Theodosius on the eve of the Vandal expedition. It was this adoption that led to trouble.[5]

Antonina accompanied her husband during the campaigns because she wanted to keep her husband in tight control by means of her womanly charms. In the course of the voyage to Carthage Antonina developed an insatiable lust towards Theodosius, her adopted son. First she had sex with him in secret, and then publicly in the presence of servants of both sexes. Belisarius caught the two in the act in Carthage, but bought the explanation put forth by Antonina that they were just hiding the most valuable part of the booty so that the emperor would not learn of its existence. This in itself is important because it proves that Belisarius and Antonina were both in the habit of stealing part of the loot. The scandal grew even worse as time went by. When the 'family' was in Syracuse after the conquest of Sicily, a servant girl called Macedonia and two bedroom attendants approached Belisarius and told him what Antonina and Theodosius had been up to. Belisarius ordered Theodosius killed, but Theodosius was able to flee to Ephesus because the execution order had been exposed by those who knew Belisarius's weak vacillating nature towards his wife. Indeed they knew Belisarius better than he did himself – one may imagine that they included Procopius, who certainly did everything to please the *domina* of the house because he involved Antonina in all of the decisions when he was subsequently sent to Naples (see later). Antonina used her womanly wiles to convince Belisarius that Macedonia and the bedroom attendants had lied. Belisarius handed them to Antonina who duly had their tongues cut out, after which she cut them up bit by bit with the help of a servant called Eugenius and then placed their pieces in sacks which she tossed into the sea. After that Constantinus sympathized with Belisarius and said to him that he would have rather killed the woman than the youths. Antonina heard these words and never forgave Constantinus. She bided her time to exact vengeance as we shall see.

The beginning of all-out war in early 536: Conquest of Dalmatia and Liburnia[6]

When Justinian learnt of these events, he dispatched Constantianus, the commander of the Royal Grooms, to Illyricum to assemble an army from the units posted there, after which he was to take the city of Salona. Belisarius was ordered to land his forces in Italy and treat the Goths as enemies. Constantianus assembled the available forces at Epidamnus/Dyrrachium and then sailed to Epidaurus (Ragusa Vecchia) where he anchored his ship. The Gothic spies/scouts who had been dispatched there by Gripas observed this and to them it seemed as if the whole of the land and sea were full of soldiers. When they returned to Gripas they told him that Constantianus was bringing an army consisting of myriads of men. This was undoubtedly true because at the time of the *Notitia Dignitatum* the paper strength of the field army of *Illyricum* consisted of about 1,000 cavalry, 36,200 legionary infantry, and 6,000 *auxilia palatina* 'medium infantry'.[7] There would also have been sizable forces of regular *foederati* and *bucellarii* to bolster these figures, in addition to which the galleys would have had sizable crews,[8] so there is no reason to doubt the existence of myriads of men. One wonders whether Procopius wanted to show the discrepancy in the size of force given to Constantianus and Belisarius.

The news frightened Gripas. He feared it would be impossible to hold Salona against the Romans when the Romans had mastery of the seas, its defences in ruins and the populace hostile. So he withdrew from the forts and pitched his camp in the plain between Salona and Scardon (Sebenico). Constantianus sailed his ships from Epidaurus to the island of Lysina (Lesina). From there he sent some men to scout the whereabouts of Gripas and to find out what his plans were. When the scouts brought back the news of the Gothic withdrawal, Constantianus sailed straight to Salona. He disembarked his men close to the city and then selected 500 placing them under Siphilas, one of his bodyguards, and dispatched them to seize the narrow pass west of the city. When Siphilas had achieved this, Constantianus and the main army entered the city on the following day, and the fleet was anchored close by. Constantianus rebuilt all the walls that had collapsed due to neglect. Seven days after their arrival, Gripas retreated to Ravenna so that the Romans gained possession of all Dalmatia and Liburnia. These events took place when the winter was coming to a close, which means March 536.

The landing in Italy and the siege of Naples in late spring 536[9]

After the short campaign to secure Carthage against the rebels of Stotzas after Easter 536 and possible pacification of the mutinous army in Sicily (see Chapter 10), Belisarius was ready to put into effect the orders of Justinian. In late spring 536 he left garrisons in Syracuse and Panormus and crossed with the rest of the army from Messana to Rhegium. His fleet carried a massive amount of grain taken from Sicily to enable him to conduct his operations. According to the speech put into the mouth of Totila by Procopius, the fleet of Belisarius carried so much grain that it sufficed to feed the Roman army and the entire population of Rome for an entire year after Belisarius had captured Rome.[10] This makes it very likely that Belisarius had previously prevented shipments of grain to Rome from Sicily so that he was able to undermine the position of the Goths while also making it certain that he would appear as the man who fed the Romans. The Italian Romans welcomed the Romans with open arms because they hated the Goths. The cities were also unfortified so that even if they had wished, they wouldn't have been able to resist the invaders. On top of this, one of the Gothic leaders, called Ebrimous/Ebrimuth, deserted with his followers. Ebrimous was married to the daughter of Theodahadus. Belisarius dispatched him immediately to Justinian who made him patrician. From Rhegium, Belisarius marched through Bruttium and Lucania to Campania with the fleet sailing along the coast. In Campania the forces of Belisarius faced their first resistance. Naples was both well fortified and heavily garrisoned with Goths. Theodahadus had ensured the loyalty of the garrison by keeping their families as hostages. Belisarius anchored his fleet in the harbour just outside the range of missiles and placed his camp near the city. His first action was to take by surrender a fort in the suburb. After this he allowed the citizens of Naples to send an embassy. At first the negotiator Stephanus tried to convince Belisarius to continue his march to Rome because the Gothic garrison would not surrender because their families were held hostage, but his views changed when Belisarius bribed him. Consequently, Stephanus did his best to convince the citizens to surrender. He was assisted in these efforts by Antiochus, a shipping magnate originating from Syria. It is clear that this Antiochus should be seen as yet another member of the Roman spy organization in the area just as the merchant in Syracuse with whom Procopius had conversed had been, and the merchants that the Vandals had imprisoned at Carthage. The use of businesses as cover for spying activities is not new. It is not a coincidence that

Procopius accompanied Belisarius on this trip. He was the man who handled contacts with the East Roman spies posing as businessmen during this reconquest.[11]

However, there were two men, Pastor and Asclepiodotus, who were trained orators and who sided with the Goths. These two managed to convince the Neapolitans to put forth a number of demands for their surrender. Belisarius agreed to these demands with the result that the local populace started marching towards the gates to open those up. The Goths did not attempt to prevent this because their numbers were too few. This shows how sizable the populations of major cities were. However, the two demagogues managed to halt this by calling both the citizens and Goths to a joint meeting. This time two rabble-rousers found the right words. They asked, what if the Goths win the war and the populace had betrayed them? What would happen then? And even if Belisarius won, how would he treat those who had betrayed their previous lords? After this the two men brought forward local Jews who promised that the city would not lack supplies, while the Gothic garrison promised to protect the circuit wall. This turned the heads of the Neapolitan populace against the surrender. The Jews naturally opposed the arrival of the East Roman oppressors.

Belisarius had no option but to besiege the place both by land and sea. The Romans made many futile and costly attacks against the circuit-wall with the result that Belisarius lost many of his bravest soldiers. This suggests that the defenders had at their disposal siege artillery and other machines used in defence. It is probable that these were operated by the Neapolitans because they sided with the Goths at this time. Belisarius also cut the aqueduct, but the wells inside the city ensured a sufficient supply of water. Furthermore, the blockade was not complete thanks to the smallness of the Roman army and because of this small groups of people including envoys were able to pass through undetected. Theodahadus however, ever the vacillating coward, made no preparations to assist the Neapolitans. However, he did one correct thing, which was to dispatch envoys to the Franks with the promise of handing over the Gothic part of Gaul to them together with a sizable sum of gold in return for military assistance against the Romans. The Franks promised to do this despite having just concluded an alliance with Justinian. In fact it is probable that the Franks had already assembled their forces for the invasion of Gothic Gaul before Theodahadus had dispatched his envoys, so their arrival put a stop to this invasion before it really started.

Procopius claims that Theodahadus's inactivity resulted from his cowardice, but at the same time he states that some people claimed that Theodahadus had asked one of the Hebrews who was famed for his skills in prophecy to forecast what would happen in war and that this had been unfavourable to the Goths. Procopius found the story unbelievable and so do I because it is clear that Theodahadus was making preparations for war with the diplomatic moves he was making in Gaul, and because such prophecies always promised victory to those who sought them. I have included this account only because it once again shows how good the relationship between the Goths and Jews was, and it also suggests that Theodahadus was listening to the advice given by Jews. This is by no means surprising because the Goths had protected the Jews and they had every reason to fear the reconquest of Italy by the Christian Romans who were likely to launch a persecution. It is clear that commercial interests were also involved. As we have seen the Jews had enough provisions to feed Naples, which means that they were

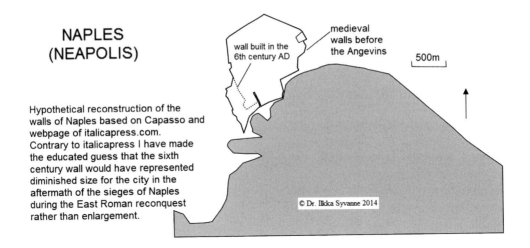

NAPLES (NEAPOLIS)

wall built in the 6th century AD

medieval walls before the Angevins

500m

Hypothetical reconstruction of the walls of Naples based on Capasso and webpage of italicapress.com. Contrary to italicapress I have made the educated guess that the sixth century wall would have represented diminished size for the city in the aftermath of the sieges of Naples during the East Roman reconquest rather than enlargement.

© Dr. Ilkka Syvänne 2014

probably in control of the grain trade in that city. The Roman merchants who were also simultaneously Roman spies obviously wanted to take control of this lucrative trade. It was therefore advantageous for them to be involved in the trade of spying as well.

Belisarius was in a tight spot: he had to reach Rome before the winter season. He had already given orders to continue the march when one Isaurian soldier noted that it was possible to penetrate the city via the aqueduct, if one enlarged one rocky gap. He brought the news to his fellow Isaurian Paucaris who served among the bodyguards of Belisarius. The delighted Belisarius instructed Paucaris to choose Isaurian soldiers who were then sent to cut out a passage not by using picks or mattocks but by scraping. Belisarius gave the Neapolitans one last chance to surrender. According to Procopius, he told Stephanus that if the soldiers captured the city it was typical that the men would be slain, women raped, children taken as slaves, and buildings torched. He would be unable to control the fury of his soldiers many of whom were of barbarian origin and had lost relatives before the walls of the city. The Neapolitans did not surrender and Belisarius sent two trumpeters (their loud call would throw the city into confusion and serve as a sign for the attackers to attack) and 400 men armed with swords and shields under Magnus (commander of a *katalogos* of cavalry) and Ennes (leader of the Isaurians) to the aqueduct. Belisarius also ordered the men to stay awake in the camp, which on the basis of this account was located north of the city, while he with a large chosen force stood in readiness with ladders near the northern wall. However, then things took an unwelcome turn. Magnus's men turned back in fright. They were clearly not as brave the Isaurians. Belisarius had to choose 200 men to replace them, after which the frightened men, ashamed, re-joined the attackers. Photius, the stepson, was also eager to join the attackers, but Belisarius prevented this. The value of the Isaurian infantry in tight quarters is evident in comparison with the cavalry. Belisarius ordered Bessas to speak Gothic with the guards of the nearest tower so that they would not hear the clanging of the weapons as the men moved inside the aqueduct.

When the soldiers in the aqueduct reached a spot where there was no roof, they faced a problem. They had not brought with them the necessary equipment for descending.

Then one brave man set an example: using both hands and feet he descended to a deserted house where he found a woman squatter living in poverty. The man threatened her silently and then fastened to the olive tree a strong strap the other end of which he threw up to the aqueduct. The soldiers used the rope to get into the house and then into the city after which they proceeded toward the northern wall where Belisarius and Bessas were and captured two towers by killing their defenders. The trumpeters summoned the army. When the ladders were placed against the wall, it was discovered that the engineers had miscalculated the height of the wall – they had been built secretly so the builders had not seen the wall. None of the ladders reached the parapet so the Romans had to bind two ladders together. Now the Romans entered the city and began the typical massacre.[12] The stiffest resistance came from the Jews who occupied the wall facing the sea. They resisted until sunrise. In daylight, those Romans who had mounted the wall were able to shoot at them from behind. The Jewish resistance collapsed. By then all of the gates had been thrown open and the Roman army entered the city from every direction except from the east where the advance was delayed because the soldiers there had no ladders at all. They had to wait until the unguarded and torched gates (the defenders had fled) had collapsed. The soldiers entered the city in fury and allowed their basest instincts to take over. After the soldiers had vented their anger enough to calm down, Belisarius was able to reconcile the citizens with the army by releasing the women, children, and slaves from captivity. The Goths who were captured and not killed amounted to 800 men who were all unharmed and put under guard. The siege had lasted for twenty days. When Pastor heard the news, he died from apoplexy. Asclepiodotus however was bold enough to defend his actions before Belisarius, who pardoned him; but the populace did not and he was torn to pieces once he left the quarters of Belisarius. His body was impaled and placed on the outskirts of the city. Belisarius pardoned the citizens who committed this act.

As I have noted in my doctoral dissertation, this siege shows well how effective the Isaurian infantry specialists were in sieges as well as the importance of daylight to archery. This siege also proves that the Roman siege engineers accompanying Belisarius were not up to the task. Furthermore, it shows that the Jews were the greatest losers if the Romans conquered the city and were therefore the most effective fighting force inside the city.[13]

Vittigis voted new king and the Gothic defensive strategy

When news of the fall of Naples was brought to the Goths who were in Rome, they started to wonder why Theodahadus had done nothing and began to suspect that Theodahadus was collaborating with Justinian. This was unfair because the Goths had three fronts to deal with: the Franks in Gaul, Constantianus in Dalmatia and Belisarius in the south of Italy. Theodahadus's plan was to solve the Frankish problem first and with this in mind he had sent envoys to the Franks which promised the south of Gaul to them in return for military alliance. The Franks had promised this. Those who opposed Theodahadus assembled at Regata 280 stades (ca. 52 km) from Rome where the plains provided good pasture for the horses. They chose Vittigis as their new king because he had acquired great fame as result of battles fought against the Gepids near Sirmium when Theoderic ruled. When Theodahadus heard of this he attempted to flee to Ravenna, but was captured and killed.

Vittigis and the Goths marched to Rome and put Theodahadus's son under guard. Vittigis thought that it was not wise to confront Belisarius in Rome because the Gothic war preparations were incomplete. Vittigis took most of the Roman senators with him as hostages as he went north, with the idea of securing Rome with this measure. He also exhorted both the populace and Pope Silverius to stay loyal to the Goths. He left a garrison of 4,000 men under Leuderis at Rome and then withdrew north with the idea of assembling all the Gothic forces from Gaul and Venetia. The Gothic forces were scattered: some were garrisoned south of Gaul against the Franks under Marcias while others were in Venetia to oppose Constantianus. Vittigis wanted to assemble all of his forces against one foe at the same time and to use the inner lines to gain a numerical advantage. His plan was to march against Belisarius, but only after the war with the Franks had first been settled. In practice he therefore adopted the same policy as had been followed by Theodahadus and so it was that he sent envoys to the Franks that suggested the very same things that Theodahadus had, and the Franks accepted them. However, since the Franks had only just previously concluded an alliance with Justinian, they decided to maintain the policy of plausible deniability, so they sent only soldiers from allied nations to assist the Goths. Vittigis was now able to recall Marcias.

The reconquest of Rome on 9 December 536[14]

Meanwhile things had gone from bad to worse for the Goths. Belisarius had selected 300 footmen to serve as a garrison of Naples under Herodian and he had dispatched a large garrison for Cumae. These were the only two fortified cities in Campania and Belisarius thought this was a sufficient safety measure when he with the rest of his army advanced to Rome to reconquer it.

Reconquering Rome was easily done because the inhabitants had decided to desert the Goths to avoid what had happened in Naples. They were urged to do so by Pope Silverius, which is not surprising because he preferred Orthodox/Catholic East Rome over the Arian Goths. The citizens of Rome dispatched *Quaestor* Fidelius to Belisarius to invite him into the city, which opportunity Belisarius eagerly grasped, marching his army along the Latin Way instead of the Appian Way. Procopius does not state why Belisarius chose to do this, but one may imagine that the Goths were expecting him to use the Appian Way because he could have sailed his fleet alongside it so Belisarius's intention would have been to use the road that the enemy did not expect him to use. This appears to have worked because the Goths learnt of his approach only when he was already close to Rome. Belisarius's forces were very small, consisting of only about 5,500 regulars[15] and his own bodyguards.

The citizens of Rome fooled the Gothic garrison so skilfully that they learnt of the decision taken by the Romans only when Belisarius was already at the gates. The Goths were at a loss what to do. They had too few men to engage Belisarius and they could not defend the city when the populace opposed them. The stalemate was solved when the Romans allowed the Goths to leave the city unharmed and flee to Ravenna. With the exception of Leuderis, who chose to remain to be taken captive, the rest of the Goths departed through the Flaminian Gate at the same time as the emperor's army entered the city through the Asinarian Gate on 9 December 536. Rome was once again Roman.

Belisarius dispatched Leuderis and the keys of the city to Justinian and started to strengthen the defences of the city which had fallen into decay. He added to each merlon of the battlement an additional protective wing. See the illustration. He also had a moat dug around the wall. According to Procopius, the Romans applauded Belisarius for the measures he had taken, especially the one concerning the battlement, which indeed showed great skill. One wonders whether this was the trend of the day in the east or whether he or his siege engineer came up with this idea.

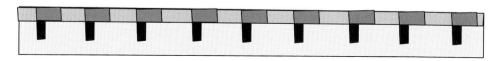

The battlements of the city of Rome from above. Belisarius' additions to the merlons shown with black

The Romans, however, were worried. They feared that the city could not be defended: it was difficult to provision because it was located inland, it was impossible to defend because it was located on a level plain, and it had a wall with so huge a circumference that there were not enough defenders to man it. Belisarius was unmoved by these complaints and continued to make preparations for a siege. He stored the grain which he had shipped from Sicily in public granaries and placed them under guard and forced the reluctant Romans to bring all their provisions from the surrounding countryside into the city. Procopius has failed to describe what the fleet of Belisarius did while he marched along the Latin Way, but it must have sailed to Portus to unload its cargo.

The success of Belisarius brought desertions from enemy ranks. The Calabrians and Apulians had already deserted to him because there were no Goths in the area, but other more serious desertions followed soon. Pitzas and all the Goths who followed him deserted with the result that Belisarius gained possession of half of Samnium without a fight. Belisarius gave Pitzas a small number of troops to guard the portion of Samnium which was in his hands. It is probable that this Pitzas is the Pitzias who had previously fought against the Romans in the Balkans. The name Pitzias or Pitzas is not Gothic so that it is possible that he was native Roman, but both Ennodius and Procopius call Pitzias/Pitzas a Goth – perhaps he was what was called a half-breed, one of his parents a Goth, the other Roman.[16] Belisarius was now in possession of all of Italy from the south up to Rome and Samnium and Constantianus of Dalmatia up to Liburnia. The Goths were being pushed into corner. However, they still had subjects that they could assemble for their support against the forces of Constantianus. According to Procopius the Goths were the overlords of the Siscii (the inhabitants of the city of Siscia), Suevi (a splinter group), Carnii, Norici, Dacians and Pannonians (possessed Singidunum and Sirmium).

Belisarius exploited the inactivity of the Goths by sending Constantinus together with a large number of his *hypaspistai* and *doryforoi* (i.e. his *bucellarii*), including Massagetae Zarter, Chorsomanus and Aeschmanus, and an army of regulars to conquer Tuscany. The Thracian Goth Bessas was ordered to take control of the city of Narnia in Tuscany. The inhabitants of Narnia welcomed Bessas and his men. In the meantime Constantinus gained control of Spolitium (Spoleto), Perusia (Perugia) and some other towns. The Tuscans welcomed him with open arms. Constantianus garrisoned Spolitium and established his headquarters at Perusia. The conquest of these areas gave Belisarius defensive depth. Vittigis dispatched Unilas and Pissas against Constantianus, who engaged them in the outskirts of Perusia. The Goths had a numerical advantage but were decisively defeated; most were killed and the commanders captured. Constantianus sent both enemy commanders to Belisarius.

The Gothic counter-attack in early 537[17]

Now Vittigis, who had lost face with the loss of Rome and other territories, was forced to take action prematurely despite the fact that Marcias and his army of Gaul had not yet arrived. The humiliation was increased when Vittigis learnt from natives who came from Rome that the army of Belisarius was small and he had therefore made a mistake by withdrawing. Vittigis dispatched a great army under Asinarius and Uligisalus to recover Dalmatia. They were to advance first to the country of the Suevi and reinforce their army with the local barbarian tribesmen after which they were to march straight to Salona. Vittigis gave them a sizable fleet, presumably the royal fleet of Ravenna, with which to besiege Salona from the seaside. If necessary the fleet was to engage the Roman fleet. Vittigis then marched with his main army against Belisarius. According to Procopius, the Gothic host consisted of cavalry and infantry and numbered not less than 150,000 men, and most of these consisted of cataphracts (men and horses clad in armour).

The figure of 150,000 men is often doubted, but there is no reason to. The Gothic army was a national army in which all men were required to perform military service, and the siege of a city the size of Rome required a massive army. As we shall see even this number of men was not enough to cover the entire length of the wall.[18]

The Goths who were advancing against Constantianus in Dalmatia committed an unforgivable blunder. When Asinarius marched to collect an army of Pannonian Suevi and other local tribesmen,[19] Uligisalus did not wait for him but went straight to Liburnia where Constantianus engaged and defeated him at a place called Scardon. Uligisalus withdrew to the city of Burnus where he awaited the arrival of Asinarius. When Constantianus learnt of the imminent arrival of Asinarius with a massive force of tribesmen, he withdrew all of his forces, including those in the surrounding fortresses, into the city of Salona and prepared the city for siege in every way including the digging of a moat around the circuit wall.

The siege of Salona in about February 537[20]

When the very large combined army of Suevi under Asinarius arrived in Burnus, the commanders united their forces and advanced to Salona. The Goths then made a stockade around the circuit wall of Salona and used their ships to blockade the city. When this happened, the Roman fleet made an attack and defeated the Gothic fleet. Many of the Gothic ships were sunk or captured, but, according to Procopius, the Goths did not raise the siege. The naval action once again demonstrates the Roman superiority in naval warfare. The Goths had similar ships, but their crews were not of the same standard as the Roman ones. Unfortunately Procopius does not tell us what happened next. Regardless, it is clear that Constantianus's defence of Salona proved effective in the end and the besiegers were defeated. This may have been because it was impossible to blockade the city after the Goths had lost the naval battle, or it may have been from some other encounter not mentioned by Procopius. The Goths were so inept as besiegers that it is not surprising they were unable to recapture Salona. The siege ended in all probability during the summer of 537, and it was definitely over by 539 because the Gothic general Uligisalus was then stationed in Tudera. The successful conduct of these operations is also clear because Constantianus replaced Belisarius in Italy in 540. This shows how Procopius downplayed the successes of other generals and concentrated his praise solely on Belisarius.[21]

These encounters and sieges show the importance of the navy. The holding and besieging of a coastal city required the use of the navy. Battlefield successes alone were not sufficient to conquer the land. The Gothic counter-attack in 536 also demonstrates that the Goths possessed ships and were ready to use them to blockade the enemy. The Romans, however, were the masters of the sea. One can say with good reason that Roman military power was entirely a reflection of their naval capabilities.

The cavalry skirmish in front of Rome on 20 or 28 February 537 and the beginning of the siege on 21 February or 1 March 537[22]

Belisarius learnt almost immediately that the massive Gothic main army was on the move, so he was forced to contemplate what strategy to adopt in this situation. He faced a serious problem. His army was too small to face the enemy and too small to defend Rome effectively. He needed to bolster his numbers by any means possible and this would have required the withdrawing of the garrisons from Tuscany. On the other hand, he was unwilling to abandon these strongholds to the enemy who could use them against the Romans. Consequently he adopted the mid-course, and ordered both Constantianus and Bessas to leave garrisons in such places that required them and withdraw with the rest back to Rome. Belisarius also wished that Vittigis would waste time in besieging these very strong fortifications so that he would gain time to organize the defence of Rome. This would enable him to bring more provisions into the city and it also bought time for the arrival of reinforcements from the emperor, which Justinian had already dispatched. Constantianus acted as ordered and left garrisons in Perusia and Spolitium and retreated back to Rome. Bessas acted more slowly. He was still in Narnia when the Gothic vanguard reached it. When Bessas saw the Goths, he sallied out and attacked and routed them, but was then forced to retreat back to Narnia because of the vastly superior numbers of the enemy. It was only then that Bessas obeyed the orders of Belisarius and, leaving a garrison in Narnia, returned to Rome. There he reported that the Goths could arrive at any moment because the distance to Narnia was only 350 stades (ca. 65 km) and cavalry could cover that distance in a day if necessary. Vittigis was indeed intent on marching to Rome as fast as possible and did not stop to besiege either Perusia, Spolitium or Narnia, all of which possessed natural defences in addition to their fortifications.

The Goths arrived soon enough but were forced to halt about 14 stades (ca. 2.6 km) from the city because Belisarius had built a huge tower with gates and a garrison to protect the Milvian Bridge. Belisarius knew that this would not stop the Goths because they could cross the Tiber at other places or use boats. His plan was just to gain time. Belisarius had estimated that it would take about twenty days for the Goths to build the required number of boats. The Goths built a camp in front of the bridge and were planning to attack the tower the next day. Procopius stated that twenty-two barbarian deserters from the '*katalogou hippikou*' (cavalry troop) of Innocentius arrived in the Gothic camp during the night. The fact that the regular *katalogoi* included barbarians is important because it shows that not only were the *foederati* full of native Romans but that the regular army was full of barbarians. At the same time, the frightened garrison of the tower and bridge deserted their post and fled to Campania. They did not flee to Rome either because they feared that Belisarius would punish them or because they were ashamed to show their faces to their comrades. This suggests that the barbarian deserters came from the same garrison. On the following day, 20 or 28 February 537, the Goths destroyed the gates of the tower and the Gothic cavalry crossed the Tiber.

Belisarius was unaware of these developments and was planning to build a camp near the Tiber River with the idea that these forces could be used to delay the crossing even more. He took with him 1,000 horsemen, which he led to the tower with the idea of reconnoitring where to place the camp.[23] Then he suddenly had the Gothic cavalry forces right in front of him. Belisarius did not hesitate. He ordered his 1,000 horsemen into the attack. According to Procopius, Belisarius was originally behind the line in safety where the *strategos* was supposed to be, but he was not content to stay there and began to fight like a soldier in the front ranks thereby endangering the whole war. Even if not mentioned by Procopius, this may imply that the first Roman line had been forced to retreat so that Belisarius had been forced to charge forward in person. Belisarius had an experienced and easily recognizable warhorse. The stallion's whole body was dark grey, but its face from the top of his head to its nostrils was the purest white. The Greeks called this type of horse *phalios* and the barbarians *balan*. The horse was so easily recognizable that when the Roman deserters told this to the Goths they were able to target Belisarius with javelins (*akontia*) and other missiles (*belē*). Subsequent analysis of this battle provided by Belisarius to his officers and friends (see later) proves that the missiles of the Goths were not arrows shot by the Gothic cavalry, but in all probability arrows shot by their infantry.

Belisarius fought with great skill and determination. With the help of his well-trained horse, which allowed him to turn from side to side, he was able to kill the onrushing enemies and then with the help of his bodyguards he was able to defend himself when the Goths surrounded him. The bodyguards surrounded Belisarius and protected him from the missiles with their *aspis* shields.[24] More than 1,000 Goths died and Belisarius lost many of his bravest bodyguards, including Maxentius, but Belisarius did not even receive a wound, nor was he hit by a missile. Inspired by the personal example of Belisarius, the Romans defeated the Goths and pursued them until they reached the Gothic infantry. The footmen withstood the attack without any difficulty and the Romans fled with Gothic cavalry hot on their heels. The Romans fled to a certain hill, but the Goths made straight for them. The Romans held their positions for a while, but then fled again towards the walls of Rome. The personal sacrifice of Valentinus, who charged alone against the Goths, bought enough time for the Romans to flee to the Salarian Gate. The citizens of Rome, however, were unwilling to open the gates because the barbarians were hot on their heels and Belisarius was forced to make one final desperate counter-attack. The long pursuit and darkness of the approaching night had disordered the Goths and thanks to this the Roman counter-attack succeeded. The ever cautious Belisarius did not pursue but returned to the safety of the city immediately.[25]

The great Gothic assault of the walls in March (possibly 10 March) 537[26]

When Belisarius reached the safety of the walls, he ordered the soldiers and almost all of the populace to the walls. He ordered them to burn fires and keep watch throughout the whole night. After this Belisarius made an inspection of the fortifications and organized its defence so that the defence of each gate was designated to a specific commander. At this point, Bessas, who had been assigned in charge of the Praenestine Gate, sent a messenger to Belisarius bearing the news that the enemy had broken through the Gate of Pancratius across the Tiber. Bessas urged Belisarius to save himself by fleeing through another gate. Belisarius was unmoved. He declared the news false and dispatched cavalry across the Tiber and found no enemy there. He then dispatched messengers to the commanders in charge of the gates ordering each to stay at his post and not to go to the assistance of any other commander regardless of what they heard. Belisarius would take care of such emergencies in person. Procopius does not state why the Gothic Bessas was not suspected of treason at this time, but perhaps he was above suspicion, and future events prove that he stayed loyal to the Romans throughout. What this incident shows is that in the darkness of night panic resulting from rumours spread fast and easily. Vittigis tried to exploit the initial confusion of the Romans by dispatching one of his commanders, Vacis, to exhort the Romans at the Salarian Gate, but since nobody answered he withdrew. Meanwhile the Romans ridiculed Belisarius for his confidence that he would be able to defend the city. The ever dutiful Belisarius had not even had time to eat; it was finally in the middle of the night that his wife and friends managed to convince him to eat some bread.

On the following day both armies prepared their forces for the siege. Since the Goths did not possess enough men to besiege the entire city, they built six well fortified camps (trenches, rampart with a palisade) from the Flaminian to the Praenestine Gate. Each of the camps had a separate commander. In addition, they built a seventh camp on the other side of the Tiber in the Plain of Nero so that the Romans would not be able to isolate them on the one side. This last mentioned camp was commanded by Marcias who had arrived from Gaul, and was therefore presumably the largest of the lot. The Goths later built an eighth camp, which is shown on one of the accompanying maps. They cut open all of the aqueducts, but the Tiber and the wells inside the city provided enough water for the Romans. See the accompanying maps of Rome, one which is included in the maps section and others in the text. I have purposely included two different reconstructions of the walls of Rome because there is no consensus regarding, for example, the location of the Vivarium.

Belisarius guarded the Pincian and Salarian Gates in person because these parts of the wall were both assailable while they also enabled the making of sallies. Bessas guarded the Praenestine Gate. Constantinus controlled the Flaminian Gate, which Belisarius had closed and blocked with stones because the enemy camp was so near it. Constantinus also held command of the Tomb of Hadrian and was responsible for the defence of the wall between that and the Flaminian Gate. The wall next to the Tiber was only lightly garrisoned because it was considered easily defended thanks to the presence of the river. The rest of the gates were delegated to infantry commanders. The aqueducts were blocked so that the enemy would not be able to enter them as the Romans had done at Naples. The breaking of the aqueducts meant that the mills could no longer be operated because the Romans did not possess enough animals to replace the water power. Belisarius solved the problem by placing boats below the bridge where he then placed the mills and water-wheels to grind the flour for the besieged. The deserters informed the Goths of this with the result that they sent large trees and corpses of killed Romans downstream to break up the mills, but Belisarius fastened iron chains across the Tiber so that the floating objects were gathered and then brought to the shore. According to Procopius, Belisarius adopted

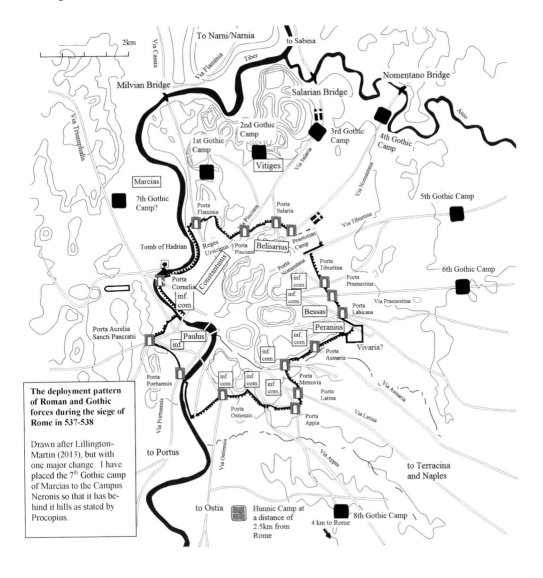

The deployment pattern of Roman and Gothic forces during the siege of Rome in 537-538

Drawn after Lillington-Martin (2013), but with one major change. I have placed the 7th Gothic camp of Marcias to the Campus Neronis so that it has be-hind it hills as stated by Procopius.

this measure primarily to prevent the Goths from using boats to get themselves onto the bridge and from there to the middle of the city and only secondarily to protect the mills. He did not need to protect the sewers because these emptied themselves into the Tiber.

These measures were quite adequate for the moment, but Belisarius faced another problem which was that the Roman populace was unaccustomed to war and sieges. They were distressed because they could not bathe and there was a scarcity of provisions, on top of which they were deprived of sleep from their guard duty on the circuit-wall. The populace was also distressed by the fact that they could see the enemy plundering their possessions outside the walls. They started to assemble in groups and voiced their dissatisfaction openly and reproached themselves for their stupidity in allowing Belisarius to enter the city with so small a force. Members of the Senate also voiced their hostility secretly towards Belisarius. When Vittigis learnt of this from a deserter, he dispatched envoys to Belisarius who then presented their case before Belisarius, the officers and the Roman Senate. Vittigis promised the Roman army an opportunity to retreat with all their possessions and promised to address the grievances of the Senate after regaining possession of the city. Belisarius answered that as long as he lived he would not give up the city. With the exception of Fidelius, who had been appointed Praetorian Prefect by Belisarius and who taunted the envoys, the rest of the Romans sat in silence. This made it clear to the Goths that Belisarius was determined to fight to the end, but the offer had served its main purpose which was to sow dissent among the defenders. This was a standard formula in sieges. The attackers always offered lenient terms of surrender.

When the envoys brought the news, Vittigis had no other alternative than to start preparations for the assault of the walls. Procopius calculates the siege to have started on 1 March 537. It is possible that he meant this day because it was then that Vittigis started his actual preparations for the siege. The other possibility is that Procopius counts the start of the siege from the date when the Goths crossed the Tiber and engaged Belisarius and then besieged the city. This latter alternative is the one adopted here. The Gothic engineers calculated the height of the walls on the basis of the layers of stones and then constructed wooden siege towers equal to its height. They placed wheels on each of the corners and yoked oxen together to draw the towers to their intended locations. They also prepared great numbers of ladders and four battering rams. The rams were four-sided with four wheels on the corners and covered with hides to protect the men inside. They also prepared large quantities of faggots of wood and reed to fill the moat.

Belisarius in his turn placed on the towers torsion ballistae that shot short thick darts with twice the range of a bow and could pierce trees and even rocks according to Procopius. He also placed onagri (sing. onager, wild-ass) stone throwers along the parapet of the wall. Outside the gates he placed lupi (sing. lupus, wolf) which consisted of two timbers that reached from the ground to the battlements on which they fitted beams which projected like beaks. When the enemy approached the gate, the defenders would push the two timbers so that the beaks fell on the enemy below. This device obviously worked well against battering wells.

At sunrise on the 18th day (10 or 18/19 March 537?) the Goths were finally ready to begin their assault. The Goths concentrated their forces at four locations: 1) the Salarian Gate; 2) the Praenestine Gate/Vivarium; 3) the Aurelian Gate (possibly a mistake – could be the Porta Cornelia), the Tomb of Hadrian, and the wall along the Tiber between them;

4) the Aurelian Gate also called the Pancratian Gate. Vittigis ordered his siege towers forwards against the Salarian Gate where Belisarius stood. The populace was frightened at the sight of the advancing towers, but when Belisarius saw them he started laughing and ordered his men to remain inactive until he gave the signal. The Romans started to insult and abuse Belisarius but he did not tell them why he had laughed. As the Goths approached the moat, Belisarius drew his bow and killed with a neck-shot one of the armoured men leading the Goths forward. The Roman army raised a shout. Belisarius repeated his action and the shouting became even louder. It was then that Belisarius gave the signal for the whole army to start using their bows. Those near him were ordered to target the oxen. Belisarius had immobilized the towers by allowing the oxen to draw them near the moat. It was because of this folly that Belisarius had laughed. In comparison to Belisarius the Goths were novices in the art of siege warfare. Vittigis left a large force of Goths opposite the Salarian Gate and arrayed it as a deep phalanx with orders not to advance under any condition but to use only missiles so that Belisarius would not be able to sally out. However, one of the Goths refused to remain in the ranks. He wore a corselet and helmet and used a tree as a partial cover so he could shoot arrows at the parapet. The Roman artillerist from the tower to his left put a stop to this. He shot a dart from his ballista that went right through the Goth's corselet and body halfway into the tree so that the corpse of the man was suspended from it. This sight frightened the Goths to such an extent that they retreated outside the range of the missiles, although they still retained the cohesion of their deep phalanx. Meanwhile Vittigis went to the Praenestine Gate with a great force with the aim of piercing the defences at Vivarium. The wall here was assailable as it had crumbled at this point. A new wall that had been built outside it was strengthened with towers. The Goths had already assembled towers, ladders and rams opposite it.

However, according to Procopius, the Goths had already started their assault against the Aurelian Gate (Porta Aurelia) and the Tomb of Hadrian (Mausoleum Hadriani) and the wall between the Aurelian Gate and Flaminian Gate (Porta Flaminia), and a separate attack against the Pancratian Gate (Porta San Pancratius). The translator Dewing suggests that Procopius has made a mistake here and that we should interpret the Aurelian Gate to be Porta Cornelia which was located right next to the Tomb of Hadrian. This, however, appears to be a mistake. Procopius's names were correct for the time he was writing. The name of the Porta Cornelia was then Porta Aurelia Nova to separate it from the old Porta Aurelia, which had been renamed the Pancratian Gate (the other name for this gate, the Porta Aurelia Sancti Pancratii, combines both). In short, the Gothic attack was directed against Porta Cornelia or Porta Aurelia Nova, however one likes to call it, and the Tomb of Hadrian and also across the Tiber against the lightly defended section of the wall, and simultaneously against the Pancratian Gate. When it was reported to Constantinus that the Goths were preparing boats for the crossing of the Tiber, he became frightened because this section of the wall was lightly defended, so he went there in person while he left most of his forces at the Flaminian Gate and Tomb of Hadrian. Procopius states that the Goths began their assault against both the Flaminian Gate and the Tomb of Hadrian while Constantinus was reinforcing the wall next to the Tiber. The Goths had not prepared any siege engines for the assault of these locations but used massed volleys of archery to suppress the Roman defences while they brought forward their ladders. There was serious trouble at the Tomb because the Goths advanced hidden below the colonnade from the church of the Apostle Peter and surprised the Romans by emerging from it suddenly. The Romans could not use their ballistae effectively because the enemy was already too close and their bows proved ineffective against the large *thureos*-style shields that the Goths carried and which Procopius likened to the large Persian shields. The *thureos* signifies either the long oblong *scutum*-type shield or the old legionary/murmillo-style rectangular *scutum*. It is impossible to be certain which of these was meant because the Persians had been using the rectangular murmillo/legionary style *scutum* since the third century and this type continues to be depicted in Roman works of art until the sixth century, which means that we cannot preclude this alternative from the equation.[27] The Romans were also in trouble because the Goths had almost surrounded them so that they faced arrows from all directions. The Goths were about to set their ladders against the walls when someone among the Romans came up with the idea of breaking up the statues on top of the battlements to thrown them with both hands on the heads of the enemy. The rain of these heavy objects forced the Goths back with the result that the Romans, raising a mighty shout, started killing their enemies with bows and then with the ballistae.

Meanwhile Constantinus had reached the Tomb, having frightened and driven off those who had attempted to cross the river in boats. The Goths had not attempted to attack the *Reges* (likely to be the *Auxilia Palatina Regii*) under Ursicinus who were posted at the Flaminian Gate because its defences were too strong. Similarly, the Goths did not assault the strong defences at the Pancratian Gate so the infantry *katalogos* under the command of Paulus had an easy time. For some unknown reason the Goths also did not attempt to attack the so-called Broken Wall between the Flaminian and Pincian Gates. This section of the wall was called broken because it leaned both one way and the other. Belisarius had planned to tear it down so that he could rebuild it, but the Romans had prevented this by saying that the Apostle Peter guarded it. According to Procopius, for some unknown reason this seemed to be true because nobody attempted to break through it even when the Goths assaulted the walls during the nights as they did many times.

When Vittigis began his assault against the Praenestine Gate and Vivarium, the Romans were in particular trouble in the area of Vivarium because its wall had collapsed and the new wall outside it was weak because it had no towers. It had been used to house lions and other wild animals. Bessas and Peranius summoned Belisarius to their assistance. Belisarius left one of his friends in charge of the Salarian Gate and hurried to the scene. Belisarius found the defenders of Vivarium in a state of fright, but he managed to restore their confidence with his own demeanour and words that the soldiers should look at the enemy with contempt. Vittigis prepared the siege engines and ordered his men to start mining the wall of the Vivarium with the idea that if he could break through here he would then be able to capture the main wall with ease. When Belisarius observed that the enemy was undermining the wall while simultaneously attacking the fortifications in many places so that only very few men were able to stay on the wall to defend it under the bombardment, he realized that it would be impossible to prevent the enemy from penetrating the Vivarium. Ever resourceful, Belisarius struck the right plan for the situation. He ordered the men to stay below the gates with their corselets and use only swords. When the Goths then made a breach in the wall and got inside the Vivarium, Belisarius sent Cyprian together with others to the attack. The Romans butchered the

Goths inside the Vivarium easily because they were crowded together in a small space. Belisarius exploited this chaos by opening up the gates of the circuit wall and sent out his entire army (presumably those near him and the bodyguards accompanying him) against the enemy. The Goths panicked and fled without any semblance of order so that the pursuing Romans were able to kill with ease all they came across. The pursuit was long and bloody because the Goths who were assaulting this section of the wall had built their camps far away. The Romans did not attempt to force their way into the camps but returned and Belisarius ordered the Gothic siege engines to be burned.

The same thing happened at the Salarian Gate. The friend (Procopius?)[28] who had been left in charge of it ordered the men to sally out with the result that the deep Gothic infantry phalanx opposite it collapsed immediately. This proves that the failed assault of the walls and the sight of the man nailed to the tree had demoralized the Goths completely because the deep infantry phalanx should have been able to oppose the Romans with relative ease. It was once again easy for the pursuing Romans to butcher the helpless fugitives after which they torched the siege engines the Goths had left behind. The flames of the torched Gothic siege engines rose as high as the walls and the men on the walls shouted loudly in support of their men pursuing the fugitives. The fighting had lasted from early morning until late afternoon and had proved a disaster for the Goths. According to Procopius, the Romans learnt afterwards from the Gothic leaders that the Goths had lost 30,000 killed and a larger number wounded thanks to the massing of large numbers of men for the assault so that the Romans could not miss them with their missiles and because the Romans who had sallied out could kill the fleeing and helpless Goths in droves. I would suggest that the reason Procopius was so well acquainted with this information is that he was a spy in charge of interrogating enemy prisoners.

Immediately after the fighting had stopped Belisarius wrote a report of the action to Justinian in which he urged him to dispatch reinforcements immediately, because he had been forced to leave so many men in Sicily and in the cities and fortifications that he had only 5,000 men left in his army (*strateuma*), which must mean the regular army, while the walls of Rome were so long that even myriads of men would not suffice. He urged Justinian to send to him so many arms and soldiers (*hopla te kai stratiôtai*) that he could engage the enemy with equal strength. The inclusion of arms in the request proves that Belisarius also needed bows, arrows, armour, shields, swords, spears, javelins, ballistae etc. and not only soldiers. The reason for Belisarius's urgent request was that the reinforcements that he had been awaiting had not yet arrived, and the reason why this had not happened was that the 1,600 horsemen that had been dispatched under Valerianus and Martinus had sailed only as far as Greece where they had then wintered in Aetolia and Acarnania. When Justinian read Belisarius's letter he dispatched an order to Valerianus and Martinus to proceed immediately to Rome while he informed Belisarius of this with another letter. As we shall see, the messengers achieved this exchange of letters with amazing speed.

Procopius gives us a good example of how the Roman upper classes continued their superstitious pagan practices despite being officially Christians. In this time of crisis, some of the patricians brought out the Sibylline Oracles for consulting and declared that the siege would last until July. Procopius notes that none of their predictions proved correct. The same kinds of superstitions were also followed in Naples where they claimed to read omens from a mosaic image of Theoderic. Crises always brought forth the superstitious fears of the populace. These superstitions have never subsided in the Mediterranean region despite the arrival of Christianity and tourists in the area are still amazed to find collections of talismans for use against the evil eye in these countries.

The reorganization of the administration of Sicily and Italy in 537[29]

The conquest of Sicily together with the conquest of Italy up to Rome enabled Justinian to begin the reorganization of the newly won territories. Sicily was placed under a praetor directly responsible to Constantinople, and its revenues were paid to the *Comes Patrimonii per Italiam*. Justinian also appointed a Praetorian Prefect for Italy with the idea of making Italy pay for the war. In the opinion of A.H.M Jones the ability of the Prefect to collect revenues was limited by the ongoing war so the collection would have been very irregular. In my opinion, however, this solution was still a success because the details given below suggest that Belisarius was indeed able to support his military operations with the supplies brought from south of Italy.

The siege of Rome continues[30]

On the morning after the Gothic assault had been repulsed, Belisarius ordered the citizens of Rome to remove their women and children to Naples together with such domestics that were not needed for the guarding of the wall. He gave the same order to his soldiers who had male or female attendants with them. The reason for this was of course the scarcity of provisions, and this was one of the standard procedures adopted by most of those who were besieged in such situations. It was easy enough to achieve because the Goths had left the southern part of the city unguarded and were also not in the habit of leaving their marching camps because they feared that the Roman cavalry would sally out to destroy them, in particular the Moors who hunted in the darkness of the night. Consequently, the unnecessary populace marched out as a great throng into Campania and on foot along the Appian Way. The more fortunate secured for themselves a boat from the harbour of Rome called Portus. Some of the fugitives settled in Campania while others fled all the way to Sicily or any other place where they thought they would be safe from the Goths.

Belisarius solved two other problems at the same time. He did not have enough men to defend the walls and be rotated and rested. Most of the populace of Rome consisted of the poorer classes who worked with their hands and possessed only what they earned from their daily work. These men had been without work from the start of the siege and were therefore starving. Belisarius enrolled them into service by giving each man a fixed salary per day after which they were mixed with the regular *katalogoi* so that the soldiers on duty could be rotated with those who rested. Thereby Belisarius gained enough men to defend the walls while the poor got a living so that they did not starve to death.

Belisarius was a man well-versed in the wiles of the art of war and healthily suspicious and cautious by nature. In his *Wars* Procopius implies that it was the Roman spy network and network of informers that Belisarius, probably with the assistance of Procopius, employed in Rome that discovered the subversive activities of Pope Silverius. It was claimed that he was engaged in treasonous negotiations with the Goths. Silverius was duly imprisoned and sent to Greece. He was replaced by an aptly named successor,

Vigilius, who may have been the man who betrayed Silverius. However, we find an entirely different account of the affair in Procopius' *Secret History* (*Anek.*, 1.14, 1.27) and *Vita Silverii* (1.146, tr. and comm. by Dewing, *Procop.*, *Anek*, xix-xxi) and other sources, which put the blame of the affair squarely on Theodora and Antonina. Theodora had quarrelled with Silverius with the result that she employed the deacon Vigilius as her messenger to Belisarius. Her orders to Belisarius were that he was to seek some excuse for the removal of Silverius from office. Belisarius then obtained false witnesses apparently with the help of his wife Antonina that put forth the claim that Silverius had sent messages to Vittigis. This then gave Belisarius the needed excuse for the exiling of Silverius and his replacement with Vigilius. Justinian later ordered Silverius to be returned to Rome for another investigation, but with the result that Belisarius handed him over to Vigilius whose men starved Silverius to death. It was rumoured that Vigilius had offered Belisarius 200 lbs of gold for his support and it seems clear that Belisarius accepted this bribe because it coincided with the wishes of his wife. The affair had another important result which was that it increased Antonina's value in the eyes of the empress so that after the later John the Cappadocian affair Antonina was her most trusted accomplice, allowed to do anything even against the wishes of her husband.[31]

However, it is possible that there were also real reasons for the removal of Silverius from office, which Procopius and the *Vita Silverii* were reluctant to admit because according to Procopius's *Wars* Belisarius found out that some of the senators were engaged in similarly treasonous discussions. These were likewise exiled to Greece, but were later allowed back to Rome when the siege had ended. This suggests the possibility that Silverius may have been doing the same and that the simultaneous arrival of the order of Theodora was just a coincidence. Belisarius also devised other precautions to make certain that the defences that he had organized could not be overcome by the enemy through treachery. He feared that the enemy could try to corrupt the guards guarding the gates and because of this had the keys of the gates changed twice in each month. He rotated the guards to other posts that were far away from their previous posts so that they could not betray the posts they were guarding. In addition to this, he placed different officers in charge of those posts every night and these men had the duty of checking that every guard was at his post and to write down their names. If they found that someone was not at his post, they were to replace him with another man, and then they were to inform Belisarius of this in the morning so that he could order a fitting punishment for the culprit. As if this was not enough, Belisarius ordered musicians to play on the walls at night, presumably to make sure the soldiers were awake and that the enemy knew it. The noise also made it difficult to converse with the enemy. Belisarius posted soldiers, especially Moors, and also guard dogs outside the walls to patrol the moat at night. This had a triple purpose. The guards and dogs outside made it difficult for the enemy to approach undetected, it made it difficult for Romans to desert, and it enabled the Romans to capture any Goths who were foolish enough to venture close to the walls.

According to Procopius, some unknown Romans once again showed their foolish superstitiousness by attempting to secretly open the doors of the temple of Janus. The attempt failed and the culprits were not found.

The failure of the assault was obviously embarrassing for Vittigis, who vented his anger by dispatching his *doryforoi* to Ravenna with orders to kill all the Roman senators that he

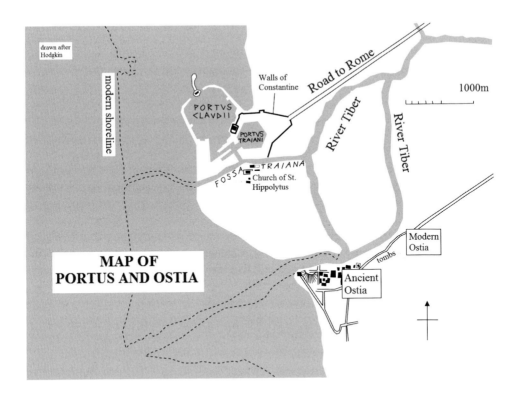

MAP OF
PORTUS AND OSTIA

had taken there. However, some of them learnt of his intent in advance and were able to escape, but the rest were butchered to satisfy Vittigis' anger. Those who managed to save themselves included Vergentinus and Reparatus, brother of the Pope Vigilius. These and others who managed to flee hid themselves in Liguria. This suggests a probability that the Catholic/Orthodox Church was at this time operating a network of spies through which the Pope and others learnt of the hostile intent of Vittigis and that this network was able to use priests as messengers and go-betweens. The ability of the Romans to leave the city unhindered and their ability to bring supplies in was also something that Vittigis could not tolerate. Consequently, he decided to capture Portus so that the Romans could not ship supplies unhindered. The Romans had two harbours, Portus and Ostia, but only the former was usable at this time. Ships brought supplies to the walled Portus where their cargoes were unloaded onto the barges which were then drawn by oxen along the Tiber to Rome. The Romans had built a road from Portus to Rome which facilitated this. Ostia did not have walls and its harbour and the road from there had been neglected for so long that it was impossible to draw barges along the Tiber. Consequently, the Roman ships no longer anchored at Ostia but anchored at Anthium a day's journey from Ostia. Vittigis dispatched soldiers to occupy Portus on the third day after his assault had failed. It was undefended because Belisarius had left it without garrison. Procopius was of the opinion that a mere 300 men would have been sufficient to hold Portus against the Goths, but now that it was undefended the Goths were able to establish a garrison of 1,000 men there and the Romans had to ship their supplies either to Ostia or Anthium and then bring their supplies with great difficulty to Rome.

April 537: The reinforcements arrive and Belisarius resumes the offensive[32]

The Roman reinforcements consisting of 1,600 horsemen under Martinus and Valerianus arrived twenty days after the Goths had taken possession of Portus. The horsemen consisted mostly of the Huns, Sclaveni and Antae. Belisarius was pleased with their arrival and thought that it was now time to resume the offensive with cavalry skirmishes.

On the following day Belisarius ordered one of his bodyguards called Trajan to take with him 200 *bucellarii* and to go near to the enemy camp opposite the Salarian Gate to challenge them, after which he was to retreat to a small hill nearby. Belisarius ordered Trajan and his men to use only arrows until they ran out, after which he was to flee as hard as he could to the safety of the city and its ballistae. According to Procopius, Trajan was an impetuous and active fighter which made him an ideal officer for such a venture. Belisarius clearly knew the qualities of the men serving under him. The plan worked as intended. The Goths equipped themselves in haste and charged out of their camp, on which Trajan and his men retreated to the hill from which they shot arrows at the dense enemy formation. Most of their missiles hit either men or horses thanks to the crowding of the enemy. After Belisarius's bodyguards had shot all of their arrows they fled straight towards the walls of Rome where the ballistae stopped the pursuit of the Gothic cavalry. According to Procopius, not less than 1,000 Goths succumbed under the showers of arrows.

A few days later Belisarius dispatched 300 *bucellarii*, this time under Mundilas and Diogenes, both of whom Procopius calls exceptionally capable warriors. They were instructed to do exactly the same as Trajan. Even more Goths fell in this action. After this Belisarius sent a group of 300 of his bodyguards, this time under Oilas, with the same instructions and with exactly the same result. According to Procopius, 4,000 Goths met their end in this way. The Goths just did not learn their lesson; in fact they drew the wrong lesson from it.

Vittigis and the Goths took these cavalry skirmishes as affronts to their manhood, and he and his Goths wanted to make their own demonstration of the awesome power of the Gothic cavalry. However, what Vittigis and his Goths did not understand was that the reason for the successes of the Roman cavalry over the Gothic spear-armed cavalry was their archery. Therefore Vittigis once more gave a demonstration of his lack of military expertise by sending 500 horsemen on a high place just beyond the range of missiles in full view of the city – and we have to remember that Vittigis was known for his military skills among the Goths, which shows that the general standard had fallen quite a bit after the death of Theoderic the Great. Belisarius, the military genius, made a response which one could expect from a man of his quality. He sent a numerically superior force of 1,000 men under Bessas to engage them. The Roman cavalry circled around the hill and shot arrows at Goths always aiming to shoot from behind them so they would lack the protection of their shields and their ability to see the oncoming arrows.[33] This punishing barrage forced the remaining Goths to descend onto the plain. In the ensuing hand-to-hand battle, most of the outnumbered Goths were killed, though some few managed to get through and flee with difficulty.

Vittigis reviled the Goths who survived as cowards. He had not learnt his lesson. The foolish Vittigis renewed his mistake three days later by choosing 500 men from all of the camps, and sent them to do the same again. He clearly thought that the reason for the defeat was cowardice and that he would have to choose the very best men from all of the camps. When they had come quite close to the Romans Belisarius responded by sending 1,500 men under Martinus and Valerianus. The cavalry battle took place immediately so the Romans had fewer chances of decimating the Goths with the archery, but still the result was the same. In this case, the overwhelmingly superior numbers allowed the Romans to rout the enemy without any trouble, most of whom were killed.[34] In this case, the Romans probably used the standard formation of two lines (two commanders!) especially because it would have been impossible to send all the men out simultaneously. The details of this battle prove one thing, which is that the Goths had finally realized that the principal reason for the Roman ability to decimate them had been mounted archery.

The Goths' next move was to advance near to the gates and engage the Romans immediately they had come out. However, what they once again failed to understand was that Belisarius could respond to this at his leisure by observing their approach from the parapet and then sending superior numbers of men against them. Vittigis and his staff of chieftains were clearly witless. After this the Goths no longer ventured outside except in strength and did not pursue any longer distances than was necessary to keep the Romans away from their camps. On the other hand, and not unnaturally, Belisarius received a public vote of praise from the Romans.

Belisarius' friends asked him why he had been so confident that the Goths could be defeated, after the first battle in which he and his 1,000 men had been completely defeated. Belisarius responded:

> 'And he [*Belisarius*] said that in engaging with them at the first with only a few men he had noticed just what the difference was between the two armies, so that if he should fight his battles with them with a force which was in strength proportionate to theirs [*smaller but equal in strength*], the multitude of the enemy could inflict no injury upon the Romans by reason of the smallness of their numbers. And the difference was this, that practically all the Romans and their allies, the Huns, are good bowmen, but not a man among the Goths has had practice in this branch, for their horsemen are accustomed to use only spears and swords, while their bowmen enter battle on foot and under cover of the heavy-armed men [*hoplitai – the meaning is uncertain; it can mean either the cataphracted cavalry or the spear-armed footmen*]. So the horsemen, unless the engagement is at close quarters, have no means of defending themselves against opponents who use the bow, and therefore can easily be reached by the arrows and destroyed; and as for the footsoldiers, they can never be strong enough to make sallies against men on horseback. It was for these reasons, Belisarius declared, that the barbarians had been defeated by the Romans in these last engagements.' Procopius, *Wars* 5.27.25–9, tr. by Dewing 259–61.

The above text is important because it proves that Gothic combat practices had changed after their arrival in Italy. It is obvious that the Goths still possessed men able to use bows while mounted, as they had when they had entered Italy under Theoderic the Great, but all the same Procopius's text makes it clear that the Goths had after that largely abandoned mounted archery as a form of combat and rather concentrated on the use of massed charge. It is actually quite probable that this change in tactics had resulted from their very successful use of the lancer charge from the 480s until the early sixth century. In other words, the Goths had drawn the wrong conclusion from their successes and had concentrated only on the use of one tactic at the expense of versatility.

The great battle before Rome in 537[35]

However, the Goths were not the only ones making mistaken conclusions. The successes that Belisarius had achieved with his cavalry skirmishes caused too much joy among the Roman populace, soldiers and officers, and led to overconfidence. The latter demanded that Belisarius lead them out to fight a pitched battle with the whole army. According to Procopius, Belisarius was reluctant to do this because he considered the numerical difference between the armies too great. Belisarius therefore busied himself by ordering additional sallies and by planning new ones. In the end the pressure from the soldiers became such that Belisarius capitulated and promised to lead them out. His plan was to begin the battle with a surprise attack. Belisarius attempted this several times in one day, but always found out to his surprise that the enemy had been warned in advance, so he postponed the attack to the following day. Procopius tells us that the Goths had been warned of the attacks by deserters. In my opinion there is every reason to suspect that Procopius was the man who was in charge of conducting these investigations and that he found out the reason through his network of operatives and informants, which now obviously included new members from the ranks of the Roman Senate and Church. Belisarius yielded under the pressure, as he usually did when the soldiers became restless so that he would not entirely loose control of them. This was obviously wiser than the stubborn unyielding policy followed by his former bodyguard Solomon in Africa which resulted in mutinies.

Belisarius's plan was complex. It took into account the geography, the location of the enemy forces, and the relative fighting power of each of his different arms of service. The main attack was to take place in front of the Pincian and Salarian gates under his leadership. His initial plan was to use only cavalry, because he did not have confidence in the fighting ability of his infantry for two reasons: 1) the cumulative evidence suggests that Belisarius was primarily a cavalry commander who did not trust in the fighting ability of infantry and who did not know how to use it most effectively; 2) the regular professional infantry force accompanying Belisarius was too small to be of importance. The regular footmen accompanying Belisarius appear to have understood the mind and thoughts of their commander so most had mounted themselves with the captured horses and had thereby become cavalry. Procopius also states that the Roman infantry had already demonstrated that it lacked the numbers to form a phalanx of any consequence and had never had any courage to engage the barbarians, so Belisarius did not think it wise to deploy it at a distance from the fortifications. This is actually a relatively accurate description of the general quality of the Roman infantry of that period if one judges on the basis of its combat performance after ca. 468 which was not encouraging, for which see volume 5 in this book series together with the analysis of the battles of Dara and Callinicum in this volume. The Romans were acutely aware that they owed their greatness to their legions and that Greco-Roman military theory and practice required the use of infantry forces.

It was because of this that there was hot debate in upper echelons of society and the military regarding the relative roles of cavalry and infantry in warfare, which is visible to us from Vegetius but even more so from the texts of Procopius and anonymous *de politica dialogus* (Book 4). The fact that the Roman infantry performed well under other generals, who knew better how to use them effectively, cautions us against drawing too far-reaching conclusions regarding the quality of the Roman infantry. It is quite possible that the reason for the poor combat performance of the infantry lay with the officers put in charge of them rather than with the soldiers. This was the view adopted by two (*doryforoi*) bodyguards of Belisarius: Principius the Pisidian, and Tarmutus the Isaurian who was the brother of Ennes, commander of the Isaurians.

These two pleaded with Belisarius to include an infantry phalanx in the battle because he was about to engage tens of thousands of Goths. They noted that the Romans owed their empire to their footmen and claimed that it had performed poorly only because their commanders were not up to their job. The infantry commanders rode to the battle and did not take their places in the battle array on foot, but rather fled on horseback even before the fight started. The two bodyguards urged Belisarius to enrol infantry commanders among his cavalry and to put them, Principius and Tarmutus, in command of the infantry on foot. It is clear that the place of origin of these two had a role in their eagerness to show the value of infantry as a fighting force. Pisidia and Isauria were famous for their infantry and both men wanted to prove their worth in combat. At first Belisarius opposed this request for two reasons. First, he liked the men and knew them to be good fighters whom he did not want to put at risk needlessly. Secondly, he thought the infantry force too small for the task. But the men kept pleading their case and in the end Belisarius consented. He divided his infantry so that he left only so many footmen behind to man the walls together with the Roman populace as was necessary for the defence and gave the rest to Principius and Tarmus. However, he ordered these two men to array the infantry in regular combat formation (i.e. as a phalanx) behind the cavalry with orders that they were merely to serve as a place of refuge for the cavalry so that the cavalry could reform and renew combat if it was forced to retreat. It is possible that the infantry was actually divided into two phalanxes so that each of the two gates had one phalanx and one commander, but since Procopius refers only to a single *taxis* it is safer to assume that there was only one phalanx under two commanders and that it was drawn in front of the Pincian Gate.

Belisarius posted other soldiers in front of the Aurelian Gate to the Plain of Nero with orders not to attack but tie up the enemy in front of them with their threatening presence so that they would not be able to cross the Tiber to help their comrades, which were targeted by Belisarius. This force was put under Valentinus, a commander of a cavalry *katalogos*, which presumably means that the men under him consisted primarily of his horsemen which had been strengthened at least with some Moors. If there were any regular infantry present, these were probably posted behind the cavalry. The Roman populace was not content to be left behind and also took up arms and demanded to join the combat. Belisarius did not put any trust in their ability to fight and did not want to mix them with his regulars, so he ordered the populace to take up positions outside the Pancratian Gate and form up their phalanx there and not make any move before he gave them the signal to do so. This very sizable force presumably consisted of the citizen militia deployed as an infantry phalanx. Most were unarmed. Belisarius thought this a lucky break because he was certain that the two forces, the Roman citizen phalanx and the force under Valentinus, would be enough to keep the enemy forces on the other side of the Tiber preoccupied. Once Belisarius was out of the gate to lead his army, the sailors (presumably those that seconded as marines) and servants joined the populace in their eagerness to fight.

After Belisarius had formed his plan for the battle, he harangued the soldiers who served under him. Belisarius knew that he needed to say something about the numerical disadvantage and also about the financial worries of the soldiers. He pointed out that wars were won not by numbers but by the enthusiasm of soldiers. He also promised that he would personally see to it that the soldiers would be compensated with new horses, bows or any weapon if these were lost, so the soldiers were not to spare their horses or weapons in combat. This shows how important it was that the soldiers knew that their possible financial losses would be compensated. The professional Roman soldiers of this era fought for the money and their morale and combat performance were a reflection of this, so the effectiveness of the army depended on the punctual arrival of salaries, compensation for lost property, prospect of booty and fair division of the booty acquired.

The Great Battle Before the City of Rome in 537

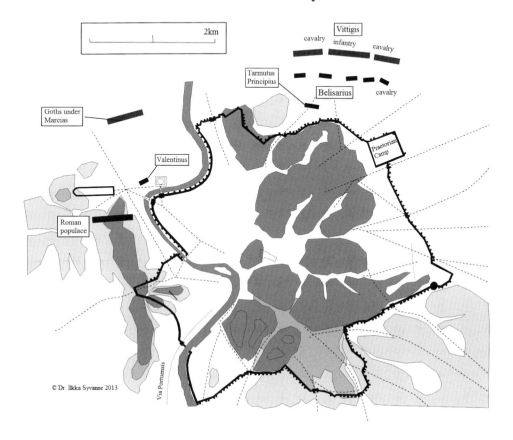

Belisarius knew the hearts and minds of his men and how far he could push them. After this, Belisarius led his men outside the gates.

Vittigis had ample warning of what was to come and, with the exception of those posted in the Plain of Nero under Marcia and those unfit for combat, he collected his entire force opposite Belisarius. He also encouraged his men with a speech, after which he arrayed his army with cavalry posted on the flanks and infantry in the middle. The Goths were deployed close to their camps so the defeated Romans would have to flee a long distance back to the walls of the city. He was confident that he would win in the plain because he had an overwhelming numerical advantage.

The battle began in the early morning. Belisarius and Vittigis remained behind their men urging them to greater achievements while the forces on the other side of the Tiber remained where they stood. The Moors sallied out of the array and harried the Goths with thrown javelins. These must have been horsemen. The Goths did not dare do anything because they feared if they attacked they would be exposed to a flank attack by the Roman populace. At first the main battle progressed favourably for Belisarius because Roman mounted archery felled large numbers of the enemy. The Romans did not attempt to pursue them because the Gothic cavalry was massed in such numbers that those who had fallen were readily replaced with the result that the Gothic line remained unbroken. This proves that the Roman cavalry targeted the foremost Goths with powerful shots aimed straight at their target rather than volleys of arrows at a higher angle. By midday the archery had forced the Goths right in front of their camps, and the Roman cavalry were completely exhausted by the archery which had continued for so long. According to Procopius they were ready to retreat on any pretext. During this first period of combat three Romans – Athenodorus (*doryforos* of Belisarius), Theodoriscus, and George/Georgios (*doryforos* of Martinus) – distinguished themselves in combat by repeatedly advancing beyond the front of the cavalry phalanx. They killed with spear many barbarians in the course of their heroics. They were not the only ones who engaged the Goths with spears, because we find later that most of the Roman cavalry had lost their spears either as a result of combat or from throwing them away. In other words, the numerically inferior Roman cavalry forced the Gothic cavalry to retreat with a combination of archery and lancer charges. It is probable that the Roman cavalry was deployed in a far shallower formation than the Gothic – which was possible because the Roman cavalry consisted of elite horsemen.

At midday the Roman army on the other side of the Tiber suddenly launched an attack at such a pace that the Goths fled without attempting to fight or even to protect their camp. Procopius fails to state who gave the order for the attack, possibly in an effort to exonerate Valentinus, but the way Procopius narrates this suggests that the attack was launched by the populace, sailors, and servants who had been eager to fight, with the implication that it had been some of their leaders that had launched the sudden unexpected attack. Valentinus attempted to gain control of this horde which now consisted of the populace, sailors, servants, Moors and his regulars, but to no effect. It was because of this that the throng of men allowed the Goths to flee without pursuit and regroup at some nearby hills, and they did not attempt to destroy the bridge connecting the Goths, and they did not attempt to cross this bridge and attack the Goths from behind. Procopius was of the opinion that had the populace crossed the bridge, the Goths would have been utterly routed. Instead of this, the whole throng started pillaging the enemy camp without any order whatsoever. The Goths then regrouped and attacked with great fury and shouting. The Goths killed many of the pillagers and forced the rest to flee back to the city. This incident shows that Belisarius failed to exploit fully the numerical advantage that the Roman populace, sailors and servants would have given him. It is clear that he could have used the citizen militia as an infantry force to overcome the enemy, admittedly with the risk that he could have lost control of his cavalry as he had at the battle of Tricamarum. Professional soldiers of the era were just as difficult to control as the populace when there existed the possibility of pillaging an enemy camp – so perhaps Belisarius after all knew better how to use the citizen militia than we do today.

In the meantime, the main army of the Romans had continued its assault against the Goths who had retreated close to their camps. The Goths protected themselves with their shields and massed formation while the Roman cavalry kept charging against them. Increasing numbers of Romans lost their lives and an even greater number their horses. It is probable that one of the main reasons for the loss of the horses was the fact that the Gothic infantry used archery even if the Gothic cavalry at this time did not. The loss of horses also suggests that most of the Roman horses were unarmoured while the vast majority of the Gothic horses were armoured because most of their cavalry consisted of cataphracts. The battle lasted for so long that it is clear that the Roman cavalry units were rotated so that the Roman cavalry units kept up constant pressure against the enemy by having some units advancing (these shot arrows and/or fought with spears) while other units stayed behind as reserves. The latter could thereby rest and refill their quivers. Those Romans who had been wounded or had lost their horses naturally retreated with the result that their already small numbers became even smaller. When this discrepancy became apparent to the right wing of the Gothic cavalry, it charged at a gallop against the Roman cavalry posted there. The Romans were unable to withstand their spears and fled headlong to their infantry support. The infantry proved unable to hold its ground and joined the fleeing cavalry with the result that the rest of the Roman cavalry joined the flight because their left flank had been exposed. The Goths pursued hot on their heels and the flight turned into a rout. However, Principius and Tarmutus and some of their men did not join the rout. They fought doggedly against the pursuers and stopped the Goths in front of them. This heroic fight bought enough time for most of the Roman horsemen and footmen to retreat to a safer location. Principius was hacked to pieces where he stood and with him died forty-two foot-soldiers. Tarmutus, however, kept on fighting and killing with two Isaurian javelins, one in each hand, by turning from side to side until he fell to the ground wounded several times.[36] His brother Ennes then came to the rescue with cavalry and Tarmutus rose to his feet and ran covered with wounds and gore, holding the two javelins in his hands all the way to the Pincian Gate. When he reached the gate he fell and his comrades thought he had died and carried him on a shield. He was not dead, but died two days later as a hero remembered fondly by the Isaurians and the rest of the army.

Meanwhile the Romans who defended the gates refused to allow the Roman fugitives inside. So the fugitives crossed the moat and packed against the wall where they turned and faced their pursuers. They trembled with fear and were so tightly pressed together that they could not use their bows. Most had also lost their spears either in combat or

Belisarius leading his men against the Goths as envisaged in the 19th century Ward Lock's Illustrated History.

in flight so were utterly unable to do anything against the Goths. When the Goths saw this, they tried to attack the helpless mass of men, but then desisted when they saw the multitude of Roman soldiers and populace at the wall. The Goths then rode off while shouting insults to the frightened Romans. This battle proves Belisarius's judgment correct. He had too few men and his infantry force was too small and unreliable to use in pitched battle. Regardless, it is still clear that he did the right thing in caving in to the will of his soldiers and populace to fight, because otherwise he could have lost control of his forces. Belisarius did the best he could in these circumstances. The ironic thing in all this is that his successful use of cavalry skirmishes against the Goths forced him to commit his army to a pitched battle which was not successful.

Cavalry battles and skirmishes continue unabated in front of Rome in 537 AD[37]

The result of the battle convinced the Romans to follow the commands of Belisarius once again, and they started making sallies out of the city to fight cavalry battles. Most ended favourably for the Romans, however there was now one difference with the previous cavalry fighting which was that Belisarius now sometimes sent infantry together with the cavalry – not separately as a phalanx but together with the cavalry, which means that the infantry in question was trained to fight alongside the cavalry. This implies that the infantry consisted of light-armed men who either rode pillion with the cavalry or ran beside the horses, perhaps holding the mane or something similar. This was a standard fighting tactic with cavalry when the commander had either a numerical or a qualitative disadvantage – in this case it was former. The inclusion of infantry enabled the Romans to fight against numerically superior cavalry forces so that their enemies were actually at a disadvantage in close-quarters combat because the Roman footmen (did these consist primarily of Moors?) could fight almost unnoticed between the horsemen when the horsemen were fighting against each other.[38]

One such cavalry skirmish involved only the Huns under Constantinus in the Plain of Nero one late afternoon. When Constantinus realised the Goths were winning, he led his Huns to the nearby stadium where gladiators had fought in the past (*Circus Neronianis*?) because he could not reach his own lines. Constantinus dismounted himself and all his Huns, who were then arrayed together in one of the narrow passages of the stadium with the result that they could shoot the Goths with impunity. The Goths stayed there for a while in the hope that the Huns would exhaust their arrows, but when this did not happen and they had lost more than half of their number and the sun was setting, the Goths started a headlong flight. This resulted in only greater disaster because the Massagetae Huns remounted, pursued and now shot arrow after arrow at the backs of the fleeing men. Consequently, Constantinus was able to return to the Roman lines at night.

Peranius led a similar sally outside the gates a few days later, but he was accompanied by Roman foot-soldiers in the manner specified above. Procopius records this incident because one of the footmen accompanying the attack fell into a deep hole built as a grain store, when the Goths regrouped and attacked the Roman pursuers with the result that the Romans fled. The man, still in the hole, did not dare to make any noise, and on the following day the Goths were put to flight and now a Goth fell into the same hole. These two men befriended each other and promised to save the life of the other if their comrades found them first. Then the two men started to shout and it was heard by the Goths. The Goth kept his word and his comrades respected this so the Roman was released unharmed. This shows how even in the midst of fighting it was possible for the enemies to show respect to each other. It also shows that the infantry accompanying the cavalry during skirmishing included at least some native Romans.

According to Procopius, after this the horsemen continued to attack each other in small numbers, but in such a way that they always ended in single combats, all of which Roman champions won. If this is true and not flattery, then it proves that Roman horsemen were on average better trained in the use of weaponry. In light of the numerical disadvantage that the Romans were fighting under, this is indeed likely to be true. The Roman cavalry and their mercenary forces had to be expert fighters for them to be able to defeat numerically superior foes repeatedly.

And then 'a little after this' a remarkable incident took place in the Plain of Nero worth recounting in greater detail. Many small groups of horsemen were pursuing fleeing Goths in various directions.[39] One of these groups included Chorsamantis, a *doryforos* of Belisarius and by birth a Massagetae Hun. This group was pursuing about seventy Goths, but when the Romans had advanced far into the plain, the other Romans (presumably also bodyguards of Belisarius) retreated while Chorsamantis continued his pursuit. When the retreating Goths noticed this, they turned about and charged against him. Chorsamantis, however, charged right into the middle of them and killed one of them with a spear with the result that the Goths turned again to flight while Chorsamantis continued his pursuit. When they got close to their own encampment the Goths turned around again, as it would have been dishonourable to have done otherwise. Chorsamantis now killed one of their best men, upon which the Goths continued their flight inside their camp with Chorsamantis in pursuit. When the Goths reached the safety of their stockade Chorsamantis turned and rode back to the Roman fortifications alone as a hero who had humbled the Goths with his personal fighting skills. A little later in one of the skirmishes Chorsamantis was wounded in the left shin, which left him unable to fight for a number of days. According to Procopius, he did not bear this patiently because he was a barbarian and he vowed to exact revenge for the insult that the Goths had done to his shin. A little later, when he was drunk at lunch time as was his habit, he went alone against the enemy to get satisfaction. At the Pincian Gate he claimed that he had been sent by Belisarius to the enemy camp. Since this man was known as the best bodyguard of Belisarius the guards did not doubt his words and allowed him to pass through. When the Goths saw Chorsamantis they thought that he was a deserter and sent twenty men to receive him. Chorsamantis drove them off with ease and then turned back to the Roman lines. But then the Goths dispatched more men and he turned against them too. The Goths surrounded him, and even though Chorsamantis fought with great valour he paid the ultimate price for his drunken bravery. When Belisarius and the Romans learnt of this, they mourned for the loss of the great fighter who failed to achieve his full potential thanks to the drunken stupidity. This incident shows how superb individual members of the *bucellarii* could be. They were worth easily more than 100 men as individual fighters and warriors.

The arrival of salaries in mid-June 537[40]

At about the spring equinox (June 537), a certain Euthalius came to Taracina from Constantinople. He was bringing the salaries of the soldiers and therefore wrote to Belisarius that he needed safe passage to the city. Belisarius dispatched 100 of his *hypaspistai* together with two *doryforoi* to protect Euthalius while he planned to distract the Goths. The latter he did by pretending to prepare his army for a pitched battle. The threat of the imminent pitched battle kept the Goths in place so that they did not go to seek provisions or reconnoitre the approaches to the city from the south, which meant that they could not find out about the imminent approach of Euthalius. When Belisarius learnt that Euthalius would arrive on the following morning, he arrayed his entire army in battle formation in front of the city. The Goths did the same. Belisarius kept his army close to the gates for the entire morning and then ordered his army to eat lunch. When the Goths did the same, Belisarius dispatched Martinus and Valerianus with about 1,600 men to the Plain of Nero where they attacked the Gothic camp, while 600 men under three of Belisarius's bodyguards, Artasires (Persian), Bochas (Massagetae Hun), and Cutilas (Thracian), sallied out of the Pincian Gate. The Goths advanced to meet them. For a long time, the Goths and Romans opposite the Pincian Gate advanced and retreated in turn without coming into close quarters. However, after a while tempers rose and both engaged each other in mêlée in which many of the best fighters from both sides fell. One of those wounded in this action was Cutilas who was struck in the middle of the head by a javelin. He did not die but continued to fight and pursue with the javelin waving about. At sunset he returned to the city, but the doctors pulled the javelin violently from his head and Cutilas died not long afterwards from inflammation of the brain (phrenitis).

Another remarkable incident in this battle concerns Arzes, a bodyguard of Belisarius. He was hit by an arrow shot by a Gothic archer between the nose and the right eye so that the point of the arrow penetrated the neck but did not go through. This means that Arzes was wounded when he had pursued the fleeing Goths up to their infantry. Arzas also continued to fight, with the arrow waving about as he rode, but he survived without any harm when the physician Theoctistus removed the arrow. This shows the high quality of the Roman medical professionals – it was for good reason that Roman doctors were sought after by the Persians.

Support came to both groups from the rear, from the camps and from the city. Ultimately, the Romans gained the upper hand and routed the Goths and it was presumably then that the abovementioned Arzes was wounded. The practice of sending reinforcements from within the city represented a system of deployment in depth with reserves posted in a safe place. The fact that Bochas with his rested men was sent next to save the men of Valerianus and Martinus who were in trouble shows that he had retreated with his men in the course of the battle while the reserves from the city had advanced to engage the enemy. In other words, this was a cavalry battle in which the reserves were posted inside the city.

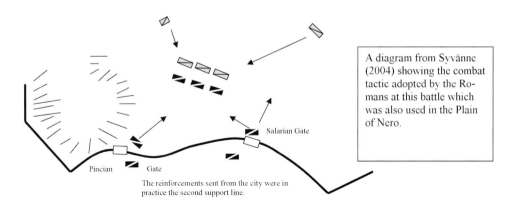

A diagram from Syvänne (2004) showing the combat tactic adopted by the Romans at this battle which was also used in the Plain of Nero.

Salarian Gate

Pincian   Gate

The reinforcements sent from the city were in practice the second support line.

The fact that Valerianus and Marinus with their 1,600 horsemen were in trouble in the Plain of Nero is not surprising because they faced overwhelming odds. When Belisarius saw this from the parapet, he ordered Bochas to advance against the Goths on the Plain of Nero. By then it was late in the day. When the Goths saw Bochas charging with his men, they fled, but in the process Bochas became separated from his men and was surrounded by twelve spear-carrying Goths. The Goths thrust their spears at him, but did not cause any serious damage because the corselet (thorax) withstood them easily. But then one of the Goths hit Bochas from behind at a spot above the right armpit very close to the shoulder which did not have armour (a joint in different parts of armour?)[41] followed by a slanting cut directed at the left thigh which cut its muscles. Bochas clearly did not wear any effective protection for his thigh – although it is possible that he could have had pteruges because these offered limited protection which would fit the description. When Valerianus and Martinus saw what was happening, they came to his rescue, which again shows how the Roman cavalry units alternated in fighting and retreating and regrouping.

This attack demoralized the Goths who now fled back to their camp. Valerianus and Martinus then took hold of the bridle of Bochas's horse and led him to the city. Sadly the wounds of Bochas proved fatal because he had lost too much blood from the slanting cut to the thigh. He died three days later.

The death of Bochas and the other losses caused grief among the Romans but when they heard on the following day that many of the men of greatest note had been killed among the Goths during the first charge of Bochas, they got at least some comfort. Despite the loss of many valuable men, the battle had been a success. The Goths had been distracted so that Euthalius with his money was able to enter the city the following night. Moreover, the Romans had won all of the cavalry battles that had taken place. Belisarius was a master in the art of war and his horsemen were probably the best fighters of their day.

Famine and pestilence in summer 537[42]

Despite the arrival of salaries, the situation in Rome took a turn for the worse in June. Although the soldiers possessed enough grain for themselves, the populace did not. The result was famine and pestilence. When the Goths realized this, they no longer sought decisive battle but settled on starving the Romans. The Goths dispatched 7,000 men to a place where two high aqueducts met between the Latin and Appian Ways (Torre Fiscale, 5.5 km from Rome) and walled the lower arches of the aqueducts with stones and mud so that they had a fort there. The idea was to isolate the city completely, which begs the question why the Goths had not attempted this in the first place. It is clear that the Gothic leadership was quite incompetent.

This did not prevent the most daring of the Roman soldiers from going out of the city at night to collect grain from the nearby fields. They loaded grain on the horses and carried it back to the city where they sold it for exorbitant prices to civilians. Only the rich could afford to buy it; the rest of the populace lived by eating herbs which grew in abundance both outside and inside the fortifications. This abundance of herbs, that grew year round, also allowed the soldiers to pasture their horses. The most enterprising of the Roman soldiers made sausages of the mules that died in Rome and sold them secretly. This and other accounts of greed show how the Roman soldiery of the time were primarily motivated by money – which is only natural because they were essentially a heterogeneous group of paid mercenaries. However, this did not mean they were poor soldiers; on the contrary, they were the best soldiers of the era as long as they got their salaries and fair share of the booty.

When the corn ran out the Romans (meaning the upper classes) surrounded Belisarius and tried to force him to fight a decisive battle. This put Belisarius in a difficult spot. He answered these demands by stating that he would never put the cause of the emperor and populace at risk because of reckless demands. He also pointed out that the help the civilians promised was too risky in a situation in which he was expecting reinforcements (army and fleet) from the emperor to arrive within a few days.

The guerrilla war against the besiegers results in armistice in about mid-December 537[43]

After this Belisarius dispatched Procopius to Naples because it was rumoured that the reinforcements had arrived there. His orders were for Procopius to load as many ships as possible with grain and to assemble all soldiers who had arrived from the east or who had been left behind in Naples and other garrisons of Campania and then to convoy the grain to Ostia. Procopius in the company of Mundilas the *doryforos* and some horsemen left through the Gate of the Apostle Paul (Porta Ostiensis) secretly at night. When Procopius had bypassed the Goths safely and reached Campania, the guardsmen returned to the city. The guardsmen had also observed an important thing which was that the Goths did not venture outside their camp at night.

This news delighted Belisarius. He decided to exploit it by sending detachments of horsemen to the neighbouring strongholds with instructions to sally out of these positions to make ambushes against enemy convoys which were bringing supplies to the Goths. The idea was to besiege the besiegers, and he sent Martinus and Trajan with 1,000 horsemen to Tarcina. Belisarius's wife Antonina was dispatched together with them with orders for her to go with a few men to Naples where she was to await the outcome of the siege in safety. Magnus and Sinthues, the *doryforos*, were dispatched with about 500 men to the fortress of Tibur at a distance of 140 stades (26 km) from Rome. He had already sent Gotharis with some of the Heruls to the town of Albani, but the Goths had driven them away. The Goths had left the Church of the Apostle Paul unoccupied because of respect for sanctuaries. The church was located beside the Tiber 14 stades from Rome and was connected to the city with a colonnade. This means that it was not located on the Vatican Hill but south of it along the Via Portuensis which began at the Gate of Portuensis, then known as the Gate of Apostle Paul. Belisarius ordered Valerianus to take all the Huns there and build a stockade by the bank of the Tiber with orders to prevent the Goths from venturing far from their camps. Belisarius took the Huns there in person and then returned to the city.

After this Belisarius no longer offered battle but settled on guarding the walls. The sending of the soldiers to carry out a guerrilla campaign enabled Belisarius to distribute grain to the populace. It is clear that Belisarius feared that the populace would betray the city to the Goths. In the meantime, Martinus and Trajan had spent the night between the camps of the enemy after which they had marched to Taracina where they sent Antonina to Naples. After this they occupied the fortified locations in that district and started to use these as their bases of operation against the enemy supply columns as instructed. Magnus and Sinthues hastily rebuilt those sections of the fortress of Tibur that needed repairs, after which they too started their operations. The Huns did likewise so it did not take long for the Goths to run out of food supplies, and they too started to suffer from famine and pestilence. The situation was particularly bad in the camp that the Goths had built at Torre Fiscale. When some had died, they retreated back to their main camps. The Huns were likewise affected and returned to the city.

In the meantime Procopius had collected 500 soldiers in Campania and loaded a great number of ships with grain. At that moment Antonina arrived and assisted Procopius in his tasks. Soon after, a fleet carrying 3,000 Isaurians under Paulus and Conon arrived in the harbour of Naples. Another force landed at Dryous. This army consisted of 800

Thracian horsemen (meaning Gothic settlers) under John, the nephew of Vitalian, and 1,000 regular cavalry under various commanders which included Alexander and Marcentius. The overall commander appears to have been John who is called *magister militum* by Marcellinus Comes (538.1). According to Marcellinus, the commanders that arrived now included Batzas and Rema who are not mentioned by Procopius. Still another force of 300 horsemen under Zeno had already reached Rome via Samnium by using the Latin Way. John was provided with wagons by the inhabitants of Calabria which he then took to Campania together with his 1,800 horsemen. These forces were united with the 500 men already collected by Procopius. This combined force was marched along the coastal road. The wagons were loaded with grain and could be used as a defensive circle of wagons if the enemy threatened. Procopius and John ordered Paulus and Conon to sail with their 3,000 men straight to Ostia with orders to meet them there. The ships were loaded not only with grain but also with wine. John and Procopius expected to meet Martinus and Trajan at Taracina where they were to join their forces together, but when John and Procopius reached Taracina they found they had already been recalled to Rome, presumably for the same reasons as the Huns.

When Belisarius learnt of the approach of John's forces, he became fearful that the Goths could attack them with far superior forces. So he again devised a distraction. The enemy had built a camp very close to the Flaminian Gate which Belisarius had blocked up at the very beginning of the siege, so the enemy did not expect an attack from there. He tore down the masonry secretly during the night and then assembled most of his army behind the gate. Then at daybreak he sent Trajan and Diogenes from the Pincian Gate with 1,000 horsemen against the enemy camps to shoot arrows, with orders to flee back to the city if the enemy attacked. Belisarius posted reserves behind the Pincian Gate in readiness. When the men under Trajan and Diogenes started to harass the camps, the Goths gathered forces from all of the camps (meaning presumably those north of the Pincian Gate). When this happened the Romans galloped towards the fortifications as fast as they could with the Goths in pursuit.

As soon as Belisarius saw this, he knew that his diversion had worked as planned, so he now gave the order for the soldiers posted behind the Flaminian Gate to charge out. The Gothic camp was located along the road and in front of it was a narrow passage between steep banks. This was presumably a separate defensive moat with a narrow passage built in advance of the camp and its defences. When one of the barbarians clad in a corselet saw the Romans charging, he advanced there and took a stand, urging his fellows to follow, but Mundilas killed him before the other Goths could reach it, and then held it against the Goths. The Romans were therefore able to cross the narrow passage and attack the camp. However, its very deep trench and defences proved sufficient to prevent the Romans from taking it even though there were only a few defenders left inside. One of the guards of Belisarius called Aquilinus then performed an amazing stunt by seizing his horse by the bridle and bestriding it so that it leaped from the trench into the camp. There he killed some of the enemies, but when the Goths gathered around him and hurled many missiles at him his horse fell and he was forced to flee from the camp. After this, Aquilinus went on foot together with his mounted comrades towards the Pincian Gate so that they were able to target the Gothic troops that had pursued Trajan and Diogenes from behind with arrows. It is probable that this had been planned from the start and it is probable that Aquilinus and his comrades were protected by the rest of the troops that had been previously posted behind the Flaminian Gate so that the Goths in front of it could not attack Aquilinus. By this time Trajan had been reinforced by the reserves posted behind the Pincian Gate so he was able to attack his pursuers with reinforcements. The Goths were now caught between two Roman cavalry forces with the result that the Romans were able to kill exceedingly large numbers of them. According to Procopius, only very few of the Goths managed to flee back to their camps with great difficulty; the rest of the Goths stayed inside their camps terrified. Trajan, however, received a serious wound in this action, presumably somewhere close to the enemy camp and its infantry archers. A barbed arrow hit him above the right eye near his nose. The iron point disappeared completely inside his head, but the rest of the arrow fell to the ground because the iron point had not been fastened securely to the shaft. Trajan paid no attention to the wound but continued to pursue and kill the enemy. The doctors did not dare to do anything to the barbed head. According to Procopius, the iron head started to emerge from Trajan's head of its own accord five years later and was still in the process of coming out three years after that. It did not hinder the man in any way. The fact that Trajan and Arzas were both wounded with arrows dropping from a high angle[44] means that it is unlikely that either would have been wearing a helmet with a long projecting visor (e.g. the Corinthian type depicted in sixth century art) protecting their faces from missiles coming from above. These men probably used either typical ridge or segmented helmets, or the so-called Pseudo-Attic helmets which could also be ridge helmets.

The results of this battle and the famine and pestilence demoralized the Goths completely. In the exaggerated words of Procopius, their numbers had been reduced from the myriads to the very few. They felt more besieged than besiegers. When they then learnt that reinforcements had arrived from the east both by land and sea, they became frightened and started to make plans of departure. They did not know that the reinforcements were not large – in their fear they imagined that the emperor had sent a huge force. Consequently, the Goths sent three envoys to Rome. The Goths promised to give the Romans Sicily in return for peace. Belisarius answered this insult with an insult and promised to give them Britain. After this the Goths added Campania and Naples to the concessions, which Belisarius answered by stating that he had no right to transgress the wishes of the emperor. The Goths then promised to pay the Romans a yearly sum of money, and Belisarius answered that he could do nothing else but guard Italy for its rightful owner the emperor. The envoys then said that they should send envoys to the emperor. Belisarius agreed to this and an armistice was signed and hostages exchanged.

While these negotiations were going on, the fleet with the Isaurians landed at Ostia and John's forces marched there without any interference from the Goths. The Isaurians dug a deep trench near the harbour while John made a barricade of wagons inside it. Marcellinus claims that the army pitched their camp at Portus Romanus, but Procopius's version is to be preferred here because he was present in person. The following night Belisarius went there with 100 horsemen. He told them of the agreement reached and ordered them to take the cargoes to the city. At daybreak he returned to the city, while Antonina and the officers started to plan how to take the cargoes to the city, their oxen having been overworked. It was also dangerous to travel the narrow road with wagons because the wagons could not be formed into defensive circle, and it was impossible to tow the barges on the river because the road on the opposite bank was now held by the enemy. So they improvised in a manner that could have been taken straight out of siege treatises. They took small boats from the ships and built a wall of planks on all sides. Then they embarked archers and sailors on them and waited for a favourable wind so that they could sail the vessels along the Tiber towards Rome. They placed a *meros* of Roman soldiers on the right bank which marched along and protected the boats. A large number of the Isaurians were left to guard the ships. Belisarius was to adopt this same organization again during the second siege of Rome.

It is unfortunate that we do not know whether we should take this *meros* in its literal sense to mean about 6,000 men or whether we should think it to refer to just some unit/ group of soldiers. Both are possible because the Romans could have bolstered the cavalry and Isaurians with servants and sailor-marines so that the overall size of the force could have reached the figure of 6,000 men. The sailing was easy where the river was straight, but in other places the sailors were forced to row with great difficulty against the current. The Goths could have easily attacked the Romans, especially those posted at Portus, but they did not make any hostile move so the Romans were able to make the trip several times and bring the necessary supplies to Rome. This shows nicely how all Roman operations relied on their navy and its forces of sailors and marines. Without them the Roman armies would not have received their salaries and supplies and without the presence of the naval personnel many of the operations would have been just impossible. Once this had been accomplished the fleet retreated at full speed because it was already about the time of the winter solstice in 538. Paulus remained at Ostia with some of the Isaurians but the rest of the soldiers entered Rome. According to Procopius, it was only after this that the two parties gave hostages to each other to secure the armistice. The Romans gave Zeno and the Goths Ulias after which they agreed that the armistice was to last for three months. In other words, the expectation was that three months would suffice for the exchange of messages even in the wintry conditions. It is no wonder that the Romans had taken all the precautions described above.

These two images depict the fortifications built on top of rafts in siege treatises that could have inspired the use of the similar fortifications also on boats. It is probable that the walls looked somewhat like depicted in these images. However, it is possible that the naval practice alone would have sufficed in this case because the sailors added parapets also to ships when this was thought necessary (see e.g. Syvänne, 2004).
Left: The parapet built on a raft in Apollodoros (2nd century).
Right: The parapet built on a raft in Heron of Byzantium (10th century)

Belisarius violates the terms of truce and enlarges Roman territories with a naval blockade[45]

The Romans then escorted the barbarian envoys to Constantinople while Ildiger, the son-in-law of Antonina, came to Rome from Libya with cavalry forces. At about the same time the Goths posted at Portus abandoned their positions because they ran out of supplies. The reason for this was that the Romans controlled the sea. When Paulus saw this he and his Isaurians marched from Ostia and took possession of Portus. The naval blockade also forced the Goths to abandon Centumcellae, which the Romans likewise proceeded to occupy. Following this the Romans also took possession of the town of Albani. The Romans were clearly taking advantage of the armistice to enlarge their domains. This naturally angered the Goths. They dispatched envoys to Belisarius to complain about this violation of truce. They demanded that Belisarius return Albani and Centumcellae or face war. Belisarius laughed and sent the envoys back empty-handed.

This incident appears to have given Belisarius an idea when saw that Rome now had abundant supplies of soldiers. He decided to send many horsemen to places far distant from Rome. The most important of these was the decision to send John the nephew of Vitalian with his 800 horsemen to pass the winter at Alba in Picenum. Under John served 400 horsemen of Valerianus who were placed under Damianus, the nephew of Valerianus, and 800 chosen bodyguards of Belisarius himself who were placed under Suntas and Adegis. Belisarius's instructions for John was that if he found the armistice broken, he was to make a sudden raid into Picenum where he was to visit every district before the news of his arrival could reach it. This area was almost defenceless because most of the Goths had marched against Rome leaving their women and children vulnerable to attack. John was instructed to take them as slaves (i.e. as hostages) while not harming any of the Romans who lived there because the conquest required their goodwill. If John met resistance in any of the fortified places, he was to attack with his whole force. If John managed to conquer it, he was instructed to press on, but if he failed, he was ordered to march back because Belisarius considered the leaving of such fortifications in the rear too dangerous. John was also ordered to keep all of the booty intact so that it could be divided fairly among the whole army.

At about the same time in early 538, Datius, Bishop of Milan, and some notables from the same city arrived in Rome. They pleaded with Belisarius to send them some of his guards so that they would be able to betray their city to the Romans. Belisarius promised this, but kept the men in Rome for the duration of winter presumably with the idea of not exposing his plans to break up the armistice in the spring.

During this winter break in hostilities Belisarius and Constantinus quarrelled with dire results. The quarrel resulted from the theft of daggers from Presidius, who was a native Roman from Ravenna. He offended Vittigis at the time when Vittigis was about to march against Rome. Presidius fled together with some of his domestics. He carried with him two daggers with scabbards adorned with gold and jewels. When Presidius then entered Spolitium, Constantinus, who was posted there, stole these two daggers. Both Constantinus and Presidius fled to Rome, where Presidius maintained silence as long as the city was under serious threat, but when the two sides signed armistice, Presidius made a complaint to Belisarius. Belisarius duly asked Constantinus to return the daggers, but did not put any pressure on Constantinus at this moment because it was then that Belisarius travelled to Campania to collect supplies (Marcellinus 538.1). When nothing happened Presidius resorted to a desperate measure. When Presidius met Belisarius, who was then riding, he got hold of the bridle and shouted his case with a loud voice. This forced Belisarius's hand because he needed to retain the goodwill of the Roman populace. Consequently, Belisarius assembled Constantinus and many of the commanders in the palace. There Belisarius told Constantinus what had happened the day before and urged him to return the daggers, but Constantinus refused. This angered Belisarius who now asked who was the superior officer. Constantinus promised to obey him in everything else except this. Belisarius then gave the order for his guards to enter, which Constantinus naturally interpreted as an order to kill him, with the result that he drew his dagger and attempted to stab Belisarius in the stomach. Belisarius stepped back and threw his hands around Bessas and thereby saved himself. At that moment Ildiger and Valerianus grasped the hands of Constantinus who was attempting to go after Belisarius and dragged him back. Then the bodyguards of Belisarius arrived, took the dagger and led Constantinus to another room. Procopius states that Constantinus was executed soon after.[46]

According to Procopius's *Secret History* (*Anecdota* 1.15ff., esp. 1.28–30), Belisarius was prepared to forgive the man, but his wife Antonina, who hated Constantinus for the comment he had made earlier regarding the infidelity of Antonina, convinced her husband to execute him. The killing of Constantinus had far reaching consequences for Belisarius because it angered the emperor and all of the Roman notables, and this despite the fact that it had been the greed of Constantinus which had endangered the project to retain the goodwill of the Roman populace which was needed for the smooth conquest of the cities.[47]

The Goths exact revenge against the faithless Romans in March 538[48]

The breaking of the armistice by the Romans naturally angered the Goths who started to make plans for the breaking of the armistice through subterfuge as the Romans had. The first attempt was to send men with lamps and torches by night into the aqueduct that was close to the Pincian Gate to check whether it would be possible to attack through it. They duly advanced to the middle of the city where there was a passage to the palace. This Belisarius had blocked at the beginning of the siege. One of the Romans posted at the gate saw the lights, but his comrades ridiculed him that he had seen the eyes of a wolf inside the aqueduct. When the soldiers then spread this story, it came to the ears of Belisarius who did not take it lightly but had the aqueduct investigated. When the truth was found out Belisarius posted guards there and the Goths abandoned their plan.

The next plan was to make an open attack with ladders against the Pincian Gate at lunchtime. Ildiger and his men, who were on guard duty at that time, saw this and noticed that the attackers were in disorder. They attacked the Goths before they managed to put their lines in order and killed many. The commotion aroused the Romans to action and they manned the walls. The Goths again abandoned their attack. This was an open act of hostility so now Belisarius dispatched envoys to the horsemen posted far away from Rome, which included also the forces under John nephew of Vitalian.

The next ploy of Vittigis was to bribe two Romans who lived near the Church of Peter the Apostle to take wine with a sleep-inducing drug to the guards in charge of the wall on the bank of the Tiber which had been poorly constructed. This section of the wall was without towers and was lightly guarded because it was believed that the Tiber would offer protection. Vittigis prepared skiffs and ladders and waited for the men to do their job. One, however, betrayed the plan to Belisarius, who tortured the other to get a confession and cut off his nose and ears. The man was then sent on an ass to the enemy's camp as a warning.

The operations in Picenum and the end of the siege of Rome in mid-March 538[49]

When John the nephew of Vitalian received Belisarius's orders he at first acted as ordered and plundered Picenum and captured the Gothic women and children as 'slaves'. Ulitheus, the uncle of Vittigis, led an army against John, but John defeated and killed the whole army in battle in which he personally killed Ulitheus. Possibly the men fought a duel. After this none of the Goths dared to face him and his 2,000 horsemen in battle. However, when John reached Auximus (mod. Osimo), he found it was defended by a strong garrison with good defences. Consequently, he decided not to besiege it and marched forward contrary to the instructions of Belisarius. John found Urbinus (mod. Urbino) likewise too well defended and continued his march to Ariminun (mod. Rimini), because its Roman inhabitants invited him to come there. Its Gothic garrison opted to flee to Ravenna, one day's march away. According to Procopius, John had not forgotten what Belisarius had ordered him to do, but had taken a calculated risk in the expectation that the news of the presence of the Roman army so close to Ravenna would lead to the breaking up of the siege of Rome. He was not betrayed in his hopes, because when the Goths learnt of this, they abandoned their siege. According to Procopius, John received great fame as a result. Belisarius, however, appears to have preferred to keep the Goths opposite the city of Rome where he could slowly destroy them through guerrilla warfare. When Belisarius learnt of the exploits of John, he appears to have dispatched Conon with Isaurian infantry and Thracian (Gothic) cavalry to occupy Ancon, the so-called harbour of Ariminum. In the meantime Matasuntha, wife of Vittigis, had sent messengers to John and he back to her about the possible betrayal of Ravenna to the Romans. The reason for Matasuntha's hostility towards her husband was that he had taken her as his wife with violence.

It was about the time of the spring equinox (mid–March) 538 when the Goths started their preparations for the abandonment the siege of Rome. By then the armistice had already ended, but the envoys had not yet returned. The Goths torched all of their camps and then began their march at daybreak. When Belisarius saw his enemies in flight, he was at first at a loss for what to do because he had dispatched most of his cavalry far away from Rome. However, he still decided to exploit the opportunity. He armed all of his infantry and cavalry and waited until more than half of the enemy force had crossed the Tiber, after which he attacked those who were behind. The Goths withstood the initial attack but then turned to flight. According to Procopius, two of Belisarius's *doryforoi*, Longinus the Isaurian and Mundilas, distinguished themselves in this combat. Mundilas killed four barbarians, but the real hero was Longinus who was the chief cause of the rout of the enemy. He fell where he fought. This suggests that Longinus charged into the middle of the enemy array and broke it with a heroic if suicidal attack. When the Goths then panicked it was every man for himself. They fled as a mass into the bridge and vast numbers died at Roman hands, or in the crush, or when they fell into the Tiber in their heavy equipment. The Goths lost most of those who had been on the Roman side of the bridge when Belisarius launched his attack. Nevertheless, subsequent events prove that the Goths still retained a numerical advantage.

The manoeuvring in 538[50]

Vittigis retreated towards Ravenna with the intention of placing Ariminum under siege. En route he posted garrisons in important places presumably with the intention of protecting his rear. He posted 1,000 men under Gibimer at Clusium (mod. Chiusi) in Tuscany. In Urviventus (Urba Vetus, mod. Orvieto) he placed 1,000 men under Albilas. Uligasus was posted in Tudera (mod. Todi) with 400 men. He left at Petra 400 men who had previously formed its garrison. Auximus was strengthened with 4,000 men under Visandus, while Urbinus was strengthened with 2,000 men under Moras. The cities of Caesana and Monteferetra (mod. Montefeltro) were garrisoned with 500 men each.

Belisarius appears to have been unwilling to commit enough men for the defence of Ariminum because John had acted contrary to his orders. It is also possible that he was jealous of John's success because John was certainly correct in his expectation that the Romans could have reinforced him by sea because Ariminum was a coastal city. According to Procopius, Belisarius dispatched 1,000 horsemen under Ildiger and Martinus with orders to reach Ariminum before the Goths. They were ordered to remove John from the city together with all those with him and place an infantry force there to guard the city. They were also ordered to collect the infantry from Ancon where Conon had taken them. Procopius claims that Belisarius's hope was that the Goths would not besiege the city if it was defended by a commander of no importance with infantry, and he also expected that the supplies would last longer if the city was defended by infantry. This sounds like an excuse to remove John. Ildiger and Marinus reached the city easily before the Goths because the Goths avoided the fortresses of the Flaminian Way and the cities of Narnia, Spolitium and Perusia which were in Roman hands.

However, the Romans under Ildiger and Marinus still faced obstacles because they started their journey after the Goths started theirs. When they reached Petra, they attacked it. The place was basically an impregnable tunnel in a pass. However, the Romans managed to defeat its defenders both in the tunnel and in the nearby houses by climbing the cliff above it from which they dropped rocks on the tunnel entrances and houses causing the Goths to surrender out of fear. Some were enrolled into the Roman forces, some were left there with their families while some of the Romans were posted there as a garrison. After this the Romans marched to Ancon where they collected a force of infantry which they took to Ariminum, which they reached on the third day of their travel. John, however, refused to leave and kept his 800 Thracian Goths together with the 400 men under Damianus. Ildiger and Marinus were therefore forced to leave the infantry there and to take only the 800 bodyguards of Belisarius with them. They retreated in haste before Vittigis arrived. John had once again disobeyed Belisarius, but there were certainly good reasons for this because as the Romans controlled the sea it would have been very easy to supply the city from the sea. The real reasons for Belisarius's actions must have been anger and jealousy.

The siege and relief of Ariminum in 538: The defeat of the Goths without a battle[51]

When Vittigis reached Ariminum, he duly besieged the city because the Roman presence in it posed a threat to Ravenna. There was never any chance of Vittigis not besieging the place in these circumstances, unless of course the Romans had visible support for the defenders from the sea. The Goths built a siege tower which was higher than the walls, but this time they did not make the mistake of using oxen to draw it but used men inside the tower. When the tower reached the small moat in front of the walls when it was becoming dark, the Goths halted in the expectation that they would be able to leave the tower there and then use it in the morning. This was a serious mistake, which John exploited. John led a force of Isaurians outside the wall to dig the trench deeper so that the earth was placed on the side with the wall. The enemy guards were not up to their job so that the Isaurians were able to do this unobserved for a long time. By the time the Goths finally noticed it and attacked, most of the work had already been accomplished. When Vittigis saw the result, he executed some of the guards and then ordered the trench filled with faggots. This was duly done, but when the Goths then pushed their tower into the trench the faggots gave way under its weight and it tilted. Vittigis, quite rightly fearing that the Romans would make a sally at night and torch the tower, ordered it dragged back. John was eager to prevent this and armed his men. John noted that he never expected to be besieged in this city because it would have been easy for the Romans to send reinforcements by sea, but now there was no alternative but to fight bravely. With the inclusion of the speech which stated this Procopius clearly implies that the real reason for the troubles was the jealousy of Belisarius. John led his men out. The fight was hard, but in the end the Goths managed to drag the tower back to their lines late in the day. The fight, however, had been so hard that the Goths no longer planned to attack the walls with the tower and settled on besieging the city because its supplies had already run out.

In the meantime Belisarius had dispatched 1,000 Isaurians and Thracians (Goths and natives) to Milan. The Isaurians were commanded by Ennes, the Thracians by Paulus, while Mundilas was their overall commander. The Praetorian Prefect Fidelius was dispatched with them because he was a native of Milan with influence in Liguria. This force set sail from Portus and put in at Genoa. There they loaded the ships' boats on wagons so they could be used to bridge the Po if necessary. They did indeed cross the river with the help of these boats. Procopius does not state whether the boats were used to build a pontoon bridge or whether they were just used as boats. When they reached Ticinum (mod. Pavia), the Goths engaged them in battle, but the Romans once again defeated the Goths despite the fact that these Goths were more numerous and also known as excellent troops. The Goths fled to the city. The Romans continued their march but Fidelius remained behind at a temple where he prayed. He was the last man to leave. Fidelius then mounted his horse, but as he did so it stumbled for some reason and he fell.

The Goths saw this and charged out of the city and killed him. This caused much grief, but the Romans continued their journey and duly arrived at Milan. They secured the city and the rest of Liguria without a battle. When Vittigis learnt of this, he sent a request to Theudibert, king of the Franks, to dispatch the forces he had promised. Theudibert dispatched 10,000 Burgundians under the pretext that they operated independently of the Franks. These forces were then added to the army of Uraias, nephew of Vittigis, which had been dispatched against Milan. The Goths and Burgundians then besieged Milan before the Romans could collect enough provisions. On top of this, Mundilas had posted most of his soldiers in the surrounding fortresses, Begomum, Comum, Navaria and some other fortresses, so he had only 300 men left in Milan. This meant that the defence of the city was mainly in the hands of its inhabitants. This was the situation at Milan at the end of the winter 538/9.

It took until about the time of the summer solstice for Belisarius to begin his march towards Vittigis. Subsequent events suggest that he had been coordinating his actions with the emperor and other officers who were en route to Italy or already in Italy. Belisarius left a garrison at Rome and dispatched other men against the cities of Tudera and Clusium while he marched with the rest behind them. When the Goths in these cities learnt of this, they surrendered without a fight. Belisarius sent these Goths to Sicily and Naples and established garrisons in the cities after which he continued his march towards the enemy's main army.

In the meantime Vittigis had sent another army to Auximus with orders to join forces with those posted there after which they were to attack Ancon. Ancon was a sort of pointed rock and was therefore called 'elbow'. The defences were placed on this rock, but all of the houses lay outside it. When the Goths approached, Conon made the mistake of leading his men outside where he posted them as a shallow phalanx as if the men were being led on a hunt to surround the entire mountain. When these men then witnessed the size of the enemy host, they fled straightaway to the fortress. The Goths pursued and managed to kill large numbers of the Roman army and came close to taking the fortress with their ladders, and they would have done so had there not been two men present there: the *doryforos* of Belisarius called Ulimuth the Thracian Goth, and the Massagetae *doryforos* of Valerianus called Gouboulgoudou who had come by ship to Ancon a little before. These two warded off with their swords all those Goths who had managed to scale the walls and thereby saved the city even if by the time the enemy had been defeated they both were half dead from the many wounds they had received. This proves that Belisarius had reinforced Ancon by sea when he had failed to do the same for Auximum.

Belisarius was informed at the same time that a great army under Narses the Eunuch, guardian of the imperial treasury, had arrived from Byzantium and was now in Picentium. Narses had with him 5,000 men under several commanders, the most notable of whom were Justinus the *Magister Militum per Illyricum*, and Narses the Armenian deserter. The brother of the latter, Aratius, had already arrived with another army and was now accompanying Belisarius. Aratius commanded about 2,000 Heruls whose leaders were Visandus, Aluith and Phanitheus. These were the loyal Heruls because most of the Herul nation appears to have been in revolt against the Romans at this time. It was actually very wise to take these Heruls to Italy rather than attempt to use them against their fellows.[52] This means that Belisarius had been in touch with these commanders and emperor before this so that he knew of the arrival of these forces. It is unlikely to be a coincidence that the reinforcements arrived in Picentium or nearby at the right moment.

The two armies met each other near the city of Firmum (mod. Fermo), one day's march from Auximus. The commanders of the army held a council there to discuss future plans. Belisarius at least officially feared that if they marched to relieve Ariminum, the Goths of Auximus would attack them from behind. It is indeed possible that this fear was real because Belisarius was an extremely cautious commander who had ordered John not to advance past strong enemy positions. However, it is also clear that the anger and jealousy of Belisarius against John also played its part. Most of the officers were hostile towards John and accused him of disobedience which had caused his problems and that they should besiege Auximus instead of helping him. However, Narses, who loved John, disagreed. In his opinion Auximus was of secondary importance in comparison with saving John, the army and Ariminum, and Belisarius should be able to look past his own hurt feelings. Narses pointed out that if the Goths, who had numerical superiority, gained this victory, their fighting spirit would also return. An envoy from John arrived at this same time with the news that John would have to surrender within seven days. This together with the fact that Narses was close to the emperor forced Belisarius's hand, but true to his character he came up with a superb plan to save the disobeying commander.

Since the Roman position was threatened by the presence of the Goths in Auximus, Belisarius left Aratius to protect the rear with 1,000 men who were encamped by the sea. The 2nd army under Herodian, Uliaris and Narses the brother of Aratius, he dispatched by sea to Ariminum. The commander of that force was Ildiger. Their orders were not to make a landing near the city before the land forces had taken their positions. He posted still another army under Martinus, which was to march along the coast, keeping near the ships with instructions to light a great number of campfires to fool the enemy into believing that a large army approached. I have speculated in *The Age of Hippotoxotai* that this army was probably expected to receive supporting fire from the ballistae of the ships in case the Goths decided to attack. The combined use of fleet and army side by side shows the advantage that the Romans had over all their enemies after the Vandals had been defeated. Belisarius with Narses went further inland by another route. Belisarius advanced his forces through the city of Urvisalia/Urbs Salvia (mod. Urbisaglia) and nearby mountains because he was greatly inferior to his opponents and did not wish to engage them in open battle. Belisarius's intention was to scare the enemy away by surrounding them from three sides and by leaving one route open for flight. The leaving of an open route for fleeing was a standard method used against fortified camps and cities, which Belisarius now adapted for use against besiegers.

At one day's distance from Ariminum, Belisarius's vanguard encountered a small force of Goths. The Romans killed most of them by missiles, but some managed to flee. In their fear they exaggerated the size of the Roman army and informed Vittigis that Belisarius was about to attack them immediately. As a result, Vittigis deployed the army to the north of the city of Ariminum to face Belisarius, but nothing happened because this was not Belisarius's plan. The following night the Goths then saw a large numbers of campfires to the east of the city. In the morning, they saw the fleet approaching which finally tilted the scales and caused them to panic and flee. According to Procopius, if the besieged defenders of Ariminum had had any energy left in them they could have ended the war then and there. The first to arrive at Ariminum was the fleet under Ildiger. They proceeded to enslave all those who had stayed behind in the camp and to pillage the valuables that the fleeing Goths had left behind. When Belisarius arrived at midday, he told John and his men to be grateful to Ildiger. John answered that he felt no gratitude to anyone but Narses. The seeds of quarrel had been sown.

This stands as an excellent example of the tactics adopted when one did not want to engage the enemy in combat, which used all of the branches of service (navy, infantry, cavalry) and employed a skilled use of successive psychological shocks to produce the flight of the enemy.[53] Furthermore, to succeed, this manoeuvre demanded excellent cooperation between the different sections of the army and therefore shows the remarkable ability of the troops and commanders at this time.

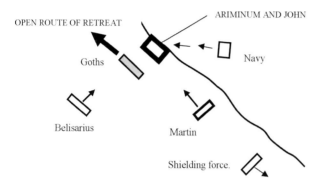

Left: a diagram showing the general principle behind Belisarius's master plan (source: Syvänne, 2004)

The officers quarrel over strategy in 538–9[54]

After the relief of Ariminum John and the other officers who were displeased with Belisarius started to flatter Narses and called it a disgrace that a man who shared the secrets of the emperor should obey a mere *strategos* (general). Narses was ready to listen to this flattery because his judgment had just been proved correct. Consequently, whenever Belisarius suggested something this was blocked by Narses. When Belisarius perceived this, he assembled the officers. He warned of overconfidence and pointed out that the enemy had a numerical advantage and had been defeated so far only because they had been outgeneralled. He pointed out that the Romans were now actually surrounded by the Goths. Vittigis was with myriads of men at Ravenna. Another army was at Auximus. Still another army was at Urviventus, and Milan was besieged by the Goths and Franks. Belisarius's plan for the situation was to send a relief army to Milan and to besiege Auximus with the rest of the army. Narses opposed the division of the army and demanded that they should conquer Aemilia and then harass Ravenna. He opposed the besieging of Auximus because the Goths of Ravenna could then attack them from behind. On paper this looks good, but as we shall see it did not take into account the logistical problems facing the Goths at Ravenna and it left Milan to its own devices. Subsequent events prove that Belisarius was correct. When Belisarius heard Narses's comments he showed a letter of Justinian which stated that the emperor had sent Narses to Italy to serve under Belisarius and that all were to obey the commands of Belisarius in the interest of the state. Narses responded that Belisarius's plans were contrary to the interests of the state and he would not follow him.

Therefore the army and commanders were now divided, but Belisarius acted as if this was not yet the case and dispatched Peranius to Urviventus/Urbs Vetus with instructions to besiege it while he left the rest of the army against Urbinus/Urbinum at one day's distance from Ariminum. Narses, John, Justinus, Aratius and others who opposed Belisarius still followed but pitched their camp separately from that of Belisarius so that the Roman army that besieged the city which was located on a hill consisted actually of two armies under two commanders. The hill on which Urbinus was located was round and very high and the garrison placed inside was strong and well provisioned. It could be approached easily only from the north. Consequently, Belisarius gave his men orders to collect poles and build a long protective *stoa* (colonnade), called *vinea* in Roman military parlance. This was a protective shed that the soldiers carried where desired. In this case Belisarius ordered it to be taken against the gates of the city where the ground was level so that the soldiers could break that spot of the wall with their tools.

When the soldiers of Belisarius were preoccupied with this, the friends of Narses pointed out to him that John had already attempted to capture the place and had found it impossible. In their opinion it was better to recover Aemilia for the emperor as Narses had suggested than waste time here. Narses accordingly abandoned his camp at night and marched fast to Ariminum. When the Gothic commander Moras saw this in the morning, he taunted Belisarius, but he did this too soon. Belisarius was still determined to storm the place, but little did he know that he did not need to do it because luck was on his side. The spring which had provided the defenders with water dried up and the Goths were prepared to surrender. Belisarius who did not know this armed his entire force and posted it in a circle around the hill and then dispatched his *vinea* against the wall, but when the men inside it approached the wall, they were met with pleading. The Goths were prepared to surrender. Belisarius duly accepted the Goths as subjects of the emperor with complete equality with the Roman army, which presumably implies that he enrolled perhaps about 2,500 Goths (original garrison plus 2,000 reinforcements) into his army. This took place around the winter solstice (mid-December) 538.

When Narses heard of this, he was obviously surprised and depressed. He decided to stay in Ariminum while he put into effect his plan to conquer Aemilia. He dispatched John against Caesena, which he attempted to storm with ladders. The Goths defended themselves well and many Romans died. These included Phanitheus, commander of the Heruls. John decided to abandon the attempt and march on with Justinus. He managed to capture Forocornelius/Forum Cornelii (mod. Imola) and the whole of Aemilia because the Goths refused to fight against him and retreated.

In the meantime Belisarius had decided to postpone the siege of Auximus to the next year because it was already winter. He dispatched Aratius to winter at Firmum with orders to prevent the Goths of Auximus from harassing the Romans, while he marched to Urviventus to assist Peranius in his siege of the place because he had heard from deserters that the Goths were suffering from a lack of supplies. This siege had lasted a long time. According to Marcellinus, the siege was over before the end of 538, but it is possible that it actually lasted into 539.

In summer 539 much of Italy suffered from famine. The war had caused the farmers to flee from their fields which therefore did not yield any harvest. The result was famine and pestilence, which hit particularly badly Tuscany, Aemilia, Picenum and north of the Adriatic Gulf. According to Procopius, at least 50,000 farmers died in Picenum and many more in the north of the Adriatic Gulf. Procopius provides us with a particularly sad description of how the famine stricken people looked and how the corpses lay on the ground because there was nobody to bury them. He also gives us a gruesome story of two women who lived above Ariminum. They were the only inhabitants who survived there, and gave lodging to travelling strangers. They then killed the guests in their bed during the night and ate them. They did this to seventeen travellers, but when they were attempting to kill their eighteenth traveller, the man woke up and killed them both after interrogating them.

At some unknown time in late 538 when Belisarius had learnt of the plight of Milan, he dispatched Martinus and Uliaris with a numerous army to relieve the city, but these two men did not dare to cross the Po because they feared the size of the enemy host. Belisarius ordered John and Justinus to assist them because they were closest to the scene of operations, but the two men told him that they would obey only Narses. Belisarius then asked Narses to order John and Justinus to do so. Narses agreed and ordered the men to go to the assistance of Milan. John went to the sea coast to obtain boats for the crossing of the Po, but then at least officially fell ill so that his army became immobilized. All of this took so much time that the situation became desperate in Milan, with the result that its small garrison surrendered on terms and abandoned the population to its fate. The Goths butchered the entire male population (according to Procopius, 300,000 males) and gave the women as presents to the Burgundians for their support. A man called Vergentinus, however, managed to flee with his followers to Venetia and from there to Dalmatia and from there to the emperor where he told him the entire story. One wonders if this man was a member of the Roman spy organization and that his name is included for this reason? The garrisons in the neighbouring cities all surrendered rather than faced the prospect of destruction. This was a massive disaster and clearly a result of the divisions among the Roman leadership.

The siege of Urviventus was presumably over by the end of 538 or February 539 because Belisarius then marched his entire army into Picenum. Martindale (*PLRE3/Belisarius 1*, p.204) has speculated that Belisarius spent the winter of 538/9 in Rome because according to Marcellinus Comes (a.538), he captured Urbinum and Urbs Vetus and then on his way back to Rome he captured an island in the *lacus Volsiensis* (Lago di Bolsena). It was then in about March 539 en route to Picenum that Belisarius heard the sad news that Milan had fallen. He was so angry over the behaviour of Uliaris that after this he never allowed him to come into his presence. Belisarius also wrote a letter to the emperor telling him what had taken place. Justinian did not punish anyone, but recalled Narses to Byzantium and reinstated his previous order that Belisarius was the *autokrator* (commander-in-chief) of all forces in Italy. The dismissal of Narses from service resulted in the desertion of the Heruls who were particularly fond of Narses and they refused to fight under anyone else. Belisarius tried to lure them to stay with all kinds of promises but to no avail. The Heruls packed their things and went to Liguria where they sold slaves and animals to the Goths and promised never to fight against them. However, when they reached the lands of the Veneti, they met Vitalius and started to repent their behaviour and betrayal of Justinian. They decided to leave some of their number behind under Visandus while the rest went back home with the idea that this would remove their guilt.

The Goths seek allies in 539[55]

When Vittigis and the Goths heard of the approach of Belisarius, they became frightened because they did not think it possible to defeat him unaided in pitched battle. They also considered the Franks too untrustworthy as allies so that they started seeking new ones. They dispatched envoys to Vaces, king of the Lombards, but to no avail because he remained a steadfast ally of Justinian. At this time, the Lombards were located north of the Danube and Vittigis's idea was clearly to invite them across to the area of Noricum and Pannonia, which were later granted to them by Justinian. Their next plan was to urge Chosroes, the ruler of Persia, to attack the Romans because they thought that the Romans would never be able to conquer Italy if they were fighting against the mighty Persia. They convinced two priests from Liguria, who hated Belisarius, to act as their envoys so that they could go unhindered all the way to Persia. Chosroes was indeed persuaded because he was angry over the fact that his enemy was achieving great successes as a result of the peace. The Romans learnt of his jealousy from their spy network well in advance so Justinian was able to start planning for the recall of Belisarius to the east and also to make plans for the ending of the war in Italy. Because of this Justinian then finally released the envoys of Vittigis and dispatched them back to Italy. Belisarius, however, did not allow them to leave before the Goths had released the Roman envoys Athanasius and Peter. These two men had been previously sent to negotiate with Theodahad on behalf of Justinian in 535. Justinian rewarded Athanasius with the position of *praefectus praetorio* and appointed Peter as *magister*.

The year 539 saw another development in the Balkans which was that the Gepids exploited the fact that the Goths had been forced to abandon Sirmium and Dacia to the Romans. This had created a power vacuum and the Gepids filled it by invading. Up to that time the Gepids had been allies of Justinian but this invasion of Roman territory changed it. Justinian dispatched *magister militum* Calluc against them. He was at first successful, but then suffered a defeat and was killed. Thus the Gepids obtained Sirmium with the province of Dacia from where they started to conduct raids against Roman territory.[56] On the face of it, it could be possible to suggest that the Goths also suggested an alliance to the Gepids, their enemies, but since none of the sources mention such a diplomatic move, it is clear that the Gepids merely exploited the opportunity offered to them by the war between Romans and Goths. Thanks to the defeat of Calluc, the ongoing war in Italy, the Hunnic invasion of Thrace in about 539/40 and then the renewal of the war with Persia in 540, Justinian was in no position to exact vengeance against the Gepids let alone to prevent their raids.

The siege of Auximum from April/May to October/November in 539[57]

In May 539, Belisarius decided to capture Auximum/Auximus (modern Osimo) and Fisula/Faesulae (modern Fiesole) to secure his rear before advancing against Ravenna.

He sent Cyprian and Justinus together with their own men, some Isaurians and with a detachment of 500 footmen taken from the detachment commanded by Demetrius to besiege Fisula. They encamped close to the city and set out to starve the Goths. The city was unassailable. The Goths made several sallies, but were repulsed. Another army under Martinus, John and John Phagas (the Glutton) was sent to the Po River to act as a shielding force for the Romans besieging Fisula against the Goths at Milan under Uraias. They established their headquarters at Dorthon/Dertona (modern Tortona). Belisarius himself went to the city of Auximum with 11,000 men. His army was protected by the garrison of Ariminum and also by the fact that the Gothic army at Ravenna was unable to acquire provisions for campaigning against him since the land of Picenum was devoid of provisions as a result of the ravaging. The Romans, in contrast, were able to ship supplies from Sicily and Calabria and store them at Ancon.

Auximum was about 84 stades (ca. 15 km) from the sea on a hill about 275 m above the sea. The flower of the Gothic army garrisoned the city. Belisarius judged the place unassailable and set out to starve the Goths. The army was commanded to encamp in a circle around the base of the hill. While the army was doing this, the Goths observed that the Roman camps were too far apart from each other to be able to assist each other quickly. So, in the late afternoon they sallied out from the east side of the city against Belisarius and his guards who were engaged in the building of the camp. The guards hastily formed their ranks and forced the attackers back until they reached the middle of the hill. There the Goths turned and made a stand. The higher ground allowed the Goths to kill many Romans with missiles. The battle continued until the night. The speed of the Roman advance against Auximum had taken the Goths by surprise when they had sent some men to gather provisions at dawn. When these foraging parties then returned and saw the camp fires, some of them courageously passed through the Roman lines undetected while others became frightened and attempted to hide themselves with the idea of fleeing to Ravenna, only with the result that all were captured and killed by the Romans. In this case being courageous clearly paid off.[58]

There was a place close to the walls which allowed the Goths to gather forage for the horses and herbs for the men. The Romans engaged and defeated the Goths each time they tried to gather the forage. The Goths devised countermeasures. At first the Goths rolled wagon wheels at the Romans, but the latter were able to open up their ranks so that they caused no harm. The details prove that we are here dealing with footmen, either regular ones or dismounted horsemen. Then the Goths placed an ambush, which succeeded for the following reason. When one part of the Roman army was attacking, those left behind saw the Gothic attack and tried to warn their comrades, but were unable to do so because of the distance separating them and because the Goths made loud noises. According to Procopius, Belisarius was at a loss what to do until he, Procopius, told Belisarius that the ancients had had men who could use the trumpet (*salpigx*) with two different strains to urge the men forward or to retreat as needed. However, since this skill had been lost, Procopius urged Belisarius to use cavalry trumpets (made of leather and thin wood) to order the men to attack and to use the infantry trumpets (made of thick brass) to order the men to retreat back to their camp. Belisarius accepted the plan. The above indicates that the level of training of the army musicians and footmen had fallen well below the ancient standard. On the basis of this it would be all too easy to draw the conclusion that at this time infantry was not expected to be able to withdraw because it was always posted behind the cavalry as a defensive bulwark. However this is actually completely wrong because the above also indicates that the infantry could be ordered to make an orderly retreat but at this time it was always done with the vocal command and not with the trumpet as it had sometimes been done in the past.[59]

Consequently, when the Roman soldiers saw the Goths next time gathering fodder and herbs, they once again attacked and killed some of the Goths. One of the Moors (this means that the Romans consisted of footmen) saw that one of the Gothic corpses was adorned with gold. He grabbed the corpse by the hair and started dragging him. At that moment one of the Goths threw a javelin which passed through both of his legs just behind the shins so that both of his legs were pinned together. Even then the Moor was unwilling to let go of his catch and continued to drag the Goth by the hair. It was then that the Goths launched their ambush, which was seen by Belisarius who duly ordered the trumpeters of infantry to sound the retreat. The Romans duly retreated taking up and carrying the Moor with his javelin and loot. The Goths did not dare to follow the retreating Romans.

When the Goths were running out of supplies, they naturally thought it wise to inform Vittigis, and devised a stratagem to enable their envoy to pass through the Roman lines. In the middle of a moonless night, the Goths suddenly raised a loud shout from many parts of the circuit wall. The ever cautious Belisarius reacted by ordering all Romans to stay inside their camps because he feared that the Goths were attempting a stratagem of some sort against the Romans. Thanks to this the Gothic envoy managed to pass through the lines and inform Vittigis of their plight. Vittigis promised help but then later decided not to send any because he feared to place his army between the forces of John posted at Ariminum and those besieging Auximum under Belisarius, and even more importantly he feared that he would not be able to feed his expeditionary army because it could not live off the land if it advanced against the Romans. The besieged, however, did not know this. When the promised help did not materialize, they wanted to urge Vittigis to fulfill his word. They managed to convince one Roman who belonged to the Vesi tribe (i.e. he was a Visigoth) to deliver a message to Vittigis in return for a large sum of money. This man accomplished his mission and Vittigis once again promised to send a relief army to keep up the morale of the defenders. As the siege went on Belisarius was disturbed by the fact that the city had not surrendered despite its precarious situation. Consequently, he wanted to obtain a prisoner. The prisoner, taken by a Slav soldier (Slavs were specialists in capturing prisoners), disclosed that they had a traitor among their ranks who had delivered messages from Vittigis that he would bring help to the city. The traitor was given to his comrades who burned him. The usefulness of the Slavs as footmen is clear. They were among the best light footmen of their era and the Romans recognized this.

As the siege dragged on and on, Belisarius decided to destroy a water cistern close to the walls to hasten the surrender. He drew up his army in a circle around the city in the *foulkon/testudo* order. Five Isaurians were concealed below the shields. Their duty was to go to the cistern and destroy it. The Goths perceived that the Isaurians were trying to destroy the water supply and hurled stones and missiles. The Romans, except the five, retired on the run. The vault of the cistern protected the Isaurians. The Goths sallied, but the Romans counter-attacked. The battle became a fierce mêlée involving pushing and shoving (*othismos*) in which the Goths had the upper hand because of their advantageous position. Despite suffering casualties, the Romans held their ground while Belisarius encouraged them from behind. During the fight, one of Belisarius's bodyguards saved his life by placing his right hand in front of an incoming arrow. Even sixth century bodyguards appear to have gone to great lengths to protect their employer. Finally, seven Armenians ran up the steep part of the hill and killed those who had made a stand against them. This encouraged the rest of the army who also attacked. The rout of the Goths became decisive. The fight had lasted from the early morning until midday. However, the troubles had been in vain, since the Isaurians had not been able to destroy the cistern. So Belisarius poisoned the spring with dead animals, herbs and asbestos and the Goths had to make do with the scant supply of water they obtained from the well inside the fort.

In the meantime, Martinus, John, and John Phagas had been facing the Goths under Uraias who had advanced to Ticinum until the Franks under King Theudibert/Theodebert had arrived to exploit the situation. The Frankish army consisted of 100,000 men of which only a small proportion consisted of cavalry. It was with good reason that Marcellinus Comes (539.4) called this force an enormous army. The footmen did not have bows or spears but were armed only with a throwing axe and sword. At the beginning of the battle the axes were thrown at the shields of the enemy to shatter them after which the Franks finished the defenceless enemies with their swords. Furthermore, according to Procopius, despite the fact that the Franks had converted to Christianity, they still continued to practice old pagan ways, sacrificing humans etc. The Franks defeated in succession the Goths who mistakenly believed that the Franks were friends and then the Romans who mistakenly believed that Belisarius had arrived because the Goths were fleeing. Both the Goths and Romans were at loss what to do, but the supply problems caused by the large size of the army together with the ravaged land took care of the problem for them. The spread of dysentery and diarrhoea primarily caused by the water of the Po killed a third of the Frankish army causing it to withdraw. According to Marcellinus Comes (539.4), Theudibert made an agreement with Belisarius so that he could return his disease-stricken army to Gaul. The Goths and Romans were now able to resume their previous positions.

The end of the siege of Fisula caused by famine solved the problem of the siege of Auximum for Belisarius. The prisoners were paraded in front of the besieged. The Goths were now ready to surrender, but on condition they could leave with their property. However, Belisarius was unwilling to let such good soldiers as defended Auximum join their brethren at Ravenna and he knew that his soldiers were also unwilling to concede the property to the Goths. On the other hand, he also feared that the Franks would soon send another army into Italy to assist the Goths, which required a fast end to the siege. So he suggested a compromise. The solution was that the Goths gave one half of their property to the Romans and joined the Roman army. As a result, Belisarius was now in a position to blockade Ravenna and end the war. For this purpose he also employed two shielding armies to protect the Roman besiegers.

Siege of Ravenna in about late 539/early 540 to May 540[60] (see the Maps section)

With the exception of garrisons posted at strategic locations and two shielding forces, Belisarius assembled the rest of his army to besiege Ravenna. Magnus was dispatched with a large force beyond Ravenna with orders to move along the bank of the river Po to guard it against a possible relief army of Goths from the other side of the river. By then Vitalius had also advanced from Dalmatia with an army to join Belisarius. Belisarius ordered this army to guard the northern bank of the Po for the same purpose. The Romans also had a very lucky break. The Goths had in the meantime collected a large number of boats in Liguria, which they had brought down to the Po, where they had filled these with grain with the idea of sailing them to Ravenna. However, then happened something that nobody remembered as having happened before, namely that the level of the water dropped so much that the river became impossible to navigate. Consequently, when the Romans reached the Po, they were able to capture boats with their cargoes, after which the river became navigable again. The Po may have become impassible in the autumn of 539 and become navigable again as a result of the melting of snow and rainfall in the spring of 540. By then the Goths in Ravenna were already starting to run out of supplies because the Romans had command of the seas.

When the Franks had learnt what had happened, they dispatched envoys to Vittigis with a suggestion that they would assist the Goths if they would divide Italy with them. Belisarius learnt of this from the network of spies and dispatched his own envoys to Vittigis. This embassy included Theodosius, who was the head of Belisarius's household. This shows how important this mission was. Belisarius trusted it to his most trusted man. The Franks bragged that they had not less than 500,000 men who had by then crossed the Alps and that they would bury the entire Roman army with axes. The figure of 500,000 is plausible only for the size of the entire Frankish army, but obviously not for a single campaigning force. Belisarius's envoys responded by stating that the emperor had a greater multitude of soldiers than any of his enemies. They also noted how treacherously the Franks had behaved previously. Vittigis and the Gothic nobility agreed with the Roman view and started negotiations with Belisarius.

The ever cautious Belisarius knew that peace negotiations were one of the means that the ancients had used to lull their enemies into a sense of false security. He did not make this mistake, and remained vigilant. He also ordered Vitalius to march to Venetia with the purpose of bringing to the Roman side as many towns as possible, while he together with Ildiger, who had already been sent forward, guarded both banks of the Po now that Vitalius had been ordered away. Belisarius had also learnt that the Goths still possessed a large amount of grain in storage in public warehouses of Ravenna. He bribed one of the inhabitants of the city to set these warehouses on fire. Procopius does not name the person, but merely states that some people claimed that it was Matasuntha, the wife of Vittigis. This claim appears to be correct, because Procopius had already stated that Matasuntha had been in secret communication with John the nephew of Vitalian when the latter had captured Ariminum. The Goths, however, did not know the truth, so their opinions were divided. Some of them believed there was a plot behind the fire while others believed it was caused by lightning. The latter suggests that the fire took place in the spring of 540. The end result of this was an ever-increasing sense of helplessness because both Vittigis and the nobles no longer trusted in the loyalty of their compatriots.

Being well aware of the threat posed by the Franks Belisarius's next move was to attempt to gain possession of the Cottian Alps where there were several strongholds still in Gothic hands. These garrisons were now ready to surrender. Belisarius sent one of his officers called Thomas to accept their surrender. When Thomas reached the Alps, one of the commanders, Sisigis, duly surrendered to him and urged the other commanders to follow his example. This took place at the same time as Uraias was in the region. He had selected 4,000 men from Ligurians and local garrisons with the intention of marching to relieve Ravenna. When the news of Sisigis's surrender reached them, the men became fearful for their families, so they demanded that Uraias first advance against Thomas. Now Uraias had no other alternative than to besiege Sisigis and Thomas with his entire force. When John the nephew of Vitalian and Martinus, who were very near the Po, learnt of this, they came to the rescue as fast as possible. John and Martinus knew exactly what to do. They captured some of the fortresses in the Cottian Alps, those which housed the families of the men serving in Uraias's army. These women and children were now used as hostages to bring about the desertion of Uraias's soldiers. Uraias and his few remaining men were forced to return to Liguria.

It was then that Justinian's envoys Domnicus and Maximinus, both members of the senate, arrived on the scene. The threat of the Persian invasion had made Justinian ready to seek a compromise peace with the Goths so that he could send Belisarius with reinforcements against the Persians. Vittigis would be allowed to keep the land north of the Po together with half of the royal treasure. Vittigis and the Goths accepted this treaty with great eagerness because they were hard pressed by famine, but this time Belisarius was not prepared to follow the emperor's will. He wanted the glory of having reconquered all of Italy and he wanted to lead Vittigis as a captive to Constantinople. Consequently, when the envoys returned, he refused to sign the treaty. When the Goths learnt of this, they suspected treachery and demanded that Belisarius sign the treaty and take an oath to keep it. As a result of this the commanders criticised Belisarius openly and accused him of plotting against the emperor. Belisarius's response was to assemble his officers together with the emperor's envoys. Belisarius then asked the opinion of his officers. They unanimously supported the emperor and declared that it would be impossible to take Ravenna. Belisarius then asked the officers to put all of this in writing and then sign the document. This they did. This means that at that time Belisarius had already been in secret discussions with the defenders of Ravenna and knew that the city would surrender to him very soon after this. He wanted it to be absolutely clear to everyone that the conquest of Ravenna and Italy was his achievement and his alone.

When these discussions were going on, those Goths who were hostile to Vittigis but unwilling to surrender to the emperor decided to make Belisarius the King/Emperor of the West. They sent envoys to Belisarius secretly and urged him to don the purple robe. Procopius claims that Belisarius was unwilling to become the emperor against the will of Justinian because he loathed the usurpers and because he had taken an oath never to do that. Belisarius therefore made it appear that he accepted their suggestion gladly. It is clear that this discussion must have taken place before the officers signed the document declaring that they could not take the city. When Vittigis learnt of this, he too sent similar messages to Belisarius.

Belisarius was now ready to assemble the envoys and officers again. He asked if the men present would consider the capture of Vittigis and the royal treasure, together with Italy, to be of the greatest importance for the Romans. Their answer was that if that was indeed possible then Belisarius should do that by any means possible. Belisarius sent some of his intimates to Vittigis and nobles. The famine was now so bad that the Goths had no alternative but to surrender. They sent envoys to Belisarius with orders to bring pledges from Belisarius that he would not harm the Goths but would become the Emperor/King of the Goths and Italians. Procopius claims that Belisarius swore everything else except the pledge to become King, which he would swear only in front of Vittigis and the Gothic nobility. Subsequent events show that Belisarius swore this oath too and broke it when it no longer served his interest. But Procopius's idea must have been to present Belisarius in the best light by not making him an oath breaker. In preparation for the taking of the city Belisarius took a series of precautionary steps. He dispatched Bessas, John (the nephew of Vitalian?), Narses and Aratius to different places with the claim that there were not enough supplies for them so they had to feed their armies elsewhere. The recently arrived Praetorian Prefect Athanasius was given similar instructions. The real reason for this was that these men were hostile to Belisarius and could prove to be a hindrance if Belisarius swore the oath of becoming King of the Goths. Once these men had been sent elsewhere, Belisarius was ready to take the city. He ordered a fleet filled with grain and other provisions to sail into the harbour of Classes after which he entered the city. The numerically superior Goths surrendered to the Romans without having fought any decisive battle. This was a masterful achievement and it is no wonder that Procopius also wondered how on earth this could be so. Caesena surrendered at the same time as Ravenna. Belisarius placed Vittigis under guard and sent those Goths who lived south of the river Po back to their homes. This was a safe move because the Goths would be scattered and in the midst of strong Roman garrisons. As a result of this move the Romans were also no longer outnumbered in Ravenna. After this, Belisarius took possession of the money in the Palace for the purpose of carrying it to the emperor, but did not touch the private property of the Goths. Subsequent details given by Procopius prove that Belisarius did not give the entire treasury to the emperor but took a sizable portion of it for himself.[61]

The family triangle of Belisarius, Antonina and Theodosius had continued during the Italian campaign and it was apparently after the Pope Silverius affair that Antonina had become emboldened enough to send messages to Theodosius in Ephesus which urged him to return to her arms. Theodosius's answer was that she needed to get rid of her biological son Photius first because Photius hated to be in Theodosius's presence. According to both John of Ephesus and Procopius, Photius was utterly corrupt and detested anyone who had more influence than he. He was claimed to have plundered as much as 10,000 lbs of gold from the palaces of Carthage and Ravenna. This once again proves how Belisarius and his family enriched themselves illegally with loot and how it was possible for Belisarius to maintain 7,000 bodyguards out of his own pocket. Belisarius must have looted considerably more than his stepson. The sums that the Romans paid for the maintenance of peace with Persia pale in comparison. However, as we shall see, Belisarius's corruption can still be considered patriotic. Antonina was so madly in love with Theodosius that she now started to plot against her own biological son with the result that Photius fled to Constantinople while Theodosius sailed to Italy to be beside his *domina*. According to Procopius, Theodosius there enjoyed the full attention of his mistress Antonina and the simplicity of Belisarius and later accompanied both of them to Constantinople.[62]

When the Gothic commanders of the other major towns learnt of the surrender of Ravenna and Vittigis, they expressed their eagerness to surrender. Belisarius gave his pledges to all, and thereby took over Tarbesium (Treviso) and other strongholds in Venetia. The commanders and their forces duly went to Ravenna where they surrendered to Belisarius. The only one who did not surrender was Ildibadus who commanded the garrison of Verona. He had also dispatched envoys to Belisarius, but only because Belisarius now after the surrender of Ravenna held his children captive. The previous policy of Vittigis to keep the families of the nobles as hostages now served Roman interests.

The actions of Belisarius naturally raised hostility among those who already hated him. These men now accused Belisarius of usurpation. According to Procopius's *Wars*, the emperor recalled Belisarius, not for this reason but for the reason of the Persian war. Regardless, it is still clear that these hostile rumours and the actions of Belisarius made the emperor jealous and resentful, because Belisarius was denied a triumph of the kind that Justinian had previously given Belisarius after the Vandal war. However, according to Marcellinus Comes (539.3–6), the order for Belisarius to return to Constantinople came through the *Magister Officiorum* Marcellus which presumably signalled to Belisarius that he was under suspicion. Justinian ordered Bessas and John nephew of Vitalian, the sworn enemies of Belisarius, to take charge of Italy when Belisarius left. It is therefore clear that Justinian lent his ear to the accusations these men levelled against Belisarius. Constantianus was also ordered to march from Dalmatia to Ravenna, while Bessas marched from Ravenna to Placentia to oppose Ildibadus and Uraias/Oraios (Marcellinus Comes 539.3–6). When the Goths who lived north of Ravenna and of the Po learnt of the summoning of Belisarius they did not pay any heed to it because they assumed that Belisarius would prefer to be the King/Emperor of Italy rather than a subject of Justinian. This proves that Belisarius had indeed assumed the kingship of the Goths and Italy publicly – otherwise it is very difficult to see how he could have sent the Goths living south of the Po to their homes and how the Goths north of the Po believed Belisarius to be their king. There was a good reason why the enemies of Belisarius accused him of usurpation. When the Goths realized that Belisarius was making preparations to leave, the Goths north of the Po asked Uraias to become their king. Uraias refused and suggested that they should make Ildibadus their ruler because he was a brave soldier and because his uncle Theudis, King of the Visigoths, would be sure to assist him. Ildibadus left Verona and was duly clothed in purple, but very soon after having assumed power he changed his mind and asked the Goths to dispatch envoys to Belisarius with the idea of convincing him to remain King of the Goths. The fact that the Romans held his children hostage undoubtedly had a role in this request. The Goths accepted the suggestion and dispatched envoys to Belisarius in which they all promised to surrender if Belisarius kept his promises. It was only after Belisarius flatly refused and departed to Byzantium at the end of the winter of 540/1 that the Goths realised that they had been duped and readied themselves to fight under Ildibadus.

The return of Belisarius to Constantinople[63]

Belisarius took with him Vittigis, notables of the Goths, children of Ildibadus, the royal treasure together with the forces of Ildiger, Valerianus, Martinus and Herodian, and the forces drawn from the ranks of the captured Goths. As usual, as cavalry lancers the last-mentioned proved particularly useful in the forthcoming campaign against the Persians.

Justinian was jealous of the success of Belisarius and probably also angry over the fact that he had disobeyed and it was because of this that Justinian did not grant Belisarius a triumph nor did he bring out the treasure of Theoderic for the common people to gaze at – he only allowed members of the senate to view it in private in the palace. This, however, did not diminish the reputation of the man in the least because his name was on the lips of all, as Procopius describes it. The populace followed Belisarius whenever he went from his house to the market place and back. The procession looked like a festival in which Belisarius was escorted by bodyguards consisting of Vandals, Goths and Moors while the people gazed in amazement. It is unlikely to be a coincidence that Belisarius chose men of these nations as his retinue. He clearly wanted to remind the audience of his successes. According to Procopius, Belisarius was a tall and handsome man, which made the processions eye candy for those who liked that sort of thing. Belisarius also knew how to behave in public. He was amicable to all, and humble so that he seemed like a poor man and not a man of great repute.

Procopius provides us with a very good description of why Belisarius had been so effective as commander during the Vandal and Gothic wars:

‘As commander the love ever felt for him both by the soldiers and peasants was irresistible, seeing that, in his treatment of his soldiers on the one hand, he was unsurpassed in generosity; (for when any had met with misfortune in battle, he used to console them by large presents of money for the wounds they had received, and to those who had distinguished themselves he presented bracelets and necklaces to wear as prizes, and when a soldier had lost in battle horse or bow or anything else … another was … provided in its place by Belisarius); and in his treatment of the peasants … he won their affection because … it never fell to their lot to suffer any violence when Belisarius was general – nay, rather, all those whose land was visited by a large body of troops under his command unexpectedly found that they were enriched; for they always set their own price upon everything sold to the soldiers. And whenever any crops were ripe, Belisarius used to watch closely that the cavalry in passing should not damage any man's grain. Also, when the fruit was ripe on the trees, not a single man was permitted to touch it. Furthermore, he possessed the virtue of self-restraint in marvellous degree; and hence it was that he never would touch any woman other than his wedded wife. [*Procopius highlights the above because these ensured the loyalty of the soldiers and the goodwill of the populace towards Belisarius. The latter was particularly important in defensive wars and also in the reconquest of former Roman territories.*] And so, although he took captive such great numbers of women from both the Vandals and the Goths, and such beautiful women [*Procopius and presumably most of his fellows therefore appreciated the Nordic looking women because this list does not include the Moorish women*]… he refused to allow any of them to come into his presence or meet him in any other way… he was also remarkably shrewd, and in difficult situations he was able with unerring judgment to decide the best course of action. Furthermore, in the dangers of war he was both courageous without incurring unnecessary risks and daring to a degree without losing his cool judgment, either striking quickly or holding back his attack upon the enemy according to the requirements of the situation. Nay more, in desperate situations, on the one hand he showed spirit which was both full of confidence and unmoved by excitement, and in the fullness of success, on the other hand, he neither gave way to vanity nor rushed into indulgence; at any rate no man ever saw Belisarius intoxicated [*this was very rare for soldiers of the time*].

Now as long as he was in command of the Roman army both in Libya and in Italy, he was continually victorious... But when he had been brought back to Byzantium by imperial summons, his ability was recognized still more fully than in previous times and received most generous appreciation. For since by his own outstanding merit in every field he was prominent above all his fellows, and surpassed the generals of all time in the vastness of his wealth [*This means that Belisarius took a very sizable portion of the loot for himself possibly illegally!*] and the number of his *hypaspistai* [*rank-and-file bucellarii*] and *doryforoi* [*officers*], he was naturally looked upon by all officers and soldiers alike as a formidable person. [*This implies that Belisarius used his great wealth and especially his vast numbers of personal bodyguards for the maintenance of discipline in the army.*]. For no one, I am sure, had the hardihood to resist his commands, and his men never refused to carry out whatever orders he gave, both respecting as they did his ability and fearing his power. [*As we have seen, this was only partially true because examples above have shown that Belisarius faced several refusals to obey his commands.*] For he used to equip 7,000 horsemen from his own household, and... each of them could claim to stand first in the line of battle... Indeed, when Rome was beleaguered by the Goths, and the Roman senators were watching... they marvelled greatly and cried out that one man's household was destroying the power of Theoderic.' Procopius, *Wars* 7.1.8–21, tr. by Dewing (pp.153–7), changes and comments by author.

The above demonstrates how Belisarius was able to retain the goodwill of the soldiers and populace for the Roman cause. Belisarius was head-and-shoulders above his fellow officers in generalship and military skills, but he still needed his personal bodyguards to force his will on the quarrelling and greedy officer cadre – and he was not above quarrelling himself. As we have seen Belisarius was himself partially to blame for the problems that he had with his officers, but this was clearly not the only reason why he needed 'muscle' to coerce them to obey his commands. The narrative accounts make it clear that period officers consisted of greedy and disobedient men intent only on personal glorification. Such men had to be forced into line with the threat of violence. Belisarius had these same qualities. He would not have become so rich had he not been so, but in his defence one can say that he was better as a general than anyone of his generation and he also needed the bodyguards bought with this money to force the other officers to obey his commands – the second of the reasons being that Justinian gave Belisarius too few resources so he needed his own. Most importantly, Belisarius was wise enough not to be too greedy. He clearly helped himself only by taking money from the royal treasuries that he had captured; he did not fleece the soldiers or civilians. On the contrary, he was generous towards both and retained their goodwill. This was why he had been able to reconquer both Libya and Italy for the Roman Empire. We need to coin a new term for Belisarius's corruption – it was patriotic corruption.

Chapter Ten

Era of Military Revolts in North Africa in 536–46

The reasons for the mutiny of the Roman army in 536[1]

While Belisarius spent the winter of 535/6 in Syracuse, things were taking an ugly turn in North Africa. The reasons for this were manifold. Many Roman soldiers had married Vandal wives or their daughters when their husbands had either been killed or sent away. These women urged their husbands to demand the return of the lands that they had previously held. Solomon and the emperor did not accept this, because these lands were now added to the imperial domains which were used for the upkeep of state structures. Those that were not had been returned to the mighty men who had lost them previously to the Vandals. The fact that some of the Romans, namely the higher ranking officers, had become unbelievably rich also worked to agitate the soldiers when they themselves had received so little in comparison and also in comparison with the barbarian Vandals who had previously occupied the lands. In addition, the Roman army included about 1,000 men who were of the Arian faith. Most were of barbarian origin and these also included some Heruls. The Vandal priests urged these men to mutiny because they were forbidden to practise their religion. This problem came to boiling point in the Easter period of 536 when the soldiers could not baptize their children nor practise their religion in any way. In addition to this, the Romans had formed five *katalogoi* of cavalry out of the Vandals that Belisarius had taken to the east, the so-called Vandals of Justinian, which served loyally against the Persians in the coming years, but the destiny of the remaining 400 Vandals was different. When they reached the island of Lesbos, they forced their sailors to sail first to the Peloponnesus and from there to a deserted place in Libya, where they abandoned the ships and marched to Mt. Aurasium and Mauretania. The news of their exploits encouraged those soldiers who were planning to mutiny, and so it happened that the Arians decided to launch their revolt during the Easter of 536.

The plotters planned to kill Solomon in the church on the first day of the feast. This time the entire Roman leadership was clueless of what was about to happen because, according to Procopius, the plotters kept their tongues in check despite the fact that the mutiny involved many people. One of the reasons for this was that the plotters included even *doryforoi* and *hypaspistai* of Solomon and most of his domestics/household had also joined the plot because they desired to obtain the lands that their women had previously possessed. Procopius's account makes it clear that the men whose duty it would have been to prevent the plotting were actually the prime movers in the plot. These men were also careful to hide these things from Procopius, who, as I have noted above, was the man charged to conduct spying operations in the area. The fact that so many *bucellarii* and domestics of Solomon joined the revolt suggests that his presence – after all he was a eunuch – did not command the respect of his subordinates. This was not the first example of this happening (see above the battle of Ad Decimum) and neither it was to be the last.

When the appointed day came, the plotters urged each other on and put their hands to their swords, but did nothing for some unknown reason. It would have been dead easy for them to kill Solomon because as bodyguards and domestics they stood right next to him. When the rites were over and everyone was returning to their homes, the plotters started accusing each other, and then agreed to kill Solomon the next day. When the same happened on the following day and the men were departing from the Church, they started accusing each other openly so that the plot was exposed. Then because of this most of them went out of the city as quickly as they could, and started to plunder the Libyans as if they were in enemy territory. Those who remained in the city pretended to be ignorant of the plot. When Solomon finally learnt what was taking place in the countryside, he exhorted the remaining soldiers to remain loyal. However, when on the fifth day the remaining soldiers learnt that their compatriots in the countryside were doing just fine, they gathered in the hippodrome and insulted Solomon and the other commanders without restraint. Solomon sent Theodorus the Cappadocian to the soldiers with orders to win them over with words, but only with the result that these soldiers elected him general because it was known that Theodorus was hostile against Solomon and was suspected of plotting against him. This piece of information suggests that Theodorus may indeed have been party to the plot. The soldiers and Theodorus then marched to the palace where they killed *Comes Excubitorum* Theodorus (there may have been several counts of the Excubitores at this time) and after him everyone they met if he was friendly with Solomon or had money, after which they started to plunder those houses which did not have soldiers billeted in them. This continued until the night when drunkenness put a stop to it.

Solomon managed to save himself by hiding inside the Great Church in the palace. Martinus joined him there in the afternoon and they all, including Procopius, remained in hiding until night. In the darkness of the night, they went into the house of Theodorus the Cappadocian, who forced them all to dine with him, after which he took all of them to the harbour where there was a ship prepared by Martinus. Solomon, Martinus and Procopius then put out from the harbour and when they reached the safety of Misuas, the shipyard of Carthage located about 300 stades (55.5 km) from the city, they stopped. Solomon dispatched Martinus to Numidia to secure the loyalty of Valerianus and other officers there with money or any other means. He also sent a letter to Theodorus the Cappadocian in which he confirmed his de facto position by ordering him to take care of Carthage on behalf of the emperor. In the meantime, he and Procopius sailed to Syracuse to seek help from Belisarius.

Procopius reported that it was in this same year, 536, that a horrible portent took place. The sun stopped shining brightly for a whole year, as if it was an eclipse lasting for a year. This suggests a massive volcanic eruption. In the grim words of Procopius, this was a portent after which the men were not free from war or pestilence or any other unwelcome thing that led to death.

The battle of Membresa/Bagradas River in 536[2]

The rebels who had left Carthage assembled in the plain of Bulla where they chose Stotzas/Stutias, one of the guards of Martinus, as their leader. He assembled all the rebels, which amounted to 8,000 men, and asked the more than 1,000 Vandals who had returned to North Africa to join them. They did so eagerly, as did many slaves because this offered them a chance to liberate themselves. Stotzas led this force against Carthage, but Theodorus and those inside the city declared their loyalty to the emperor and refused to obey him. Theodorus sent Joseph as his envoy to Stotzas. This man was of humble origins, a secretary of the emperor's guards and a member of Belisarius's household who had been sent to Carthage on some mission, as Procopius puts it. It is therefore clear that Joseph was a member of the secretive spy organization and that he had been sent there by Belisarius when he learnt of the revolt. When this Joseph presented the demand that Stotzas should put a stop to the revolt, Stotzas killed him and besieged the city. It was then that Belisarius together with 100 men and Solomon arrived with one ship at about dusk. He arrived in the nick of time because the rebels expected that the city would be surrendered to them on the following day. When they then learnt at daybreak that Belisarius had arrived, they broke their camp and retreated in disorder.

Belisarius gathered 2,000 horsemen and bribed them with large gifts of money to secure their loyalty and then started the pursuit. Belisarius overtook the fugitives at the city of Membresa, 350 stades (c.65 km) from Carthage. Neither side entered the city because it was without walls, so Belisarius built a fortified camp for his army at the River Bagradas while the enemy entrenched itself on the nearby heights. This means that Belisarius managed to isolate the enemy from the best source of water in the area. On the following day both sides deployed for combat opposite each other. Belisarius encouraged the men with a speech, which stressed the justice of their cause – they had come to exact vengeance against the rebels and barbarians who had killed their Roman comrades. He also told them that the enemy was no longer a disciplined force and that it was discipline, order and bravery that brought victory. Stotzas in contrast stressed the fact that they had broken free from the Roman yoke and were now freemen. When the armies were about to fight, a violent wind rose which blew straight into the faces of the rebels. Belisarius clearly knew where to deploy his men and how to exploit the wind, but Stotzas realized right away that he had deployed his army in a position which gave Belisarius's mounted archers an advantage and tried to move his army towards the flank (Procopius unfortunately fails to state which flank). However, this manoeuvre to outflank Belisarius was performed without order with the result that Belisarius gave his men the order to attack immediately. The attack caught the disordered rebels by surprise and they panicked and fled. They continued their flight until they reached Numidia, but their casualties were small and mostly consisted of Vandals. Belisarius did not pursue them as he had too few men for this. The rebel camp was captured without a man inside, but with all the women and money, which were duly given as booty to the soldiers. After this Belisarius returned to Carthage where he learnt that his army in Sicily had revolted. Consequently, Belisarius left Ildiger and Theodorus in charge of Carthage while he sailed back to Sicily. However, since Procopius fails to mention the mutiny of the soldiers in Sicily in his books devoted to the Gothic Wars, it is quite possible that there was no revolt at all, but that Belisarius used this as his excuse for leaving. He would not have wanted to disclose publicly the plan to invade mainland Italy.

The non-battle of Gazophyla in 536[3]

When the Roman commanders in Numidia learnt that the rebels had fled there, they assembled their forces and prepared for battle. The commanders of the *foederati* were Marcellus and Cyril. The commander of the *stratiotai* was Barbatus and the commanders of the infantry were Terentius and Sarapis. The overall commander was Marcellus. If we estimate that each cavalry unit had 400 men, then the total for cavalry was 1,200 horsemen, and if we estimate that each infantry commander had about 1,000 or 2,000 men, then the size of the infantry force was 2,000–4,000 men. Marcellus had learnt that Stotzas was at a place called Gazophyla, two days' march from Constantia, and was assembling there the remnants of his forces. Marcellus's plan was to attack him before he could assemble his entire force. Things, however, did not go as Marcellus had planned, because when the two armies had assembled for combat, Stotzas approached the Romans and spoke to the troops. He reminded the soldiers that the emperor had not paid their salaries, on top of which he had deprived them off their rightful spoils, on top of which there were others who lived in the lap of luxury brought about by their hard work and toil. The soldiers not unnaturally responded with eager shouts of support. When the officers saw this, they fled to the local church of Gazophyla while their men joined the rebels. Stotzas promised the generals safety, but killed them all once they had surrendered.

The above shows nicely what the emperor and the generals did wrong when they had conquered North Africa from the Vandals. They had not paid the soldiers' salaries while they and other upper class figures lived in the lap of luxury right in front of them. Had they done otherwise, it is possible the soldiers would have found it easier to swallow the fact that they had not received the lands previously held by the Vandals. There would certainly have been enough money to pay the soldiers their salaries had the emperor not built so many churches or had he chosen to spend less on luxurious living or had the officers given a part of their spoils to their men.

Germanus takes charge of the war in 536–7[4]

When Justinian learnt of the above disasters, he dispatched his cousin the patrician Germanus with a small army to take charge of the war. It was impossible to send a large army as the reconquest of Italy needed all available resources. Justinian also sent two senators with him. Symmachus replaced the previous prefect, because the latter had died of disease, and Domnicus took command of the infantry forces. On his arrival Germanus made a headcount of how many men he had available for war. When Germanus learnt that he had only about a third of the Roman forces in the cities under imperial control and the enemy had two thirds plus the Moors as allies, he started a propaganda campaign to undermine the loyalty of the enemy forces by stating that he had been sent to Libya by the emperor to defend the soldiers who had been wronged. It is also probable that he had already initiated negotiations with the Moors at this stage to bring about their change of sides which took place later. The ploy to undermine the loyalty of the rebel army worked like a dream and Germanus started to receive a steady flow of deserters from the enemy ranks. When Stotzas realized this, he assembled his men and advanced against Carthage with the aim of fighting a decisive battle. Stotzas built a marching camp

35 stades (6.5 km) from the city and Germanus led his forces out. Thanks to the presence of spies inside the enemy camp Germanus knew exactly what Stotzas was planning so he was able to address his men with exactly the right words: he promised in the name of the emperor pardon for all soldiers for the crimes they had committed. He also noted that he had had no role whatsoever in the wrongdoings that had caused the mutiny. As his final words, Germanus stated that all those who disagreed with him were free to join the enemy.[5] These words undermined whatever promises Stotzas could make.

The armies stood opposite each other for some time, but when the mutineers realized that there were no desertions and Stotzas's promises did not come to fruition, they retreated back to Numidia where they had deposited their women and booty. After a short hiatus during which Germanus had prepared his forces for the march with wagons, Germanus followed after them. The Romans overtook the rebels at Scalae Veteres.

The Roman hero Germanus at the battle of Scalae Veteres (Cellas Vatari) in 537[6]

Germanus deployed his army by using the standard lateral phalanx array with the wagons deployed behind it and the cavalry on the flanks. The infantry phalanx was commanded by Domnicus. The *strategos* Germanus commanded the left wing where he posted the best horsemen that he had brought from Byzantium. The right wing cavalry was not arranged as one body but in three bodies (*lochoi*) under Ildiger, Theodorus the Cappadocian, and the largest under John, brother of Pappus (= John Troglita/Troglyta). The implication is that John led the defenders and the others the *koursores*. We can calculate the size of the army commanded by Germanus on the basis of Procopius's statement that the right cavalry wing consisted of three *lochoi* and on the basis of the battle array used. The three *lochoi* of the right wing mean about 3,000 horsemen on the basis that Procopius equated the *lochos* with a chiliarchy when he discussed the strength of the Vandal army (*Wars* 3.5.18), but obviously with the caveat that one of the three *lochoi* was larger than the rest. Regardless, the equation of *lochos* with the chiliarchy gives us a rough figure for the total so that one may estimate the flank *lochoi* of *koursatores* (runners) to contain about 800 men (2 x 400 horsemen *bandon*) each and the centre *lochos* of *defensores* about 1,200 men (5 x 400 men *bandon*). It is probable that the left wing had about the same number of horsemen so that the total number of horsemen was about 6,000. The use of the standard lateral infantry phalanx with the wagon rear means that it was far more numerous than the cavalry. In such cases the usual relationship between cavalry and infantry forces was that the cavalry consisted at most of a quarter to a third of the entire force with the implication that the infantry consisted of at least about 10,000–12,000 footmen.

The mutineers took their stand opposite, not in the manner of the Romans but in the scattered formation of the barbarians.[7] Along with the mutineers followed myriads of Moors who were posted behind under a number of leaders of whom the most notable were Iaudas and Ortaias – this proves that it had been Ortaias who had previously attempted to mislead the Romans into destruction. The Moors had already promised to Germanus that they would betray the rebels. It is probable that the rebel force still consisted of the same number as previously, namely of 9,000 horsemen and the freed slaves with the probable addition of some Roman infantry, because even if they had received deserters after that the generosity of Germanus had caused most of these deserters to flock back to the emperor's side.[8] Procopius's reference to the use of the barbarian formation implies that Stotzas posted his entire cavalry force at the front, and left whatever infantry he had behind to guard the camp.[9] When Stotzas was about to attack Germanus, the Heruls prevented it and persuaded him to attack the men of John while others faced Germanus. The advice proved well founded because Stotzas with the Heruls routed the men of John with their wild charge. After this, Stotzas divided his victorious wing in textbook manner so that some of his men pursued the fugitives while the rest attacked the flank of the Roman infantry that had already began to disintegrate when they saw their horsemen in flight. However, on the other side of the field, Germanus with his elite cavalry had routed his opponents and then attacked the flank and rear of Stotzas's men while Ildiger and Theodorus regrouped their men and counter-attacked. This resulted in great confusion because Germanus's forces that attacked from the rear, Stotzas's forces in the middle and John's regrouped forces were all equipped in like manner and spoke the same language. This suggests general uniformity in equipment that could result only from standardized production. However, Germanus had already solved the problem in advance by requiring his men to ask everyone they captured the watchword. The confusion also enabled one of the enemy horsemen to approach Germanus unnoticed and kill his mount. Germanus fell to the ground, but his bodyguards saved his life by forming a protective cordon around him and then gave him a new mount. It is clear that many men died needlessly in this confusion, but it did not change the end result. When attacked from two directions the rebel force collapsed and started to flee. The confusion also enabled Stotzas to flee to the camp.

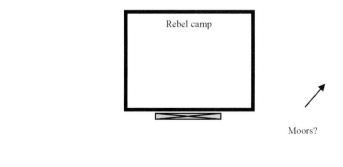

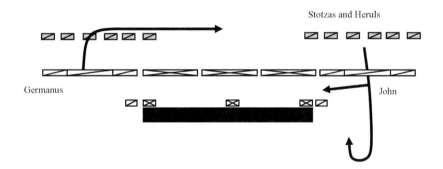

After the enemy's wing had collapsed, Germanus directed his men towards the rebels' camp where the enemy had fled. The rebel infantry put up a spirited resistance at one of the entrances and came close to forcing the Roman army back, but Germanus sent some of his followers to attack the camp from another position. These men found an undefended point in the defences and penetrated into the camp. According to Corippus, the leader of these men was John Troglita who charged into the enemy camp with sword in hand and slaughtered the enemies. When the mutineers saw these men inside the camp, they panicked and fled with the result that Germanus and his men dashed inside. It was at this point that Germanus lost control of most of his men who charged inside to loot and pillage without any order despite the pleas of Germanus. In desperation Germanus together with a few of his men took a stand in front of one of the entrances to protect his men inside. When the rebels had lost their camp, the desperate Stotzas rode towards the Moors who now showed their true nature and betrayed him. When this happened Stotzas fled, but was still able to regroup some of his men for one final attempt, that failed. This shows that Germanus still had enough men left who obeyed his orders. The rebels were crushed and the remnants changed sides so that Stotzas was forced to flee with only a handful of men to Mauritania. The desertion of the Moors ensured the total destruction of the rebels. The Moors joined the Romans in the looting of the camp. The fact that Germanus allowed his men and Moors to keep the loot they had taken from the enemy camp was a wise decision. The other commanders in North Africa were not quite as sensitive to the needs of the moment. Germanus, however, was. He knew what had caused the troubles and how to keep his men happy. However, his own troubles were not yet over.

The conspiracy at Carthage in about 538/9[10]

When Germanus returned to Carthage he faced a conspiracy initiated by a certain Maximinus, who was a bodyguard of Theodorus the Cappadocian. He managed to gather around him a large following of collaborators who sought to raise this Maximinus as their emperor. However, then he made the fatal mistake of confiding his plan to Asclepiades of Palestine who then exposed the plot to his friend Theodorus and then to Germanus. Germanus decided to get rid of the conspirators with a ruse. He summoned Maximinus, praised him for his bravery and asked him to join his bodyguards, which was a high honour and likely to lead to higher commands. Consequently, he was enrolled among the *bucellarii* of Germanus.

Then at about lunch time during some general festival when Germanus was entertaining his friends and Maximinus was standing beside the couches with the other bodyguards, some of Maximinus's followers advanced before the door of the palace where they claimed that the government owed them their pay for a long period. This suggests that the soldiers had once again been left without their payments. When this information was brought to Germanus, he ordered his most trusty guards to keep a close watch on Maximinus so he would not realize what was happening. When the conspirators were unable to enter the palace they ran to the Hippodrome where their fellows joined them. They were expecting that Maximinus would soon arrive there to lead them against Germanus. This suggests a probability that Germanus had manipulated these men to take this action, for example by using Asclepiades, because it is clear that Maximinus and some others of his followers were unaware of what was taking place. Germanus had prepared a trap for the men who had entered the Hippodrome, which was launched when enough of them had entered it. The conspirators panicked. Most were killed and those who surrendered were brought before Germanus. Maximinus and presumably also those who had been captured were impaled near the fortifications of Carthage as a warning, but Germanus did not make any search for those conspirators who had not entered the Hippodrome presumably because this could have led to further disturbances.

Soon after this the emperor summoned Germanus together with Symmachus and Domnicus back to the capital to receive their well deserved reward. It seems probable that he took with him the forces that he had brought to Libya, because Solomon arrived with another army.

Solomon's second command in 539–44

Justinian once again put Solomon in charge of Libya in about 539 now that the crisis had been solved by Germanus. He gave Solomon an army and officers to enable him to perform his duty. The officers included Rufinus, Leontius, Zaunas, and John son of Sisiniolus. According to Procopius, Solomon ruled Libya with moderation and defended it well, but on close inspection this is not true but rather an expression of Procopius's own view or his attempt to endear himself with those who held a positive view of Solomon. My own suggestion is that Solomon was a member of the same secretive spy organization as Procopius, because Solomon was clearly tasked with a mission to purge the army of suspect elements. Solomon sent all suspect elements either to Belisarius or to Constantinople, and then enrolled new men into the army to replace them. He also collected all remaining Vandals, especially the women, and removed them from Libya. All of the cities were now surrounded with walls and the laws were strictly implemented.

Solomon's second campaign on Mt. Aurasium in 540[11]

In 540, Solomon was again ready to face the Moors. Solomon put Gontharis, one of his own bodyguards, in charge of the vanguard. When Gontharis reached Abigas River, he built a camp near the deserted city of Bagaïs, but was then defeated by the Moors so he had to flee back to his camp. Solomon, who followed in his footsteps, pitched his camp at 60 stades' (c.11 km) distance from Gontharis and sent a detachment (of horse?) to his rescue. The Moors shut off all the water channels so that the whole stream flowed into the Roman camp, but Solomon arrived next day in the nick of time to save his vanguard. The Moors fled and pitched their camp at Babosis, at the foot of Mt. Aurasium. Solomon followed, engaged the Moors and defeated them decisively.

The Moors scattered. Most escaped to Mauritania or the desert south of Mt Aurasium, but Iaudas and 20,000 Moors stayed behind. Iaudas retreated to the fortress of Zerboule on Mt Aurasium. Solomon did not want to besiege the place but marched his army to the grain fields of the city of Tamougade with the idea of forcing the enemy into surrender by ravaging the surrounding territory and burning the grain to starve his enemy into submission. Iaudas left a garrison at Zerboule and fled to Toumar (a very rocky place) before the Romans returned. The Romans then besieged Zerboule for three days using their bows. It is clear that the army was very proficient in the use of archery since the arrows killed all the leaders of the Moors. The Moors quietly left the fortress during the night unbeknownst to the Romans, which means that they had not surrounded the place effectively. The Romans found this out the following morning, when they were planning to march on foot towards Toumar. The terrain was clearly not favourable for this, and Roman cavalrymen detested marching on foot. The fort of Zerboule was garrisoned so that the Moors would not be able to reoccupy it.

The terrain around Toumar favoured the defenders.[12] The Romans had to encamp in so bad a position that they had to limit the water ration to one cupful per man per day. After a while the soldiers started openly showing their discontent, but this Solomon managed to calm them with words. While Solomon was pondering how to take the fort in these circumstances, he had a lucky break. A certain Gezon, an *optio* of the *katalogos* to which Solomon belonged (does this refer to the spies or to the *bucellarii* of Belisarius? The former is probably likelier), began to make the ascent alone and he was followed by some of his comrades. Three Moorish guards came to confront him. The narrowness of the path allowed him to dispatch them one at a time. When those who were following Gezon saw this, they advanced with much shouting. And when the rest of the Roman army heard this, they too joined the disorderly attack without waiting for orders. The Roman army ran against the enemy's camp, and the Moors were so terror-stricken that they did not attempt to defend themselves but fled. A javelin wounded Iaudas in the thigh, but he still managed to flee to Mauritania. After plundering the camp and surrounding area, Solomon built fortresses which he then garrisoned so as to make Mt. Aurasium inaccessible to the Moors. This campaign demonstrates quite well that the Romans possessed military superiority both in the open and in difficult terrain against the Moors.

After Toumar had been taken, the Romans searched the rough country of Aurasium to find where the fugitives and their treasury were. During one such search the Romans arrived at a location which the natives called the Rock of Geminianus which was a perpendicular rock surrounded by rock faces that had a single tower built on it. Unbeknownst to the Romans, a few days before Iaudas had deposited his money and women there under the care of an old Moor. One Roman soldier attempted to climb the cliff and the women and the old man taunted the soldier that he was attempting something impossible. The soldier however, using both his hands and feet, climbed and then leaped forward as quickly as he could and cut off the head of the old man with a sword. When the head fell on the ground, the rest of the Roman soldiers were encouraged. They held one another and ascended to the tower and captured both the women and the money. Solomon used this money well. It was used for the building of the walls for several cities.

When all of the Moors had then been forced to flee from Numidia, Solomon added a new province to the Empire, which was called the land of Zabe beyond Mt. Aurasium, and which received the name First Mauretania with a metropolis located at Sitifis. With the exception of Caesarea, Mauretania Caesarensis remained in Moorish hands under the chief Mastigas. It was because of this that the Romans had to travel to Caesarea on ships.

The battle of Tebeste in 544[13]

The next four years were peaceful, but then in 543 the plague arrived and resulted in a massive disaster in which not only Roman civilians died, but large numbers of soldiers as well. It is also clear that this destroyed the local tax base. It is probable that this was one of the root causes of the disasters that followed. However, according to Procopius the main cause was actually a decision made by Justinian. He sent the sons of Solomon's brother Bacchus to take charge of some of the cities in Libya. Cyrus, the eldest of the brothers, became the ruler of Pentapolis (Cyrene), and the youngest, Sergius, was given charge of Tripolis. The third brother, Solomon the Younger, was also sent there, but Procopius does not state which area he ruled. The Moorish confederacy called Leuathae or Laguatan marched before Leptis Magna with the purpose of obtaining the customary gifts and insignia of office in return for peace and alliance. Pudentius, however, persuaded Sergius to invite eighty leading Laguatans inside the city while the rest would stay in the suburbs. These men were invited to a banquet. Procopius states that it was claimed that these eighty men had come inside the city with treacherous intent and that their real plan was to kill Sergius. When the men had assembled at the banquet, the Moors charged that the Romans were guilty of wrongdoings and that they had plundered their crops. It was then that Sergius rose up with the intent of leaving the banquet. One of the Moors grabbed his shoulder to prevent him leaving which in turn led one of the bodyguards of Sergius to draw his sword and kill the Moor. This led to an uproar among the banqueters after which Sergius's bodyguards killed all of the Moors except one who managed to flee unnoticed.

There are three possible explanations for what happened. Firstly, it is possible that the Moors indeed had hostile intent, but this is the least likely of the alternatives. Secondly, it is possible that the whole incident was just an accident resulting from the fact that Sergius's bodyguard protected his employer. This is a possible scenario, but not as likely as the third one which Procopius does not mention even if he does imply it with the reference to Pudentius's role in these matters. The third alternative is that the Romans had from the start planned to assassinate the entire tribal leadership at the banquet and had invited them for this purpose. This is indeed a clever way to get rid of the enemy leadership, but this begs the question why would it have been in Roman interest to destroy the Laguatan leadership when the Laguatans were Roman allies. Furthermore, it begs the question why was such an action undertaken without the prior acceptance of Justinian, if that indeed was the case. One possible answer is that the Roman leadership, or at least Pudentius and Sergius, considered the Laguatans to be too powerful for their own good and that they had to be destroyed before they grew even more powerful.

The one Moor who managed to escape from the massacre warned his comrades who then duly took up their arms and advanced before Leptis Magna. The Romans in their turn marched out of the city and engaged the enemy in hand-to-hand combat which ended in Roman victory. This is not surprising in light of the fact that the Romans were better equipped, better protected and better trained and almost all of the enemy leaders had just been massacred. The Romans plundered the enemy camp and captured large numbers of women and children, but then in the midst of the joy came sad news. Pudentius had pursued the enemy too recklessly and was killed. After this, Sergius led his army back inside the city because it was becoming dark.

Unsurprisingly the end result of the Roman treachery was the uprising of the Laguatan Confederacy against their overlords, and this time the Confederates collected a massive army. As if this would not have sufficed, Solomon had also managed to turn Antalas into an enemy. Solomon had denied the customary payments and had had his brother killed. According to Corippus, the real reason for the revolt of Antalas was the killing of his brother and that he only delayed his revolt because he was still too frightened to attack the Romans in 543 because they were suffering from the plague and there existed a danger that the Moors could also be infected with it.

The denial of subsidies suggests a policy decision made at the top, by which I mean the emperor, but obviously this is not conclusive because such decisions could also have been made at the local level. It would seem that the root problem was the plague which had entered the Roman Empire from Egypt in 541 and which had then resulted in the loss of revenue, which in its turn caused economising in salaries and in payments to the allies. In North Africa this had disastrous consequences. The state certainly had enough money to bribe the Moors had it decided to tap the money of the wealthy citizens for this purpose. Antalas became the leader of the Laguatan Confederacy.

When the news of the uprising was brought to the authorities it forced the Romans to assemble all of their available forces from the cities of Pentapolis up to Carthage. According to the version preserved in Procopius, when the news of the trouble was brought to Sergius, he marched to join his uncle. When they then joined forces, he found that his brother Cyrus had already arrived before him. This is an odd detail, because Procopius had previously stated that Cyrus was the ruler of Pentapolis (Cyrene), and implies that he had been marched to the scene of operations past his brother. Solomon marched the united Roman force against Antalas and engaged the Moors close to the city of Tebeste at a distance of six days' march from Carthage. Solomon, Cyrus, Sergius and Solomon the Younger pitched a marching camp on the site. Solomon was frightened by the size of the enemy host and suggested peace negotiations. The Moors mocked him because they no longer trusted Roman oaths after what Sergius had done. So on the following day Solomon attacked a party of Moors who were carrying booty and defeated them. After this, he committed an unforgivable plunder. He kept the plunder under guard and did not distribute to the soldiers their share of it because he claimed that it should be distributed only after the war was over. This answer did not satisfy the greedy soldiers. The Moors then attacked with their main army and lured the Romans to follow them into a forest. It was then that the Roman soldiers showed their dissatisfaction so that some of them stayed behind while the rest entered the combat without any enthusiasm. According to Corippus, Gontharis was one of those who betrayed Solomon in this battle. At first the two sides were equal, but in the end the Moors' superior numbers gave them victory. The Romans fled and left Solomon and those nearest him behind. Solomon and his men held out for a while, but eventually Solomon was forced to flee. When Solomon reached a ravine, his horse stumbled and threw him to the ground. His bodyguards lifted him up and placed him on his horse, but the fall had injured him so badly that he was unable to hold the reins, with the result that the Moors overtook him and many of his guards and killed them. Solomon the Younger was at the same time captured by the Moors, but they did not know who they had captured.

Sergius in Charge in 544[14]

The death of Solomon left Sergius in charge of North Africa and his position was confirmed by Justinian. According to Procopius, Sergius was the man who bore the blame for the disasters that ruined the people of Libya. In his opinion Sergius was young in both character and in years and exceptionally stupid. Procopius also calls him the greatest braggart who insulted his subordinates for no reason and disregarded others by using his official position and personal wealth as excuses for doing so. The soldiers disliked him intensely because he was unmanly and weak, and the Libyans disliked him for the same reasons and also because he proved himself strangely fond of the wives and the possessions of others. Most importantly, John the son of Sisiniolus hated him intensely because Sergius failed to reward him for his services even though he had proven himself an able warrior with unblemished repute. Because of this John and the other military men were unwilling to fight on behalf of Sergius against the enemy. And this in a situation in which Antalas had summoned Stotzas to join him and both were ravaging the territory unhindered. Antalas wrote directly to Justinian to explain why he had revolted. Antalas put the blame squarely on Sergius and Solomon. Antalas complained that Sergius and Solomon had treated him unfairly and had not given him and his people the payments promised by Belisarius, on top of which Solomon had murdered his brother. He promised to end the revolt if Sergius was recalled and another general sent to replace him. Justinian, however, even after he had learnt that Sergius's subordinates hated him and Antalas was prepared to surrender, still decided to keep Sergius in office.

While these things were taking place, Solomon the Younger managed to convince his captors that he was a Vandal by birth and that his friend in the city of Laribus would be willing to ransom him. The Moors bought the story and Solomon's friend Physician Pegasius ransomed him with fifty gold coins. Once inside the fortifications Solomon started to insult his captors for being stupid as they had just released Solomon the son of Bacchus. This proved in fact to be very stupid of Solomon. The Moors assembled their men and besieged Laribus, which lacked adequate supplies to withstand a siege. The Moors, however, did not know that and since they were themselves poor besiegers they accepted the ransom of 3,000 pieces of gold in return for ending the siege. It is likely that Procopius includes this episode because it demonstrates well that not only Sergius was stupid but that also his brother Solomon the Younger can be included in this category. It proved very costly for his saviours to have ransomed him. Antalas and his Moors and Stotzas with his soldiers and Vandals were once again assembling in Byzacium for the purpose of continuing their ravages. Procopius and Corippus provide us with two slightly different versions of what happened next.

According to Procopius, the Libyans begged John the son of Sisiniolus to intervene, and this time he agreed despite his hatred of Sergius. John assembled his men and marched against the enemy. He ordered Himerius/Himerus the Thracian, the commander of the *katalogoi* in Byzacium, to bring his men and all the commanders of the *katalogoi* to a place called Menephesse, which was located at Byzacium, and join forces with him. However, when John learnt that the enemy had reached the area first and was encamped there, he sent another letter to Himerius and directed him to another place. This letter, however, did not reach him with the result that Himerius and his men were captured. The only

Roman who fought was Severianus, son of Asiaticus, a Phoenician and native of Emesa. He was a commander of a *katalogos* of fifty men. He and his men engaged the numerically superior enemy and were forced to flee to a hilltop where there was a fort. Once they realized that their position was hopeless, they too surrendered. The Moors kept Himerius under guard, but gave all his men to Stotzas who united them into his forces. The Moors forced Himerius to help them to gain possession of the city of Hadrumentum on the sea. The Moors used a ruse. Himerius and some of the soldiers of Stotzas were sent in advance and they dragged in chains what appeared to be Moorish captives. Himerius was the commander (archon) of the *katalogoi* of Byzacium so the men in charge of the gates opened them when Himerius ordered them to do so. Once inside the men drew their swords and forced the guards to leave the gates open so that the entire Moorish army was able to enter. The Moors duly sacked the city, after which they left some guards behind and departed. At this stage some of those who had been captured by the Moors managed to flee to Carthage because it was not difficult to flee from the Moors if one wanted to, as stated by Procopius. Those who escaped included Himerius and Severianus.

According to Corippus, the capture of Himerius/Himerus was the result of a skilful ruse by Stotzas. He sent Sinon with a letter which claimed to come from John to Himerius who was headquartered at Hadrumentum. It ordered Himerus to march to a plain where Stotzas and Moors had placed an ambush. When the men neared the place, Sinon went in advance to inform the ambushers who duly surrounded the Romans when they arrived. The Romans fled to a nearby fortress where the horsemen dismounted and formed a circle. Stotzas approached them and managed to convince the Romans to join his forces. The Romans then helped Stotzas and Moors to take Hadrumentum. After that the storyteller in Corippus, who is claimed to be Liberatus, one of the men captured (Corippus 2.52ff.), and many of his comrades, decided to return to their own standards in small groups. Liberatus fled and was united with his wife, and so did his friend Maturius and others separately. Hadrumentum was then retaken when a friendly citizen opened a gate for the Roman army.

The discrepancy between Corippus and Procopius is easy to explain with the fact that Corippus provided an eyewitness account by a local officer called Liberatus while Procopius had access to information which recorded the actions of the high command at Carthage which was not made available to Libyans. The other discrepancy in their accounts would be the result of Procopius's hero Severianus fleeing to another place while the main force fled elsewhere.

Procopius provides us with a longer account of how Hadrumentum was retaken. Soon after this, one of the priests called Paulus, who had been put in charge of caring for the sick, came up with a plan to liberate the city. He conferred his plan with the local nobles and promised to bring an army to the rescue. He was lowered into a fishing vessel which then sailed to Carthage. Once in the city the priest asked Sergius to send a large army to recover the city, but Sergius was not pleased because he did not have that many men in the city. Paulus then begged Sergius to give him at least some soldiers. Sergius gave only eighty men. The ever-resourceful Paulus formulated a plan how to overcome his lack of resources. He collected ships (ships/*neōn* and small merchant galleys/*akatoi*) and loaded them with Libyan civilians dressed in Roman military uniforms. After this he sailed at full speed for Hadrumentum. When he reached a place close by he anchored the ships and sent some men inside the city secretly to inform the local nobles that the emperor had sent his cousin Germanus to Carthage and that Germanus had now dispatched a substantial army to help the citizens of Hadrumentum. The nobles were to open a small gate for them the following night. The nobles did this and Paulus and his men got inside. They then duly killed all the Moors and recovered the city for the emperor. Paulus the priest had shown himself a better commander than the professional Roman commanders whose duty it would have been to defend and recover such cities, and it is probably at least partly because of this that Procopius dwells upon the details of this incident. Paulus's story gained a life of its own. Soon after this the Carthaginians and others learnt that Germanus had arrived. The fame of Germanus was such that Antalas and Stotzas became frightened and fled to their hideouts, but when they learnt the truth, they thought that they had made a terrible mistake in sparing the citizens of Hadrumentum. Consequently, when they resumed their raiding, they no longer spared anyone regardless of age or sex, but killed all. This calculated campaign of terror caused the Libyans to flee to the cities or islands, which only emboldened the Moors and Stotzas even more. According to Procopius, almost all of the nobles, Paulus among them, fled to Byzantium (Constantinople). The flight of Paulus and those who assisted him can be excused on the grounds that they had committed such an act that would mean their death if ever captured by the Moors or Roman turncoats serving under Stotzas, and the fact that the Roman army stayed inactive during this entire time must have frightened them. However, for the rest of the nobility there is no excuse. They acted like rats leaving a sinking ship and left the defence of their homes in the hands of the poor Libyans. John son of Sisiniolous remained inactive thanks to his personal hostility towards Sergius.

Diarchy: Areobindus and Sergius in 544–46[15]

After he had heard of the disasters from the refugees Justinian resorted to compromise which ended up satisfying no-one. He dispatched Areobindus together with some soldiers to Carthage, and with him Athanasius who had just arrived from Italy to serve as his prefect. He was accompanied by some Armenians led by Artabanes and John, both sons of John and of the royal Arsacid line. These two Armenians had just defected from the Persians. The idea was undoubtedly to send them to a place from which they could not desert back to the Persian side. Areobindus was a senator and descendant of the famous Gothic namesake generals, but unlike them he was not at all skilled in matters of warfare. See *MHLR* vols. 3–5. He was accompanied by his sister and by his wife who was a daughter of Vigilantia, the sister of Justinian. It is therefore clear that he had received his command as a result of his family relations.

The problem with this was that Justinian did not recall Sergius but gave the two commanders equal powers. Sergius was put in charge of Numidia and Areobindus in charge of the war in Byzacium. The resulting diarchy did not work because the two men failed to cooperate and coordinate their efforts, which meant that the Roman efforts were paralyzed. When Areobindus then learnt that Antalas and Stotzas were encamped near the city of Siccaveneria three days' march from Carthage, he ordered John the son of Sisiniolus to choose the most warlike from the soldiers present and then advance against the foe. At the same time he asked Sergius to unite his men with those of John, but

Sergius did not pay any attention to him. The end result was that John was forced to engage the enemy alone with only those forces that he had which were too small for the task.

The battle of Siccaveneria or Thacia in 545[16]

What happened next is described by Procopius and Corippus, but the latter offers us a far more detailed account of what happened, clearly based on an eyewitness account. On the basis of Procopius and Corippus the principal reasons for the readiness of John son of Sisionolus to engage the enemy were the command of Areobindus and his personal hatred of Stotzas. Procopius places the battle at Siccaveneria while Victor Tonnensis places it at Thacia (Thaciae, Taceae, Taccae), which is located 38 km from Siccaveneria.

Corippus divides the battle into three distinctive phases.[17] When the armies came face-to-face with each other they were separated by river, behind which lay a plain, and behind it hills. Initially the Moors used the river as their line of defence. John and his *duces* led an attack against the enemy which failed and the Romans were forced to flee, but were then regrouped by John who encouraged them with a speech (4.103–135). It is possible that this was actually a Roman attempt to lure the enemy to cross the river, and if it was, it worked. Now the Moors crossed the river and the Roman cavalry shot at it a volley of arrows. The Moors feigned flight and John pursued with his men. It was then that the rebels under Stotzas launched their ambush from a nearby valley and caused the rout of the army. In pure hatred, John advanced without noting the flight of his men and attacked Stotzas. His idea was also to keep the men in the field with his personal example. John killed Stotzas with a well-placed shot to the groin. According to Corippus, the arrow penetrated the bone marrow and went through so far that even the feathers disappeared into the flesh. Stotzas and John both knew that the wound was fatal. Stotzas, who was transfixed to his horse, turned it and fled, after which his comrades lifted him up to rest beneath the thick leaves of a tree from which he observed the battle. It was then that John looked back and saw that his own men were fleeing. He galloped after them and tried to convince them to return to the battle but failed. The river which the Romans had crossed turned the defeat into disaster because it slowed down the fugitives so that large numbers of them were cut down in the riverbed. John himself died when his horse stumbled in this ravine and he was unable to mount it in time to save his life. John the brother of Artabanes died in this battle. Corippus has preserved for us the survival story of one Roman officer whose name was Marturius, who fought his way through the enemy with his men. When Justinian learnt of the disaster, he realized his mistake and recalled Sergius, and put Areobindus in charge of the whole of Libya. The rebels appointed still another John as successor of Stotzas.

The events of this battle may suggest the use of a single cavalry line but this is uncertain because it is equally possible that the Romans deployed two cavalry lines and that when the first attack had failed it had been united with the second line by assuming its place in the interval (if there were two reserve units) or on both sides of the single reserve unit if the Romans employed only one reserve unit. The battle was an unmitigated disaster for the Romans. They had lost their best commander and most of their best men.

The plot thickens: Gontharis/Guntarith assassinates Areobindus in 545[18]

It was at this point in time that Gontharis, who was the commander of the *katalogoi* of Numidia, and his closest friend, confidant and advisor Pasiphilus both started to dream of the possibility that Gontharis could become either King or *Magister* of Libya. Gontharis convinced the Moors of Numidia, who were commanded by Cusina and Iaudas, and the Moors of Byzacium who were commanded by Antalas, to march against Carthage. The Roman rebels under their new leader John marched in the army of Antalas. Gontharis appears to have communicated only with Antalas who then convinced the other Moorish leaders to join him. When the Moors advanced towards Carthage, Areobindus ordered Gontharis and other commanders to retreat to Carthage for its defence just as Gontharis had expected.

According to Procopius, Gontharis at first had sent one of his servants, a cook, who was a Moor, to Antalas. Gontharis promised to share Libya with Antalas. Antalas answered that such matters are not discussed with cooks. This must have happened before the Moors began their advance. Gontharis then sent his trusted bodyguard Ulitheus who then promised Antalas that he would receive Byzacium together with the half of the money of Areobindus and 1,500 Roman soldiers while Gontharis would rule Carthage and the rest of Libya as a king. After this Ulitheus returned to Carthage where the Roman army had been encamped in front of the city walls to protect its gates so that each commander was responsible for one of its nine gates.[19] The Moors acted as promised and marched to Ad Decimum where they pitched their camp, and then on the following day continued their march towards the city itself. It was then that some Romans surprised and killed a small number of Moors with the result that Gontharis ordered them to retreat after which he reprimanded them for their reckless daring – this was obviously only his excuse in this situation.

In the meantime, Areobindus had not been idle but had managed to convince the half-Roman Cusina to betray his fellow Moors[20] so that he would suddenly turn against Antalas in the middle of a combat. Areobindus reported this to Gontharis who was naturally worried about it. However, he managed to convince Areobindus that he should demand the children of Cusina as hostages because the Moors were inherently unreliable, with the idea of delaying the alliance. Gontharis in turn warned Antalas of this, but the latter chose not to act upon it, quite possibly because he did not fully trust Gontharis. There always existed the possibility that the Romans could attempt to turn the Moors against each other. Antalas was a player who did not trust anyone. This is Byzantine plotting at its best. Gontharis's plan was to have Areobindus killed by the Moors so that it would appear as if he had been compelled to become the *strategos* because the soldiers demanded it. With this in mind, Gotharis convinced Areobindus to lead the army out against the Moors on the following day. The plan failed, because Areobindus did not have any experience of military matters and therefore spent the entire day in the making of preparations with the result that the battle was postponed to the next day. This delay frightened Gontharis into thinking that Areobindus had discovered his plan with the result that he decided to revolt openly against him.

On the following day, Gontharis opened the gates that had been entrusted to him, placing a huge rock to make it impossible to close them, placing armoured men with bows on the parapet to protect them, and then took a stand between the gates. Gontharis's plan was not to invite the Moors inside the city – because he knew that they did not trust the Romans and were therefore unwilling to do so – but to make Areobindus believe that he had done so so that Areobindus would flee from the city and leave it to him. According to Procopius, it was the winter (of 544/5) that frustrated this plan. This implies that the weather was not suitable for sailing so Areobindus feared that more than he did Gontharis. Consequently Areobindus assembled Athanasius, some of the notables together with Artabanes and two other commanders. These encouraged Areobindus to attack Gontharis immediately with all their men. However, Areobindus the coward rather sent one of his friends called Phredas to test Gotharis, and it was only after this had failed that he ordered his men to prepare for battle.

In the meantime, Gontharis had undermined the loyalty of the soldiers by calling Areobindus a coward who was just intent on fleeing in a ship at the first opportunity while the soldiers died for the state. He also stated that Areobindus was responsible for the fact that they had not received their salaries and that Areobindus was also unwilling to pay them, but that he, Gotharis, would pay their salaries from his own pocket. This is once again a good example of the foolish behaviour of the emperor and top brass. The emperor economized on salaries preferring to spend money on unnecessary building projects (e.g. most of the new churches or monasteries). Moreover the nobility were so wealthy that a single notable like Gontharis would have been able to pay the salaries that the state owed to the men. Areobindus and his wife certainly possessed enough personal wealth to be able to pay the salaries if needed, but chose not to. It was this attitude that made it possible for a succession of rebels to foment mutinies. Areobindus and Artabanes then arrived and attacked Gontharis and his men at the gate and parapet where they had taken their stand. The battle was even, but the mutineers faced certain defeat because the Romans who had stayed loyal were leaving their camps and marching to the scene of combat to crush the revolt. But then Areobindus, who had never seen any combat or bloodletting, lost his composure completely and fled from the scene of combat because he could not endure the sight. He fled to the walled monastery which had been built by Solomon by the seashore where he had left his wife and sister. When Artabanes saw this, he and the rest of the soldiers fled from Carthage as best they could while Gontharis took control of the city.

Athanasius managed to save himself by flattering the usurper, who considered Athanasius to be no threat to him because Athanasius was already an old man. However, Athanasius was cleverer than he looked and appears to have started to hatch a plot to kill Gontharis at the first possible opportunity. Gontharis managed to convince Areobindus to abandon his safe haven with the help of a priest called Reparatus who took an oath that Gontharis would spare Areobindus. At first it appeared as if Gontharis would do so because he gave a dinner in honour of Areobindus, but when the night came he sent Ulintheus and others to kill him in his bedchamber. Pasiphilus had advised Gontharis to do this so that Gontharis could then blame Ulintheus while claiming innocence. Gontharis then forced Areobindus's widow Prejecta/Praeiecta to write to Justinian that Gontharis had not approved the murder. The deluded Gontharis thought that Justinian would then appoint him *magister* of Libya and allow him to marry Prejecta. Gontharis was a heavy drinker and it is not impossible that he had drunk a few too many glasses of wine for his own good.

On the day after the killing of Areobindus, Gontharis dispatched the severed head of Areobindus to Antalas, but then refused to hand over the money and the soldiers. Antalas was furious. He had been double-crossed. Antalas left Carthage immediately and decided to support Justinian. When he learnt that Marcentius, who was commander of the *katalogoi* of Byzacium, had fled to one of the islands, he allied himself with him so that Marcentius joined his army. The soldiers at Hadrumentum also stayed loyal to the legitimate government. However, when the Roman rebels under John realized what was happening, they left Antalas and went to Carthage where they pledged loyalty to Gontharis. At this point, these rebels consisted of not less than 1,000 men: 500 Romans, about eighty Huns and the rest Vandals. The Moors of Cusina also separated from Antalas, which is not surprising in light of their previous agreement with Areobindus, which Gontharis now used to his own benefit by allying himself with Cusina against Antalas. Gontharis also sent envoys to Artabanes and managed to convince him to return to Carthage. Procopius makes Artabanes the principal mover in the plot to kill Gontharis, and claims that Artabanes confided his plans with his nephew Gregorius and his bodyguard Artasires. However, it is likely that Corippus is here correct to claim that the primary mover was Athanasius and that it was Athanasius who encouraged Artabanes to take the decisive step. After this Artabanes involved Antalas in the plot to kill Gontharis, as Corippus states and Procopius implies.[21] After the diplomatic moves had been completed, Gontharis ordered Artabanes to lead an army against Antalas and to join his forces with those commanded by Cusina.

The Battle of Hadrumentum in early 546[22]

The army under the *strategos* Artabanes consisted of his Armenians, the Roman rebels under John, the Moors of Cusina, and the bodyguards of Gontharis under Ulithaeus. The two armies met near Hadrumentum, with the implication that Antalas's army was supported by the loyalist army of Marcianus which was garrisoning the city. Artabanes built a camp close by and then advanced to fight a battle on the following day. Artabanes deployed his army in two lines. John and Ulithaeus with a detachment of the army (*moira*)[23] stayed behind while Artabanes and Cusina with their army (*strateuma*) advanced against Antalas. John and Ulitheus were clearly the commanders of the two reserve divisions. The Moors under Antalas did not withstand the charge and fled, but Artabanes who was secretly loyal to the emperor's cause stopped the pursuit and withdrew from the battle. As a result, Ulithaeus wanted to kill him when he returned to the camp. However, Artabanes had a valid excuse. He claimed that he feared that the *dux* Marcentius could come out of Hadrumentum to assist Antalas. He also claimed that it was because of that that Gontharis should lead his entire army against the enemy. At this point, Artabanes was unsure what to do next. He pondered whether he should join the loyalists at Hadrumentum or return to Carthage. He decided to return and assassinate Gontharis.

Hero of the Hour: Artabanes the Arsacid in 546[24]

As noted above, the elderly Athanasius had encouraged Artabanes to assassinate Gontharis and so did his nephew Gregorius who noted that this would bring Artabanes greater glory than the achievements of Belisarius because whereas Belisarius had had a large army, a fleet and a large cavalry force with lots of money, Artabanes would achieve the same with clever trickery. So he returned to Carthage with the aim of assassinating Gontharis. Gontharis accepted Artabanes's excuse and decided to lead the campaign in person, leaving his trusted friend Pasiphilus behind to protect Carthage. After this he decided to entertain his friends with a banquet and march against the enemy on the following day.

Gontharis entertained at his palace Athanasius, Artabanes, and Peter the Thracian (former bodyguard of Solomon) and noblest of the Vandals, while Pasiphilus entertained John (Stotzas's successor) in his own house and each of the other leaders in other places. The end result was that the men and followers of Gontharis were scattered around the city. Artabanes decided to kill Gontharis now. He confided his plan to Gregorius and Artasires and three other bodyguards and ordered Artasires to strike the first strike. Gregorius was to choose the most daring of the Armenians, take them to the banquet and then leave them at the vestibule. The leaders were allowed to take their bodyguards to the banquets where they were to stand beside or behind them, but they were not allowed to wear any weapons other than their swords and no protective gear at all. The men who were left behind at the vestibule were not told anything of the plan, but rather were told that there could be a plot against Artabanes and that it was because of this that they had been taken along. They were told to act as if they were playing – they would take hold of the shields carried by the bodyguards of Gontharis and wave them about – and then if there was any tumult coming from inside, they were to take these shields and come to the rescue with all speed. Artasires also came up with a plan. He cut some arrows in two, tied them to his left hand between the wrist and elbow and hid them with a sleeve of his tunic. The idea was to use this as an improvised shield. Artasires also asked his master to kill him if his strike failed to kill Gontharis so that Artabanes would appear innocent.

When Artasires had said these things to Artabanes, Artasires, Gregorius and one of the bodyguards then entered the room with the couches to stand behind Artabanes. Artasires was nervous. He wanted to carry out the attack too soon and grasped the hilt of his sword, but Gregorius prevented him saying in Armenian that Gontharis had not yet drunk enough wine. Gregorius had nerves of steel unlike Artasires. The drinking continued and the drunken Gontharis started to feel jovial. He gave his bodyguards portions of food with the result that one after another these guards left the palace to eat outside the building. Soon there were only three bodyguards left, one of whom was Ulitheus. It was then that Artasires went to take his food, which he also took outside. Once there he unsheathed his sword, placed it under his arm and beneath his cloak, and rushed back in to Gontharis. When Artabanes saw this, he became excited so Peter realized what was happening, but did not say anything because he was very pleased to see this. When Artasires approached Gontharis, a servant pushed him so that the sword became visible. The servant cried out and asked what he was doing and Gontharis put his hand on his right ear to hear what was being said. It was then that Artasires cut so that part of Gontharis's scalp together with his fingers flew off. Peter urged the man on and Artabanes drew his two-edged *machaira* (short sword or long dagger) which was hanging on his thigh as Gontharis was attempting to rise to his feet, and thrust it into the tyrant's side up to the hilt and left it there. Gontharis still tried to get up, but the wound was fatal and he fell on the spot. Evidently Artabanes had better nerves than his bodyguard. At that moment Ulitheus attempted to strike Artasires with his sword, which Artasires blocked by raising his left hand so that the arrows in his sleeve deflected the sword cut. He then used his own sword to kill Ulitheus. Then, Peter taking the sword of Gontharis and Artabanes taking the sword of Ulitheus, they attacked and killed the remaining bodyguards. When the Armenians in the vestibule heard the commotion, they picked up the shields and ran to the banqueting room as planned and killed all the Vandals and friends of Gontharis. Procopius does not say what the Armenians did to the bodyguards when they did this, but since he states that after the killing of Gontharis the bodyguards joined the Armenians because most of them were former bodyguards of Areobindus, it is possible they did not make any serious attempt to prevent the Armenians doing what they wanted.

After the deed had been done, Artabanes told Athanasius, who was present at the scene, to take charge of the money of the palace. When the bodyguards had united with the Armenians they started to shout in unison and claimed the Emperor Justinian triumphant. This shouting was loud enough to be heard in the greater part of the city and encouraged all those who had been secretly supporting the legitimate government to run into the houses of the mutineers and kill them in a spontaneous burst of revenge. Pasiphilus was killed in this manner but John and his Vandals managed to flee to a sanctuary. Artabanes managed to convince them to surrender after which they were sent to Constantinople. The tyranny had lasted for thirty-six days.

This exploit won Artabanes immortal fame. Prejecta rewarded him with large sums of money and Justinian appointed him *magister* of Libya, but Artabanes asked to be relieved of office and permission to come to Constantinople. The grateful emperor fulfilled this wish and appointed the highly qualified John Troglita as his successor.

Chapter Eleven

East: The Persian War in 540–45

Important Places of the Persian War 540-545 (see also the Lazic War)

drawn after Katarzyna Maksymiuk with some changes based on Barrington Atlas

100km

Satala · Pharangium · Bolum · Doubios

Theodosiopolis · Anglon

Armenia · Chorzanene · Citharizon · Persarmenia

Martyropolis · Arzanene · Adarbiganon

Sophene · Samosata · Amida · Corduene

Dara

Cilicia · Batnae · Edessa · Sisauranon · Nisibis

Hierapolis · Beroea · Rhesaina · Beth Arbaye · Singara

Antioch · Daphne · Obbane · Callinicum · Chaboras · Soura

Seleucia · Chalcis · Beth Balash · Sergiopolis · Circesium · Mesopotamia · "Assyria"

Apamea · Syria · Euphratesia · Zenobia · Tigris

Orontes · Emesa · Dura Europos · Euphrates

Natural Disasters: Earthquakes, Bubonic Plague and Famine 540–65[1]

According to modern calculations, despite the multiple wars the East Roman Empire had actually enjoyed population growth and increasing wealth from about 305 until 540. This meant that Justinian was easily able to fund his projects during the first half of his rule, even with his spendrift habits, but this was to change. The years from 540 onwards were marked by continual fighting on almost all of the fronts (these will be dealt in greater detail below), earthquakes, periodic bouts of bubonic plague, and years of crop failures.

From 540 onwards the intensity of the earthquakes increased, and there were other natural disasters. In September 543 Cyzicus was partially destroyed. In 544 the Black Sea coast of Thrace experienced a tsunami. Between 543 and 548 a series of catastrophic earthquakes hit many regions and resulted in bad harvests and famines. The Cydnus River in Cilicia flooded in March 550. In July 551 the diocese of Oriens was hit by earthquakes along the Aegean Sea. Many people died in Constantinople and on the island of Cos, and Phoenicia was also effected, Beirut and Batroun being hit particularly hard. Beirut suffered 30,000 killed with the result that its law school was transferred to Sidon.

In August and September 554 there were more earthquakes, which hit Constantinople particularly hard, as well as Nicomedia and other cities in the area. Between 14 and 23 December 557 Constantinople was hit again and entire quarters were levelled. These natural disasters were very costly for the economy.

The worst disaster that hit the Roman Empire was bubonic plague. It arrived in Pelusium in Egypt in autumn 541 from where it progressed along the coast to Palestine, Syria, and Asia Minor in 542, reaching Constantinople in 242. It continued its ravages in the Balkans and passed through Mesopotamia into the Persian Empire, and continued its advance westward into Italy, Africa and Gaul. It is estimated that 10 to 30 per cent of the Roman population lost their lives in this pandemic. It continued to recur at irregular intervals after this in a less virulent form. New outbreaks are recorded for the years 558, 560, 561, 573–74, 592, and 599. This massive culling of the population hit the Roman economy very hard. It became increasingly difficult for the Empire to collect enough taxes and revenues for the upkeep of the administration and military forces, which in turn increased the hardship of the taxpayers who were required to pay the taxes previously paid by those who had died. The fact that the Empire, its administrative system and the armed forces survived these disasters is a testament to its endurance.

As if this was not enough, the Romans also faced crop failures, resulting not only from wars and plague but also resulting from weather, animal plague and locusts. The sources list crop failures for the following years: 534–6 cold weather and locusts; 537 bad harvest of grapes and fruits; 547 bad harvest of wheat; 551 bad harvest of wheat in the spring and fruits in the autumn after which followed a cattle plague; 552–3 cattle plague; 568 drought results in poor harvest in the spring and autumn. These disasters worsened an already bad situation and continued after the reign of Justinian, but as we shall see the Empire rebounded.

The background to the Second Persian War: The storm clouds gather in 532–40

The conclusion of the so-called Eternal Peace with Persia in 532 did not only free troops for the reconquest of the west, it also gave Justinian the chance to restore its defences with fortifications and organizational changes.

The fortification programme included the rebuilding, restoration and strengthening of existing forts, fortresses and cities and the rebuilding of new forts in the Balkans and the East. This was a continuation of the policy which started under Anastasius, but if we are to believe Procopius, and there is no reason not to, the scale of Justinian's fortification programme was more far reaching than those of his predecessors.[2] The aim was the same, namely the protection of strategic locations, the blocking of invasion routes and the protection of the populace and property. Procopius describes the programme for us in great detail in his *Buildings*. Subsequent events, however, prove that whatever fortifications were built or rebuilt during 532–40 were insufficient to deter the Persians and the enemies in the Balkans. Furthermore, as we shall see, Justinian relied far too much on the treaty he had concluded with Chosroes and neglected the implementation of the necessary defensive measures until it was too late.

Soon after the conclusion of the Eternal Peace, Chosroes faced an attempted coup as a result of his reforming policies, of which his religious tolerance towards the Manicheans was most obnoxious to the magi. The magi plotted together with the magnates who had by then become aware of Chosroes's plans to weaken their position (see below) and sought to place Cabades/Kavadh, son of his brother Zames, on the throne with Zames as regent (he was not allowed to be ruler because he had a disfigurement of the eye). The plot was discovered and Chosroes executed Zames and all the rest of his brothers together with their male offspring and their fellow plotters. Kavadh, however, was reared by the Kanarang/Chanaranges Adergoudounbades, as was the Persian custom according to Procopius. Chosroes ordered this Kanarang to kill the son, but Kanarang could not bring himself to, and only claimed that he had done so. The only persons who knew that the Kanarang had not killed the son were his own son Varanes and one of the servants. This was to have consequences later. Chosroes is also known for having crushed the Mazdakite religion once and for all and it is possible that this took place during this same time period. We know that the *mobadh* (the chief magus) remained loyal to Chosroes, which means that Chosroes was supported by a significant section of the magi.[3]

Chosroes's reform of the armed forces consisted of three major pillars, which were meant to diminish the power of the nobility while improving the efficiency of the armed forces. Because of this the office of *Iran-Spahbed* (supreme commander of the armed forces) was broken up into four regional *spahbods/spahbeds/spahbadhs* (north, south, east, west); the offices were not hereditary. See also the discussion concerning the abolishment of the position of *Adrastadaran Salanes* (*Arteshtaran-salar*). It is entirely possible that both took place at the same time. This removed the threat that a single commander could become too powerful. The second of the important reforms was the raising of the position of petty nobility *dehkan* vis-à-vis the nobility *azadan*. The *dehkan* were now allowed to serve in the elite heavy cavalry called *asavaran/savaran* and were thereby made equals of the nobles. The third of the major reforms was the regularization of the military reviews/inspections of the cavalry so that all horsemen were required to possess at least the following set of martial equipment: helmet, hauberk, breastplate, mail, gauntlet, girdle, thigh-guards, *contus*-spear, sword, battle-axe, mace, bowcase, two bows and bowstrings, a quiver with thirty arrows, two extra bowstrings, a lasso, a sling and stones, a shield, and horse armour (either metal or leather). The result was more efficient Persian armed forces.[4] The subsequent wars make it clear that Chosroes improved the efficiency of the Persian infantry markedly. The fact that Chosroes did not like the strengthening of the Roman Empire, because this posed a potential threat to him, made it certain that the Romans would soon have a taste of how well the new reformed Persian army operated.

Chosroes appears to have been dissatisfied with the terms of the Eternal Peace from the start, because when he learnt of the reconquest of Roman North Africa in about 534, he sent a messenger to Justinian in which he demanded a share of the spoils from Libya on the grounds that Justinian would never have been able to defeat the Vandals if they had still been at war with Persia. Justinian duly dispatched a present of money to Chosroes. This was a case of highway robbery and blackmail, but it is still easy to see that it was wise for Justinian to pay the money when his plan was to reconquer Italy after this. It is also possible that there was another reason for Justinian's readiness to act in this manner, if the usurpation attempt mentioned by Procopius took place roughly at the same time.

According to Procopius, a certain John, who served in a *katalogos* of infantry at the city of Daras, usurped power. He occupied the palace and declared himself emperor. However, on the fourth day of the usurpation some soldiers decided to kill this John because the local priest Mamas advised it. According to the first version of events, they killed the bodyguards at the door of the courtyard, entered the apartment and captured the usurper. According to the second version, the soldiers hesitated at first and stayed in the courtyard so that the initiative was taken by a sausage-vendor who was accompanying them. He rushed in and hit John with a cleaver, but the wound was not fatal. John ran into the courtyard where the soldiers captured him and then torched the palace. John was taken to prison where one of the soldiers on his own initiative killed him to restore order.[5] If Justinian had learnt of this (it took only three days for a fast courier to travel to Constantinople, for which see vol.3), he would certainly have wanted to keep the Persians happy because he would have known that his soldiers were in a state of confusion in the east (possibly caused by the actions of Alexander the Snips).

When Chosroes then learnt that Belisarius had begun the reconquest of Italy, presumably in about 537/8, he wanted to find some pretext for the breaking of the treaty.[6] So he asked Alamoundaros (Al-Mundhir) to provide him with an excuse for war, and Alamoundaros set out to do this, probably in about late 538 to early 539. Alamoundaros accused the phylarch of Roman Arabs, Arethas, of having violated the boundary in an area called *Strata*, and then Alamoundaros started to overrun Roman territory on this pretext while declaring that he was not violating the treaty because there was no mention of the Saracens in it. This was literally speaking true because the treaties the Romans and Persians had made had always included the Saracens under the names of Persians and Romans. Arethas's claim to the area was that the name *Strata* (a paved road in Latin)[7] meant that it belonged to Rome. Alamoundaros countered this by claiming that the owners of flocks in that area had paid him for the right of pasturage in the past. Justinian dispatched Strategius, a patrician and administrator of royal treasuries, together with Summus, the former *Dux* of Palestine, to mediate in the conflict. Summus had been reappointed as *Dux Palaestinae* in about 537/8 with the additional title *MVM* (honorary?). He was a brother of Julian who had served as envoy to the Aksumites and Himyarites, and he was advised by a trusted Arab in all matters.[8] Strategius advised Justinian to hand over the unproductive and insignificant tract of land to the Persians so that they would not have the pretext for war they desired, while the former soldier Summus advised the exact opposite: that the Romans should never surrender the land. Justinian temporized. According to Procopius, it was then that Chosroes accused Justinian of breaking the treaty by sending Summus to Alamoundaros with the intention of bribing him with large sums of money to join the Romans. He also accused Justinian of an attempt to bribe the Huns to attack Persia and of having sent a letter to the same effect – according to Chosroes he had proof of this because the Huns had shown him Justinian's letter. Procopius claims that he was unable to state whether the claims were true or false – in my opinion it is more than likely that the claims were accurate and that Justinian had once again engaged in diplomacy to create diversions for the Persians. The Huns in question are likely to have been those who invaded the Balkans in 539 because the above implies that they discussed the matter with Chosroes and it is not impossible to think that Chosroes then paid them to attack the Romans, even if Procopius does not state this.

Coins of Justin/Iustinus I struck in Constantinople, Thessalonica and Nicomedia. Source: Warwick Wroth, British Museum. Malalas (17.1) describes Justin I to have been a man of medium height with a good chest, curly completely grey hair, a good nose, with a handsome and ruddy complexion. He was also a veteran of many wars, generous by nature but unlettered.

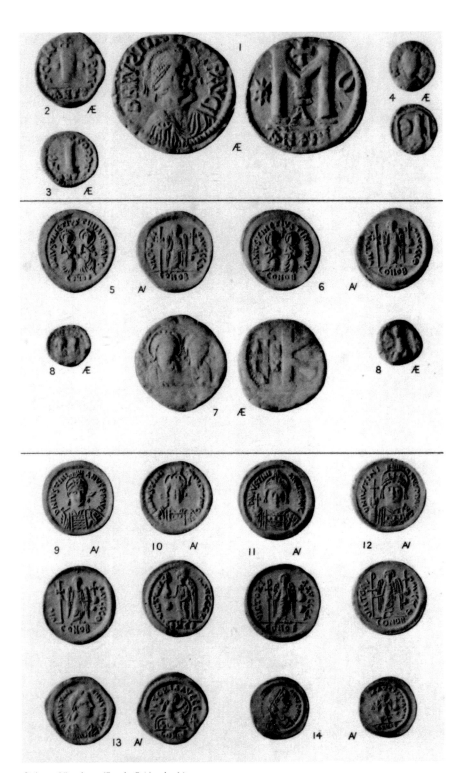

Coins of Justinus/Justin I (Antioch).
Coins of Justinus/Justin I and Justinianus/Justinian I (Constantinople and Antioch).
Coins of Justinianus/Justinian I (Constantinople).
Source: Warwick Wroth, British Museum.

Coins of Justinianus/Justinian I minted in the areas reconquered (Carthage, Sicily, Rome, Ravenna, uncertain). Source: Warwick Wroth, British Museum

Above: A bust of an empress claimed to represent Theodora. Source: Joseph Wilpert.

Left: Gold medallion depicting Justinian in the British Museum. Photo by author. Note in particular the fancy helmet with the peacock feathers. The narrative sources like Corippus make it clear that whenever possible those Romans who could afford to wear richly decorated clothing, armour, shields, swords, helmets etc, did so. Soldiers and officers were peacocks like they always have been. One of the reasons for this would obviously have been to show off to women.

Above: Mosaic in S. Apollinaire Nuovo variously claimed to represent Justinian or Theoderic the Great. The latter claims that the mosaic depicted originally Theoderic, but that this was then adopted as the basis for depicting Justinian after the reconquest. (*Public domain*)

Justinian (or Anastasius) depicted in a diptych. Source: public domain. Note the equipment worn by the emperor and the officer depicted on the left. The Romans could still be clearly distinguished from the barbarians bearing gifts and tribute below. The barbarians on the left are probably Goths while those on the right are probably Indians. According to Malalas (18.106), Justinian received in January 549 or 550 an Indian ambassador who brought an elephant for him. It is probable that this event is depicted in this scene so that we can add to the list of gifts brought also a tiger and elephant tusks. If my interpretation is correct, then we can pinpoint the carving of this diptych to the period after 552.

Mosaic in San Vitale, Ravenna, depicting Justinian with his court. Justinian is in the middle and it is usually assumed that the man left of him (on Justinian's right hand side) is Belisarius, while the man right of him (on Justinian's left) is Narses, but the identifications are obviously uncertain. The identification of Narses in particular is suspect, because the man in this image has a beard. In my opinion some patrician, e.g. Liberius, would be more likely. The men carrying the bejewelled Chi-Rho shields on the far left are probably to be identified with the Scholae and/or Candidati rather than with the Excubitores. (*Public domain*)

Mosaic in San Vitale, Ravenna, depicting Theodora with her court. Theodora is in the middle and it is usually assumed that the woman to the right of her (on Theodora's left) is Antonina. This is indeed probable. The 'man' to the left of Theodora (on her right side) is likely to be a eunuch and in my opinion he is to be identified with Narses the Eunuch as he actually sometimes has been. (*Public domain*)

Belisarius and his horse Phalios/Balan.
(*Author's painting*)

A mosaic in San Maggiore, Ravenna, ca. 500. Note the use of traditional equipment. (*Public domain*)

A mosaic in San Maggiore, Ravenna, ca. 500. Note above the large round shields which are almost as large as recommended by Syrianus Magister in the sixth century *Peri Strategias / Strategikes*. (*Public domain*)

A mosaic in San Maggiore, Ravenna, ca. 500. Note the use of the spike in the shield as recommended by Syrianus Magister in the sixth century *Peri Strategias / Strategikes*. (*Public domain*)

Typical sixth century heavy-armed line footman. (© *Jérémie Immormino*)

A Roman officer and other members of the military in the background, sixth century. (© *Jérémie Immormino*)

Roman infantry in light gear. (© *Jérémie Immormino*)

A mosaic depicting Roman cavalry in San Maggiore, Ravenna, ca. 500. Note the fancy helmets including the so-called Phrygian one in the background. (*Public domain*)

This image depicts a Gothic/Ostrogothic cataphract of the type used against Belisarius during the siege of Rome in 537-8. Note that he does not use bows and arrows. It was this that made the Gothic cataphracts impotent against Belisarius's *bucellarii* and regular cavalry. I have depicted the Goth in scale armour, but he could equally well have worn chain mail or lamellar armour. The shield emblem is generic and is not intended to represent any unit or group. The Romans used Goths who had surrendered both in their regular forces and among the *bucellarii*.

The period Romans used stirrups just like they had at least since the first century AD (see Gawronski available online at academia.edu), but at this time their use was a matter of personal preference, which is proven by the works of art depicting the Romans without these. This changed by the time the *Strategikon* was written. This treatise demanded that each horseman would use the stirrups.

Therefore in this case I have depicted the horseman without the stirrups.

cavalry *kontarion / contus* (ca. 3.74m)

Lorica squamata (scale armour) after the sixth century Egyptian ivory

javelin-quiver

The horse and its harness drawn partially after Mattesini

A fully equipped multipurpose trooper from Thrace who could be a regular *stratiotes / kaballarios* from the *katalogoi,* or *bucellarius / hypaspistes / doryforos* in the service of some officer.

I have here depicted the man in such gear as can be seen in the period works of arts which I have combined with the information provided by the textual sources.

arrow-quiver

round shield

a spatha and a composite bow in a holster behind the back

greaves

Lightly equipped Hun. This image represents those Huns who did not wear armour but specialised in archery. They were, however, always prepared to charge into contact when necessary. The Huns saw service also as *symmachoi*, *foederati* and *bucellarii*.

© Dr. Ilkka Syvanne 2018

Cabades/Cavades/Kavadh, son of Zames. Zames was the eldest son of Cabades I and his legitimate successor, but Cabades chose Chosroes as his successor so Cabades the younger was forced to seek a place of refuge from Constantinople. He served as commander of a cavalry unit consisting of Persian deserters in Italy under Narses the Eunuch. I have modelled the drawing after a relief variously claimed to depict either Peroz or Chosroes II. The position of the legs suggests the use of stirrups. I have also made the educated guess that Cabades would have continued to wear royal gear as a sign that he had a claim to the Persian throne. The rest of his men would have been equipped in like manner as heavy dual-purpose cavalry but probably in less fancy manner. The Roman regulars, *foederati* and *bucellarii* could wear similar gear when equipped heavily. In fact they could even wear Persian equipment if they had captured it as war booty. Similarly the Persians could wear Roman gear if they had captured it. Persian deserters would obviously have worn whatever mix of equipment they had access to.

Roman officer gesturing with his hand. (© *Jérémie Immormino*)

Re-enactors in the process of forming the *foulkon* and wearing typical gear of the period. (© *Jérémie Immormino*)

Roman soldiers at rest. (© *Jérémie Immormino*)

A sixth century Roman heavy-armed footman and other members of the military in the background. Note the Persian style jacket and the Germanic style helmet. The equipment soldiers wore reflected their multi-ethnic backgrounds and the booty captured from the enemy. (© *Jérémie Immormino*)

A dashing Roman officer enjoying a moment of rest. (© *Jérémie Immormino*)

Typical sixth century Roman heavy infantry. (© *Jérémie Immormino*)

A dashing Roman officer in in fancy gear. (© *Jérémie Immormino*)

It was then that the envoys of Vittigis, the bribed Ligurian priests (the envoys of Vittigis were Ligurian priests who had been bribed), arrived in the Persian court.[9] According to Procopius, the envoys noted the achievements of Justinian and warned Chosroes of the danger that Justinian would soon be strong enough to turn his arms against Persia and advised him to launch a pre-emptive strike before the Romans became too strong. The advice was actually sound and it fell on a receptive audience because according to Procopius Chosroes agreed with the assessment of the situation and was already seeking an excuse for the breaking of the treaty, on top of which Chosroes envied Justinian for the great military successes he had achieved. A little after this, presumably in the autumn of 539, the envoys of the Lazi and Armenians arrived. Both had serious grievances against the Romans and were seeking help from Chosroes, and in him they found a receptive audience.

The growing problems in Lazica in 532–40

The Lazi and their king Gourgenes were angry over the fact that Justinian had put them under a Roman *strategos* Peter and had sent a Roman garrison into the area. The Lazi were particularly hostile towards Peter because he was treating them highhandedly and was also prone to avarice. When Justinian became aware of the hostility he replaced Peter with other officers who included John Tzibus. According to Procopius, the only virtues of John were to be the greatest villain in the world and the cleverest person in discovering unlawful sources of revenue. It was John who persuaded Justinian to build the city of Petra on the sea where John then stayed and plundered the property of the Lazi. John established a monopoly in Petra over all the necessary goods including the salt that was shipped for the Lazi so that he himself became the retail dealer and overseer of all trade. The monopoly enabled him to charge exorbitant prices, to the great annoyance of the Lazi. The Lazi also detested the presence of the Roman garrison in the area and because of this they dispatched envoys to Chosroes begging him to come to their assistance. It is possible that the Lazi actually sent two sets of envoys to Chosroes because Procopius mentions them both before the war and then again for the year 540.[10]

The Armenian Revolt in 538–9[11]

Armenian grievances resulted from the administrative changes that Justinian made in 536 and from the abuse of power by those put in charge of one of the provinces. The situation was aggravated by the fact that the Armenian Church was not happy with the reinstatement of Orthodoxy under Justin, a policy which was continued by Justinian. It was then in 536 that Justinian abolished the Armenian satraps and satrapies and organized them as regular provinces so that a Fourth Armenian province was added, as he had previously done to the military forces of these provinces which had been enrolled into the regular army at the same time as Justinian had created the office of *Magister Militum per Armeniam* in 528. This naturally caused resentment among those who lost their hereditary rights, but there was more to it than that. Justinian had made Symeon, who had previously given Pharangium (the gold mine in the Armenian canton of Sper) into Roman hands, the title 'lord of the Armenian villages'. This title meant that Symeon became the ruler of one of the new Armenian provinces. His province was called Inner Armenia or Great Armenia. The previous owners of these villages, two brothers, sons of Perozes, murdered him and then fled to Persia.[12] Justinian then gave the villages and governorship of the Armenians to Amazaspes, nephew of Symeon. In due course, one of the friends of Amazaspes 'Acacius' denounced him to Justinian and claimed that he was oppressing the Armenians and planning to hand over Theodosiopolis and other fortresses to the Persians. When Justinian learnt this, he gave Acacius his blessing to murder Amazaspes, which he duly did with the reward of being nominated as Amazaspes's successor. Acacius proved particularly cruel to his subjects, plundering their property without any excuse and inventing new taxes. The Armenian nobility of Inner Armenia could bear him no longer and assassinated Acacius and then fled to Pharangium for a refuge. This took place in about 538/9.

Armen Ayvazyan is correct to point out that the assassination of Acacius in the midst of his bodyguards stands as a good example of the great skills that the Armenian forces possessed for special operations at this time, and this was by no means the only such operation. Assassination operations and stratagems were trademarks of the Mamikonean House, who still held a position of prestige among the Armenians as the House with hereditary rights for the position of *sparapet* (see *MHLR* Vol.1). This was a national uprising led by one of the branches of the Mamikoneans. The other major princely houses involved were the Arshakunis and Bagratunis (Aspetuni or Aspetians), but it is likely that other noble houses were also involved even if not mentioned by the sources. Furthermore, it would be strange if there were not contingents from the so-called satrapies present in this rebel army because Justinian had abolished them just two years before. It is clear that the rebel forces consisted primarily of the former field army of Armenia, which had previously consisted of at least 15,000 horsemen (see the battle of Satala) and some of the forces that garrisoned the forts and fortresses in Armenia. One can therefore assume that the rebel force included a very significant portion of this army under their own lords, even if it is clear that the other three Armenian provinces remained loyal to the Empire. Armen Ayvazyan (p.58) suggests that the Armenian rebel army consisted of about 10,000–20,000 horsemen. I would put the figure lower because the other three Armenian provinces appear to have remained loyal to the Empire. I would estimate the size of this force to have been about 5,000–10,000 horsemen plus whatever other forces there were in the forts and fortresses but which did not take part in the actual battle.

The battle of Oinochalakon/Avnik 539[13]

The revolt of Inner Armenia took place at a bad time because Justinian had only just sent 7,000 men under Narses the Eunuch and others to assist Belisarius in Italy in 538. The Romans were also acutely aware that Chosroes was possibly seeking an excuse for a war, so there was a need to crush the Armenian rebels as soon as possible. Because of this Justinian sent one of his best commanders, Sittas, to deal with the rebels. Subsequent problems in the Balkans are strongly indicative that Sittas was given a very sizable army to deal with the rebels and that this army was mostly drawn from the forces posted in the Balkans. This makes it likely that Sittas was the commander of the praesental army of the Balkans. Ayvazyan suggest that Sittas may have had as many as 30,000 men in his army because there existed the danger of simultaneous Persian invasion. This is a plausible figure for the entire force sent to the scene, but in light of the details provided by Procopius it is clear that Sittas used only cavalry. This figure was certainly lower, but if one assumes that Sittas was able to add some of the Armenians (who had stayed loyal) and also some of the other cavalry units posted on the eastern frontier into his force one may assume that he could face the Armenians with at least about 15,000–20,000 horsemen.

Sittas wisely wanted to calm the situation without a fight and promised to persuade the emperor to remit the new taxes. He had served in the area and had been the first *MVM per Armeniam* in 528–30, so he knew what he was up against. Adolius, son of Acacius, slandered Sittas to Justinian and urged him to order Sittas to put an end to the conflict with greater speed. Justinian agreed and ordered Sittas to act. Even then, according to Procopius, Sittas was reluctant to attack immediately and tried to cause desertions among the enemy with promises.

It was then that the Aspetiani (Bagratuni) sent envoys to Sittas. They promised to betray their kinsmen in the middle of a battle if Sittas would give them pledges in writing that they would retain their possessions. Sittas was pleased and gave them the promises in writing. According to Procopius, something strange then happened. The Aspetiani envoys supposedly did not find the Aspetiani and the Roman vanguard came across a contingent of the Aspetiani and attacked them, on top of which Sittas found some of the Aspetiani women and children in a cave and had them killed in anger. The only logical explanation for this is what Armen Ayvazyan has stated, which is that the Bagratuni were deceiving Sittas, probably because Vasak the Mamikonean had ordered them to do so. The other alternative is that all of the above resulted from the fog of war, but this is not nearly as convincing as the alternative suggested by Ayvazyan. The main aim was clearly to gain time so that the Armenian army could retreat from Sper in an effort either to feign fear so that the Romans could be lured to follow the retreating Armenians to their chosen battlefield, or just to flee to the Persian side of the border. The killing of the women and children in the cave (probably a cave fort in Sper) would therefore have been an act of revenge by Sittas when he realised that the Bagratuni had fooled him and the enemy had fled from Sper southwards.

The retreating Armenians fled first south from Sper and then across the Persian border into Oinochalakon, which is to be identified with the city/fort of Avnik, where they halted because this was a suitable location for them to face the pursuing Romans. This makes it clear that the Armenians wanted to make certain that the Romans would commit a hostile act against Persia if they followed them. This, however, had not usually served as a casus belli in the past because both had committed such acts when they had pursued Armenian rebels. Regardless, it is still clear that the Armenian plan was masterly in a situation in which the Persian ruler was looking for an excuse to break the 'Eternal Peace'.[14]

The Roman army then caught up the retreating Armenians at Avnik; they had chosen it as the ideal place to face the Romans. The terrain close to Avnik consisted of ridges and ravines which forced both the Armenians and the Romans to adopt a scattered formation. This was part of the Armenian masterplan. Ayvazyan is absolutely correct in his analysis regarding the reasons why the Armenians chose this location for the battle. The Armenians had fewer men than the Romans so they wanted to break up the cohesion and command structure of the Roman cavalry forces so they could not exploit their greater numbers. Therefore the resulting battle consisted of a series of scattered cavalry encounters. Procopius describes one such encounter where Sittas was present with a few of his horsemen. He saw Armenians on the other side of a ravine and charged them across the ravine with the result that the Armenian cavalry fled a short distance to the rear. The Heruls (as *koursores?*) conducted a short pursuit, but Sittas pursued no further and rested the remainder of his men. The Armenians apparently stopped their retreat and forced the Heruls back. As this was happening, one of the returning Heruls rode his galloping horse into Sittas's spear which was resting on the ground, shattering it. According to Procopius, the Armenians, who were not far away, noticed Sittas because he did not wear his helmet, and charged. Sittas drew his sword and tried to escape back across the ravine with a few of his men. During this flight, someone hit him in the head with a sword but failed to kill him, after which Artabanes the Arsacid killed him with a spear thrust from behind. Ayvazyan has correctly pointed out that it is more than likely that the targeting of Sittas formed a part of the Armenian plan from the start, the overall plan being to break up the command structure of the Roman army. Ayvazyan is correct to point out that the Armenians would surely have been aware where Sittas was because he was surrounded by his personal standards. The initial flight by the Armenians would therefore have been meant to lure Sittas and his men to cross the ravine so that he could be killed more easily. Therefore, in my opinion, the detail where the Armenians recognized Sittas because he was not wearing a helmet belongs to the stage when the Armenians had already counter-attacked (note the fleeing Herul) and were seeking out Sittas to kill him. The fact that he could be recognized only because he was not wearing any helmet is interesting because it proves that he did not wear any uniform or equipment which would have made him easily recognizable. The fact that Belisarius could also be recognized only from his horse suggests the same. The Roman officers undoubtedly wore better equipment that separated them from the rank-and-file, but they did not usually wear equipment that would have made them easily recognizable or equipment that would have made it clear to everyone that they were the generals (*magistri, comites, duces*) – unless of course they did so purposefully. The rest of the Roman cavalry would have been defeated in similar encounters between scattered units of cavalry in which the Armenians were able to match the Romans with equal numbers of men. Armenians won most of them.

The endgame: Bouzes/Buzes vs. Armenians in 539[15]

When Justinian learnt the news, he dispatched Buzes/Bouzes to take charge of the war. Even though this is not mentioned, it is probable that Justinian gave Bouzes reinforcements quite possibly again drawn from the armies posted in the Balkans. Bouzes promised reconciliation with the Armenian nobles and asked them to send representatives to meet him, but most of them did not trust him. However, there was one man called John the Arsacid, the father of Artabanes, who trusted Bouzes because he considered him a friend. He and his son-in-law Bassaces and some others went to meet Bouzes. When they then arrived at the meeting place, they realized that they were surrounded by a Roman army. Bassaces realized what was afoot and urged John to flee. John refused, but Bassaces and all the rest managed to elude the Romans and flee. When Bouzes then arrived, he showed his true colours. John was killed. After this, the Armenian rebels realized that there was no chance for reconciliation and fled to the Persian side of the border under the able leadership of Bassaces and offered their services to Chosroes. It was therefore because of Justinian's unwise policies and the greed of his representatives in Inner Armenia that Rome lost a very significant part of its eastern army and that the Persians were able to employ these elite forces against their former masters.

In my opinion, it is similarly clear that the revolt of Inner Armenia had other unwelcome consequences elsewhere. It is unlikely to be a coincidence that there were troubles in the Balkans precisely in 539 when Sittas and then Bouzes were fighting against the Armenians. It is clear that the combined effects of sending men to Libya and then to Italy in 538 and then to Armenia in 539 created a power vacuum in the Balkans, which was soon enough exploited by the Gepids and Huns.

The speech which Procopius puts into the mouth of the Armenian envoys when they pleaded help from Chosroes after their flight to Persia includes important pieces of evidence for the size of the Roman Empire at this time and for the strategy adopted by Justinian. The Armenians warned that Justinian would attack Persia after he had accomplished the conquest of the west. Justinian was turning the whole world upside down. He had already abused the rights of the Armenians and imposed a new tax on them; placed a Roman magistrate in charge of the Lazi; conquered Bosporus from the Huns; formed a defensive alliance with the Ethiopians; annexed Himyar, Red Sea and the Palm Groves; and added the Libyans and Italians as his subjects. The whole earth was not enough for Justinian. He was looking about the heavens and searching beyond the ocean to find other worlds to conquer. The last mentioned is particularly interesting because it is probably the truth. Justinian very likely sent naval expeditions to the Indian Ocean and possibly even to the Atlantic in search of new worlds.[16]

According to Procopius, it was then after hearing the arguments put forth by the Armenians that Chosroes assembled his nobility to discuss the question of war and peace. Chosroes disclosed to the nobility what the envoys from Vittigis and the Armenians had told him and put the question under discussion. The nobles expressed many views but in the end it was decided that the Persians would launch an invasion in the spring of 540. This decision is not surprising because the Persians had now been strengthened by the Armenian fugitives and the information that the Armenian commanders provided for Chosroes came from such men who had previously served in the Roman army and certainly knew many of their defensive secrets.[17]

According to Procopius (*Wars* 2.3.57), the Romans did not suspect that Chosroes had such plans and thought that the Persians would never break up the 'Eternal Peace' even when they knew that Chosroes charged Justinian of having attempted to bribe Alamoundaros to change his allegiance and of having attempted to use the Huns as his proxy and that he envied the successes achieved by Justinian in the west. Procopius does not blame the emperor here but it is clear that he meant Justinian and his advisors by 'the Romans'. On the basis of Procopius's text it is clear that the Romans and the emperor Justinian in particular were still operating under the same false view of international politics as previously which was based on legalistic concepts. It just did not occur to them that the enemy, who also usually operated by following legal niceties, would suddenly stop doing so without any specific warning.

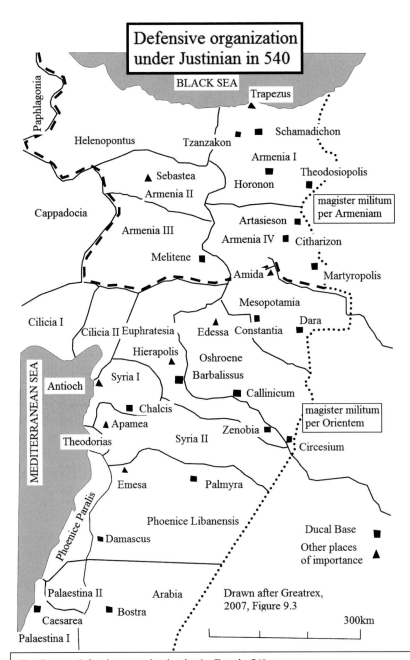

Defensive organization under Justinian in 540

BLACK SEA

Paphlagonia

Trapezus

Helenopontus

Tzanzakon

Schamadichon

Armenia I

Sebastea

Horonon

Theodosiopolis

Armenia II

Cappadocia

Artasieson

magister militum per Armeniam

Armenia III

Armenia IV   Citharizon

Melitene

Amida

Martyropolis

Mesopotamia

Cilicia I

Dara

Cilicia II Euphratesia   Edessa Constantia

Hierapolis

Oshroene

Syria I

Barbalissus

Antioch

Callinicum

Chalcis

Apamea

Zenobia

magister militum per Orientem

Theodorias

Syria II

Circesium

Emesa

Palmyra

Phoenice Libanensis

Ducal Base

Other places of importance

Damascus

MEDITERRANEAN SEA

Phoenice Paralis

Palaestina II   Arabia   Drawn after Greatrex, 2007, Figure 9.3

Caesarea   Bostra   300km

Palaestina I

The Roman defensive organization in the East in 540
The attached map shows the command structure of the Roman forces posted in about 540. On paper the Roman army covered the entire length of the frontier but in practice the economising in salaries and the corruption of the auditors had destroyed this entire defensive system.

Justinian's blind belief in the treaty caused other very serious problems, as I noted above. Procopius states in no uncertain terms in his *Secret History* (*Anekdota*, 24.12–29, 30.1ff.) that Justinian destroyed the defensive system in the east as a result of the Eternal Peace. The peace had given him the reason and excuse to fleece soldiers so that the remaining soldiers were now few in number and unwilling to fight. The economizing in public posts and the reduction of the intelligence-gathering organization in the east show that the Romans were operating blindly. In sum, Justinian's trust in the Eternal Peace was sheer stupidity, and this is particularly strange considering Justinian himself failed to follow his treaties and promises in the west. This was particularly true of his relationship with the Goths of Italy. He pretended to be their ally and then conducted a surprise attack, just as Caracalla had been in the habit of doing.[18] The only logical answer to this is that these areas were considered parts of the Roman Empire so that the emperor's promises were not legally binding in Justinian's eyes while his treaty with Persia was concluded with a foreign power. Or perhaps Justinian and his advisors just failed to grasp the difference in their own *modi operandi* or just fell victim to wishful thinking.

However, it is clear that Chosroes himself was not entirely free of similar tendencies. The best proof of this is the above list of things that he did before this war. He was seeking an excuse for the breaking up of the peace, which shows he was also operating within the legal framework and sought loopholes within the contract. It is clear that neither Justinian nor Chosroes could be considered military geniuses on a par with the great Caracalla. They operated under the legal framework of international politics and sought legal loopholes for their actions – this includes war by proxy. This would have been ridiculous for a military genius like Caracalla who did not need any excuses for his actions. He rather fooled those who believed in such things with promises or vows to convince them of his goodwill so that they could then be massacred.[19] It didn't occur to Chosroes that he could have made a surprise attack without warning (in truth he gave his enemy plenty of warnings) or excuse, and it didn't occur to Justinian that Chosroes would break up the treaty without warning, even with the evidence right under his nose. Chosroes, however, has one mitigating circumstance on his side. It is possible that his soldiers needed an excuse to make the war just in their eyes.

The Persian 'surprise' attack in 540[20]

When Justinian grasped that Chosroes was eager for war, as Procopius puts it, he dispatched one Anastasius with a letter to dissuade him from this in the spring of 540. On the basis of Procopius's statement in *Wars* 2.3.57, it is clear that Justinian still did not expect that Chosroes would invade, so there was time for diplomatic negotiations. The abovementioned abolishment of the spy network undoubtedly contributed to this blindness. Chosroes imprisoned the envoy and forced him to remain with him until the Persians launched their invasion at the beginning of spring 540. Chosroes basically prevented Anastasius from warning the Romans that an invasion was imminent.

The Romans were ill-prepared. The army on the scene was utterly demoralized as a result of the economizing and their underpayment; Justinian had sent forces to Italy and North Africa both from the east and the Balkans; the only field army in the Balkans, under Calluc, had been destroyed in 539; the Huns had devastated the Balkans at the turn of 539/40 and it is clear that some forces from the east had been dispatched there; and as if this was not enough, the Armenian revolt had destroyed the Army of Armenia so that Romans needed to keep Armenia garrisoned with large numbers of forces that could have been used elsewhere. Excluding the defeat of Calluc, Justinian bears much responsibility for all of the other matters that affected the ability of the Roman Army of the East to face an invasion. There is also no doubt that the stingy Justinian was the man who bore the blame for the troubles that the Roman armies had in North Africa and Italy where salaries were constantly in arrears. It is no wonder that the soldiers either refused to fight or even mutinied. Had Justinian prioritized the army, he would not have faced so many troubles all over the empire. The arrears in payments and the lowered salaries also meant that the soldiers were all too eager to plunder, and when the commanders then made the mistake of denying this from the soldiers, because this lowered the emperor's share, the soldiers were naturally ready to mutiny. For this, see especially the chapter dealing with Solomon's exploits in North Africa.

When the Persians then launched their surprise invasion, Chosroes kept the Euphrates on his right so that the Roman city of Circesium was on the opposite side of the river. In other words, the invasion route did not follow the typical route. Chosroes bypassed the city because it had strong walls, and the siege would also have required him to cross the river. His plan was to march straight to Syria and Cilicia. It is possible that it was only then that the Romans learnt of the invasion, because this is the first event that Procopius includes. If this is the case, then the Roman defences and intelligence-gathering networks were in a really sorry state. After this Chosroes came to Zenobia and attempted to force the place to surrender, but when this failed he continued his march so as not to waste time taking an unimportant place. When Chosroes reached the city of Sura, he stopped his army close by, after which he consulted the magi. When they promised success (presumably as instructed), the Persians encamped and assaulted the walls. The garrison led by its Armenian commander Arsaces fought bravely and killed many of the attackers. Late in the day, the Romans were struck by disaster. Arsaces was killed by an arrow, but the Persians withdrew to their camp because it was nearly nightfall.

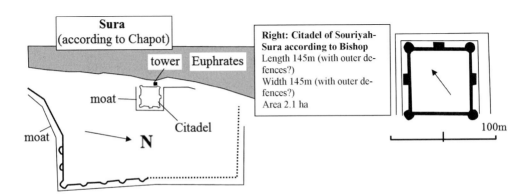

On the following day the leaderless Romans were at loss what to do and decided to offer a ransom for their freedom through a priest. Chosroes was not willing to accept this because the Romans had killed large numbers of his notables. He wanted to make Sura a warning example of what would happen when they resisted the Persians. He pretended to accept this and then dispatched the priest back to the city, giving him an escort of Persian notables. Chosroes instructed the notables to go as far as the gate and then when the guards opened the gate the notables were to throw a stone or block of wood between the threshold and the gate so it could not be closed. In the meantime Chosroes prepared his army, giving it instructions to attack on the run when given the signal. When the Roman guards duly opened the gate wide to receive the priest and the envoys, the notables acted as instructed and the guards could no longer close the gate. Chosroes then gave the signal for the attack and the Persians stormed the place. Large numbers were killed and the remaining 12,000 were enslaved. The houses were plundered and set on fire. After this, Chosroes released Anastasius the envoy so that he could take the message to Justinian. This was not the end of the story for the citizens of Sura because, according to Procopius, Chosroes later decided to show kindness to the enslaved people. Procopius states that the reason was either love for a beautiful local woman called Euphemia, whom Chosroes married, or humanity, or avarice. The first is the likeliest and is certainly not the only example of lust affecting destiny. Chosroes sent a message to Candidus, bishop of Sergiopolis, that he could ransom the inhabitants of Sura for two centenaria. Candidus didn't have enough money but promised to pay later or be dismissed from the priesthood. Chosroes agreed to this and released the prisoners.

According to Procopius, just before the above had taken place, Justinian had divided the command structure in the east so that Buzes was responsible for the portion east of the Euphrates and Belisarius for the territory west of the Euphrates, but in such a manner that Buzes was in charge of the whole until the return of Belisarius from Italy. Buzes resided in his headquarters at Hierapolis until he heard what had happened to Sura in about mid-summer 540. Then he assembled the leading citizens of Hierapolis and told them what his strategy was. He noted that if he was to remain in the city when the Persians possessed a numerical advantage this would mean that if they besieged it they would eventually take it because provisions would run out sooner or later. Buzes stated that he would therefore leave a garrison for the city while taking the rest of the forces with him to the surrounding heights from which they would then conduct attacks against the enemy to prevent them obtaining supplies. This was a sound strategy, but according to Procopius Buzes chose the best soldiers after which he disappeared so that neither the Hierapolitans nor the enemy knew where he was. This, however, appears to be a purposely misleading statement because later on, as we shall see, he was at Edessa when the Persian army marched there. Procopius (*Wars* 2.12.31–4) claims that it was the fear of supernatural protection provided by Jesus Christ for the city of Edessa in combination with the appearance of suppuration in Chosroes's face that caused him to abandon his plan to take Edessa. It is clear that Procopius is here at pains to hide the shadowing warfare conducted by Buzes. It was the presence of Buzes with his chosen men that caused Chosroes to abandon his plan of taking the city and not some supernatural intervention.

When Justinian learnt of the Persian invasion, he improvised and hastily dispatched his cousin Germanus with 300 sworn followers to Antioch with the promise of dispatching a sizable army soon after. Germanus took with him his son Justin to school him in the art of warfare. The figure of 300 men is pitiful in the circumstances and begs the question: Was this the entire force? If the 300 men represent the bodyguards of Germanus, then it was the entire force, but if the 300 men consisted of the bodyguards of Justinian, then we should add to this figure the personal bodyguards of Germanus. Even though both are possible my own educated guess is that the figure of 300 men should be interpreted as the *bucellarii* of Germanus and that this indeed was the entire force available to him on so short a notice because Procopius implies this when he refers to the disorderly sending of Germanus with so few men. However, as we shall see, this was not the entire force available for the defence of Antioch, because the local *duces* had also been ordered there with their fast moving cavalry forces – though it is probable that it was actually Germanus who ordered them to do so. The idea was clearly to use the great military skills of Germanus to best effect. Justinian probably had little choice because Germanus was probably the only skilled commander available in Constantinople at the time. It was lucky he had recalled him from North Africa in 539 (Marc. Com. a.539.5, a540.1).

When Germanus reached Antioch, he inspected the circuit of the wall and found every part to be defensible except the section located on the highest peak which was called Orocasias. With his keen eye he noticed that the wall was easy to assail at that point as there was a rock which stood as high as the wall. Therefore he ordered the architects either to cut off access to the wall from the rock by digging a deep trench, or to build a great tower on top of the rock which would then be connected to the wall of the city. However, the architects of the public works stated that they could not accomplish either of these in the time available, and if they started and did not finish they would only show the enemy where to assault the walls. Germanus agreed, but did not yet despair because he was still expecting the arrival of the promised army from Constantinople. However, when this did not materialize, he began to fear that Chosroes would target Antioch in particular because of his presence there. The Antiochenes, who feared the same, held a council and decided to send Megas Bishop of Beroea as their envoy with orders to offer money to Chosroes in return for not attacking. This had the opposite effect. It made Chosroes even more eager to advance against Syria and Cilicia because the offer demonstrated the weakness of the Roman defences. Chosroes told Megas to follow and advanced to Hierapolis.

On arrival Chosroes realized that the city had strong fortifications and a sizable garrison, so he settled on demanding money rather than assaulting the place. One wonders whether Buzes had any role in this which Procopius refuses to acknowledge. Chosroes sent Paulus the interpreter as his envoy. This Paulus was a native Roman who had attended an elementary school in Antioch. This proves that Chosroes had in his entourage men that knew the local circumstances well. In fact, it is quite possible or even probable that this Paulus was a member of the Persian intelligence services. The Hierapolitans agreed to pay 2,000 lbs of silver as their ransom. The abovementioned Megas was also active on behalf of all of the inhabitants of the east and persisted in his efforts for so long that Chosroes finally agreed that he would depart from the Roman Empire after having received ten centenaria of gold. When Megas got this promise, he travelled to Antioch while Chosroes continued his march to Beroea.

Chosroes repeated his demand for ransom through Paulus when he reached Beroea, but this time he doubled the sum because the wall was vulnerable in many places. The inhabitants were glad to accept this, but when they had collected 2,000 lbs of silver they claimed they had no more. This did not please Chosroes. The frightened inhabitants and the garrison abandoned the walls and fled to the fortress located on the acropolis. On the following day, Chosroes ordered his men to assault the city with ladders and since there were no defenders this was easily accomplished. Chosroes was enraged and ordered the city torched after which he proceeded to the acropolis and ordered his men to assault the fortress. The Romans defended themselves valiantly, but owing to a blunder their situation was hopeless. The Romans had brought their horses and other animals inside the fortress and they had exhausted the only well.

In the meantime, Megas had reached Antioch. On his arrival he was met by the envoys John son of Rufinus and Julian, the *a secretis* (Justinian's private secretary) sent by Justinian. These two refused to carry out the terms negotiated by Megas. Julian specifically forbade the paying of money and the ransoming of cities. He also implicated Ephraemius, the chief priest of the city, as Chosroes's collaborator. This means that Julian was a high-ranking member of the intelligence services with the duty of assisting Germanus in the fulfilment of his duty. Megas returned to Chosroes with the bad news. Procopius claims that it was because of the fear of Persian attack that Ephraemius fled to Cilicia, but it is more likely that he feared Germanus's reaction to the accusation. Whatever the truth, Germanus soon after followed in his footsteps because he did not want to be at Antioch when the Persians arrived. Germanus took with him some of the soldiers, but left the vast majority behind. The sources do not tell us what Germanus did after this, but it is practically certain that he collected whatever forces there were present in Pamphylia and Cilicia and that he garrisoned at least the Cilician Gates to defend the main route that the Persians could take if they decided to invade Asia Minor.

Megas reached Chosroes when the latter was about to attack the fortress. The two exchanged accusations, but in the end Megas managed to persuade Chosroes to send him to the acropolis to negotiate. When Megas learnt that the well was dry, he returned to Chosroes and begged with tears in eyes to grant the Beroeans their lives because they had no money left. The Beroeans were allowed to depart from the acropolis unharmed. Some of the soldiers fled with them, but most deserted to the Persians. The reason for this was that the state had not paid them for a long time. The stupid economising policies of Justinian paid great dividends for the enemy.

The siege of Antioch in the summer of 540

After this, Chosroes led his entire army against Antioch. Some of the citizens fled with their money, and the rest would have followed had not the *duces* of Lebanon, Theoctistus and Molatzes, arrived with their 6,000 horsemen. As noted above, it is probable that they had been ordered to do so by Germanus. The Persians arrived soon after this and built a marching camp by the River Orontes. Paulus was again sent to demand ransom, and the Roman ambassadors went to meet Chosroes after which they retired back to the city. On the following morning, the populace started to shout insults at Chosroes and when Paulus approached the wall they almost killed him with arrows. Chosroes was incensed and decided to storm the city. On the following day, Chosroes ordered a portion of his army to attack the city from different points along the river, while he himself led most of the army together with the best men against the vulnerable section on the heights. Chosroes was therefore well aware of the weak spot, either thanks to Antiochene traitors or thanks to his siege engineers. The spot which the Romans defended had only a narrow parapet so they needed to widen it to enable more men to assume a defensive position on it. Therefore, they hastily bound together long timbers which were suspended between the towers. The Persian attack began with showers of arrows all along the walls, the most effective attack being directed against the vulnerable section. Chosroes was personally in charge of the attack against the heights and urged his men forward from behind. The Romans defended themselves bravely, not only the soldiers (*stratiotai*) but also the youths (*neaniai*) belonging to the factions. This suggests that the military training of the paramilitary forces and youth was now performed by the circus factions, at least in Antioch. The fighting was hard because thanks to the rock the fighting was almost as if it had been on level ground. Procopius's opinion is that if 300 Romans had had the courage to go outside the fortifications to seize the rock, the Persians would not have been able to take the city because all approaches to it and to the wall close by could have been easily defended by missiles. Should we take this as a veiled accusation against Germanus who had 300 followers? Be that as may, Procopius notes that this alternative occurred to no-one and because of this the Persians captured the city. Then suddenly the ropes that had kept the timbers together broke and the beams and the men standing on them fell to the ground with a mighty crash. The Roman engineers had clearly miscalculated. When the crash was heard in the adjoining towers they did not know what had happened but assumed that the wall must have collapsed, so they abandoned their positions and fled.

The youth of the factions retreated from the fortifications and descended into the city where they formed up a defensive line and refused to budge. The soldiers of Theoctistus and Molatzes however, fled to their horses and rode away to the gates where they claimed that Buzes had come with an army and that they were there to receive this army into the city. This claim and presumably the collapse of the defence on the heights caused the Antiochenes to rush to the gates at the same time as the soldiers attempted to get there. The soldiers spared no-one and trampled under hooves anyone in their way. In the meantime, the Persians had reached the abandoned battlements with ladders, but did not descend from them either because they feared the rough ground below in front of them, or because Chosroes forbade it. According to Procopius, some claimed that when Chosroes saw how difficult the ground was he decided to let the Roman soldiers go from the city so that the Romans would not put up a fight, and that he therefore ordered the soldiers opposite the gate leading into Daphne to give the Roman soldiers an unopposed way to flee. This age-old trick worked as anticipated. When the Persians opened an escape route, the Roman cavalry together with their officers and some civilians fled towards Daphne. After the soldiers had fled, Chosroes gave the order to enter the city, but this was not the end of the resistance because in the middle of the city they came face-to-face with the brave youths. Some were fully armoured and equipped but most were forced to use only stones as missiles. For a while it seemed as if the youths would prevail because they forced the Persians back and started shouts proclaiming Justinian triumphant. Then Chosroes sent forward his best men that he had kept in reserve, but their efforts were not needed because the Persian regulars had meanwhile broken through the enemy lines with great slaughter. The Persians slaughtered everyone they met regardless of age or sex until their bloodlust had been satisfied. After this, the rest of the population were enslaved.

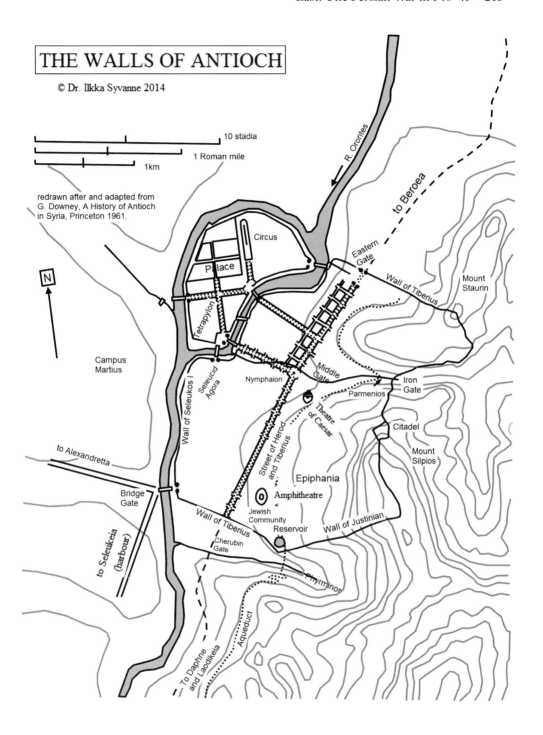

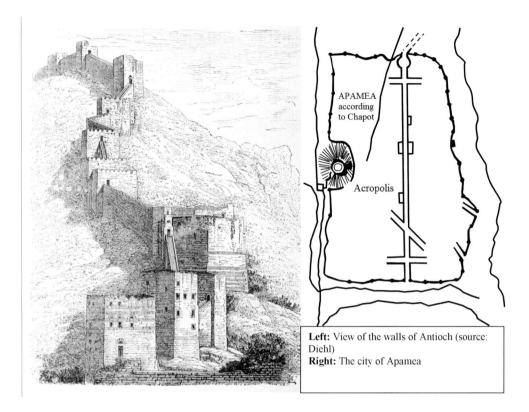

Left: View of the walls of Antioch (source: Diehl)
Right: The city of Apamea

When the city had been taken, Chosroes spoke to the envoys dispatched by Justinian. According to Procopius, he was the cleverest of men in lying so was able to accuse the Romans of the wrongs he had himself committed. Basically, Chosroes hypocritically claimed that it was Justinian who was responsible for all the bloodshed and not he. He presented the letter that had been sent to Alamoundaros and stated that the Romans had broken the peace while the ambassadors made the excuse that it had not been done by the emperor but by one of his subjects. Then he finally presented his demands, which were the paying of a large sum of money immediately and then after that an annual sum. The excuse for the latter was that the Persians maintained a garrison at the Caspian Gates. According to Procopius, Chosroes also noted that he would no longer feel resentment on the account of the fortification of Dara/Daras if the Romans paid the money.[21] If true, and there is no reason to doubt it, it is no wonder the Romans sent reinforcements precisely to Dara – the treacherous Chosroes had named the place so it was therefore clearly in danger. This was a foolish thing for Chosroes to say. The Roman ambassadors accused Chosroes of an attempt to make the Romans appear to be subjects of Persia, which Chosroes countered by saying that the Romans actually had the Persians in their service as soldiers in the same way that the Romans paid the Huns and Saracens to guard Roman territory. This means that Chosroes recognized the sticking point and wanted to make it appear as if the payments were for services rendered rather than payments obtained under duress. This does not mean that he would not have then represented the Romans as his tributaries to his own populace for propaganda reasons. It merely means that Chosroes knew why the Romans were unwilling to pay. The Romans did not want it to appear that they were a tributary state of Persia. It should be noted, however, that the Roman reluctance to pay was not based solely on pride; on the basis of the past, the Romans knew that such payments did not secure the border. It was then that the ambassadors and Chosroes made an agreement. The envoys agreed that the Romans would immediately pay 50 centenaria of gold (a centenarium was 100 lbs so the total was 5,000 lbs) to the Persians and after that a yearly tribute of 5 centenaria, in return for leaving Roman territory immediately without causing any more harm. The ambassadors gave hostages as a guarantee of the terms of the treaty. The hostages were to be released once the Persians reached their native land where they were to be met by envoys sent by Justinian who would then confirm the peace.

Chosroes extorts more money

After this Chosroes visited the city of Seleucia where he bathed in the sea and sacrificed to the sun and other divinities. When he returned to the camp, he stated that it was his intention to visit the city of Apamea. See the accompanying map. The ambassadors granted this request on condition that Chosroes march back without harming the city after which he would receive 1,000 lbs of silver, but the envoys and everyone else knew that Chosroes was merely seeking an excuse to plunder the city. Chosroes then marched to Daphne, where he burned the sanctuary of Archangel Michael and some other buildings. The reason for this was that Aeimachus the butcher killed a Persian nobleman who rode after him. The young man turned suddenly and threw a stone which hit him on the forehead knocking the Persian off his horse, after which the butcher butchered the Persian with a sword, stripped him of his weapons and gold, leaped on his horse and rode away. This is quite typical of the period. The civilians are the ones who perform the brave deeds and not the soldiers, who were readier to desert than to fight thanks to the economizing policies of Justinian.

It is probable that the reason for Chosroes's march to Apamea via Daphne was to make certain that the cavalry that had fled through the Daphne Gate would not make the mistake of attempting to harass him when he returned home. In other words, the probable aim would have been to force the Roman fugitives to flee further south if they had regrouped in Daphne or Apamea and also to extort more money in the process.

When Chosroes reached Apamea, Thomas the priest negotiated on behalf of the city. The Persian army was encamped in front of it and Chosroes was admitted inside with 200 of his best soldiers. However, once inside, Chosroes demanded that the citizens hand over all their possessions, which the inhabitants did. After this Chosroes acted as if he were the emperor and organized races at the hippodrome while he watched. When the Blue (Venetus) chariot took the lead, the *Shahanshah* took this as an insult because the Blue Faction was supported by Justinian and ordered the Green Faction to win. The citizens of Apamea also exploited the occasion, just as if the real emperor was present, and voiced their complaints. One of the Persians had entered a house in the city and violated the maiden daughter. Chosroes duly ordered the man impaled, but the populace thought this too harsh a punishment. Chosroes promised he would release the Persian but then impaled him anyway secretly to maintain discipline in his army. This shows him as a strict disciplinarian – it is no wonder the Persian army performed so well under him.

After this Chosroes continued his policy of extortion by marching to Chalcis, which he threatened through Paulus. The inhabitants were required to hand over any soldiers in the city and pay a ransom. The citizens hid the soldiers and then swore that none were present and paid 200 lbs of gold. We should not wonder what Buzes was doing while Chosroes was extorting money from the Roman cities, because the ambassadors had concluded a treaty with Chosroes which the Romans considered to be in effect even if Chosroes failed to follow it. The not-so-veiled accusation of Procopius that Buzes disappeared and did nothing to protect the Roman cities is in all probability an attempt to contrast Belisarius and Buzes with each other by blackening the latter's reputation with no good reason.

Chosroes naturally wanted to avoid the route he had taken and marched to Mesopotamia to extort more money. He built a bridge at Obbane which was 40 stades (c.7 km) from Barbalissus. The Persians were ordered to cross the Euphrates in three days because he was going to break up the bridge on the third day. Those left on the other side after this were forced to find their way back to their native land as best they could. Chosroes was a disciplinarian. The march was continued to Batne/Batnaea with the idea of continuing against Edessa; he wanted to capture it because it was claimed to be under the protection of Jesus Christ. Procopius (*Wars* 2.12.31ff.) claims that Chosroes attempted to continue his march to Edessa but his army lost its way twice and was forced to encamp close to Batne, and when then a suppuration set in his face, Chosroes sent Paulus to demand money from the citizens of Edessa in return for not ravaging the countryside around it. The Edessans gave 200 lbs of gold for this. A more rational explanation for the above is that Buzes was performing his duties admirably by shadowing Chosroes so that the latter decided that his best policy was to agree to a small ransom. The reason for this conclusion is that we find Buzes at Edessa (Procop. *Wars* 2.13.1–7).

At about the same time, Justinian's ambassadors arrived at Chosroes's camp. They had been sent by Justinian to confirm the terms of the treaty. Chosroes duly released the hostages and started to make preparations for the return. Because of this Chosroes announced that he wanted to sell all the captives he had taken from Antioch. The citizens of Edessa were overjoyed and everyone contributed their possessions for this purpose – even the harlots, as Procopius notes. They amassed a great amount of gold and silver but all to no avail because Buzes prevented the transaction in the hope that it would earn him the emperor's gratitude. I would suggest that this actually means that Buzes was following the terms of the treaty, even if Procopius does not say so. The peace was to be obtained with the terms agreed, and I would suggest that the terms included a clause for the release of the captives taken in return for the first payment of gold, even if Procopius does not refer to it. It is also clear that Chosroes had by then broken the terms agreed because he was still on Roman soil and not in Persia.

Some time after May 540, Belisarius, Valerianus, Martinus, Ildiger and Herodianus were recalled from Italy. They reached Constantinople by about midsummer. Belisarius and possibly also Valerianus, Ildiger and Herodianus stayed there but Martinus was immediately dispatched to the east with his men to reinforce the strategic city of Dara just in case Chosroes didn't respect his promises, as indeed happened. This was a wise decision, but we do not know why Justinian failed to dispatch Belisarius with his men; he was after all the official *Magister Militum per Orientem* for the area west of the Euphrates. It is possible that Belisarius was now under suspicion because of his actions and was therefore not sent to the front, or that when Germanus was still in the east the arrival of Belisarius would have caused a conflict between these two men, or that Justinian just did not think it necessary to send Belisarius to the scene thanks to the treaty he had agreed to sign and because the Persians were already withdrawing. It is possible that all of these matters influenced the decision, but the likeliest is the last alternative.

Consequently, Chosroes led his army and the captives east towards home. En route he was met by the envoys of the citizens of Carrhae who promised him a ransom, but Chosroes refused to accept this money because the money did not belong to him on the grounds that the majority of the populace of Carrhae were pagans and not Christians. Chosroes wanted to appear as the protector of the pagans to cause divisions among the Romans. When the citizens of Constantina offered a ransom, he accepted it because he claimed that the city belonged to him as it had previously been captured by his father Cabades/Kavadh in 502 (see vol.5).

The siege of Daras/Dara in late summer 540[22]

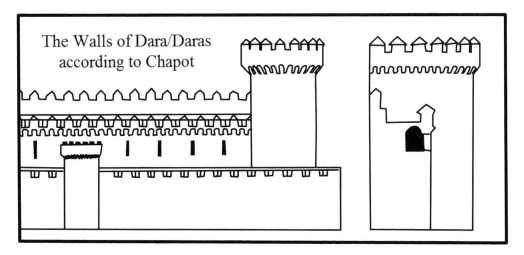

When Chosroes reached Daras/Dara, he besieged it. The Romans were under Martinus, who had brought reinforcements there from Italy. Chosroes clearly did not have any intention of respecting his promises and the treaty agreed. Thanks to its strategic location close to the border and Nisibis, Daras had always been a thorn in the Persian eye ever since it had been built under Anastasius. By now the city was surrounded by two strong walls, which enabled the populace to place their cattle between them during sieges. See the attached map and the drawing of the walls. The first Persian assault was directed against the western section. The Persians forced back the defenders by overwhelming numbers of arrows and burned the gates of the small wall. However they did not dare go inside. Next, the Persians made a tunnel secretly against the eastern side of the city.

According to Procopius, the Persians would have succeeded had there not been someone from the Persian army (probably a Roman deserter) who revealed this to the Romans. Thanks to this Theodorus (a skilled engineer) built a crosswise trench between the two walls and when the Persians then reached it the Romans killed those in front, but allowed the rest to flee back to their camp because they did not want to follow the Persians into the dark tunnel. The Persians now despaired of attempting to take the city so that Chosroes opened negotiations. It was now the late summer and it is certain that Chosroes was now also aware of the arrival of the Roman reinforcements from Italy. Chosroes agreed to leave after receiving a ransom of 1,000 lbs of silver so that he could return home while the season was favourable. This siege demonstrates the value of civilian engineers in defence as well as the value of sympathizers among the enemy ranks. According to Procopius (*Wars* 2.13.29), when Justinian learnt of the siege of Dara/Daras during a truce, he was no longer willing to abide by the agreement reached with Chosroes. This means that Chosroes had taken his policy of hoodwinking the Romans one step too far, unless it had been his plan all along to continue the war next year on the basis of the news that he had learnt from envoys sent by the king of Lazica. Justinian had clearly been willing to accept the previous instances of extortion of ransoms, but the unprovoked attack against Dara after the terms of the treaty had been confirmed was too much.

On his arrival at home Chosroes built a city for the captives taken from Antioch at a distance of one day's journey from Ctesiphon. He constructed for them a bath and hippodrome together with other Roman luxuries so that it included charioteers and musicians like any Roman city. These inhabitants were made direct subordinates of Chosroes so that there were no magistrates to rule over them. Under Justin I Antioch had lost 300,000 people in the earthquake of 526 and now the survivors had become subjects of Chosroes in a city which was named 'Antioch of Chosroes' or 'Better Than Antioch' or the 'City of the Romans'.[23]

Return of Belisarius from Italy and the downfall of John the Cappadocian in 540–41[24]

As discussed above, when Belisarius returned from Italy officially to take charge of the Persian War, he did not receive a triumph or any other form of formal thanks from Justinian due to the behaviour he had demonstrated in Italy. However, all others looked upon Belisarius with great admiration. But there was one exception: Praetorian Prefect John the Cappadocian. He did not care much about his schooling; he appreciated more the practical side of life in which he excelled. He knew how to obtain money for the emperor by both legal and illegal means and how to enrich himself in the process. He had a daily routine. John plundered the property of the subjects with any means possible until lunchtime, after which he spent the rest of the day in drunken revelry. He was also in the habit of eating so much food that he vomited like a bulimic.

John hated Belisarius and Theodora and slandered both at every opportunity. He even insulted Theodora in public, despite the fact that Justinian loved her blindly. Because of this Theodora started to seek ways of getting rid of the man, but was unable to do so because Justinian thought the services of John too valuable. John, however, feared that

Theodora would attempt to assassinate him and with this in mind surrounded himself with thousands of *bucellarii*.

The next stage in the family drama of Belisarius took place when he had returned to Constantinople in the summer of 540. The reason for the family drama was that Antonina was no longer able to conceal her passion towards Theodosius so Theodosius became frightened and fled to Ephesus. Antonina was grief-stricken. But she managed to draw her husband into the same mood so that Belisarius wept for his adopted son Theodosius and even entreated the emperor and empress to recall Theodosius from Ephesus. It is very likely that both the empress and emperor knew the truth of the matter, unlike Belisarius. Theodosius, however, refused to return and claimed to be a monk, but in truth he had other ideas because he joined Antonina immediately after Belisarius had departed to the Persian front. This time Antonina did not join her husband because she lusted after Theodosius and wanted to spend every spare moment having sex with him. In addition to this, Antonina made certain that there would not be anyone preventing this and convinced Belisarius to take Photius with him to the front. Photius was annoyed and took every opportunity to slander his mother to Belisarius.[25]

After the departure of Belisarius to the eastern front in the spring of 541, Antonina the wife of Belisarius and the closest friend and confidant of Theodora came up with a plan to get rid of John the Cappadocian – Antonina certainly felt compelled to make herself useful to the empress in return for her silence regarding Theodosius. She befriended herself with Euphemia, the daughter of John of Cappadocia, and let it be known through her that Belisarius would be ready to support John's usurpation of the throne with military force. John loved his only child dearly and was ready to believe her words. He was encouraged in this by sorcerers and oracles who promised him the imperial throne. Antonina promised to meet John in the suburb of Rufinianae, at a house which was owned by Belisarius. The excuses were that Antonina wanted to discuss the details at a place where others could not overhear them and that Antonina was on her way to be beside her husband in the east which would explain her travel there. Antonina claimed that she would tell her husband the plan by travelling to the east after the two agreed on the details. Antonina then told the empress and she dispatched Narses the Eunuch, Marcellus the commander of the palace guards (presumably the *Comes Excubitorum*) together with numerous soldiers (*stratiôtai* meaning presumably the *excubitores*) to investigate. Meanwhile the empress went to meet the emperor to tell him what was afoot. According to one story, the emperor sent a messenger to John which warned him not to go to the meeting, which was ignored by John – Procopius claims that this was because Justinian loved John too much, but if the account is true, it is also possible that it was a test of some kind. Antonina posted Narses and Marcellus behind a curtain wall so that they could hear what was being said. When enough had been said, the two men rushed in to capture the culprit, but the bodyguards of John fought back so that John was able to flee. Procopius was of the opinion that Justinian would have spared John had he fled to him, but John chose to flee to a sanctuary so Theodora was able to convince the emperor to punish the plotter. John's property was confiscated and he was made a priest in Cyzicus, but soon after this he was exiled to Egypt in 542 and John's house was given to Belisarius. Theodora, Antonina and Belisarius could be happy. They had got rid of their worst enemy within the inner circle of the emperor.

John the Cappadocian's 'reforms' scaled back[26]

The downfall of John the Cappadocian meant also the scaling back of his 'reforms' which had proved disastrous. The uniting of civilian and military duties in a number of provinces had not worked as expected because bandits had been able to cross from one province to another and when there were no longer vicars there was no-one to coordinate efforts for such situations. In 542 the *Comes Orientis* received back some of his duties over his diocese, and in 548 the vicariate of Pontica was revived to act as police officer with duties to control brigandage crossing provincial borders. At about the same time, the administration also created a new office called *biocolytes* (preventer of violence) with the duty of maintaining law and order in the five provinces of the Asianic diocese: Lycaonia, Pisidia, Lydia and the two Phrygias. This solution worked becase in 553 Pisidia and the two Phrygias were considered pacified enough to be removed from under *biocolytes*. Justinian also recognized the mistake that had been made in Thrace and restored its vicariate. He did not stop at this; the string of new legislation shows that he continually attempted to make adjustments and improvements in the collection of revenue and administration of justice.

The principal financial advisor of Justinian during these years was Peter Barsymes who was appointed *Comes Sacrarum Largitionum* in about 540 and *PPO* in 543. He made himself very unpopular in this office and Procopius accuses him of being a corrupt rogue. This may be an exaggeration, but corrupt he certainly was. On the other hand he was able to collect the revenue that Justinian needed for his administration and armed forces. Barsymes was dismissed from office in 546 , but Justinian soon recalled him to service as *Comes Sacrarum Largitionum* after which he was again appointed *PPO* in 554/5. He held this office at least until 562 but it is likely that he held it until Justinian's death. Barsymes gained additional notoriety with the creation of the state monopoly in silk fabrics and with the selling of monopolies in other categories of goods to unscrupulous guilds of merchants/shopkeepers. He sold these monopolies first in Constantinople, but then extended the scheme to other cities as well. The natural result of this was a rise in prices. According to Procopius, prices tripled. In addition to this, it appears likely that Barsymes revived the practice of selling the offices. Justinian did get the money he wanted and needed for his wars and other projects, but at the cost of the taxpayers and those who had to pay higher prices for goods.

Belisarius takes the offensive in 541

Chosroes's strategy for 541[27]

What is notable about the course of the war in 541 is that Chosroes retained the initiative despite the arrival of Belisarius together with reinforcements from Italy. After Germanus had returned to Constantinople, Justinian dispatched Belisarius to the east together with the officers, soldiers and Goths that he had brought with him from Italy. Valerianus was appointed *MVM per Armeniam* while Belisarius commanded all of the forces south of him as *MVM per Orientem*. According to Procopius, the orders were just to fight against the Persians. Once put in charge in the spring of 541 Belisarius acted fast because he wanted to be on the scene before Chosroes invaded. This begs the question why the

Romans remained passive. Subsequent details of the campaign provide an answer. The destruction of the intelligence gathering organization in the east and economising in the state postal system had made the Romans blind so it was very difficult to make plans in advance. However, there was at least one lucky break for the Romans which was that *Dux Mesopotamiae* John Troglita managed to capture one of the envoys who had previously been dispatched by Vittigis to Persia near the boundaries of Constantina. The fact that Justinian dispatched Belisarius with his men to the east only in the spring of 541 and not in the autumn of 540 also influenced the course of events because Belisarius was able to start gathering necessary information for the strategy he would adopt only after he had been given command.

In the meantime, Chosroes had received another set of envoys from Lazica/Iberia who were annoyed by the presence of the Roman garrison in their territory at the newly built fort of Petra and by the establishment of monopolies to satisfy the greed of John Tzibus. This time King Gourgenes had found the right way to convince Chosroes. Gourgenes noted the strategic advantages that the Persians would gain if they possessed harbours and a fleet on the Black Sea. The Persians would also gain possession of the strategic passes over the Caucasus, which would enable them to open them for their Hunnic allies. In short, they could threaten the Roman capital with a fleet and Huns. Chosroes, however, was worried about the terrain because he had heard that it was heavily forested and difficult to traverse. The envoys promised to show the way through which Chosroes could lead his army, if they cut down the trees to build a road. Chosroes was delighted and assembled a great army and then spread disinformation that the plan was to march to Iberia which was in Persian hands to fight against a Hunnic tribe that had invaded. This was a superb double feint. The Huns had indeed crossed into Iberia so their arrival could be confirmed, but not as enemies of Persia but as their allies. The invasion of Armenia by these Huns served as a diversionary operation to keep the Army of Armenia preoccupied while Chosroes marched to Lazica/Colchis.

When Belisarius reached Mesopotamia his first actions were to send spies into Persian territory while assembling forces from every quarter possible. His plan was to meet the enemy invasion there if it took place. The Roman army was in a sorry state. Most of the soldiers were without arms and armour, in addition to which they were in a state of fear. Consequently, the very first thing that Belisarius did was to equip them with arms and armour while attempting to raise their morale. When the spies returned they declared that Chosroes would not be invading because he was fighting against the Huns in Iberia. In other words, the spies believed the disinformation that Chosroes had purposely spread. It is impossible to know if this would have been the case if Justinian had not abolished the spy organization in the east, but it is clear that Procopius (*Anek.* 30.12–14) was of the opinion that the disinformation would not have fooled the Romans had Justinian retained the intelligence gathering organization intact. In other words, he claimed that the Romans had infiltrated the Persian Royal Palace so well before the abolition of the organization by Justinian that they knew the innermost secrets of the Persians. As a member of this spy organization he was undoubtedly in a position to know. When Belisarius learnt that Chosroes would not be invading, he decided to invade the enemy territory immediately.

Belisarius assembled the officers in Dara to discuss how to do this. He wisely flattered those present and stated that he needed advice because he had only just returned from the West and since he was only human he could not know what had happened in the long interval during which he had been absent. Peter and Bouzes urged the taking of the offensive and their advice found favour among all those present excepting Rhecithancus and Theoctistus, the *duces* of Lebanon. They feared that if they abandoned their posts, Alamoundaros would invade Phoenicia and Syria. It was only then that Belisarius openly showed his knowledge of local affairs. He stated that both were mistaken because it was then the season of the vernal equinox when the Saracens did not undertake wars because they devoted two months to the worship of their god. So Belisarius promised that he would release the two *duces* and their men back to their stations within sixty days. Now all were prepared to invade.

The assembled army consisted of the local forces that Belisarius had reinforced with his own bodyguards, Germanic Federates (Goths and Vandals), Thracian troops, and Saracens under Arethas. The size of the force must have been considerable. The two Lebanese *duces* had previously had 6,000 horsemen and it is probable that this was the size of their force now, and one may also assume that the army would have included the *duces* of Mesopotamia, Oshroene and Euphratensis, each of whom would have brought at least 3,000 horsemen with them. These would total 15,000 horsemen. Belisarius's own bodyguards must have consisted of a minimum of 7,000 horsemen as previously, and the Gothic contingent he had brought from Italy must have been at least 6,000–10,000 horsemen strong. The Vandal contingent would have consisted of at least 3,000 horsemen and the Arab contingent of Arethas perhaps about 5,000 as previously. The local Army of the East and the reinforcements taken from Thrace (Goths and other Federates posted in Thrace, Praesental Forces, Army of Thrace) would have added perhaps 10,000 cavalry and 30,000 to 40,000 footmen to the figure. It is likely that most of the *Limitanei* infantry forces posted in the east would have been left as garrisons. The likely total would therefore have been about 43,000–48,000 horsemen and 30,000–40,000 footmen of variable quality because most of the unarmed men would probably have belonged to the infantry. The reason why Procopius fails to mention the size of the army this time is that it was so large and its achievements were rather puny.

The battle of Nisibis in vernal equinox 541[28]

When the preliminaries for a campaign had been completed satisfactorily Belisarius led his army in good order from Dara towards Nisibis. This is known with certainty, but then we face a problem. There are two versions of the events that took place before Nisibis, one by Procopius and another by Corippus. These two texts provide us with slightly different accounts of the resulting battle because Corippus fails to mention any setbacks suffered by his hero John, while Procopius claims that John was saved by Belisarius. Procopius's account is inherently more likely to be true, but it is still clear that he has left out the heroics of John which can be added to his account. The following account therefore reconciles and combines these two accounts as one.

Belisarius chose an open and level terrain with an abundance of water springs suitable for cavalry warfare. The other officers voiced their disapproval loudly; they wanted to get closer to the city. Belisarius, who wanted to keep his plans secret as long as possible, was forced to state his case. He noted that if the engagement was close to the walls, the

Persians would be bolder in attack, having a place of refuge nearby. However, if the battle was fought in his chosen place, the Persians would have a long distance to flee back, which would either enable the pursuers to take their city through pursuit, or force the Persians to flee away from the city so that it would be easier to take.

According to Procopius, Belisarius's words fell on deaf ears. Peter and John Troglita encamped 10 stades (1,850m) away from Nisibis. Belisarius knew that this meant trouble and warned the two commanders to be in readiness at midday because the Persians habitually attacked when the Romans ate their food. Belisarius prepared his forces for combat, but according to Procopius the two commanders chose not to follow the order and let their soldiers go about in a disorderly fashion and eat. When the Persian commander Nabedes observed this, he attacked immediately. Peter and John hastily collected their forces and sent to Belisarius to ask his help. The disordered forces of Peter and John were easily routed, but Belisarius's men were already on their way. It is this setback that Corippus has left out of his account. The pursuing Persians were unable to withstand the charge of the Roman cavalry. The Goths charged in close order in front of the rest with their long spears. The sight frightened the Persians. They did not wait for the attack but fled straightaway back to Nisibis. The Goths had once again proven their great value as lancer cavalry against the Persians. During the short pursuit, the Romans and Goths killed 150 Persians. Casualties among the men of Peter and John were 50 and the standard of Peter was captured. In short, the whole encounter proved to be a skirmish.

Corippus (1.58–69) mentions no setbacks, but states that the brave John Troglita had charged through the showers of arrows shot by the Persians and attacked their commander Nabedes in the broad fields of Nisibis with the result that Nabedes was forced to seek safety from inside the central citadel of Nisibis. According to Corippus, the Persians had been scarcely able to close their gates behind them and prevent the Roman horsemen from entering the city. It was then that the brave John advanced up to those tall gates and struck them with his spear in apparent frustration and a show of bravado. Nabedes was second only to the king of kings in the ranking so this feat earned John praise.

It is therefore clear that there is a distinct difference in the accounts of Corippus and Procopius. However, it is quite easy to reconcile them. Procopius is certainly right that Peter and John had disobeyed Belisarius and had been routed and Belisarius had advanced to save them. It was then as a result of this that at least John had been able to regroup his men so fast that he had actually charged ahead of all the rest in pursuit of the defeated foe, and that this pursuit had been performed with such speed that the enemy was scarcely able to flee inside the city. The Romans clearly deployed at least two cavalry lines in this battle, the first under Peter and John, the second under Belisarius, but it is possible that there were actually three cavalry lines if Belisarius deployed his own forces in two lines; none of the sources mention any personal involvement for him in this battle. If he did, it is possible that he could have deployed it in an unusual manner so that his first line would have consisted of four divisions to make it easier for the forces of Peter and John to retreat as if it were a training exercise. Belisarius presumably left his infantry behind in the marching camp when he had deployed his forces for combat because it is clear that he had infantry forces present for the planned sieges.

This small battle shows the typical time of attack chosen by the Persians, the relatively small numbers of casualties in cavalry skirmishes, the fleeing of one party before contact and the number of casualties in pursuit. It also shows how important it was for the cavalry to have sufficient distance for pursuing the enemy so that it could be decisively defeated. This encounter is a good example of the worst kind of disobedience that the Roman commanders sometimes showed towards their superior officers. It is probable that in this case Belisarius's situation was aggravated by his slavish relationship with his wife Antonina and by the apparent envy of the other commanders. Practically the only Roman commander during Justinian's reign to have an easy relationship with other officers was Narses the Eunuch, but we should not overstate the difficulties arising from the strained relationships between the officers, since no army is without them. The true testament to the ability of the Romans to conduct their operations, despite personality clashes, is that most of their operations were still successful.

The siege of Sisauranon/Sisarbanon and raid into Assyria[29]

Belisarius was unwilling to attempt to besiege Nisibis because its defences were strong and he had failed to destroy its garrison. He wanted to bypass the city and cause damage to the enemy by some other action, so he next advanced his army in front of Sisauranon, which was a day's march from the border. According to Procopius, it was a populous city with a garrison of 800 elite soldiers under Bleschames. If the modern identification of the area by Anthony Martin Comfort is correct, then Procopius exaggerates. Sisauranon was certainly not populous, as is suggested by the small number of defenders, but it was strategically located right opposite the Roman fortress of Rhabdion. However, if Procopius's description is accurate then it is possible that the identification is incorrect or that there were outer defences that are not visible from the satellite image unless they are located alongside the minor hills – in fact it is possible that the hill was just the acropolis/citadel of the city, which has not yet been subjected to a thorough archaeological study. Belisarius pitched his camp close to the city and ordered his men to assault, but the wall was strong and the Roman attack failed and they lost many men. Belisarius therefore called together an assembly of officers in which he reiterated his reasons for not advancing further in a situation in which there were enemy garrisons behind that could have endangered his lines of communications. He suggested that the Romans persist in their efforts against Sisauranon while Arethas conducted a reconnaissance in strength to Assyria, the area around the Persian capital Ctesiphon. He feared that if the Romans advanced any further the garrisons of Nisibis and Sisauranon could shadow and harass them, and that they could also face another enemy force in front of them. The Arabs were useless in sieges and could therefore be used for this intelligence gathering operation, and if the Romans were able to capture Sisauranon and the intelligence gathered by the Arabs showed that it would be possible to invade Assyria, Belisarius stated it was then that the Romans could advance with their whole army against Ctesiphon. As we shall see, Procopius gives us entirely different reasons for this reluctance to advance any further in his *Secret History* – namely that the marriage problems of Belisarius made him unwilling to advance far from border. But this is unlikely to have been the main reason. The reasons given here fit the character of the typically cautious Belisarius.

This time the officers voiced their approval, despite some apparently thinking that the real reason for Belisarius's reluctance to advance any further was his marital problems.

Consequently, Belisarius dispatched Arethas with his Arab *foederati* to reconnoitre the route to Assyria. Procopius does not give any number for the Arabs, but it is probable that Arethas had about 5,000 horsemen, as previously. Belisarius reinforced these by 1,200 *stratiotai*, most of whom were drawn from his own bodyguards, placing two of his guardsmen in command of them, Trajan (Traianus) and John the Glutton (Ioannes ho Fagas). His orders for these two men were to obey Arethas, and his orders for Arethas were to pillage everything on the route and then return to the camp to give a report of the military forces present in Assyria. Arethas and his men thereby crossed the River Tigris and entered Assyria. Arethas passed through the area fast and was able to gather vast amounts of booty thanks to the fact that it had not been pillaged for ages. Meanwhile Belisarius's forces captured some of the Persians, who told Belisarius that the Persians in this area were not in constant combat readiness and were not gathering supplies in store-houses to prepare themselves for possible sieges.

So the Romans put Sisauranon under siege, and sure enough the defenders lacked the necessary provisions to hold out. Belisarius dispatched his confidant George to offer terms of surrender, and unsurprisingly the city surrendered. Belisarius released all the inhabitants because they were Christians of Roman origin, razed the fortifications to the ground, and then sent the Persian garrison together with its commander Bleschames to Constantinople. Justinian despatched these Persians to Italy where they were used against the Goths.

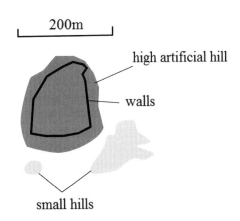

Sisauranon/Sisarbanon
A rough hypothetical reconstruction of the fortress based on a satellite image. The fortress was built on top of an artificial hill with an elevation of 545m

According to Procopius's *Wars*, it was then that the greedy Arethas betrayed the Romans. He had gathered vast amounts of booty and feared that if he returned to the camp, the Romans would take it from him, so he came up with a ruse to keep his booty. He dispatched some of his men to reconnoitre with orders to return immediately with the news that there was a large force of Persians at the crossing of the River Tigris. He then instructed Trajan and John to take another route to the Romans. Trajan and John kept the River Euphrates on their right side and did not come anywhere near Belisarius until they reached Theodosiopolis-Resaina. In the meantime, Belisarius and the Romans became nervous because Arethas's force appeared to have vanished from the face of the earth. On top of this, many of the soldiers had developed a fever because the area controlled by the Persians in Mesopotamia was dry and hot and the Romans – in particular those from Thrace – were not accustomed to this. According to Procopius's *Wars*, a third of the Roman force was lying half-dead because they could not withstand the summer heat and the whole army was eager to return to Roman territory as quickly as possible. The most eager to leave were the *duces* of Lebanon, Rhecithaneus and Theoctistus, because the three month long Sacred season of the Saracens had already passed. Belisarius therefore assembled his officers. John son of Nicetas was the first to speak. He recommended withdrawal because: 1) the Saracens and the elite Romans must have suffered a terrible disaster because they had been unable to dispatch any messengers to them; 2) The *Limitanei* of Lebanon were about to leave; 3) The rest of the army consisted of the sick and of those who were needed to take care of them. These comments met with approval and when the officers demanded an immediate withdrawal, Belisarius consented. The sick were placed in carts, which were put in the van while the rest of the army under Belisarius followed after them. When Belisarius reached the Roman territory, he learnt what Arethas had done, but was unable to inflict any punishment because Arethas never came into his sight again. According to the *Secret History* of Procopius the real reason for the withdrawal of Belisarius was his eagerness to return to Roman territory to exact punishment on his unfaithful wife Antonina, but as the above has made clear, that was only hostile gossiping. Belisarius was by nature a cautious commander and when his scouting forces under Arethas failed to bring any report of the enemy strength in Assyria he was naturally unwilling to take any risks.

Chosroes invades Lazica[30]

It is probable that Chosroes met the Sabir Huns he had invited when his forces reached Iberia and that it was then that he dispatched these Huns towards Armenia to distract the forces serving under *MVM per Armeniam* Valerianus so that he could invade Lazica without having to fear Roman counter-attack. Valerianus defeated and annihilated this Hunnic force.

The Lazican envoys leading the way, the Persian army cut trees where necessary and threw them to enable them to pass through the rough places and so they reached the centre of Colchis. In his *Wars* Procopius states that the road became easy to march thanks to these measures, but in his *Secret History* (*Anekdota*), he states that the roads were so bad that many Persians died as a result of these operations. Goubazes met Chosroes there and made obeisance, and told him of the Roman garrison posted at Petra under John Tzibus. When Chosroes learnt of this, he dispatched an army under Aniabedes against them. When John heard of their approach, he armed all of his men and posted them near the gates in readiness to charge out, but with orders not to make a sound. When the Persian scouts approached the city and they did not see or hear anything, they thought that the city was abandoned. Consequently, the general sent a message to Chosroes who dispatched most of the army forward to make a general assault with ladders while one officer was ordered to take the battering ram against one of the gates. After this Chosroes seated himself on a hill near the city to observe the attack. Then the Romans threw the gates open and assaulted the Persians. The Romans killed large numbers of Persians especially around the ram. The rest beat a hasty retreat as best they could. The enraged Chosroes had either Aniabedes or the officer in charge of the ram impaled as a punishment – there were two versions.

After this Chosroes led his entire force to the scene, built a camp and began a proper siege. On the following day, Chosroes inspected the fortifications and came to the conclusion that the Romans would not be able to withstand a strong attack. He ordered the Persians to shoot arrows on the Romans, to which the Romans responded by using their artillery pieces (*mechanai*) and bows. Despite the great quantity of arrows shot by the Persians the Romans had an advantage thanks to their elevated position, but then a disaster struck. One of the Persian arrows hit John in the neck, killing him. This demoralized the Romans, but the Persians did not know it and withdrew to their camp. They planned to renew their attack on the following day by digging a tunnel beneath the fortifications. Petra could be approached from only one direction where the terrain was level. The Romans had built two walls each with one tower to protect this vulnerable spot. The Persians dug their tunnel secretly against this section, their tunnel finally reaching one of the towers. The Persians placed wood to support the structure and then burned it with the result that the whole tower collapsed. When the Romans posted on the tower realized what was happening they fled inside the city wall before the tower collapsed. Realizing their situation was now hopeless, they started negotiations. The end result was that the Romans surrendered and were enrolled into the Persian army and Chosroes got possession of the city together with the treasury of John.

The treasury of John was obviously substantial, but according to the *Wars* and *Secret History* of Procopius, the conquest of Lazica had been very costly to the Persians because they had lost many men to the difficult terrain and even more to the pestilence affecting the area and the difficulties in provisioning the army in this area. This is not surprising because the Romans had faced similar difficulties even though they had had access to the sea. For this see, vol.5. It was at this point in time that certain Persians arrived in Lazica with the news of the successes of Belisarius and Valerianus. This frightened the Persians who started to fear that the Romans would block their retreat route or that the Romans would attack their homes in Assyria and kill their families while they were still in Lazica. They complained to Chosroes and charged him with the accusation that they were in trouble because he had violated his oaths and invaded Roman territory during a truce – this presumably refers to the siege of Dara. The Persians were on a point of mutiny, but Chosroes found a remedy in the form of a letter that the empress Theodora had sent to Zaberganes. He read the letter to the nobles and stated that this proved that the Roman Empire was not a real state because women acted in this manner. This calmed the Persians' anger and Chosroes placed a garrison at Petra and then led his army homewards. Chosroes feared that Belisarius might have blocked the route of retreat, but when this fear did not materialize he was glad to lead his army back home.

There were two fortresses, called Pityus and Sebastopolis, two days apart from each other along the coast that the Romans still garrisoned even after they had abandoned their other possessions in the lands of 'Saginae'. When the Romans in these two cities learned that Chosroes intended to dispatch an army against them from Petra, they anticipated this by burning their houses and razing the walls to the ground, after which they embarked in small boats and sailed to Trapezus. The Persians were forced to return to Petra. This means that the two garrisons did not expect to be able to withstand a siege so that they rather adopted the policy of denying them to the Persians.

When Chosroes was campaigning in Lazica he learnt from Varanes, son of the Kanarang, that Adergoudounbades had not killed Kavadh, son of Zames. The goal of Varanes was to become the Kanarang instead of his father. Consequently, when Chosroes was returning from Lazica he sent a flattering message to Adergoudounbades in which he instructed the latter to come to meet him so that they could invade Roman territory with two divisions, the other of which would be placed in the hands of the Kanarang. He was now an old man. The journey proved difficult for him and he fell from his horse breaking a bone in his leg. Chosroes came to meet him and told him to go to a nearby fortress to receive treatment. However, the retinue which escorted the Kanarang killed him, and Varranes became the new Kanarang. This was how Chosroes lost an able commander who could have been of great use to him, because Kanarang Adergoudounbades had never been defeated in combat. He had marched against twelve barbarian nations and subjected all for *Shahanshah* Kavadh, and as we have seen he had also served well under Chosroes himself. The son of Zames, Kavadh/Cabades, managed to escape and flee to Constantinople. Procopius was uncertain whether the man really was Kavadh/Cabades, but Justinian treated him as if he was. Not long after, another of Chosroes's military commanders died, Mebodes. He was killed by Chosroes himself as a result of plotting by Zaberganes. Procopius gives Mebodes the title of *magister*, which presumably means *Magister Officiorum*, the Persian equivalent of which was *Hazarbed*.

Belisarius's family affairs

According to the *Secret History* of Procopius (*Anek.* 1.2.1ff), the real reason for the failure of Belisarius to achieve anything of any importance was that he was eager to meet his wife Antonina at the first opportunity when she came near to the border region. Because of this Belisarius neither advanced against Ctesiphon nor attempted to block the route of retreat from the Persians. Procopius claims that during the Persian campaign Photius constantly slandered his mother Antonina to Belisarius and when a certain person arrived from Constantinople with the news that Theodosius was secretly staying with Antonina, Photius brought this news immediately to Belisarius. Belisarius was enraged and asked Photius to exact vengeance on Antonina because her behaviour cast a shadow on them both. Photius was at first hesitant to act because he knew how weak Belisarius had been in the past, but when Belisarius swore on oath, they formed a plan. When Antonina travelled from Constantinople to meet Belisarius, Photius was to capture Theodosius while Belisarius would imprison Antonina. It was then when Belisarius had just captured Sisauranon that he learnt from a messenger that Antonina had just started her journey to the east, with the result that he led the army straightaway back to Roman territory. However, Procopius (*Anek.* 2.18–19) was still forced to admit that this was not the only reason for Belisarius's decision to retreat. There were other reasons too. He merely states that the marital problems made this decision easier. In my opinion it is clear that in this case Belisarius did not subject the interests of the state to the needs of his personal life. It would have been dangerous for him to lead an illness-stricken army deep into the enemy territory in a situation in which he did not possess any intelligence of enemy forces. However, this did not prevent those who envied Belisarius from exploiting this situation, because according to Procopius 'all Romans' accused Belisarius of having subordinated the vital interests of the state to those of his family. The accusation ran that Belisarius had been unwilling to advance further than a day's distance from the border after which he withdrew immediately to punish his wife. The accusers, who included Procopius, claimed that he could have invaded Assyria up to Ctesiphon with his whole army and rescued the prisoners from Antioch. They also accused him of not having blocked the route of retreat from Lazica so Chosroes was able to retreat unpunished. However, as noted, these accusations were unfounded. In hindsight it is clear that Belisarius could have achieved the successes that Procopius and the other accusers state but it would have meant taking a massive risk because Belisarius would have had to do this without having any intelligence of the enemy forces – Belisarius was not in the habit of taking such unnecessary risks.

Belisarius's problems, however, did not end with the slander. When he returned to Roman territory, he put the adulteress Antonina under guard in disgrace with the intention of killing her, but every time he set about to kill her, his heart softened. He also sent the army to its winter quarters, which in the case of his bodyguards meant Cilicia. In the meantime, Photius set out for Ephesus and took with him Calligonus, one of Antonina's eunuchs, who was a confidant of Antonina. Photius tortured Calligonus until he broke and revealed all the secrets. However, Theodosius had meanwhile learnt what had happened so he was able to flee to the Church of Apostle Paul. This proved insufficient because Photius bribed the chief priest who duly handed him over. By now Theodora had also learnt what had happened and she summoned Belisarius and Antonina to Constantinople. When Photius learnt of this, he realised what was afoot and sent Theodosius to Cilicia so that Belisarius's *doruforoi* and *hypaspistai* could guard the prisoner in some secret location. After this Photius took Theodosius's money and Calligonus and went to Constantinople; Theodora rewarded her loyal friend Antonina most handsomely. She handed over to Antonina friends of Belisarius and Photius who they tortured despite the fact that no charges were brought against them. Some were killed and others were exiled. One of the men to suffer this treatment was another Theodosius, who held senatorial rank, but because he was a friend of Photius he was forced to stand in a dark underground chamber for four months of tortured existence until he died. Theodora also forced Belisarius to become reconciled with Antonina and then tortured Photius. According to Procopius, Photius withstood the torture and revealed nothing, but the whereabouts of Theodosius was still found out. Theodora housed Theodosius in her palace for Antonina's physical enjoyment until the day came when Theodosius died of dysentery. Photius was also imprisoned in Theodora's quarters. He managed to flee twice, only to be forcibly taken back, but on the third occasion three years later he managed to flee to Jerusalem where he became a monk, where he managed to avoid being detected by Theodora's agents. Subsequent events make it clear that the treatment Belisarius had received from Theodora and Antonina turned him against them and Justinian.

The Campaign Season 542[31]

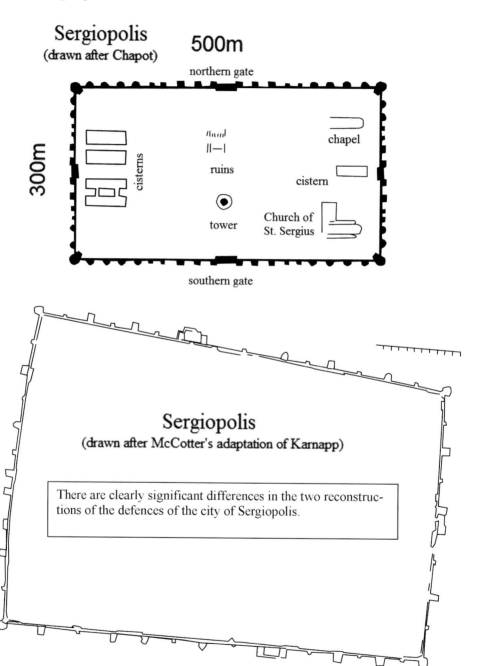

Sergiopolis
(drawn after Chapot)

500m

northern gate

300m

cisterns

ruins

chapel

cistern

tower

Church of
St. Sergius

southern gate

Sergiopolis
(drawn after McCotter's adaptation of Karnapp)

There are clearly significant differences in the two reconstructions of the defences of the city of Sergiopolis.

Siege of Sergiopolis 542

In 542 the Persians retained the initiative. Chosroes I invaded again. Candidus, the priest of Sergiopolis, went to meet Chosroes because he had not paid the *Shahanshah* the ransom he had previously promised. He promised the treasury of the sanctuary as a compensation for his failure. After receiving the money, the king did not consider it sufficient and decided to send men to take the city on the pretext of seeking further wealth from it. The plan was betrayed by a Christian Arab, Ambrus, and the gates remained closed. Chosroes sent only 6,000 men to besiege the city because it was in the desert, while he marched on with his main army keeping the Euphrates on his right. The situation was opportune because there were only 200 regular soldiers in the city. At first the citizens fought bravely, but they were on the point of giving up when Ambrus again informed them that their supplies had failed and they would leave after two days. So the thirsty Persians were forced to flee in disgrace thanks to the presence of a Christian traitor in their ranks. The desert terrain and Christian sympathizers amongst the enemy proved helpful in defence. The two attached slightly different reconstructions of the defences of the city show what type of obstacle these were for the Persians and their Arab allies.

Belisarius defeats Chosroes without a fight in 542

Chosroes's plan was to avoid the lands that he had plundered in 540 and would lead his army straight to Palestine and Jerusalem. Chosroes speeded up his progress by bypassing several places, which had the added benefit of making it difficult for the Romans to assemble their forces. When his army reached Commagene/Euphratesia, Justinian sent Belisarius in haste to the scene. The likely reason for the absence of Belisarius from the front is that his relationship with Theodora and Justinian was now strained at best. Chosroes also appears to have invaded early in the year. The Roman commanders on the scene did nothing. They and their soldiers stayed inside their fortifications in great fear of what Chosroes might do.

The situation was pressing so Belisarius used postal horses to get to Euphratesia as fast as possible. En route he received a letter from Justus, cousin of the emperor, Bouzes and others who had sought a place of refuge from Hierapolis. They asked him to join them, but Belisarius didn't accept their advice but rode only as far as Europum/Europus and then started to collect the scattered forces. Once there, he dispatched an order for the officers at Hierapolis to join him further north. They obeyed and left Justus with his men at Hierapolis. It is clear that Belisarius considered Hierapolis too exposed in this situation for him to enter. When Chosroes learned of Belisarius's presence and his actions he halted his advance and sent an ambassador to spy on him. Belisarius used the age-old stratagem of showing the ambassador only his best men. He chose 6,000 elite fighters to go on a fake hunting trip. He posted Thracians, Illyrians, Goths, Heruls, Vandals and Moors to go about his pavilion tent in a casual manner as if leaving for a hunt, the men not wearing cloaks but only linen tunics and trousers. They carried horse-whips, some carried only a sword, one carried an axe and another a bow. In addition, he sent 1,000 men under his bodyguard Diogenes and Adolius across the Euphrates to threaten the retreat route of the Persians. Adolius was an Armenian *silentarius* who had been put in command of Armenians, which probably means that we should not think this 7,000 strong corps to have consisted solely of Belisarius's bodyguards. It is probable that Adolius had been posted on the scene at the same time as Justus to make certain that everyone followed Justinian's orders. It is also probable that haste had had a role in this so that Belisarius had not been able to transfer all of his own bodyguards to the scene before the arrival of the Persians. For the use of a somewhat similar stratagem by the emperor Carus, see my *Aurelian and Probus. The Soldier Emperors Who Saved Rome*, also published by Pen & Sword.

When the Persian ambassador saw this show, he became convinced of the need to withdraw. The envoy also noted that if Chosroes won he would defeat only a slave of the emperor, while the Romans would still be able to flee to the safety of their cities, but if Belisarius won it would be a great disgrace to the Persians. Chosroes agreed, but it is likely that the threat of the plague which had reached Palestine and Syria at about this time influenced his willingness to abandon the campaign. He did not want to come in contact with it. Nevertheless, Belisarius again showed his brilliance in manoeuvres that did not include any combat. Now Chosroes had the problem of how to retreat from Roman territory. The trick of showing the forces of Diogenes and Adulius on the other side of the Euphrates caused the Persians to fear that it would be impossible to cross the river. Belisarius, however, knew that he wouldn't be able to prevent the crossing even if he had 100,000 men, because the Persians always carried with them hook-shaped irons with which they fastened together timbers to build an improvised bridge in a very short time. Therefore, Belisarius ordered his men to open up the route of retreat, which Chosroes exploited immediately by building the bridge and leading his entire army to the other side of the river so that there was now a river between him and Belisarius – this shows how frightened he was of Belisarius's reputation. Once across, Chosroes dispatched an envoy to Belisarius in which he stated that he was doing a favour to the Romans by withdrawing and that therefore the Romans should send envoys to him.

Belisarius then crossed the river too and sent messengers to Chosroes. The idea behind the crossing of the river was clearly to put pressure on Chosroes. Chosroes promised to conclude peace on the same terms as before if the emperor sent envoys to him promptly. Chosroes promised not to harm the Romans during his retreat if they sent one of their notables as a hostage. When the envoys returned, Belisarius went to Edessa where he chose John son of Basilius as the hostage, much against his will, and then dispatched him to Chosroes. In the meantime, however, Chosroes had continued his retreat and reached Callinicum. Its defenders had abandoned it because portions of its walls had been torn down for repairs and the city now lay open to attack. Those who remained there were enslaved by the Persians contrary to the agreement made with Belisarius. A little after this the Romans gave Chosroes the promised hostage, and the Armenian rebels who had previously deserted to Persia in 539 were allowed back to Roman territory without suffering any harm. This suggests a possibility that the handing of the hostage to the Persians even after their treacherous behaviour was connected with this and with the suggested peace negotiations. However, it is equally possible or even more likely that the Armenian deserters simply fled from Chosroes's field army on their own accord without any permission from Chosroes. In this case it is possible that the Armenian *silentiarius* Adulius had a role in this. It is easy to see that the handing over of the hostage even after Chosroes had betrayed his promises could be used against Belisarius later, but it is possible that Belisarius was unaware of the sack of Callinicum at the time he had dispatched the hostage and that his men just followed the order. The other alternative is that the deserters were actually in Persarmenia and that they had negotiated with the local Roman commanders there.

According to Procopius's *Wars* Belisarius's stratagem earned him the praise of all. He had forced Chosroes back without a fight when before his arrival the Roman forces had been too frightened to fight. However, Procopius contradicts himself in his *Secret History* and claims that Belisarius acquired a reputation for cowardice because on his way home Chosroes captured Callinicum. I would suggest that the version preserved by Procopius in his *Wars* is more accurate in this case. It is clear that when Belisarius and the officers discussed the situation after this campaign season had ended, the other officers were not criticising Belisarius at all – the fact that there was a hole in the defences of Callinicum explains quite well why Belisarius did not attempt to protect it. However, it still leaves open the question of why Belisarius chose to hand over the hostage after the sack of the city contrary to the agreement.

After the campaign had thus ended, Belisarius and other officers heard that Justinian had contracted the bubonic plague. Some of the rumours even claimed that he had died. They started to voice their discontent towards Justinian by stating that they would never allow the setting of another Justinian on the throne. This shows nicely that the other officers were not unhappy with Belisarius's performance of his duties during the campaign season of 542. They were unhappy with Justinian's rule. When the news then arrived that Justinian had survived the plague, the frightened generals started accusing each other, Peter (Petrus) the *Strategos* and John the Glutton saying that they had heard Belisarius and Bouzes saying those things. When the empress Theodora learnt of this, she summoned the men to her Palace. Belisarius and Bouzes could do nothing but obey because the officers had not concluded any conspiracy against Justinian that would have secured them the support of the other officers and army. All that they had done was to voice their discontent, and the principal source of discontent was actually Theodora's position as empress because her support for Antonina had angered most of the officers in the east. Procopius is utterly wrong to criticize Belisarius of unmanly behaviour. Belisarius did not have a conspiracy of officers behind him against Theodora and Justinian – the other officers had implicated both him and Bouzes to save themselves. He was alone and he knew it. Theodora threw Bouzes into the dungeon under the women's apartment where she kept him in a dark pit for two years and four months. Then she started to pity Bouzes and released him. Bouzes, however, suffered from poor eyesight and poor health for the rest of his life.

Belisarius was not convicted of any charges but was still relieved from office at the insistence of Theodora, and Martinus was appointed as his successor. The *doruforoi* and *hypaspistai* of Belisarius were confiscated and distributed to the officers and eunuchs who cast lots for them and divided them up. The friends of Belisarius were forbidden to meet him ever again. Belisarius was frightened and expected to be killed at any moment by some assassin. The relationship between Belisarius and Antonina had also not returned to normal and Theodora set out to change this too. She pretended that it had been Antonina who saved Belisarius's life. Belisarius bought the story and kissed the ankles of Antonina while promising to be her slave from that date onwards. After this, Theodora returned Belisarius's property to him except 30,000 lbs of gold which she gave to her husband Justinian. According to Procopius, Justinian and Theodora had always suspected that Belisarius had kept most of the Vandal and Gothic treasure himself, but had never found any evidence for this so that they now grasped the opportunity of confiscating at least some of it. Theodora sealed the new relationship by marrying her grandson Anastasius to Belisarius's only daughter Joannina. This gave Belisarius the opportunity to ask for another favour, namely that he would receive back his previous command and be allowed to march against Chosroes. This was opposed by Antonina who did not want to return to the area where she had been publicly insulted and shamed. Therefore Belisarius was appointed *Comes Sacri Stabuli* (Commander of the Royal Grooms) and dispatched to Italy for the second time. To gain this appointment Belisarius had promised that he would never ask any money from the emperor, but that he would use his personal funds for the waging of the war. Procopius claims that everyone expected Belisarius to attempt a usurpation the very moment he got outside the circuit wall of Constantinople and that he would punish his adulterous wife at the same time. It was a great disappointment that he did not do that but meekly followed the 60-year-old woman who had caused all his troubles. This criticism is unfair. Belisarius did not have adequate forces at his disposal for such an attempt even if he had wanted to follow such a course of action.

The great plague in 542[32]

Procopius provides us with a vivid description of the arrival of the bubonic plague in East Rome. His description is based on Thucydides's description of the plague which hit Athens in the fifth century BC, but it is still likely to be accurate in its details, as has often been noted. The plague was a massive disaster, but as will be seen it did not prevent the Romans from achieving their military aims when the commanders were up to their jobs.

The plague arrived at Pelusium in Egypt in about 541 and advanced from there to Alexandria and the rest of Egypt, from there to Palestine and thence to the rest of the world. It arrived first in ships to the coastal cities and from there inland. This means that the plague arrived through the Red Sea trade route, originating either in Asia or Africa. As is natural, the plague hit the cities worst where the people were in closest contact with each other. When the plague reached Constantinople in the middle of the spring of 542, it devastated the populace. According to Procopius, the illness plagued Constantinople for four months, its greatest virulence lasting for three months. After a slow start the number of dead rose to 5,000 a day, then to 10,000, then even higher. This means that well over 300,000 persons lost their lives in Constantinople alone, so the number of deceased in the whole empire must have risen to several millions. The death toll in Constantinople was so high that normal life ceased to function; all work stopped and people were no longer buried. Justinian ordered Theodorus, the *referendarius*, to see to it that the dead were buried and gave him money and soldiers from the palace for the task. The members of the circus factions also helped. When the burial grounds were full, the corpses were shipped to Sycae where the roofs of the towers of the fortifications were torn off so that the bodies could be thrown into them. When they were full of corpses, they were roofed again to hide their contents. This of course created a new problem as the rotting corpses spread their stench across the bay whenever the wind blew from that direction. As noted above the emperor Justinian caught the plague too, but he survived to rule for another twenty-three years. No nation was spared the horrors of the pandemic.

The Campaigns in 543–44

The battle of Anglon 543[33]

In 543 Chosroes advanced from Assyria to a place called Adarbiganon, which had a great sanctuary of fire. This is likely to be the sacred fire temple of the Warrior Class. Chosroes's plan was to invade Roman Armenia. When Chosroes had reached the place, he was met by an envoy dispatched by Justinian with the news that Justinian's envoys would arrive shortly to negotiate the terms of peace. There were two major reasons for Justinian's readiness to negotiate. Firstly, the Romans had been severely weakened by the plague while it had not yet hit the Persians with the same severity. Secondly, Justinian needed resources especially against the Goths after their new king Totila had managed to defeat the Romans at Faventia and Mugello in 542. See the relevant chapter. However, the Roman envoys never arrived because one of them fell ill. It was then that the Persian army also contracted the plague and Chosroes received the news that his son had usurped power. Chosroes duly retreated back to Assyria where the pestilence had not yet become an epidemic. Then because of this the local Persian commander ('*dux*' of Persarmenia) Nabedes dispatched the *Catholicos*/Priest of Dubios as an envoy to Valerianus, the Roman commander in Armenia. The priest took his brother with him and he betrayed to Valerianus the real reasons for Chosroes's reluctance to advance any further, namely that one of Chosroes's son had risen against him and his army had caught the plague. Valerianus dismissed the envoys and promised that the Romans would soon send envoys.

When Justinian learnt this, he immediately ordered the *Magister Militum* of the east, Martinus, and others to invade Persarmenia. He ordered all commanders to assemble in one place for the purpose of invading the defenceless Persarmenia. Martinus appears to have had overall command. Valerianus, the *Magister* of Armenia, and Narses with Armenian and Herul troops encamped close to Theodosiopolis (Erzurum) where they waited for the arrival of the others. Martinus, Ildiger and Theoctistus encamped by the fortress of Citharizon, four days' march from Theodosiopolis. Adolius, Peter and some other commanders arrived there soon after. The local commander of the area was Isaac (the brother of Narses). The Heruls of Philemuth and Beros, who served under Isaac, came into the territory of Chorziane soon after this. They were not far from the camp of Martinus. Justus the emperor's cousin, Peranius, John the son of Nicetas, Domentiolus, and John the Glutton encamped near Phison, which was located in the boundaries of Martyropolis. It is possible that they acted as a shielding force for the main army or that the intention was to use it as a separate invasion force even if this is not mentioned by Procopius. The invading army totalled about 30,000 men, but according to Procopius did not cooperate effectively. If true, this was because Martinus lacked authority, but it is most likely that Procopius exaggerates the disorder.

Procopius claims that the invasion of enemy territory began without any planning when Peter advanced (as a vanguard?) and the rest followed.[34] Excepting those under Justus, the rest united with each other and proceeded for Doubios/Dubius, which was suitable for cavalry action and had ample supplies available. The coordination of movements suggests that the plan was to mislead the enemy with an invasion along a wide front so that the different columns met where planned for the actual strike against Dubius. The target of the attack was well-chosen. Dubius was one of the most important commercial centres where the merchants from India, the Persian Empire and the Roman Empire met and conducted transactions. Dubius was also the place from which Christian envoys came who were likely to side with the Romans. It is in fact possible that the bishop/priest/ *Catholicos* and his brother had planned the operation together with Valerianus. The size of this army is uncertain, but was probably over 20,000 men. The Persians opposed it with 4,000 men under Nabedes. His plan was to ambush the Romans, so he shut his army inside the village of Anglon, which lay beside a mountain and rough terrain, he blocked the entrances to the village with stones and carts, in front of the village he dug a trench, and he filled the houses with footmen (probably dismounted cavalry) in ambuscades.[35]

When the Romans were one day's march from Anglon, they captured a Persian spy who informed them that Nabades had fled. In my opinion it is probable that the capture of the spy was not an accident but part of the Persian plan. The intention was to mislead the Romans with false intelligence. According to Procopius, the Roman soldiers moved forward in complete confusion and the troopers were mixed in with the baggage train. However, he seems to have exaggerated this confusion, because he then related that when the army reached Anglon, scouts were sent ahead. These scouts then informed the commanders of the presence of the enemy, and the Romans, improvising on the spur of the moment, hastily disposed their army in three divisions. Valerianus commanded the left, Peter the right and Martinus the centre. This suggests the use of a single line, but is not conclusive. It is entirely possible that the left wing had one cavalry division as a reserve, the centre two divisions, and the right wing one division as standard combat formation required. When the army came close to the enemy they halted because they faced difficult ground ahead.

When the two sides began to fight, the Persians feigned flight through the town and into the fortress above with the Heruls and regulars under Narses in pursuit. The probable sequence of events is that when the Persian cavalry feigned flight the Heruls and others pursued as *koursores* into the town where the Persians had hidden footmen (probably dismounted elite cavalry) inside the houses. When this occurred, the rest of the army joined in hot pursuit. When the Heruls and others reached the site of the Persian ambush between the houses in the narrow alleys, they faced the enemy archers in cramped conditions with no cover. The Heruls, who did not use helmets or armour, only shields and thick jackets, suffered terribly. The Herulian servants/squires suffered even more because they were not allowed to use shields before they had proved their manhood in battle. Narses was mortally wounded and his brother Isaac carried him back.[36] So when the Persians launched their counterattack from the houses and engaged the Romans in the alleys and rough ground, the disordered and scattered Roman cavalry formation which had foolishly entered the trap was doomed. The Persian ambush was a great success and the Romans fled in complete disorder. The Persians, however, did not pursue beyond the rough terrain, because they feared the possibility that the numerically superior Romans would decide to fight. But the Romans fled at full speed, throwing off their armour and weapons, while they rode their horses to death. As a result, the casualties were huge and the number of prisoners taken by the Persians considerable. The Romans also lost their baggage train.

The other Roman army under Justus and Peranius however had more success, possibly because it was under better leadership. They had invaded the region of Taraunon and taken some plunder before returning.

Corippus (1.70–109) gives us two otherwise unknown instances in which his hero John Troglita distinguished himself during the Persian war, one at Theodiopolis and the other at Daras. The first of these refers to the siege of Theodosiopolis (Karin, Erzurum), which had been besieged by the Persians under Mermeroes. One may make the educated guess that Chosroes would have dispatched Mermeroes with an army to take the city when he learnt of the result of the battle of Anglon. The Persians had isolated the city completely by building a palisade around it, but then John came to the rescue. John's headquarters appear to have been at Daras, so he would have advanced north immediately when he learnt of the threat to Theodosiopolis. John attacked the enemy in the middle of the night, burst through their lines and brought help to the tottering city with Mermeroes retreating in terror from the area. The likeliest date for this incident is in the immediate aftermath of the defeat suffered at Anglon because the Armenian army of Valerianus had clearly suffered terribly at that battle. This would date it to late 543 or 544.

The Persian invasion in 544

The second of the instances in which John Troglita distinguished himself as *dux* of Daras must have taken place in 544. It was once again Mermeroes who caused trouble. According to Corippus, he advanced his dense array against Daras to tempt the Latin phalanx to fight a battle. It is quite possible that Mermeroes's mission was to keep John and his forces at Daras so he would not be able to harass Chosroes from behind. Beside John stood the wise Urbicius, who appears to have been either the *Magister Officiorum* (this is likelier) or *praefectus praetorio* at this time on the basis of Corippus's text. Justinian had tasked Urbicius to assess the military situation on the eastern front. John first ascended to the parapet to observe the approach of the enemy, after which he led his forces out without delay and attacked the enemy head on. The enemy forces were routed. The fleeing Persians and their tribal allies threw their swords, spears, shields, and scabbards all over the fields in their panic, and the fields were covered with corpses and dead horses. Mermeroes would also have been killed, but John had ordered him to be taken alive. When Urbicius witnessed this from the parapet he praised the Lord and the bravery of John. I would suggest that Mermeroes's invasion either coincided with the invasion conducted by Chosroes in person against the city of Edessa, or it took place towards its end so that it caused the retreat of Chosroes from Roman territory; or alternatively that it took place after Chosroes had retreated, the intention being to catch the Romans unawares. The latter two are likelier because it would be odd if John had not exploited his victory over Mermeroes by harassing Chosroes during the siege of Edessa. The likeliest is probably the last.

Siege of Edessa in 544[37]

In 544, Khusro again invaded Roman territory. His main target was Edessa, because this was the city that had previously escaped his clutches. The size of the army was huge and it was accompanied by elephants. The claim that Christ protected Edessa irritated both Chosroes and the magi. The Romans, however, were well prepared for the invasion and Edessa was defended by both the militia and regulars. The generals Peter, Peranius and Martinus were in charge of the defence. When the Persians approached the city, Chosroes sent some of his Hunnic allies against it with the purpose of seizing the flocks of sheep close to the wall in that portion of the city where the hippodrome stood (location unknown). The shepherds put up a brave fight and the Persians came to assist the Huns. At that moment, Roman soldiers and some of the populace sallied out and engaged the enemy in hand-to-hand combat. Procopius noted that during the combat one rustic heartened the Romans by landing a good shot on the right knee of a Hun with a sling causing him to fall from his horse. After fighting from the morning until the midday, both sides withdrew.[38]

After this the Persians pitched their camp 7 stades (c.1.3 km) from the city. True to form Chosroes asked the citizens to pay a huge sum of money to avoid the siege, but his proposal was refused. On the eighth day, the Persians began to build an artificial hill/mound. They cut down many trees, which were then laid out in a square without bothering to remove the leaves. They then heaped great amounts of earth and stones and additional trees to raise the mound as fast as possible. This part of the mound was placed outside the reach of Roman missiles with the intention of advancing it then towards the walls. Peter sent some of his Huns in sudden attack against the mound. The attack was a success and they killed large numbers of Persian engaged in the work. The Huns had proved their worth once again and one Hun in particular distinguished himself. This man was a guardsman (*doryforos*) called Argek. He killed twenty-seven Persians. Argek was clearly a guardsman serving under Peter, but the fact that Procopius names him suggests that he had previously served under Belisarius. It is clear that Belisarius had an eye for military talent. After this the Persians kept a careful guard over the building site. Next the Romans tried to stop the building by using slings and bows, but the Persians used a hanging canvas with attached pieces of long wood to protect the workmen. In desperation, the Romans sent envoys to Chosroes, but his conditions were unacceptable. Not even the words of one of the envoys, called Stephanus, could turn his head – Stephanus was a doctor who had saved the life of Kavadh/Cabades. Next, the Romans tried to elevate their wall to the height of the mound, but realised that this was too slow. Consequently Martinus decided to employ a stratagem. He went to meet the Persian commanders in person to discuss the terms of putting a stop to the siege. While he negotiated with the Persians, the Romans dug a tunnel underneath the embankment, which was directed against the central portion of the mound. However, the Persians found this out and began to dig. The Romans answered this by filling up the end of their tunnel, directing it now against the end portion closest to the wall. The Romans hollowed out the structure and in haste placed dry tree trunks saturated in cedar oil with sulphur and bitumen underneath the mound. The negotiations between Martinus and Persian commanders continued until the mound reached the wall. It was then that the Persians put a stop to the negotiations. This suggests a likelihood that the Persians had been negotiating only because they intended to play for time and mislead Martinus – in short, both negotiated only to betray the other, but it was the Romans who came out on top. When that night the Persians prepared to attack, the Romans ignited the trunks and smoke began to rise from the embankment. The Romans shot small pots filled with coals and fire onto the mound to hide the smoke from the subterranean fire. At sunrise Chosroes mounted the mound and it was he who realised what was happening. He ordered his men to extinguish the fire, but water only made the fire spread faster. By late afternoon the smoke was so voluminous that it was visible as far away as Carrhae. The Romans, however, were still worried that the Persians would be able to extinguish the fire so that they attacked the Persians by going up into the embankment where they engaged them in hand-to-hand combat. The Romans drove the Persians off the mound and the flames finally rose above the embankment, at which point the Romans retreated while the Persians fled.

Six days later, the Persians attempted to surprise the Romans at dawn by using ladders against the Fort/Acropolis, but one farmer was awake and shouted the alarm. At midday, Chosroes sent his men to storm the wall near the Great Gate, but Roman regulars, rustics and populace went out of the gate and repulsed the Persians. The Romans pursued the defeated Persians, but Chosroes put a stop to this with a stratagem. He sent his interpreter Paulus to confront the Romans with the message that the Roman envoy Rhecinarius had arrived in the Persian camp to negotiate on behalf of Justinian. In truth, Rhecinarius had arrived some days ago, but Chosroes had decided to take Edessa before that. As a result of this the Romans stopped their pursuit and Rhecinarius entered Edessa. Chosroes then demanded that the Romans immediately dispatch envoys to discuss terms of peace, but the Romans said that they would send them only three days later because the *strategos* Martinus was unwell.

Chosroes suspected that this was a lie so he decided to throw his whole army against the city. A great mass of bricks was thrown on the collapsed mound and the army was ordered to assault the city two days later. Chosroes stationed some of the commanders with their forces at every gate. Ladders, siege towers and other war-engines were readied. In the rear were placed all the Saracens and some of the Persians to catch any fugitives from the city, and one may assume that the other purpose was to catch any Persian who fled. The attack began early in the morning. Procopius (*Wars* 8.14.35ff.) mentions that at some point during this siege Chosroes sent his elephants mounted with his best fighters close to the circuit-wall. One of the assaults of the wall mentioned here would be the likeliest occasion for that. At first the Persians had the advantage, but when the whole population were brought to the walls the Persians were repulsed. The civilians distinguished themselves, and even women, children and the elderly did their best by bringing stones and other things for the men to throw. One may guess that the initial advantage could also have resulted from the use of elephants as siege towers to clear the parapet of defenders, if it took place now. The Romans resorted to an ancient stratagem, which can be found in military treatises, of suspending a pig from a tower. The squealing of the pig frightened the Persian elephant with the result that it turned. But once again Chosroes forced his men forward. Towers, ladders and other war-engines were brought against the walls, but the Roman missiles and their sheer dogged determination turned the tide. Only at the Soinian Gate were the Romans in trouble, but Peranius with large numbers of soldiers and some of the citizens readdressed the situation by advancing out

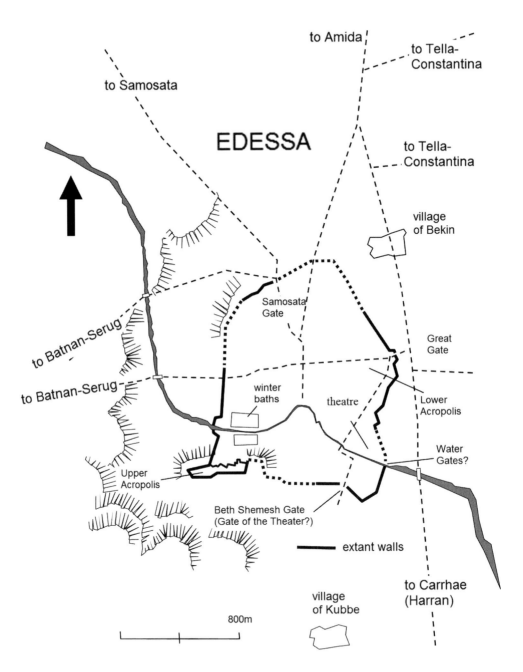

to Amida

to Tella-Constantina

to Samosata

EDESSA

to Tella-Constantina

village of Bekin

to Batnan-Serug

to Batnan-Serug

Samosata Gate

Great Gate

winter baths

theatre

Lower Acropolis

Water Gates?

Upper Acropolis

Beth Shemesh Gate (Gate of the Theater?)

extant walls

to Carrhae (Harran)

village of Kubbe

800m

of the city. They defeated the Persians in battle and drove them off. The general assault had lasted from morning until late in the afternoon. The Romans prepared for the next one by collecting stones and by placing them in readiness on the parapets. Two days later, the Persians assaulted the Gate of Barlaus but were once again decisively beaten by the Roman sally. The Persians retreated back to their camp and Chosroes dispatched Paulus to arrange a truce. Martinus went out and negotiated with the Persian commanders the terms of Persian withdrawal. The Romans gave 500 lbs of gold to the Persians in return for their leaving. This siege shows clearly the great variety of means in the arsenal of the Romans for the defence of their cities and also the importance of the urban and rural militias. The latter had distinguished themselves.

The Truce for five years in 545[39]

Very soon after the siege of Edessa ended, the Romans lost two commanders. Justus succumbed to a disease while Peranius fell from his horse while hunting and suffered a fatal rupture. The emperor sent his nephew Marcellus, who was just reaching the age of manhood, and Constantianus as replacements. Constantianus and Sergius were also ordered to go and meet Chosroes to arrange the truce. They met Chosroes in Assyria where the two major cities built by the Macedonians, Ctesiphon and Seleucia, were located. The two sides concluded a truce for five years in 545. The Romans paid 2,000 lbs of gold and allowed Chosroes to be treated by a Greek physician. Lazica, however, was left out of the truce, because Chosroes thought that he had the advantage there. In short, the two sides agreed to restrict their military activities only to Lazica, but in practice the Romans did not conduct any military operations there until much later because they had more pressing problems elsewhere.

Chapter Twelve

West: Italy 540–44:
Greed, Corruption, and Incompetence

Justinian divides the command and causes chaos in Italy in 540–41[1]

I t is clear that the stratagem Belisarius had used to bring about the surrender of the Goths (i.e. he became their king) had frightened Justinian that something like that could really take place in practice, and that because of this Justinian did not nominate a successor for Belisarius but divided the command between three commanders, Bessas, John the nephew of Vitalian, and Constantianus. The division of command proved to be a grave mistake. Being equal in power, these three ambitious and greedy men fell into squabbling and quarrelling. After Belisarius had left they started to enrich themselves by unleashing their soldiers on the Italian populace like hyenas. They made no efforts to defeat the remaining Goths but concentrated solely on plundering as much as possible as fast as they could. This behaviour in its turn loosened their hold on their soldiers because the widespread plundering of the civilians, which was contrary to the military law, loosened the traditional discipline that had been upheld while Belisarius was in charge. Consequently, in a very short space of time these three commanders managed to undermine the loyalty of the Italian populace towards the Roman Empire.

The situation became even worse thanks to the second mistake that Justinian made. He dispatched a man called Alexander the Snips from 'Byzantium' (Constantinople) to audit the taxes in Italy. He held the office of *logothete* (auditor), a senior officer in the state treasury. He had received the nickname Snips from the 'Byzantines' because he was apparently corrupt to the bone and known for cutting off the edges around gold coins. According to Procopius, Alexander had made his fame by constantly making accusations against soldiers for the losses they had supposedly caused to the state treasury. He managed to collect vast amounts of money for Justinian while enriching himself on the side by 'snipping', and in doing so he became the chief reason why the soldiers were few and poor and unwilling to fight. It was this man that Justinian unleashed on the Italians and soldiers serving there.

On his arrival at Ravenna, Alexander immediately published an utterly idiotic audit of taxes. He launched an investigation of Italians for the claimed tax frauds they had committed under the Gothic rulers and forced them to pay to Justinian what they were claimed to have owed to the Goths. The second of his actions was to reduce the rewards given to the soldiers for their wounds and bravery. The inevitable result was the alienation of the Italian populace and Roman soldiers. The former started to regret changing rulers while the latter refused to fight so the Goths were free to do whatever they pleased.

When Ildibadus learned that Belisarius had departed, he started to gather around him all the barbarians and those from the Roman army who were ready to desert. With this recruiting drive he was able to assemble an army of 1,000 horsemen. Initially he held only the city of Ticinum but thanks to the abuse of power by the Roman commanders he managed to convert little by little the inhabitants of Liguria and Venetia to his side. When the other Roman commanders were paralyzed by their quarrelling and poorly motivated soldiers, the only one who took action against the advancing Goths was Vitalius whose territories the Goths targeted when they advanced into Venetia. He had a numerous army composed of many different parts including a sizable host of Heruls. Vitalius feared that if he did not act immediately the Goths would become too powerful and advance against them. The two sides fought a battle near Tarbesium (Treviso) in which Vitalius was severely defeated. Vitalius lost most of his men but still managed to flee in the company of a few men one of whom was Theudimundus, son of Mauricius, grandson of Mundus. The brave Heruls suffered particularly badly losing large numbers of their men including their commander Visandus. This victory made the name of Ildibadus and it was only now that Justinian learned of his existence.

   Gothic joy was short-lived because Ildibadus soon after this murdered Uraias solely because Uraias's wife had insulted Ildibadus's wife, with the result that Ildibadus's wife wanted revenge. The murder of Uraias for no good reason angered the Goths some of whom started to plot against Ildibadus. According to Procopius, Ildibadus was then murdered for another reason, namely that Ildibadus married to another man a woman who Velas the Gepid desired to be his wife. Velas, who was one of the bodyguards of the king, killed Ildibadus during one dinner by cutting off his head. However, it is also possible that this Velas was only used as an assassin because of his hatred of Ildibadus by those who desired to get rid of Ildibadus; at least this was subsequently suspected by the Goths. The Romans were unable to exploit any of this because their leadership was in a chaotic state.

The Gothic resurgence under Totila in 542–44

The death of Ildibadus was immediately exploited by Eraric, who was by birth a Rugian. At this time the Rugi/Rogi belonged to the Gothic nation because Theoderic the Great had managed to convince them to join him, but they had retained their tribal purity by marrying only Rugian women and now formed a power block among the remaining free Goths. Eraric exploited this and was nominated King of the Goths by his Rugian followers. The 'native' Goths naturally resented this and many of them also suspected that Eraric was behind the murder of Ildibadus. Eraric remained inactive for the next five months, which enabled the disgruntled Goths to gauge their options. One of these was Totila who had been put in charge of the Gothic garrison of Tarbesium by Ildibadus. When he learned that Ildibadus had been murdered he wanted to surrender to the Romans together with his men and the city. Constantianus was glad to hear this and the two sides agreed to a fixed day. However the Goths, who were dissatisfied with Eraric, wanted to make Totila, who was a nephew of Ildibadus, their king. They sent envoys to Totila who did not hide his agreement with the Romans. He made one condition for his kingship which was the murder of Eraric. In the meantime Eraric had not remained entirely idle. He had convinced the Goths to send envoys to Justinian with the request of granting the Goths the same terms as before. His secret message, delivered by his trusted man Caballarius, was that he was ready to betray the Goths in return for a sizable sum of money together with the position of *patricius*. Before this could take place however, the Goths had managed to assassinate Eraric, so Totila was able to take the throne in about May 542.

The battle of Faventia (Faenza) in 542[2]

When Justinian learnt of the death of Eraric he censured his commanders and ordered them to act more resolutely. John nephew of Vitalian, Bessas, Vitalius, and others gathered in Ravenna where Constantianus and Alexander the *logothete* were already quartered. They collectively decided first to march against Verona and then move against Totila and Ticinum. The size of the army was 12,000 men under eleven commanders, of whom the first were Constantianus and Alexander. This and the subsequent details make it clear that the Romans now finally had Constantianus as their commander-in-chief, but unfortunately for the Roman cause he lacked authority (read adequate number of bodyguards) and skill to force the other commanders to obey him.[3]

When the Romans reached a site about 60 stades (ca. 11km) away from Verona, they were met by a local man called Marcian who promised to deliver the city to the Romans. The commanders decided that one of them with a few men should advance in front of the rest to the city to occupy a gate, but when none of the commanders showed any enthusiasm to be the one, a brave Armenian commander Artabazes volunteered. Belisarius had dispatched this man together with Bleschames from Persian territory after the capture of Sisauranon. Artabazes chose 100 men and was admitted inside the city at night by a guard bribed by Marcian. Artabazes's men occupied both the gate and the wall on both sides and killed the guards. The Goths panicked and fled through another gate to a great height overlooking the city where they remained through the night. The Roman army camped 40 stades away from the city where the commanders fell into quarrelling amongst themselves over their shares of the loot with the result that the army did not advance into the city. At daybreak the Goths observed the situation and returned to the city by the same gate they had used when fleeing, after which they attacked the men of Artabazes who retreated to the parapet. By then the commanders had finally agreed how to share the loot and were marching to the city. However, now they found all the gates closed with Goths opposing them. So the army started to withdraw while the men of Artabazes begged them not to abandon them, but to no avail. Artabazes and his men tried to save themselves by jumping from the wall. Some like Artabazes were lucky and landed on smooth ground but others were not and were killed. When Artabazes then managed to catch the fleeing Romans he heaped justified abuse on them. After this debacle, the Romans crossed the Eridanus (modern Po) and entered the city of Faventia (Faenza).

When Totila heard what had happened in Verona, he advanced against the Romans with his whole 5,000-man army. When the Romans learned of his approach, they held a council. According to Procopius, Artabazes wisely recommended letting half of the Gothic army across the river before attacking them.[4] However, the opportunity was lost as the commanders disagreed amongst themselves. They were completely incompetent. Totila's plan for the battle was simple. He sent 300 chosen men by a roundabout route across the river to attack the Romans from behind their camp while he himself crossed the river with the rest of his army and engaged the Romans. When both armies had advanced close to each other, the Goths played for time by challenging the Romans to a single combat. Artabazes killed Valaris the champion of the Goths with his long spear, but was mortally wounded in the process because he pushed forward with his horse against the upright spear. The medics carried him to the rear to tend his wounds in vain; he died three days later. This was a serious blow to the Romans because they lost an able commander. Then the battle began. When the engagement was at its hottest, the 300 Goths suddenly appeared behind the Roman army. The Romans panicked and fled.

Procopius doesn't give enough details to make any certain conclusions concerning the Roman battle formation, but the numbers of commanders together with the size of the army imply a first line of five commanders (3 divisions, 2 wings) and a 2nd line of four divisions plus *strategos*, and Alexander in charge of supplies. However, this is by no means conclusive and the use of the single line is also possible, although it is difficult to see how the Romans would have failed to outflank the enemy at the first onset if they had used a single line. In sum, it is very probable that the Romans employed two lines while the Goths employed their typical one cavalry line plus the 300 ambushers. The fact that the second Roman line fled without even attempting to fight shows that their morale was very low, which is not surprising in light of the events that preceded this battle.

The Battle of Mucellium/Mugello 542[5]

After the Battle of Faventia, Totila sent an army under Vledas/Bleda, Roderic/Ruderit, and Uliaris/Viliarid against Justinus in Florentia (Florence). Justinus had failed to collect provisions into the city before the enemy advanced against him so his position was desperate. Consequently, the Romans collected an army under Bessas, Cyprian, and John the nephew of Vitalian to relieve Justinus. Learning this from the scouts, the Goths broke up the siege and withdrew to a place called Mucellis (mod. Mugello) one day's march from Florentia. The Romans combined their forces and advanced towards the Goths.

The Roman commanders decided amongst themselves that the most advantageous plan would be to send one in advance of the others to attack the enemy suddenly with chosen elite troops while the rest followed at a more leisurely pace. In other words, the Roman plan was to deploy their army in two cavalry lines with the frontline consisting solely of their best men. However, when the time came to put the plan into effect and the lot chose John, the other commanders were no longer willing to give their best soldiers for John. So John was forced to rely only on his own men, who were a mixed lot.

According to Procopius, the Goths, learning of the approach of the Roman forces, decided to abandon the camp on the plain and to occupy a hill to gain the advantage of terrain. John and his men followed, charging impetuously up the hill all the while shouting loudly. When a javelin killed one of John's bodyguards, the troops panicked because they believed their commander had been killed. The remainder of the army was deployed on the plain as a phalanx (presumably meaning two divisions), but failed to support the retreating troops because it was rumoured that John had been killed. Hearing this, the commanders joined in the headlong flight in the course of which Bessas was wounded by the pursuing enemy. The reason for the flight was simple. When the other commanders believed that the first line would not join the support line in the ensuing combat because it was leaderless (John survived but they did not know that), it was not wise to stay and fight. When the first line had been defeated, the success in cavalry battle depended upon the determination of the support forces to engage the pursuers.

The Romans continued their flight for many days despite the fact that the outnumbered Goths did not follow them. The panicked Roman commanders entered whatever fortress they came to during the flight so the entire force became scattered and the commanders were no longer in any contact with each other. Meanwhile Totila showed great kindness to the Roman prisoners and managed to convert them to his side during the winter of 542/3. Totila knew how to win the hearts and minds of the enemy.

Totila triumphant and the siege of Naples in 543–44[6]

After defeating the Romans at Faventia, Totila took the fortresses of Caesena and Petra. Then he entered Tuscany, but none of the towns was willing to surrender. Then Totila moved southwards to isolate the Roman armies from their supporting bases. He advanced into Campania and Samnium and with no trouble won Beneventum. The walls were razed to the ground so that any Roman army coming from the east would be unable to use it as a base. Next he advanced against Naples. The inhabitants were ready to oppose him because they had a garrison of 1,000 Romans and Isaurians under the leadership of Conon. Totila pitched a camp near the fortifications. He was content to blockade the city with his army and fleet. Since no hostile force was operating against him, he was constantly sending small detachments to conquer the south of Italy. Cumae and some other strongholds were captured together with the wives of the senators. These he actually set free to obtain the goodwill of the Italians. Totila was seeking to win the senators to his side. His forces conquered the Brutii, Lucani, Apulia, and Calabria with ease. It was now Totila who collected the public taxes and the revenues of the estates from these areas. This meant that the Roman soldiers no longer got their customary payments, which in turn immobilized the entire Roman army in Italy. They stayed inside their cities and refused to fight. Totila's game plan was clever. He knew how to win deserters from the enemy army, how to win the goodwill of the populace and senators, and how to immobilize the enemy army.

Justinian's response to this crisis was to appoint the militarily inexperienced Maximinus with the title of *eparch* (prefect) of Italy as supreme commander of the armies in Italy. The emperor gave him a fleet and Thracian, Armenian and Hunnish troops to support them. However, after reaching Epirus in Greece the timid Maximinus wasted precious time by staying there. Later Justinian sent *strategos* Demetrius to Sicily. He had previously served as a general of infantry under Belisarius. On reaching Sicily, Demetrius learnt of the danger facing Naples. Since his forces were too small for the task, he gathered as many ships as possible from all Sicily and filled them with grain and other provisions. However due to the presence of the Gothic navy, he was still unwilling to take a risk by steering right into Naples. Procopius is quite correct to call this a grave mistake because the Goths would surely have panicked if he had done this; they did not know that the actual fighting force on board was small. Therefore Demetrius sailed first to the harbour of Rome to recruit men from there, but to no avail. The soldiers there were just not willing to face dangers when they had not got their salaries and because they now held the Goths in great awe. When Demetrius then finally sailed to Naples, the Goths had already learnt of the small number of fighting men aboard the ships. Totila placed many of his swift dromons in ambush. The Goths seized all the ships with their cargoes. The importance of having a full complement of marines or soldiers on board shines through. Demetrius managed to escape in a small boat. After this, Maximinus finally put in at Sicily with his fleet. He sent the whole army to Naples with Herodian, Demetrius, and Phazas. However, the violent winter winds destroyed the fleet. This times the action roughly to November 543–March 544. Most of the Roman ships were carried to the shore where the Goths were encamped. The Goths boarded the ships and sunk them. They also captured Demetrius. He was paraded to the defenders of Naples and told to shout to them that they could expect no relief from the emperor, which was actually true. Totila promised the defenders the freedom to leave with their possessions and an amnesty to the populace. The besieged asked for a thirty-day truce after which they would surrender if no relief army had appeared. Totila gave them three months. However, hunger drove them to surrender before the appointed date.

Totila treated his enemies uncommonly humanely for the time. He kept his word and wanted everyone to know it so that it would be easier to convince his enemies either to surrender or to change sides. The Roman soldiers were at first given ships, but because the stormy weather prevented them from leaving, Totila provided them with horses and provisions and sent them on their way. Totila also issued food sparingly to the starved populace, increasing their daily allowance only gradually so that they would not kill themselves by eating too much. He also executed one of his bodyguards because he had raped a local girl. His strategy was to win the hearts and minds of the people through kindness. Totila razed the walls of Naples so that the Romans would be unable to use it as a base again. He wanted to fight his enemies in pitched battles. Totila was one of the best commanders of his era and certainly the most humane, a person who deserves our full admiration.

While these things were taking place in the south of Italy, the Roman commanders and their soldiers in central Italy continued their old practices of abusing the Italians. The Italians now started to see the Goths of Totila as liberators. Constantianus had had enough. He sent a letter to the emperor saying that he was unable to hold out against the Goths and asked to be relieved of duty. The other generals expressed the same view. They too wanted to be relieved of duty. Meanwhile Totila sent letters to the senators in Rome upbraiding them for their behaviour and promised pardon if they would desert to the Gothic side. When the Romans in charge of Rome learnt of this, they actively prevented the delivery of the messages, but then these same messages started to appear in public places during the night. The authorities suspected the Arian clergy was behind this, so they were expelled from the city. When Totila heard of this, he marched his army into Calabria where they attempted in vain to take Dryus (Hydruntum mod. Otranto) so it was put under siege. After this, Totila advanced with his main army near to Rome. He posted the naval vessels of the newly created Gothic navy at Naples and at the so-called Aeolian Islands (Liparean Islands) and other islands along the coast of Italy to intercept any Roman vessels sent from Sicily to Rome. The blockade proved effective and the Goths were able to capture all the ships with their crews.[7]

Some time between 542 and 547 Justinian made a diplomatic coup in the Balkans. As noted above, the Gepids had conquered Sirmium and Dacia in 539 after which they had started to raid Roman territory. Justinian lacked the resources to counter this so he needed to find some other solution to the problem, which was to invite the allied Lombards/Langobards across the Danube into Noricum and Pannonia to serve as a counterbalance against the neighbouring Gepids. However, true to their predatory nature, the Lombards then proceeded to plunder the population of Dalmatia and Illyricum as far as Epidamnus/Dyrrachium and took captives. When some of these escaped, the Roman authorities helped them to apprehend the escapees from the Roman territory because they were officially Roman allies (*foederati/symmachoi*). In short, the emperor Justinian overlooked their banditry so that he could keep them in his service against the Gepids.[8] None of the sources mention other uses for these Lombards, but since their domains were located in Noricum and Pannonia, it is clear that the Lombards were also used to isolate the Goths in Italy.

A copper coin of Totila according to Diehl.

Chapter Thirteen

West 544–48: Belisarius's Second Italian Campaign

Belisarius dispatched to Italy in 544[1]

When the news of this was brought to Justinian, he decided to resend Belisarius to Italy despite the fact that the Persian war was still unfinished. He was appointed *Comes Sacri Stabuli*. Belisarius, however, was no longer in imperial favour because of his previous actions. He no longer possessed his outstandingly effective combat-proven bodyguards and had also been forced to promise to wage the war out of his own pockets to get the command. This meant two things: He had to find money for the waging of war by illegal means when he reached Italy, which caused opposition to his policies; he no longer possessed enough personal bodyguards with superb fighting skills to force his will upon the other commanders and soldiers and which he could use for fighting the war.

The first order of importance for Belisarius was therefore the collection of a new army of *bucellarii*. With this in mind he travelled through Thrace and Illyricum offering money for anyone who fulfilled the physical requirements and was prepared to join his force. He was accompanied by Vitalius the *MVM per Illyricum* who had only recently returned from Italy. Vitalius had left the Illyrian soldiers behind in Italy and was also collecting a fresh force of recruits because of this. The two men managed to collect a force of 4,000 men after which they went to Salones/Salona. However, the force that they collected was not combat-ready, consisting mostly of fresh recruits with no combat experience. The situation was aggravated by the fact that Justinian had expected that the Roman forces posted in Italy would receive their upkeep from Italian taxpayers and now that the Goths had gained possession of the taxes the Roman forces had not received their pay. Because of this most of the Roman soldiers had deserted to the Gothic side and those who had remained loyal were unwilling to fight until they received the salaries the state owed them. On top of this, the remaining Roman soldiers lacked horses and equipment because they had abandoned them during the defeats, and the defeats had completely demoralised them. Vitalius advised Belisarius that it was impossible to make a landing near Rome thanks to the naval blockade and thanks to the fact that the Goths were encamped both in Calabria and Campania, and it was also impossible to defeat the Goths in battle because they possessed too few men for this. Vitalius's advice was therefore that they would sail to Ravenna.

However, before that they had one pressing problem: the siege of Dryus by the Goths. The defenders had run out of provisions and had agreed to surrender on a definite day if the Romans did not bring relief to them before this. Belisarius therefore dispatched ships under Valentinus loaded with a year's provisions to relieve the city. His orders were to exchange the garrison with fresh forces and then return. Valentinus sailed in favourable winds to the city where the harbour was unguarded because the Goths had settled on waiting. When the Goths saw the fleet, they abandoned the siege, fled and reported the event to Totila. Some of Valentinus's men were eager for plunder and sallied out of the city, but they encountered the enemy close to the shore. The Goths defeated the Romans badly and most were forced to flee into the sea. The Romans lost 170 men and the rest fled back to the city. After this Valentinus replaced the garrison with fresh forces and returned to Salona/Salones.

When Valentinus had returned Belisarius was ready to begin his campaign and sailed to Pola where he stayed for a while to drill his forces. When Totila learned of the presence of Belisarius at Pola he resorted to an ingenious stratagem to obtain intelligence. The Roman garrison at Genua was commanded by Bonus, the nephew of John, and Totila wrote a letter in his name which he then dispatched to Belisarius. The letter was carried by five men who had instructions to observe what they were up against. Belisarius was gullible enough to believe them and promised Bonus help once he arrived in Italy, and the five Goths were able to bring the news back to Totila that Belisarius did not possess enough men to fight against him. Totila's clever way to obtain intelligence was just one example of his brilliance as a commander. In the meantime, Totila had captured the city of Tibur thanks to the fact that some of the inhabitants who had quarrelled with its Isaurian guards had invited the Goths in. The Isaurians, however, fought with dogged determination and most of them managed to fight their way out of the city to safety. The citizens were not so lucky. Totila massacred the entire population with such inhuman cruelty that Procopius did not want to leave a description of it for posterity. The capture of Tibur blocked the supply route from Tuscany to Rome.

When Belisarius arrived at Ravenna, his first action was to promise pardon for the deserters and for those who had refused to fight or who had committed any wrongs, in an effort to cause defections in the enemy ranks, but with no result. This meant that Belisarius lacked the means to achieve the goal of reconquest. The soldiers (both Goths and regulars) that he possessed in Italy were unwilling to fight because they had not received their salaries and the men he had brought from the Balkans were too few and inexperienced to achieve anything. Regardless, Belisarius still decided to use what he had got as well as he could. He dispatched his bodyguard Thurimuth and some of his own *bucellarii* together with Vitalius and the Illyrian soldiers into Aemilia with orders to retake the cities there. Vitalius led this force to a position near Bononia (Bologna). He captured some of the surrounding fortresses by surrender and then Bononia too. After this he remained inactive there, apparently because his soldiers refused to fight – soon after this the whole Illyrian corps left the city secretly during the night and returned to their homes in Illyricum. The reasons for their desertion were that they had heard that a Hunnic army had attacked Illyricum and enslaved women and children, plus the Illyrian soldiers had not received their salaries for a long time and were suffering from a scarcity of supplies in Italy. The invasion by this Hunnic army took place at the same time as the Antae and Slavs were raiding in 544 and it is probable that the Huns in question were the Bulgars. When they reached Illyricum they sent a letter to Justinian in which they reiterated their complaints. Justinian was naturally angry but he forgave them because he knew that the soldiers had good reasons for their complaints.[2]

The second of the decisions of Belisarius was to replace the commander in Rome, John the nephew of Vitalian, with Bessas. When John reached Ravenna, Belisarius dispatched him to Constantinople with instructions to beg the emperor to send them a large army and a large sum of money with arms and horses. The other alternative is that Belisarius kept John with him until the spring of 545 and dispatched him to the emperor only then. This is actually the timescale given by Procopius, but it is equally possible that it is a mistake because Procopius refers to the long time John spent in Constantinople and fails to even mention the replacement of John with Bessas. My own educated guess is that Belisarius dispatched John to the emperor in 544 once he realised the situation was hopeless. Belisarius asked Justinian to return his spearmen and guards to him reinforced with a very large force of Huns. Belisarius also gave John a letter in which he reiterated all the problems and how it was impossible for him as general to achieve anything without soldiers. Belisarius also bound John on oath to return as fast as possible, but John spent a long time in Constantinople in the course of which he married the daughter of Germanus, cousin of the emperor. Procopius claims that John achieved none of the objectives, but as I shall make clear this is not true. Justinian did not give Belisarius back his *bucellarii*, but he did give him a plentiful supply of men and money. Belisarius no longer had Justinian's full trust so it is unsurprising that he did not get back his bodyguards.[3]

According to the *Secret History* of Procopius, when Belisarius reached Ravenna he became greedier than any other man for money because the emperor had not given him any for the waging of the war. He plundered and extorted everything he could from the Italians of Ravenna, Sicily or any place still under Roman control. His excuse was that he made the men pay for the wrongs they had committed in the past.[4] This means that he actually made the corrupt Roman officers pay back the money they had plundered from the Italians, but it was paid to him and not returned to the Italians. In short, this was not really a form of corruption but rather a necessary evil in the situation in which Belisarius had to pay the cost of waging war from his own pocket. He used the money to maintain his *bucellarii*, which in turn were used against the Goths. This was patriotic corruption!

When Totila learnt of the withdrawal of the Illyrians, he sent an army against Bononia, but Vitalius and Thurimuth laid ambuscades in several places destroying a significant portion of the attacking army and forcing the rest to flight. According to Procopius, an Illyrian man of note called Nazares, who was a commander of *stratiotai* in Illyricum, distinguished himself in these actions. This is a good example of the high fighting quality of the Illyrian troops when they were motivated – it was a great shame for the Roman Empire that their authorities had failed to pay the salaries of these excellent soldiers and had failed to protect their families. After this, Thurimuth returned to Belisarius. Belisarius dispatched him and two other bodyguards called Ricilas and Sabinianus with 1,000 soldiers (*stratiotai*) to Auximus, which was besieged by the Goths. They managed to slip past Totila and the enemy's camp at night to support its garrison under the commander Magnus. On the following day about noon they sallied out when they learnt that there were enemies nearby. However, they did not attack them immediately but decided to send scouts first. It was then that Ricilas, who was drunk at the time, forbade others to take this task and rode out alone at full speed. He encountered three Goths and prepared to fight them, but the Goths rushed at him from all sides. Ricilas attempted to flee, but then his horse stumbled in a rough place. The enemy raised a shout and hurled javelins at him. The Romans heard this and galloped to the rescue but too late. Thurimuth's men routed the Goths, lifted the corpse of Ricilas on horseback and returned to Auximus.

After this Thurimuth, Sabinianus and Magnus came to the conclusion that their presence at Auximus was actually detrimental to the Roman cause because they consumed the provisions too fast and were still no match in combat against the numerically superior enemy. Therefore, they decided that the forces of Thurimuth and Sabinianus would break out of the city. One of the soldiers, however, betrayed the Romans and deserted secretly to the Goths so that Totila was able to select 2,000 men who were ordered to post an ambush at a distance of 30 stades (c. 5.5. km) away from Auximus. When the Romans then reached the spot at about midnight, the Goths launched their ambush and managed to kill 200 of them, but the rest managed to flee to Ariminum under cover of night. The Goths, however, captured all the pack animals, servants, weapons and clothing which the soldiers had been forced to leave behind.

Belisarius's next plan was to send Sabinianus and Thurimuth to Pisaurus (mod. Pesaro). Pisaurus and Fanus (Fanum Fortunae, mod. Fano) were located between Auximus and Ariminum and were therefore strategically situated, but the defences of both had been dismantled by Vittigis. The plan was to occupy Pisaurus first because the cavalry under Sabinianus and Thurimuth needed pasturage for horses. So Belisarius sent some of his men secretly to obtain measurements of the breadth and height of each gateway. Then the workers constructed gates according to these measurements and they were loaded onto boats. Sabinianus, Thurimuth and their men then boarded the vessels and sailed to Pisaurus where the gates were put in place and the other defences were repaired as well as possible. Orders were to remain inside the circuit wall. When Totila learnt of this he marched there, but was unable to achieve anything and was therefore forced to retreat back to his camp at Auximus. The Romans there were no longer making any sallies, but stayed inside their defences.

Belisarius's next move was to dispatch two of his *doryforoi*, Artasires the Persian and Barbation of Thrace, to Rome to assist Bessas in guarding it. His orders to the commanders were that they were to stay inside the walls and not make any sallies against the Goths. The probable reason for this was that the new *bucellarii* of Belisarius were not combat-ready forces but recent green recruits. These were no good in open conflict but sufficient for fighting from within the walls.

By now Totila was convinced that Belisarius could do nothing to stop him so he decided to start reducing the strongest of the cities still in Roman hands. Therefore he pitched a camp in Picenum before the cities of Firmum (mod. Fermo) and Asculum (mod. Ascoli) and started a siege. This took place in the winter when the tenth year of the war ended, meaning 545. The two cities appear to have surrendered in the spring of 545 so Totila was able to advance into Tuscany where he began the sieges of Spolitium (mod. Spoleto) and Asise (mod. Assisi). The garrison of Spolitium was under Herodian/Herodianus. He agreed to hand over the city to Totila if the Romans did not send him assistance within thirty days. As a guarantee he gave his son. No help arrived and Herodian duly surrendered. Procopius, however, in his *Wars* notes that there were some who claimed that Herodian surrendered because he feared Belisarius on the grounds that Belisarius had threatened to call him to account for his previous record, and in his *Secret History* he elaborates this further by stating that Herodian found the demands for money too much for him to bear. This is indeed possible. Relationships between the officers were complex. The commander of the garrison of Asise was Sisifridus, who was a Goth but very loyal to the Roman emperor. He made a sally out of the city with the result that he and most of his men were killed. The inhabitants of Asise duly surrendered. After this Totila ordered Cyprian, the Roman commander at Perusia, to surrender. Totila used a combination of threats and promises of rewards, but this failed to convince the loyal commander. Therefore Totila bribed Ulifus, one of Cyprian's bodyguards. Ulifus managed to kill his employer and then flee to Totila, but this did not result in the hoped-for outcome. The soldiers steadfastly refused to surrender and kept Perusia for the Romans.

After this, Totila was ready to begin the siege of Rome in earnest. His orders for all of the farmers of Italy were to continue to live their lives as usual and pay their customary taxes to the Goths. This enabled Totila to maintain his forces during the siege. When Totila arrived before Rome, and some of the Goths approached the walls, Artasires and Barbation sallied out of the city contrary to their instructions and contrary to the orders of Bessas. At first their attack met with success because the Goths apparently employed the tactic of feigned flight and then when the Romans in their folly pursued them they were ambushed and lost most of their men. The Romans were also starting to suffer from a lack of provisions by this time, which means that Totila's strategy of blockade from a distance was already working even before he arrived in front of the city. The Roman commanders started to suspect that the leader of the Roman Senate, the Patrician Cethegus, was entertaining treasonous plans. Cethegus, however, learned of these suspicions and was able to flee to Centumcellae (mod. Civita Vecchia). This probably means that the Roman security apparatus in Rome had been compromised. Totila also sent an army into Aemilia with orders to take Placentia. It was the only city still in Roman hands in this area. The Goths at first offered terms, but when the request met with no success, they began a siege. They knew that the situation was opportune and that the besieged were already suffering from lack of victuals.

According to Procopius, it was at this point in late 545 that Belisarius despaired and decided to journey to Dalmatia to stress the urgency of the situation. The other possibility is that Procopius is here purposely misleading readers and in truth Belisarius went to Dalmatia to lead the already assembled forces, and I would in fact say that this is the case. Procopius claims that at this stage Belisarius had begun to have regrets about having adopted the plan suggested by Vitalius which had been to sail to Ravenna. This had resulted in Belisarius being shut inside the city without any ability to affect the outcome of the war. Procopius claims it was because of these thoughts that Belisarius put Justinus in command of the garrison at Ravenna, while he himself went through Dalmatia and the neighbouring lands to Epidamnus (Durazzo, Dyrrachium). Procopius goes on to claim that Belisarius then wrote another letter to the emperor in which he gave a report of the current situation, and in response the emperor sent him John the nephew of Vitalian and Isaac the Armenian, brother of Aratius and Narses, together with an army of barbarians and Roman soldiers. In addition to this, Justinian dispatched Narses the Eunuch to the rulers of the Heruls to persuade them to send most of their soldiers with him to Italy. His words were convincing because many of the Heruls under Philemuth and others joined him. They marched to Thrace with the intention of passing the winter there so that they would be in readiness to be sent to Belisarius at the onset of spring. Narses was accompanied by John the Glutton so that he, John and Philemuth served as the main commanders of this force. En route they came across a large force of invading Sclaveni Slavs who had crossed the Danube and enslaved large numbers of Romans. It is quite probable that Narses was purposely leading the Heruls against these invaders even though Procopius claims that the resulting encounter took place by accident. Despite being outnumbered the Heruls inflicted a crushing defeat on the Slavs so that the Roman captives were freed. Then Narses came across a man who pretended to be a Roman commander called Chilbudius. He exposed the pretender and took him in chains to Constantinople. See below.

The false Chilbudius and invasions in the Balkans in the early 540s

According to the version preserved by Procopius (*Wars* 7.14.7ff.), at some unknown point in time after 533 the Antae and Slavs fought against each other with the result that one young man with the name Chilbudius was captured by the Slavs. On the basis of the fact that Procopius states (*Wars* 7.11.14–16, 7.13.21ff., 7.14.6) that after the death of Chilbudius the general the Danube was crossed freely by enemies, it is clear that the Antae, Slavs and Bulgars all raided Roman territory separately. But he mentions specifically only two such raids conducted by the Slavs and Antae, and by the Hunnic army in about 544, and he mentions the invasion of the Antae in about 544 only because it was then that they captured a crafty Roman who managed to convince his master that Chilbudius, who then lived among the Slavs, was actually the famous Roman general. His idea was to use this as his means of escaping back to the Roman territory. The captor of this Roman man then duly bought Chilbudius from the Slavs, and the Roman captive managed to convince the rest of the Antae that Chilbudius really was the general. According to Procopius, 'Chilbudius' eventually thought it wise to assume the garb of an imposter so that when the envoys of Justinian arrived in about 544/5, the Antae demanded that this Chilbudius be reappointed general in return for their alliance. Justinian's proposal was that the Antae would settle in the city of Turris on the northern side of the Lower Danube with the duty of protecting the frontier against the Huns in return for subsistence and money. Thereby the Antae became the allies of Rome, but Chilbudius did not get what he desired.

As noted, when 'Chilbudius' was en route to Constantinople, he was met by Narses the Eunuch in late 545. Justinian had just before this dispatched Narses to the rulers of the Heruls for the purpose of obtaining soldiers for the war in Italy. Many of the Heruls flocked to his service under Philemuth and others and Narses took these men to Thrace. En route they luckily came across a vast invading horde of Slavs and defeated them despite being outnumbered. It was then that Narses met Chilbudius the impostor. Despite the mannerisms and ability to speak Latin, Narses was not convinced that Chilbudius was the general and forced him to confess, after which Narses brought him to Constantinople. This account means that it is probable that the Bulgars, Antae and Slavs continually raided Roman territory during the years 541–45 even if this is not specifically mentioned by the sources. The Balkans saw no peace at all and it obviously influenced Roman ability to send forces to the other fronts in Italy, North Africa and the east.

Rome 545–6 (defensive siege)[5]

Totila began his siege of Rome probably in late 545 by blockading Rome closely with his army. The Roman garrison consisted of 3,000 men under Bessas and some civilians.

The Romans occupied the port of Portus while the Goths occupied Ostia. Totila had already stationed a strong fleet at Naples and in the Liparean Islands to cut off the sea route to Rome. Totila supported his forces from the regular taxes paid by the civilians. As noted above, the small forces sent by Belisarius were insufficient to break up the siege. Furthermore, Bessas and the other officers profited from the selling of grain and other foodstuffs to the hungry civilians and later received a ransom from those allowed to leave the city. The soldiers profited from the distress of the population by selling their food rations and by selling the oxen that they could capture outside the city. The man who profited most was Bessas. Despite the fact that the Goths blockaded the city from the sea, the Sicilian grain ships had sometimes managed to make their way to Portus, and Bessas made sure that the bulk of the supplies that arrived ended up in his secret storage rooms.

Belisarius was aware of the urgency of the situation and dispatched whatever extra forces he had available to him from Epidamnus/Dyrrachium in winter 545/6. The commanders of these were Valentinus and one of his *doryforoi* called Phocas. It is clear that Belisarius always placed one of his personal retainers in each force to make it certain that his commands were followed. They were dispatched to the fortress of Portus, which at the time was commanded by Innocentius. Their orders were to make sallies from there to assist Rome. Consequently, when Valentinus and Phocas reached Portus they sent an envoy to Bessas to coordinate their actions with him. They asked Bessas to assist their sallies with sallies from the city. Bessas, however, was not willing to do that. Therefore, when Valentinus and Phocas then attacked the Goths with 500 horsemen all they could achieve was the killing of a few men inside the enemy camp before they had to retreat, which happened when they realised that Bessas had not sent any help. Therefore they sent another messenger to Bessas, but he still refused to cooperate. This time Valentinus and Phocas took a larger force with them, but their plans were betrayed by a soldier of Innocentius who deserted to the Goths. Because of this the Goths were able to ambush the men. Both commanders and most of their men died. This took place in about March 546.

The pope Vigilius, who was at that time in Sicily, tried to alleviate the hunger by dispatching a fleet of grain ships, but this ended in disaster when the Goths spotted them. The Goths entered the harbour of Portus and hid their ships inside the walls. The Roman garrison of Portus saw them, mounted the parapets and tried to warn the approaching ships by waving their cloaks, but the crews interpreted this as a welcome and entered the trap. All the ships were captured without a fight. Bishop Valentinus was taken prisoner but all the rest were killed. Totila interrogated Valentinus in person and when he did not believe what Valentinus said he had his hands cut off. Meanwhile the Pope had been summoned to Constantinople by Justinian.

The hoarding of all the extra grain enabled Bessas and the other officers to make a profit. Eventually the other officers and soldiers ran out of their extra food with the result that Bessas was the only person with extra supplies, which he then sold at exorbitant prices to the senators. The populace attempted to seek terms from Totila but in vain so they were doomed to live in famine. The populace attempted to reason with Bessas, Conon and other officers, but in vain. It was just too profitable for them to keep them in hunger. Those who could not afford the prices demanded by Bessas were forced to eat nettles which grew in abundance in the city; some ate mice, dogs or whatever they could; some resorted to cannibalism, others ate each other's dung or killed themselves. Eventually Bessas and other imperial commanders allowed those Romans who could not pay their exorbitant prices to depart from the city so that only a few remained. Some who attempted to flee died, some were captured and killed by the Goths, and some were able to make their way to freedom. The soldiers, however, still had enough for their needs and because of this Bessas and his subordinates could continue their project of fleecing the rich.

The army that Justinian had assembled to serve under John and Isaac reached Epidamnus/Dyrrachium in late spring 546. As I have already noted in my doctoral dissertation this army was not as small as it would seem at first notice. Subsequent details make it clear that it consisted of the land forces which Belisarius commanded and of the forces brought by Isaac. His navy consisted of at least 200 dromons and of an unknown number of transport ships. This means that the dromons carried a minimum of 22,000 rowers, sailors, marines and soldiers on board if we estimate that each had about 100 rowers and ten other sailors. The minimum land fighting component of such force would have been at least 8,000 men,[6] but it is clear that the figure was even higher because the cargo ships could also carry soldiers besides the horses. Procopius even states that the land army consisted of more than 20,000 men.[7] Their strength could be bolstered with marines and rowers if necessary. This means that Belisarius had at least 42,000 men at his disposal plus those forces that had been used to garrison Portus and Rome once he arrived there. In addition to these there was a separate fleet under John the nephew of Vitalian. His forces consisted of the hired barbarians who appear to have been horsemen; the first thing they needed to do after landing was to obtain horses locally. It is unfortunate that we do not know what tribes made up these 'barbarians', but one may assume that the vast majority would have consisted of Hunnic tribesmen, because Belisarius had asked them, and some other barbarians from the Balkans, which included Heruls, Antae and Armenians as these are mentioned, and may also have included Gepids, Lombards, Slavs and others.

John suggested to Belisarius that both sail straight to Italy after which they would proceed on land to Rome. Belisarius opposed this because he knew the urgency of the situation. His plan was to sail straight to Rome to save it because in favourable winds it could be possible for him to reach it in five days; marching on land would take much longer. Therefore, he ordered John to sail to Italy and then march through Calabria and other lands to Rome while driving out the Goths from those areas. However, things did not go as planned because adverse winds forced Belisarius's fleet to put in at Dryus which was being besieged by the Goths. On seeing Belisarius's fleet, the Goths fled to Brundisium (Brindisi) and informed Totila. Totila in his turn readied his army to oppose Belisarius and ordered the Goths in Calabria to guard the passes.

According to Procopius, when favourable winds returned Belisarius continued his journey and reached Portus. En route he probably made a stop at Sicily to gather provisions for Rome.[8] However, there exists a possibility that Procopius has misplaced the order of events either by accident or on purpose so that it is possible that John's campaign in Italy actually presaged Belisarius's, because John cleared the straits of Messina of Goths which would have been the right thing to do in advance of the passage of Belisarius's fleet to Rome. I have interpreted the evidence in this way in my doctoral dissertation, but in this account I have given Procopius the benefit of the doubt and presented the events in the order Procopius states. If one accepts the account of Procopius, the reason for Belisarius's ability to pass through the Straits of Messina was that the Gothic fleet in the south of Italy was just too small to stop a fleet of 200 dromons, which is indeed quite possible.

In the meantime John the nephew of Vitalian had disembarked his troops in Calabria.[9] His men captured two Gothic scouts. One was killed to induce the other to betray where the Goths (near Brundisium) had pasturage for their horses. Those who had horses mounted them and the army advanced at full speed upon the Gothic camp. The Goths were utterly surprised and defeated. As a result, John captured Brundisium and the whole of Calabria. Thence he advanced into Apulia, where he captured Canusium (Canosa). There he met Tullianus from Cannae. This man held great power among the Brutii and Lucani and promised to help the Roman cause if the Romans promised to treat them well, unlike before. John promised this, just as he had previously calmed down the fears of the Calabrians. The aim was to win the goodwill of the population and this worked. Most of the territory in the south of Italy was now in Roman hands. When Totila heard of this, he dispatched 300 horsemen to Capua with orders to shadow John unobserved if he marched towards Rome. In his *Wars* Procopius claims that John learnt of this and therefore no longer continued his march towards Rome but marched to the territory of the Bruttii and Lucani.

The Goths had a garrison at Bruttium under Rhecimundus whose mission it was to prevent the Romans from passing through the Strait of Scylla (Messina). It is this piece of information that has led me to suspect the order of events. John surprised this force of Goths, and Roman and Moorish deserters under Rhecimundus. He pursued the Goths up the mountain where the desperately-fighting Roman and Moorish deserters were killed while the Goths surrendered in despair. According to the *Secret History* of Procopius, John remained inactive after this and did not join Belisarius in Rome out of fear of Antonina, wife of Belisarius. It was only after Antonina had returned to Constantinople that John found the courage to meet Belisarius face-to-face again. The thing that had compromised John's position was his marriage with Iustina, the daughter of Germanus. Theodora hated Germanus so much that nobody had dared to marry his daughters with the result that they were all spinsters. Because of this Germanus had approached John, whose rank was below him, with his proposal to marry his daughter. This had angered Theodora, who ordered Antonina to assassinate John.[10] In light of what had happened to Silverius in 536, Constantinus in 538, and Buzes/Bouzes and Photius in 542, there was every reason for John to fear the pair Antonina and Belisarius. Antonina was known as an effective operative of Theodora and it was well-known that Belisarius followed her wishes.

Belisarius's situation in Portus was not good. He needed to relieve Rome and the numerically superior Gothic army was posted between them. On top of this, Totila had built a wooden bridge with high wooden towers at both ends, and each of the towers had 200 men inside. This bridge blocked the Tiber at its narrowest point and in front of this he had placed a chain which was protected by additional Gothic forces. Belisarius could not challenge the Goths in open battle because he had too few men for this. The rowers/ marines were needed to transport supplies so these could not be used to bolster numbers, and John failed to arrive with his elite barbarian cavalry. Therefore Belisarius decided to break through the enemy formation by using the combined and joint arms approach. He intended to march to Rome with ships loaded with men and supplies. With this in mind Belisarius ordered Bessas to make a sally, but Bessas refused because he wanted to cash in on the siege and it was not in his interest for it to end or for supplies to arrive for the besieged.

The Goths with their bridge, chain, and towers proved no obstacle for the ingenious Belisarius, the expert of siege warfare. First he measured the height of the enemy towers by sending some of his men as false deserters to the enemy. Then he attached two skiffs of unusual size together and had a higher tower built on that structure. See the illustrations accompanying the siege of Naples.[11] On the tower he placed a small boat filled with pitch, sulphur, resin and other flammable substances. He also erected wooden parapets to protect the archers and sailors in his 200 dromons. Infantry and cavalry forces were stationed on both sides of the river in strong positions near the mouth of the river to protect Portus in his absence. Isaac was put in command of the forces in Portus with orders to stay there regardless of what news arrived so that Portus could serve as a place of refuge. Antonina was left there too. After this Belisarius advanced against the bridge with the tower skiffs and 200 dromons which were towed from the shore. He also placed a strong infantry contingent on the right shore presumably to protect the men who pulled the ships.[12] When they reached the iron chain in front of the bridge closing the river, the Romans killed some of the guards with arrows forcing the rest to flee. The combination of archery and close order infantry made it impossible for the Goths to stay. Then the Romans lifted the chain. Next, they cleared the opposition on the bridge with arrows so that they could bring the ships with the tower close to the northern tower, then they dropped the flaming boat killing all 200 men in the garrison. By then the entire Gothic force had been alerted and was on its way to the scene, but too late. However, Isaac who had been left to guard Portus decided to show personal initiative and attacked the nearest Gothic camp, but he was defeated and captured. When this was reported to Belisarius, he mistakenly thought that the Goths had captured Portus with his wife Antonina. Belisarius panicked and ordered the fleet to return to Portus. He could have still changed the situation but he fell seriously ill and was unable to conduct any operations. In fact he came close to losing his life.

As a result of Belisarius's illness the Goths were able to take the city. This resulted from Bessas's failure to enforce guard duty. This enabled four Isaurian soldiers to betray the city to the Goths. Bessas's scouts had even captured some Goths who divulged the plot, but he and Conon neglected to do anything about it. When the Goths entered their section at night, Totila kept his men together because he feared an ambush and let the Roman army flee through the other gates. Bessas and other Roman officers had amassed their wealth, only for Totila to capture it. In the morning, Totila occupied the city, preventing his men from carrying out excessive slaughter of those very few people still left in the city. The city fell on 17 December 546. He even prevented his men from raping the women. His behaviour was uncommonly humane for the period. The capture of Rome gave Totila the chance of attempting to negotiate peace with Justinian. Totila threatened to carry the war to Dalmatia unless peace was agreed, but Justinian dismissed the envoys and stated that Belisarius was in charge of the war.

Manoeuvring in the south of Italy in 547[13]

As noted above the local Italian strongman named Tullianus had handed over both Bruttium and Lucania to John and the Romans in 546. John had given Tullianus 300 Antae to assist him, which Tullianus had strengthened with the local rural militia. Of particular note is that Procopius considered the Antae the best soldiers of the era for fighting in difficult terrain. On the basis of the later *Strategikon*, the Slavs and Antae were indeed superb light infantry and apparently the best of that time for use in difficult terrain. This force Tullianus posted in the strategic pass leading into Lucania. Totila decided it was unnecessary to send an army against them. Instead he collected a multitude of Gothic rustics and gave them some of his soldiers as support. These were sent against the Lucanians. In the ensuing fight, the Antae and the Lucanians defeated their opponents in a violent struggle. Procopius does not give the exact composition of the Lucanian force or its battle array, but it is easy to imagine that the centre would have consisted of a phalanx of Lucanians and, on the flanks and on the slopes, of the Antae and some Lucanian archers or slingers. The Italian rural militia and Antae demonstrated their efficiency in the difficult terrain.

When the news of this defeat was brought to Totila, he decided to march against them and John in person. It was then that Totila tore down a third of the walls of Rome and demolished all its gates. He also planned to burn the finest buildings to make the city of Rome sheep pasturage. When Belisarius learnt of this, he sent a letter to Totila in which he reminded him that posterity would judge Totila if he destroyed the beautiful buildings of Rome. Totila was convinced to leave the buildings standing. This proved a serious mistake. Belisarius had recovered from his illness and could exploit it to his own benefit. Totila was a typical Goth who did not understand siege warfare and its possibilities. However, Totila left most of his forces behind at Algedon, which was 120 stades (ca.22km) from Rome. Their mission was to prevent the freedom of movement of Belisarius and his forces which were located at Portus.

When John learnt of Totila's approach, he abandoned Apulia and fled to Dryus. As regards the Lucanians under Tullianus, Totila's plan for the campaign was to crush them with a stratagem. He had taken with him several Roman senators and their families as hostages. They were forced to send their domestics into Lucania with orders to promise their lands to those tenants who would abandon the defence and return to till the fields. This worked and Tullianus and the Antae were forced to flee together with John to Dryus. Thus Totila had regained the entire south of Italy at a single stroke. The Goths, however, became over-confident and scattered about to plunder. When the news of this was brought to John, he exploited it and sent a large force against them, managing to kill large numbers of Goths. This taught Totila a lesson. Henceforth he kept his army united and assembled in the neighbourhood of Mt. Garganon (mod. Gargano) in the centre of Apulia. According to Procopius, the Goths encamped in the former fortified enclosure of the famed Hannibal and remained there quietly.

At about this time, one of the men who had fled from Rome together with Conon came to Belisarius with a suggestion. His name was Martinianus and he was a famous duellist, a Byzantine (Constantinopolitan) by birth. He asked for permission to pretend to be a deserter. Belisarius agreed to the scheme. When Martinianus reached Totila, the latter was very pleased because he had heard that Martinianus had won great fame in his youth in single combats. Totila also had the wife and two sons of Martinianus among his captives. He released the wife and one of the sons as a reward, but kept the other hostage just in case. After this he dispatched Martinianus together with some others to Spolitium, which had previously been surrendered by Herodian. The Goths had razed its entire circuit-wall to the ground, but had afterwards built walls in front of it to keep animals. They used these walls as a defence when they posted a garrison of Goths and Roman deserters there to control the surrounding area. When Martinianus reached the city, he managed to win the friendship of fifteen soldiers whom he persuaded to return to the Roman army. Then he sent some of the men to the commander of the Roman garrison in Perusia asking him to come to Spolitium because he intended to betray it. The garrison was now under Odalgan the Hun, after the murder of Cyprian, and he agreed to the plan. When he then brought his forces close by, Martinianus and his fifteen accomplices killed the commander of the Gothic garrison and opened the gates. They killed most of the Goths and brought the rest as prisoners to Belisarius. Procopius fails to tell what happened to the son who had remained hostage, but one may assume that Totila had him killed. Martinianus surely paid a steep price for his actions, but at the same time it is clear that he was a true patriot and that it had been his plan from the start to save as many members of his family from captivity as he could. The presence of Martinianus's family in Italy suggests three possibilities: It is possible to use this as a proof that the soldiers of the time could be allowed to take their families with them to the scene of operations; and it is possible to think that Martinianus had married a local woman; and it is possible to think that the presence of the family in Italy merely reflected the fact that after the conquest the area was considered a normal part of the empire so that the soldiers were allowed to transfer their families there. The last two alternatives are the more likely.

John had also not been idle. The Tarentines invited him and his army to come to the rescue. Tarentum lay on the road from Dryus to Thurii and Rhegium at a distance of two days' journey so the plan was feasible. John took a small force with him and marched there. On arrival he realized that the city was exceedingly large and entirely without defences and that it would be impossible to defend it with a small force. However, he showed his resourcefulness by noting that a part of the city was located on an isthmus separating two bays. This enabled him to divide the city in two by building a wall with a deep ditch on the isthmus. The Tarentines and the inhabitants of the surrounding countryside were then transferred to the isthmus behind the protective wall and he left them a considerable garrison for their protection. In the meantime, Totila occupied a strong fortress called Acherontis situated near the border of Calabria. He left there a garrison of 400 men and then left another force of barbarians in Campania after which he started to march towards Ravenna. The force which was left in Campania was for guarding the senators, their families and other Roman prisoners.

The Romans reoccupy Rome in about February 547[14]

It was in about January-February 547 that Belisarius decided to lead 1,000 selected soldiers to Rome to inspect its defences with the idea of reoccupying it. However, before this took place some unknown Roman went in haste to the Gothic camp at Algedon.

This enabled the Goths to post several ambushes. When Belisarius reached this spot, the Goths rose from places of hiding and attacked. According to Procopius, there was a fierce battle in which the Romans defeated the Goths through their courage and then retreated back to Portus. One wonders whether this retreat hides a setback, but in light of the previous combat performance of the men serving directly under Belisarius it is probably safest to accept this account at its face value.

As a result of his reconnaissance, Belisarius decided to reoccupy Rome. He left a small garrison at Portus and led the rest of his army into Rome with their provisions, and used those provisions to lure the civilians back into the city. When Totila learned of this he immediately turned his force towards Rome. Belisarius had the demolished sections of the wall simply filled with rocks and debris and spent the next twenty-five days improving the defences, but he was unable to replace the destroyed gates because there were too few artisans in the area. When Totila arrived, Belisarius ordered caltrops thrown in front of the gates, while chosen men in close order were placed between the openings. The rest of the army was placed on the battlements to give support to the men guarding the gates. The Goths built camps along the Tiber after which Totila threw his men against the gates but was defeated in bitter fighting lasting from morning until night. The Goths withdrew to their camps and the Romans rotated the men on guard duty during the night. During the next day Totila again threw his forces against the gates. This time the assault was conducted by his entire army at the same time. He may have attempted the tactic of feigned flight because when the Romans sallied out the Goths almost surrounded them. Only the arrival of the reserves sent by Belisarius saved the day. Several days later, the Goths made yet another attempt, but now the Romans arrayed themselves in front of the city to fight a true pitched battle. The fact that Belisarius probably had more than 20,000 men made this quite possible. The decisive moment appears to have been the death of Totila's standard-bearer. He fell off his horse and threw the standard to the ground. Those of the Romans who were in front charged forward to seize the standard, but the Goths got there first. This probably means that the Romans had killed the standard-bearer with an arrow and when this was seen by the cavalry posted in front they charged forward. In the ensuing rush to capture the standard, the Goths managed to save it, but were still defeated and pursued for a long distance. The sequence of events suggests a cavalry battle in which the Romans used two lines. The Goths withdrew to the city of Tibur and tore down all of the bridges except one which they could not demolish because of its strength. This bridge was the famous Milvian Bridge. They fortified it so that the Romans would be unable to follow them. Belisarius fitted gates to the wall, bound them with iron and then sent the keys to the emperor. Rome was again Roman.[15]

Belisarius was unquestionably the best Roman commander of the era despite the ranting of Procopius against him in his *Secret History*. Totila was no match for him when Belisarius had enough men. Belisarius was undoubtedly corrupt, and even more so now that he needed to pay a part of the cost of the war. He sought to enrich himself by extorting money from corrupt Roman officers with threats of punishment for their misconduct, but then again he needed this money for the upkeep of his bodyguards who were after all the best soldiers of the era and the men who usually decided the battles in favour of Belisarius and the Roman Empire. There would not have been a need for this if Justinian had paid the soldiers enough money and in time. Furthermore, Belisarius's corruption in this case was not really corruption at all because he extorted money from corrupt officers for the upkeep of his army. It was also not detrimental to the achievement of the overall goals of the emperor, as had been the case with the corruption of the officers who had been left in Italy after the year 540.

Totila continues his campaign to retake Italy[16]

Before the abovementioned events in front of Rome, Totila had sent an army to besiege Perusia. The besiegers learnt that the Romans lacked provisions and informed Totila who duly started to make preparations for leading his whole army there. Totila's soldiers were no longer willing to obey him after the disastrous loss of Rome which had culminated in a lost pitched battle, but he managed to regain their trust with a speech.

In the meantime, John the nephew of Vitalian had continued his siege of the fortress of Acherontis. When this did not bring the desired outcome, John came with a daring plan, as he was apt to do. He decided to rescue the Roman senate from the Goths. When John heard that Totila was besieging Rome (see above), he led 1,000 chosen horsemen to Campania. The Roman cavalry rode there as fast as possible without resting either day or night and so were able to surprise the Gothic guards. Totila, however, had in the meantime started to ponder that he had left too few guards to guard the hostages, so he dispatched a cavalry army to Campania. When these reached the city of Minturnae (mod. Traetto), they stopped to rest because their horses were tired. They dispatched 400 men with the least tired horses to scout the situation in Capua, about 300 stades away. It was at this precise moment that the army of John reached Capua so the two forces had a chance encounter and fought against each other on the spur of the moment. The fight ended in a complete Roman victory and they killed most of the Goths immediately. Only a few managed to flee to Minturnae. When the Goths there saw the panic-stricken fugitives dripping with blood and looking like porcupines thanks to the arrows, they joined them in flight. They reported to Totila that they had encountered an innumerable force of Romans, as befitted their panic.

In the meantime, seventy Roman deserters who were in Campania joined John, while John found only a few members of the senate among the hostages because most of them had managed to flee when the Goths had taken Rome. However, he found almost all of the wives of the senators because they had not been able to join their husbands in flight. According to Procopius, John then sent the seventy deserters together with the senators to Sicily. One may guess that the wives were sent there too.

When Totila learnt of this, he left a small guard behind to continue the siege of Perusia and then marched his main body against John whose camp was located at Lucania. John had posted scouts to guard all the main roads, but he had made the mistake of thinking that it would be impossible for the enemy to march through the mountains. It was this route that Totila took. The scouts, however, had become aware of the presence of the enemy army and marched towards the Roman camp, but they arrived too late to give a warning because both the scouts and the Goths arrived at the same time, at night. The Continuator of Marcellinus Comes' Chronicle (a.547/8.1), however, claims that the surprise resulted from the treachery of Bulgars in John's army. As noted by Procopius, Totila then made a mistake. He could have surrounded the Romans with his 10,000 horsemen, but instead he ordered an immediate attack so that, despite being surprised, most of the Romans were able to save themselves in the darkness by fleeing as fast as they could to the mountains. Among the survivors were John and Arufus (one of the Herul leaders). The Romans continued their flight to Dryus. The Goths managed to kill only 100 of their foes. The Goths also captured *strategos* Gilacius who was an Armenian in charge of a small force of Armenians. The notable thing about this is that this Gilacius did not speak Greek, Latin or Gothic so the captors were unable to communicate with him. The Goths killed him soon after. This proves that the Romans employed units and officers who could be commanded only by using interpreters. The Goths plundered the Roman camp and then returned.

Roman response[17]

Belisarius kept sending letters to Justinian, which related the troubles and pleaded with him to dispatch another army against the Goths. It was actually the success of Belisarius that created this strategic problem. Belisarius needed to post sizable garrisons for the protection of Rome and Portus and any city he was able to take, and after the reconquest of Rome Belisarius no longer had enough men to face the Goths elsewhere. Typically Justinian reacted to these pleas by sending reinforcements piecemeal, so he dispatched first Pacurius son of Peranius together with Sergius nephew of Salomon with a few men. These were immediately incorporated into the Roman army on their arrival. After this, Justinian dispatched Verus with 300 Heruls, Varazes the Armenian with 800 Armenians, and recalled *MVM per Armeniam* Valerianus from his Armenian command and ordered him to travel to Italy with his *bucellarii*, who numbered more than 1,000 men. Verus was the first to arrive at Dryus. He left the ships there and refused to stay there because he was a reckless drunkard. He led his forces on horseback close to Brundisium and encamped his 300 men there. When Totila learned of this he stated that Verus either had a powerful army or was a fool, after which he led a sizable army against him. When the Heruls saw this they retreated to a nearby forest. The Goths surrounded them, killed 200, and were about to capture Verus who was hiding with the remaining men among the thorn-bushes, when fortune intervened. The ships of Vatazes the Armenian arrived and put in at the shore there. Totila thought the ships carried more men than they did in reality so he withdrew his army immediately. Verus and the remaining 100 men were lucky to escape with their lives. They ran to the ships, but Vatazes decided to land his army there. After this they marched to Tarentum, where soon after he was joined by John the nephew of Vitalian.

In about December 547 Belisarius received a letter from Justinian, telling him that he had sent a large army to assist him and that he should unite his forces with them in Calabria after which he was to engage the enemy. The reference to the sending of a numerous army was clearly a lie or an intentional insult unless it includes the forces already dispatched before. Subsequent events, however, prove that Justinian's 'large army' to assist Belisarius consisted of only about 2,100 men, which was not even a medium sized army. Valerianus had reached the Adriatic coast, but he decided not to cross because it was already the winter solstice. However, he sent a vanguard of 300 men in advance with the promise that he would follow after the winter had ended. One wonders whether Valerianus had heard of the invasion of Illyricum by the Sclaveni/Slavs (see below) in advance so that he stayed in Illyricum to protect it against these invaders during the winter 547/8. This would be at least as good an explanation for his stay in Illyricum as was the winter weather and I would suggest that this was indeed one of the reasons for his decision to stay behind. When Belisarius read Justinian's letter, he selected 700 horsemen and 200 footmen and left the rest behind to guard Portus, Rome and the surrounding district, putting Conon in charge.

After this he sailed to Sicily and from there across the Straits of Messina to Tarentum. However, a violent storm threw his ships from their course so that he was forced to put in at the harbour of Croton. The location had no fortress and there were no provisions for the soldiers available. Therefore Belisarius decided to stay there with his infantry so that he could, if necessary, summon and organize John's army, while the horsemen would encamp in the passes close to the city of Thurii leading into the country. The horsemen were put under Phazas the Iberian and the guardsman Barbation. The idea was that the horsemen could find provisions for themselves and their horses while they also protected the passes against the enemy. There was a fortress close to this area at a distance of 60 stades (ca. 11km) built by the ancient Romans and John had established a garrison there. Totila had dispatched an army to take this fort, and the horsemen of Belisarius now engaged and defeated them, killing more than 200 men in the process even though the enemy outnumbered the Romans. They reported this to Totila. He selected 3,000 horsemen and went against the Romans in person. Phazas and Barbation failed to follow the proper safety protocols so Totila was able to surprise them completely in their encampments. Phazas and some of his men fought bravely and managed to save some of their comrades by sacrificing their own lives. This was a bad blow to Roman morale because they had put most of their trust in this elite fighting force. This is one of the rare instances in which they performed poorly. Barbation with two others were the first to reach Croton. When Belisarius learned of the defeat, he rushed to the ships and set sail using the prevailing wind to sail to Messana in Sicily.

The Slavic Invasion in 547–48 and other troubles[18]

The Sclaveni (Slavs) crossed the Danube and invaded Illyricum in strength in about December 547–January 548. They spread destruction and mayhem as far as Epidamnus/ Dyrrachium. They killed or enslaved all who came in their way regardless of age or sex and plundered their property. They also managed to capture large numbers of fortresses that were regarded as strong but which could now be captured with ease because there were no defenders. This shows that Justinian had previously dispatched their garrisons to Italy probably at the same time as the commander of the Illyrian armies, Vitalius, campaigned there. However, there was an army present in Illyricum at this time and it consisted of 15,000 men, but according to Procopius their commanders merely followed the enemy but did not engage them because they lacked the courage.

It is probable that this is one of those instances in which Justinian forbade his generals from engaging the retreating enemy because he planned to use them as allies against the Goths or some other enemies. In the example that Procopius gives in his *Secret History* (*Anek.* 21.26) the enemies are the Huns, but it is probable that under this heading he includes the Sclaveni because according to Procopius the Sclaveni followed the Hunnic lifestyle. Furthermore, it is known that Justinian employed the Slavs against the Goths. In the abovementioned example the farmers took matters into their own hands and gathered together and attacked the invaders, killed many and captured their horses together with all the booty, but this resulted only in difficulties for them. Justinian sent men to punish them for their initiative. They were mutilated, fined and the captured horses were taken from them. This was a shameful act for which Justinian bears full responsibility.

Procopius lists several other disasters that struck the Roman Empire at this time which certainly affected its ability to overcome its enemies. There were several earthquakes of extraordinary severity in Constantinople and elsewhere, and the Nile remained flooded in places so that seeds rotted.[19] The superstitious of course interpreted these events, as they always did.

Roman troubles in Italy multiply in 548[20]

In March 548, when Totila learnt that the Romans in the fortress near Rusciane were running out of supplies; he marched there to besiege it. Justinian had not been completely idle in the meantime. He dispatched not less than 2,000 footmen by sea to Sicily and ordered Valerianus to set sail immediately and join Belisarius. Valerianus landed at Dryus where he found both Belisarius and Antonina, which means that they had just sailed there from Sicily. Belisarius sent his wife to Constantinople to beg Theodora to send greater resources for the waging of this war. This proves clearly that Belisarius was at this stage entirely disillusioned with Justinian's strategy regarding Italy and did not trust his promises. The arrival of Valerianus with only about 700 men must have been the last straw, bordering on insult. It did not bring the desired outcome because on 28 June 548, by the time Antonina arrived in Constantinople, Theodora had already passed away.

Meanwhile the siege of Rusciana was reaching its climax. The Romans were so hard pressed by famine that they opened negotiations with Totila. They agreed to surrender the fortress in the middle of the summer if they had not received any help by then. This fortress was strategically important because it possessed many Italian notables of whom Procopius mentions by name Deopheron the brother of Tullianus. The Roman garrison consisted of 300 Illyrian horsemen sent there by John. Their commanders were Chalazar the Massagetae and Gundilas the Thracian. Belisarius had strengthened the garrison with 100 footmen.

The situation in Rome was also reaching a culmination point. Conon, the commander of the Roman forces there, had engaged in trafficking of grain and other provisions to the detriment of the garrison with the result that the soldiers killed him in the summer of 548. After this, the soldiers dispatched priests as envoys to Justinian with the message that they should be forgiven for this murder and that the emperor should send them the salaries he owed them. The message also contained an ultimatum: if he did not do as requested, the soldiers would join the Goths without the slightest hesitation. Justinian had little choice. The soldiers were pardoned and the salaries sent. This proves nicely that the money had always been there, it had just not been sent to the soldiers. Justinian bears a strong responsibility for this and it is easy to see why Belisarius had despaired and sent his wife to meet Theodora. Justinian was an avaricious ruler who failed to grasp military realities. It is very likely that he wanted to delay the payments so that if the soldiers died he would not have to pay them. The often claimed difficulty of sending money to Italy cannot be used as an explanation for the arrears because Justinian was always able to send money when he had to. As regards the reluctance of Justinian to dispatch more men to Italy than he did there is another probable explanation: he wanted to retain as many men in the East as possible because there was a threat of imminent Persian invasion in 548. I would suggest that this was the case now, and since Justinian was reluctant to spend money on soldiers he did not raise more men than he thought necessary, which were far too few for the Italian theatre.

Belisarius summoned John to Dryus to combine all the available forces. This was now possible because Antonina had departed to Constantinople. Belisarius gathered a great fleet and put all the available forces on board and then sailed for Rusciane to bring help before the city had to surrender. When the defenders saw the approaching fleet, they were filled with hope, but then it evaporated right before their eyes. A storm broke out which scattered the fleet. A considerable amount of time was wasted in collecting it back together again in the harbour of Croton. However, even the mere sight of the Roman fleet over the horizon had been enough because now the besieged Romans decided to break their previous treaty with the Goths and continue to wait for the arrival of reinforcements, regardless of the fact that the terms now required surrender.

The fleet set out for the second time for Rusciane. When the Goths saw them approaching, they mounted their horses and came down to the beach to prevent the landing. Totila spread out his cavalry armed with spears and bows along the entire length of the beach with the result that the Romans stopped their ships at a great distance, gave up the whole idea of landing and sailed back to Croton. According to Procopius, the reason for the failure to make the landing was that the Romans lacked the courage to do so, but in my view it is probable that the main reason was that this place lacked suitable harbours for the ships that Belisarius had (Procop. *Wars* 7.30.11) so that the landing was actually impossible when contested by the enemy. These Gothic cavalry forces were clearly better equipped to deal with the Roman forces than before as they possessed mounted archers which had not been the case during the initial stages of the conflict. It is clear that many of the mounted archers were Roman deserters, but it is equally likely that the Goths had relearned the art of mounted archery, a skill for which they had once been famous.

After the relief of Rusciane had ended in failure, the officers gathered together to plan what to do next. It was decided that it would be best if Belisarius went to Rome immediately. The city and its soldiers certainly needed attention after the murder of Conon. It was agreed that after Belisarius had set matters in order, he would bring in provisions. Meanwhile John and Valerianus were to disembark their men and horses, after which they were to march overland to Picenum against the Goths who were besieging fortresses in that area. The idea was to create a diversion so that Totila would abandon the siege of Rusciane and march to Picenum. As agreed John carried out this plan with his 1,000 horsemen, but Valerianus feared to march overland and sailed to the Adriatic Sea, landing at Ancon with the idea of then uniting his forces with those of John. This plan did not work because Totila sent only 2,000 horsemen to Picenum while he continued the siege with the rest. Totila was a veteran commander who was not fooled by such tricks.

The besieged opened negotiations. Totila's terms were lenient as usual. He required only the punishment of Chalazar who had broken his word. The fortress was surrendered. Totila cut off both of Chalazar's hands and then his private parts after which he killed him. The Roman soldiers were allowed either to join the Goths or leave without their arms and possessions. Only eighty chose the latter option and went to Croton. The Italians were not harmed but all of their possessions were taken.

The recall of Belisarius in late 548

There are two versions of this in the texts of Procopius. According to the *Wars*, when Antonina reached Constantinople after the death of Theodora, she asked the emperor to summon her husband back from Italy, which the emperor gladly did because the Persian war was at this time worrying him. The worry was the result of Chosroes's attempt to take the city of Dara through subterfuge, which proved that Chosroes intended to invade Roman territory very soon. According to the *Secret History*, Belisarius had himself asked to be relieved of duty in Italy and when he received permission he did so with great eagerness abandoning Perusia in Tuscany to the Goths by not attempting to relieve it so that it fell to the Goths who stormed it while he was still on his journey.

Belisarius had amassed a vast fortune and when he reached Constantinople he settled there as a rich man. The misfortunes of the last campaign had not diminished his fame in the eyes of the populace who still admired him for his past successes. It is indeed probable that it was Belisarius who had himself asked to be relieved of duty rather than his wife. It is clear that Belisarius had become disillusioned with Justinian and did not believe that he would ever grant him enough men or money to complete the conquest of Italy. And who could blame him for having arrived at such a conclusion? Justinian was clearly reluctant to give him enough resources after 542. Regardless, when Belisarius returned Justinian treated him with great honour, undoubtedly because the Artabanes plot (see below) had proved that Belisarius was loyal to Justinian. Justinian appointed him once again *MVM per Orientem* and gave him the title of Commander of the Imperial Bodyguard. Since it is known that Marcellus was *Comes Excubitorum*, it has been speculated that Belisarius held the title *Comes Protectorum*, but the former is still possible because this title appears to have been purely honorary, or at least modern historians have assumed it was. In spite of giving Belisarius the official command of the Armies of the East, Justinian kept Belisarius in Constantinople for the rest of his career.[21]

The Artabanes Plot in late 548/early 549[22]

The plot came about as a result of grievances caused by both Theodora and Justinian. The great hero of the African wars, Artabanes the Arsacid, had returned from Libya in 546. On his arrival Justinian bestowed on him the offices of *MVM Praesentalis*, *Comes Foederatum* and honorary consulship. Artabanes and Prejecta/Praeiecta, the widow of Areobindus, both wanted to marry each other, but there was a problem. Artabanes already had a wife from childhood who was his relative. The marriage had grown sour so that Artabanes had repudiated her. She had accepted the situation, but then when Artabanes rose to the high positions he did in 546, she came to Constantinople where she went to meet the empress who was known as an ardent protector of women. Theodora forced Artabanes to accept his wife back against his will and at the same time married Prejecta to John, the son of Pompeius. Artabanes did not take this lightly. He was now forced to share a bed with a woman he hated. When Theodora then died, the overjoyed Artabanes sent his wife away immediately.

Germanus, the cousin of Justinian, had a brother called Boraides. When Boraides died he left most of his property to his sons and brother Germanus. He had a wife and daughter too, but he ordered that the daughter should not get more than the law required. Justinian chose to support the daughter's cause so that Germanus had to back down. It is probable that Theodora had a hand in this too. Germanus was angry and this was known to everyone.

There was also an Armenian who was related to Artabanes who became the primus mover behind the subsequent events. His name was Arsaces and he had been convicted of treason because he had negotiated with Chosroes the Persian King of Kings. It is probable that he sought Persian help for his native Armenians. Justinian punished him only mildly by having him beaten on the back after which he was paraded through the city on a camel. This only angered Arsaces more and he started to stir up anger in Artabanes against Justinian. He reminded Artabanes of his own treatment and of the treatment of their native Armenia with the result that Artabanes finally agreed to a plan to murder Justinian. Arsaces then dispatched another Armenian called Chanaranges to meet Justinus/Justin, the eldest son of Germanus, with the idea of convincing him to join the plot to kill Justinian. Justinus/Justin flatly refused. When Justinus reported this to his father Germanus, the latter contacted the *Comes Excubitorum* Marcellus. Marcellus, however, was not prepared to act on mere hearsay. According to Procopius, he was also incorruptible and austere in his lifestyle. So it was decided to obtain the necessary incriminating evidence. Germanus told his son to organize a meeting with Arsaces, but this was now impossible. Justinus then approached Chanaranges who agreed to talk to Artabanes. It was agreed that Chanaranges would meet Germanus in person. Marcellus duly placed his trusted man Leontius behind a curtain to hear what was being discussed. The plan was to wait until Belisarius arrived and then kill Marcellus, Belisarius and Justinian all at the same time and then place Germanus on the throne. Marcellus was reluctant to react even after this, so Germanus decided to secure his own position by revealing everything to Bouzes/Buzes and Constantianus.

Only when it was reported that Belisarius was approaching did Marcellus finally act. He reported everything to Justinian and Justinian ordered everyone involved in the plot thrown into prison where they were duly interrogated under torture. When everything had been revealed, Justinian convened a session of the Senate to act as a court. The senators attempted to involve Germanus in the plot, but Germanus managed to save himself by presenting the testimony of Marcellus and Leontius, and then that of Constantianus and Bouzes. As a result the senators released him and his sons. However, this was not enough for Justinian. He blamed Germanus for being too slow in disclosing the plot and the emperor's view was backed by two officials of the court. It was then that Marcellus intervened on behalf of Germanus and saved his life. Justinian's punishment of Artabanes was very lenient. He just removed Artabanes from office, and confined him and the other plotters in the gilded cage of the Imperial Palace. Justinian was clearly a man who was ready to overlook the greatest offences while punishing others for the smallest, as was noted by Procopius.

The barbarian dominance in the West and invasions of the Balkans in 549[23]

Procopius paints a bleak picture of the state of affairs in the west for 549. In his opinion the barbarians had become the masters of the whole West by then. The Romans had lost not only Italy, but practically all of Illyricum and Thrace was also ravaged and destroyed by the barbarians. Before that the Franks had captured all of Gaul with the excuse of alliance. When Totila had gained the upper hand in Italy, the Franks took control of most of Venetia in about 549 because the Romans and Goths were unable to prevent it. The Romans had lost Sirmium and most of Dacia to the Gepids when the Goths had been driven away from there in about 538/9. The Romans of these areas had been enslaved. The Gepids then went on to pillage other Roman territories.

Justinian's answer had been to grant Noricum and Pannonia to the Lombards in about 542–47 to act as a counterbalance against the Gepids. The Lombards duly crossed the Danube and took control of these areas but then pillaged Roman Dalmatia and Illyricum up to Epidamnus. This was in about 547/48 but the date is not known with certainty. It is possible that this was one of the instances in which Justinian forbade his generals from engaging the invaders so that they could be later used against the Goths or other enemies.

Justinian had also granted Singidunum (mod. Belgrade) with some cities in Dacia to the Heruls. These faithless federate soldiers of Justinian did the same as the Lombards and pillaged Illyricum and the cities of Thrace despite their status as Roman soldiers.

In about 549, the Lombards under Audouin and Gepids under Thorisin quarrelled and prepared to fight a war against each other. Both asked Justinian to assist them, but Justinian chose to assist the Lombards. He dispatched 10,000 horsemen under Constantianus, Bouzes and Aratius. Their orders were to destroy the Gepids first after which they were to march to Italy. In the meantime, John the nephew of Vitalian had also been summoned from Italy. Justinian's orders to John were to join this army, and fight a decisive battle against the Gepids after which he was to march to Italy. The Romans added to their strength 1,500 Heruls under Philemuth and others who had stayed loyal to the Romans while 3,000 other Heruls had revolted and joined the Gepids in about 537. When a *moira* of Romans was marching to join the Lombards, it had a chance encounter with Heruls led by Aordus, the brother of the king. The Romans achieved a complete victory, killing Aordus and large numbers of Heruls.[24] However, the Gepids and Lombards had in the meantime concluded a peace agreement to the great disappointment of Justinian. The Roman generals were in a difficult spot. They could not advance into Italy while the Gepids and Heruls had not been defeated decisively because this would have opened Illyricum for their invasion so they decided to stay in place and inform Justinian about the new development. The Gepids, however, feared that Justinian would later take revenge against them and allied themselves with the Kutrigur Huns.

Chapter Fourteen

John Troglita: The Roman Hero in 546–52

John Troglita comes to the rescue of Libya in 546–47[1]

When Justinian received the plea from Artabanes to recall him, he faced the problem of whom to send as his replacement. His choice fell on John Troglita, who was eminently qualified for the post. He had arrived in Libya with Belisarius and after that served with distinction under Solomon and Germanus after which he had been recalled to fight against the Persians in about 540. John distinguished himself against the Persians on three occasions. In 541 he was one of the commanders that fought under Belisarius against Nabedes in Nisibis. Some time between then and 545 he fought against the great Persian commander Mermeroes. He relieved Theodosiopolis when Mermeroes was besieging it and then he defeated and captured Mermeroes when the Persians advanced against Dara. The name of John Troglita was on everyone's lips when Artabanes's request arrived.

So Justinian recalled John from the east together with some of the troops that he commanded. These included obviously John's *bucellarii/armigeri* under the Persian Recinarius/Ricinarius, but it is possible that the men who were sent with John to North Africa also included regular units that had served under him in the east. John first reported to the emperor on his activities in the wars that he had just concluded. Justinian gave John an army that included regular cavalry (*stratiotai* and *foederati*) and infantry, the numbers of which had been bolstered by new recruits. They were loaded into the ships at Constantinople where Justinian gave his last instructions to John who then threw himself on the ground before the emperor and kissed his feet while watering them with his tears.

Justinian's instructions were to liberate the Libyans and punish the Laguatan rebels. As John approached the fleet he was received with the cheers of the sailors. John then gave the order to unfurl the sails and was on his way to make a rendezvous with destiny. The fleet sailed through the 'Thracian Straits' where they sailed past Sestos and Abydos after which they sailed past the ancient shore of Troy. There the soldiers recited the stories of the Trojan War to each other and to Peter, son of John Troglita. The heroic stories of this war were still vividly and fondly remembered by the soldiers as lofty examples to be emulated. The fleet sailed across the Aegean and Adriatic seas to Sicily and from there to Caput Vada where John had once made a landing with Belisarius. John recognized the shore with delight and ordered the fleet to sail on to Carthage. The troops were disembarked and then assembled and organized in the city's open spaces as units by their *duces*. These forces were then united with the local units which appear to have included Armenians serving under Gregorius the nephew of Artabanes and possibly also Artasires, the man who struck Gontharis first, if Corippus's Arsacis is to be identified with him and not with Arsaces the Armenian. Then the army was led out through nine gates. John rode around the army and encouraged the men and recalled their battles fought in Persia.

The battle of Antonia Castra 547[2]

John was not a man to hesitate or temporize. He marched immediately against the Moors in Byzacium. He had at his disposal an army of about 12,000–15,000 infantry and 9,000–12,000 cavalry. However, as a former veteran he knew that he needed to bolster their numbers with Moorish allies to obtain additional manpower. Therefore he obtained the services of Cusina and Ifisdias through diplomacy. This had the additional benefit of diminishing the numbers of Moors he had to face on the enemy side. According to Corippus, both had a *caterva* of troops, which meant about 6,000 men in formation or alternatively a very crowded formation of barbarians with considerably more men. I use here the figure of 6,000 men per *caterva* as the likeliest.[3] Therefore I estimate that the overall strength of the Roman army was about 33,000–39,000 men. We know that the Moors possessed a large army, but Corippus fails to say what the size of this army was on this occasion. However, on the basis of Procopius's text we know that Antalas had 20,000–30,000 warriors and his Laguatan ally is unlikely to have had fewer men. There were over twenty-five tribes involved, in addition to which came the Moorish ploughmen, which means that the Moorish army was massive.[4] I have previously estimated the size to have been about 35,000–45,000 fighting men, but my current view is that this is an underestimation. A more realistic figure would be about 70,000–80,000, which would have given the Moors a clear numerical advantage. But this was not enough in a situation in which they were qualitatively weaker. It was thanks to the numerical advantage and the overconfidence resulting from the previous victories that Antalas was ready to fight against the Romans.

At first the Moors withdrew before the advancing Roman army, which they continued to do until they could concentrate their forces in the western and wilder parts of the province.[5] Two Roman *duces* led a strong reconnaissance party to seek a safe marching route for the army. The Moors burst out of the forests and mountains, surprised the advance guard and forced them to flee to a nearby forest. The surrounded Romans managed to push their way up the hills where they held on until help arrived from the Roman camp. When the swift messenger brought the news, John ordered all horsemen out of the camp to help their comrades. He spearheaded the attack and his *duces* and horsemen followed behind him in close-ranked formations. John's leadership was heroic, rather than cautious like Belisarius's by-the-book style of generalship. The sight of the approaching Roman cavalry frightened the Moors who fled back to their camp. After this fiasco, John observed where the enemy was and ordered his army to build a marching camp with trenches close to it. The outer defences consisted of spears fixed on the ground with shields rested against them. Some of the Romans raised the snowy white tents and others raised the taller tents of the commanders in the centre of the camp by using towering poles. Some refilled their quivers after the previous battle and restrung their bows; some piled up missiles and other weapons; some fitted heavy *loricae* (armour) and helmets; some rounded up the horses and brought them fodder; some prepared meals on cauldrons heated on the fire; some brought cool spring water; some prepared curved couches on the grass and set out all the platters in their places having washed them in running water. Everyone performed the tasks that had been assigned to them. The army prepared to face the enemy next day. The guards were rotated during the following night so that they could get some sleep, but even so the expectation of combat the next day caused many to have a sleepless night. The allied Moors pitched their camps separately.[6]

The Moorish camp on a hill was protected by a circle of pack animals, hostages and a stockade, which enclosed their women, children and baggage inside. The camels were formed eight deep, the hobbled mules and asses were deployed as the second protective tier, and the innermost defences consisted of two-pronged forks, spikes, and rocks. In addition, the Moors prepared traps. These defences provided the Moors with a maze-like protection which only they knew how to get through safely. The two armies faced each other at a place called Antonia Castra, which was located in Byzacium but is otherwise unknown.

The situation was complicated by the fact that the Moors had African hostages. Ricinarius, the commander of John's bodyguards, advised his superior to send an embassy to Antalas so that John could wash his hands of the fate of the hostages. John offered Antalas an amnesty on condition of returning the prisoners. When Antalas refused, John could proceed to attack. This proves that the fate of the hostages mattered and the commander was required to take it into account. It is actually probable that the Moors posted these prisoners as human shields among their camels, even if this is not mentioned by Corippus, just as the Romans did with their prisoners. Corippus just did not want to remind his audience that the Roman attack had also meant the butchering of their own countrymen.

The ever dutiful John Troglita had a sleepless night. He assembled the *duces* in a circle around him in his tent and conversed with them. Firstly, he instructed the tribune Caecilides Liberatus, who was from Libya, to tell the *duces* why the war had begun, presumably in an effort to justify the righteousness of their cause to the officers. When he had told the story, the *duces* started to voice their views to each other, but this was cut short by John who waved his hand and ordered silence. Now he told the *duces* his plan of battle after which he exhorted the commanders, reminding them that they were surrounded by the Moors and the result of the fighting would depend solely on their bravery. After this he ordered the *duces* to prepare their men for combat. The interesting point here is that the Roman high command spent a sleepless night, unlike their soldiers. It is impossible to know if this resulted in any problems, because it is entirely possible that the excitement of the coming battle kept them all wide awake and motivated.

When John Troglita had finished his speech to the officers, he leaped on his horse. He was wearing a gleaming reddish *lorica*-armour, gleaming helmet, a sword, several *hastae* (presumably in a holster) and a *clipeus*-shield (a circular shield akin to *aspis*). The *duces* and tribunes saluted him, after which the horsemen of the cavalry '*cohors*' (meaning presumably John's personal bodyguard unit drawn from the ranks of his *bucellarii/ armigeri*) leaned upon their strong *hastae* and mounted their horses with a leap, while others held the necks of the tall steeds. This may suggest that these horsemen had a leather loop on their spears, or the cross-bar in their *hastae* as depicted in the attached nineteenth century drawing by Ginzrot.

The battle array which John Troglita adopted is as follows. On the extreme left, John posted the Moors of Ifisdaias and Ifisdaias' son Bibipten whose mission it was to protect the left flank. On the basis of Corippus' account, it is probable that the Roman cavalry wings seem to have been deployed in two divisions each and that each of these was

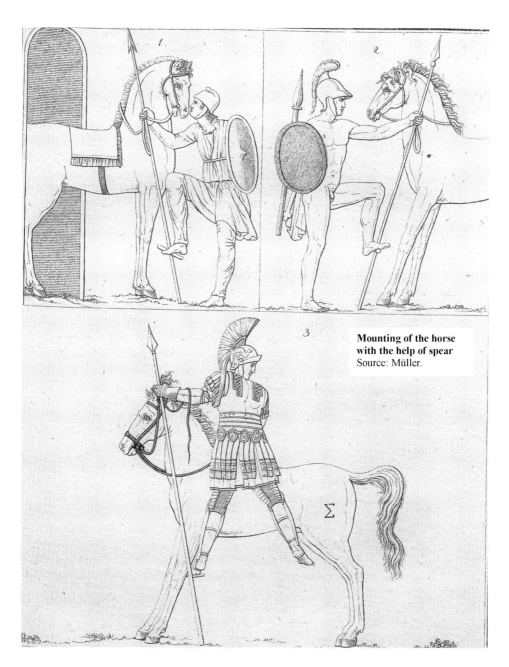

Mounting of the horse with the help of spear
Source: Müller.

divided into *koursores* and *defensores*. See the diagram stage 1. John posted his infantry under Tarasis between the wings. The infantry was ordered to link their *clipei* shields. They hid the bodies of the footmen with a wall of shields so that only the tops and crests of the helmets and the two-edged *bipennis* battle axes and *hasta* spears were visible. The double-edged axes were needed for the breaking of the camp defences. Corippus fails to mention the bows in this context, but it is obvious that the infantry carried these and that

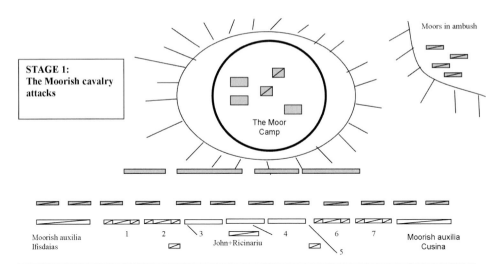

STAGE 1:
The Moorish cavalry
attacks

Moors in ambush

The Moor
Camp

Moorish auxilia
Ifisdaias

1   2   3

John+Ricinariu

4   6   7

Moorish auxilia
Cusina

5

Probable order of the first line from left to right based on equipment and position during the action. 1) Ulitan?, Liberatus, Marcentius?; 2) Unknown, Fronimuth, Unknown; 3) Commander of the left wing, John Sr.; 4) Tarasis; 5) Commander of the right wing, Gentius; 6) Putzintulus, Gregorius, Geiserith; 7) Marcianus?, Marturius, Senator. See Syvänne, 2000, 42-3. Alternative order would be to group 4 cavalry commanders in the center of the wings as *defensores* and two flank commanders (including those assigned here as wing commanders) as *koursores*, but the commanders assigned as wing commanders would appear to have had the wings under their leadership and the equipment given would also suggest the first order of battle. However, both are still possible.

when Corippus refers to the use of bows in general this included the infantry archers. John's bodyguards, who were commanded by Ricinarius, formed the reserve behind the centre. The camp behind the infantry served as a place of refuge.[7] The formation used the single phalanx infantry formation (or the mixed formation) with additional Moorish forces on the outer flanks. I have previously assumed that the Moors would have been deployed as wedges to protect the flank, which is one of the battle formations included in the *Strategikon*, but since every time Corippus describes Cusina or Ifisdais in action they fight mounted, I have here made the assumption that they used only cavalry and if there was any Moorish infantry present they were left in the camp.[8]

And what of the battle array of the Moors? Practically all we know is that their battle line was divided into two sections, one under the command of Antalas and the other under Ierna. Antalas appears to have commanded the left wing, Ierna the right. The battle plan seems to have revolved around the method the Arabs were to call the *al-karr wa al-farr*, which meant a quick attack with cavalry followed by withdrawal repeated until the enemy had had enough after which the army as a whole would attack. The light javelin-armed Moorish cavalry had two places of refuge behind which to renew their attacks. The first consisted of their light infantry, the front sections of which were deployed as a shield wall. Therefore, despite their light equipment, the Moorish infantry can be considered the equivalent of heavy infantry when fighting against Roman cavalry, but the lack of armour made them less well able to face the heavily equipped Roman infantry. The other place of refuge for the Moors consisted of the camp with its reserve forces and barricades. For the battle they used a mixed order of light infantry and cavalry, which could operate together or separately, the cavalry charging out of the formation for the attack and retreating behind the infantry for protection. The flanks were held by the cavalry alone. The key to understanding the Moorish deployment is that one of their leaders, Bruten, seems to have occupied the centre of the line; another, Sidifan, commanded the cavalry of the right wing; and Antalas had posted cavalry forces in hiding behind the rest in the hills.

The battle began with the Moors deploying right in front of their camp while the Romans advanced against them until they came within bow range, after which the Romans halted and readied their bows and other weapons. By conjecture, one may assume that at this moment the Romans had completed the tightening of their lines into compact formations. This was followed by another typical feature of the age, the challenge to single combat. Antalas came to the front of his line and apparently by his presence challenged John Troglita, who was in the centre leading his troops forward like the rest of the *duces/merarchai*. The heroic John accepted the challenge eagerly with the result that Antalas immediately fled. John taunted the enemy leader and laughed at his cowardice. This naturally lowered the enemy's morale while it undoubtedly aroused the spirits of the Roman army. The Romans were led by a MAN with capital letters. Belisarius would have considered – as would Roman combat doctrine, one may add – this sort of behaviour to be highly irresponsible, but it certainly encouraged the men. After this the Moors let loose a 'magical bull' from the centre of their battle line to represent the divine presence of Ammonian Gurzil in the presence of Iarna, the chieftain and priest of the Laguatan. A Roman cavalryman pursued it when it turned towards the Moorish lines and killed it with a quivering spear. After this the horns sounded the battle call. The Moors shouted to their gods Sinifere, Mastiman and Gurzil, while the Romans shouted 'May the brave do battle for your arms Justinian, inspired by the divine power of Christ. Preserve, Almighty Father, the rule of our Emperor.'9

This was followed by the attack of cavalries towards each other while the Roman infantry and cavalry shot volleys of arrows at the approaching Moorish cavalry. In this exchange of arrows and javelins, the horses of both sides, but especially the horses of the Moors, suffered terribly. In the text of Corippus the Roman horsemen then started pursuing the enemy horsemen. The effectiveness of Roman archery can be attributed to three things: 1) the help of the wind; 2) the wide-open spaces; 3) the better quality of Roman bows, arrows and training. The Roman infantry of Tarasis opened their ranks so that John's *armigeri* (arms-bearers) under Ricinarius could spearhead the cavalry charge while the other half, under the personal command of John Troglita, was left behind. This precaution of keeping a cavalry reserve behind was there just for the eventuality that occurred next. Corippus fails to note what the Roman cavalry wings and their Moorish allies next to them did at this point, but subsequent details make it clear that the Roman and allied cavalries also pursued their foes. The fleeing Moorish cavalry stopped their flight and wheeled back to face the pursuing Roman cavalry and managed to force the pursuing horsemen of Ricinarius (and presumably also the Romans on the flanks) back to their own lines. However, the Moorish success was short lived, because it was now John's turn to cut his way through the disordered pursuing ranks of the Moorish cavalry with his reserve cavalry. The possible presence of the allied Moorish infantry and the certain presence of Roman infantry would have enabled the cavalry wings to regroup in the space between them, which would also have been helped by the presence of the *bucellarii* of the wing commanders. John's horsemen were deployed in dense formation as was expected from the *defensores* while the other half of his bodyguards under Ricinarius undoubtedly regrouped themselves on the flanks or behind his men. John's men let loose a storm of iron-headed arrows on the enemy, which stopped the enemy pursuit in its tracks, after which John and his men rode through the enemy lines.

It is probable that John and his men had at first advanced at a trot/canter, which probably involved stages in which they were close to a standstill and in which both sides exchanged blows, and periods of faster advance at a canter and gallop. Corippus lists the personal heroics of John, and the heroics of all the commanders and notables in this battle, but I will here restrict the description only to the things that John did to save space. Unlike all too often assumed, the heroic details are by and large accurate. Had Corippus invented them, he would have insulted John before his audience who knew better. Some of the names of the killed were undoubtedly invented while some of the details of combat were only hazily remembered, but it is still clear that everyone knew that the officers had killed droves of enemies in the course of the combat. It is not a coincidence that Procopius also sometimes listed the number of killed. Those interested to read all about the heroics and combat details are advised to read Corippus and/or the English translation of Corippus by Shea.

John led the attack with sword in hand, and killed his first foe by cutting off his head. The next enemy he killed by thrusting his sword through his temple and brain, finishing the job by cleaving his helmet and forehead in two so that eyes and long locks of hair tilted different ways. John then threw a spear at the enemy horse, which hit it on the left shoulder and transfixed the rider through his right foot. The horse collapsed on top of the rider. After this John cut another enemy in two up to the waist in an ultimate show of swordmanship. He then hit the neck of Iartus, and cut off his hand holding his weapon at the same time. Mazana galloped forward and threw a spear at John and then turned away. John deflected it with his *clipeus* and charged after the foe and killed him. By this time John had reached the enemy infantry lines, or he faced a dismounted enemy, because Mazana's brother Gardius attempted to exact revenge by advancing, jumping up and down with his spears and shield. This time John used a spear, because he did not want to attack the enemy infantry head on. He threw the spear with such force that it penetrated Gardius's armour. The quivering spear hit his ribs and pinned the Moor to the ground. Following this, John pursued Cullan and other Moorish horsemen, throwing several *hastae* at Cullan, the last of which pierced his back. By now the Moors were completely demoralized and fleeing back to their camp. This was the usual result when loosely organized lightly equipped cavalry faced the tightly arrayed Roman heavy cavalry.[10] John took a risk leading his men from the front, but then he was a man always quite prepared to put his life on the line, and it undoubtedly encouraged his soldiers.

However, the Roman advantage proved short-lived. Bruten managed to turn his Moors back into combat with his own personal example and exhortation. He appears to have faced the pursuing bodyguards of John, and his example was enough to make all the Moors wheel back into the fight all along the front. In the meantime Antalas had retreated to the hills where he had hidden some of his forces in small groups. When Antalas saw Bruten's counter-attack, he ordered his fresh reserve forces to attack downhill and go through his own men against the Roman right wing cavalry. The fact that the Roman attack had faltered at this point enabling the enemy to regroup was only natural in this situation because the pursuing Roman cavalry had now come close to the barricaded Moorish camp and their momentum would have faltered. Furthermore, it is probable that the Romans now came face-to-face with their fellow countrymen, the Libyan prisoners, who were used as human shields, even if this is not mentioned by Corippus. The subsequent small respite allowed both sides to reorganize their battle formations. In the case of the Romans this meant the bringing up of the infantry to take the enemy camp, and the posting of the cavalry to its original places in the formation. The Moors in their turn regrouped and reorganized their forces into wedges (*agmina densatur cuneis*) in the spaces between the animals. In this case the *cuneus/cunei* clearly mean the column array.[11]

After both sides had reorganized their forces, the Moors attacked and tried to force the Romans back with their wedges or columns. The Moors appear to have made an all-out attack along the entire front, because Corippus's text has detailed accounts of both cavalry and infantry action. The cavalry attack of the Moor Sidifan, on the right wing, seems to have caused a partial collapse of the Roman left wing infantry and possibly parts of the cavalry, which, however, was addressed by John and his bodyguards who led his reserves where needed. In the centre of the battlefield, the Roman infantry advanced into contact with the Moorish infantry and the men packed together shield on shield until it became difficult to move. They therefore fought as if in a rugby match, with one mass of men shoving another – which the ancient Greeks called *othismos* – and trying to stab each other. Corippus describes how in this type of close combat men were unexpectedly stabbed with weapons they couldn't see. The Romans had the better of this fight because in close-order battle when someone managed to thrust his weapon past a shield, only helmet or armour could block it. The Romans literally pushed the enemy backwards, but the Moors were not fighting only for their lives, but also for the lives of their loved ones behind them. They also knew that they could not hope for mercy after what they had done to the hostages.

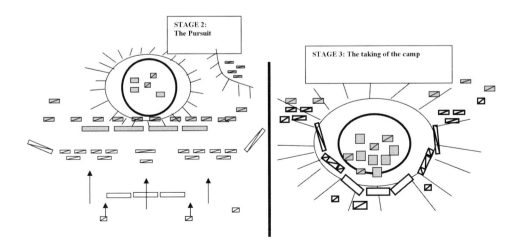

The Romans, both infantry and cavalry (possibly by dismounting), tried to force their way through the spaces the Moors had left between the camels and other barricades, and when they attempted it, the counterattacks of the Moors forced them back. John tried again and again to encourage his soldiers. In the end, late in the day, he came up with the most effective way of encouraging his men: he promised them the contents of the entire enemy camp as booty. He then once again led the men forward in person, cutting a way through the camels. The infantry axes were now used to great effect as the defences were broken with axes and swords. The Romans massacred everyone inside the camp, excepting those women and children that the soldiers took as slaves once their bloodlust had been satisfied. They pursued relentlessly, killing the fleeing foes until sunset, and then retreated back into their camp. The Romans recovered the lost standard of Solomon from the enemy camp and thereby wiped out their shame.

This campaign and battle stand as good examples of typical late Roman campaigns and fighting in which infantry participated and in which each branch of service was used for its particular role on the battlefield. Before the battle the Romans scouted, pitched the fortified camp, the commanders held a pre-battle council, the wind was favourable, troops were exhorted, and the battle lines were arrayed, after which the ground was scouted by the officers in person while the army advanced. The untrustworthy allied Moors were kept outside the real contest on the flanks, the infantry received the charge of the Moorish cavalry after which the cavalry pursued them in the manner the military manuals instructed. The brunt of the taking of the camp was born by the infantry, and the commanders boosted the morale of their soldiers by personal example, although the heroics of John Troglita went against Roman military doctrine and were by no means typical for commanders of that time.

According to the text of Corippus, John Troglita analyzed the peculiar features of the battle that they had just fought for the officers with the intention of praising and flattering them for their bravery. John Troglita was amazed by the resilience the enemy had shown in the combat saying he had never before seen the like, not even in savage Persia. He had never before seen people who were so prepared to look death in the eyes and fight their enemy face-to-face. Every time the Romans beat back the Moors, they had returned to the combat shouting wildly and jumping up and down with fearsome rage in their eyes. It had taken a great effort from the Romans to defeat such a foe. There is no reason to doubt the contents of this speech. Corippus had certainly learnt of it from the participants, on top of which the reasoning behind it is confirmed by the *Strategikon*. Once defeated the Persians did not usually return to the combat, whereas the Moors clearly did so repeatedly again and again.[12] It is no wonder that the Romans found the Moors useful as allies. They were brave and hardy folk.

After the battle John Troglita divided his army into two separate armies. The first he sent to occupy the forts in Byzacium. Unlike before, this force was now divided between two *duces*. The aim was to re-establish the defensive system so that the Moors of the desert could be starved into submission. The second of the armies John led in person back to Carthage where he organized a sort of triumph in which the prisoners were paraded. Of note is the fact that the prisoners (women and children) included blacks from further south and that their presence caused amazement among the audience who assembled to gaze at this strange sight.

The Battle of Gallica near Marta/Martae in the summer 547[13]

The Laguatan were distraught with the defeat. They had lost their families and were yearning for revenge. Carcasan used this anger to his advantage, having himself declared the new chieftain of the Laguatan. He travelled to the lands of the Marmaridae where he sought advice from the oracle of Ammon. The omens were good, as one would expect when the intention was to unite the tribes behind his cause. It was also during this trip that he allied himself with the Nasamonians and many other tribes. Once Carcasan had gathered the harvests of the year 547, he invaded Tripoli in late 547 with the intention of advancing to Carthage.

Pringle (35–6) has noted that John faced serious troubles at this time. The Laguatan invasion was not the only one he faced. The Visigoths had made an amphibious landing in North Africa in early 547 with the intention of taking the city of Septem/Ceuta. This problem, however, did not require his attention. According to Isidore of Seville (42), the Visigoths attacked in great strength, but then on the following Sunday they put down their arms so that they would not pollute the sacred day with fighting. This was a serious mistake, because the Romans did not care for such formalities, but exploited this 'God given' opportunity. They made a surprise attack, and thanks to the fact that the Goths were trapped between land and the sea, killed every one of them.

When John learnt of the invasion of Tripoli from Rufinus, the *dux* of Tripolitania, he assembled his officers to discuss the situation. He asked his officers whether they would be prepared to fight before the enemy reached Byzacium so that they could protect the next harvest. John noted that the previous harvest had been so bad that on campaign the Roman army would face serious logistical problems and the soldiers would suffer from shortage of food, because, as John and Corippus put it, the Romans had a huge army. John still urged his officers to accept his plan of attacking the enemy immediately to limit the damage it could cause. The officers agreed eagerly and claimed that they could endure the relentless heat of Libya and shortage of food. So John assembled his cavalry and infantry and added the Moors of the loyal Cusina to its strength. After this John marched south towards the enemy. By this time the Laguatan had already advanced into Byzacium and when they learned of the imminent approach of John they fled through the dry wastes of the western Tripolitanian desert towards Fezzan. The Romans were unaccustomed to fighting in the deserts and so suffered terribly. On top of this their provisions of food and water proved quite insufficient and they lost a number of cavalry horses. John was forced to withdraw to the coast to save his army where the scouts led them to a river somewhere close to the city of Tacapes. This area was then controlled by the Astrices who were frightened enough to send envoys to renew their vows of loyalty to the emperor. While the envoys were discussing this, the soldiers were openly speaking about the hunger and troubles, which naturally angered John beyond measure. He dispatched Ricinarius to silence the men. Fortunately for John, the envoys had probably not heard the words because they concluded an alliance and were sent away to bring children as hostages.[14]

The weary Laguatan were close by and were also suffering from thirst so they too faced the unwelcome prospect of destruction. Consequently, they turned back against the Romans. The Roman scouts soon saw the glow of fires on the horizon in the darkness of night. They did not know whether these were the Astrices or the Laguatan. John was unsure what to do, but then Cusina recommended that the Romans take possession of a river in the plains of Gallica which lay on the route to Lepcis Magna. Which river is unknown, but Pringle locates it somewhere near the city of Martae. The reason for Cusina's recommendation was that as a Moor he guessed that the Laguatan were tired and suffering from thirst so that the Romans could deny them sorely needed access to water. John approved of the plan, broke the camp and set his army in motion.[15]

Both armies reached the river at the same time, but the Moors retreated and left it in Roman hands. John ordered his men to postpone the fighting until the next day and build trenches and camp. However, his order was not followed by some of the cavalry units that crossed the river and pursued the Moors in disorder. The men were clearly sick and tired of pursuing the elusive enemy in the desert and were eager to fight it out. This was a very grave mistake because in truth the Laguatan had reached the site first and had placed an ambush on their left flank and in the surrounding hideouts. When John saw this he ordered his men to assume fighting order and advance to the river bank again. Cusina occupied the right flank and had under him both his own Massyles and Roman regulars. The details of the subsequent action suggest that all of Cusina's Moors were mounted – although it is possible that some were meant to fight as infantry and used camels for travel. Next to him was Fronimuth and after him the commander's namesake John. The huge Putzintulus held the left flank together with the bowman

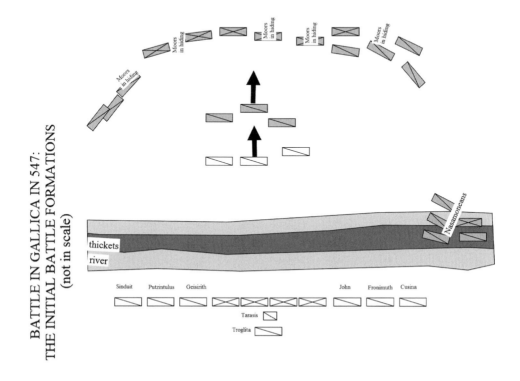

Geisirith (clearly in charge of the *koursores*) and Sinduit (probably also in charge of the *koursores*). The close-order infantry under Tarasis was placed in the centre and arrayed for battle while the mounted Tarasis protected it with his shielding force of cavalry, which presumably means that Tarasis had his own *bucellarii* for this. John took his place behind Tarasis.

It was then that a messenger came from those who had pursued the enemy with a message claiming that the enemy was in flight. John was unmoved and intent on holding the river line, but then two of his bodyguards, Ziper and Ariarith, managed to turn his head with their pleas.

Consequently, John gave the fateful order for his men to advance. This advance took place at the same time as Carcasan regrouped his men and counter-attacked. The river where the Romans now advanced had a thick grove which blocked the view while it also prevented the Romans from using their bows and arrows and their long spears effectively. The thick foliage also prevented the Roman cavalry from manoeuvring because it was next to impossible to turn the horses. So the Romans halted. John then approached with his guards the place where he was planning to make the crossing, and the Moors launched their ambush. The Nasamoneans attacked the allied Moors of Cusina with the result that they fled in headlong flight. When the news of this was brought to John, he dispatched Paul and Amantius to the rescue, but they could not find the allied Moors. At the same time, the *duces* behind them and their subordinates fled so that the chain of command was broken. At that very moment the Laguatan launched their ambush at every point so that their men burst forth from all of the ravines and advanced across the wide plain. They surrounded both the Moors of Cusina and the *duces* and their forces. Only pitiful remnants of them managed to save their lives by flight. When John saw the flight, he managed to rally the remaining men, and the two armies fought at close quarters. Corippus fails to mention how the Romans managed to regroup, but it is quite obvious that he ordered his infantry to assume the hollow square array, which served as a place of refuge for his cavalry and that the cavalry then sallied out of this array as opportunity presented itself and retreated back inside when the opposition proved too strong. It is this action that Corippus narrates when he describes the heroics of cavalry officers. Ziper and Solumuth fought through the enemy lines with their long *conti* and swords while in another part of the field Bulmitzis, Ariarith, Dorotis and *armiger* John killed enemies with sword, spear, arrow and skill.

This is a description of cavalry sallying out of the hollow infantry square from different points simultaneously. This description actually fits well what the tenth century East Roman manuals state, namely that in emergencies the hollow square was to limit the number of gaps: there was expected to be only four in a serious emergency. These later so-called Byzantine military treatises were based on old practices. For this, see *Military History of Late Rome Vol.2*. Corippus states above that there were two separate groups of horsemen charging against the enemy. One can imagine that Ziper and Solomuth charged out of two openings on one side, and that Bulmitzis, Ariarith, Dorotis and *armiger* John from two other openings on the other side of the square, even if in the latter case Corippus names four persons. This is depicted in one of the accompanying diagrams.

According to Corippus, this would have brought a victory for John but for the fact that it was now that the Laguatan infantry reached the scene and attacked. The Moorish infantry threw javelins and stones and then fought at close quarters with the result that the men were tightly pressed together, which presumably means that the infantries now fought shield to shield in a mass shoving action. John and his bodyguards appear to have charged out of the square from whichever side did not have enemy infantry close to it, so they charged the enemy infantry from the flank. The two armour-bearers of John, Ariarith and Ziper, fell in this attack, and John's horse was killed under him with a spear. It is notable that the two bodyguards who fell were the two who were claimed to have urged John to commit the blunder. This raises two possibilities. Firstly, since the two could not claim otherwise, it was possible to use them as scapegoats. Secondly, it is possible that these two knew that it was they who had urged John to commit the mistake and so had fought with extraordinary bravery and died as a result. The latter is actually more likely, because there were certainly other bodyguards present when these two men urged John to attack. John's bodyguards brought him another horse, which he mounted and then renewed the attack. This attack was successful. John cut a path through the enemy force with his sword and then charged straight at the heart of the enemy formation with the result that the enemy fled. This suggests that John attacked only from one side with all of his bodyguards at the same time, but this is not conclusive because Corippus's interest was to extol the achievements of his hero. It is possible that John actually ordered his bodyguards to attack from two sides simultaneously, as before. However, I have in the accompanying diagram reconstructed this as an attack from one side. After this John reorganized his troops beneath their banners and kept the enemy at bay with his arrows. If anyone attempted to reach John, John killed him forthwith with an arrow. This obviously means that the cavalry was now arrayed outside the infantry square to protect it with arrows while the entire formation marched. The Laguatans regrouped and encircled the Romans with their cavalry, but were unable to prevent the retreat of the Romans because this would have required them to break through the tight infantry formation which was the last line of defence for the Roman force, but they were not even able to attack the infantry because the cavalry outside it was enough to prevent the Moors from trying this. Consequently, John and the Roman army marched and joined their forces with the regrouped Moors of Cusina after which they marched to the safety provided by the walls of a nearby town. The army was now fed and rested and the horses given water.

John and his officers had clearly overestimated the ability of their men and horses to withstand hunger and thirst in desert conditions when they decided to advance into the desert and this is partly to be blamed for the disaster. However, it was ultimately John who bore the responsibility. Granted, his cavalry had disobeyed him and charged over the river, but it was still John who then ordered the army to cross the river which enabled the Nasamoneans to launch their ambush on the Roman right flank.

As a result of this, the Roman army was isolated from its baggage and servants that had been left behind when the army advanced. Corippus fails to say what happened to these, but one can make the educated guess that when the servants saw what was happening they fled by mounting whatever horses and mules and camels there were. It is possible that a fair number were able to flee, but it is clear that Moors were able to catch a fair number of them and almost the entire baggage train. It is also clear that Corippus lost most of the horsemen who had crossed the river without his permission and a fair number of those who had remained behind. He bears no responsibility for those who had disobeyed

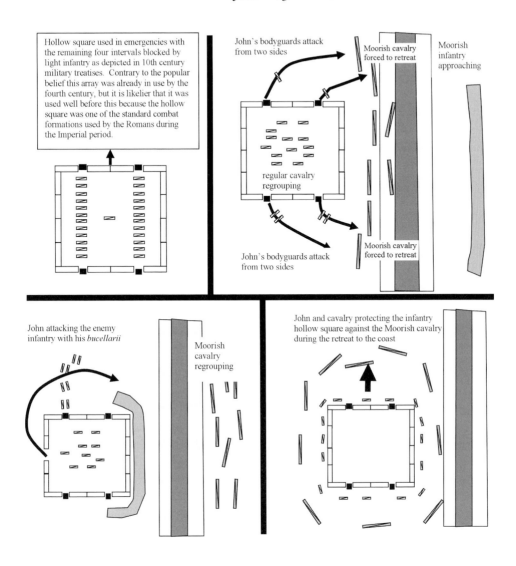

Hollow square used in emergencies with the remaining four intervals blocked by light infantry as depicted in 10th century military treatises. Contrary to the popular belief this array was already in use by the fourth century, but it is likelier that it was used well before this because the hollow square was one of the standard combat formations used by the Romans during the Imperial period.

John's bodyguards attack from two sides

Moorish cavalry forced to retreat

Moorish infantry approaching

regular cavalry regrouping

John's bodyguards attack from two sides

Moorish cavalry forced to retreat

John attacking the enemy infantry with his *bucellarii*

Moorish cavalry regrouping

John and cavalry protecting the infantry hollow square against the Moorish cavalry during the retreat to the coast

him, but he bears responsibility for those casualties that resulted from his ill-conceived advance into the river. However, he was a general who was able to maintain his self-discipline even in the midst of disaster and he was a man who could organize his army in such a manner that it could be withdrawn safely from the scene of combat. It is also clear that his footmen were well drilled and able to assume a new combat formation in the midst of an enemy attack. John and the cavalry knew what to do when this happened: they protected their infantry while it assumed its hollow square array; and they knew how to operate from within such a formation.

The battle of Campi Catonis at Latara in the summer 548[16]

Once safely in the city near the previous site of battle, John rested his army, but spent the next night without sleep pondering what to do next. The loyal confidant and friend Ricinarius comforted John who groaned and wept for the death of so many men. John's initial plan was to regroup his forces and then attack as soon as possible while the enemy was still jubilant over its victory. Ricinarius managed to convince his commander to reconsider. His advice was that the soldiers were too shaken after the previous defeat for an immediate attack. John was also to collect the scattered remnants of his army and add Moorish allies to it; only then after all had been assembled in one place and supplies brought for them was John to make another attempt. The facts that the Moorish allies brought with them flocks of animals, and that the weather had now opened the sea for sailing and the bringing up of bread and wine, meant that John would be able to feed his army. This can be used to place the previous campaign to have taken place between late 547 and March 548. Ricinarius's advice was sound and John accepted it. It was also the advice of Maurice in his *Strategikon* (7.2.11.1ff.). After a defeat, the general was not to attempt to renew the battle within the next few days because it was always very difficult to win after having suffered a defeat. The Persian Ricinarius was the cool and calculating man in this case, and his commander the bold commander that he always was, but John was still wise enough to recognize good advice when he heard it, so he did not commit his army to battle now.

John dispatched swift messengers everywhere to assemble the remnants of his forces and to bring new tribes to his assistance. Then when the sun rose, the general washed his hands and face and prayed through tears to the Almighty to help the Roman army and destroy the enemy. It was in the midst of praying that John received the first piece of good news. The scouts informed him that many of his allies had survived the carnage and had assembled at Iunci where they were waiting for their leader. This gave the general some joy. He then assembled his army and told them this good news. He also promised that the soldiers would get back their property and additional booty from the Moors in the future. After this he ordered the army to assume its marching formation, and it set off along the coast to Iunci and from there inland to Laribus, the latter of which had been fortified by Justinian. John ordered his allies and forces to assemble at this place for the coming campaign. In the meantime, news of the defeat had reached John's wife at Carthage, but there was no information regarding the survival of John so his wife collapsed in grief and wept for her dead husband.

When news that John had survived reached Carthage, the Praetorian Prefect Athanasius put in motion the imperial machinery for the renewal of the war. He ordered everyone needed to march to Laribus to assist John, and ordered supplies to be collected and allies assembled. Peter, the young son of John, participated by sending attendants as envoys to his father, and was thereby given important lessons in his youth about governing. The smiths had been ordered to make more arms because many of these were lost in the defeat and in the flight. After this the loaded wagons started to make their way to Laribus loaded with supplies of grain and arms. While there, John learnt that Ifisdaias and Cusina were moving towards civil war. He dispatched John, son of Stephen, to mediate. He was successful. Consequently, according to Corippus, Cusina brought 30,000 men, and Ifisdaias 100,000 men. In addition to these, Iaudas and his son sent 12,000 men, who were soon joined by the cattlemen led by *praefectus* Bezina.

I am usually reluctant to challenge the figures given by the sources, but in this case there are good reasons for it. Firstly, it is very unlikely that the Romans would have accepted this many allies into their army, because the allies would have outnumbered them significantly. Secondly, in the first battle at Antonia Castra, Cusina had a *caterva* of troops. This term means a unit consisting of 6,000 men, which, when combined with the information that Cusina had lost significant numbers of men in the previous battle in Gallica, would imply that he had fewer than 6,000 men now. In light of this, it is preferable to take one zero from the total given to him and to the others so that Cusina would have had 3,000 men, Ifisdaias 10,000 men, and Iaudas 1,200 men strengthened by Bezina who brought cattlemen. My assumption is that Bezina's cattlemen did not participate in combat but were used for the herding of the cattle, the food reserve, and for guarding the camp. All Moors participating in the combat proper were likely to be mounted on camels during the marching and then on horses during combat. One may estimate that after the reinforcements had been collected John would have had approximately the same number of regulars and *bucellarii* as in the first battle, namely about 12,000–15,000 infantry and 9,000–12,000 cavalry, and about 14,200 Moorish horsemen.

Once the preparations were complete, John led his army towards the enemy, which at the time was pillaging the plains around Mammes and Byzacium. Antalas had also joined the enemy. The Roman army expelled Moorish tribes along their route of advance with the result that the Moors learnt of John's imminent arrival. Carcasan wanted to engage John immediately, but Antalas warned against this, and advised him to avoid fighting in open terrain in the initial stages of the conflict because the Moors could not withstand the Roman attack. His sound advice was to retreat before the Romans while destroying any fields which had ripened crops and engage them only after they had been completely worn out by marching, heat, thirst and hunger. Carcasan accepted the advice, broke up his camp and started to flee in front of the Romans. John attempted to catch the fugitives by doubling his marching speed, but to no avail. The Moors were too fast. Later when they were close to achieving their goal, the Sirocco wind rose and John abandoned his planned attack so that his men could quench their thirst. However, the spring from which they drank proved insufficient for the needs of the army and some of the soldiers who came later pressed their lips against the wet sand which had been fouled by the horses and their dung.

The situation was not easy for the retreating Moors either and even less so for their captives who were dying in throngs; it is unlikely there were many captives left by the time of the battle to be used as human shields. The power of the wind was such that it threw the Moors into heaps, but the Moors persisted and continued their flight into the desert for fifteen days while the sun grew hotter. Then the Moors arrived in the fields near the city of Iungi by the sea. The Moors were torching the farms and fields when John ordered the tribune Caecilides Liberatus to reconnoitre the enemy positions. He was well placed to do this because he was Libyan and knew how to operate in this terrain. Caecilides and his men performed their mission admirably. First he reconnoitred the enemy camp and its gates and defences in person after which he slipped past the enemy into Iungi itself. The city was unfortified and all the dwellings were open, but miraculously none of the Moors had entered it. Caecilides found there a single priest who soothed the people and kept their spirits up. This priest urged John to come to the rescue and he was confident that Romans would win if he did. After this, Caecilides departed but was not yet satisfied with the results. He wanted to capture prisoners to interrogate. When he was saying these words to his comrades, it happened that the Moors led by Varinnus saw them and attacked. Caecilides and his men charged straight at the enemy and started killing them. The Moors turned and the Romans pursued, killing some. The tribune however aimed to take prisoners rather than kill, so he used his lance butt to strike their limbs. He chose four out of the enemy band and captured and tied their arms. Most importantly, he grasped their commander, Varinnus, by the hair, lifted him from his horse and threw him on the ground, after which he leapt agilely from his horse, fell upon the breast of the Moor, twisted him around and tied his hands. Consequently, Liberatus brought to his superior a very detailed report of the enemy together with a prisoner who could divulge the secrets of the enemy, which Varinnus indeed did. He told that Carcasan had adopted Antalas's advice and tried to tire the Romans with a guerrilla campaign before engaging them. John had all five prisoners killed by hanging their necks on five wooden stakes with two-pronged ends erected for this purpose.

According to Corippus, when John heard of the enemy plans he devised a counter-strategy. This is surprising if true. It is very odd that John would not have realised what the enemy was attempting to achieve with its retreat and torching of the fields before he heard it from the prisoner, but this is what Corippus claims so we should accept it. John's counter-strategy was simple but effective. He advanced to the middle of the fields at Iunci. If the enemy stayed it would be defeated in the level plains because it could not withstand the Roman cavalry attack with javelins and arrows. If it chose to retreat to the desert, the Romans would take possession of the coastline to prevent the Moors from getting supplies with the result that the enemy would perish through hunger or be forced to fight. In contrast, the Romans would be provided with plentiful supplies of food and drink because they could use the port of Lariscus, as they then did.

The allied Moors encamped on both flanks with the Romans in the middle to spread out the army so that they could control as wide a frontage of the coastline as possible. Then a disaster struck. The Roman regulars mutinied. According to Corippus, the reason for this was very pathetic. There were some soldiers who began to slander the commander to other soldiers with statements like how far would the soldiers follow John when he promised only toil, hardship, thirst, heat, hunger, Sirocco winds, death and one crisis after another without any rewards. If true, this suggests that the soldiers, most of whom were not native to these lands, felt the hardship and toil of marching in these desert conditions quite unbearable, and now that they had reached the area where they had suffered a defeat a short while ago the bad memories and hardships proved too much for them. The rest of the men assembled around these ringleaders, and eventually their grumblings became so loud that they were heard in the commander's tent. The *dux* Tarasis was the first to go out to see what was happening. He tried to calm the men with words, but they started to stone him. Tarasis sent a messenger on foot to John, who then grasped his weapons and assembled his guards, *duces* and all those soldiers who were still loyal, and sent orders to Cusina and Ifisdaias to bring their men too. He took a stand on a mound and addressed the men, and threatened the mutinous ones with the Moors who were advancing towards the camp from two sides. At first the mutineers just manned the defences, but in the end the entreaties of John and in particular those of Ricinarius convinced them to abandon their plans so that the men voluntarily handed over the ringleaders to be executed. Corippus likens this incident to one in which Julius Caesar was involved, which proves that Caesar's exploits were well-known.

John's first reaction to the revolt was to attempt to force a battle with the enemy by advancing to the fields of Cato (Campi Catonis) where they had pitched their camp. However, when he realized that the allied Moors were suffering from hunger and had been forced to resort to the eating of their herds, and that the enemy actually held an advantageous position thanks to the presence of forests and dangerous terrain, he started to retreat to avoid having to fight. He retreated for some days, his plan being to increase the enemy's difficulties and force them to come onto the level plains, and in the end the enemy was forced to do so. When this happened, John assembled his forces before him and addressed and exhorted his men from a mound. It was now time to fight the enemy and crush them. The soldiers showed their eagerness by waving their standards and banging their shields. They were to prepare to fight tomorrow. Then the *magister*, the *duces* and the priests performed the holy rites after which the soldiers were sent to eat their food rations. John instructed the *duces* not to let the horses go too far to graze, because his plan was to move the camp after the soldiers had eaten their meal. His plan was to fight the Moors in the neighbouring Lataris/Latara (an unknown place close to equally unknown Campi Catonis) on the following day, the idea being that the soldiers would not have to march far from their marching camp. The *Strategikon* (12.2.23.28ff.) recommended that the general was not to march the infantry battle line more than two miles from their camp on the day of battle, so John's actions were well in keeping with Roman combat doctrine.[17]

The enemy was also making plans for the battle. The Moors adopted the plan of Autilien. He advised the Moors to first attack the camp of John, after which they were to attack the Latin band, and then after that Garsana/Guarsana was to attack Cusina. In my Master's Thesis I interpreted this to mean that the Moors were to attack first John and then Cusina and that Guarsana could be a mistake for Carcasan. This is indeed possible, but it is also possible that the extant text of Corippus has just omitted to mention the attack of Antalas and the Moors of Iaudas against the Roman left wing under Ifisdaias. The fact that the Roman regular cavalry are later found pursuing the enemy together with John and his *bucellarii* implies that someone had attacked them (Corippus: '*has sequitur Romanus eques fortesque tribune armigerique ducis*'). My educated guess is that these attackers would have been the Moors of Antalas and Iaudas. In short, I would suggest that the Moors planned to attack John in the centre first, followed by the attack against the Roman left wing, after which followed the attack against the Roman right wing under Cusina, but so that Cusina probably made a pre-emptive charge against the enemy to buy time for the Romans to form their battle line.

The Romans spent the following night in the same manner as before. The soldiers were rotated on guard duty while John and the *duces* spent a sleepless night in conversation and planning. On the other hand, the Moors spent the night making sacrifices to their gods. They set up altars and sacrificed cattle to Gurzil, horned Ammon, and Sinifer the god of war. Still others sacrificed for Mastiman, which required both human and animal sacrifices, so the Moors would have killed quite a few of the surviving Roman captives at this time.

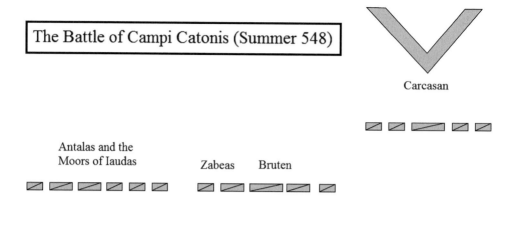

The Battle of Campi Catonis (Summer 548)

Carcasan

Antalas and the
Moors of Iaudas

Zabeas   Bruten

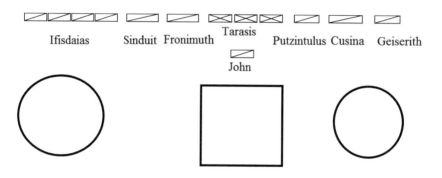

Ifisdaias   Sinduit Fronimuth   Tarasis   Putzintulus Cusina Geiserith

John

When the sun rose the Romans assumed their customary places before the Christian altar that had been placed in the centre of the camp where the tents of the commander, *duces* and priests were. The acolytes formed a choir and sang hymns. When the general then entered the area, the soldiers burst into tears and started to beat their guilty breasts again and again with their fists while chanting 'Forgive our sins and the sins of our fathers, we beseech You, Christ.'[18] John kneeled and cried and beat his chest with his fist while he prayed God to crush the enemy and preserve the Roman soldiers in combat. John, Ricinarius, *duces* and soldiers all prayed together, and the high priest placed gifts on the altar, prayed and sobbed. Now that the army had been sanctified and cleansed for combat, the commander and *duces* rose and the commander gave his orders to the *duces*. Putzintulus was to link his forces with those of Cusina. Corippus does not state where Cusina was but it is probable that he was on the right as before. Geisirith was also to join his forces with Cusina. Subsequent details make it clear that Cusina was between the two. Sinduit was to join his forces with Ifisdais, and Fronimuth was to stand beside him, with the implication that Ifisdaias led the outermost left wing. It is probable that both allied Moors left some sort of reserves behind to protect their camps. Tarasis with his infantry and bodyguards, and John with his bodyguards, assumed their traditional positions in the centre. The reserve of the centre would therefore have consisted of the bodyguards of both Tarasis and John Troglita.

As noted above, the Moors planned to surprise the Romans by attacking first and they did indeed charge onto the plain first with shields in hand, but their surprise was only partial. The details that Corippus gives – Cusina protecting the forming of the Latin array (which is ambiguous) and Putzintulus without armour – suggests that the speed of the enemy attack did come as something of a surprise, although Corippus fails to say so.

In the description of Corippus, Zabeas and Bruten led the cavalry attack against the Roman centre, but the subsequent text makes it clear that at least the right wing of the Moorish line attacked simultaneously with their centre. The Moors sent a thick volley of spears (*lanceae*) into the air. The Roman soldiers blocked them with their shields and their armour groaned underneath this assault. However, none of the spears found their mark. The Roman infantry had clearly assumed the *testudo/foulkon* array to receive this attack with the result that the enemy spears fell uselessly on the Roman shields. The Moorish attack had now failed and had been brought to a halt in front of the Roman infantry. It was now time for John to lead the counter-attack, which he did in person. Corippus gives us a description of his heroics together with the names of the killed, which I summarise because it is entirely believable that a superb fighter like John could kill such a large number of enemies when they were fleeing. John charged into the centre of the enemy array with his *hasta*-spear in hand as befitted his heroic leadership style and killed the first foe by striking him in the chest and unhorsing him. The rest of the Moors were now fleeing and the general pursued and struck one man in the back at the spot where spine meets the ribs with the result that he grasped the spear that was stuck in his bones while some of the Moors turned to help him. John grasped the enemy's spear from him and threw it at the first man approaching him and hit him in the heart. After this, John unhorsed another Moor with an enormous *hasta*, and then he cut off another's hand with a sword, hit another in the throat, and still another in the neck and thrust another in the groin. Then he hit a man in the face shattering his teeth, nose and cheeks. Not far from there he killed another man with a javelin and almost immediately after this he stabbed another 'foolish' Moor in the chest. Then he took a spear and thrust it through a Moor from one side to another, and then with a *contus*-spear unhorsed another Moor who he finished off from above. John continued his pursuit and killed another man with a thrown spear and after that killed a further eight during his relentless pursuit.

The Moors exploited the absence of John and his men by launching their attack against Cusina as they had planned. The Nasamoneans were formed up as a wedge (*cuneus*) while Cusina prepared his men to receive its attack by making a counter-attack with all three cavalry *moirai*. Cusina was in the centre of the attack and galloped through the enemy's closely packed units while the tribunes prepared the Latin arms (Romans) for battle. The Romans then received the shock of the Nasamonean *catervae* attack in their customary manner by pointing their spears and aiming their javelins (*hastaque parent et specula tendunt*). This is a fitting description of an infantry array used against cavalry. At that same moment the sky was blackened with clouds of missiles (javelins and arrows). The Marmaridans were pressing their attack and fought at close quarters so that only help from John could save the Romans. This account requires the making of several educated

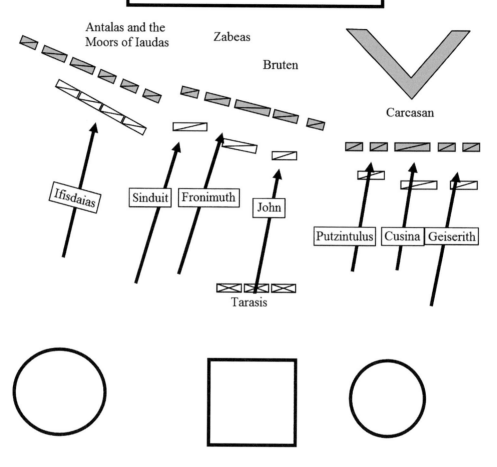

conjectures. The reference to the *cuneus* is likely to mean an infantry formation. The fact that the Romans were still marshalling their lines at the time Cusina made the charge means that Cusina bought time for the Romans to complete some manoeuvring. This means either that Tarasis's infantry was still in the process of deploying itself into combat formation so that Cusina's charge would have presaged the above Moorish attack against the Romans, or that Cusina also had some Roman infantry in front of his own camp, or that Cusina was attempting to protect John's right flank by tying up the enemy in front of him while John was pursuing the enemy. The first and last are inherently more likely, so it would have been Cusina's very timely charge that had enabled Tarasis to array his infantry to confront the enemy attack and then for John to exploit the success of his infantry, or that it was Cusina's attack that protected the right flank of John's pursuing cavalry. It is ultimately impossible to know, but the third alternative is probably the most likely on the basis of the order of accounts in Corippus. The fact that Cusina charged together with

Putzintulus and Geiserith and then burst through the enemy array and was still forced to flee means that the Moorish wedge was preceded by a cavalry screen so that the presence of the Moorish infantry *cuneus* behind their cavalry came as a nasty surprise for Cusina. This would have forced Cusina and the *duces* under him to flee behind the infantry of Tarasis and past them, while the infantry of Tarasis then received the pursuing enemy cavalry by poising their spears while those behind them used either javelins or bows.

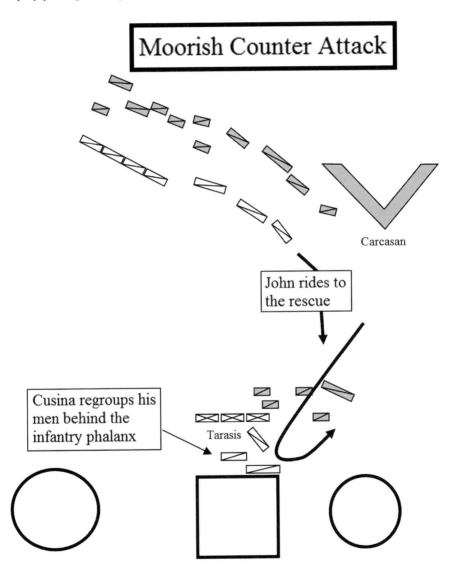

When John then learnt from a messenger that the hero of the hour Cusina was in trouble, he turned his cavalry forces right against the Moors. It is probable that John divided his cavalry forces at this point even though Corippus fails to say so. It is more or less probable that Ifisdaias continued the pursuit of the defeated enemy forces and the same may also be true of Sinduit and Fronimuth, because Corippus doesn't mention these in the context of John's next attack whereas he lists John together with a number of men belonging to John's *armigeri*. The sight of John's flank attack encouraged Putzintulus, Cusina and Geiserith to return to the combat. Putzintulus attacked with mad fury. When the *duces* of the Ifuraces tribe saw this, they formed up a battle line consisting of thousands of men, which must mean the infantry behind the pursuing Moorish cavalry. I would suggest that this was the left flank of their infantry wedge, which was now arrayed as a separate formation against Cusina while the other half of the infantry wedge was arrayed against John Troglita and his cavalry. When Putzintulus came close to this array he (and undoubtedly his men) received a volley of spears. Putzintulus did not wear any breastplate and received a deadly wound. He asked his soldiers to avenge his death, which Corippus likened to the self-sacrifice of the Decii. This suggests that Cusina and the Roman cavalry under him had charged against the enemy so hastily that some of the men had been unable to equip themselves with armour.

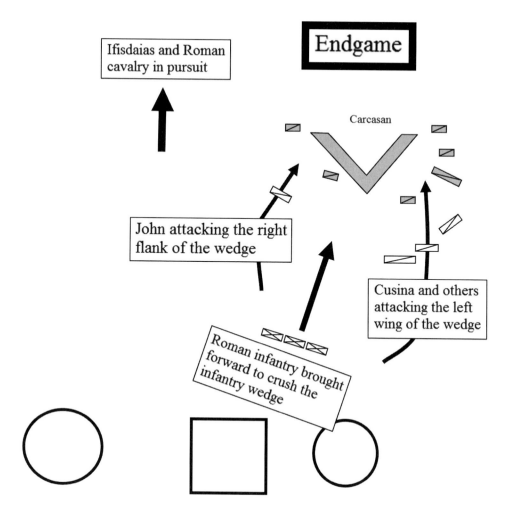

John's flank attack toward the Moorish left wing was received by Moorish cavalry that had retreated there. When it gave way the Romans shot hissing arrows from their twanging bowstrings which means that there was some distance between them and the fleeing enemy cavalry. The pursuing Roman cavalry soon reached the enemy infantry lines where their attack faltered. This would have been the right flank of the previous infantry wedge. It was then that a Roman unit armed with *pila*-javelins (the *pila*-armed unit '*pilata manus*' clearly refers to Roman infantry that was brought to the scene to attack the enemy infantry) advanced against the Moors. This unit slaughtered the opposing forces with the result that the Roman cavalry could once again renew its pursuit of the enemy. At this point in his narrative Corippus notes that it was impossible to name all of those that John killed because the common enemy soldiers died nameless and unknown, but he still named a few of those that he had learnt from the enemy. On the previous occasions in which I have left the names out, Corippus named those killed, and so did he after this, but in this case I only offer a summary.

Now John cut through the enemy cavalry and infantry formations and killed thirteen Moors that Corippus names and captured one Camalus who he handed over to his bodyguards and continued his pursuit of the enemy *turmae* and then received the surrender of still another Moor called Labbas. John was clearly a regular killing machine. Corippus also gives us a list of the killed and captured for his bodyguards, including Ricinarius. At some point the pursuers were once again stopped by some infantry formation: an *armiger* called John came face to face with Fastita whose horse he killed with a thrown spear with the result that Fastita fled to safety behind a closely arrayed formation consisting of thousands of warriors. This would be the left flank of the infantry *cuneus*, which had stopped Putzintulus just before this. Carcasan appears to have been in charge of this array, because Corippus states next that Carcasan turned the standard under his command around to attack through the heart of the Roman formation, which is where John Troglita was. Carcasan's aim was to fight his way to safety by attacking those who were behind him. When John Troglita recognized Carcasan, he took a javelin from the hand of his namesake *armiger* (the John from whose hands Fastita had fled) and attacked Carcasan. The javelin hit its mark and killed the enemy commander with the result that the remaining Moors panicked and their cavalry turned and fled and the infantry with them. The Romans followed hot on their heels and John continued to cut down the fleeing enemies as if he was mowing a lawn. The field was level and it was dead easy for the Romans to kill and kill. The end of Corippus' poem is missing, but it is clear that this was the battle that decided the fate of Roman North Africa and Libya.

John Troglita and his successors in 548–65

The victory at Campi Catonis/Latara proved decisive so the remainder of John's stay in Africa was peaceful and he could consolidate the Roman conquests with fortifications and garrisons and good governance. The peace enabled John to dispatch a fleet to retake Sardinia in 551, which together with Corsica had in the meantime been captured by Totila's Huns. The Hunnish garrison defeated this amphibious force at Caralis and it returned to Carthage. This operation was clearly one part of the coordinated Roman effort to retake Italy from Totila at this time. John dispatched another force next year, which this time captured the island with ease. The capable prefect Athanasius had in the meantime been replaced by Paul who is mentioned for the first time in September 552. John remained in command of Africa at least until 552. The sources are silent about events after this, which shows how successful John had been. All we have are two laws, a letter of Pelagius and references to troubles in Malalas and Theophanes for the year 563. The laws name Paul as prefect in September 552 and John as prefect in 558. Pope Pelagius I (555–60) mentions Boethius as a prefect in a letter. Agathias claims that during the latter part of his reign Justinian reduced the strength of the Roman armies from 645,000 to 150,000. The implications of this are difficult to assess for Africa.[19] Perhaps we should interpret this to mean that Justinian did not pay salaries to the *Limitanei*, which would explain the military revolts after 536, but in light of the general lack of revolts after John Troglita assumed command, it would seem probable that salaries were paid under him, probably from local sources, and that the crisis that had caused the so-called reduction in the size of the army had passed at least in Africa.

The silence of the sources suggests that North Africa saw a period of relative peace until 562/3 when troubles with the Moors surfaced again. Cusina/Cutzinas/Koutzines/Koutzinas, the trusted Moorish chieftain who held the title of *magister*, was murdered by John (Ioannes) Rogathinus for reasons unknown when Cusina arrived to collect the tribute paid in gold to the Moors. Malalas calls Cusina 'exarch' so it is possible that he held an even higher position than that of *magister*. John held either the title of *Praefectus Praetorio Africae* so he should be identified with the addressee of the law in 558, or he held the title of *MVM per Africam* in which case it is not known whether he should be identified with the addressee of the law in 558. Whatever the case, he seems to have lacked adequate forces against the Moors, who naturally revolted after this.[20]

When the news of the murder of Cusina was brought to his sons, they rose against the Romans conquering and pillaging parts of Roman North Africa. When the news of this was brought to Justinian in December 562 he dispatched his nephew the *magister militum* Marcian (Marcianus/Markianos) with an army to pacify the Moors. The Moors went over to Marcianus and Africa was pacified. This presumably means that Marcianus negotiated with the Moors and addressed their grievances somehow, probably that he arrested John and put him on trial for his actions, but ultimately we do not know how the pacification was achieved. What we do know is that the troubles with the Moors renewed under Justinian's successor Justin II in 569 when they killed *PP Africae* Theodore.[21] This suggests that the troubles were always related to the payments of tribute, and that it is also probable that the abovementioned John Rogathinus had been *PP Africae*. We do not know whether the refusal to pay the tribute was a policy decision, corruption of the prefect, or inability to pay. In my opinion the last can be discarded because the Romans always found the money when they really needed to. This leaves the two other options, probably their combination: the prefect wanted to pocket some of the money meant for the Moors and made a policy decision to this effect. On the basis of the constant references to the corruption of the imperial officials and officers, this would have been the typical modus operandi for most of the office holders. The Roman Empire and its populace and soldiers were ill-served by these corrupt men.

Chapter Fifteen

East: The Wars of the Arab Federates in 545/6–562/3

The Wars of the Arab Federates. Phase 1 (545/46–550/51)[1]

In her seminal study of Arab Federates, Irfan Shahid has brought to the attention of the scholarly world the fact that the area of Lazica was not the only area where there were confrontations between Rome and Persia after 545. The federates of both Rome and Persia fought against each other almost continuously from about 545/6 until about 562/3, and even if neither of the superpowers provided direct assistance to them it is clear that they fought against each other as allies of the superpowers. Because of this they were later mentioned in the terms of peace.

Shahid divides the wars between the Ghassanids of Arethas and Lakhmids of Alamoundaros into three distinct phases: 1) the first phase in 545/6–550/51; 2) the second phase in 551–556/7; 3) the third in 556/7–561, but Shahid's subsequent discussion of events proves that there was probably still fighting in 562/3.

According to Procopius, very soon after the conclusion of the truce, it received its first test and this time the legalistic thinking present in both empires worked to their mutual advantage. When the two Arab sheiks, Alamoundaros/al-Mundhir and Arethas/al-Harith, then fought against each other neither of the superpowers assisted their ally. The war began with Alamoundaros capturing the son of Arethas with a sudden raid when he was pasturing his horses. Alamoundaros sacrificed the son to Aphrodite. According to Procopius, this proved that Arethas had not betrayed the Romans and was not working for the Persians. It also proves that Arethas's previous actions under Belisarius had indeed made him suspect in Roman eyes even though the real reason for Arethas's misbehaviour was merely his greedy Bedouin nature which was not that different from the behaviour of the Roman soldiers in general. The murder of the son resulted in full scale war. Later both assembled their armies and met each other in battle. Arethas achieved an overwhelming victory over his nemesis, killed large numbers of his foes and came close to capturing alive two of Alamoundaros's sons. Shahid suggests that this meant the famous battle of 554 in which Alamoundaros was killed, but I do not agree with this view. In my opinion, Procopius's reference to the attempted capture of the sons should be seen to mean that Arethas wanted Alamoundaros to witness the death of his sons as he had been forced to witness the death of his own son. There is no reference to the death of Alamoundaros for this reason so the traditional dating for the writing of Procopius's texts should be seen to be still valid.

Shahid is correct to note that by fighting Alamoundaros Arethas was also protecting the Roman Empire, so this fighting should not be seen merely in terms of tribal warfare or banditry. Had Arethas lost, Alamoundaros would surely have started plundering Roman territories proper. Furthermore, it is clear that if Alamoundaros had defeated Arethas, the Persians would hardly have been able to resist the opportunity to join the raiding of the territories of the weakened Romans. Furthermore, it is clear that both superpowers were forced to keep their own forces in the area just in case the fighting spilled over to their territories, so the Arab wars also tied up resources from other theatres of war. This was also a war between the Christians and pagans in which both sides fought for their religion. The Arabs of Arethas were sort of crusaders who exacted vengeance on the evil pagan Saracens who robbed, raped, tortured and killed Christians regardless of age or sex. These were naturally seen as Christian martyrs by the Ghassanids.

The first phase of the war concluded with the signing of the truce between Rome and Persia in 551. The two sides agreed to a truce of five years during which their envoys would continue to negotiate the sticking points which were the disagreements concerning Lazica and the Saracens. This means, as Shahid has noted, that the Saracen question was constantly on the table when the two superpowers negotiated.

Chosroes's treachery in 548

According to the well-informed Procopius, in the third year of the truce in 548 Chosroes formed a plan to use it for a surprise attack. He had most probably been dishonest from the start. It means that Chosroes was not satisfied to restrict the fighting to Lazica or to the fighting between the Arab allies of both empires. The first part of Chosroes's plan was to assassinate Goubazes and to transfer the entire population of Lazica because they were unreliable and replace them with the loyal Persians. The idea was to use Lazica as a launching pad for an invasion of Asia Minor and Constantinople. The second part of his plan was to capture Dara with a surprise attack. The capture of Dara would have enabled Chosroes to use neighbouring Nisibis as a secure base for an invasion of Roman territory in the central section of the frontier. Chosroes chose the brothers Phabrizus and Isdigousnas as the men to carry out this operation. They were officially dispatched as envoys to Justinian. However, they were given an escort of 500 men and were instructed to make a stop at Dara. When the Romans would let them in, they were to set several houses on fire to keep the Romans preoccupied while they would then let the Persian army inside. The latter consisted of the men secretly dispatched for this purpose from the garrison of Nisibis. The plan was betrayed to the Roman commander George by a Roman deserter (former *doryforos* of Martinus). George duly met the ambassador at the border and ordered that the massive retinue accompanying the envoys was to be housed at Ammodios and that he would allow only twenty men to enter Dara. Thus the Persian plan was foiled and the envoys were forced to undertake a futile trip to Constantinople where Justinian entertained them for a long time: their trip lasted for ten months. Justinian gave them as presents valuables worth 1,000 lbs of gold, clearly meant as a bribe to keep the Persians happy. The fact that Justinian kept the Persian envoys in Constantinople for so long also suggests that he was playing for time to amass resources for the possible war against Persia.[2] This incident once again proves the greater readiness of the Persians to betray their agreements than was the case with the Romans of the time.

The Wars of the Arab Federates: Phase 2 (550/51–555/6)[3]

The five year truce which the superpowers signed in 551 did not put a stop to the fighting between their Arabic allies. The only area where there was quiet was the Mesopotamian front. The era saw the climax in the fighting between Arethas and Alamoundaros. The decisive moment came in 554 when Justinian had committed most of his forces available for the east to Lazica where he had dispatched an army of 50,000 men. It was then that Alamoundaros invaded Roman territory proper, advancing as deep as Chalcis/Qinnasrin where he was met by the Arab forces of Arethas. This time Alamoundaros was pillaging Roman territory and not the tribal lands of Arethas so it was of paramount importance for Arethas to decide the question quickly and decisively. The details that we have of the decisive battle Chalcis/Qinnasrin in June 554 suggests that it was fought immediately after two holy months for the pagans had ended. The exact location is not known, but it was fought close to Chalcis/Qinnasrin, and there was a spring and hill. The battle was fought between two cavalry forces. Alamoundaros had the advantage and broke the Ghassanid ranks with a charge. Arethas's oldest son Gabala died, but then Arethas regrouped his forces and inflicted a decisive defeat on the Lakhmids killing Alamoundaros in the process possibly in person. The abovementioned hill may have served as a place of refuge for Arethas where he regrouped his forces, even if this is not stated by the sources. After the battle Arethas buried his son in a *martyrion* and some of Arethas's men went to St. Simeon's monastery where they thanked the saint for his help in the battle. Some chose to remain in the monastery. The Christian Ghassanids had invoked St. Simeon's help and also the help of Jesus, Job and Du'miyy (meaning not known) during the battle so this behaviour is not surprising. The victory was so complete that the Lakhmids ceased to be a serious threat for a while, which was recognized by Justinian who gave Arethas the Patrician title and rank. Now he belonged to the upper echelons of the Roman military and society. However, we should not forget that even though Arethas's victory over Alamoundaros was complete, it did not prevent the surviving Lakhmids from launching raids in revenge in the following years; the Arabic sources prove that the son of Alamoundaros did launch retaliatory wars. However, these were no longer as threatening as they had been when Alamoundaros lived.

The victory had another less welcome consequence, which was that the other federate Arab allies of Rome, the Kindites posted in Palestine, appear to have started fighting against each other, presumably because the Monophysite Ghassanids came to the Holy Land to give thanks to Jesus while the Kindites themselves were strongly Chalcedonian. Arethas appears to have punished the Kindites for this because he is known to have established peace in the area which usually means the use of violence. This fighting between the Roman federates took place apparently in about 554/5 and it is also possible that the Samaritan and Jewish revolt of 555 was somehow connected with these events because at least Simeon the Younger was involved in it with his efforts to make Justinian inflict punishment on the Samaritans. In my opinion it is also possible that the Persians or the Lakhmids had incited the revolt.

According to Malalas (18.119), in July 555 the Samaritans and Jews of Caesarea rioted and then united together against the Christians of the city and killed many of them. They also plundered the churches of the Orthodox. The governor of the city, Stephanos, reacted by coming to the assistance of the Christians, but the Samaritans attacked and killed him in his *praetorium* and looted it. When Justinian learnt of this, he ordered *Comes Orientis* Amantios to investigate the events and the murder. Amantios acted as instructed and found the culprits. Some were hanged, others beheaded, others had their right hands cut off, and still others lost their property. Amantios's action proved successful because Malalas states that after this there was great fear in the city of Caesarea.

The Romans and Persians concluded a new truce in 557, but this time without any payments to the Persians from the Roman side. The defeats the Persians suffered in Lazica were only one of the reasons for this. It is equally clear that the resounding victory of Arethas over the Lakhmids contributed to this situation. Chosroes may also have desired to turn his attention against the Turks at this time.

The Wars of the Arab Federates: Phase 3 (556/7–562/3)[4]

The Arabic sources suggest that Alamoundaros's son and the Lakhmids continued to wage wars of revenge after the truce of 557, but at the same time it is clear that the defeat at Chalcis had weakened the Lakhmids so badly that they appear not to have posed any serious threat. Partly because of this the Romans were able to put a stop to the payments to the Persians in 557 and solely because of this they could put a stop to the 100 lbs of gold per year payments to the Lakhmids. It was also because of this that when the Romans and Persians finally concluded a peace in 561, which included the Arabs of both sides in the agreement, the Romans refused to pay any money to the Lakhmids while they paid protection money to the Persians in return for peace. The Lakhmids were not happy about this state of affairs. They had already complained about it to the Persian negotiator Zikh during the peace negotiations so that he had raised the issue in his discussion with the Romans, but the latter had flatly refused to pay. The Lakhmids complained again and this time to Chosroes so that Chosroes raised the issue in his discussions with the Roman envoy Peter in 562 when the two sides discussed the status of Suania in the previously agreed treaty. Once again the Romans refused to pay. This answer did not satisfy the Lakhmids who then raided the territories belonging to Arethas to apply pressure. Arethas appears not to have reacted to this because the peace treaty prevented it, and only raised the issue in his discussions with the emperor Justinian when he had been called to Constantinople to meet him in 563. Justinian promised to settle the matter, but how we do not know for certain. However, Shahid has pointed out that there exists evidence for the Romans paying money to Amr the Lakhmid in 567, which does suggest that Justinian may have started to pay money to the Lakhmids once again in 563 in return for peace and that it is probable that he did this secretly so that Arethas would not become upset. This is indeed the most likely alternative.

Chapter Sixteen

East: The Lazic War in 549–57

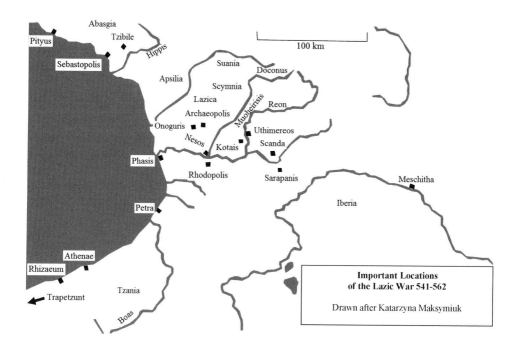

**Important Locations
of the Lazic War 541-562**

Drawn after Katarzyna Maksymiuk

Justinian's diplomatic moves in about 547–48[1]

The Abasgi of Georgia had converted to Christianity during the reign of Justinian, which signified that they had become allies and clients of Rome. Before this, the Abasgi had been ruled by two kings who earned income by capturing boys who were then castrated and sent to Constantinople. The emperor had managed to make the area his clients with a clever manoeuvre. He converted the Abasgi to Christianity, built a church there and most importantly dispatched one of the eunuchs of the Palace called Abasgus, and Abasgian by origin, to the two kings with the order to stop mutilating males forthwith. The common people received this with eagerness and dethroned their kings. The idea was clearly to undermine the position of Goubazes and the Persians in Lazica.

When the Tetraxitae Goths, who dwelled in Crimea close to the Roman-held city of Cherson, learnt of this they dispatched four envoys to Justinian in 548 with the request that he give them a bishop, because they had learned that Justinian had given a bishop to the Abasgi. The Tetraxitae feared that the Utigur Huns might hear their discussions in Constantinople, so they asked for a secret audience. They advised Justinian secretly that it would be very advantageous for the Romans if the Huns (presumably meaning

Utigurs and Kutrigurs) who were their neighbours were on hostile terms with each other. The Tetraxitae and Utigurs were allies so this advice was treacherous in its intent. But it was undoubtedly something that Justinian was glad to hear. He now knew that the Utigurs could not put any trust in their alliance with the Tetraxitae. It is probable that this treacherous behaviour influenced the results of the subsequent fighting between the Utigurs and Kuritgurs, just as the Tetraxitae and Justinian wanted.

The cause of the resumption of hostilities in 549[2]

Procopius gives us an admirable list of the reasons why the Persians considered the keeping of Lazica in their hands to be of the greatest strategic importance: 1) The possession of Lazica/Colchis secured Iberia; 2) It secured the passes over the Caucasus so that the Romans could not use the Huns against the Persians, while the Persians could use the Huns against the Romans; 3) It gave the Persians access to the Black Sea which gave the Persians the chance to conquer Asia Minor and Constantinople.

Sicgc of Pctra in 549 (offensive siege)[3]

In 549, the Persians planned to assassinate the king of the Lazi, Goubazes. When the plan was revealed to him by a native Lazi who had been tasked with the murder by the Persians, he changed his allegiance to the Romans. Justinian eagerly accepted the proposal and sent Dagisthaeus with 7,000 soldiers and 1,000 Tzani to assist Goubazes. They put Petra under siege. In response, Chosroes sent a great army of horse and foot consisting of 33,000 men under Mermeroes against the besiegers. Goubazes learned of the imminent arrival of the enemy and advised Dagisthaeus to send a strong detachment of men to guard the pass below the River Phasis while he himself would guard the other strategic pass north of the River Phasis, which was located opposite Iberia. Goubazes also allied himself with the Alans and Sabirs to whom he promised that the emperor Justinian would send money. Justinian indeed promised to send money even though Goubazes had promised it without his prior permission, but he sent it late and it did not arrive at the time promised. Regardless, when the Alans and Sabirs subsequently received the promised money, they made a diversionary attack against Iberia to keep the Persians occupied. The inexperienced Dagisthaeus sent only 100 men while he with the rest of the army tried unsuccessfully to assault the city.

In the meantime, the Romans and Lazi had decimated the 1,500-strong Persian garrison defending Petra with missiles, but the Persians hid this fact from the Romans by keeping their dead within the walls despite the stench so that the besiegers would not gain courage from this fact. The Romans made a trench along the wall for a short distance and managed to bring down the circuit wall at that spot. However, this did not bring about the desired outcome because there was a separate building behind the downed wall that now became a new wall for the defenders. This did not discourage the Romans because they knew that they could bring down the wall in some other place, and Dagisthaeus sent a message to Justinian in which he promised to take the city soon. Dagisthaeus ordered a general assault, but the Persians withstood this contrary to his hopes, so he resorted to undermining the wall. The Romans mined the circuit wall for a great distance so that a significant portion of the foundations no longer stood on solid ground and the city could have been taken almost immediately had Dagisthaeus ordered the foundations torched. When the foundations were fired a portion of the wall fell down and fifty Roman volunteers rushed inside the fort under an Armenian, John the Gouzes, son of Thomas. This John had built many fortresses about Lazica on behalf of Justinian and was the commander of the Roman soldiers in Lazica. John was wounded by the defending Persians and he was immediately taken to the camp. His men then withdrew from the fortress because nobody had come to their assistance. Mirranes (Mihran), the Persian commander of the fort, was now in a state of despair and ordered the garrison to guard the walls diligently while he went in person to meet Dagisthaeus. Mirranes promised to hand over the city soon and with this ruse he managed to fool Dagisthaeus so that the Romans did not repeat their attack against the defenceless fort.

When Mermeroes's army arrived in Lazica, the 100-man garrison fought valiantly at the pass. According to Procopius, the Romans killed more than 1,000 Persians, but the Persians did not withdraw. Those who fell were constantly replaced by others, and the Persians kept advancing until the exhausted Romans saved themselves by running up to the heights of the mountain. According to Procopius, when Dagistheus learnt of this, he panicked and abandoned the siege immediately without giving any orders for the army and marched to the River Phasis where the Romans followed. The hasty flight meant that the Romans had left their possessions inside their marching camp, which the Persians from Petra proceeded to loot. The Tzani, however, had not followed after the fleeing Romans because they had not been given any orders. So they attacked and defeated the Persians, looted the Roman camp and withdrew to Tzanica via Rhizaeum, Athens and the territory of the Trapezuntines. The Tzani therefore exploited the opportunity they had been given and retreated to their own territory with the loot. Procopius has exaggerated the disorder among the Romans because subsequent events prove that the Romans and their Lazi allies occupied the passes leading into Lazica to isolate the defenders of Petra. Nevertheless, it is clear that there was some confusion in the ranks because the actions undertaken by the Tzani prove it. Dagisthaeus had clearly panicked for no good reason because Mermeroes arrived only nine days later.

The Persians arrived indeed only nine days after the flight of the Roman army. On his arrival Mermeroes learnt that he had arrived in the nick of time. The 1,500-strong garrison under Mirranes had lost 1,000 men dead and 350 wounded; only 150 remained unhurt. The siege had been a close run thing and shows how effective the Roman and Lazican missile attacks with bows, slings and artillery fire had been. It was only the clever ruse of Mirranes and gullibility of Dagisthaeus that had saved the Persians.

Before that, Justinian had not been idle. He had already sent another army under Rhecithancus to Lazica, but this army had not yet arrived when Dagisthaeus and Gubazes were engaging in guerrilla warfare against the Persians. Mermeroes was unable to provision his 30,000-strong army so was unable to tarry in the area. One of the Lazi notables, Phoubelis, with Dagisthaeus (with 2,000 Romans) made a successful night attack/raid against Mermeroes's camp when the Persians were en route home. Mermeroes left 5,000 men to protect the reinforced 3,000-strong garrison of Petra while he withdrew his main army. In Lazica, the Persians placed 1,000 men in advance (or rather in the rear) of their camp to act as a covering force. However, Dagisthaeus and Goubazes with 14,000 men surprised both the advance guard and then the camp (at night) in succession. Their pursuit of the enemy led them into Iberia where they defeated another Persian force. Afterwards, the passes leading into Lazica were more firmly defended. These events not only show the defensive strategy of guerrilla warfare but also the aggressive strategy of isolating an enemy fortress by blocking the advances (passes) to it in preparation for the forthcoming new attempt.

Justinian's diplomatic manoeuvres against Persia in 548–50

According to Malalas (18.106), in January 549 or 550 an Indian ambassador arrived at Constantinople and presented an elephant to Justinian. See also the Plates. On the basis of this it is possible that Justinian and the Indian ruler who had sent the ambassador and gift were negotiating to form a joint alliance against Persia. It is impossible to know how he had made the initiative, but since Justinian had known since 548 that the Persians were planning a war and he knew that the five-year truce would end in 550, it is probable that he had been the man who had started the negotiations. We do not know whether these negotiations brought any tangible results, but we do know that the Persians were ready to renew the peace in 550–51, which may mean that they had brought some troubles for the Persians in the east.

Battle of Hippis River in 550[4]

In 550, a vast Persian army, including Alans, under Chorianes invaded Lazica. The large army means that there were at least 30,000 Persians and Alans. In addition to this, Chosroes dispatched another army under Nabedes to Lazica where he marched to Abasgia which at this time had revolted from the Romans. It is possible that the intention was to put pressure on the Romans to conclude a new peace which would be more favourable to the Persians, but it is equally possible that it was just a Persian attempt to regain land lost.

 The Persians encamped in a fortified camp near the River Hippis. Gubades king of Lazica and Dagisthaeus the commander of the Roman army in Armenia opposed him. They encamped their army on the opposite side of the Hippis River and proceeded to cross it. The Lazi were eager to fight and demanded the right to fight in front. Consequently, the Lazi horsemen were posted in front. Behind them were posted the Roman horsemen under Philegagus the Gepid and John Guzes. The use of two commanders may imply the use of two lines (or divisions) behind the Lazi. Behind them were the combined infantry forces of Gubazes and Dagisthaeus. The Persians sent a 1,000-strong heavy cavalry vanguard. The Lazi horsemen fled immediately and galloped to take refuge between and behind the two Roman cavalry divisions. When the vanguards of both armies came face to face, they did not join battle but made threatening advances to test the mettle of the enemy. This continued until Artabanes,[5] one of the Persarmenians serving in the Roman army, with two others engaged the Persians in single combat and won causing the retreat of the Persian vanguard.

 When the Persian cavalry came into sight, Philegagus and John withdrew their cavalry to the safety of their infantry, which had just arrived. The Lazi and Romans were dismounted to form a very deep phalanx bristling with spears. According to Procopius, the reason for this decision was that they considered their numbers too few to face the Persian cavalry and the Romans did not have trust in the ability of the Lazi horsemen to withstand the onslaught of the Persian cavalry. The deep phalanx undoubtedly refers to the flanks of the so-called *epikampios opisthia* formation rather than to the depth of a single lateral phalanx. Consequently, the Romans adopted one of the standard methods to be used against enemy cavalry. The Persian cavalry was unable to break down the tight infantry phalanx. The points of the spears and the clashing of the shields distressed the horses. The Persians tried to break up the formation with arrows, but the Romans and Lazi responded in kind. The Persians and the Alans shot much faster than the Romans, but most of the arrows were checked by the shields (showing that the Roman and Lazican cavalry were equipped with shields). The battle was decided by a single arrow shot which killed the Persian commander Chorianes. After he fell, the Persians fled towards their camp with the Romans in pursuit. The Romans captured the camp despite the personal heroics of one Alan who only delayed the inevitable. The Persians fled as they could. For the sequence of events, see the following diagrams.

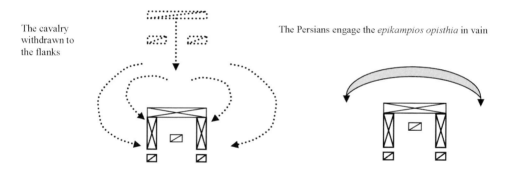

The cavalry withdrawn to the flanks

The Persians engage the *epikampios opisthia* in vain

Despite the successful use of guerrilla tactics against the Persians and the success at the Battle of Hippis River, Dagisthaeus was dismissed because of his failure at Petra. The Lazicans accused him of betrayal when he had stopped the attack at Petra when the Persians were defenceless. Justinian imprisoned Dagisthaeus and appointed Bessas as his replacement.

Nabedes invades Lazica, Apsilia and Abasgia in 550[6]

As noted, in the meantime the Persians had also invaded Lazica with another army which was led by Nabedes. His object was the land of the Abasgi which had revolted from the Romans and the Lazi, and his secondary object was Apsilia just south of Abasgia. The Apsilians had revolted against the Lazi because their ruler *magister* Terdetes had quarrelled with Goubazes. He promised to lead the Persians into Apsilia and hand over the fortress of Tzibile to them. Terdetes captured the fortress through subterfuge. He went there with his Lazi forces and the defenders could not prevent an entrance from their superior. After this, he handed it over to the Persians.

En route, in the land of the Apsilii, Nabedes managed to capture Theodora, wife of Opsites, who was uncle of Goubazes. He took her to Persia. It was a rule among the royals of Lazica to marry Roman women and Goubazes was half Roman. This and Christianity naturally tied the Lazicans and Iberians to the Romans.

Once in Abasgia, Nabedes took from them sixty noble-born children as hostages after which he retreated. The Abasgi had revolted because the Roman soldiers who had been sent there treated the locals harshly with the result that the Abasgi put their rulers back in power with Opsites ruling the eastern half and Scaparpas the western half. One may make the educated guess that the Roman garrison was butchered at the same time as the Persians arrived, but this is obviously not stated.

Battle of Trachea in 550[7]

When Justinian learnt of the revolt of the Abasgi, he ordered Bessas to reconquer Abasgia and Lazica. Bessas selected a large number of men for this task (apparently 9,000) and appointed Wilgang/Uligagus (a Herul) and John the Armenian as their commanders. This force was sent by sea against the Abasgians. Scaparpas was in Persia so that all Abasgians were now under Opsites. The Abasgians under king Opsites occupied a strong fortress built on a lofty ridge gradually sinking into the Black Sea on the border facing Apsilia. The only path to the land of the Abasgi and to this fortress lay in a gorge. It was passable only on foot for men marching in single file. The Roman army was disembarked on the border and advanced on foot along the coast while the navy followed. The whole Abasgian army protected the pass. The Romans were in a quandary until John had an idea. He left Uligagus with half the force behind while he with the rest embarked the ships and landed behind the enemy. The Romans raised their standards and attacked the enemy from two sides. The Abasgi fled in disorder to their fortress, the pursued and pursuers reaching it on the run almost simultaneously. The surviving Abasgi occupied the roofs of their houses and threw at the Romans anything they could lay their hands on. The Romans responded by setting the houses on fire. Opsites with few of his men fled, but the rest were either burnt or captured. The fortress was razed to the ground and the land rendered desolate around it. Thus ended the revolt. Naval supremacy again proved its worth.

The return of Apsilia to the Roman fold in about 550–51[8]

The revolt of the Apsilii (south of the Abasgi) and Terdetes against the Lazi ended when the Persian commander fell in love with the wife of the commander of the Apsilii garrison of Tzibile. The husband slew the Persian commander and his men. Goubazes sent 1,000 Romans and Lazi under John son of Thomas against Tzibile. Now John managed to convince the defenders to admit them inside. Love and a few persuasive words conquer all before them.

Chosroes's problems in 550–51[9]

Chosroes was at this time preoccupied with personal problems which undoubtedly affected his ability to conduct operations in Lazica. According to Procopius, Chosroes punished his eldest son Anasozadus with exile at Belabaton which was located a distance of seven days from Ctesiphon. The reason was that he had committed many breaches of conduct, the most serious of which was that he had slept with the wives of his father. It is not surprising that in these circumstances Chosroes fell violently ill. He was by nature sickly so any setback such as this was bound to affect him. He was treated by a succession of Roman doctors, one of whom was the already mentioned Tribunus the Palestinian. When Anasozadus learnt of his father's illness, he started to stir up a revolt to usurp power, but then his father recovered. It was now too late to back down so the son usurped power in the city of Belapaton. Chosroes dispatched an army under Phabrizus the *strategos* against the rebel son. The two sides fought a battle which ended in the defeat of Anasozadus. He was captured and brought before Chosroes. Chosroes disfigured his eyelids so that the son's outward appearance was not only ugly but also such as he could no longer become ruler. The Persian law forbade the enthroning of disfigured persons.

The negotiations to renew the truce in 550–51[10]

When the five-year truce between Rome and Persia was reaching its end, Justinian dispatched *Magister Officiorum* Peter to Chosroes to negotiate its renewal, but Chosroes sent him back with the promise that he would send his own envoy soon. The negotiations lasted until autumn 551 so the following events took place during the negotiations. The two sides now agreed to another five-year truce which left Lazica out of it. This time the Romans agreed to pay 2,600 lbs of gold to the Persians in return for this. This was intensely disliked by the populace. They resented the paying of tribute and the fact that the Persians had not been forced out of Lazica so that the Persians formed a real and present danger for Constantinople. The honours given to the Persian envoy also irritated the populace. However, in my opinion Justinian did the right thing because there was not really any imminent threat for Constantinople and also he needed resources for the reconquest of Italy.

Siege of Petra in 550–51[11]

In 550, while diplomatic negotiations for peace with Persia were going on, Bessas began the siege of Petra. He had 6,000 men while the Persians had 2,300. First, he attempted to cut off the water supply to the city by cutting the water pipeline on the surface. However, it was soon found out that the city still received water. This caused the Romans to dig the ground. They found a second pipeline but failed to realize that the Persians had hidden a third pipeline even deeper. Bessas decided to undermine the wall where the ground allowed it (most of the circuit wall rested on rock), which was the same place that had been undermined previously under Dagisthaeus's leadership. However, after the previous Roman attempt to retake the city, the Persians had reconstructed the wall so that gravel and heavy timber supported the structure, and when the ground gave way the wall simply lowered into the empty space without breaking up. Bessas was at loss what to do. The slopes prevented them from bringing their battering rams against the walls, but one of the allied Sabiri Huns came up with a novel idea for how one could build a light ram built out of thick wands bound together that could be operated by forty men even against a wall on a slope. Did he get the idea from the way they built their yurts? Procopius (*Wars*, 8.11.27–31) stressed the novelty of this ram and wondered how the Persians and Romans who had great numbers of siege specialists and engineers had not made this simple innovation. The Sabiri built three of these novel rams, and with them the Romans in groups of forty began to break the wall. Others on each side of the engines loosened and pulled down the stones with long poles with hook-shaped irons. The Persians countered by placing on top of the wall a wooden tower from which they threw pots filled with sulphur, bitumen and naphtha on the ram sheds. Bessas responded by ordering a general attack. Bessas (over 70 and fat) was the first to mount the ladder. He fell to the ground but his bodyguards protected him by forming a *foulkon* and then dragged him away from the danger under the protective cover of shields. Once outside the range of missiles, Bessas got to his feet and ordered the attack to be renewed. He was once again among the first to set foot on the ladder. The renewed attack frightened the Persians. They asked for free passage out, but Bessas suspected trickery and agreed only to designate a place where they could conduct negotiations. The Persians declined.

Then suddenly part of the wall that had been undermined collapsed. Both sides rushed to the spot. The battle became very fierce, most of the participants receiving wounds, and continued until John Guzes, the son of Thomas, took some of his Armenian followers and forced his way in at the place which all considered impregnable. He killed with a spear thrust the first opponent on the top of the wall, but was subsequently killed in action. At about the same time the Persians in the wooden tower accidentally burned themselves to death when the wind spread the fire from the burning ram sheds into the tower. In the end, the numerical advantage of 6,000 Romans against 2,300 Persians proved decisive. The city was captured, but 500 Persians took refuge at the acropolis. These elite soldiers refused to surrender and were burned to death when the Romans hurled fire into the acropolis. The Romans had taken 730 prisoners of whom only eighteen were unhurt. The rest of the Persians were killed in action. These Persians consisted clearly of elite fighters. Bessas razed the circuit wall to the ground so that the Persians could not use it again.

Siege and Battle of Archaeopolis in 551[12]

The Persians under Mermeroes had collected an army consisting of Persians and allied Sabiri Huns. Sabiri Huns had originally sent 12,000 men, but fearing their numbers Mermeroes had sent the rest back home so that 4,000 Sabiri remained. Procopius claims in a speech put into the mouth of a Lazi traitor that Mermeroes had more than 70,000 Persians plus the Sabiri. In light of the inability of the Romans to challenge them this figure seems credible indeed. However, the Persian relief army arrived too late to save Petra and was therefore directed against Archaeopolis. The Roman forces that he faced were divided at this time. Bessas had withdrawn his 6,000 men to the Pontici in Armenia, which, as Procopius (*Wars* 8.13.11–14) noted, had left the easily defensible passes between Lazica and Iberia defenceless and had allowed Mermeroes to invade. According to Procopius, the reason behind this decision was Bessas's avarice. He and his men apparently wanted to secure their considerable loot from the siege of Petra. According to Agathias, Bessas also visited the cities under his control to collect money

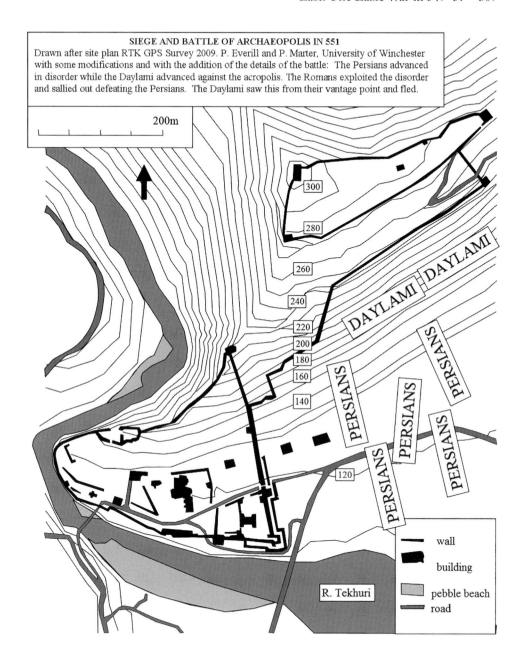

SIEGE AND BATTLE OF ARCHAEOPOLIS IN 551
Drawn after site plan RTK GPS Survey 2009. P. Everill and P. Marter, University of Winchester with some modifications and with the addition of the details of the battle: The Persians advanced in disorder while the Daylami advanced against the acropolis. The Romans exploited the disorder and sallied out defeating the Persians. The Daylami saw this from their vantage point and fled.

200m

DAYLAMI   DAYLAMI

PERSIANS

PERSIANS

PERSIANS

PERSIANS

PERSIANS

R. Tekhuri

wall
building
pebble beach
road

instead of protecting the passes. This means that Bessas engaged in corruption, as had been his habit while in Rome.

The Romans had another army consisting of 8,200 men under Venilus and Uligagus with 800 Tzani under Varazes the Persarmenian to protect the other side of the Phasis River, which left only 3,000 men under Odonachus and Babas to protect Archaeopolis. When Mermeroes learned of the presence of the army by the Phasis River he advanced against them, but they fled. Thereupon he advanced against the city. Most of Mermeroes's army consisted of cavalry, as was typical for the Persians, but he also had elite Daylamite infantry together with eight elephants that he could use as siege towers. The Daylami were sent against the precipitous parts of the city, while the rest prepared to use the new rams constructed by the Sabirs. The heavily outnumbered 3,000 Romans opened two gates and sallied out of the city, completely surprising the Persians. Small numbers of Roman soldiers remained behind because a traitor had set the grain storage on fire. The Persians were not in battle array and were spread apart, some unarmed and others armed only with bows. The Romans kept slashing, turning from side to side. Additionally, one of the elephants became enraged and wheeled around. The Persians fled and the Daylami joined in the rout. According to Procopius, 4,000 Persians and three commanders fell, four standards were captured and 20,000 Persian horses perished from the lack of fodder. This was a major loss for the Persians.

Mermeroes withdrew to Mocheresis, which according to Procopius was one day's journey from Archaeopolis. Most of Lazica still remained in Persian hands so he planned to continue his campaign. He intended to rebuild a fortress called Cotiaon/Cotais/Cotaecon, but this proved impossible because he lacked equipment and the winter had already set in. So Mermeroes merely settled his army there with the idea of blockading a nearby fortress, Uthimereos, that had a garrison of Lazi and Roman troops.

Desertions to the Persian side in late 551[13]

In spite of the setback at Archaeopolis, the Persians had the upper hand at this time thanks to the large army that Chosroes had given Mermeroes, and the unruly behaviour of Roman soldiers and their commander Martinus which had convinced many locals to rethink their loyalties. Goubazes remained loyal to the Romans because he knew that Chosroes had planned to kill him, but his subjects reacted only to what they saw.

One of those subjects was Theophobius. He sent secret messages to Mermeroes in which he promised to betray Uthimereos. He could easily communicate with the Persians because the Romans and Lazi were hiding by the Phasis River, or had enclosed themselves inside Archaeopolis and other fortresses, while Goubazes and his men were hiding in the mountains. This Theophobius then went inside Uthimereos and told its garrison consisting of the Lazi and Romans that the Persians had annihilated the entire Roman army. The situation was supposed to be hopeless because now Chosroes had come to Lazica in person with a large army which he had now united with that of Mermeroes which consisted of more than 70,000 Persians and vast numbers of Sabiri. The garrison was convinced and Theophobius promised that Chosroes would guarantee their safety if they surrendered. Mermeroes duly dispatched men who gave money and pledges to the men of the garrison and received the surrender of the fortress.

We learn from Procopius and from later peace negotiations preserved in the fragments of Menander the Protector that Suania, the inland mountain district of Lazica, deserted to the Persian side in about 551 and then obtained a Persian garrison for its protection. Suania was garrisoned by the Romans under Ditatus but thanks to the quarrel between the Roman *MVM* in Lazica, Martinus, and Goubazes, the Lazi did not send the customary supply of grain to Suania. This angered the Suani so they asked the Persians to come to their country, while they told Ditatus and other Romans that a huge Persian army was approaching and they did not have enough men to oppose them. The Romans bought the story and evacuated Suania so the Persians were able to take over the country. Procopius likewise states that Scymnia deserted to the Persian side at this time, but does not provide any details. The capture of these areas together with the fortress of Uthimereos secured Iberia against any possible Roman attempts.

The Lazicans and Romans appear not to have made an attempt to regain these areas, because at least Suania was subject of the negotiations between the Romans and Persians later. Furthermore, Procopius notes that the Romans and Lazi did not even dare to descend from the mountains or strongholds to attempt this.

Persian campaigns in 552–53[14]

In winter 552 Mermeroes was continuing his interrupted campaign by building a wooden wall at Cotais so that he could put a garrison of 3,000 Persians there. He also placed a sufficient force of men to hold Uthimereos. After this he built new fortresses in an area called Sarapanis and stayed there. This was possible because Chosroes was not niggardly in his actions. Mermeroes had been given a sizable army so he could simultaneously control the open terrain while capturing fortresses where he could then place garrisons. Numbers mattered. The Persians now had the initiative on their side.

When this was going on the Romans attempted to assemble an army at the mouth of the River Phasis late in 552. When Mermeroes learnt of this he marched there immediately, and when the Roman commanders learned of this, they scattered and fled, while Goubazes once again retreated to the mountains with his wife, children and followers. Goubazes and his followers were ready to face the hazards of winter in the mountains because they were confident that the Romans would eventually win.

In the meantime, Mermeroes continued his project of securing the area by building houses in the villages of Mocheresis, by establishing stores of supplies everywhere, and by sending deserters to the mountains to convince the Lazi to change sides. These attempts found many who were ready to desert to the Persian side, but they did not include Goubazes.

Justinian had also not been entirely idle during these events. According to Procopius in winter 552/3 Justinian received certain monks from India who promised to bring him silkworms. Justinian accepted this so that Romans would not have to buy their silk from the Persians. The monks fulfilled their promise and the Roman silk industry was created. Procopius does not say when the monks returned with the silkworms, perhaps it was about two years later. This obviously did not change the trade balance immediately because it took some time to set up the silk industry, but it is clear that it eventually brought significant savings to the Romans while it hurt the Persian economy.

It was only in early 553 that the Persians got the money promised to them in the armistice treaty. Chosroes put the money to good use immediately using it to hire a vast horde of Sabiri Huns which he dispatched together with some Persians to Mermeroes. This presumably means that Mermeroes's field army once again had at least 70,000 Persians and the Sabiri. When the reinforcements had arrived Mermeroes together with the elephants marched from Mocheresis and advanced against the remaining strongholds in Lazi hands. Martinus did not attempt to oppose the Persians but posted his forces in a location that had natural defences close to the mouth of the Phasis. Goubazes and his Lazi were with him. When Mermeroes learnt that the sister of Goubazes was in a certain fortress he decided to attempt to capture it together with the sister to gain leverage against Goubazes. His attempt failed thanks to the strength of the location and bravery of its defenders. After this he marched against the Abasgi. The Romans who were posted there kept guard in the abovementioned fortress of Tzibile which was impregnable against the Persians because the Persians did not have a fleet in the area and it was impossible for them to force their way through the pass which had room for only a single man at a time. There were enough brave and skilled Romans to hold this pass. After this failure, Mermeroes turned against Archaeopolis. He attacked the circuit wall but was once again repulsed and forced to retreat. This time the Romans followed the retreating Persians and attacked them in a dangerous pass killing many of the Persians together with the Sabiri and the commander of the Sabiri. A fierce battle was fought over who would possess the corpse, but the Persians finally gained the upper hand at dusk and forced the Romans to flee. After this the Persians retreated to Cotais and Mocheresis.

Goubazes subsequently criticized the Roman commanders for their inactivity, but it is clear that Martinus and those under him were right to decide to hide inside strongholds. The Persians had a vast numerical advantage which the Romans needed to compensate for with defences. The results speak for themselves. All Persian attempts were defeated and the pursuit conducted by the garrison of Archaeopolis was a first class operation. The retreating Persians were engaged in a pass that evened out the odds. However, Goubazes may have been correct in one respect. It is possible that if the pursuers had been joined by the forces under Martinus, the Persians would have been completely defeated. However, we are not in a position to know all of the details so it is impossible to know who was correct: Martinus by remaining where he was or Goubazes who demanded more action.

The ruse of Mermeroes in 554[15]

In early 554 Mermeroes conceived a plan to march from Mucheirisis/Mocheresis and Cotais through the difficult terrain around the fortress of Telephis so that he could advance as far as the river Phasis. The fort of Telephis was held by Martinus and the rest of the approaches that he could use were also guarded by Romans. It was impossible to clear the difficult route (gorges, woods etc.) if it was opposed by the Romans. Therefore he devised a stratagem. He was an old man with crippled feet and was always carried on a litter behind the soldiers, even when he encouraged them during fighting. So it is entirely plausible that when he pretended to fall ill and disappeared from sight, it was believed. The news naturally reached the Romans, via those who sold information, and caused them to relax their vigilance. When Mermeroes then pretended to die and the informants in his army spread the news to the Romans they became entirely careless, no longer caring to guard the chokepoints or send scouts. It was then that Mermeroes appeared before his troops and led them forward. He had a massive army so it did not take long for them to clear the woods and other obstacles. When this news was brought to Martinus, he was dumbstruck and retreated with his men to the nearby plain called Ollaria/Chrysopolia where the forces of Bessas and Justin were. The generals decided that they would not retreat but fight, and dispatched 500 Tzani under Theodore to reconnoitre. They stayed near Telephis to observe the situation and then retreated. En route back Theodore came across some Roman soldiers who had not gone to Ollaria but were pillaging the huts of the local Lazi. He reproached them. This may have delayed him too long: he had no chance of delivering his report. In the meantime some Persians had attacked some of the Roman pillagers who fled to the Roman camp where they infected the soldiers and generals with panic. The Romans fled, not stopping until they reached Nesos, 150 stades (ca. 28km) from Telephis. When Mermeroes reached Chrysopolia he did not follow the Romans but built a pontoon bridge across the Phasis and retreated to Cotais and Mucheirisis. However, then Mermeroes caught a disease, this time for real, and had himself carried to the city of Meschitha (Mtskheta) Iberia.[16] He died there, also for real. He was greatly mourned by the Persians because he had been an exceptionally gifted and brave commander. Chosroes replaced him with Nachoragan.

The quarrel between Goubazes and Roman commanders in 554[17]

As noted above, the problems between the Romans and the Lazi started in 551 because the Roman soldiers had mistreated them, but the last straw for Goubazes was the inactivity shown by the Roman officers in 553–4. Goubazes sent a report of his views to Justinian in which he accused the Roman commanders of negligence of duty and cowardice, singling out in particular Bessas, but he also named Martinus and Rusticus. The latter was a *sacellarius* whose duty it was to reward those soldiers who performed their duties using the emperor's personal funds. This gave him tremendous influence over the officers and soldiers. Justinian's intentions were clearly admirable, namely the boosting of morale with money, but the influence of Rusticus on the officers had proved disastrous. In light of Bessas's previous history Justinian readily accepted what Goubazes said and removed Bessas from office, confiscated his property and assigned him to Abasgia. Martinus was now made supreme commander (*strategos*), Justin son of Germanus was made his second-in-command (*hypostrategos*), followed by Bouzes/Buzes and the rest in descending order.

The Roman officers who had been accused reacted to the report and hostility of Goubazes by forming a plot to get rid of him. With this in mind they sent John the brother of Rusticus to Justinian. He falsely claimed that Goubazes had been found to collaborate with the Persians. Justinian was dumbstruck but in the end handed to John a letter which gave them permission to kill Goubazes if he could not be safely apprehended. When this letter was brought to Martinus and Rusticus, they summoned Justin and Bouzes to discuss how to put into effect Justinian's orders. Justin and Bouzes naturally obeyed the order and asked Goubazes to meet them near the banks of the River Chobus to discuss how to attack the Persians at Onoguris. When they met, John the brother of Rusticus feigned a quarrel, drew a dagger, and stabbed Goubazes in the chest. Goubazes, whose legs had been crossed over his horse's neck, fell to the ground. This was not fatal, but the next attack was. The conspirators had instructed Rusticus's bodyguards to kill Goubazes and one of them now hit him in the head with the sword. Justin and Bouzes were deeply distressed by this, but as they believed it had been the emperor's order they said nothing. The murder angered the Lazi who from this date onwards refused to fight alongside the Romans. They buried their king and withdrew to the mountains.

Siege and Battle of Onoguris in 554[18]

In the meantime, Martinus had continued his preparations for the siege of Onoguris. He had 50,000 Romans, which shows that Justinian was finally paying attention to this front. Narses had reconquered all of Italy up to the Po, and the Balkans saw a period of relative peace at this time. Martinus was the *strategos* and Justin the *hypostrategos*. Under them served Bouzes and others. Nachoragan commanded the Persian army.

When the Roman army was besieging Onoguris employing wicker roofs, ballistae and other siege equipment, a captured Persian told of the approach of the Persian relief force under Nachoragan. In the resulting council of officers, Bouzes and Uligagus/Wilgang leader of the Heruls recommended a full-scale attack against the relief army. However, Rusticus's opinion to send only 600 men under Dabragezas and Usigardus to ambush them was put into action. They surprised the 3,000 horsemen of the Persian relief force (a vanguard?) and routed them, but when the Persians noted the smallness of their opposition they turned about and routed their pursuers. When both parties reached the Roman lines, the Roman army panicked, which was further aggravated by the sally of the garrison of Onoguris. The Roman cavalry galloped away and left their infantry to face the inevitable. The flight was hampered by a bridge. However, Bouzes realized this, returned with his horsemen and covered the retreat.

Because of a badly chosen strategy, the Romans had now suffered a terrible defeat and the land of Lazica was in turmoil. The commanders had again shown remarkable stupidity. As Agathias noted, the magnitude of the defeat was tremendous when a mere 3,000 horsemen had defeated 50,000 men. This battle shows the effect the rout of a small cavalry force could have on the morale of a huge army. The flight of the small force and the uncertainty caused mass hysteria among the ranks and officers. The first to flee were the cavalry and officers, which naturally caused the flight of the infantry.

Justinian intervenes on behalf of the Lazi[19]

The Lazi held a secret meeting in the mountains to discuss how to react to the murder of their king. The pro-Roman opinion prevailed. The Lazi decided to stay loyal and seek justice from Justinian. They sent envoys to the emperor, who stated what had happened. Justinian agreed to crown Tzathes/Tzath, the younger brother of Goubazes, as their new king. Justinian also sent a leading senator, Athanasius, together with imperial bodyguards to conduct a full judiciary inquiry into the matter and then settle the case according to Roman law. Athanasius imprisoned both Rusticus and John, but apparently did not arrest Martinus because he was at the moment needed for his generalship qualities. Justinian also dispatched Soterichus with a plentiful sum of money to pay the yearly distribution to the allies and subjects of Rome and the Lazi. When Soterichus together with two of his sons reached the land of the Misimians, he quarrelled with them with the result that they killed Soterichus and his sons and looted the gold. The Misimians feared the Roman reaction and so sought help from the Persians. The Roman generals were unable to answer this affront because they knew that Nachoragan was already advancing towards Nesos at the head of a 60,000-strong army.

Siege and Battle of Phasis in 555[20]

In 555, after the horrific defeat at Onoguris, the Roman army was mustered near Nesos. This time the Persians were prepared to advance towards Nesos, however the Romans had placed 2,000 Sabirs near the plain of Archaeopolis to act as guards/guerrilla troops against any Persian surprise attacks against Nesos. Nachoragan sent 3,000 Daylami footmen to surprise them during the night. Instead, the Sabirs ambushed the Daylami when they entered the empty Sabir encampment. The Sabirs killed 800 of their enemies and when the defenders of Archaeopolis saw what had happened in the morning they sent their cavalry in pursuit and they managed to kill more than 1,200 men.

Next, Nachoragan decided to attack the vulnerable town of Phasis. It only had wooden walls. The Persians crossed the river in secrecy by using a pontoon bridge and got a head start. The Romans responded by sending all the triremes and 'thirties' (*triakontoroi* – 30 oars) downstream. However, the Persians had blocked the river with boats and and timber structures and also placed elephants behind them. Seeing this, the Romans immediately began to back water. However, two of the thirties failed to do this and their crews abandoned their ships and swam to safety. The Persians captured both of the ships.

After leaving Bouzes to guard Nesos, the Romans took the overland route and reached Phasis before the Persians. At this time the fort consisted of a wooden wall that had partially collapsed (so it cannot be the fortress depicted in the accompanying map, but probably a larger wooden fortification built around it). The Romans had built a massive rampart for its protection with a moat in front of the walls.[21] They had also diverted water from the nearby lagoon to fill the moat with water. Large merchant ships were anchored by the seashore and the mouth of the River Phasis. Boats were placed on their masts to act as towers and soldiers and sailors were instructed to use bows. Artillery[22] was also readied. On the other side of the town, up the river, ships were outfitted similarly to protect that flank so that the Persians would face missiles both from the walls and from the ships posted on the other side of the river. In addition, there were the forces of Dabragezas the Ant and Elminegeir the Hun on ten skiffs (equipped with fore and aft rudders) to protect the riverfront. They also had luck on their side. The Persians who operated the captured Roman 'thirties' slept on one night and they had moored the other so poorly that it got loose and was carried by the current to the Romans. According to Agathias, the men of Justin and Martinus protected the sea walls; Angilas's Moors armed with small shields and spears, with Theodorus's Tzanian heavy infantry (hoplites) and Philomathius's light Isaurian infantry protected the middle part of the walls; and Gibrus's Lombards and Heruls and Valerianus's eastern *tagmata* protected the eastern quarters.[23] See the accompanying map for the likely locations.

At the beginning of the siege, Angilas and Philomathus sallied out with 200 men on their own initiative, which forced Theodorus to follow them with the Tzanians. The Daylami that were ranged in battle formation at that point awaited their approach calmly and then encircled them. This caused the Romans to attack in desperation back towards the walls in a compact body with spears levelled.[24] Through sheer desperation, they succeeded in gaining the safety of the walls. This sortie shows how the commanders were capable of acting on their own initiative when they considered it appropriate, but the downside of this was that it could jeopardize the rest of the army if done foolishly.

Martinus came up with a stratagem that encouraged his men while weakening the enemy.[25] He announced that a relief force was on its way and that if the soldiers wanted to plunder the Persian camp they had to take it before their arrival. The soldiers agreed. The news of the imminent arrival of the relief force was also heard by the Persians, which caused them to send a large holding force against this imaginary foe. Nacharagan decided to attack immediately. However, Martinus had sent Justin the son of Germanus, with the pick of cavalry and 5,000 additional horsemen to a nearby church in ambush. When the Persians brought up their siege engines against the walls and tried to undermine them, the Romans responded by throwing huge rocks that crushed the sheds. Slings, bows,

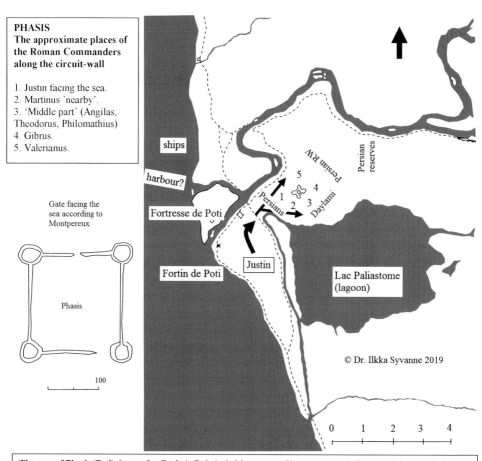

The map of Phasis (Poti) drawn after Frederic Dubois de Montpereux (*Voyage autour du Caucase* Vol. 3, 1839), but with the addition of the details of the siege by author.
- It is clear that the small square fortress depicted by Montrepeaux is not the wooden fortress that the Romans had now on the site. This would have been far larger in size. The map shows with the box Justin and arrows the direction of his cavalry attack against the Persians.

javelins, and ballistae were used to great effect: the Persians were unable to approach the walls. Then the Romans launched their ambush. Justin's cavalry in regular order, with accompanying war cry, attacked the rear of the left wing of the Persian army. With pikes (*sarisai*), spears (*kontoi*), swords and shields they broke the Persian formation into pieces in a series of charges. The Persians thought that this was the relief army they had heard about, closed their ranks in panic and started to retreat.

When the Daylami in the centre perceived what was happening, they left only a small force to guard the position and went to relieve those in distress to their left. Angilas and Theodorus sallied out when they noticed the movement of the Daylami. Now their personal initiative served to benefit the Romans. When the Daylami on their way to rescue the Persians saw this, they turned back, but with such speed that it looked as if they were fleeing. When the Persians next to them saw this they fled and the Daylami who saw it fled in their turn. While the panic spread, more Romans sallied out causing the retreat to turn into a rout. Only the Persian right wing continued to resist. I would suggest that this right wing would probably have meant the place where I have put the Persian RW on the map.

Into this mess Nachoragan sent his reserves, show on the map as Persian reserves. In front were the elephants and behind the elite cavalry. The elephants and their archers wrought havoc among the Roman infantry in the middle and the sorties of the cavalry between the elephants only increased the disorder among their ranks. The Roman infantry retreated, but Ognaris, a bodyguard of Martinus from the Roman right wing cavalry serving under Justin, became trapped in front of an elephant, which forced him to act. I would suggest that this right wing had been formed on the right by advancing through the former Daylamite positions. The left cavalry wing would have been formed to the side facing the river Phasis. It was then that a powerful spear thrust by Ognaris enraged the elephant, which threw the Persian ranks into disorder.[26] The horses of the Persian cavalry shied away from this beast. When this occurred, the rest of the Romans sallied out and with the others formed a tight phalanx and shield wall between the two cavalry wings and proceeded towards the disordered enemy who fled in disorder.

The pursuit was continued until Martinus sounded a retreat. When the Persians finally reached their camp they had lost at least 10,000 men, according to Agathias. The Romans burned the siege equipment, which caused the Persian servants sent to cut wood to come to the scene in the vain hope of loot. The sight of fire and smoke caused them to think that the Persians had managed to gain entrance to the city. Two thousand of them perished in this folly. The Romans had lost 200 men in combat and they were buried as the regulations expected. On the following day, the Persians fled while the Daylami protected their flight.

This victory proved to be quite decisive since it resulted in a lull in hostilities and in the execution of Nachoragan through torture. Furthermore, Chosroes sought an armistice by sending an envoy to the Romans, which he got in 557 on condition that both keep what they held in Lazica, but this time the Romans did not pay any money for the truce. The most obvious reasons for this were the successes achieved by Arabs in Roman service, the defeat suffered by Nachoragan at Phasis and probably also Chosroes's own plans to attack the Turks.

The campaigns in Lazica involved great numbers on both sides, which is also demonstrated by the fact that this defeat at Phasis finally caused the Persians to put a stop to their active operations in Lazica. The building of the roads from Iberia to Lazica had enabled the Persians to use numerous armies, but at a greater cost than to the Romans, who could provision their armies by ships. The war was just too costly to continue, especially when the men were needed for war against the Turks.

The last actions in Lazica and the siege of Tzacher/Siderun 557–58[27]

The Persian defeat at Phasis resulted in a lull in hostilities, which allowed the completion of the judicial inquiry into the matter of Goubazes's murder. Justinian had decided that it would have to be made in full public view so that the Lazi would be satisfied, while he also ordered that Martinus should not be found guilty because the soldiers loved him and it was dangerous to remove so skilled and popular a commander while the war continued. Consequently, only John and Rusticus were executed. The Romans spent the winter of 556–7 in the towns and fortresses of the region. In the meantime, the Misimians had given Nachoragan in Iberia money so that the Persians would send them help in the spring 557.

The Romans decided to attack the Misimians immediately after the winter ended in 557. They collected an army of 4,000 cavalry and infantry for this purpose. The commanders included Maxentius and Theodorus the leader of the Tzanian contingent. The army was put under the combined leadership of the Armenian Barazes and the Lazi Pharsantes until Martinus arrived to take overall command. These commanders lacked authority over the rest of the officers. When the Romans reached Apsilia, they found that the Persians had arrived first. Both armies remained inactive, except for a small skirmish in which Maxentius and Theodorus with 300 horsemen wiped out almost the entire 500-strong Sabiri contingent in Persian service who had encamped carelessly. The wall of the Sabir encampment was so low that the Roman horsemen were able to use their bows and javelins to annihilate the Sabirs inside. Only forty Sabirs managed to flee.[28]

While this standoff continued, Justin sent one of his commanders, Elminzur the Hun from Nesos, to Rhodopolis with 2,000 horsemen. He was very lucky because the Persian garrison had for some reason left the town when he arrived so he was able to enter it unopposed. After this he made raids against the Persians and allowed the Lazi to live in peace because they had not joined the Persians of their own free will.

At the first onset of the winter, the Persians withdrew to Iberia to their winter quarters. This had been the Roman plan from the start. They knew the Persians would be forced to leave when the winter set in and it was this that opened up the route for the Romans. The Romans advanced to the fort of Tibeleos which marked the border between Apsilia and Misimia. It was there that Martinus arrived but was unable to take command because of an illness. He may have brought reinforcements, but this is not mentioned. The army marched on. They dispatched some Apsilians as their envoys with an offer of peace, but the Misimians killed the ambassadors. The Misimians had too much trust in the impregnability of their territory and neglected to guard the route leading there. Consequently the Romans, who were occupying the strategic mountaintop, descended to the open plains. The Misimians burned most of their strongholds and assembled the entire population at the fortress of Tzacher/Siderun.

During the approach march to the site forty Roman officers went to reconnoitre the terrain ahead of the main body. They were attacked by a mixed cavalry and infantry force of 600 men. The Romans fled to a nearby hillock from which they charged downhill and then galloped back uphill, repeating this several times. The Misimians fled when the main army appeared over the horizon. Most of the Misimians who had attacked the Roman officers died in the encounter. The multipurpose Roman cavalry composed of their officers was just too effective for the lightly-equipped Misimians in the open.

As a result of their divided command structure, the Romans remained inactive and encamped far from the enemy fortification. Martinus sent John Dacnas (the emperor's 'spy' in charge of payments) to take the command. He besieged the fort. Most of the dwellings of the Misimians were not inside the fortified enclosure but on top of a nearby rock. The rock was flanked by deep gorges. The Romans proceeded to destroy this place after one Isaurian soldier found an accessible route there. One night 100 chosen men, probably under Theodorus's leadership, climbed there in single file and surprised the guards. The soldiers massacred the men, women, and children. The children were hurled on the rocks, or tossed in the air and then speared. Agathias mentioned the killing of the children because he considered it a monstrous act.

At dawn, 500 Misimians sallied out of the fortress. Most of the Romans that had participated in the horrible bloodbath were either killed or wounded as they fled (but it is possible that this claim is just moralizing on the part of Agathias because the Romans certainly had enough men left to crush the remaining Misimians). Now the Romans resorted to using siege engines and bows. The Misimians attempted to destroy the Roman siege works by using a wicker-roofed shed, but a well-placed spear throw by a Slav soldier toppled the structure revealing all to be butchered by arrows. Now the Misimians were desperate. Everything around the fort had been razed to the ground. Most of the civilian population had been killed. The situation inside the fort was untenable. The entire nation was facing extinction. The Misimians asked for forgiveness. John granted the request. He was unwilling to continue the war in winter. After taking hostages and a considerable amount of booty, and the 28,800 gold pieces that were still left of the emperor's money, John and his army returned in triumph. He had lost a total of only thirty men.

Despite being a minor incident, this war against the Misimians demonstrates the value of the Lazi, Armenians, Isaurians, Tzani, and Slavs in mountain warfare. To succeed in the Caucasus, the Romans needed local knowledge, mountaineers and other lightly-equipped swift-footed infantry. It is also clear that it was the brutality and determination of the Romans against a small nation that brought success. The ability to fight in winter was also important.

In 557, after the above campaign, Justinian relieved Martinus of his office and made him a common civilian. He thought that this was a sufficient punishment for the murder of Goubazes in his case. The many services he had made for the state and his military ability were reasons for his merciful treatment. Justinian appointed Justin son of Germanus as Martinus's successor. Justin was undoubtedly an able general but was also corrupt and one of his first actions as supreme commander was to hire a corrupt person who filled his pockets with money while the soldiers lacked adequate supplies. Justin's corruption was not patriotic, but plain greed.

In the autumn the Persians and Romans concluded the abovementioned truce for five years, which still left Lazica out but this time without monetary payments from the Romans. When Justin was in Lazica envoys arrived from the Avars under Candich who wished to establish relations with the Romans. Justin sent the envoys to Constantinople where they were received by Justinian between December 557 and February 558. Justinian gave the Avars presents and stated that he would take their request into consideration if they would attack his enemies. This the Avars proceeded to do. The Avars crushed in succession Unigurs (i.e. Utigurs), Zali (a Hunnic tribe), then the Sabirs, and later the Kutrigurs and Antae too. Justinian continued his policies of using barbarians against barbarians apparently with great success, but as we shall see in this case the Avars were eventually too successful and became an even greater threat than the others had been.[29]

Rhizaeum 557[30]

In 557, most of the Tzani were in revolt and raiding the Pontus. One may guess that they could have been incited to do this by the Persians before they concluded their truce with Rome. Consequently, Theodorus, who was by birth a Tzani, was sent to deal with them. He moved his forces from Lazica to Rhizaeum, where he built a camp with a rampart. From this strongpoint he summoned the friendly among the Tzani to negotiate. However, those opposing him occupied a nearby hill, threatening the camp. The Romans attacked them in a disorganized fury without waiting to draw them out onto the lower ground. The Romans advanced up the hill in irregular formation with shields tilted over their heads. The Tzani poured stones, arrows and spears down on them in such quantities that the Romans were easily put to flight when the Tzani attacked downhill. They killed forty Romans on the way. The Tzani pursued the Romans to their camp where fierce hand-to-hand fighting took place. Theodorus observed that the enemy had attacked without a leader, did not use reserves and were concentrated in a single mass; this enabled him to send some of his men to attack the enemy from behind. When they appeared behind the enemy, they shouted a loud war cry to scare the enemy. This caused the Tzani to panic. The fleeing Tzani made themselves easy prey for the pursuing Romans who killed 2,000 and ended the independence of the nation for good.

This battle shows how an able commander after he had lost control of his men was able to use the camp as a place of refuge and then turn the tables by using his reserves and the hidden position of the rear of the camp to defeat his leaderless foe. The battle also shows why the Romans put so much importance in the defences of the camp and the great variety of methods in use. The Roman commanders needed to be able to improvise. The local knowledge of this commander was clearly appreciated when he was appointed to his post.

The peace for fifty years in 562

After the conclusion of the five-year truce in 557, Chosroes and Justinian both sought peace; Chosroes probably because he was beginning his final campaign against the Turks, and Justinian because Roman resources had been exhausted by the continuous wars. The negotiations began immediately in 557, the two powers finally signing a peace accord for fifty years in 562. It is not known why it took a whole five years to achieve this. This time the Romans agreed to payments of gold in return for peace. Both sides agreed to protect the other against the Huns and other barbarians, and this time the agreement mentioned the Arabs by name. They also made agreements regarding how commercial transactions were to be conducted and many other things. With the exception of Suania, the Persians handed over to the Romans their possessions in Lazica. The exact terms of the peace have been preserved in full in the fragments of Menander together with the details of the negotiations.

A late Roman mounted archer and legionary.

Drawn after a 6th century Egyptian ivory (slightly simplified).

The shield emblem identifies the legionary as a member of the *legio V Macedonica*

Chapter Seventeen

Italy after Belisarius in 548–51

Justinian and Italy after Belisarius had returned[1]

A fter Belisarius had returned and settled in Constantinople, the question of who would lead the Romans in Italy was acute. Pope Vigilius and other Italians present in the city attempted to convince Justinian that Vigilius was their man, but the man who had most influence on Justinian was the patrician Gothigus. Justinian promised to make the problems of Italy his first priority, but according to Procopius Justinian actually neglected this question because he was preoccupied with finding a satisfactory settlement to the problem of Christian doctrine. In short, Procopius accused Justinian of neglect of his duties as head of state. In light of what had happened and what took place after this, or rather what did not take place (he was unable to make any decisions), it is clear that Procopius is correct in his criticism. The apparent reason for this is that Justinian was convinced that if he gained the favour of God, he would also take care of the matters of state because it was God who granted victories over enemies. This is so silly on so many levels that there is no need for further comment beyond what I state next: there is another reason for Justinian's neglect of Italian matters during 548–50 which is that he mourned the loss of his beloved wife Theodora so deeply that it affected his ability to guide the affairs of the state. It took a couple of years for Justinian to recover.

Justinian's religious policy ca. 540–65[2]

Justinian continued his previous religious policies after 540. He persecuted pagans, Monophysites and other heresies while attempting to find a way to reconcile the views of the Chalcedonians and Monophysites. John of Ephesus, a Monophysite, hunted down Hellenes in Asia, Phrygia, Lydia and Caria in 542. He destroyed temples and built 96 churches and 12 monasteries while converting 70,000 souls. Since this took place in the middle of the Persian war it is probable that Justinian considered this persecution of pagans to be one way of gaining the goodwill of God against the Persians. There were two major persecutions of pagans in the capital, the first conducted by John of Ephesus in 546 and another in 559. These persecutions, however, did not concern all of the pagans because there were many distinguished persons in Constantinople whose behaviour was intentionally overlooked by Justinian.

The 530s also saw a revival of the old heresy of Origen in Palestine. Nuncio Pelagius and Patriarch Menas sought Justinian's help against it, and the Patriarch of Antioch Ephraim convened a synod in 542 to condemn the heresy, but the heretics won the day. Pelagius and Menas then convinced Justinian to intervene in person. He issued an Edict which condemned ten opinions of Origen. The emperor's view was decisive. All accepted the Edict, even Theodore Ascidas who was probably secretly a Monophysite and Origenist.

The Monophysites considered the texts of Theodore of Mopsuestia to be the most offensive religious text in existence, and now Ascidas, with the backing of Theodora, decided to move against them. Theodora convinced Justinian that it would be possible to reconcile the Chalcedonians and Monophysites by anathematising the writings of Theodore of Mopsuestia. Justinian accepted this and proclaimed the so-called Edict of Three Chapters in 546 which condemned 1) Theodore of Mopsuestia and his works; 2) some texts of Theodoret; 3) the letter of Ibas. This was to become a major problem for the rest of Justinian's reign and took up too much of his time. The eastern patriarchs were initially unwilling to accept it, because the deceased could not defend themselves, but eventually signed it when Justinian put pressure on them. In the meantime, Pope Vigilius had been taken from Rome on 22 November 545 to go to Sicily with the intention of continuing on to Constantinople. The authorities apparently made it look as if they had forcibly taken Vigilius away from the besieged city, but in practice it was only to remove him from danger. During his ten-month stay in Sicily Vigilius organized the sending of supplies to Rome. He also learnt of the Edict of Three Chapters and what was the opinion of the western patriarchs to it. The western patriarchs were uniformly against it, so Vigilius was too. He began his journey to Constantinople in autumn 546 and reached it on 25 January 537, settling in the Palace of Placidia.

While in Constantinople Vigilius failed to formulate a clear opinion on the matter of the Edict because he could not decide between the opinions of the emperor and his western patriarchs. In the end however, he decided to follow his flock and excommunicated Menas and his followers, but was then again reconciled with them when Theodora intervened. Regardless, Vigilius still refused to sign the Edict because that would have conceded to the emperor the right to make religious decisions. As a compromise he issued a Iudicatum (pronouncement) on Easter-eve 548, which condemned Theodore of Mopsuestia while still upholding the text of Chalcedon. This resulted in turmoil in western Christendom, some of the bishops and patriarchs dissolving communion with the Pope. This frightened the Pope so he decided to convene a General Council, which Justinian accepted as a way to solve the schism. It was these matters that occupied Justinian's thoughts when he should have been thinking about Italy.

Justinian did not wait until the Council convened, but removed the patriarchs of Alexandria and Jerusalem from their offices and then issued another similar edict in 551. On the same morning that it was published, Theodore Ascidas and other members of the Greek clergy visited the Pope. Vigilius urged them to wait until the Council, which they refused to do with the result that Vigilius excommunicated both Ascidas and Menas, and then together with the Archbishop of Milan sought a place of refuge from the Church of Saints Peter and Paul near the Palace of Hormisdas. Justinian sent soldiers to drag him away in August 551. The soldiers grasped him by his feet and beard with the result that the altar onto which he was clinging fell on him. Those who saw it shouted in horror and the soldiers and their commander departed.

Justinian then decided that it was better to attempt to find a way to convince the Pope to return to the negotiating table, but this time Justinian placed his soldiers around his residence so that he was in practice under house arrest. Then on 23 December 551 Vigilius managed to elude his guards and flee to the Church of St. Euphemia in Chalcedon during the night. This time Justinian sent Belisarius to turn Vigilius's head because these two knew each other. Belisarius promised on oath that Vigilius would be honourably treated, but Vigilius answered that it was now too late for oaths. He also told the emperor to abandon Menas and Ascidas. Justinian replied with a letter full of threats and insults. Then followed a period during which Vigilius lived in the church while composing an Encyclical Epistle, which he then published. Justinian responded by offering guarantees of safety once again on 4 February 552, but the Pope once again published an excommunication of Ascidas and Menas and their followers. This headstrong behaviour wore out Justinian and he sent a humble submission to the will of the Pope through the Patriarch and clergy. This convinced Vigilius to return to the Palace of Placidia.

Menas died in August 552 and his successor Eutychius sent a letter to the Pope who then accepted the convening of the Council. Justinian agreed to it but manipulated the situation so that only those who supported him were able to come to Constantinople. When Vigilius realized this he attempted to temporize, but the first session began on 5 May 553. The participants required that the Pope make an appearance but he refused and stated that he would make an independent written judgment. The text was ready on 14 May 553 and Belisarius went to the Palace of Placidia to meet the Pope, but when Vigilius asked him to take this document to the Council Belisarius wisely refused. Vigilius then dispatched it to the emperor using his own courier, but this time Justinian refused to receive it. In the session of the Council which followed, Justinian presented documents in which the Pope had approved the Three Chapters Edict and then stated that the name of Vigilius should be struck out of the diptychs because he refused to attend the Council. The Council did as requested. The resulting degrees of this Fifth Ecumenical Council duly condemned Vigilius together with Theodore of Mopsuestia and the works of Theodoret and Ibas so the will of the emperor carried the day. Some of the bishops who opposed this in the West were banished from their sees and Pelagius was imprisoned. Vigilius was now alone, and after six months, on 8 December 553, he signed the formal document recognizing the Three Chapters and then issued a formal judgment on 26 February 554 which confirmed this. Justinian then allowed him to return to Rome. It is probable, as Bury stated ages ago, that Vigilius's change of heart resulted from the reconquest of Italy by Narses. Vigilius, however, never reached Rome, because he died en route in Syracuse on 7 June 555. His successor was Pelagius who was prepared to accept the Three Chapters in return for being nominated Pope by Justinian – indeed it was Justinian who decided who was the pope and not the clergy.

Despite Justinian being able to force his will on everyone at the Fifth Ecumenical Council, it did not result in unity in the east. It only created a new schism in the west which lasted in some cases for the next 140 years. In the east the activities of the Monophysite Bishop of Edesssa, Jacob Baradeus, ensured that the Monophysite faith would survive and prosper. He spent his life going around the provinces of the east disguised as a beggar. He strengthened the resolve of the Monophysites who continued to follow their practices in secret. The secret underground Monophysite Church that Jacob organized was so effective that he was never found out by the authorities and because of it his Monophysite Church came to be known as the Jacobite Church. There was a limit to what the emperors and authorities could achieve, even with their secret services and military forces. From the point of view of ecclesiastical history and imperial power the Three Chapters controversy had taken control of the church and its doctrines to new levels. Not even the *Henoticon* of Zeno went as far. Basically Justinian usurped power to make doctrinal decisions with imperial edicts.

This, however, was not the end of the controversy created by Justinian's religious policies. In his last years Justinian adopted the dogma of aphthartodocetism and published an edict to this effect, which the Chalcedonian clergy considered a Monophysite view. Patriarch Eutychius condemned it and was arrested on 22 January 565 and condemned to exile in a monastery. The other patriarchs and bishops condemned it too and when they protested to the emperor he planned to exile the lot of them, but his death on 14 November 565 put a stop to this.

All of these religious policies of Justinian to gain the favour of God were more or less detrimental to the achievement of military goals. Much time, effort and money was spent on these religious projects while important matters of state were neglected. The soldiers who actually fought cared very little about these matters. There is no reference to soldiers abandoning their posts because of some religious stance of Justinian excepting the Arians who were persecuted or that the soldiers would have fought for the Orthodox Chalcedonian faith against the barbarians. What mattered was that their salaries arrived on time and that they had commanders they respected and who did not mercilessly fleece them. This should not be a surprise because the Roman forces consisted basically of foreign mercenaries and native professionals who were primarily motivated to fight for money and booty. Justinian had quite probably drawn the wrong conclusion from the revolt of Vitalian, which had become a pivotal event that had influenced his whole thinking.

The Lombard question and Venetia in 549[3]

In about 548/9 important developments took place in the royal family of the Lombard kingdom. Risiulfus, nephew of the ruling king Vaces and according to the law the crown prince, had been forced to flee in a situation in which Vaces sought to ensure that his own biological son would succeed him. Risiulfus fled first to the Varni, having been forced to leave his children behind. Vaces bribed the Varni to kill Risiulfus, who learnt of this and fled to the Sclaveni/Sklavenoi. Then one of the sons of Risiulfus died, officially of disease but probably of poison, while the other boy, Ildiges, managed to flee to the Sclaveni. Soon after this, Vaces died of disease and was succeeded by his son Valdarus. However, since he was very young, Audouin was appointed regent. This Audouin seized power after Valdarus conveniently died 'of disease'.

Then in 549 arose the war between the Lombards and Gepids. Ildiges, together with his Sklavenoi and Lombard followers, joined the Gepids. However, then the Lombards and the Gepids concluded peace, so Audouin demanded the handing over of Ildiges. The Gepids refused but ordered Ilgides to depart with his followers. Ildiges complied and added to his retinue some Gepids and then joined Totila with not less than 6,000 men. When he reached Venetia, he came across some Romans commanded by Lazarus. Ildiges defeated them but then decided not to join Totila after all. Instead he crossed the Danube and joined the Sclaveni.

The Goths invade Dalmatia in 549[4]

In 549, the former bodyguard of Belisarius, Indulf, deserted to the Goths. Totila sent him with a large army and fleet against the Romans in Dalmatia. Indulf continued to pretend to side with the Romans so he was able to plunder Mouicurum near Salona. Next he plundered the fortress of Laureate. Claudian, the commander of Salona, sent dromons against him. They engaged the Goths at the harbour but were overwhelmingly defeated. The Romans abandoned their ships at the harbour so the Goths were able to take them as prizes together with other boats/ships laden with grain and provisions. After this the Goths returned to Totila. This invasion was basically only a raid, but it is clear that it was still very costly in casualties and damage to the Romans.

Totila's siege of Rome summer 549–16 Jan 550[5]

Totila led his main army against Rome in 549 and settled on blockading the defenders. Rome was protected by a garrison of 3,000 chosen men commanded by Diogenes, a *doryforos* of Belisarius. He had been appointed by Belisarius before he left. There were also Roman garrisons nearby at Portus and Centumcellae, but these failed to support the Romans effectively. The siege became prolonged because Diogenes had sowed grain in all parts of the city inside the circuit wall, and because he maintained strict discipline the enemy was unable to cause damage to walls or storm the city, which it attempted several times only to be repulsed every time. However, the Romans fared less well in Portus, which the Goths soon captured. This meant that the Romans could no longer expect help and provisions from there.

Justinian had started to make plans to send another army to Italy immediately after Belisarius had returned, but as noted above he then became distracted by religious matters. Procopius goes so far as to claim that had Justinian acted then, he could have saved Rome. This sounds like an accurate judgment of the situation. However, the end result would obviously still have depended on the number and quality of the forces dispatched and the skills of their commander, so it would not have been a foregone conclusion. According to Procopius (Wars 7.36.6), Justinian first chose the elderly patrician Liberius from Rome as commander and ordered him to prepare for the campaign, but then because some distraction claimed his attention he lost interest in the matter. This would be the abovementioned religious disputes (*Wars* 7.35.11). It is abundantly clear that Justinian was neglecting his duties as head of state.

When the siege of Rome had already continued for a very long time, some of its Isaurian guards at the Gate of Paul the Apostle grew tired of the fact that the emperor owed them several years back pay when they could see their Isaurian comrades who had previously betrayed the city to the Goths being rewarded amply by Totila. Because of this they opened secret negotiations with Totila. Undoubtedly this was the result of Totila's clever use of Isaurians in his service. He had clearly instructed them to communicate with their Isaurian compatriots and brag about their wealth. The two sides agreed to a date when the Isaurians would betray the city. Totila came up with a plan in which he created a diversion by launching two long boats (*ploia makra*) in the Tiber during the first watch of the night filled with men who knew how to use the trumpet. The rest of his army he posted opposite the Gate of St. Paul and in ambushes along the Via Aurelia leading to the coastal city of Centumcellae north-west of Rome with the idea of destroying the fugitives. The Gothic trumpeters rowed straight across the Tiber, got close to the circuit wall and then blew the trumpets loudly. When the Roman guards heard this they panicked, most rushing in the direction of the trumpets. This gave the Isaurians the chance they needed. They opened the Gate of St. Paul and let the Goths in who launched a great slaughter of those inside. Thanks to the darkness many of the Romans managed to save themselves by fleeing through other gates, but most of those who tried to flee to Centumcellae were killed in the ambushes. Those who survived included Diogenes who was wounded.

Paulus, a former head of Belisarius's household (possibly a *maior domus*), was a commander of a *katalogos* of cavalry in Italy, and was one of the commanders present in Rome at this time. This Paulus and 400 horsemen under him fled into the Tomb of Hadrian and seized the Pons Aelius in front of it. The Goths under Totila attacked them at the first light of dawn, but were repulsed with heavy losses. Totila duly settled on starving the defenders. The only source of food the Romans had were their horses, which they decided to use for this purpose on the following day, but then hesitated and finally decided that it was preferable to sally out and die fighting. After this they hugged and kissed each other goodbye. However, this was observed by Totila, who realised what was about to happen. He hastily offered the Romans two options: 1) surrender horses and arms and be free to leave; 2) join the Gothic army and keep arms, horses and all possessions. These proposals were God-sent in the eyes of those who had just said their goodbyes. At first most were for the first option, but then because they feared the Goths would kill them once they'd handed over their arms and horses they decided to join the Gothic army. The other major reason for this was that they felt that the Roman state had betrayed them because they had not received their salaries for years. Only Paulus and one of the Isaurians called Mindes chose to leave because both had wives and children in their native land. Totila gave them travelling money and an escort for their safety. There were also 300 other Romans soldiers who had sought a place of refuge from the churches of the city. Totila gave them the same pledges and all joined the Gothic army.

This time Totila decided he would never again abandon Rome. It was because of this that he settled there both Goths and Italians together with the Senate. According to Procopius (*Wars* 7.37.1ff), the reason for this was that the Frankish king had refused to hand over his daughter in marriage to Totila because Totila was not a king of Italy and would never be so. Totila needed Rome as his capital to gain the respect of his neighbours. However, in my opinion it is more likely that the most important reason for the decision to keep Rome was that the previous sieges had proved its strategic importance. Therefore Totila summoned the senators and others that he kept under guard in Campania to Rome. This proves that John had not managed to release all of the senators and their families who were being held by the Goths during his previous operation, or that some of them had returned from Sicily afterwards only to fall into Gothic hands again. Totila then organized horse-races in the city over which he presided as if he was Roman emperor. After this, he prepared his army for a campaign against Sicily.

Totila's diplomatic manoeuvres and preparations for the invasion of Sicily in 550[6]

In 550, Totila prepared a fleet of 400 warships and a fleet of large cargo ships for the invasion of Sicily. The large cargo ships had previously been captured from the Romans together with their crews and cargoes. This means that Totila had a truly sizable force at his disposal. The fleet consisted of at least 42,000 men (rowers, mariners, and marines) in addition to which we should count the crews manning the large cargo ships and the land army put on board. The land army must have consisted of at least 20,000 horsemen. At the same time as he was making these preparations, he dispatched a Roman called Stephanus as an envoy to Justinian to make a peace treaty. The idea was to use the threat of invasion of Sicily to put pressure on Justinian to sign the treaty. Justinian refused to receive the envoy. When Totila heard this, he decided to complete his preparations. The first part of the plan was to attack the coastal city of Centumcellae, after which he would launch his invasion of Sicily. Totila besieged the city, then challenged Diogenes to fight a battle with the Goths, and then offered them the option of joining the Gothic army or leaving unharmed. Diogenes refused the challenge saying that it was impossible for him and others to return home without a plausible excuse. So the two sides agreed to a date for surrender if no Roman relief force had arrived by then. They exchanged hostages after which Totila broke the siege and sailed to Sicily.

When the Goths came to Rhegium opposite Sicily, Totila decided to attempt to take it before crossing the straits. The garrison was commanded by Thurimuth and Himerius who had been appointed to their posts by Belisarius. When the Goths assaulted the city, the Romans repulsed the attack and then made a sally which forced the Goths to retreat but was not sufficient to break the siege. When Totila learnt that the Romans lacked adequate provisions, he left a portion of his army there to blockade them and dispatched another army against Tarentum, which his forces took without any difficulty, while he himself proceeded to cross the Straits of Messina. The force which he had left in Picenum captured the city of Ariminum at the same time.

Justinian's reaction in 550[7]

When Justinian heard the bad news, he appointed his cousin Germanus to lead an expedition against the Goths. He was now free to do so because Theodora was not there to oppose him. When news of the appointment of Germanus reached Italy, the Goths became anxious – Germanus was a brilliant commander. The Romans in Italy were likewise emboldened: the soldiers suddenly started to fight with greater ardour than before. Then Justinian changed his mind and replaced Germanus with Liberius. Liberius completed the preparations fast – after all, he had already started doing so last year – and was ready to sail, but the emperor again changed his mind and nothing happened. So Totila was free to do as he wanted. It is possible that the reason for Justinian's sudden indecisiveness was the invasion of the Balkans by the Sclaveni in 550 (see below). He may have wanted to retain the soldiers that had been assembled by Liberius in the Balkans just in case they were needed.

Meanwhile Verus, who had gathered an army of excellent soldiers, fought an engagement with the Goths of Picenum near Ravenna with the result that he lost many of his men and his own life. He is the drunkard commander who previously brought 300 Heruls to aid Belisarius in 547, but what his position was now is not known and we do not know why the battle took place. Had the Goths who had previously taken Ariminum now advanced against Ravenna so that Verus attacked them, or was Verus himself making a counter-attack against the Goths of Ariminum?

The Sclaveni invade the Balkans in 550[8]

In 550 a force of 3,000 Slavs crossed the Danube without encountering any opposition and advanced to the Hebrus River (mod. Maritza). There they divided their army into two parts, consisting of 1,800 horsemen and 1,200 horsemen. The separate Slav divisions defeated the vastly numerically superior Roman armies both in Thrace and Illyria. One of the enemy divisions then proceeded to defeat a numerous force of Roman elite cavalry *katalogoi* (*numeri*) led by Asbadus (a *candidatus*) stationed at Tzurullon. They killed most of the Romans during the pursuit and captured Asbadus. He was tortured by flaying strips of flesh from his back and then burned to death. As noted by Procopius, these defeats, especially the one by the elite cavalry, were shameful for the Romans. They show that the invading Slavic horsemen were superb fighters. It was not only the light infantry of the Slavs that was of very high quality, but also their cavalry.

Though not stated by Procopius, it is possible or even probable that it was this that caused Justinian to cancel the sending of the forces to Italy under Liberius after he had already assembled them. The defeat of the armies of Thrace and Ilyricum together with the Roman elite cavalry by the very small force of Slavs must have frightened Justinian senseless so that he wanted to retain all the men he could in Constantinople. It is in fact very likely that after the defeats the size of the invading force had been magnified in the telling to make the situation look worse than it really was.

The force which had defeated Asbadus plundered everything as far as the sea and advanced against Topirus, twelve days' journey from Constantinople. The Slavs hid themselves in the rough ground close to the city and then some went to the enemy gate to harass the Romans so that they would attack with the idea of leading them with a feigned flight to the place of ambush. The Romans swallowed the bait and pursued past the point of ambush. The ambushers blocked the route of retreat while those who had fled turned around. The Romans were killed to the last man. After this the Slavs attacked the city which was now defended only by its inhabitants. The population defeated the first attack with stones and heated oil and pitch. The Slavs responded with missiles, which must mean arrows, forcing the defenders to abandon the walls so that they were able to place their ladders against the fortifications and take the city by storm. The Slavs killed everyone regardless of age or sex to the number of 15,000, but then once their bloodlust had been satisfied, they took the remaining children and women as slaves together with their property. The Slavs had pursued a systematic policy of killing everyone they came across to spread terror among the defenders and it had worked like a dream – very small Slavic forces had achieved unbelievable successes.

The way the Slavs spread terror is described in detail by Procopius. According to him, the Slavs impaled their victims by planting them on stakes which had been driven between the buttocks. The Slavs also tied their hands and feet and then planted them on the ground after which they beat them over the head with clubs killing them like dogs or snakes. This was unheard of in the Roman Empire. Others they placed inside huts which they then torched. Once they had satisfied their bloodlust, they started to take slaves.

The Slavs would repeat the invasion next year with greater forces.

Totila invades Sicily in 550: Justinian's response

After crossing the straits, Totila first proceeded against Messina/Messana. The sally, led by Domnentiolus nephew of Buzes, effectively stopped the assault before it even began, because the Goths had advanced too carelessly against the city. So the Goths proceeded to plunder the rest of Sicily. Rhegium surrendered on terms. When Justinian heard of these disasters, he again appointed Liberius to take the command of the fleet sailing to Sicily, but then repented because Liberius was not only very old but also lacked military experience, so he appointed Artabanes to replace him.

Artabanes was therefore freed, appointed *MVM per Thracias*, and ordered to take command of the fleet. Germanus was appointed supreme commander of all operations in Italy. Justinian did not give him many men, but he gave him plenty of money with orders to gather a great army from Thrace and Illyricum after which he was to proceed to Italy. He was also instructed to take with him Philemuth with his Heruls and the *MVM per Illyricum* John, nephew of Vitalian (now Germanus' son-in-law and posted in Salona). On the basis of this it is possible that it was John who was defeated by the Slavs in 550 (see above), but it is more likely that he had actually been recalled to Salona after the defeat.

Germanus proceeded to fulfil his instructions with great care. He wanted to be known as the man who saved both Libya and Italy. His first move was as masterly as one would expect from a superb military commander. He married Matasuntha the granddaughter of Theoderic the Great because Vittigis had died. The intention was that Matasuntha would accompany the army and undermine the loyalty of the Goths on the other side. This resembles the strategy Germanus adopted against the Roman rebels before and during the battle of Scalae Veteres in 537. In that case he negotiated with the Moors that they would betray the rebels in the middle of the battle. Germanus was a wise commander who realized that it was easier to win if the enemy was not united.

On top of this, Germanus easily managed to assemble together a very large force of warlike men in a very short time. He was able to do this because of his generosity and his excellent reputation. He used more of his own money than had been given to him by Justinian. The *bucellarii* in the service of other officers in Constantinople, Thrace and Illyricum simply deserted their employers and joined him. Thrace and Illyricum undoubtedly provided a good recruiting ground for Germanus (and to others before and after him) because the constant state of war in this area was bound to produce hardy men in need of a livelihood, which they could obtain only in the army or in the retinue of some officer or noble. His sons Justin (Iustinus) and Justinian (Iustinianus) also played an important role in the recruiting process. In addition to this, Germanus enrolled some *katalogoi* of cavalry from Thrace with the emperor's permission. Furthermore, barbarians from the Danube region flocked into his army thanks to his fame and promise of wealth. In fact, Procopius states that barbarians flocked to serve under his colours from the whole world, suggesting that they arrived from very far flung places. The king of the Lombards also promised to send 1,000 heavy-armed *hoplitai* (in this case, meaning cavalry cataphracts). When the rumours concerning this arrived in Italy, they raised Roman morale. Those Roman soldiers who were serving unwillingly under the Goths sent a messenger to Germanus promising that they would desert to his side once he arrived. In addition, all those Romans who had previously been defeated and scattered, as happened when Verus engaged the Goths, now assembled together at Histria/Istria and waited quietly for the arrival of Germanus. The Roman garrisons in Ravenna and elsewhere were also reinvigorated by the news, while the morale of the Goths suffered both from the reputation of Germanus and from the presence of Matasuntha. The Goths would now have to fight against the house of Theoderic the Great.

It was at this time in winter 550/1 that the time limit set for the surrender of the garrison of Centumcellae terminated. Totila commanded that Diogenes surrender the city, but Diogenes stated that he no longer possessed the authority do so because Germanus had been appointed commander-in-chief. He suggested that both sides return their hostages and then prepared to defend the city until Germanus arrived. The mere news of the appointment of Germanus was clearly enough to change the strategic situation in Italy. So why had Justinian failed to do this before? It seems probable that he was cautious about using Germanus in case he became too powerful.

The Slavic invasion in 551[9]

While Germanus was collecting and organizing his army in Serdica/Sardica (mod. Sofia), the Slavs invaded in greater strength than the Romans had ever seen before. The success of previous attacks with a mere 3,000 horsemen had encouraged the rest to invade similarly. Military weakness always invites predatory behaviour. When the Sclaveni reached Naissus (mod. Nish), some of them scattered to plunder and the Romans managed to capture those who wandered alone. It is important to note that Naissus lay on the route that Germanus would have to take to reach Italy so that when he had assembled his army at Sardica, he simultaneously blocked the invasion route to Thrace from the invaders. The Romans interrogated the prisoners to find out the size of the enemy force and their plan. The prisoners told that their intended target was Thessalonica and the cities close to it. When Justinian heard this, he wrote a letter to Germanus ordering him to postpone the invasion of Italy and defend Thessalonica and other cities.

Germanus acted as ordered, but when the Sclavenoi learnt from their own captives that the feared Germanus was at Sardica and that he had a large army for use against Totila, they changed their plans immediately and decided not to advance to the plain. This suggests that Germanus had previously crushed the Antae on the plain with the same combination of heavy infantry and superior numbers of cavalry that he had used against the Roman rebels at the battle of Scalae Veteres in 537. The Sclavenoi turned and marched to the mountain ranges of Illyricum and from there into Dalmatia. Germanus decided to ignore them and made ready to march to Italy in two days, but then disaster struck. Germanus fell ill suddenly and died. Procopius quite rightly calls him a man endowed with the finest qualities, known as a general who was not only most able in his profession but also resourceful and able to operate independently. In civilian life he was known as a man who upheld the laws and institutions of the state. He was indeed one of the most able men of his age and absolutely loyal to his cousin despite the treatment he received from him and Theodora. In short, he was an admirable person, and it was to the detriment of the Roman Empire that Justinian failed to use his high gifts more often and instead relied on men who were utterly corrupt.

When Justinian learnt of Germanus's demise he was deeply moved and commanded John, nephew of Vitalian and son-in-law of Germanus, to take with him Germanus's other son Justinian and lead the army to Italy. With this in mind John led his army to Dalmatia with the intention of spending the winter in Salona. On the basis of this I would suggest the secondary aim was to drive out the invaders from Dalmatia – it is also entirely possible that this had been Germanus's plan when he likewise intended to lead his army into Italy. It is easy to see that he could have adopted the same route as was taken by John. When John reached Salona he found out that there were no ships available, so he stayed there through the winter.

Roman counter-attack in Sicily 550–51[10]

In the meantime, however, the plan of Justinian for Sicily did not work because Liberius had already sailed in 550. In 551 Liberius forced his way through the Goths who were besieging Syracuse and sailed his fleet into the harbour. When Artabanes reached Cephallenia he found out that Liberius had already left. Artabanes, however, did not remain idle but crossed the Adriatic Sea with his ships, but then near Calabria a storm scattered the fleet. Most of the ships were forced back to Peloponnesus. The ship which carried Artabanes lost its mast and was forced to land on the island of Melita (mod. Meleda). Liberius considered his forces too small to engage the enemy in sallies or battles, and when he then came to the conclusion that there were not enough provisions for his men, he eluded his enemy and sailed to Panormus. In the meantime, Totila had plundered most of Sicily, the booty had been loaded onto ships and he had returned to Italy. The threat posed by the army under John against the women and children of the Goths in Italy made this necessary.

After this, with the help of the navy Liberius's successor Artabanes reduced the remaining Sicilian cities in Gothic hands to surrender (the Goths had consistently failed in their sallies against the Romans). The Goths clearly understood the importance of the navy. They used fleets to cut Roman supply lines, but the Romans were better sailors. This gave them the ability to break through the blockading Gothic fleets. The Romans were also able to collect new armies and fleets to send against the Goths.

The Sklavenoi invasion continues in 550–51[11]

Meanwhile John faced a new problem in Salona. The Sklavenoi reappeared, both those who had previously invaded and others who had crossed the Danube after that. The death of Germanus undoubtedly encouraged them to do so. The Slavs now started to plunder Roman domains with impunity. According to Procopius, it was claimed that Totila had bribed them to do so, but Procopius said he didn't know whether the claims were true. The Sklavenoi divided their force into three divisions and caused irreparable damage across all Europe. This was not a mere raid: the Slavs stayed in the area throughout the winter 550/1.

Justinian responded slowly, presumably because there were not enough men available for all of the fronts in Lazica, Salona and Italy. When a considerable force of men had finally been assembled, he put it under the command of Constantianus, Aratius, Nazares, Justinus son of Germanus and John the Glutton. The commander-in-chief was Scholasticus, one of the eunuchs of the palace. When the army came upon one of the three Slav raiding columns near Adrianople five days' journey from Constantinople, the Slavs, who were hindered by their booty, took refuge on a hill while the Romans were on the plain. This situation resulted in a long stalemate and blockade of the enemy, which made the Roman soldiers resentful as their supplies ran low while their commanders enjoyed abundance. This suggests that the Romans had used a cavalry army without a large baggage train to catch up with the raiders. It also shows how incompetent the Roman commanders were. They should have known better than to live in the lap of luxury when the men suffered from want of provisions. Consequently the generals were forced to engage the Slavs in a battle in which the Romans were decisively bested by the Slavs. According to Procopius, many of the best soldiers were killed in this folly. Considering the area, the use of dismounted cavalry would seem likely but we don't know for certain. Only with difficulty did the commanders save themselves, while the standard of Constantianus was captured. This allowed the Slavs to continue their ravages, so that they pillaged Astica, the area between Adrianople and Constantinople. However, the Romans were able to destroy a portion (*moira*) of their force in an ambush and consequently able to free a vast number of captives and recover the standard. *Moira* in this case probably means one of the three divisions rather than a *moira* of 3,000 soldiers. This saved the Romans from complete humiliation. The remaining Slavs returned with their booty.

The Lombards, Gepids, Huns and Slavs in 550–52[12]

In 550, when the peace negotiations between the Lombards under Audoin and the Gepids under Turisindus had resulted in nothing, both sides prepared for battle. The simultaneous invasion of Roman territories by the Slavs appears not to have had any influence on these intertribal conflicts. The resulting war proved a non-event because when the two huge armies came close to each other, both forces panicked simultaneously before even seeing each other so that only the personal retinues of the kings were left in the field. The two kings therefore agreed to another two-year truce. It was during the same year that Audoin promised to send men to the army of Germanus.

The Gepids feared that the Romans would array themselves with the Lombards, and because of this they allied themselves with the Kutrigur Huns who sent them 12,000 men under Chinialon. These, however, arrived too early because the truce was still in force. This implies that the Kurtigurs arrived in 551. Consequently the Gepids decided to send them against the Romans. However, the Romans defended the Danube line effectively, evidently with their fleet, so the Gepids had to ferry the Huns across themselves at the point which belonged to them. This shows how important it was to possess the entire length of the river. Thanks to the fact that the Roman army had at this time advanced west under John the nephew of Vitalian, the Huns could pillage at will. This was one of the famous occasions on which Justinian forbade his generals from engaging the invaders because he now played a stratagem against the Kutrigurs by following the suggestion earlier made by the Tetraxitae.

Justinian dispatched a message to the Utigur Huns in which he urged them to demonstrate their friendship with the Romans by invading the Kutrigur territory. They did so under Sandichl. His army, which included 2,000 Tetraxitae, crossed the Don, defeated the Kutrigurs, and took their children and wives as slaves. When the news was brought to Justinian he sent one of his generals to the Kutrigurs to inform them of what had happened. The invasion appears to have lasted until early 552 so the Huns delayed Narses and advanced as far as Thessalonica and Constantinople. Justinian gave them a large bribe to leave Roman territory. Justinian also promised that if they were unable to wrest back their lands from the Utigurs he would give them land in Thrace. Soon after this the Kutrigur Hun Sinnion arrived with 2,000 Huns and asked for land. Justinian granted the request and settled them in Thrace. Sinnion was the man who had served under Belisarius. This angered the Utigurs. Justinian had given their enemies greater rewards. Justinian calmed the Utigurs with sizable bribes. This was superb diplomacy on Justinian's part – a textbook example.

The Sklavenoi invaded Illyricum in 552 and inflicted a lot of damage, so Justinian dispatched Justinian and Justin, the sons of Germanus, against them. The Slavs outnumbered the Romans so the Romans could only shadow and harass them. When the Slavs then retreated from Roman territory, they were shipped across the Danube by the Gepids in return for payment so the Romans still could not inflict any damage on them.

In 552 the Lombards and Gepids finally fought the war that had been in the books from the start. The Gepids asked Justinian to renew their alliance, which Justinian promised to do. Then the Lombards asked Justinian to fulfil the requirements of alliance with the result that Justinian now revoked his promise to the Gepids because they had helped the Slavs. Justinian ordered Justinian and Justin with Aratius, Suartuas and Amalafridas to lead an army to assist the Lombards. However, there was a revolt in Ulpiana resulting from Christian doctrinal matters. Justin, Justinian, Aratius, and Suartuas marched there and suppressed the revolt so the only commander who reached the Lombards in time was Amalafridas. The Lombards crushed the Gepids in battle so Audoin sent a message to Justinian in which he admonished the Romans for having failed to help him despite the fact that he had provided large numbers of soldiers for the Italian campaign during the same year.

Italy, Dalmatia and Greece 551–52[13]

John the nephew of Vitalian had spent winter 550/1 in Salona with the intention of advancing into Italy in the spring of 551. However, Justinian prevented this because he dispatched Narses the Eunuch as new supreme commander. Procopius notes that nobody knew why Justinian did so but that it was suspected that he feared that the other commanders would not obey John while they would obey Narses. This indeed appears to be the more likely reason. However, the abovementioned invasion of the Balkans by the Kutrigur Huns caused a further delay to the operation because when Narses reached Philippopolis he could not advance any further because of these Huns, but when they continued their advance near Thessalonica and Byzantium, Narses resumed his journey.

Totila's campaigns and Roman response in 551–52[14]

In the meantime, Totila had divided the Roman senators between Campania and Rome, after which he conducted two major operations. These consisted of the naval expeditions to Corsica and Sardinia under his command while a separate fleet of 300 ships was dispatched to ravage the coasts of Greece. In addition to this, Totila dispatched an army with a small fleet to besiege Ancona/Ancon. The fleet which was dispatched against Greece plundered the island of Cercyra and the islands called Sybotae (mod. Sybota islands) after which they crossed to the mainland and plundered the country about Dodona, and in particular the cities of Nicopolis and Anchialus. Then they sailed along the coast and captured many Roman ships including those meant to bring supplies for Narses's army.

The fleet which Totila led in person advanced first against Corsica, which was captured with ease because it was undefended. From there Totila sailed to Sardinia, which also fell to him. These islands belonged to the jurisdiction of Libya; John Troglita reacted by sending a large force in ships to Sardinia. The Romans landed near Caralis, but they felt unable to take the city because the Gothic garrison was large. The Goths noted the demoralization of the besiegers and made a sally. The Romans were routed and fled to their ships.

Meanwhile Justinian attempted to convince the Franks who held the Cottian Alps and some parts of Liguria and Venetia (the Romans held the coast) to join him against the Goths, but to no avail because the Franks had concluded a non-aggression treaty with Totila.

The naval battle of Sena Gallia in 551[15]

In the meantime, the Goths under the leadership of Scipuar, Gibal and Gundulf (Indulf)[16] had besieged Ancon on the Italian coast. The Gothic navy also took part in the blockade. Valerianus, who was at Ravenna, informed John, the nephew of Vitalian, of the situation. The news prompted John, who was at Salones, to intervene before it was too late. He did this despite the emperor's explicit order not to act on his own initiative. The Romans had to react to this threat. They needed the city between Ravenna and Dryus to be able to transport troops across the Adriatic Sea.

The Romans united their forces and landed near Sena Gallia. The Goths boarded their ships and advanced against the Romans so that the two sides engaged each other in a naval battle there. John had 38 warships[17] and Valerianus 12. The Goths had 47 warships under Gibal and Gundulf. After both sides halted and arranged their ships in line, the Goths attacked the Roman fleet. Procopius divides the naval battle into stages. In the first stage, both navies advanced head-on, bow against bow, while launching missiles. The bolder captains advanced close enough to touch each other and then fought on the decks with swords and spears. This means that some of the ships advanced into contact while others stopped short and engaged the enemy with missiles. Those that advanced into contact undoubtedly used boarding bridges and grappling hooks while the archers and spearmen tried to clear the enemy decks so that the boarding party could advance. The fighting at this range was intense and exhausting as the men stood face-to-face on unsteady platforms on ships swaying in the waves. Attacks via boarding bridges were conducted two abreast so that the front rank placed their shields in front and succeeding ranks placed their shields on the sides.[18] While jumping onto the enemy ship the shield was always placed in front to provide cover. It is not certain what types of ships were involved in this action, but most appear to have been smaller warships. Some may even have lacked forecastles and full decks. Those that lacked decks were vulnerable to attacks from the side since the narrow catwalks on the sides did not allow the deployment of men in depth. Once the boarding crew had fought its way there, it was likely to be able to advance even further. Those ships that lacked forecastles or had shorter ones were also at a disadvantage in frontal combat. In this type of action it was likely that the more numerous crews of the larger ships with higher forecastles would succeed over the smaller crews.[19]

Schematic representation of the battle. Left: The probable deployment of the navies in two lines. The guess has been made that the admiral of the fleet was John and that he took his place among the reserves. The guess has also been made that the Romans employed separate wing guards. Right: The Gothic navy disordered and outflanked.

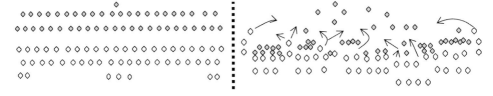

In the second stage the Goths, through lack of experience in sea-fighting, disordered their fleet. Some of them separated from one another giving the Romans opportunities to ram them singly, while others drew together in large groups. These latter the Romans engaged with missiles since these Gothic ships were a helpless mass unable to move as a result of the mess that their oars were in. It is likely that some of the ships were burned with their crews. Since the Gothic ships were sometimes pushing their prows into the crowded space, and sometimes backing off at a distance, it appears likely that the second line of the Goths had advanced into their first causing even further disorder. In contrast, the Roman ships coordinated their actions perfectly, all the time maintaining the proper distances. This allowed the ships to support one another. This was particularly important because the effective ramming of an enemy ship demanded approach from the side. Only eleven of the Gothic ships managed to escape to the nearby shore.[20] The rest were either sunk or captured by the Romans. This probably implies that the Gothic navy was outflanked, perhaps by the specially chosen wing units. The general standard of the Roman navy remained high. This naval battle was truly decisive for the outcome of the war because it allowed the Romans to continue their naval operations and even more importantly because, as Procopius specifically states, it lowered the morale of the Goths just before Narses's arrival. It was also important because the Goths lost large numbers of their elite fighters.

The Roman success in this battle relieved Ancon.

It is notable that neither of the Roman commanders had any particular training or experience in naval warfare, yet could be expected to be able to lead navies in combat. This shows the generally high standard of the commanders at this stage and also the high standard of seamen and captains.

Sicily, Croton and Thermopylae[21]

In the meantime, Liberius's replacement as commander in Sicily, Artabanes, had performed his duties with characteristic effectiveness. He besieged Gothic forces in the fortresses, defeated all sallies made by the enemy and took all of the fortresses through surrender. This and the defeat at Sena Gallia demoralized the Goths greatly.

The inhabitants and soldiers in the city of Croton had been besieged by the Goths for a long time. They were running out of provisions and asked Artabanes to help them, but he did nothing. Justinian was also informed of this and he decided to act. He ordered the garrison of Thermopylae to embark in ships and relieve the city. This they did. When the besiegers saw the Roman fleet, they broke the siege and fled in ships to the harbour of Tarentum while others fled to Mt. Scylaeum. The morale of the Goths sunk to new lows, and the Gothic noble Ragnaris, commander at Tarentum, and Moras, commander at Acherontia, opened negotiations with Pacurius son of Peranius, commander of the Romans at Dryus. The Goths promised to surrender if Pacurius brought pledges of safety from the emperor. Pacurius promised and the Goths handed hostages as their pledge.

Warlord on the loose in the Balkans in 552[22]

The mercenary Ildigisal/Ildiges and his warbands caused numerous defeats to the Romans in the course of his adventures, although he too had been ready to join the Romans for money. His career was colourful. In 549, Ildigisal (a personal enemy of Audoin, king of the Lombards) with his followers and some Slavs fled from the Lombards to the Gepids. From there he fled to the Slavs and then with 6,000 followers marched to join Totila. In Venetia he defeated the Romans commanded by Lazarus, but then again decided to withdraw to the land of the Slavs across the Danube. Then with 300 followers he fled to the Romans. He was appointed commander of a *lochos* of the *Scholae* while his 300 followers lived together at Apri in Thrace. The Lombard king complained and demanded that Ildigisal should be handed over to him, but Justinian refused. Ildigisal, however, was dissatisfied with his rank and salary and decided to leave together with Goar (a Gothic captive) in 552. They joined the 300 Lombards and then looted the horses of the imperial horse pastures nearby. Justinian ordered the commanders in Thrace and Illyria to engage them immediately. The Kutrigur Huns (2,000 men plus families probably led by Sinnion) engaged them in battle in Thrace but were defeated.

Now Ildigisal and Goar moved into Illyria. The Illyrian army under Aratius, Rhecithangus, Leonianus, Arimuth, and others had gathered against them. However, their horses were tired after a day's march. Upon reaching a wooded place at about nightfall, the commanders ordered the soldiers to care for their horses, then they took three or four bodyguards each and went to water their horses beside the river in a concealed place. Sadly for them, the scouts of Ildigisal were nearby. The fugitives surprised and killed the commanders and their bodyguards. Without the commanders, the Illyrian army was paralyzed and decided to withdraw. Consequently, the route was left open for the fugitives to continue their journey to the land of the Gepids. The career of Sinnion the Hun from being an ally of the Romans to their enemy and then to the position of federate also shows the nature of these adventurers and their war bands. They were adventurers.

Soon after this Audoin and Justinian both demanded that the Gepids should extradite Ildigisal, but the king of the Gepids, Turisindus/Thorisin, was unwilling to do this and demanded in return the extradition of a fugitive from Audoin's realm. No result was therefore reached, but subsequently both managed to assassinate their opponents by stealth. This appears to have been the last serious disturbance in the Balkans until the Kutrigur invasion in 559. The inciting of the Kutrigurs and Utigurs against each other by Justinian therefore proved very successful.

The reconquest of Spain in 552–54[23]

Justinian's strategy for 552 consisted of two parts. The first was the sending of Narses with a strong force to crush the (Ostro)Goths of Totila while Liberius took a fleet to Spain to assist a usurper against the legitimate Visigothic king with the idea of beginning the reconquest of Spain.

The Visigoths were an easy target because they were divided and weak. Theoderic the Great had left his general, Theudis, in charge of Visigothic Spain, and when the king, Amalric, then suffered a defeat in a war against the Franks of Childebert in 531, it was easy for him to have Amalric killed and take power himself. The Franks invaded Spain but were this time unexpectedly defeated by Theudis's general Theudigisel who blocked the passes of the Pyrenees behind the invaders and inflicted a defeat. The Franks offered money to be allowed through, which Theudigisel accepted but gave them only one day and one night to do it. The rest were killed. Theudis was also an enemy of the Romans so in about 547 he dispatched an expedition against the Romans who had taken Ceuta/Septem with disastrous results for the Visigoths, as already mentioned. This made the Visigoths enemies of the Romans. In 548, soon after the failed campaign, Theudis was murdered in his palace. According to Isidore, the murderer was a man who had pretended to be insane for a long time and was thus able to get close enough to Theudis to stab him mortally. Isidore also claims that Theudis forbade his followers from punishing the man because it was only fair that Theudis should suffer such fate because he had killed his own commander when he was a private citizen. In my opinion, it is also possible that the assassin escaped punishment because his action was well received after the failed campaign against Ceuta. The circumstances of the murder also make it possible that the assassin had been sent by the Romans with Theudigisel assisting them because the murder of Theudis was so soon after his attack against Ceuta, but there is no concrete evidence for this in the sources.

Theudis's successor was Theudigisel, the man who had defeated the Franks. However, he seduced the wives of many of his followers and may even have raped some with the result that there were powerful men who wanted to see him killed. A conspiracy was formed and his throat was cut in the midst of feast in Seville in 549. The fact that Theudis's successor Theudigisel was a man with clear personal weaknesses lends further support for this conclusion because it is easy to see how the Romans could have used this as their leverage in such circumstances.

Theudigisel's successor was Agila. Among his first actions was to begin a persecution of Catholics, so he faced a civil war against the citizens of Cordoba. Agila lost the fight and his son was killed in action. He was forced to flee to Merida. The Visigoths were Arians so there was a schism between the two groups to begin with, but this attack against the Catholics, the followers of the Chalcedonian doctrine, can also be invoked as further evidence for possible involvement of Roman agents in the murder of Theudis. Furthermore, Athanagild revolted soon after this against Agila and dispatched a plea for help to Justinian. This is also highly suggestive of the presence of Roman agents and their collaborators among the Visigoths and natives and Catholic clergy. One wonders if Athanagild had been in charge of the defenders of Cordoba. In my opinion it seems probable. When Justinian then received the plea for help either in late 551 or in early 552, he dispatched a fleet and a small force under Liberius, who had just returned from Sicily to Constantinople. Liberius acted as instructed and escorted the reinforcements to Athanagild and was back in Constantinople by 553 where he took part in the negotiations with Pope Vigilius. Liberius was eminently suited to all of these missions because he was an experienced and influential Italian senator and patrician who had served with distinction under Theoderic the Great.

Athanagild and his army of Roman reinforcements occupied Seville where Agila then dispatched his army, but Athanagild and the Romans defeated them. It was then that the loyalist Visigoths came to the conclusion that the Romans could take all of Spain if they continued to fight against each other so they killed Agila in Merida and then surrendered themselves to Athanagild. Athanagild asked the Romans to hand back to him the areas they had conquered, but in vain with the result that he attempted to force them to do so, but this effort was also defeated. The Romans had thereby gained possession of at least Baetica and parts of Carthagiensis, so they held at least the cities of Carthagena, Corduba Assidonia and probably also Hispalis (Sevilla). The conquered areas appear to have been organized in a regular manner with *limitanei* and *comitatenses*. The former were commanded by a *duces* and the latter by a *magister*. It has been speculated that the Roman forces in Spain would have been placed under the *Magister Militum per Africam*, but this is not certain. It is entirely possible that Spain already had its own *Magister Militum Spaniae* which is recorded for the first time for the year 582. However, it is still obvious that in practice the fleet and garrison posted at Ceuta opposite Gibraltar would have been used in support of these forces when needed. It is also possible or even probable that Justinian posted a separate detachment drawn from the regular Roman navy in Spain and used the local ships in the coastal cities as corveed forces when needed.

The conquest of Spain was probably very profitable. It had not required large forces or vast quantities of money and it had secured North Africa from the Visigoths. The control of the Straits of Gibraltar also had strategic advantages, as did control of the coastal regions of Spain, which secured the Romans better control over the trade routes of the western Mediterranean.

Chapter Eighteen

Narses the Eunuch and the Return of the Roman Glory Days 552–65

Battle of Taginae/Tadinae/Busta Gallorum in 552[1]

Probably in April 552, Narses the Eunuch finally reached Salona and was ready to begin his campaign. He had initially refused the appointment unless Justinian gave him adequate resources and this time Justinian acted energetically. Narses was given a sizable force, together with a massive amount of money: for the hiring of men, for the paying of the arrears of salaries owed to the soldiers in Italy, and to lure Roman deserters back from the Goths. He had been finally given an adequate force to deal with the Goths once and for all. The army consisted of the soldiers Narses and Germanus had collected: there were forces from Byzantium, Thrace, Illyria, and the soldiers under John nephew of Vitalian and John the Glutton. In addition, there were 2,500 Lombard 'knights' and 3,000 of their servants/esquires, 3,000 Herul cavalry commanded by Philemuth and others, Huns, Dagisthaeus with his followers (he was released from prison to take part in the campaign), Cabades (the grandson of the *Shahanshah* Cobades/Cabades) with Persian deserters, Asbadus with 400 Gepids, and Aruth with large numbers of Heruls. Furthermore, the generosity of Narses endeared him to his soldiers and his barbarian allies. According to Procopius, this army was extraordinarily large and befitting of the Roman Empire.

Since the road to Italy through Venetia was controlled by the Franks, Narses asked their permission, but was denied. There was also the problem that Teias with the best of Gothic forces was stationed at Verona and he had built obstacles to prevent the easy crossing of the Po, so he was nearby with his forces to attack when the Romans attempted to cross the river. To avoid these obstacles, Narses adopted the plan suggested to him by John the nephew of Vitalian who knew the area well: to march along the coast with the fleet of ships and boats sailing alongside, and whenever there was a river-mouth to cross the army could be shipped across in these. This took time, but the Roman army was able to reach Ravenna safely.

At Ravenna, Narses was joined by Valerianus, Justinus and the remnants of Roman forces. Narses left Justinus with a garrison at Ravenna and marched towards Ariminum. The Gothic commander of Ariminum, Usdrilas, had taunted and insulted Narses, but his plan was not to engage him but to march directly against Totila who was then at Rome, to fight a decisive battle with all forces available. However, the marching route took Narses close to Ariminum, so he and his Heruls advanced to reconnoitre the bridge that the Goths had destroyed. The Gothic commander came to the opposite shore and one of the men following Narses shot an arrow, which hit and killed one of the enemy horses. The Goths fled to Ariminum, but then came in greater strength out of the other gate with the idea of attacking the Roman army that had already arrived. However, then one of the Heruls by chance happened to kill the Gothic commander, and brought his head to the Roman camp for Narses. This could have given Narses the chance of taking Ariminum, but he was not distracted and built a bridge and continued his march. However, he was forced to avoid Via Flaminia because it was blocked by a Gothic garrison at Petra Pertusa. He marched his forces a longer way, with Via Flaminia on their left.

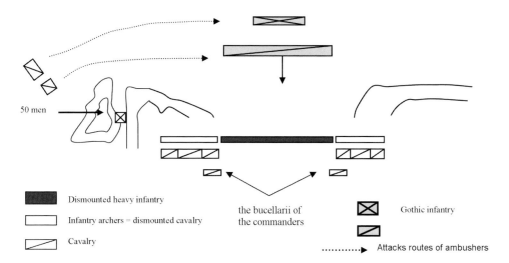

Dismounted heavy infantry

Infantry archers = dismounted cavalry

Cavalry

50 men

the bucellarii of the commanders

Gothic infantry

Attacks routes of ambushers

When Totila heard that Narses had reached Ravenna he was forced to recall Teias and his men to engage him. When all but 2,000 soldiers had returned he moved his forces towards Narses and pitched his camp at Taginae. Narses pitched his camp 100 stades (ca. 18.4 km) distant from the camp of Totila in the Apennines. The Romans numbered probably 35,000–40,000 men or more while the Goths probably had only about 20,000. Procopius states in no uncertain terms that the Romans had a great numerical and qualitative advantage over Totila which was made even worse by the advantage the Romans had in equipment. Totila had the same strategic dilemma as Belisarius before: if he wanted to keep Portus with its fleet and Rome in Gothic hands, he needed to post garrisons in each, with the result that his field forces were diminished. Narses's army occupied a strong defensive position at a place called Busta Gallorum, named after an ancient battle fought against the Gauls. Narses dispatched an envoy to Totila in which he urged him to surrender or choose the day for battle. Totila stated that they would fight in eight days, but Narses guessed correctly that they would fight immediately.

The next day both armies faced each other two bowshots apart. Between the armies there was a small hill that gave its occupant safety against any flank attacks. It had a single narrow path with a watercourse in front of it. The Goths tried to seize it with the idea of outflanking the Roman position, but their attempt was anticipated by Narses who sent fifty infantrymen to occupy it in advance. Totila sent a cavalry wing (*ilê, ala*) against them (Procopius, *Wars* 8.29.16ff., tr. by Dewing):

'The Gothic horsemen… charged upon them with great shouting… but the Romans drew up together into a small space, and making a barrier with their shields and thrusting forward their spears, held their ground… the fifty, pushing with their shields and thrusting very rapidly with their spears, which were nowhere allowed to interfere one with the other, defended themselves.'

The above text is important because it shows the Roman infantry using several ranks of spears in such a manner that the spear thrusts were coordinated so well that they did not interfere with each other. It also shows the infantry phalanx advancing against the crowded enemy cavalry in a coordinated manner.

When the Goths grew tired, Totila replaced the attackers repeatedly with others, but then gave up the effort when they had all been repulsed. Two Romans, called Paulus and Ansilus, had shown exemplary bravery in this encounter by advancing out of the formation to fight like the earlier *antesignani* or *lanciarii* or club-bearers or like the much later tenth century *menavlatoi*. They used their bows to very great effect when the situation allowed and then used shields and swords when required so that whenever the Goths thrust their spears they cut the spearheads and killed their wielders. In the end the sword of Paulus bent and became useless, so he started to seize enemy spears with both hands which he then threw to the ground. After he had wrenched only four spears from the enemy, the Goths lost their morale and stopped their attacks. Narses rewarded Paulus by making him his own personal guard.

After the Goths had failed to outflank the strong Roman position, both sides readied themselves for combat. Narses himself held the left wing with John near the hill with the regular soldiers, the Huns and the bodyguards. According to Procopius, the forces posted on the left wing were the best troops in the army. On the right were posted Valerianus, John the Glutton, Dagisthaeus and all the rest of the Romans. On the wings were posted about 8,000 dismounted bowmen on foot, 4,000 on each flank. The dismounted archers were actually dual purpose soldiers which could be used simultaneously as a pike/spear phalanx and foot archers. The cavalry wings that remained mounted were posted behind the footmen. The minimum figure for the mounted force would have been about the same number as there were dismounted archers in front, but since the foot archers would have in all probability been deployed in a shallower formation than the cavalry one may assume that the mounted portion of each wing was greater. My educated guess is that archers were probably deployed four deep with a width of ca. 1,000 metres while the cavalry behind them was deployed with a depth of six men on average so that there were 6,000 horsemen per wing behind the footmen; but there could have been even more of them. I have merely made this guess on the basis of a standard depth of ten ranks so that four ranks of them would have been dismounted to form the wings of foot archers. The wings were probably posted on rough or higher ground or on some other similar terrain that provided them with additional protection.

In the centre of the phalanx, Narses posted the dismounted Lombards, the Heruls and the rest of the barbarians to bear the brunt of the forthcoming Gothic cavalry charge. In addition, Narses posted 1,500 horsemen at the extreme left flank at an angle, apparently behind the small hill. One thousand of these were directed against the enemy infantry that was posted behind the Gothic cavalry, and 500 were to attack the flank of the Goth cavalry if any of the Roman forces were forced to retreat. Consequently, this battle array made the centre of the Roman army static. The different dismounted Germanic tribesmen could not be trusted with any complicated battlefield manoeuvres. They were only to hold their ground. In essence, the only manoeuvrable sections of the army were its wings composed of the Romans. The flanks of the Roman formation, the archers on foot, would have been protected by some terrain features, and possibly caltrops. The cavalry of the Roman wings undoubtedly shot over the heads of the foot archers.[2] The purpose was to defeat the enemy cavalry by volleys of arrows. Of note is the fact that Procopius leaves out the infantry from his list of units in the phalanx. The only unit he lists is the 50-man group that came from the infantry units (*ek katalogou pezous*). It is therefore clear that there were other infantry units besides. There are two possibilities: 1) the Roman infantry were deployed in the centre together with the dismounted barbarians so that the dismounted barbarians were in the middle of this infantry phalanx; 2) the Roman infantry were left in the camp, or in front of the camp. Both are possible, but the first is the more likely. Totila arrayed his cavalry in front of his infantry. See the diagram.

A Roman deserter in Gothic service challenged the Romans to a duel. This call was answered by an Armenian in Roman service. They charged against each other with lances. The Armenian avoided the spear thrust of his foe by veering to the left, and unhorsed and killed him with his own spear. The Romans raised a mighty shout. After the single combat had gone in favour of the Romans, Totila played for time by performing a lance play on horseback. He wanted to postpone the engagement until the reinforcements of 2,000 men arrived. When they did, he withdrew the army back to its camp to eat and then suddenly arrayed his forces again in the hope of surprising the Romans. Totila's battle plan was simple. He aimed to crush his opponents with a wild cavalry charge against the centre of the phalanx. The cavalry was ordered to use only spears. The use of bows was forbidden. Procopius is correct to criticize this decision. The infantry was used only as a place of refuge. The battle plan of Narses was also simple. He planned to put the Gothic cavalry into crossfire as it approached the centre of the Roman formation. When the Goths advanced, the Roman infantry wings composed of the archers gradually moved forward to form a crescent. See the diagram. The Gothic infantry was unable to respond to this move because it was posted behind only as a place of refuge for the cavalry. And besides, Narses had 1,000 horsemen in reserve to engage the infantry if it moved. Totila was outgeneralled. The Goths lost many men and horses in the crossfire, but they continued their futile attempts until late afternoon. Then the Romans counter-attacked.

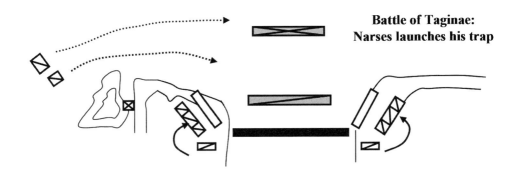

**Battle of Taginae:
Narses launches his trap**

The disorderly rout of the Gothic cavalry caused the rout of their infantry. In the carnage of the battle and in the ensuing pursuit, 6,000 Goths were killed and many others were made prisoners, only to be massacred later. Only darkness put a stop to the killing. Totila perished in this encounter, either during the retreat or from an arrow wound. The story of the arrow wound relates that when Totila consequently withdrew from the battle, the morale of the army finally collapsed and that it was because of this that the rout began.

Battle of Mons Lactarius on 1 or 30 October 552[3]

After the Battle of Taginae, Narses gave thanks to God and then got rid of the outrageously behaved Lombards by sending them away loaded with gifts. Lombard behaviour had indeed been outrageous. They had pillaged the Italians, torched their houses, and raped even those who had sought refuge in the churches. Valerianus and his nephew Damianus were tasked to escort the Lombards away. Their assignment was to make certain that the Lombards would not commit any more outrages while on Italian soil, and they were given an army for this purpose. After this, Valerianus pitched a camp near Verona with the intention of taking the city through surrender, but when the Franks in Venetia learned of this, they prevented the surrender of the garrison. So Valerianus retreated.

Meanwhile, the surviving Goths had retreated to Ticinum where they chose Teias as their new king. Totila had placed some money in Ticinum while the rest had been deposited at Cumae. This gave Teias a war chest which he could use to continue his war against the Romans. He dispatched envoys to the Franks to ask them to form an alliance against the Romans. The Franks refused, because they wanted the Goths and Romans to wear themselves out so that they could then conquer Italy. When Narses learned of the regrouping of the Goths, he ordered Valerianus to keep watch on the crossings of the Po while he himself continued his march to Rome. When Narses reached Tuscany, he took Narnia by surrender. He left a garrison at Spolitium with orders to restore the demolished walls. He also sent some soldiers against Perusia. It was held by Roman deserters Meligedius and Ulifus. Ulifus had been a bodyguard of its former commander Cyprian, but he had then killed his superior after which he had fled. This had not resulted in the immediate surrender of Perusia to the Goths, as we have seen, but Ulifus was apparently able to change their minds later. Meligedius wanted to surrender to the Romans, while Ulifus was opposed to this. The two sides fought: Ulifus lost and Meligedius surrendered the fort to the Romans.

Narses continued his march to Rome. There was no longer sufficient manpower to guard the entire length of the circuit wall, so Totila had hastily built fortifications around the Tomb of Hadrian to create a separate fortress for which there were enough Goths to man the walls. The Goths, however, chose to test the Romans by manning the length of the circuit wall as best they could. They did not have enough men for this, and neither did the Romans. It was because of this that Narses dispatched separate divisions around the city to make separate attacks while the Goths opposed them with separate forces. This left large sections of the wall undefended, so when the fighting was going on Narses dispatched Dagisthaeus with some men against one of these sections; they were able to place their ladders against the wall unopposed and then open up the gates. The Goths fled to their ersatz fort in the Tomb of Hadrian and to Portus. The Romans entered the city, but the barbarians in their midst treated the local populace as they usually did those in a conquered foreign city: many Romans lost their lives or were raped. Narses sent the keys of the city to Justinian.

When the Goths learnt of the loss of Rome, they started killing their hostages. The Goths in Campania killed the senators and their families while Teias killed the 300 children that Totila had collected from the magnates of the different cities. In addition to this, they started killing all Italians who had the misfortune of meeting them. Ragnaris, who had promised to surrender Tarentum, changed his mind when he heard that Teias had become the new king and that he was negotiating with the Franks. He wanted his hostages back, so he sent a message to Pacurius and asked him to send fifty Romans to lead his men to Dryus. When he got them, he dispatched a message demanding an exchange of hostages. Pacurius's answer was to lead his army against Ragnaris. The armies fought, the Goths lost, Ragnaris fled to Acherontis, and Tarentum was captured by the Romans.

Meanwhile, the Romans captured Portus and Nepa. Valerianus had marched south where he captured Petra Pertusa, and after this Narses dispatched men against Centumcellae and Cumae. Both places were strategically important, Cumea more so because the main war chest of Totila had been left there. This move frightened Teias, not least because his brother was the commander at Cumae. Thus he prepared to march immediately to Cumae, thirty days march away. Narses attempted to prevent this by ordering John nephew of Vitalian and Philemuth to guard Tuscany. Teias learned of this and made several very long detours, finally reaching the Adriatic coast and continuing until

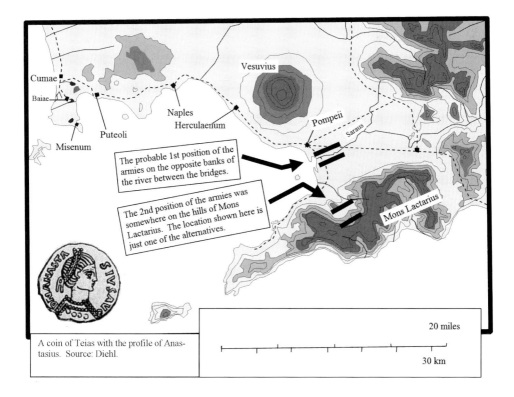

The probable 1st position of the armies on the opposite banks of the river between the bridges.

The 2nd position of the armies was somewhere on the hills of Mons Lactarius. The location shown here is just one of the alternatives.

A coin of Teias with the profile of Anastasius. Source: Diehl.

20 miles

30 km

he turned inland to Campania. When Narses learnt of this he immediately summoned John and Philemuth together with Valerianus and marched to Campania.

When Narses reached Campania he managed to block Teias near Vesuvius because he marched there by the direct route. Both armies encamped at the base of Mt. Vesuvius, a small stream separating them from each other. See the attached map. The Goths protected the only existing(?) bridge over the river by erecting two towers with ballistae. Both armies skirmished using bows or fought single combats. The standoff lasted for two months until the Romans cut off the supply route of the Goths by bringing up their fleet and taking the boats of the Goths through the treachery of the Gothic 'admiral'. The ring around the Goths was further tightened by setting wooden towers along the river to face the Gothic ones. As a result, the Goths suffered from starvation.

The Goths withdrew, but noted soon enough that their situation had worsened. However, their withdrawal had lured the Romans into rough ground exposing them to the sudden surprise attack of the Goths on 1 or 30 October 552. The Romans held their ground, but without any order because of the difficult terrain. The first to dismount were the Goths who formed a deep phalanx or column. The Romans also dismounted to face this attack and formed a deep phalanx as well. At the head of the Gothic forces was Teias with his followers. This suggests that he was at the apex of a wedge protruding out of the phalanx with his retinue. The Goths used shields and spears. The Romans tried their best to kill Teias, some thrusting their spears, others hurling them. Teias protected himself with his shield and by sudden charges slew great numbers. When too many spears stuck in his shield, he exchanged it with one of his followers. This movement forwards and backwards continued for the third part of the day. When twelve *dorata* (spears) were stuck in Teias's shield, he called by name one of his bodyguards to come to his side so that they could change their shields. At that moment, Teias's chest became exposed long enough for a Roman javelin to find its mark and kill him instantly. The Romans put his head aloft on a *contus* to discourage the Goths, but in vain. The Goths wanted to die fighting because this was their last battle. The fight continued till night, after which both armies separated and passed the night on the battlefield in their full gear. On the following day, they again fought till nightfall, neither army retreating nor giving any quarter. Finally, the Goths sent negotiators to ask permission to withdraw with their own money as travelling funds. John the nephew of Vitalian advised Narses to agree because it was dangerous to continue to fight against such desperate enemies. So Narses agreed on condition that the Goths leave Italy (Procopius) or stay in Italy as loyal subjects (Agathias). The rest of the Goths, all except 1,000 who fled during the negotiations, gave their oaths and were given permission to leave.

This was an exceptionally long battle, with both parties desperately engaged. The dismounted troopers fought at close quarters, advancing and retreating in turn. There would have been periods of lull in this long battle. It is also noteworthy that most of the spears were thrown rather than thrust, even though spear thrusts were also used.

The Frankish intervention: The battle of Capua/Casilinum/Casulinus River AD 554[4]

After Narses had defeated the Goths, their remnants who lived north of the Po sought the help of the Franks. Theudebald, one of the three Merovingian kings, was too young to campaign but he despatched a large army led by two Alamannic dukes, Lothar/ Leutharis and Butilin/Butilinus/Buccelin. According to Agathias, this army consisted of 75,000 Franks and Alamanni. Agathias's set piece speech put into the mouth of Narses summarizes the relative strengths and weaknesses of each side at the beginning of the invasion. The Franks had superior numbers, but the Romans had better discipline. The Romans possessed forts and supplies, the Franks lacked them.

Meanwhile, Narses had exploited his victory at Mons Lactarius by advancing against Cumae while he dispatched other forces to take the cities of Tuscany still held by the Goths. The siege of Cumae proved difficult because the city was located on a steep hill beside the sea and was well fortified and supplied with plentiful provisions and a garrison under Teias's brother Aligern.

The Romans attacked first using bows, slings, javelins, and siege engines, but with no result. The Goths responded with javelins, arrows, huge stones, logs, axes and anything else they could lay their hands on. The mention of logs and huge stones may imply the use of trebuchets. Agathias particularly extols the power of Aligern's archery by noting how he killed the high-ranking officer Palladius with an arrow that passed through his shield, breastplate and body. If this was indeed a bowshot and not a ballista shot, it proves that Aligern was indeed an extraordinarily powerful man. This fighting continued for several days until Narses realized that part of the fortification was built on top of a natural cave. This meant there was a chance of tunnelling. The Romans hid the noise by conducting further assaults until the tunnel had been propped up with wooden beams ready to be fired. However, the Roman undermining of the wall ended in failure. When the wall collapsed, the ground was full of cracks and fissures and littered with broken pieces of rocks. It was impassable. When Narses ordered the men to assault regardless, the Goths resisted all attacks. So Narses resorted to using a blockade and built a continuous line of earthworks. He expected the Goths to run out of supplies in about year. In the end Aligern chose to surrender and join the Roman cause against the Franks.[5]

By that time Narses knew of the Frankish invasion, so he knew that it was important to secure the towns of Tuscany and to post an army near the River Po. Philemuth/Filimuth, leader of the Heruls died at this time. Narses chose Fulcaris as his successor and ordered him to follow Valerianus and Artabanes who were given most of the army for their mission. Narses's instructions to them were to take their men through the Alpine range between Tuscany and Aemilia/Emilia. They would then encamp in the neighbourhood of the Po to check the enemy's advance while he captured the cities of Tuscany and Etruria.

Narses conducted a lighting campaign in the course of which he took Florence, Centumcellae, Volaterrae, Luna and Pisa by surrender. The only place which offered resistance was Lucca, which had a garrison of Franks. Its inhabitants gave Narses hostages and promised to surrender if no Frankish relief army arrived within thirty days. The thirty days passed and they did not do as promised so Narses started preparations for a siege. First he played a ruse on them by pretending to kill the hostages in full view of the populace and then claimed that he would bring them back from the dead if the inhabitants followed their agreement. The populace disbelieved Narses but all the same still voiced their approval of these terms. Narses then paraded the live hostages in front of them. The populace again broke their word, but Narses responded merely by dispatching the hostages back to the city. These actions were psychological ploys meant to confuse the defenders. The release of the hostages, who felt gratitude towards Narses, was meant to undermine the morale of the defenders.

Then Narses learnt that the shielding forces he had posted near the Po had suffered a terrible setback in Aemilia/Emilia. The Romans had until then been in the habit of using the hollow rectangle/oblong formation (*plaision*), which had enabled them to march in perfect safety, but then the impetuous Fulcaris had led his men against Parma without conducting any scouting with the result that the Franks of Butilinus were able to post an ambush in an amphitheatre near the city. When Fulcaris and his men arrived there in irregular formation they were duly surrounded. Most of his men managed to save themselves however, but Fulcaris preferred to stay and fight to the death rather than face an upbraiding from Narses. When the other officers, John the nephew of Vitalian and Artabanes, learnt of the defeat of their subordinate Fulcaris they withdrew their forces to Faventia to be closer to Ravenna.

Narses was enraged because John and Artabanes had shielded his operations against Lucca. This news had also demoralized his men. But he calmed them with a speech in which he noted that the defeat had resulted from barbarian rashness and that the Romans had nothing to fear even though they were outnumbered because they were better disciplined and the enemy's numbers would only cause them to suffer from lack of provisions. To continue his siege, Narses dispatched one of his closest associates, called Stephanus, with 200 of the bravest and best-armed horsemen to John and Artabanes. His task was to order the commanders back to their posts which they had abandoned. Stephanus and his men used forced marches and sleepless nights to avoid being captured by the roving parties of Franks. They also kept close order in case the enemy attacked. On his arrival Stephanus threatened the commanders with the words of Narses: that he would make certain the emperor's wrath would fall upon their heads if they refused to follow his orders. The commanders gave many excuses, the most poignant of which was that they claimed that *PPI* Antiochus had failed to send them adequate supplies and that he had not even shown up to give them their salaries. Stephanus therefore went to Ravenna and took the Prefect with him to meet the officers. Now that their troubles were solved, the officers promised to assume their stations and Stephanus returned to Narses with the news that the siege could continue.

Now Narses brought his siege engines, archers and slingers against the walls and firebrands and firebombs were hurled into the city. The Frankish garrison ordered the citizen militia to sally outside, but the hostages had by then undermined their morale so badly that it was easy for the Romans to force them back inside. At this point, the Franks and populace decided to surrender. Narses left a garrison under Bonus inside the city with orders to secure it.

After this he marched to Ravenna to rest for the winter. Narses believed it would be detrimental for him and his forces to engage the Franks during the winter because they were used to it. It was the heat of the summer that was the enemy of the Franks. Therefore Narses distributed his forces into the cities for the winter with orders to assemble in Rome in the spring. Narses himself went to winter in Ravenna with his general staff, the officials of which were called a *cancellis*. Zabdalas was the head of his household and he had also with him his eunuchs and the rest of the servants. The overall number of his household was 400 men of whom 300 were combat troops.

It was then that Aligern the Gothic commander of Cumae came to the conclusion that he would rather side with the Romans than with the Franks. The Franks had not come to Italy to help the Goths but to help themselves. Consequently, with the permission of the garrison he travelled to Classis, a district of Ravenna, to meet Narses. Narses was delighted and accepted the surrender, placed a garrison at Cumae while the rest of the besiegers were withdrawn to spend the winter elsewhere. He posted Aligern at Caesana to undermine the morale of the Franks when they passed by it. The Heruls also needed a new commander but were divided amongst themselves between Aruth and Sindual. Narses decided to back Sindual, after which they were dispatched to their winter quarters.

At this point, the new Gothic commander of Ariminum decided to surrender the city to Narses. Narses travelled there with his household, but when he arrived, a force of Franks consisting of about 2,000 infantry and cavalry arrived there too. Narses was reluctant to watch them from the safety of his position so he mounted his very obedient thoroughbred horse and led out a force of 300 *bucellarii*. When the Franks saw this they formed up a shallow phalanx with infantry centre and cavalry wings close to the nearby forest. The Romans charged but did not make contact with the solid enemy force but stayed at a distance and shot arrows and threw javelins. This proved ineffective thanks to the solid wall of shields which received additional protection from the trees. Therefore, Narses gave his men the order to feign flight. The Franks duly left their safe positions and pursued in disorder. When they were far enough from the forest, Narses gave the order to turn about and charge at the pursuers. The Franks fled in panic. Most of their cavalry managed to save themselves, but more than 900 enemy footmen were slaughtered like a herd of swine or cattle. Narses returned to Ravenna.

Next spring, Narses collected and trained his army thoroughly in Rome. He faced the enemy army in some minor skirmishes while allowing them to advance past Rome. The invasion force was only engaged when it was returning, as standard defensive doctrine recommended. The Franks had divided their forces into two parts to facilitate their provisioning.

Butilinus advanced along the west coast up to Bruttium while his brother Leutharis advanced along the east coast up to Apulia and Calabria. Agathias notes how the Franks respected the churches while the pagan Alamanni pillaged them. Once both had reached their destination, Leutharis sent a messenger to his brother that it was time to return home, but Butilinus wanted to respect their promises so he stayed where he was. Leutharis, however, led his army north. When he was near the city of Fanum, he dispatched a force of 3,000 scouts in advance. Artabanes and the Huns of Uldach were at this time posted in Fanum. When they saw the scouts, they charged out and killed them, most in combat, others as they fled to the sea. Those who survived rushed to their camp. Leutharis arrayed his army as a phalanx and marched against the Romans, but this time they stayed inside. The Franks had left their prisoners unattended and they now grasped their opportunity and fled. It was then that the magnitude of the loss dawned on Leutharis who duly led his forces back to his camp and then northwards until he crossed the Po. When they reached Venetia, they encamped in the city of Ceneta where they fully understood that all of their efforts had been in vain. As if this was not enough, the army caught 'plague'. Leutharis died raving like a madman foaming at the mouth. Others also died in a feverish rage, some fell into a swoon, others succumbed to delirium, others were gripped by seizures.

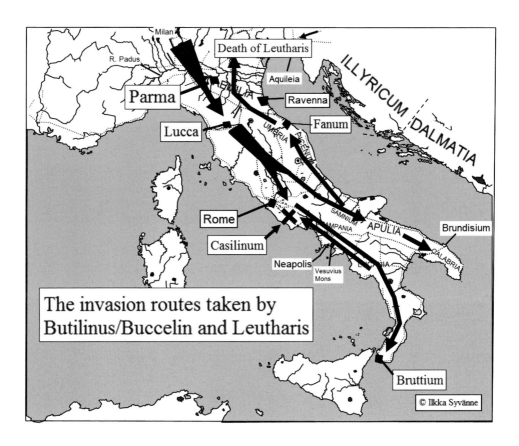

The invasion routes taken by Butilinus/Buccelin and Leutharis

Some blamed the air, others blamed a change in living conditions (campaign life vs. city life). My guess is that this was not plague but the Romans spreading contaminants into the sources of water or food.

In the meantime Butilinus and his Franks had started his march north while suffering from lack of provisions, as Narses had arranged. Therefore they sought to engage the Romans in a decisive battle before they had to succumb without a fight. The Franks encamped by the Casulinus River, where they trained and waited for the approach of Narses, who at this stage also sought a decisive battle. The situation was opportune. The Romans were in high spirits while the Franks were weakened, and the weather at the beginning of autumn was warm and uncomfortable for the Franks.

The Franks intended to fight their way through the Romans blocking their way home. Frankish tactics were based upon the infantry attack in wedge formation in which thrown missiles (*angon*-javelin and/or *francisca*-axe) were first used to cause disruption among the enemy ranks, followed by a charge. Narses planned to counter the wedge by using the classic hollow wedge and/or *epikampios emprosthia* (forward angled half-square). Agathias (2.8.5) claims that there was an empty place left for the Heruls in the middle of the phalanx because they supposedly hesitated to fight. This is actually likely to be a stratagem of Narses. He sent two Herul deserters to tell Butilinus that the Heruls would desert when the Franks attacked. The gullible Franks fell for it.[6]

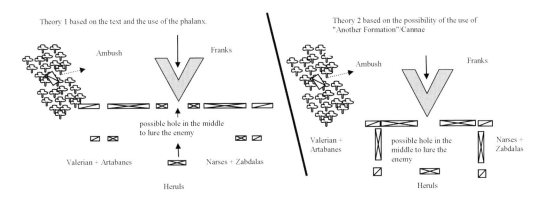

The empty space in the phalanx meant for the Heruls could mean the centre of the Roman phalanx so that it had an opening in it to lure the Franks to charge into it or it could mean that there was an empty place for the Heruls behind to form the bottom of the *epikampios emprosthia* or hollow wedge both of which could be used to counter an enemy wedge – it was the former array that the Romans used according to Agathias. In short, it is quite possible that there was no real hole in the actual array, but that 'hole' meant the place where the Heruls advanced to form up the bottom of the *epikampios emprosthia*. The hole where the Heruls were meant to advance was formed by opening the Roman array to receive the enemy attack. So the hole in the array could also refer to the use of the so-called *antistomos difalangia* which was formed by having two phalanxes wheel backwards to form an opening for the enemy cavalry and elephants to enter. This tactic could obviously be used with equal ease against infantry because it was really only a variation of the hollow wedge. The strength of the Roman army was 18,000 while the Franks/Alamanni had about 30,000 men. This discrepancy led Narses to augment his army with camp followers.[7]

The battle began when the Romans intercepted a foraging expedition, which resulted in the Romans taking the bridge which separated the armies. When the incensed Franks approached the Romans, Narses stationed his men in battle array. The Franks were allowed to cross the river so that the trap could be formed. The cavalry were placed on the wings. They were armed with short spears (*doratia*), shields, bows and arrows, and with swords. In addition, some carried pikes (*sarisae*), which may imply the use of the two-handed grip, but is not conclusive in this respect.[8] Narses posted his bodyguards and the camp followers and servants on the right wing. The infantry occupied the centre. The phalanx was formed in the standard manner. In front the heavy-armed infantry, clad in mail reaching their feet, formed a solid wall of shields.[9] Behind them were the light infantry archers, slingers and javelin throwers. The Heruls were posted behind the centre in reserve position. On the left, hiding in the woods, were cavalry forces under Valerianus and Artabanes whose duty it was to attack the flank and rear of the Franks. Narses and Zabdalas commanded the right flank. The Heruls were commanded by Sindual. Agathias does not mention any commanders for the infantry or for the centre, but the footmen undoubtedly had their own commander. It is probable that there were also reserves for the flanks. On the right, the infantry reserves were probably formed out of the camp followers while the cavalry reserves consisted of the bodyguards of Narses. The reserves of the centre consisted of the dismounted Heruls and possibly of some mounted Heruls. The reserves of the left consisted probably of the regular infantry or dismounted Germans and possibly of bodyguards of one or the other of the commanders. However, it is also possible that Narses used the so-called 'Another Formation' of the *Strategikon*. This would explain the final form even better, the forward angled half-square, than the use of the regular infantry phalanx, but the use of the regular phalanx still appears the more likely of the two. See the diagram.

The Franks formed their battle array in the typical German wedge formation as Narses had expected. The front consisted of a compact and dense mass of shields. The Franks advanced with their typical impetuous rush. This attack swept clean through the Roman phalanx without causing many casualties. Some of the Franks then continued towards the Roman camp where they were eventually faced with the bottom half of the hollow wedge/pincer which was formed out of the dismounted Heruls. At that moment, Narses launched his trap. He quietly ordered the wings lengthened and bent forward (or turned around) into the *epikampios emprosthia* formation.[10] The mounted archers poured volley after volley of arrows crosswise from either side to the backs of the enemy. The infantry also closed its trap, the *epikampios emprosthia*. The Heruls formed the bottom and the heavy regular infantry its flanks. In this case, the *epikampios emprosthia* probably refers to the final shape of the whole formation.[11] The Franks and the Alamanni panicked when they saw the trap forming around them and felt betrayed by the Heruls. The Franks became a helpless mass of men.

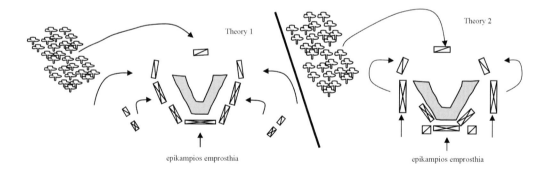

Theory 1

epikampios emprosthia

Theory 2

epikampios emprosthia

The rest of the battle resembled more butchery than battle. Of course the butchery was punctuated by periods of rest, since it was physically impossible to continue to kill for so many hours. The Franks were probably massed together so close as to have difficulty using weapons. Those Franks who had a chance of trying to fight their way through during the lulls in the fighting or in the rear of the formation were probably forced back by volleys of missiles or by cavalry charges on the vulnerable parts of their irregular groups of men. The Romans probably alternated the units doing the killing while others rested. Those Franks who managed to escape the trap were driven into the river, which made their escape even more difficult. According to Agathias, only five out of the whole army managed to escape. The rest were killed. Of the Romans, only eighty were killed. Agathias singles out Aligern the Goth and Sindual commander of the Heruls for special mention, which shows how much the Germans were appreciated for their skill and bravery in hand-to-hand combat. In fact, besides preventing the possibility of fleeing, the dismounting of the Germans in both of the major battles of Narses and their positioning in the thick of the battle shows that Narses appreciated their value in tight spots and in mêlée. This battle and its preliminaries show all the characteristic forms of what was expected from a good commander in the military treatises. Narses was a superb commander. It also shows the high standard and drill of the Romans.

Triumph of Narses and reconquest of Italy in 554–65[12]

Narses returned to Rome where he celebrated the last Triumph in Rome. He cut short the rejoicing so that the soldiers would not become soft from too much easy living. In late 554 he led his forces against the city of Compsa which was held by Ragnaris with 7,000 Goths. The siege lasted until the spring of 555 when Narses and Ragnaris held a parley. Narses refused to accept Ragnaris's demands and when the two parted Ragnaris suddenly turned around and shot an arrow. It missed its target. Narses's bodyguard responded by shooting at him. This arrow found its mark and killed Ragnaris. It is possible that this Roman version of events was just meant to cover up the assassination of Ragnaris during the peace negotiations. Now that their commander was dead the remaining Goths surrendered. Narses dispatched them to Constantinople to serve in the imperial forces against enemies in the east. All Italy south of the Po was now in Roman hands. The conquest of the north of the Po took until about 562/3.[13]

Justinian gave Narses the task of completing the reconquest as well as the reorganization and restoration of Italy as part of the Roman Empire. This meant the creation of administrative and military organizations and the rebuilding of cities, walls and public buildings. As far as the military organization is concerned, Narses's own field army became the Army of Italy while the rest of Italy was divided into duchies of *limitanei* and other forces each under its own *dux*. At this time the *duces* usually had the title of *magister militum*, but these duchies were eventually put under actual *duces*.

In about 561 Narses received a refugee from the Franks. His name was Gundovald and he was an illegitimate son of Chlotar/Lothair. He was to play an important role in the future plots hatched by the East Romans to undermine the Franks. The acceptance of foreign crown princes and royals always had a very significant role in Roman diplomacy because they could be used to foment dissent among neigbours.

The next secure information that we have of military activities took place in about 561/2. It was then that *Comes Gothorum* Widin rebelled against Narses. When Narses then marched against Widin his route was blocked at the river Attisus (Adige) by Frankish *dux* Amingus despite the fact that the Romans and Franks had a truce. Narses asked for permission to cross but Amingus did not grant it. After this Amingus joined forces with Widin, but Narses defeated both in battle. Widin was captured and sent to Constantinople, Amingus was killed. The Franks were now finally driven out of Italy altogether. It was probably in November 562 that Narses reported to Constantinople that he had captured Verona and Brixia from the Goths. However, the date is uncertain because the sources give different dates from 561 until 563. It is probable that the capture of these two cities was connected with the above revolt. In 565 or 566 the Heruls of

North Italy revolted and declared Sindual as their king with the result that the old war-gelding Narses advanced against his old comrade-in-arms and defeated and captured him in battle. Sindual was duly executed. Narses continued in his post after the death of Justinian but that account is to be found in volume 7 in this book series.

The Great Kutrigur invasion in 558–59: The battle of Chettus 559 AD[14]

The Balkans had seen an exceptionally long period of peace after Justinian managed to convince the Utigurs and Kutrigurs to fight against each other in 551 and after the episode of Ildigisal ended. This proves the effectiveness of this diplomatic ploy. In 559 Zabergan, the leader of Kutrigur Huns, crossed the frozen Danube with a huge cavalry force that included Slavs. The Romans were caught unprepared. However, according to Menander the Romans knew that Zabergan was planning an invasion and it was because of this that Justinian urged the Utigurs to attack them with a stream of embassies. The Utigur leader promised to deprive them of their horses but not to destroy them. On the other hand, it is also possible that this fragment has been misplaced and that it actually describes the situation in 551. However, there is another fragment of Menander which lends support to it, namely the one in which Justinian in 558 asked the Avars to show their usefulness to the Romans by attacking their enemies. The Avars crushed in succession Unigurs (i.e. Utigurs), Zali (a Hunnic tribe), and then the Sabirs. It would then have been the ingenuity of Justinian's policy of inciting barbarians against barbarians that resulted in the prevention of the Utigur attack against the Kutrigurs so that they were able to invade Roman territory in 559. Justinian's multiple plots clearly backfired. However, there is still another possibility which is that the urgings of Justinian to the Utigurs took place at the same time as the Kutrigur invasion, just as was the case in 551, so that the Utigurs attacked only after this campaign ended. I have included this alternative at the end of this chapter.

Zabergan divided his army into three parts. One force raided Greece and another advanced to Thrace where Zabergan divided his forces: one advanced against Thracian Chersonese while Zabergan himself advanced against Constantinople. According to Agathias, the Huns were able to pillage with impunity because Justinian in his old age neglected his army. This means that Justinian had returned to his bad habits after 552. However, this is only partially true because according to Theophanes, the Huns had first captured Sergius the *magister militum* and Edermas the *strategos*. Consequently, there had been some forces with which to engage the enemy. There exists another possible explanation for the lack of forces available to engage the enemy successfully in pitched battle or in guerrilla warfare: that is, thanks to the large scale refortification project, most of the forces that had not been sent elsewhere as reinforcements were used as garrison forces for these. This would have left too few men to engage the enemy if the emperor did not recruit them – and on the basis of the narrative sources this seems to have been the case. In short, it is very likely that most of the mobile forces of the Balkans had been sent elsewhere and no replacements had been recruited. There is no reason to suspect what Agathias states. Whatever the Romans had available for combat under Sergius and Edermas has been brushed aside with ease.

When the Huns learned that parts of the Anastasian Long Walls had collapsed as a result of earthquakes they got inside and pillaged. Zabergan advanced with only 7,000 horsemen towards Constantinople, which shows how badly the defences in the immediate vicinity had been neglected. Justinian answered by sending a hastily collected/conscripted force consisting mostly of the *scholarii*. These were badly mauled by the Huns. This explains why Agathias (5.15.1–6) criticized them so badly. According to him, they were soldiers in name only. However, the fact that they were still used for military functions shows that they were not quite as useless as one would expect from a parade corps (probably an exaggeration). The emperor also ordered that valuables were to be evacuated from the churches to the safety of the city. The rest of the *scholae* and the *protectores*, the *numeri*[15] and the whole senate[16] guarded the Theodosian Walls. In his hour of need, Justinian again asked the help of the trusted patrician Belisarius.

Belisarius rose to the occasion and collected and hastily armed every kind of horse and fighter he could lay his hands on. Most of the horses appear to have been confiscated from the horses maintained at the hippodrome. Belisarius's forces consisted of 300 first-rate heavily armed veteran troops, of the followings of some members of the senate, and of the unarmed civilians and peasants. Belisarius marched his force to the village of Chiton/ Chettus. There the unwarlike mob of civilians was used for digging a ditch for the camp. Belisarius sent spies to report to him of the activities of the Huns. Through these, Belisarius was able to formulate a plan for the battle. Since his forces consisted mostly of raw recruits/militia in small numbers, Belisarius decided to use stratagems and cunning, as was his habit. Firstly, he lit a large number of beacons to present an impression of great numbers. Secondly, for the same purpose he had his army drag felled trees behind them. Thirdly, he calmed the fire in the hearts of inexperienced men for the battle with a speech. The speech of Belisarius to his soldiers, as reported by Agathias, stressed the importance of maintaining discipline and compact formations. Furthermore, it stressed that the Romans had an advantage over the Huns in mêlée.[17]

When the scouts reported that a vanguard of 2,000 Huns was advancing towards their camp at a gallop, Belisarius led out his motley crew. He posted 200 horsemen armed with shields and javelins on either side of a woodland glen along the probable route of the Huns. The purpose of this ambushing force was to crowd the Huns in on themselves so they would be unable to use their superior numbers and bows. Belisarius ordered the massed peasants and civilians to make a lot of noise and clouds of dust to create the illusion of greater numbers. Belisarius was with his 300 elite horsemen in the centre in front of the infantry. His troopers were the spearhead of the army. Belisarius's plan worked like a dream. When the Huns galloped towards the Romans, the ambushers launched their attack. With their oblique volleys of javelins they crowded the Hunnish force together so that they were unable to use their bows or manoeuvre their horses. I would suggest that this attack with javelins was done in the same manner as the Greeks and Romans had done since antiquity, namely by sending individual files of horsemen in succession against the enemy so that each soldier threw his javelins in succession. It is probable that these horsemen consisted of the *scholarii*. When this occurred Belisarius directed his 300 men against the front of the Huns who were ripe for panic. The Huns were stunned by the shouts and dust, encircled, and faced the compact array of Belisarius's 300 cavalry while their ranks were in complete disorder. The Huns panicked and fled. Belisarius conducted the pursuit in an orderly manner thereby avoiding the risk of being surprised if the Scythians suddenly wheeled about. Four hundred Huns died in this encounter.[18]

This battle demonstrates how one could ambush the supposed masters of this tactic, the Huns. It also shows how the Romans still used the age old method of throwing javelins on horseback, retreating, and doing the same again and again as long as they had javelins left or until the enemy succumbed. And it also shows how the Huns had to employ open formations to be able to use their bows and their light cavalry tactics. When the Huns were crowded together, they became a solid target against which the Roman heavy cavalry could direct its charge, just as they could against the compact formations of the Persians.

Around about this time, one of the invading groups of the Kutrigurs advanced against the great wall of the Chersonese. Each of their attacks with ladders and siege engines was repulsed by the Romans who were led by Germanus son of Dorotheus. Subsequently, the barbarians built 150 boats out of reeds for 600 men. Germanus prepared twenty fast skiffs/trading vessels with fore-and-aft rudders against them. He manned them with rowers, helmsmen, and soldiers with breastplates, shield, bows, and halberds (reaping sickle, scythe). He moored the ships behind the wall out of sight. When the enemy boats were past the end part of the wall,[19] the ships put out to sea. The waves caused by the approaching Roman ships jolted the reed boats and threw some of their crews overboard while others had difficulty keeping steady on their feet. The Roman ships simply ran over the reed boats and broke their formation. In some cases, the Romans engaged the enemy at close quarters with their swords since they had a firm foothold in their ships, while in other cases they used their halberds to cut through the cords that bound the reeds. All the boats were sunk. A few days later, the Romans made a sortie against the besiegers. The young and impulsive Germanus led his men from the front and was struck in the thigh by an arrow, but still managed to fight until it was time to withdraw. The demoralized Huns left to join Zabergan and his forces.[20] This siege demonstrated the value of ships in naval defence. The Huns also needed the Slavs in the invading force to besiege cities.

The Hunnish threat did not end with the engagement with Belisarius. The Huns retreated to the district of Stratonikos at Dekaton and when they then learned from their scouts that the Romans had posted a great force on the Theodosian Walls of Constantinople, they went to the region of Tzouruolon, Arkadioupolis and St. Alexander of Zoupara and remained there until Easter 559. Immediately after Easter Justinian went to Selymbria, one of the praesental garrison towns in the area, and ordered everyone in the city to help in the rebuilding of the Anastasian Great Walls. Justinian stayed there until August and so did the Huns who apparently attempted to find a way to attack, but when the wall had been restored they gave this up. Justinian had also ordered double-prowed ships to be built. They were dispatched to the Danube to prevent the retreat of the barbarian invaders. When the Huns learnt of this, they sent an envoy who asked Justinian's permission to cross the Danube. Justinian agreed and sent Justin, the nephew of the emperor, to escort them away. Justin held the title of *curopalatus* (*cura palatii*) at this time and was considered superior to all other patricians in rank. Indeed he was destined to become the next emperor, Justin II, even though Justinian failed to name a successor. It is possible that Justinian induced, through skilful diplomacy, the Utigurs to destroy the Kutrigurs during their retreat, but, as noted above, it is equally possible that this diplomatic manoeuvre should be placed in a different context.

Chapter Nineteen

The Last Years of Justinian 560–65

Justinian's armed forces in 560–65[1]

In the course of his reconquests and wars Justinian had retained the basic military structures of his predecessors, but he had also made a number of modifications, the most important of which were the creation of unified command for the Long Walls of Thrace under Praetor of Thrace; the creation of the post of *quaestor exercitus* (Quaestor of the Army) to coordinate the supplying of the Danubian provinces with the taxes from the Aegean islands and parts of Asia Minor; and the creation of new field and frontier armies for Armenia, Africa, Italy and Spain. The exact organization of the Army of Spain is not known, but since a *magister militum* for Spain is recorded for 582 my educated guess is that all new field armies had their own *magister*. Another important new development for the reign of Justinian appears to be the multiplication of officers with the title *magistri* so that most of the recorded commanders of this era, even the ones with only hundreds of men, bore the title *magister militum vacans*.[2] The idea was clearly to flatter the officers with grander titles and salaries. But this was very costly and it is possible it was one of the reasons for Justinian's dearth of cash. However, if the purpose was to secure the loyalty of the officers, it was certainly a great success.

We do not know what the overall size of the army was, but on the basis of Procopius (*Wars* 6.28.10, 6.28.17), who implies that the Romans had more than 500,000 soldiers, I would suggest that Justinian had more than 500,000 men in arms at least in 540. Agathias (5.13.7) claimed that the Roman army had consisted of 645,000 men under the earlier emperors, but had dropped barely to 150,000 men by about 559. It is clear, however, that even with the larger estimates given by Procopius its quality varied greatly thanks to the niggardly policies of Justinian and thanks to the widespread corruption of the officers and civil servants.

The composition of Justinian's forces was as follows: 1) imperial bodyguards (*scholae, protectores domestici, excubitores*), mostly cavalry; 2) the regular mobile forces (the *stratiotai/comitatenses*), a mix of infantry and cavalry; 3) the Federates (*foederati*), mostly cavalry; 4) the frontier forces (the *limitanei/ripenses*), a mix of infantry and cavalry; 5) the personal bodyguards of officers and magnates (the *bucellarii*), all cavalry; 6) Naval forces; 7) the citizen militias and police forces; 8) allies (the *symmachoi*), mostly cavalry. It is also possible that the imperial bodyguards included the *optimates* under *Comes Domesticorum* which are recorded for the reign of Tiberius II, if Belisarius was their commander. It is probable that the *vigla* (*vigiles/vigiliae*) of Constantinople were commanded by *Praefectus Urbi* after the office of *Praefectus Vigilum* was abolished in 535. It is also possible that they were incorporated into the *Urbaniciani* at the same time. The Anastasian Long Walls under *Vicarius* of Thrace (after 535 Praetor) was garrisoned by a special infantry unit with the name the Walls. See the Map.

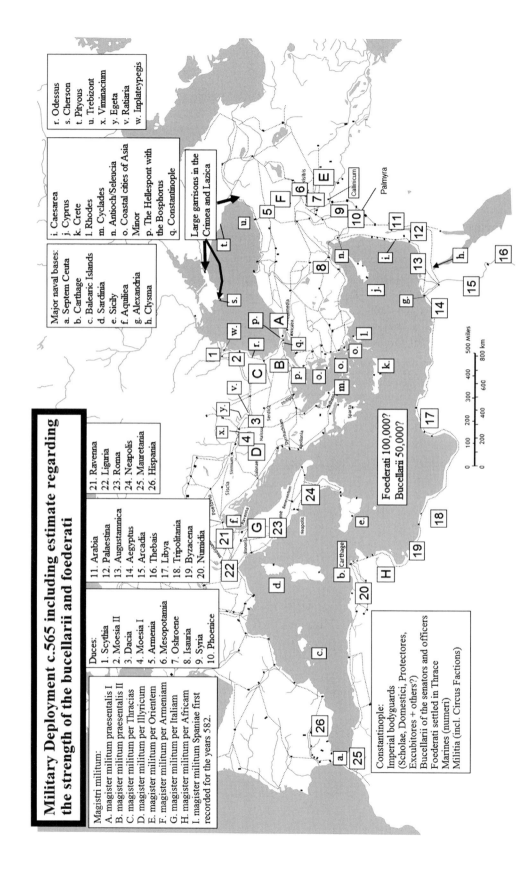

Military Deployment c.565 including estimate regarding the strength of the bucellarii and foederati

Magistri militum:
A. magister militum praesentalis I
B. magister militum praesentalis II
C. magister militum per Thracias
D. magister militum per Illyricum
E. magister militum per Orientem
F. magister militum per Armeniam
G. magister militum per Italiam
H. magister militum per Africam
I. magister militum Spaniae first recorded for the years 582.

Duces:
1. Scythia
2. Moesia II
3. Dacia
4. Moesia I
5. Armenia
6. Mesopotamia
7. Osrhoene
8. Isauria
9. Syria
10. Phoenice
11. Arabia
12. Palaestina
13. Augustamnica
14. Aegyptus
15. Arcadia
16. Thebais
17. Libya
18. Tripolitania
19. Byzacena
20. Numidia
21. Ravenna
22. Liguria
23. Roma
24. Neapolis
25. Mauretania
26. Hispania

Major naval bases:
a. Septem Ceuta
b. Carthage
c. Balearic Islands
d. Sardinia
e. Sicily
f. Aquilea
g. Alexandria
h. Clysma

i. Caesarea
j. Cyprus
k. Crete
l. Rhodes
m. Cyclades
n. Antioch/Seleucia
o. Coastal cities of Asia Minor
p. The Hellespont with the Bosphorus
q. Constantinople

r. Odessus
s. Cherson
t. Pityous
u. Trebizont
x. Viminacium
y. Egeta
v. Ratiaria
w. Inplateypegis

Large garrisons in the Crimea and Lazica

Foederati 100,000?
Bucellarii 50,000?

Constantinople:
Imperial bodyguards
(Scholae, Domestici, Protectores, Excubitores + others?)
Bucellarii of the senators and officers
Foederati settled in Thrace
Marines (numeri)
Militia (incl. Circus Factions)

With each new reconquest Justinian had modified the Roman naval organization and its dispositions so that by 565 there were naval bases in Septem Ceuta, Carthage, Balearic Islands, Sardinia, Sicily, Aquilea (and probably also elsewhere in Italy), Alexandria, Clysma, Caesarea, Cyprus, Crete, Rhodes, Cyclades, Antioch/Seleucia, coastal cities of Asia Minor, the Hellespont with the Bosporus (Isle of Tenedos, Hieron, Abydos, Lampsacus, Cyzicus), Constantinople, Odessus, Cherson, Pityous, and Trebizont. The Antioch/Seleucia fleet provided marines and sailors for the operations along the Euphrates River against the Persians. There were probably also bases along the Danube (Viminacium, Egeta, Ratiaria, Inplateypegis). It is probable that one of the praesental *magistri* acted as the supreme commander of the Roman navy, assisted by professional admirals. It is also probable that the Imperial Fleet posted at Constantinople included an elite unit of marines called the *numeri* (later *arithmoi/arithmos/noumera*), which could also be used to defend the circuit walls of Constantinople. We probably should identify this unit with the 2,000 marines accompanying Belisarius during his Vandal campaign.

When assessing the above information the readers should keep in mind that the numbers of regular forces at this time were often below their paper strengths due to the rampant corruption. Their morale and fighting quality could also be low, either for this reason or because the emperor had not paid their salaries. In short, the quality of the regular forces varied greatly. The only two groups which appear to have escaped this general lowering of quality were the Roman navy and the private retinues employed by the officers. There are some examples of poor performance by the *bucellarii*, but there is not a single instance in which the navy performed poorly, so one has to realize that wherever there were naval forces present they really posed an effective force for use against enemies. Similarly, considering the many cases in which there were not enough men to fight an enemy, especially towards the end of Justinian's reign, it is entirely possible that the size of the armed forces had dwindled from the 650,000 soldiers to 150,000 soldiers under Justinian, as claimed by Agathias (5.13.7). On the other hand, Procopius claimed that the Romans had more than 500,000 soldiers in 540. What is clear is that there was a tendency for the field armies to be smaller under Justinian than those of his predecessors or his successors just as it is clear that very small enemy forces were able to advance as far as the gates of Constantinople in 559. On the other hand, the Romans had enough men to oppose the Avars in about 562–3. The Avars fielded armies in excess of 60,000 horsemen, which means that the Romans must have had a sizable force to oppose them. This suggests that we should probably put more trust in Procopius than Agathias. Perhaps we should interpret Agathias's statement to mean that it was thanks to the policies of Justinian that the general fighting quality of the *limitanei* and other forces was so low in 559 that they did not deserve to be called soldiers? The latter was definitely the case for the *limitanei* of the period from 540 until 565 and one may assume that the same was also true of some of the *comitatenses* forces.

Justinian's twilight years[3]

As noted above, Justinian's last years were not trouble free. In Italy there was fighting under Narses, but these ended favourably for him in the conquest of the last fortresses held by the Goths and Franks so that Italy south of the Alps became really Roman in

562. In the east the peace negotiations with the Persians lasted from 557 until 562 before they were successfully concluded. In Africa the Moors revolted in December 562 so they needed to be suppressed by sending forces from Constantinople. In addition to this Justinian created his own troubles by creating religious disturbance with his Edict in support of aphthartodocetism. This schism lasted and intensified until he breathed his last.

There were other lesser troubles that he faced during his last years. On 9 September 560 there was a rumour in Constantinople that Justinian had died because he had not kept any public audience because of a headache. This resulted in a food riot with people robbing bread from the shops and bakeries. The populace was calmed when the Senate called a meeting and a prefect was sent to light the city's lights to show that the emperor was well. When he recovered Justinian launched an investigation into the cause of the rumour. Ex-prefect Eugenius accused George the curator of the Palace of Marina, and Aitherios the curator of the Palace of Antiochos, of a plot to make Theodore, son of Peter the *magister*, emperor, and that the City Prefect Gerontius was party to the plot. The accusations were found to be groundless so the emperor confiscated the property of Eugenius.

The religious fighting which resulted in deaths in Antioch also required the emperor's attention. The *Comes Orientis* was ordered to put a stop to it which he did.

On 12 October 561 there was a serious circus faction riot in Constantinople in which the Greens attacked the Blues. The emperor had to send Marinus the *Comes Excubitorum* with others to stop it, but they failed to and the rioting continued. Fires raged and many were killed. In the end the emperor used enough military force to put a stop to it.

In February 562, Justinian ordered the seven *Scholae* which had been posted at Nikomedia, Kios, Prousa, Kyzikos, Kotyakion, and Dorylaion to leave their posts and take up quarters in Thrace in Herakleia and in the surrounding cities. It is probable this is connected with the threat posed by the Huns in early 562. These had been pushed against Roman territory by the Avars who reached the Danube later in 562. The Avars had defeated the Utigurs, Kutrigurs and then the Antae in succession. Justinian's plan to use the Avars against his enemies was clearly backfiring badly. The Avars were far more dangerous than the previous Hunnic groups.

In March 562 Justinian committed a blunder which was typical of him. He abolished some of the traditional payments to the *Scholae* so they attacked their *Comes*. Justinian sent Theodore Kondocheres to appease them. He did so with a threatening speech. Did he threaten to send the *scholarii* against the Huns or Avars? This is what Justinian had done with the wealthy pampered *scholarii* in the past to make them agree to lowered salaries. These upper class primadonna soldiers were in no mood to see actual combat. I would suggest that this was indeed the reason because both Malalas and Theophanes record a Hunnic invasion for the year 562. According to them, the Huns captured Obaisipolis (text corrupt, place unknown, possibly Odessa) in about March 562 with the result that Justinian dispatched *magister militum* Marcellus, his own nephew, with a large army to rescue that city and Persis (text corrupt and place unknown). In April 562 the same Huns captured Anastasioupolis in Thrace which suggests that Marcellus was not successful in his defence of the Balkans. The identity of these Huns is not known. It is possible that they were the Kutrigurs, Slavs or Antae. The sources state clearly that the Avars were at this time unable to cross the Danube and were soon after this asking to be settled in Roman territory – a demand that they could only make if they had attacked the enemies Justinian had asked them to. I would suggest that it is probable that Justinian used the Avars against the returning Huns and that it was then after this that they approached Justin son of Germanus on the Danubian frontier where he was dispatched at about this time.

On May 562, George, the curator of the Palace of Marina, accused Zemarchos, the curator of the Palace of Placidia, of having slandered the emperor, which was always considered a crime. Both were relatives of the late empress Theodora. Zemarchos was dismissed from office and replaced by Theodore. It is easy to see that these slanders were widespread at this time. The *Secret History* of Procopius was only one of the symptoms of growing dissatisfaction towards the emperor towards the end of his life. The civic disturbances in the form of factional rioting were another.

The inability of Marcellus to protect the Danubian frontier against the abovementioned Huns is the likeliest reason for the appearance of Justin son of Germanus on this frontier zone in Menander Protector, Evagrius, and Nicephorus Callistus. Martindale in the *PLRE3* dates the arrival of Justin in the Balkans to 561, but in my opinion it is much more likely that his arrival should be dated to the period after the failure of Marcellus so that it took place in 562. Justin would also have brought reinforcements from the east at the same time to replace those lost by Marcellus. When Justin then reached the Danube, envoys from the Avars arrived to ask for land to settle. This suggests a situation in which the Avars had just before this defeated the Huns who had invaded the Balkans in 562. Justin advised Justinian to offer land in Second Pannonia where the Heruls had lived previously. The Avars stated that they were unwilling to live anywhere but in Scythia. However, Justin had in the meantime befriended Kunimon, one of the envoys. He told Justin confidentially that the Avars were planning to betray the Romans. He said that they would first present reasonable requests to lull the Romans into a false sense of security, after which they would cross the Danube, and if they managed to cross the Danube they intended to attack with their whole army. Justin informed the emperor immediately and told him to keep the envoys in Constantinople as long as possible because the Avars were unwilling to invade before their envoys returned.

Justin also posted Bonus, the commander of his household troops (*maior domus*), to guard the crossings of the Danube. Menander fails to say what Justin did himself, but one may guess that he started assembling forces from whatever sources possible. These efforts were successful: Agathias (4.22.7) states that Justin successfully prevented the crossing of the Danube.[4] The importance of the private retinues of the commander shines through once more. The *bucellarii* of the Roman officers were the real elite forces of this era. The barbarians were no match against these, and neither were the regular soldiers. The stingy policies of Justinian ensured that all too often the only effective forces available were indeed the private armies. When the Avar ambassadors finally realized that they could not obtain their objective, they received the customary gifts from Justinian. They were also allowed to buy whatever they wanted including clothing and weapons. However, the emperor sent a secret message to Justin in which he ordered him to confiscate the weapons by whatever means necessary. Justin acted as ordered. This resulted in the breaking of hostilities between the two sides. The war had already been on the horizon, but the fact that the envoys had not been released quickly despite the requests of the Khagan Baian resulted in immediate hostilities. However, as noted, the son of Germanus defeated all attempts the Avars made to cross the Danube. The dating of this conflict is difficult. It took place either in late 562 and/or in 563.

Justin was undoubtedly corrupt in his handling of the public finances but still an excellent general. The principal problem that we have in the making of any judgments regarding him or the rampant corruption of the officer cadre in general at this time is that it is clear that they all needed money for the upkeep of their private armies which they could maintain only through corrupt practices. And the maintenance of the private armies was necessary for the safety of the Empire when the emperor failed to provide adequate funds for the maintenance of the regular forces. We should not forget that the officers did not use their soldiers against their emperor but against the enemies of the empire. Therefore there were good patriotic reasons besides the personal ones for the corruption. Perhaps the best way to characterize the situation is that the corruption was a necessary evil in these times and that it was bad only when it resulted in military mutinies in situations in which the officers had stolen the salaries of the regulars, *foederati* or allies.

In October 562 there were once again riots in the capital which Justinian was required to punish. The situation became worse because there was drought in November, on top of which the north wind blew constantly so that the grain ships could not reach the capital. The arrival of good news from Italy helped: that Narses had taken Verona and Brescia. But it is clear that there is a possible connection with the rioting, drought and famine with what happened next on 25 November. There was a conspiracy to kill Justinian. The plotters were musician Ablabius, banker Marcellus, and Sergius the nephew of curator Aitherios. The plan was to assassinate Justinian when he was sitting in the *triclinium* (usually a dining room but in this case a room in the Palace) in the evening. The plotters had infiltrated the Palace staff so that there were Indians (in this case probably Ethiopians) in the office of the silentiaries in the Chapel of the Archangel and in the Harma (military quarters in the northern section of the Palace linked to the Tribunal). These were to cause disturbances so that the assassins could enter the room and kill the emperor. Ablabius had taken fifty pounds of gold from the banker Marcellus to join the conspiracy. The plot was uncovered thanks to the loose talk of Ablabius. He told of it to Eusebius, the honorary consul and *Comes Foederatum*, and also to the *logothete* John, son of Domentziolus. He told them that he and his friends intended to attack the emperor that evening. Eusebius and John informed the emperor immediately and Eusebius arrested Ablabius. A dagger was found on Ablabius. Marcellus managed to kill himself by hitting himself three times with the sword he carried. Sergius fled to a church but was dragged out and interrogated. He fingered banker Isaac/Isaacius (notably he was Belisarius's banker), banker Vitus, and Paulus *suboptio* of Belisarius. These three were arrested and interrogated by the City Prefect Procopius. They all fingered the famed patrician Belisarius himself. Justinian convened *silentium et conventus* to judge the conspirators and ordered all officeholders to be present including Patriach Eutychius, and others from the *Scholae* (they were needed in case there was trouble). The dispositions were then read aloud. Justinian confiscated Belisarius's retinue and property. He did not resist. The *Quaestor* Constantine and the secretary Julian were also suspected to have been among the plotters so they would have acted in the interest of Aitherios who also knew of the plot. Six days later the plotters were again interrogated, this time by *Comes Excubitorum* Marinos/Marinus and *magister militum* Constantianus with the result that Belisarius was held in imperial anger. It is difficult not to conclude that Belisarius had indeed been the brains behind this conspiracy of the bankers and others. Whatever the truth, the emperor proved very forgiving, as usual.

As noted before, in December 562 the Moors rose in Libya and Justinian was forced to send his nephew Marcianus there to pacify them. This he did in 563. Troubles continued in 563. Then in April the City Prefect Procopius was dismissed from office and replaced by Andrew, and then on 19 July the patrician Belisarius was restored to favour. This begs the question, had Procopius purposely forced the conspirators of 562 to finger Belisarius? We shall never know for certain. What is certain, however, is that Belisarius was restored to his positions. This does not necessarily mean that he was not guilty – Justinian was in the habit of forgiving those who had conspired against him.

There were also civil disturbances by the Greens immediately after Andrew had been appointed which resulted in the use of military force under the command of *curopalates* Justin. It was in July 563 that envoys arrived, probably from the Turks (Askel king of the Hermichiones). The Avars had been their former subjects. It is possible that Justinian wanted to use them against the Avars, but we have no information about these discussions.

March 565 was a sad month for the Empire because then the great patrician Belisarius breathed his last. His fame though will last forever.

That year saw a plethora of problems in the capital. When a member of the Green Faction was paraded before being castrated for having raped a daughter of imperial curator Akakios, the Blues hijacked the man and took him into Hagia Sofia. The emperor showed clemency and punished the Blues only by parading them for two days. But this was not all. The City Prefect Zemarchos sent some of his *commentarienses* to arrest a young man called Kaisarios in the quarter of Mazentiolus. The inhabitants of this quarter attacked the soldiers and the *commentarienses*. This resulted in serious trouble. The fighting lasted for two days and in the end Justinian had to send more soldiers and *excubitores* to the scene, but many of them were killed together with members of the Green Faction. The fighting continued as far as the Forum, the Tetrapylon and the praetorium of the City Prefect. The Blue Faction did not fight against the Greens, but they fought against the soldiers and *excubitores*. These clashed against each other in the Strategion on the same day. This was too much. Zemarchos had to go. His replacement was Julian, the *ex-magister scriniorum*, and therefore a trusted man. Julian brought more soldiers into the city so he was now able to punish the faction members, especially the Greens, very harshly. His suppression of the factions lasted for ten months. He burned, impaled, castrated and dismembered them. Julian considered the members of the factions to be murderers, robbers, bandits and pirates, and perhaps they were. Julian maintained order with an iron fist as long as was necessary. He was the man who restored complete order to the city after many years of troubles. It was high time.

On 14 November 565 the great but still very controversial emperor Flavius Petrus Sabbatius Iustinianus (Justinian) breathed his last. He was about 83 years old.

Chapter Twenty

Justinian as Emperor

Left: Copper coin depicting Justinian dated 538

source:
Diehl

Right: Copper coin depicting Justinian minted at Ravenna in 560

Justinian's legacy to posterity is mixed, but one can still say that he belongs to the great Roman emperors. It is clear that he created huge problems with his spendthrift habits, his oppression of taxpayers, his failure to pay the soldiers and by allowing rampant corruption. These problems were made worse by his religious policies. He wasted much money on church buildings and other civilian projects. Because of his economizing, the intelligence network and the postal services of the east were in such bad condition that the Romans were operating in total darkness. And it was simply idiotic to believe that the 'Endless/Eternal Peace' of 532 would really be eternal.

The numerical information that we have makes it clear that the field armies that served under Justinian were smaller than they had been before or were to be after him. Procopius and Agathias are correct in their criticism of Justinian's policies. His successors had to recruit men to bolster numbers after Justinian had left the scene.

The arrears of payments to the soldiers were the major cause of troubles mentioned repeatedly. Procopius makes it abundantly clear that these arrears resulted from Justinian's own decisions which included his inability to pay attention to any other matters than Christian doctrinal issues. On top of this it is clear that Justinian did not recruit enough men in the Balkans to replace those he had sent as reinforcements elsewhere. There would have been enough money for this had Justinian not spent so much on civilian projects. The first time the Romans could hold their own in the Balkans after ca. 539 was in the latter half of 562. It was only then that they finally managed to prevent the crossing of the Danube by the Avars. This probably resulted from troop transfers from the east after the conclusion of the Fifty Year Peace in 562. Justinian appears to have trusted that the fortifications he had built were sufficient protection so he would not need to recruit new soldiers. The fortifications indeed acted as multipliers of numbers, but they also needed a large field army to protect them.

However, he did many things right. The first was that he and his wife Theodora were courageous enough to begin the reconquest of the west against the strong opposition of both the generals and civil servants. It was the iron will of the pair that made the reconquest possible. But it was their avarice and the reduction in defence spending in the east after 532 that then made the reconquests more difficult than they should have been. The plague and the cooling of the climate were not the reasons, because the enemies of Rome were clearly able to collect large armies when the Romans were not.

Justinian deserves full credit for his masterful diplomatic policies. He was able to play one enemy against another, fool some enemies (like the Goths) into gullible inaction and form alliances with a great variety of barbarian nations. These operations dimished the need for Roman military action and often mitigated Justinian's mistakes. Furthermore, Justinian did not solely look to the possibilities offered by nearby neighbours. He dispatched expeditions to seek new lands. He dispatched monks to China to obtain the secret of silk manufacture so the Romans could start their own silk industry. He also conducted diplomatic negotiations with an Indian ruler which certainly included discussion of the bypassing of the Persians in international trade and probably also the forming of an alliance against the Persians. He was undoubtedly the best and most open-minded diplomat of his era.

Justinian was lucky that he had the services of one of the best commanders in the history of mankind to lead his armies in North Africa and Italy. This man was Belisarius.[1] It was thanks to Belisarius's great personal skills and his large retinue of bodyguards that the conquests were possible at all. By any measure, the emperor gave Belisarius far too few resources for the tasks. Even allowing for Procopius's magnification of Belisarius's achievements, it is clear that Belisarius faced huge odds in North Africa and Italy and yet he was still somehow able to overcome them with his superb strategic and tactical skills.

Justinian deserves full credit for his eye for talent. It is possible that without his great commanders, who were able to compensate for the mistakes of their emperor, we would not call Justinian great at all but rather a great disaster. Belisarius and Sittas were not the only gifted commanders he promoted to elevated positions. Others were Germanus, Mundus/Moundos, Dorotheus, Bouzes, John the nephew of Vitalian, Artabanes, John Troglita, Narses the Eunuch, and Justin son of Germanus. Of these, two have achieved ever-lasting fame: Belisarius and Narses; but Germanus should probably be added to the list. It was only the fears of Justinian and Theodora that prevented Germanus from performing greater services for the state. There is also no doubt that the dashing John Troglita, Martinus and many others deserve more appreciation than they have received. Nevertheless, Belisarius fully deserves to be called one of the most gifted military commanders of all time; and Narses fully deserves his fame for finally completing the reconquest of Italy. Narses knew that he needed enough resources and he knew how to use them to win the war decisively.

Justinian and the Roman armed forces were not responsible for the sudden collapse of fortunes under Justinian's successor Justin II. Justin II acted haughtily, refused to pay tribute/protection money and caused wars on all fronts, stubbornly ignoring the advice of civil servants and professional soldiers. Justinian would not have been that foolish; he often sought to buy peace from his enemies so he could concentrate his forces elsewhere. He was not a perfect ruler, but with the exception of Marcian and Anastasius he was much better than any of those of the previous century.

There was healthy debate in this period about the relative merits of cavalry and mounted archers vs. traditional Roman infantry tactics (in truth combined arms tactics), at least in the works of Procopius, Syrianus Magister (*Peri Strategias/Strategikes*), and *De Politica Dialogus* (see Appendix). It resulted from two things: 1) The combat performance of the Roman infantry had not been good after the 490s while their cavalry fought well; 2) Belisarius achieved amazing successes with very small forces of cavalry. This question also divided the Roman officer cadre into two schools of thought: 1) Those who neglected infantry, like Belisarius; 2) Those who sought to use combined arms tactics like Germanus, John Troglita and Narses. In spite of the successes achieved by the latter this question continued to divide officers after this era, but eventually the officers reached a consensus which is in evidence in the so-called *Strategikon* of Maurice. This treatise analysed the relative merits of each service and recommended the use of them in the most advantageous ways. The above narrative has also shown that the Roman officer cadre was divided into: 1) bold leaders like Solomon, John the Nephew of Vitalian, John Troglita and Narses who favoured aggressive decisive combat; 2) and cautious leaders like Belisarius and Martinus. Both approaches brought success when correctly applied so one cannot say that one or the other was better. It depended on the circumstances.[2]

Justinian also deserves full credit for his legislative work, the codification of laws and legal practice. It made life easier for the Romans and thereby improved their loyalty towards the authorities. This is probably his most enduring legacy, for which we all in the west can still be grateful.

In sum, in spite of his many failings Justinian fully deserves to be called great. At the time of his death the Roman Empire was the most powerful force in the Mediterranean region and beyond. What happened next will be told in *Volume Seven (565–641)* in the series *Military History of Late Rome*. It details what happened under the disastrous rule of Justin II, how the emperors Tiberius II and Maurice restored Roman fortunes, and how Roman fortunes once again resumed their fall under Phocas. Initially the Romans fared poorly under his successor Heraclius, but he managed to save the situation temporarily by winning the long Persian war, only to lose most of the fruits of his success to the Muslims. The book then details how Heraclius managed to save the Empire from complete collapse.

De scientia politica dialogus

The background

The anonymous *De scientia politica dialogus* contains important information of the state of Roman military forces during the reign of Justinian. Unfortunately we possess only a fragment of the original text, which means we lack some of the very important details that would allow us to put the text in its right context. However, enough evidence still exists for us to put this work in the same context as the texts of Procopius and Syrianus Magister. These treatises show that there existed lively discussion regarding the relative strengths and merits of cavalry vis-à-vis infantry. According to the anonymous author of *De scientia politica dialogus* (4.26, 4.38–9) the Romans had neglected their infantry forces to such an extent that the cavalry forces were the dominant arm of service. This text and Syrianus Magister promoted the traditional use of infantry, and it is clear that they were not alone in their stance: Procopius also felt compelled to defend the use of mounted archers. The advice in the treatise is presented in the form of a dialogue between Menas and Thomas. The treatise dates from the reign of Justinian, but we cannot put a precise date on it. The attribution of the treatise is also uncertain. Some have suggested that it was written by Menas, but other suggestions like Peter the Patrician have also been put forward.[1]

The training (4.1–4.53)

The text goes on to describe the proper procedure for commanders, infantry and cavalry in combat training. The commander was advised to direct the battle formation sometimes in front of the front ranks, sometimes on the wings, sometimes just behind the rear ranks (*ouragia*) and sometimes among the rear guards (*opisthofulakes*). On the basis of the way the cavalry was deployed (see Chapter One), the rear guards could mean either the reserves, if the rear was protected for example by a baggage train, or the second phalanx if the rear required additional protection. The commander was instructed to give orders to both junior and senior officers in a concise military manner. He was also advised to address each man by name.

The preparations for the day's exercises were to be completed by sunrise. The army, equipped with their weapons, took its positions and stood completely motionless. The officers were expected to be skilled at communication and also in the use of trumpets, which signalled halts, resting periods, reveille, changes of watch, when to arm and put on armour, when to march quickly or slowly, and the type of formation adopted. In training the soldiers were to be equipped as if for battle with the exception that instead of their dory-spears (*dorata*) they were to use long green staves, the tips of which had been dipped in ruddle. They were to strike each other with these and those who had marks only on their shields were considered good soldiers, those who had marks on their body or back were considered less so. This is important because it shows footmen fighting with spears against other footmen. They fought like the hoplite spearmen of the past. It shows nicely that footmen could also be used as spearmen against infantry and not only as spearmen who threw first their javelins/spears and then engaged the enemy footmen with swords as instructed by the *Strategikon*.

The *hipparchos* of the cavalry was to deploy the cavalry similarly (a rather imprecise reference, but with the *opisthofulakes* it is clear that it consisted of two lines as described in the *Strategikon*; see the attached diagrams in Chapter One) so that the horsemen were sometimes deployed on their own and at other times evenly on the wings of both phalanxes. The latter implies that the cavalry was deployed on the wings of the frontline and on the wings of the *opisthofulakes* (rear guards), which mean either reserves or the second line if the baggage train did not follow. On the other hand, it is also possible that two phalanxes actually meant the two opposing phalanxes used in training. However, the text then goes on to state in addition to the *opisthofulakes*/rear guards (could actually be interpreted to mean the second phalanx) and baggage guards (this implies that the baggage train was expected to follow) the commander was also required to detail 500 cavalry on both sides at a distance of a stade (c.184 m) to search out ambushes and traps. Mazzuchi and Bell (p.128) think that the stade in question must be a mistake for a mile (1,760 yards) and that these men should be interpreted to mean the two *banda* ('flags' of 200–400 men) that the *Strategikon* instructed to be kept a mile or two in front of the main body. In my opinion this is a mistake. These wing units should rather be interpreted to mean the outflankers and flank guards who guarded the flanks of the main formation against ambushes and traps. The vanguard which advanced in front should be considered as a separate array, which was not considered part of the battle array proper, and we are here dealing with the actual battle formation which was used in combat training. The next instructions (4.16) clarify the above. See below. These refer to two phalanxes engaging each other in mock combat. This means that we should see the cavalry array to mean the cavalry lines of the *Strategikon* (the front line and the rear guards meaning the second line with the other units accompanying it), and the infantry array to mean a single phalanx with cavalry wings outside which were extra units for its protection and which had reserves consisting of the rear guard units of both infantry and cavalry behind which was the baggage train with its guards.

The mock battle was to begin when the sun began to decline and was to last three to four hours. When the two phalanxes engaged (this means that the cavalry was divided evenly between them), the officers were instructed to order their forces as previously stated. These instructions are unfortunately lost. The general was then required to move about the battlefield as described to observe how the officers and men performed. When the mock combat had lasted three to four hours, the signal for rest was sounded. Next day at sunrise, the commander assembled the officers and soldiers for a public critical review of the training. He was instructed to reward and punish the *falaggarchai* (commanders of phalanxes) and *chiliarchoi* (*chiliarchos* was a commander of a thousand men) according to their merits. The rewards included crowns, praises, honours and gifts. The punishments included flogging, the shaving of hair, and cashiering from service.

In real war the punishments were harsher: amputation of limbs and executions. In addition, the commander was instructed to ask officers and soldiers to come forward to give evidence if someone had performed well or poorly so that these individuals could be rewarded or punished. Menas (i.e. the mouthpiece of the author) stated that these mock battles and public examinations educated the soldiers better than anything else.

The merits of infantry and cavalry: both complement each other (4.26ff.)

The author followed this with a discussion of the individual merits of each of the arms of service in which he noted that the cavalry was held in higher esteem by the military of the time while in truth the infantry should have been considered the flower of the army but so that both services complemented each other and both were equally necessary. The author drew examples from the past and also from practices of the time. The past examples that the text mentions include that the Romans sometimes placed infantry alone in the frontline so that cavalry only followed it, and that when sometimes there were 1,000 footmen there could be as few as or even fewer than 100 horsemen in the force. The contemporary examples are even more important. The author notes that the Persians at the time were using infantry forces with great effectiveness, as the events right in front of their eyes showed. This is a very important piece of evidence for the effectiveness of the Persian infantry at this time. The author claims that among the Franks only the king was allowed to stay mounted – the rest fought on foot. This is an exaggeration, but can still be considered a good generalization because the Franks relied primarily on their footmen to win their battles. All Franks could indeed fight on foot, as demonstrated by the battle of Casilinum.

The mouthpiece of the author (Menas) describes the merits of the two services as follows (4.46–4.50, tr. by Bell, 135–6):

In my opinion, the Etruscan Firminus [*unknown*] well described the infantry army properly drawn up as: 'a truly inviolate wall, a living wall, a moving wall, an intelligent wall, and iron wall, a wall not of single city, as is usual, but of the whole state'. In short, neither a lawful state nor a barbarian confederacy is known to have taken possession of, or lost territory or peoples – which are the major operations in war – or generally to have either achieved or suffered anything great without the power of infantry – except, that is, in exceptional circumstances. [*Bell, 135, notes that it has been suggested that the above quote comes originally from Frontinus's treatise.*]

The cavalry will, however, have its own place and tasks in the battle without which the infantry would not easily survive. [*The following views can also be found e.g. in Asclepiodotus 7.1, which suggests that the author may have been familiar with Asclepiodotus or with some other comparable ancient treatise.*] For example, reconnaissance and tracking the enemy, skirmishing, seizing in advance suitable places for encampment, preliminary securing of provisions and seeking out water and fodder, pursuit and follow-up of the enemy and wherever there happens to be need of cavalry assistance. Both arms combine in a complete military organization, provided, however, that the cavalry is up to its tasks. If not – and sometimes it does great damage – it itself readily both causes the horses to flee and destroys the morale of the infantry.

To guard against this, we said earlier [*Bell 136 notes: in the lost section*] that cavalrymen should display nobility and a brave spirit... It would not be unreasonable if horsemen were physically spare and neither very large nor heavy, both on account of their armament [*This implies an expectation that the horsemen were heavily armoured*] and to preserve their horses' manoeuvrability and agility where needed. [*This is actually the only treatise which refers to this very sensible instruction that I know. It would have been preferable to make certain that the horsemen were not too big for their horses to carry comfortably. It is known that this instruction was not followed, at least when the massive Maximinus Thrax served in the cavalry, and one may wonder if the above instruction is also meant to correct the period practice in which tall and heavy men were allowed to enter the cavalry.*]

Marching, encamping and misc. (4.53ff.)

The unknown author did not forget the other necessary instructions. The men were to carry all their equipment, together with five days rations, always, even when pack animals were available. The army was expected to build a fortified camp with a trench, to be filled up with water if available and with caltrops scattered around. It is probable that this practice was not always followed when discipline was lax, and because of this the instruction is included. Haircut, dress and clothes were expected to be appropriate for status and rank. Soldiers were expected to respect civilian property while in their own territory. Rations and salary should be appropriate to the level of service. The elderly were to receive a pension in retirement. The children of the fallen were to receive education and be fed at public expense and the parents of the fallen were also to be taken care of. The author also instructed the state to enrol the children of the fallen into the army so that they could receive the rations that had previously been given to their fathers. This again was expected to motivate the soldiers.

The unknown author was clearly aware of the problems facing Justinian's forces and his instructions can be considered very practical. The soldiers fought better when they were well equipped, trained and when they received just rewards, punishments and salaries and when the state took care of their children and parents. This was and is just common sense, but all too often not the case in practice.

Notes

Chapter 1

1. This chapter gives only a bare outline of these topics and follows sometimes word-by-word the introductions in *Military History of Late Rome* volumes 4 and 5. The reader is advised to consult the previous volumes in this book series for a more detailed discussion. I will include in the following text only a skeleton version of the administrative and military matters, into which I will add new fifth to sixth century material. The part dealing with military forces is based mainly on my *The Age of Hippotoxotai* (Tampere, 2004), on the appendix dealing with Urbicius and Roman tactics in *Military History of Late Rome*, Volume 5, and on the text and appendix of this book.
2. This is entirely based on Syvänne (2004) and 2013b, and on the previous *MHLR* volumes 1–5 in the series together with monographs dealing with Caracalla, Gallienus and *Britain in the Age of Arthur*.
3. It is sometimes claimed that the *scribones* (sing. *scribo*) who are for the first time mentioned in 545, were a new bodyguard unit created by Justinian, but I agree with Jones (1.658–9) that it is likelier that the *scribones* were actually officers of the *excubitores*. This means that they were probably created earlier, at the same time as the *excubitores*.
4. This interpretation has not been universally accepted because the meaning of *spithamai* varied. For a fuller analysis of the problem, see Dawson (2007), who prefers smaller alternatives. However, I do not see any compelling reasons to think that the Romans could not have used extra-large shields too because it is well-known that Goths and Persians of the period did likewise.
5. Once again see Dawson (2007) for the problems and another view. I do not consider it impossible that the length was really 3.74m because of bog finds dated to the third century (see my *Britain in the Age of Arthur*) and because the use of spears so that the first four ranks protruded in front of the front rank requires a long spear.
6. Corippus 4.489ff. 5.325ff. 6.522.

Chapter 2

1. This analysis is entirely based on Syvänne, 2004, Chapters 6.1.8, 10.4. I used Bacic, Barford, Dolukhanov and other secondary sources to back my conclusions regarding the Slavs in *The Age of Hippotoxotai*. For other sources, see *The Age of Hippotoxotai*. The most important sources for the Antae and Slavs are the *Strategikon* (11.4) and Procopius (*Wars* 7.14.21–30).
2. In fact, according to Constantine Porphyrogenitus (*De administrando imperio*, 31.71–2), the baptized Croats alone could field armies that consisted of 60,000 cavalry and 100,000 infantry. The claim of Menander the Protector (fr. 20.2.152–55) that one of the invading Slavic hordes consisted of 100,000 men also receives support from the numbers of Avars used against them. Menander (Blockley fr.21) claims that the Romans shipped 60,000 armoured Avar horsemen in double-sterned ships against the Slavs. The Slavs chose to flee to the safety of the forests. This shows that it required a major army to counter the threat of the Slavs and therefore the totals do receive additional support. The Romans were certainly in a position to make a head count of the Avars that they shipped across, although it is possible that the figure might have also included the non-combatants. It is therefore clear that the Slavs could collect massive armies when they cooperated.

3. 3,000 Slavs successful: Procop, *Wars* 7.38. See also this in the narrative.
4. The attack along the river from two directions was an old practice. See for example Ammianus 17.1.4.-10 and 30.5.13–4.
5. Based on Syvänne, 2004, Chapter 6.1.8.
6. This and the following is mostly a quote from Syvänne (2004, Chapter 6.1.8), which is based on *Strategikon* 11..4, 12.B.20–22. The use of lightly equipped troops in the difficult terrain was not new in Roman history. By simply leaving out heavy equipment one could lighten the forces. See e.g.: John Lydus 1.46, p.74.8; Zosimus 4.25.3; Eunapius fr.45.1 (Blockley ed.); the 4th century *De Rebus Bellicis* (15, 19.1); Caesar, *Civil War* 1.44.
7. Based on Syvänne (2004, Chapter 10.2) and MHLR vols. 1–5.
8. This is based on Syvänne (2004) and *Military History of Late Rome* vols. 1–5.
9. Procop. *Wars* 7.4.12 (200,000 men).
10. Based on Syvänne, 2004. See also Bachrach which was used as a secondary source for this.
11. Based on Syvänne (2004) and *Military History of Late Rome* vols.1–5.
12. Based on Syvänne, 2004 with *MHLR* vols. 1–5.

Chapter 3

1. The following analysis of the reign of Justin I is largely based on the work of A.A. Vasiliev. I depart from it only when I state it.
2. The following account is based on Vasiliev, 102ff.
3. Vasiliev, 102–8.
4. The following is based on Vasiliev, 108ff.
5. Vasiliev, 115ff., Procop. *Anek.* 7.1ff. with *MHLR* Vol.5.
6. These are my views based on Procopius's texts. The confiscation of property with various excuses was not a new phenomenon in Roman history; most emperors had done it. The same information can also be found in Evagrius 4.30ff., but Evagrius is not an independent source because he used Procopius as his primary source.
7. Vasiliev, 121ff.
8. PLRE3 suggests that he held the position of *Comes Domesticorum* before his magistracy and he was *MVM per* Thracias under Anastasius in 518 and was then exiled.
9. PLRE3; Vasiliev, 126.
10. PLRE3; Vasiliev, 126–7.
11. Vasiliev, 318ff.; PLRE2 (with sources therein) for the persons named.
12. This is based on Syvänne (2004), and Syvänne (2013). The principal sources for these were the texts of Procopius, Malalas, Marcellinus, Chronicon Paschale, Evagrius, and Theophanes. The most important secondary source was Geoffrey Greatrex's *Rome and Persia at War*, 502–32. Chippenham (1998). I used other studies as well, for which see the notes and bibliography in my studies.
13. Ilkka Syvänne, 'La Guerra Persa: 527–532', in *Desperta Ferro 18* (2013, 26–35), 26; Irfan Shahid, *Byzantium and the Arabs in the Sixth Century Volume 1 Part 1* (Washington DC, 1995), 40ff.; Malalas 17.9 in *The Chronicle of John Malalas*. A Translation by Elisabeth Jeffreys, Michael Jeffreys and Roger Scott with others (Melbourne 1986), 245–6. This contains both the Greek and Slavonic versions in a single volume.
14. Malalas 17.8 with commentary pp. 232–3 and Vasiliev, 1950, 111.
15. Malalas 17.9–10; Procop. *Anek.* 11.5.
16. Shahid, BASIC, 40ff.
17. Syvänne, La Guerra Persa, 26.
18. Procopius, *Wars* 1.11.1–39 in *Procopius in Seven Volumes*, English tr. by H.B. Dewing. Loeb 1914–1935.
19. Syvänne, La Guerra Persa, 26. A fuller discussion is in the forthcoming *Military History of Late Rome Volume 5 (457–518)*.

20. Procop. *Wars* 1.19.1ff, 1.20.1ff.; Syvänne, La Guerra Persa, 26–7; Robin (2015, 145–149); Vasiliev, 283ff. The date when the naval campaign was launched against Joseph is contested, but it is clear that it took place between 525 and 531. I prefer the former.
21. Malalas 17.16–19; Marcellinus 526.
22. This is discussed in greater detail in *MHLR5 (457–518)*, Chapter 12 Anastasius, subchapter Persian War 502–506. This book proves that the Romans achieved far greater successes against the Persians during that war than have generally been understood.
23. Lazica was the ancient Colchis, the western portion of Georgia; Iberia was the eastern portion of Georgia, so we are actually speaking about the same country with different tribes.
24. Procop. *Wars* 1.12.1ff., 1.15.18ff., *Anek.* 11.5, Syvänne, La Guerre Persa, 27.

Chapter 4
1. The following discussion adopts the same approach as in Tate (333ff.) and Moorhead (22ff.). The discussion begins with an introduction that gives a summary of the key players of Justinian's administration after which follows an analysis of Justinian's legal and administrative reforms and policies. This analysis is entirely based on PLRE2–3, Jones (226ff., but with specific details concerning the reforms also scattered elsewhere, see the index), and on the abovementioned studies. In addition, I include some observations of mine but these are clearly stated when this is the case.
2. Especially Tate, 340ff. Note also Evagrius 4.10.
3. Tate, 340ff.
4. Tate, 340ff. with PLRE2–3 for the persons named.
5. Jones, 278ff.; Moorhead, 32ff.; Tate, 423ff.
6. Malalas 18.18, 18.42; Evagrius 4.10ff. (for the building of the churches 4.30–1); Jones, 285ff.; Moorhead, 25ff.; Tate, 393ff.; Bury 2.360ff.; PLRE2 and PLRE3 with personal names of the persons named here and sources therein.
7. For this see Syvänne, *MHLR* Vol.1 with Syvänne and Maksymiuk.
8. See the discussion in Tate (365ff.) and Jones (284).

Chapter 5
1. Procop. *Wars* 1.12.9ff.; Malalas 18.10; *Chron. Pasch.* 528; Theophanes AM 6020; John of Nikiu 90.23; Syvänne, *La Guerra Persa*, 27; PLRE2 Petrus27.
2. Malalas 18.2.
3. PLRE2 Hypatius, Libelarius with the sources mentioned therein.
4. Malalas 18.6; Procop. *Wars* 6.14.33ff., 7.33.13–14.
5. Malalas 18.4–14; with Syvänne, La Guerra Persa, 27.
6. Procop. *Wars* 1.12.23–24, 1.13.1–8; Malalas 18.26; Zachariah 9.2; Discussion: Shahid, 1995, 76–9; Greatrex, 1998, 156–9; Syvänne, 2004 (Appendix Thannuris), La Guerra Persa, 28–9.
7. Malalas 18.46; Marcianus 530; Syvänne, La Guerra Persa, 28–29.
8. I have speculated about the possibility of the existence of a separate fleet for Asia Minor from the reign of Constantine the Great onwards and it is possible that these *Lykokranitai* were its marines who were billeted in Phrygia which is located inland.
9. Malalas 18.32, 18.34; Zachariah 8.5; Syvänne, La Guerra Persa, 29.
10. Syvänne, La Guerra Persa, 29.
11. Malalas 18.35, 18.54; *Chron. Pasch.* a. 530; Zachariah 9.8; John of Nikiu 93.4–9; Syvänne, La Guerra Persa, 29.
12. Malalas 18.36–44.
13. Syvänne, La Guerre Persa, 29.
14. Based on Procopius *Wars* 1.13.9ff.; Malalas 18.50; Syvänne, La Guerra Persa, 29–31; Syvänne, 2004 (Appendix Dara). My interpretation differs slightly from my previous texts.
15. Procop. *Wars* 1.15.1–17; Syvänne, 2004 (Appendix/Satala), La Guerra Persa, 31–2. For the battle of Satala see also: Greatrex, 185–190; Wass, 221–2.

16. Procop. *Wars* 1.19.1ff, 1.20.1ff.; Malalas 18.56; Syvänne, La Guarra Persa, 26–7; Robin 149–150.
17. Robin, 149–153.
18. Procop. *Wars* 1.20.1ff. A different account of the Ethiopian and Yemenite conflicts can be found in Tabari i.918ff., but Procopius's account is to be preferred here for two reasons. He was contemporary and as I have shown most likely also a well-informed professional spy.
19. Procop. *Wars* 2.3.40–41.
20. This must have taken place before autumn 547 when Abraha held a diplomatic conference in which he recognized the Romans and Aksumites as his overlords. For this conference, see Robin, 150.
21. Procop. *Wars* 1.17.1–18.56; Malalas 18.60; Zachariah 9.4; Syvänne, 2004 (Appendix/Callinicum), La Guerra Persa, 33–5; Greatrex, 1998, 193–202. Other modern accounts of the campaign and battle also in: Rubin 1.285–8; Stein 2.292; Bury 2.86–87; Shahid, 1995, 134–142, 177–179; Chassin, 35–41; Hodgkin 3.652–7; GMT Games, Cataphract; Farrokh (2017, 70). *The Peri Strategias/Strategikes* (33) warned against engaging the enemy when both had about equal numbers. This battle demonstrates the dangers well. My reconstruction of the battle (here and before) differs from other reconstructions in that it takes into account the use of the *koursores/defensores* principle and the separate deployment of allies. Kaveh Farrokh suggests on the basis of Karasulas' comments that the Persian bows were not weaker than the Roman bows and that Procopius and the *Strategikon* were both wrong in stating this. Farrokh/Karasulas suggest that the real reason was that the Hun-inspired Roman bows were more effective on the defensive when fired by foot archers while the effectiveness of the Persian archery suffered from the fact that the men were mounted. This interpretation is only partially true – the effectiveness of archery certainly suffered if the men were mounted but this was true of both the Romans and Persians. The bows used by footmen were usually more effective because their bows were indeed usually stiffer than those used by the cavalry, at least by the end of the sixth century. This was stated in the *Strategikon* which required that the bows of the Roman cavalry were to be on the weaker side. However, in the context of his descriptions of the battles Procopius does not differentiate the bows used by the infantry and cavalry, with the implication that they were probably roughly as stiff during his day. This means that there was a general change in the preferences between Procopius's day and by the time the *Strategikon* was written in the 590s. The latter text required horsemen also to learn the Persian style of archery, which required weaker bows, but apparently in the case of the Romans this did not entail the adoption of the weaker Persian bow but only a weaker version of the Roman bow. Therefore the references to the general weakness of the Persian bows vis-à-vis the Roman bows in Procopius and the *Strategikon* do not mean the difference between the bows of the footmen and cavalry but the general weakness of the Persian bows in comparison with the Roman bows. Both sources were certainly in a position to know the facts because the Roman army was full of deserters from the Persian forces. It is therefore absolutely clear that the Romans used stiffer bows as stated by Procopius and the *Strategikon*. See Syvänne, 2004, 44–5. Note, however, that the fact that the *Strategikon* required the Roman cavalry also to learn Persian archery technique means that its author (likely to be Maurice) appreciated the Persian archery technique so highly that he wanted his men to learn it too. It should also be noted that the bows were always constructed to take into account the height, length of arms and muscular strength of its user. This means that the Persian forces included specialist archers whose bows were stiffer than the average stiffness of the Roman bow and also that the Roman archers included archers that had weaker bows than the average in Roman forces. The statements of Procopius and the *Strategikon* should therefore be seen to mean only the average stiffness of the bows of the Romans and Persians. The Romans therefore had on average more muscular men with stiffer bows. It is probable that this resulted from two things: 1) the Romans selected their recruits on the basis of their physical characteristics while the Persians followed feudal practices; 2) the Romans trained their men harder.

22. Malalas 18.60.
23. Procop. *Wars* 1.18.51ff., 1.21.1ff.; Malalas 18.60.
24. Malalas 18.61; Procop. *Wars* 1.21.1ff.; Zachariah 9.5–6.
25. Malalas fails to state who of the Abgars he was. He could be the contemporary of Jesus Christ or one of his successors. Abgars were kings of Oshroene with capital at Edessa. For the role of Edessa and Oshroene in Roman times, see also Syvänne, *Caracalla*.
26. Procop. *Wars* 1.21.1ff.; Malalas 18.60–63.
27. Malalas 18.64.
28. Malalas 18.61–66 with Syvänne, 2004 (the text follows this closely) and La Guerra Persa, 35.
29. Procop. *Wars* 1.21.1–28; Malalas 18.65–70; Zachariah 9.6; REF2, 94–5; Syvänne (2004 the text follows this closely; La Persa, 35); Greatrex, 1998, 209–11.
30. Shahid BASIC 185ff.; PLRE2/Summus.
31. Malalas 18.67.
32. Procop. *Wars* 1.22.1ff.; Syvänne, La Guerra Persa, 35.
33. For the Nika riot see: Malalas 18.71; Procopius *Wars* 1.24; John Lydus *De Mag.* 3.70; Marcellinus a.532; Theophanes AM 6024; *Chronicon Paschale* a.530 and Whitby tr, 112–27, esp. 119–20; Cameron, Alan, 1976, 278–80; Bury 2.39ff.. The following account is mostly based on the interpretation of Bury.
34. Procop. *Anek.* 24.12–29, 30.1ff.; PLRE3; Jones, 284–5. Unlike Jones, I have here accepted Procopius's claim that Justinian stopped the paying of donatives every four years. Procopius was certainly in a position to know that. The negative image of John the Cappadocian is confirmed by John the Lydus (Bandy's ed., see Index John the Cappadocian and Cappadocian). He was indeed utterly corrupt and a greedy drunkard and glutton with an endless appetite for sex.
35. Jones, 280ff.
36. For the administrative changes in the areas facing the Arabs, see also Shahid BASIC, 196ff.
37. Shahid BASIC, 182–5; PLRE3/Aratius.
38. Marcellinus a.536; Shahid BASIC, 194ff.

Chapter 6
1. Procop. *Wars* 3.9.1ff.
2. Procop. *Wars* 3.10.1ff.
3. The soldiers had also been looking forward to a time of rest after the war with Persia had ended.
4. *Karabos* and *karabion* meant a boat/vessel with the implication that the fleet was named after the Greek word for ship. One may make the educated guess that the ships in question would have been cataphracted (i.e. decked) just like the single-banked *dromones* of Procopius; *karabos* also meant a beetle and a prickly crab.
5. For the *bucellarii* and their organization, see Jones, 667.
6. The following is based on Syvänne, 2004, Chapter 10.3.2; Victor of Vita 1.2; Proc., *Wars* 3.5.8–9, 3.5.18–22, 3.8.24ff., 3.9.1–3, 3.10.5, 3.14.2, 3.19.7, 4.6.5ff., 4.10.29; Proc. Secret, 18.6; Pringle, 10–11, 16–22.
7. Based on: Procop. *Wars* 3.8.25ff., 4.11.1–13.45, 4.19.5–28.52; Corippus 1.522–578, 2.1–161; *Strategikon* 6.3; Syvänne, 2000, 34ff.; Syvänne, 2004, Chapter 10.5.1; Pringle, 16–17.
8. Procop. *Wars* 3.12.1ff.
9. Procop. *Wars* 3.16.1ff.
10. Procop. *Wars* 3.17.1ff. with Syvänne, 2004. Other historians have reconstructed the battle slightly differently. Those interested in these are advised to read e.g. Hughes (90–97) and Decker (184–188). See also Jacobsen (2012, 203–8). I have based the topography of the accompanying map on his map.
11. Procop. *Wars* 3.20.1ff.
12. Procop. *Wars* 4.1.12ff. This chapter is mostly a direct quote from my doctoral dissertation *The Age of Hippotoxotai* (Tampere 2004) and contains only small changes.

13. Procop. *Wars* 3.25.1–4.8.25 (campaign), 4.2.1–3.28 (battle) esp. 4.3.1ff. Very short discussion of the battle also in Chassin, 76–77; Pringle, 21; Oman 1.29–30. For a different view of how the forces were deployed, see Jacobsen (2012, 208–11). See also The *GMT Games Cataphract* (incorrect reconstruction but still fun to play). The Roman soldiers showed their superstitious nature by observing signs that caused nightmares in sleep (Procop. *Wars* 4.2.5–7). Consequently the soldiers suffered from pre-battle anxieties and stress.

14. Procop. *Wars* 4.3.8–9. If one equates *lochos* with *moira* one could have as many as 2,000 men per *lochos*, but Procopius (Wars, 3.5.18–21) equated the Vandal *lochos* with a 1,000-man chiliarchy in exact terms.

15. Procop. *Wars* 4.3.1–7, 10–13. Pringle (p.51) has listed all of the commanders with their probable forces.

16. Dorotheus had already died during the sea voyage and Solomon had been sent as messenger back to Byzantium. It is obvious that their forces would have received new commanders and that the Federates would also have been given a new overall commander. Consequently their forces would have been among those left unmentioned.

17. The commander of the left wing was probably Martinus and the commander of the right Pappus.

18. Procop. *Wars* 4.3.10–13. This indicates that some of the bodyguard officers and soldiers remained behind in reserve. It is also notable that the procedure of attack in this case closely resembled the training ground drills in *Strategikon* 6 where the *koursores* could be sent forward singly or in groups.

19. Oman's (29–30) interpretation of the final phase of the battle was that the centres were locked in combat for a while before the Roman wings advanced and attacked the outflanking wings of the Vandals that had by then started to outflank the Roman centre. Although not mentioned by the sources, this is a plausible suggestion and has been included in the diagram.

20. The following is based on Procop. *Wars* 4.4.14ff.

21. Fuller discussion in *MHLR* Vol.1 after Procop. *Wars* 6.14.1ff.

22. Procop. *Wars* 4.9.1ff. with PLRE3.

Chapter 7

1. Procop. *Wars* 4.10.1ff.

2. Procop. *Wars* 4.11.14ff. with Syvänne, 2004 Appendix. At the next battle at Mt. Bourgaon Solomon also had infantry.

3. Based on Procop. *Wars* 4.12.1ff. and Syvänne, 2004 Appendix with some corrections and changes included here.

4. Procop. *Wars* 4.13.1ff. with Syvänne, 2004 Appendix.

5. This and the above similar tactic of posting cavalry inside a narrow pass implies that this was standard practice for the Roman cavalry when it wanted to remain in hiding and also when the aim was to make certain that it could not be outflanked.

6. Procop. *Wars* 4.17.8.

Chapter 8

1. Malalas 18.6; Procop. *Wars* 6.14.33ff., 7.33.13–14.

2. John was an ex-consul and grandson of John the Scythian. See PLRE3 with *MHLR* Vol.5.

3. Malalas 18.13–14; Nikiu 90.61–9; Theophanes AM 6020; Procop. *Anek* 25.6; Syvänne, 2004; PLRE3 for the people.

4. Malalas 18.21; PLRE3; Syvänne, 2004.

5. Marcellinus a.530; Malalas 18.46; Theophanes AM6032; PLRE3.

6. In the meantime the Romans also defeated other Hunnic groupings in the east: Sabirs invaded Armenia and Anatolia and Dorotheus, Master of Armenia, chased them out in 531 (Malalas 18.70); In 532, Bessas defeated several Hunnic raiding parties in Armenia (Zachariah 9.6). It

is clear that the Huns were no match for the Romans when the latter had adequate numbers under able leaders. The same truth held both in the Balkans and east.

7. Malalas 18.6; Procop. *Wars* 6.13.17ff., 6.14.1ff (esp.6.14.33ff.), 7.33.13ff. See the narrative for instances of different groups of Heruls serving throughout the Empire.
8. For the reforms, see Jones (280 with other references in the index) and Tate (728).
9. Tate, 728–9; Curta, 150ff.
10. For the reforms, see Jones, 280 with other references in the index.
11. Marcellinus a.539, Jordanes Rom. 387.
12. Procop. *Wars* 2.4.1ff.

Chapter 9

1. Procop. *Wars* 5.2.1ff.
2. For example, she claimed that the Romans were in debt to her and not the other way around, because she had given the Romans a market in Sicily when they had advanced against the Vandals, and that the Romans would not have been able to conquer Libya without the supplies bought there and especially without the horses that they bought from Sicily. This sounds convincing but in truth it is only partially true, because the Romans could have sailed from Egypt along the coast, but obviously they would have lost the element of surprise with that strategy.
3. Procop. *Wars* 5.5.1ff.; Marcellinus a.535ff.
4. Note also Frontinus 3.9.8.
5. This and the following is based on Procop. *Anek*. 1.11ff.
6. Procop. Wars 5.7.26ff.
7. At the time when *Notitia Dignitatum* was written, *magister militum per Illyricum* had two *vexillationes comitatenses* (2 x 500 = 1,000), one palatine legion (ca. 2,000), six *auxilia palatina* units (ca. 6,000), eight *comitatenses* legions (ca. 16,000) and nine pseudo-comitatenses legions (ca. 18,000) for a total of 1,000 cavalry, 36,200 legionary infantry and 6,000 'medium infantry' consisting of *auxilia palatina* units. The legions counted as 2,000 men, *auxilia palatina* as 1,000 men and *vexillatio* as 500 men. In practice the legions could have as few as 1,000 men, the *auxilia* as few as 500 and the *vexillationes* as few as 200–400 men. However, since the spy saw myriads of men on both land and sea it is safer to assume that the figures would have been closer to their paper strengths.
8. If we assume that there were about 100 galleys, then these could easily have had 10,000 to 20,000 men on board depending on the size of the ship.
9. Procop. *Wars* 5.8.1ff.; Marcellinus a.536; Jord. *Get*. 311, *Rom*. 370; Zachariah 9.18; Paulus Diac. *Hist. Rom.* 16.16; Zonaras 14.8 (p.281); *Liber Pontificalis* 60; Syvänne, 2004 (Appendix/ Naples).
10. Procop. *Wars* 7.16.30.
11. For Roman spies, see Syvänne 2016 with Procopius (*Anecdota* 30.1ff., esp. 30.12–14).
12. This was not a new phenomenon. In 310, Constantine the Great's army had also miscalculated the height of the walls of Marseille and used ladders which were too short. Miscalculations were always possible. See Panegyric 6.19.5–6 together with *MHLR* Vol.1, 240–241.
13. The Goths had shown great religious tolerance towards the Jews. For example, Theoderic the Great had ordered the Italians to rebuild the synagogues of Ravenna, which they had burned. See Anon. Valesianus 81–2.
14. Procop. *Wars* 5.14.1ff.; Zachariah 9.18; Lib. Pont. 60; , Marc. a.536; Jord. *Rom*. 373, *Get*. 311; Paulus Diac. 16.17; Zonaras 14.8 (p.281); Nicephorus Callistus 17.13; Syvänne, 2004.
15. Belisarius had only 5,000 regulars when the Goths besieged Rome, but before this he had dispatched soldiers to other locations, which means that he had more than 5,000 men when he approached Rome.
16. PLRE 2–3 with MHLR Vol.5.

17. Procop. *Wars* 5 16.1ff. with Syvänne 2004.
18. Jacobsen (2009, 103) accepts this figure, as I do.
19. Syvänne, 2004: 'The Pannonian Suevi consisted of infantry (Jordanes; Get. 261). Note also Jordanes, Get. 277–9; Paul, 1.21, 2.26. For a good summary of the history and siege skills of the fragmented nation of the Suevi in particular in Spain see McCotter, 1995, 235–44; Thompson, 1982, 152–87. This instance was not noted by either of them.'
20. Procop. *Wars* 5.16.12ff. with Syvänne, 2004.
21. Procop. *Wars* 5.16.8–18, 6.11.1, 6.30.2 with Syvänne 2004.
22. Procop. *Wars* 5.17.1ff. with Syvänne, 2004. For the dates, see PLRE3/Belisarius 1, p.198.
23. This and following Procop. *Wars* 5.18.1ff. with Syvänne, 2004.
24. Procop *Wars* 5.18.13. This shows that their shield was something more than a mere target shield attached to the shoulder as is all too often still assumed even after I dispelled this myth in 2004. The target on the shoulder – if even used and I doubt that it was – was only used as part of the armour. The shield attached to the shoulder was a regular small round cavalry shield which was just tied to the shoulder with straps when the horseman used his bow and then when he engaged the enemy in mêlée he loosened the straps and used it like a regular shield.
25. Procop. *Wars* 5.18.1–29.
26. Procop. *Wars* 5.18.34ff.; Marc. a.537; with Syvänne, 2004.
27. For those interested in this question, check out the discussion related to it on my Facebook page. Note that even before I stated the above, Tim Newark and Angus McBride (Plates) also accepted the possibility that the Goths could have used cylindrical and rectangular *scuta* together with the oblong *scuta* at this siege.
28. It is strange that Procopius fails to name the friend. This is why I suspect that it may have been Procopius himself; that he did not name the person was a sign of humility.
29. Jones, 283.
30. Procop. *Wars* 5.25.1ff. with Syvänne, 2004.
31. Sources collected in PLRE3/Belisarius 1, pp.199–200.
32. Procop. *Wars* 5.27.1ff.; Marc. a.537; with Syvänne, 2004.
33. The Romans exploited the techniques of the Scythian Drill and hunting *Strategikon* 6.1; 12.D. See also *MHLR* Vol.2, 44–7.
34. Procop. *Wars* 5.27.15–23. Belisarius's explanation of the events in 5.27.24–29. Note also the role of Roman populace.
35. Procop. *Wars* 5.28.1.ff.; Marc. a.537; with Syvänne, 2004. See also Boss (14–15) and Hodgkin (4.217–228) who I used as secondary sources for this battle in 2004. Note, however, that my reconstruction differs slightly from my earlier study. Jacobsen (2009, 124ff.) provides a good narrative of the events. However, he places the fighting far too close to the walls of the city. Ian Hughes (144–9), however, does place the battle to take place far enough from the walls.
36. The use of two javelins simultaneously was obviously some sort of special form of martial arts about which we know little except that it was still used also in later times as can be seen from Skylitzes folio 55r which depicts Theophilos in the ninth century checking the fighting skills of a Hagarene (Muslim) prisoner wielding two spears simultaneously on horseback.
37. Procop. *Wars* 6.1.1ff. with Syvänne, 2004.
38. See Volume I in this series for an example of the Alamanni using this tactic against the Roman cataphracts under Julian at the Battle of Strasbourg/Argentorate in 357.
39. It is clear that this description shows Roman cavalry, which included at least the *bucellarii* of Belisarius, together with the Massagetae Huns of Constantinus, using so-called irregular *droungos* formations in a fluid cavalry fight in which various different groups advanced and retreated throughout the battlefield on their own initiative. There is no doubt that the *bucellarii*, which included Huns, and the mercenary Huns were masters at this kind of fighting.
40. Procop. *Wars* 6.2.1ff. with Syvänne, 2004; Boss, 16; Hodgkin 4.233–6.

41. This may imply that Bochas had some sort of shoulder pieces possibly together with some sort of cover for the arm of the kind that the Romans used later e.g. during the so-called Middle Byzantine era. During that time, the metal shoulder pieces also had metal projections to protect the arm which were decorated to look like pteruges. The Romans definitely used metal plates to protect the shoulder at this time, but I am uncertain whether or not they used the metal projections from it that were fashioned to look like pteruges. It is definitely possible because period works of art depict shoulder pieces like this, but it is quite possible that they were actually meant to depict real pteruges.
42. Procop. *Wars* 6.3.1.ff. with Syvänne, 2004.
43. Procop. *Wars* 6.4.1ff. with Syvänne, 2004.
44. Proven by two things: the arrowhead was in Arzen's neck; neither of the arrows which hit the area between his right eye and his nose was fatal.
45. Procop. W*ars* 6.7.12ff. with Syvänne, 2004.
46. Hughes, *Belisarius*, 154–5; PLRE3/Belisarius 1, p.202.
47. PLRE3/Belisarius *1*, p.202.
48. Procop. *Wars* 6 9.1ff. with Syvänne, 2004.
49. Procop. *Wars* 6.10.1ff.; Jordanes *Get.* 312; *Lib. Pon.* 60; with Syvänne, 2004.
50. Procop. *Wars* 6.11.1ff.
51. Syvänne 2004 (Appendix/Ariminum).
52. Procop. *Wars* 6.14.33ff.
53. Syvänne 2004: 'A category of its own are the victories without a battle, which were achieved through manoeuvering and stratagems. The following two examples show how Belisarius in particular was able to achieve successes through the use of his intellect. There were also other means like the use of diplomacy that were used to achieve positive results. However, the following examples show how the military could be used without a fight. Sun Tzu 3.2 (c.500 B.C): "Subjugating the enemy without fighting is the true pinnacle of excellence" Tr. by Sawayer, 161. Belisarius' defensive strategy in 531 that ended in the battle of Callinicum should also belong to this category, but the will of the soldiers and officers to fight forced his hand on that occasion. In essence, the Italian campaigns of Belisarius as a whole belong to this category. He fought no true great pitched battles to achieve the conquest.'
54. Procop. *Wars* 6.18.1ff.; Marc. a.538–539; with Syvänne, 2004.
55. Procop. *Wars* 6.22.9ff. with Syvänne, 2004.
56. Procop. Wars 7.33.1ff. (esp. 7.33.8ff.); Marcellinus a.539; Jordanes *Rom.* 387. See also the Chapter on Balkans.
57. Procop. *Wars* 6.23.1ff. with Syvänne, 2004. The narrative follows word for word that in Syvänne, 2004.
58. Osimo 900 feet above the sea: Hodgkin 4.352.
59. Military theory divided the commands into three categories: vocal, musical and signs.
60. Procop. *Wars* 6.28.1ff.; Agnellus, *Lib. Pont. Eccl. Rav.* 62; With Syvänne, 2004.
61. Note e.g. Procop. *Wars* 7.1.18–20. Jacobsen (2009, 187ff.) accepts Procopius's version in which Belisarius postponed the swearing of an oath. As noted, in my opinion we are here dealing with Procopius's attempt to hide the oathbreaking of the hero of the narrative. However, in other respects I fully agree with Jacobsen's excellent analysis.
62. Procop. *Anek.* 1.31ff. with Dewing's quote of John of Ephesus (in *Anek.* xvii–xviii).
63. Procop. *Wars* 7.1.1ff.; Evagrius 4.21; Marc. a.540. For a list of other sources, see PLRE3/Belisarius 1, p.207.

Chapter 10

1. Procop. *Wars.* 4.14.1ff.
2. Procop. *Wars* 4.15.1ff.; Jordanes *Rom.* 369–70.
3. Procop. *Wars* 4.15.30ff.

4. Procop. *Wars* 4.16.1ff. Germanus was cousin of Justinian rather than his nephew as claimed in this section. See Martindale PLRE2/Germanus4.
5. It is more or less likely that Procopius has preserved here the real sentiments of Germanus' words. He was certainly in a position to know what words were used in the propaganda.
6. Procop. *Wars* 4.17.1ff.; Corippus 3.314ff.; with Syvänne, 2004 (Appendix/Scalae). The battle in *Wars* 4.17.1–35. The campaign as a whole in 4.16.1–17.35. For a slightly different reconstruction, see Jacobsen, 2009, 194–5.
7. Unfortunately it is not clear whether the unit order was scattered or whether the formation consisted of scattered units of close order troops or whether both the order and formation were scattered. Regardless, the Heruls were still able to rout their opposition.
8. 8,000 rebels, 1,000 Vandals and slaves: Proc. *Wars* 4.15.2–4.
9. After defeating Stotzas's cavalry, Germanus went straight for the rebels' camp where his men encountered those left behind (Wars 4.17.24–30).
10. Procop. *Wars* 4.18.1ff.
11. Procop. *Wars* 4.19.5ff. with Syvänne, 2004.
12. The following is based on Procop. *Wars* 19.20.1ff.
13. Procop. Wars 4.21.1ff.; Corippus, Ioh. 3.343ff.; Victor Tonnensis a.543–4; with Syvänne, 2004.
14. Procop. *Wars* 4.22.1ff.; Corippus 4.1ff.
15. Procop. *Wars* 4.24.1ff.; Corippus 4.81ff.
16. Procop. *Wars* 4.24.8ff. Corippus 4.136ff.; Victor Tonnensis a.545, Syvänne, 2004; Pringle, 31–32. Pringle does not give any details, but has an excellent overview of the campaign and events in general.
17. In other words, I do not agree with Pringle that Corippus would have described two separate battles that took place at Siccaveneria and then at Thacia, but rather a single battle.
18. Procop. *Wars* 4.25.1ff.; Corippus 4.219ff.
19. The number of gates in Corippus 1.426–7.
20. This is actually not surprising because Cusina had a Roman/Latin mother. See Corippus 5.451–2, 8.271.
21. In other words, I agree with Shea (p.14) that Athanasius was the prime mover and that Antalas also took part in the plot.
22. Procop. *Wars* 4.27. 23ff.; Victor Tonnensis a.546; Syvänne, 2004.
23. In this case, the word *moira* (2,000–3,000 men) may have been used in its technical sense.
24. Procop. *Wars* 4.27.11–19, 4.28.1ff.; Corippus 4.219ff.

Chapter 11
1. Based on Tate (637ff.) and Jones (287ff.).
2. Obviously Procopius wanted to flatter Justinian with his book *On Buildings*, but there is enough archaeological evidence to prove that the account of Procopius is by and large correct.
3. Procop. *Wars* 1.23.1ff., Malalas 18.68–69; Tabari i.893–4. The dating of Procopius is to be preferred in this case.
4. A good summary of the reforms is provided by Tabari i. 894ff. and Kaveh Farrokh (2007, 228ff.; 2017, 23ff.). See also Syvänne MHLR Vol.1 for the information regarding the earlier division of the Persian Empire into four defensive zones and further details concerning the tactics and equipment.
5. Procop. *Wars* 1.26.1ff.
6. This and the following account is based on Procop. *Wars* 2.1.1ff.
7. I.e. the *Strata Diocletiana* (see MHLR Vol.1).
8. For Summus and this incident, see PLRE2 with Shahid BASIC, 192ff.
9. This and the following is based on Procop. *Wars* 2.2.1ff.
10. Procop. *Wars* 2.2.1ff., 2.15.1ff.; PLRE2 Petrus 27
11. The following is based on Procop. *Wars* 2.3.1ff. with Syvänne 2004 and especially on the superb analysis of Procopius's text and Armenian revolt by Armen Ayvazyan, 28–105.

12. In my opinion it is possible that these sons of Perozes actually belonged to the Iberian nobility who were originally from Persia. See MHLR Vol.1.
13. Procop. *Wars* 2.3.8ff. with Syvänne 2004 and especially on the superb analysis of Procopius's text and battle by Ayvazyan, 28–105.
14. The identification of Oinochalakon with Avnik is by Ayvazyan. The rest of the comments are mine.
15. Based on Procop. *Wars* 2.3.28ff. and Ayvazyan, 90–94.
16. This is my analysis based on Procopius (*Wars* 2.3.32ff.) with the reference to the naval expeditions sent to the oceans at 2.3.43. The reference to the heavens is simply poetic hyperbole. The reference to the annexation of Himyar and the Red Sea is also important because it shows that Justinian extended his efforts further than usually assumed. The previously mentioned operations with the Ethiopians and the naval expeditions in the oceans are likely to refer to the operations to secure the sea routes to India and Africa.
17. Procop. *Wars* 2.3.54ff.
18. Procop. *Wars* 3.13.22ff. (esp. 3.14.5), 5.4.22f.
19. For the methods used by Caracalla, see my biography of him (Ilkka Syvänne, *Caracalla: A Military Biography*, Pen & Sword, Barnsley 2017).
20. Procop. *Wars* 2.4.14ff. with the PLRE3 for the persons named.
21. See Procopius, *De. Aed./Buildings* 2.14ff. for a description of how the city was built under Anastasius and then strengthened under Justinian.
22. Procop. *Wars* 2.13.16ff., 2.14.9; *De Aed./Buildings* 2.1.4ff.; with Syvänne, 2004.
23. The building of this city is mentioned by almost all subsequent Muslim historians that pay attention to the reign of Khosrov/Chosroes/Khusraw. A good example is the account of al-Isfahani translated by Hoyland (p.71).
24. Procop. *Wars* 1.24.11ff., 1.25.1ff.; Marcellinus a.543–544 (one year too late). For the similarly very negative view of John the Cappadocian, see John the Lydus (Bandy's ed., see Index John the Cappadocian and Cappadocian).
25. Procop. *Anek.* 1.36ff., 2.1.1ff.
26. Jones (294ff.); Tate (662ff.).
27. Procop. *Wars* 2.14.8ff. with Marcellinus a.541.1, Syvänne, 2004 and PLRE3.
28. Procop. *Wars* 2.18.1ff.; Corippus 1.58–69 with Syvänne, 2004 (sometimes word for word).
29. Procop. *Wars* 2.19.1ff.
30. Procop. *Wars.* 2.17.1ff., *Wars* 2.19.47ff., 8.4.1ff., *Anek.* 2.26ff. with the PLRE3.
31. The following is based on Procopius Wars 2.20.1–34. *Anek.* 3.30ff., 4.1.-31; Syvänne, 2004 (appendices).
32. Procopius, Wars 2.22.1ff.
33. Procop. *Wars* 2.14.1ff. with Syvänne, 2004 (Appendix/Anglon).
34. There is a strong probability that Procopius has exaggerated the disorder. It is quite likely that Peter and his men actually acted as a vanguard for the main army.
35. This battle appears to be a cavalry battle, because only cavalry action is described and the Romans were in open terrain while the Persians occupied rough terrain. Note also Procopius's (*Wars* 2.25.1–2) comments on the abundance of water, healthy climate and plains suitable for riding. However, the presence of infantry among the baggage train is still probable. See also Bury 2.107–9 and Farrokh (2017, 70–1).
36. Isaac was the local commander at Citharazon, and Narses arrived in the company of Valerianus, who was the *magister* of Armenia.
37. Procop. *Wars* 2.26.1ff., 8.14.35ff. Evagrius 4.27; Bury 2.109–113; with Syvänne, 2004 (Appendix/Siege of Edessa 1). The text follows Syvänne sometimes word for word.
38. Note also the similarities in the Roman and Persian methods. For example the Persian camp was placed 7 stades (c.1.3 km) from the city.
39. Procop. *Wars* 2.28.1ff.

Chapter 12

1. Procop. *Wars* 7.1.22ff. with Syvänne, 2004.
2. Procop. *Wars* 7.3.1ff (campaign), 7.4.1–32 (battle) with Syvänne 2004. The text follows Syvänne 2004 very closely. The source for this battle is Procopius. He was not probably present in person but was in position to know the facts.
3. That Constantianus subsequently informed the emperor that he was unable to hold out against the Goths (confirmed by other commanders) shows that he must have been commander-in-chief. As a result, Belisarius was sent again into Italy. See Procop. *Wars* 7.9.5–10.1 with Syvänne, 2004. Bury (2.229–30) held the opposite view. According to him the Romans used a divided command structure.
4. Note how Belisarius in contrast had sent his army against the withdrawing Goths when the latter began to withdraw from the front of Rome towards Ravenna in March 538 and less than half of their force remained behind. See Procop. *Wars* 6.10.12–20.
5. Procop. *Wars* 7.5.1ff.; Marc. a.542 with Syvänne 2004. The text follows Syvänne 2004 often word for word.
6. Procop. *Wars* 7.6.1ff. with Syvänne 2004. The text follows Syvänne 2004 often word for word.
7. Naval blockade: Procop. *Wars* 7.13.5–7.
8. Procop. *Wars* 7.33.1ff., (esp. 7.33.10ff.). See also the Chapter on Balkans.

Chapter 13

1. Procop. *Wars* 7.10.1ff., 7.12.3ff.
2. Procop. *Wars* 7.11.11–16, 7.13.21ff., 7.14.6
3. Procop. *Wars* 7.11.37ff. 7.12.1ff.; Marcellinus a545.3.
4. Procop. *Anek.* 5.4ff.
5. Campaign and siege: Procop. *Wars* 7.12.1–24.34; Marc. a547; Jordanes, *Romana* 380–1; Bury 2.236–44; and especially Syvänne, 2004 (Appendix/Rome).
6. This figure can be compared with the campaign force dispatched by Anastasius against Italy in 508 (Marcellinus Comes 1 Sept. 507 – 31 Aug. 508 with Syvänne *MHLR Vol.5*). He dispatched *Comes Domesticorum* Romanus and *Comes Scholariorum* Rusticus with 100 armed ships and 100 dromons with 8,000 armed soldiers (*militum armatorum*). This means that the 200 warships carried a minimum of 8,000 soldiers plus their crews of rowers which could also be required to fight.
7. Procopius (*Wars* 7.21.5). He put into the mouth of Totila the claim that after the siege the Goths had defeated over 20,000 Romans. However, as noted there clearly were other troops involved besides these, but these were needed to man the ships and would have therefore been unavailable for land combat.
8. Jordanes *Rom.* 380; Marc. a.547; PLRE3.
9. The following exploits of John, nephew of Vitalian: Procop. *Wars* 7.18.11–29, *Anek.* 5.7–15; Syvänne, 2004 (Appendix/Rome).
10. Procop. *Anek.* 5.7ff.
11. Ammianus 21.12.9: Earlier example at the siege of Aquileia in 361 (towers placed on three ships groups). Note also the 10th century treatise of Heron of Byzantium 53–54 (with figs 25–6) and 1st century treatise of Frontinus 3.9.8. See also Syvänne, 2004 (p.326) and *Military History of Late Rome Vol.1*.
12. By assigning a mere 100 men per dromon (Procop. *Wars* 7.19.5) one reaches the figure of 20,000 men for this army. However, there were other troops involved. There were 3,000 men under Bessas in Rome, but these were unwilling to take part in any action. Then there was the garrison of Portus and the sailors and soldiers left to guard the transport ships. Most importantly, there were also the infantry forces stationed on the right bank of the river. In sum, there were clearly more than 20,000 Romans involved in the operations around Rome. Confirmation for these figures comes from Procopius (7.21.5). He put into the mouth of Totila

the claim that after the siege the Goths had defeated over 20,000 Romans. However, as noted there clearly were other troops involved besides these. Procopius may have reached this figure for the size of the army on the basis of the numbers of dromons in the force. Regardless, most of the troops would have been tied to their ships and would have therefore been unavailable for land combat. Therefore, the availability of men to fight a pitched battle was considerably lower even if the total manpower probably approached the 30,000–35,000 mark rather than 20,000.

13. Procop. *Wars* 7.22.1–23.18.; with Syvänne, 2004 (Appendix/Rome/Lucania).
14. Procop. *Wars* 7.23.8ff.
15. Most of this is a quote from Syvänne, 2004.
16. Procop. *Wars* 7.24.34ff. 7.25.1ff.
17. Procop. *Wars* 7.27.1ff.
18. Procop. *Wars* 7.29.1ff.
19. However, the most interesting event is the famous story of the whale called Porphyrius, which was caught at this time. This whale had been in the habit of terrorizing Constantinople for fifty years sporadically. It sank many boats, and frightened many on others by pushing them for long distances. Justinian ordered the whale captured but nobody managed to. Then one day when the waters were calm a group of dolphins appeared at the mouth of the Black Sea and the whale went after them. It ate some but than ran aground in deep mud. When the locals saw this, they killed it. The length of the whale was 30 cubits and its breadth ten (ca. 45 x 15 ft). It would seem probable that this was a killer whale.
20. Procop. *Wars* 7.29.21ff.
21. Procopius, *Wars* 2.28.12–44; 7.30.25, 7.35.1–3, *Anek* 5.16–18; Evagrius 4.21, Jordanes *Rom.* 382. See also the chapters dealing with Persian and Lazican wars. For the titles held by Belisarius after 549, see PLRE3/Belisarius1, 216–17. Ian Hughes (229–30) follows the recent trend among historians in trying to exonerate Justinian for the sending of too few men with Belisarius to Italy with the excuse that the Empire was just too exhausted as a result of the plague. The plague is claimed to have affected the reserves of manpower to such an extent that Justinian lacked the resources to send men into Italy. This view is completely false. Firstly, Procopius states in no uncertain terms the circumstances in which Belisarius obtained his command. Belisarius promised to finance the war out of his own pocket. He was deseperate to get away from Constantinople. There was never such a lack of manpower that Belisarius could not have been given enough high quality troopers for the purpose if the emperor so wished. These men were the 7,000 bodyguards that Justinian had confiscated and it was these men that had won Italy previously. And it was these men that the emperor did not want to return to Belisarius. Furthermore, when one reads the text of Procopius carefully Justinian always somehow miraculously managed to send money and men when the situation became urgent. The best example of this happens right after Belisarius had left. It is therefore clear that Procopius is correct in criticising Justinian for his avarice and lack of support given for the soldiers.
22. Procop. *Wars* 7.31–32.51; Jordanes *Rom.* 385.
23. Procop. *Wars* 7.33.1ff., 7.35.12ff.
24. The technical meaning for the *moira* is a unit of about 3,000 men and it is quite possible that this is its meaning in this case because it would have been quite easy for 3,000 men to defeat a detachment drawn from the 3,000-strong Herul army.

Chapter 14

1. Corippus is our best source for the campaigns of John Troglita. His account is confirmed by the much shorter summary of his campaigns in Procopius (*Wars* 4.28.45–52). This chapter is based on Corippus 1.48ff. and Procopius.
2. The following account is based on Corippus 1.417–3.12, 4.247–6.20; Syvänne, 2000, 34ff.; Syvänne, 2004.

3. In tactical theory the *caterva* meant 6,000 men, for which see: Vegetius 2.2; Stelten, 302. However, Corippus (7.262–271) gives Cusina at a later date at a different battle as many as 30,000 warriors under thirty dukes, and Ifisdaias as many as 100,000 men, in addition to whom were the men of Bezina (7.272–280). It is therefore clear that both had access to far greater numbers than the 6,000 men, but I still estimate the size of the entire allied Moorish force to be about 12,000–20,000 men on the basis of this figure, for two reasons: Firstly, it is safer not to overestimate the size of the Roman army, and secondly, and even more importantly, it is probable that the Romans would not have accepted so many Moors into their service as to outnumber the Roman army significantly.
4. Corippus 2.1–161.
5. Pringle, 35.
6. The *Strategikon* (7.2.80) instructed the pitching of separate camps. The fact that the Romans and their allies had separate camps can be deduced from a later reference (Corippus 8.261–67) to this practice.
7. In the previous reconstructions I have assumed that John deployed some of his carts and wagons behind his infantry as Germanus did and the *Strategikon* instructed, but this is not mentioned by Corippus and since the fortified camp behind the line would have served the same purpose, I have not adopted this solution here.
8. The reason for the use of two cavalry divisions per wing is that in Corippus's text each commander whose place would correspond with this deployment is shown to employ missiles, while those between them are given mêlée weapons. The only odd men out are those officers mentioned next to the infantry phalanx, which makes it likely that they were the wing commanders. Similarly, the pattern of their use in combat supports this battle array. See Syvänne, 2000, 42–3.
9. English translation of the Roman shout by Shea, 131.
10. The Roman horsemen were armed with round shields, swords and spears. This is another proof that the use of the shield by the Roman cavalry had never ceased. In fact, this piece of information gives additional reason to suspect that even the ideal horsemen of Procopius (1.1.8–20) were armed with round shields. It is also noteworthy that the spear was used both as a javelin and as a thrusting weapon. The sword was used for both thrusting and cutting, but mainly the latter.
11. This proves correct Delbrück's (2.41–52) claim that a *cuneus* (wedge) meant a column of men, but this is obviously only partially true because in most cases the *cuneus* meant also the real wedge so the *turris/pyrgos* was preserved for the column. The reason for this conclusion is that, although even in this case the standard V shape is possible, the use of the column between the animals is more likely.
12. For the Persians and *Strategikon*, see Syvänne, 2004.
13. See: Corippus, Ioh., 6.492–7.6; Syvänne, 2000, 50ff.; Syvänne, 2004.
14. Pringle (36) with Corippus and Syvänne, 2000.
15. Pringle (36–7) with Corippus and Syvänne, 2000.
16. Corippus 7.1ff. with Syvänne, 2000, 56ff.; Syvänne, 2004. Note, however, that I interpret the evidence slightly differently in this study.
17. For this and other features of Roman combat doctrine, see Syvänne, 2004.
18. Translation by Shea, 197.
19. Pringle, 39; PLRE3/Ioannes 69 and 75.
20. Malalas 18.145; Theophanes AM 6055; PLRE3/Ioannes 69 and 75.
21. Malalas 18.145; Theophanes AM 6055; John Biclar/John of Biclaro a.569.

Chapter 15
1. This is based on Shahid (BASIC 236–242) except where I state otherwise.
2. Procopius, *Wars* 2.28.12–44.

3. This is based on Shahid (BASIC 242–255) except where I state otherwise.
4. This is based on Shahid (BASIC 255ff.) except where I state otherwise.

Chapter 16
1. Procop. *Wars* 8.3.18ff., 8.4.9ff.
2. Procop. *Wars* 2.28.15ff.
3. Siege and campaign: Procop. Wars 2.29.1–30.48, Syvänne, 2004 (Appendix/Petra 2). The text once again follows very closely Syvänne, 2004.
4. Procop. *Wars* 8.1.3ff, 8.8.1–39, 8.9.6ff.; with Syvänne, 2004 (Appendix/Hippis). The text follows closely Syvänne (2004) often word for word.
5. This Artabanes had deserted to the Roman side when Valerianus was *MVM per Armeniam*. He tested his loyalty by giving him fifty Romans. Artabanes took these to a fortress in Persarmenia and when he gained entrance by still pretending to be loyal to them, he and the fifty Romans gained entrance so they were able to kill the entire 120-man garrison. This show of loyalty showed his desertion to be real.
6. Procop. *Wars* 8.9.6ff., 8.10.1ff.
7. Procop, *Wars* 8.9.12ff. with Syvänne, 2004 (Appendix/Trachea, the text follows this usually word for word).
8. Procop. *Wars* 8.10.1–7 with Syvänne, 2004.
9. Procop. *Wars* 8.10–8ff.
10. Procop. *Wars* 8.11.1ff., 8.15.1ff.; Menander, Blockley ed frgs. 2, 6; Bury 2.116–7.
11. Procop. *Wars* 8.11.11ff.; Agathias 3.2.1–8; with Syvänne, 2004 (Appendix/Petra). The text is largely a quote of Syvänne, 2004.
12. Procop. *Wars* 8.13.1ff., 8.16.8; Agathias 3.2.6; with Syvänne, 2004 (Appendix/Archaeopolis). The text follows closely Syvänne, 2004.
13. Procop. *Wars* 8.16.1ff.; Menander fr. 11 (Blockley ed. fr. 6.1.239ff.); PLRE3/Martinus2.
14. Procop. *Wars* 8.16.16ff., 8.17.1ff.; Agathias 2.19.1, 3.2.1ff.
15. Agathias 2.19.1ff.
16. PLRE3/Mermeroes.
17. Agathias, 3.2.1ff.; Bury, 2.118–9.
18. Agathias 3.2.8, 3.5.6ff. The location of Onoguris is not known with certainty. There are currently several suggested sites. See also the short narrative of Rubin for the battle and campaign (1960, 360–2). In Averil Cameron's (1970, 45–6) view, Agathias has exaggerated the size of the Roman army to stress the magnitude of the defeat so that the real figures should be reduced to as low as 5,000 men. This approach does not take into account the overwhelming amount of evidence for the use of large and small armies and anything in between for which there is evidence in all of the sources. The size of the Roman army is entirely plausible when the Romans were able to concentrate their principal eastern army to the north. Furthermore, the lack of knowledge of what is happening is a known cause of panic among the soldiers and masses of people, and it is entirely plausible that a single event of seeing men in flight could cause a panic reaction. See for example the comments of De Saxe in 1732 (190–1). It is also unnecessary to criticize Agathias too much for the use of set pieces on siege preparation. The principal siege techniques continued to be the same. It is also possible or even probable that the 3,000 Persians were a vanguard.
19. Agathias, 3.8.4–17.5.
20. Agathias 3.15.1–4.1.1, 4.23.2–3, 4.30.6–10 (campaign), 3.20.8ff. (siege and battle), 4.30.6ff.; with Syvänne, 2004 (Appendix/Phasis).
21. Considering the haste that the Romans were in it is probable that these had been built before the army arrived rather than by them now. The text of Agathias would also allow the other interpretation, but this is the most likely.
22. The far shooting *sfendonai mēchanai* (Agathias 3.21.4) probably mean sling engines, ballistae or stone throwers of unknown type – perhaps onagri or trebuchets?

23. Most of the Roman army consisted apparently of cavalry: In the welcoming procession of the new king of Lazica, Tzathes, most of the soldiers rode horses (Agathias 3.15.3). Martinus chose to fight from within the walls because of the memory of the previous defeat. A short narrative of the battle and campaign also in Rubin, 1960, 362–5.
24. Agathias 3.22.1–8. In this I follow J.D. Frendo's translation p. 92: 'Forming themselves therefore into a compact body they faced about and suddenly charged with their spears levelled at those of the enemy that were positioned near town.' The word for the levelling of the spears (*ta dorata probeblēmenoi*), according to Liddell and Scott, can also mean throw forward, put before, put forward as shield, throw to, throw away. Consequently, one can interpret the sentence as the soldiers throwing their spears rather than thrusting. However, since the fighting techniques of the Tzani are not know in detail one can guess that they may have used the spears to thrust in combat just like the Roman heavy infantry did sometimes. In 134 AD according to Arrian (Ektaxis, 7), the Colchians were spearmen. On the other hand the Moors certainly threw their spears, which would support the throwing of the weapons. Perhaps both thrusts and throwing were employed as needed.
25. Averil Cameron (1970, 46–8) is once again overly critical of Agathias. The use of a rumour to cause anxiety among the enemy was one of the oldest tricks in the book. Any able enemy commander would have at least sent scouting parties in the direction of the supposed reinforcements. Furthermore, she is overly sceptical of the spreading panic among the Persian troops during the fighting. This is a similarly well-known phenomenon. However, her criticism of the covering of the use of the ambushers with a story of a visit to a church is fully justified.
26. It is noteworthy that the infantry performed poorly against the combination of the elephants and cavalry and that it was the bodyguard of Martin on horseback that decided the conflict against the elephants. The tight phalanx offered the elephants and the accompanying elite archers good opportunities. When openings in front of the elephants appeared, the horsemen behind the elephants could use the opportunity.
27. Agathias 4.1.1ff. (esp. 4.15.4–20.10) with Syvänne, 2004 (Appendix/Tzacher).
28. Agathias 3.15.2–17.3, 4.12.1–14.5.
29. Menander (Blockley ed. 2, 5); Theophanes AM6050, PLRE3/Justin4, Bury 2.315.
30. Agathias 5.1.1ff.; Syvänne, 2004 (Appendix/Rhizaeum) usually word for word.

Chapter 17
1. Procop. *Wars* 7.25.1ff.
2. Based on the discussion of religious matters in Jones, Moorhead, Tate, and in particular Bury.
3. Procop. *Wars* 7.35.12ff.
4. Procop. *Wars* 7.35.23–29 with Syvänne, 2004 (Appendix/Dalmatia).
5. Procop. *Wars* 7.36.1ff.; for the dates, see PLRE3/Totila.
6. Procop. Wars 7.37.1ff. 7.39.1–40.29, 8.24.1–2 with Syvänne, 2004 (Appendix/Sicily 550).
7. See the previous note.
8. Procop. *Wars* 7.38.1ff. with Syvänne, 2004.
9. Procop. *Wars* 7.40.1ff.
10. Procop. *Wars* 7.40.18ff. with Syvänne, 2004 (Appendix/Sicily).
11. Procop. *Wars* 7.40.30ff. with Syvänne, 2004.
12. Procop. *Wars* 8.18.1ff, 8.21.20–22, 8.25.1ff..; PLRE3, Auduin, Turisindus and persons named in the text.
13. Procop. *Wars* 8.21.1ff.
14. Procop. *Wars* 8.22.1ff., 8.23.1ff., 8.24.1ff.
15. Procop. *Wars* 8.22.1ff., with Syvänne, 2004 (Appendix/Sena Gallia). The text is mostly a quote of Syvänne, 2004.
16. Former bodyguard of Belisarius.
17. *ploia makra* = long ships = probably single banked dromons of unknown size.

18. The ancient famous Roman boarding bridge was *corvus* (raven). It was invented by the Romans to overcome their weakness against the Punic navy during the 1st Punic War. The invention and use of the *corvus* is in Polybius 1.22–3. See also Vegetius/Milner, p.149, n.8. Some kind of boarding bridge (but probably not the *corvus* proper) was also used during this period, since Vegetius 4.44 mentions the use of boarding bridges.
19. Procop. *Wars* 8.23.1–42 (campaign and battle).
20. East Roman naval manuals recommended the fighting of naval battles close to the enemy shore so that the enemy would feel inclined to flee there.
21. Procop. *Wars* 8.24.1ff., 8.25.24–5, 8.26.1ff.
22. Ildigisal: Procop. *Wars* 7.35.12–22, 8.19.7, 8. 27.1ff.. Sinnion: Procop. *Wars* 8.18.12–19.7 with Syvänne, 2004 (Warlords). For the persons named, see also PLRE3.
23. Jordanes *Get.* 303; Isidore of Sevilla, *Hist.* 41–49, esp. 46–7; PLRE3; Syvänne, 2004 (Visigoths).

Chapter 18

1. Procop. *Wars* 8.26.5ff., 8.28.1ff. (esp. 8.26.5–32.36 campaign; 8.31.1ff.,battle); Syvänne, 2004 (Appendix/Taginae). The text is largely a quote of Syvänne (2004) but contains some changes especially in the likely numbers involved. It is clear that both sides had slightly more men than I previously thought. This was a major effort from the Romans and if the Romans could assemble 50,000 men in Lazica in 554 it is entirely plausible that roughly similar numbers could also be mobilized for Italy, especially so because Procopius claims that Germanus had been extraordinarily successful in his recruiting efforts. Furthermore, since the Goths possessed a fleet of over 400 dromons, it is clear that they could easily field more men than usually thought. Even if one assigns only 110 men per *dromon* the figure would reach 44,000 men. The estimations of army strengths have varied: Haldon (Romans 20,000–25,000); Boss (Romans 28,900, Goths 18,000); Roisl (Romans 25,000, Goths 15,000); Pertusi (Romans 30,000); Thompson, 1982, 88 (Romans 25,000–30,000, Goths 15,000–20,000).
2. These wings consisted probably of dismounted cavalry as Dewing has already suggested. The 8,000 men came *ek tōn katalogou stratiōtōn* while the fifty men came *ek katalogou pezous*. This conclusion receives additional support from Agathias's description of the heavy infantry at Casilinum where the mail armour of the heavy infantry reached their feet just as was the case with the cavalry. See the battle description below. It is also possible that these were multipurpose infantry described by the *Peri strategikes* similar to the fifty men posted on the hill. The exact place of the battle is contested, but it probably possessed some terrain features to protect the Roman flanks. It is possible to interpret the foot archers as flank guards outside the cavalry wings as Boss and Jacobsen do, but it is unlikely not only because of what I state below but in light of the purpose of the flank guards. The use of the crescent seems more likely to indicate a continuous line of footmen. Furthermore, if the cavalry had been posted in front it would have been used to pursue the fleeing Goths from the start and not only in the final stages of the battle. As noted, Jacobsen (2009, 282–7 esp. 283) has interpreted the structure of the Roman battle array differently, placing the 4,000 dismounted archers as flankguards for both wings (the outermost units of the flanks). This is a possible formation because this array can also be found in the *Strategikon*. However, when one reads Procopius's text literally (*Wars* 8.21.1–7) he states that Narses and John took their places near the hill. This means that the dismounted archers could not be left of them. What he states is that both wings (LW under Narses and John, and RW under Valerianus, John the Glutton and Dagisthaeus) had 4,000 dismounted men each from the *katalogoi*. This means that they had to be posted in front of the cavalry rather than further away. Consequently I prefer to follow here Oman's and Haldon's interpretations of the battle formation.
3. Procop. *Wars* 33.1ff. (8.33.1–35.38 campaign, 8.35.15ff.battle); Agathias 1.1ff.; with Syvänne, 2004 (Appendix/Mons Lactarius). Other reconstructions: Hodgkin 4.729–41; Boss, 25; Bury 2.270–4; Pertusi, 648; Delbrück 2.363–7; Wass, 268–9. For the map of the location see also:

Roisl, 1988, 81; Pertusi, tav. 3. Roisl (77) is correct in criticizing Pertusi for making the length of the line of the armies c. 20 km, but he is unnecessarily critical of Procopius's account of the battle. This account is entirely plausible from the military point of view and the heroics and the death of the last Gothic king Teias are too. It is quite plausible that the way in which the king died was recorded and transmitted by those who saw it.

4. Agathias 1.1ff. (1.6.1–2.12.10, campaign; 2.8.1ff., battle). with Syvänne, 2004 (Appendix/ Capua/Casilinum/Casulinus). Other reconstructions with alternative and different interpretations of the battle: Hodgkin 5.29–45; Bury 2.274–81; Pertusi, 650–2; Boss, 27–8; Haldon, 2001, 40–44; Delbrück 2.369–74; Rubin, 1995, 199–200 with a map of Pertusi; Wass, 274–7; GMT Games, Cataphract.

5. Procop. Wars 8.33.1–35.38; Agathias 1.8.1.ff. (1.8.1–20.7); Syvänne, 2004 (Appendix).

6. Agathias 2.8.6–7. Agathias portrays the deserters as genuine, but it is likely that he tried to cover Narses's duplicity. For some reason (perhaps generosity) Narses was always the favourite of the Heruls.

7. Agathias 2.4.10. Boss (28) estimates the strength of the Franks at 22,000 men. His estimates of the divisions of the Roman army are incorrect. For example, he assumes that the number of Narses' bodyguards is 500 men while Agathias clearly stated otherwise. His reconstruction also leaves out the battle-ready camp followers and servants who must have numbered in thousands. Furthermore, the battle formations of both armies are clearly incorrect. See Syvänne (2004) *MHLR* vols. 1–5 and *Caracalla* with *Aurelian and Probus* for additional details of the use of this tactic.

8. The Macedonians used the cavalry *sarissa* or *xyston* with one hand which makes it possible that this only meant the regular long cavalry spear the *kontarion* while the *doratia* meant the javelin type.

9. Mail reaching the feet may imply the use of dismounted cavalry, since they wore similar armour. Boss (50) has suggested that the heavy infantry was given these heavier versions of mail armour after the success of the dismounted Germans had proved their worth. It is more likely that normal heavy infantry had these occasionally or that part of the cavalry had dismounted. See also the Battle of Taginae.

10. Agathias 2.9.2 (*epikampios emprosthia*): Rance (242–3) incorrectly calls this formation a crescent.

11. This is the final formation of Hannibal's array at the battle of Cannae in 216 BC.

12. Agathias 2.10.1ff.; Menander (Blockley ed. fr.3), Fauber, 129ff. (esp. 129–32; 141, 161–6); Syvänne (2004, 377–8); PLRE3/Narses1 (sources mentioned therein).

13. Fauber (161) suggests that there might be evidence for two Frankish invasions for the years 555 and 556. In the first case the Franks supposedly defeated a Roman army in Italy and in the latter they invaded both Thuringia and Italy. The evidence for these is so thin that e.g. the PLRE3 does not refer to them. However, I would not entirely preclude this possibility.

14. Agathias 5.11.2–25.6 (war), 5.16.1–20.4 (battle); Theophanes, AM 6051; Malalas 18.129, Menander (Blockley fr.2, 5.1–2). The text is largely based on Syvänne, 2004 (Appendix/ Chettus/Chersonese).

15. The *scholae* and *protectores* were palace guards. *Numeri* = *arithmoi* which probably means that some regular troops were present and my educated guess is that these would have been the marines of the imperial navy. See also Theophanes, 1997, p. 343 n.13. They were probably the precursors of the later *Tagmata*.

16. The members of the senate undoubtedly had their private retainers and bodyguards with them. In fact, during the Persian wars, the senate with their retinues and other reinforcements were sent to protect the cities of the east (Malalas 18.26).

17. Agathias 5.17.1–18.11, esp. 5.18.10–11. Since the contents of Belisarius's speech accurately reflected the actual advantages of the Romans over the Huns, the actual content of the speech may have been quite similar.

18. See the articles of Ilkka Syvänne (Alexander the Great, Magnesia etc.) available online at academia.edu for further details of how these files skirmished.
19. This *bracholion* continued into the sea and consisted of beams, spears, and ships' masts placed on the seabed. See *De obsidione toleranda* 51.22–52.4/Sullivan p.163.n.64.
20. Agathias 5.21.1–23.5; Theophanes AM 6051. See also Philon, *Syntaxe* C52–55.

Chapter 19
1. Based on my article (2013b) 'El ejército de Justiniano' in DF.
2. See the PLRE3 for a long list of these.
3. Malalas 8.129–152; Theophanes AM 6051—58; Agathias 4.22.5–9; Menander, Blockley frgs. 2–9; Evagrius 5.1; Nicephorus Callistus 17.34; with the PLRE3 for additional sources for the persons named.
4. This makes the dating 561 impossible.

Chapter 20
1. I fullheartedly recommend Lord Mahon's *The Life of Belisarius. The Last Great General of Rome*, Intr. by Jon Coulston, Yardley (1848/2006). It was one of the books that got me interested in late antiquity during my youth. Note, however, that my reconstruction of Belisarius's life differs from his. For a good modern assessment of Belisarius's importance for the reconquest, see also Jacobsen (2009, 259–60). I agree with him. There would not have been any reconquests without Belisarius. Robert Graves' *Count Belisarius* was the second of the books that got me interested in this period. It is an excellent work of fiction, which I whole-heartedly recommend.
2. There is a fuller discussion of this topic in Syvänne, 2004. It also explains why I prefer the sixth century date for Syrianus Magister.

Appendix
1. Syvänne, 2004, 14–16, 26; Bell, 1–27.

Bibliography and Sources

Select Primary Sources

Several of the following sources and sources mentioned in the notes are also available online. *The Age of Hippotoxotai* contains a fuller list of the sources, which have been subsumed here in the endnotes under the name of that book. *The Age of Hippotoxotai* also provides a very long and detailed analysis of period battle and combat mechanics, which has been impossible to include here. This monograph, however, provides a far more detailed analysis of the campaigns and warfare than was possible in *The Age of Hippotoxotai*. This monograph not only complements it but in some cases challenges its conclusions. An updated study of the combat mechanics sections of *The Age of Hippotoxotai* is currently in the works.

Agathias, *Agathiae Myrinaei Historiarum libri quinque*, CFHB Vol II, ed. R. Keydell, Berlin (1967). *Agathias, The Histories*, CFHB Vol. II A, English tr. by Joseph D. Frendo, Berlin (1975).

Ammianus Marcellinus, *The History of Ammianus Marcellinus*, ed and tr. by John C. Rolfe, Loeb ed. 3 vols, Cambridge, Mass.-London (1950–2/1971–2).

Anonymous, De scientia politica dialogus/see: Peri politikēs epistēmēs.

Arrian, Arrianos, Arrianus, Flavius, TEKNE TAKTIKA (Tactical Handbook) EKTAXIS KATA ALANON tr. and ed. by James G. DeVoto, Chicago (1993).

Asclepiodotus, *Aeneas Tacticus, Asclepiodotus, Onasander*, tr. by members of the Illinois Greek Club, Loeb ed. (1923). *Asclepiodoté, Traité de Tactique*, French ed. and tr. by Lucien Poznanski, Paris (1992).

Byzantine Interpolation of Aelian, in Dain, *L'Histoire du texte d'Elien le Tacticien des origins a la fin du moyen age*, Thèse pour le doctorat et lettres, Université de Paris (1946), ed. Dain, 92–100, 102–6; English tr.by Devine, A.M., Aelian's Manual of Hellenistic Military Tactics. A New Translation from the Greek with an Introduction, *Ancient World 19 (1989)*, 31–64, the Byzantine Interpolation of Aelian 59ff.

Cedrenus, George, *Compedium Historiarum*, ed. I. Bekker, 2 vols., CSHB Bonn (1838–9).

Chronicon Paschale, ed. L. Dindorf (Bonn, 1832). English Translation by Michael and Mary Whitby [TTH 7] (Liverpool, 1989). References in the notes to this translation (contains the pagination of Dindorf).

Conquerors and Chronicler of Early Medieval Spain, TTH 9, Tr., notes and introduction by Kenneth Baxter Wolf, Liverpool (1990). John of Biclar, Isidore of Seville, Chronicle of 754, Chronicle of Alfonso III.

Constantine Porphyrogenitus, Constantine Porphyrogenitus: *De administrando imperio*, Greek text edited by Gy. Moravcsik, English translation by R.J.H. Jenkins, Budapest 1949.

Corippus, *Ioannidos libri viii*, ed J. Diggle and F.R.D. Goodyear, Cambridge (1970). *The Iohannis or De Bellis Libycis of Flavius Cresconius Corippus*. Studies in Classics Volume 7, New York 1998, tr. and introd. by George W. Shea.

De obsidione toleranda, Anon, in 'A Byzantine Instructional Manual omn Siege Defense: The De obsidione toleranda', intr., tr. by Denis F. Sullivan with reprinted Greek text of Hilda van den Berg, in *Byzantine Authors: Literary Activities and Preoccupations, Text and Translations dedicated to the Memory of Nicolas Oikomides*, ed. J.W. Nesbitt, Leiden and Boston (2003).

De scientia politica dialogus, see: Peri politikēs epistēmēs.

Evagrius, *Ecclesiastical History*, ed. J. Bidez and L. Parmentier (London, 1898). *The Ecclesiastical History of Evagrius Shcolasticus*, Translated with an introduction by Michael Whitby, [TTH 33] (Liverpool, 2000). French translation A.J. Festugière, Évagre, *Histoire Ecclesiastique*, Byzantion 45 (1975), 187–488.

Fredegar, *The Fourth Book of Fredegar*. Edited and English translation by J.M. Wallace-Hadrill, New York (1960).

Frontinus (Frontin), *Strategematon*, in *Frontinus The Stratagems and the Aqueducts of Rome*, tr. by Charles E Bennett, Loeb ed.Cambridge Mass.–London (1925/1980).

Isidore of Seville, *Historia de regibus Gothorum, Vandalorum et Suevorum*, ed. T. Mommsen, MGH, AA. XI. *Isidore of Seville's History of the Kings of the Goths, Vandals, and Suevi*, English tr by Guido Donini and Gordon B. Ford Jr, Leiden (1966). English tr. of the History of the Goths also in *Conquerors and Chroniclers of Early Medieval Spain*, 81–110.

John of Biclar, *Chronicle*, ed. T. Mommsen, MGH Auct. Ant. XI. Chron Min. ii, Berlin (1893–4). English tr. in *Conquerors and Chroniclers of Early Mediaval Spain*, 61–80.

John of Ephesus, *The Third Part of the Ecclesiastical History of John of Ephesus*, tr. by R. Payne-Smith (Oxford, 1860). *Iohannis Ephesini Historiae Ecclesiasticae pars tertia*, ed. and Latin translation by E.W. Brooks, CSCO 106, Scr. Syri 55 (Louvain, 1936, 1952)

John Lydus *De Magistratibus Rei Publicae Romanae* (*John Lydus, De Magistratibus Rei Publicae Romanae*/Peri Exousiwn/Peri Arcwn thV Rwmaiwn PoliteiaV), ed., tr. and comm. A.C. Bandy, *Johannes Lydus On Powers or the Magistracies of the Roman State*, Philadelphia 1983.

John of Nikiu, *The Chronicle of John, Bishop of Nikiu*, ed and tr by R.H. Charles, London-Oxford (1916).

Jordanes, *Iordanis Romana et Getica*, ed. Th. Mommsen, Monumenta Germaniae Historica. Auctores Antiguissimi VI, Berlin 1882. *The Gothic History of Jordanes* (=Getica). Introduction, Commentary and Translation Charles Christopher Mierow, PhD. 2nd Ed. Princeton UP 1915.

Malalas, Ioannes, *Chronographia*, ed. L. Dindorf (CSHB, 1831). *The Chronicle of John Malalas*. Byzantina Australiensia 4, tr. by E. Jeffreys, M. Jeffreys and Roger Scott and others, Melbourne (1986). References in the notes to this edition/translation (contains the pagination of Dindorf and translation of the Slavonic version).

Marcellinus Comes, *Chronica, The Chronicle of Marcellinus*, A Translation and Commentary (with a reproduction of Mommsen's edition of the text) Brian Croke, Australian Association for Byzantine Studies Byzantina Australiensia 7, Sydney (1995).

Menander the Protector, *The History of Menander the Guardsman*, ed. and tr. by R.C. Blockley, Liverpool (1985).

Nicephorus Callistus Xanthopoulos, *Ecclesiasticae Historiae*, PG 145–7.

Peri politikes epistemes (*De scientia politica dialogus*), *Menae patricii cum Thoma refendario De scientia politica dialogus*, edited and translated into Italian by C.M. Mazzucchi, Milano 1982. English tr. as Dialogue on Political Science in *Three Political Voices from the Age of Justinian. Agapetus, Advice to the Emperor. Dialogue on Political Science. Paul the Silentiary. Description of Hagia Sophia*. tr. by Peter N. Bell (Liverpool 2009).

Peri strategikes/strategias, G.T. Dennis, *Three Byzantine Military Treatises*, CFHB XXV, Washington 1985, The introduction, text and tr. of the Anonymous Byzantine Treatise on Strategy, 1–135. H. Köchly and W. Rüstow, Byzantini anonymi Peri Strategikes in *Griechische Kriegsschriftsteller II.2*, Leipzig 1855, 1–209, notes 311–355.

Philon of Byzantium, *Mēchanikē syntaxis*, book V, Edition and French tr. by Y. Garlan, *Recherches de poliorcétiquegrecque*, Paris (1974), 291–404.

—— *Belopoiika*, in Marsden 1971, 106–184.

Procopius, *Wars* (*Bella*), *History of the Wars*, ed. and tr. by H.B. Dewing, Cambridge Mass., Loeb Edition reprints, 5 Vols.; *Secret History* (Anecdota), *The Anecdota or Secret History*, Loeb vol VI. Cambridge Mass. (1935/60); *Buildings* (*De aedefiis/Peri Ktismaton*), tr. by H.B. Dewing and G. Downey, Cambridge Mass. (1940/63). *Opera ed.* J. Haury, re-ed. G. Wirth, Leipzig (1963–4).

Strategikon, The Strategikon, *Das Strategikon des Maurikios*, CFHB XVII, Vienna 1981, edited by G.T. Dennis and German tr. by Ernst Gamillscheg. *Maurice's Strategicon. Handbook of Byzantine Military Strategy*, English tr. by G.T. Dennis, Philadelphia (1984). Mihaescu, *Arta Militara* (with Romanian tr.), Bucharest (1970).

Tabari, al-, *The History of al-Tabari*, ed. E. Yar-Shater, several translators, Albany New York 1985–.

Theophanes, *Chronographia*, ed. C. de Boor, Leipzig (1883–5). *The Chronicle of Theophanes Confessor. Byzantine and Near Eastern History AD 284–813*. Tr. by Cyril Mango and Roger Scott with the assistance of G. Greatrex, Oxford (1997).

Vegetius, *Flavius Vegetius Renatus, Epitoma Rei Militaris*, ed. with an English tr. by L.F. Stelten, New York, Bern, Frankfurt, Paris (1990). *Vegetius: Epitome of Military Science. Translated with notes and introduction by N.P. Milner*. TTH 16, Liverpool, 1993, 2nd ed. (1996).

Zachariah of Mitylene, *Ecclesiastical History*, tr. F.J. Hamilton and E.W. Brooks, London (1899).

Select Secondary Sources

Ayvazyan, Armen, foreword by Ilkka Syvänne, (2014) 2nd ed. *The Armenian Military in the Byzantine Empire*. 2014.

Bachrach, Bernard S., 'Procopius, Agathias and the Frankish Military', *Speculum 45 (1970)*, 435–41.
—— *Merovingian Military Organization: 481–751*, Minneapolis (1972).
—— The Imperial roots of Merovingian military organization', in *Military Aspects of Scandinavian Societies in a European Perspective*, 1997, 25–31, also available at www.deremilitari.org.
—— 'The Siege of Antioch: A Study in Military Demography', *War in History 6 (1999)*, 127–46.
—— 'Medieval Military Demography and the Methods of Hans Delbrück', in D. Kagan, ed., *Circle of War*, Woodbridge (1999), 3–20.
—— *Early Carolingian Warfare. Prelude to Empire*, Philadelphia (2001).

Bacic, Jakov, *The Emergence of the Sklabenoi (Slavs), Their Arrival on the Balkan Peninsula, and the Role of the Avars in these events: Revised Concepts in a New Perspective*, Ph.D. 1983 Columbia University.

Barford, P.M., *The Early Slavs. Culture and Society in Early Medieval Eastern Europe*, London (2001).

Blockley, R.C., '*The Fragmentary Classicing Historians of the Later Empire*', ed. and tr. by R.C. Blockley, i–ii, Liverpool (1981/3).

Boss, Roy, *Justinian's Wars: Belisarius, Narses and The Reconquest of the West*, Montvert Publications Stockport, Dewsbury (1993).

Braund, David, *Georgia in Antiquity. A History of Colchis and Transcaucasian Iberia 550 BC–AD 562*, Oxford (1994).

Brueggeman, Gary, *The Roman Army, 1994–2002*, http://webpages.charter.net/brueggeman.

Bury, J.B., *History of the Later Roman Empire from the death of Theodosius to the death of Justinian, 2 vols*, Dover Edition, New York 1958.

Cameron, Averil, *Agathias*, Oxford (1970).
—— *Procopius and the Sixth Century*, London (1985).

Dain, Alphonse, *L'Histoire du texte d'Elien le Tacticien*, Paris (1946).

Dawson, Tim (2007), 'Fit for the task': equipment sizes and the transmission of military lore, sixth to tenth centuries', in *BMGS* 31.1, 1–12.

Decker, Michael J. (2013), *The Byzantine Art of War*. Yardley.

Delbrück, *History of the Art of War*, 4 vols., translated by Walter J. Renfroe, Jr., 1975, reprint 1990.

Dolukhanov, Pavel, *The Early Slavs, Eastern Europe from the Initial Settlement to the Kievan Rus*, London and New York (1996). .

Farrokh, Kaveh (2017), *The Sassanians*. Barnsley.
—— (2007), *Shadows in the Desert*. Oxford

Fauber, Lawrence, *Narses, Hammer of the Goths. The Life and Times of Narses the Eunuch*, New York (1990).

GMT Games, *Cataphract*, The Reconquest of the Roman Empire, Dara 530 A.D., Callinicum
    531 A.D., Tricameron 534 A.D., Sena Gallica 551 A.D., Taginae 552 A.D., Casilinum 554 A.D.,
    Game Design: Richard Berg & Mark Herman,Graphic Design: Rodger B. MacGowan, also
    Campaign Game Justinian, Reconquest of Rome 528 to 558 A.D. by Rodger B. MacGowan,
    Great Battles of History Volume VIII, 1999 GMT Games, Hanford, CA 93232.
Graves, Robert (1938), *Count Belisarius*. London.
Greatrex, Geoffrey, 'Rome and Persia at War, 502–532', *ARCA Classical and Medieval Texts,
    Papers and Monographs 37*, Leeds (1998).
Haldon, John F., *The Byzantine Wars. Battles and campaigns of the Byzantine era*, Tempus
    Publishing, Port Stroud (2000/1).
Hodgkin, T., *Italy and Her Invaders, Vols. III-V*, London, Oxford (1885–95).
Hoplites, The Classical Greek Battle Experience, ed. Hanson, Victor Davis, New York (1991).
Hughes, Ian, (2009), *Belisarius. The Last Roman General*. Barnsley.
Jacobsen, Torsten Cumberland (2012). *A History of the Vandals*. Yardley.
—— (2009), *The Gothic War. Rome's Final Conflict in the West*. Yardley.
Lillington-Martin, Christopher, (2015) Forts on frontiers facing 'βάρβαροι' et al., Presentation,
    University of Oxford 28 May 2015, available online at academia.edu.
—— (2013), 'Procopius on the struggle for Dara in 530 and Rome in 537–8: reconciling texts and
    landscapes, in War and Warfare in Late Antiquity', eds A. Sarantis and N. Christie, Leiden and
    Boston.
—— (2007), 'Archaeological and Ancient Literary Evidence for a Battle near Dara Gap, Turkey,
    AD 530', in The Late Roman Army in the Near East from Diocletian to the Arab Conquest,
    Eds. A.S. Lewin and P. Pellegrini with the aid of Z.T. Fiema and S. Janniard. Oxford (2007),
    299–311.
Mahon, Lord, *The Life of Belisarius. The Last Great General of Rome*, Intr. by Jon Coulston, Yardley
    (1848/2006).
McCotter, Stephen, Strategy and Tactics of Siege Warfare in the Early Byzantine Period: From
    Constantine to Heraclius, Unpublished Ph.D Thesis, Queen's University Belfast 1995.
Moorhead, John (1994), *Justinian*. Routledge.
Oman, Sir Charles, A *History of the Art of War in the Middle Ages*, 2 vols. 2nd ed. 1924, reprint
    Methuen & Co London 1978.
Pertusi, A., 'Ordinamenti militari, guerre in Occidente e teorie di guerra dei Bizantine, saec.
    VI–X', in *Ordinamenti militari*, 631–700.
Pringle, Denys, *The Defence of Byzantine Africa from Justinian to the Arab Conquest*, 2 vols. BAR
    International Series 99 (i-ii), Oxford (1981).
Prosopography of the Later Roman Empire, edd. Martindale et al., 3 vols, Oxford (1971–92).
Rance, Philip, *Tactics and Tactica in the Sixth Century: Tradition and Originality*, Unpublished
    Doctoral Thesis, University of St. Andrews, (1993).
Shahid Irfan, B*yzantium and the Arabs in the Sixth Century, Volume 1. Part 2: Ecclesiastical History*.
    Dumbarton Oaks (1995); *Byzantium and the Arabs in the Sixth Century, Volume 1. Part 1:
    Political and Military History*, Dumbarton Oaks, (1995).
Syvänne, Ilkka, several articles available online at academia.edu which shed further light on tactics
    and other matters.
—— *Military History of Late Rome 457–518*, Pen & Sword forthcoming 2020.
—— (2020) *Military History of Late Rome 425–457*, Pen & Sword, Barnsley.
—— *Military History of Late Rome 395–425*, Pen & Sword forthcoming 2020.
—— (2020) *Aurelian and Probus. The Soldier Emperors Who Saved Rome*, Barnsley.
—— (2019) *Britain in the Age of Arthur: A Military History*, Barnsley.
—— (2019) *The Reign of the Emperor Gallienus*, Barnsley.
—— (2018) *Military History of Late Rome Vol.2 (361–395)*, Barnsley.
—— (2017) *Caracalla: A Military Biography*, Barnsley.

—— (2015) *Military History of Late Rome 284–361*, Barnsley.

—— (2013b) 'El ejército de Justiniano', in *Desperta Ferro* 18, 2013, 11–17.

—— (2013a) 'Las Guerra Persa: 527–532', in *Desperta Ferro* 18, 2013, 26–35.

—— (2004), *The Age of Hippotoxotai. The Art of War in Roman Military Revival and Disaster (491–636). Acta Universitasis Tamperensis 994*, Tampere University Press. Tampere 2004.

—— (2000), *Sixth Century Byzantine Infantry Tactics*, Unpublished Laudatur Thesis, University of Tampere December 2000.

Tate, Georges (2004), *Justinien. l'épopée de l'Empire d'Orient*. Fayard.

Thompson, E.A., *Romans and Barbarians. The Decline of the Western Empire*, Madison and London (1982).

Vasiliev, A.A., *Justin the First. An Introduction to the Epoch of Justinian the Great*. Cambridge Mass., Harvard UP (1950).

Wass, Richard Geoffrey, *Cavalry in Roman Field Armies during the Fourth, Fifth and Sixth Centuries AD*, Unpublished Ph.D Thesis February 1999, University of St. Andrews.

Whitby, M., 'Procopius' description of Dara (Buildings II.1–3)' in *Defence of the Roman and Byzantine East*, edd. P. Freeman and D. Kennedy, *BAR International Series* 297i, Oxford (1986), 737–83.

Index

Gepids, Gepidae, Germanic tribe, 13, 23–4, 113, 115–16, 119, 128, 169, 207, 245, 250, 258, 271, 304, 325, 333–4, 337–8, 340

Germans, Germanic peoples, Teutons, Germania, Germany, xi, 13, 15, 21–4, 78, 85, 97, 224, 343, 352–3, 388, 391
  see also Alamanni, Franks, Gepids, Goths, Lombards, Visigoths, Ostrogoths, Suevi/ Suebi, Thuringi, Vandals

Germanus, cousin of Justinian I, *MVM*, patrician, 35, 43, 182–6, 192, 211–14, 219, 222, 253, 259, 270, 272, 313, 316, 319, 328, 330–4, 340, 361–2, 365–6, 380, 384, 387

Germanus, general at Dara, 57

Germanus son of Dorotheus, 356

Gerontius, *PVC*, 360

Gezon, optio, 187

Ghassanids (Thlabites), 54, 81, 297–9

Gibal, Gothic general, 335

Gibamundus, Vandal commander, 90, 92

Gibimer, Gothic commander, 162

Gibraltar. Straits of, 102, 339

Gibrus, commander of Lombards and Heruls, 315

Gilacius, *MVM*, 265

Gilderich, *MVM*, 50

Goar, Gothic captive, 337

Godas, Gothic rebel, 83, 89, 96

Godilas, *MVM*, 54, 112–13

Gold, golden, gold mines, vii, 1–2, 12, 47, 54, 64, 67, 75, 78–9, 81, 111, 122, 126, 141, 159, 171, 175, 190, 203, 212, 217–18, 236, 243–4, 296, 298, 300, 307, 314, 319, 321, 362

Golden Horn, 75

Gontharis, rebel, 186, 189, 194–8, 272

Gotharis, commander of Heruls, 155

Gothigus, patrician, 322

Goths, Germanic tribal confederacy, Goths in Roman service, vii, 2, 13, 21–4, 30, 33–5, 44, 46–7, 54, 67, 76, 82–3, 89, 102, 110, 112–14, 116–78, 181, 192, 209, 222, 224–5, 227, 233, 236–7, 244–69, 271, 281, 301, 326–32, 335–49, 352–3, 359, 365, 371, 377–8, 382–3, 387–8, 391–3
  Ostrogoths, vii, 21–2, 30, 33–5, 44, 46–7, 67, 82–3, 89, 102, 110, 113–14, 116–78, 181, 209, 227, 236–7, 244–69, 271, 326–32, 335–8, 340–9, 352–3, 359, 365, 371, 377–8, 382–3, 387–8, 391–3
  Visigoths, 13, 23, 281, 338–9, 387, 391
  Tetraxitae Goths in the Crimea, 301–302, 334

Gouboulgoudou, *doryforos* of Valerianus, 164

Grassa, 90

Gratiana, 113–14, 119

Greece, 117, 139–41, 248, 334–5, 354

Gregorius, nephew of Artabanes, 196–7, 272

Grepes, king of the Heruls, 50, 112

Gripas, Gothic general, 123–5

Grod, Hunnic king of Bosporus, 112

Gubazes, Goubazes, King of the Lazi in ca.541–555, 228, 298, 301–306, 310–14, 318–19

Guerrilla Warfare, 27, 64, 155, 161, 288, 303–305, 315, 354
  see also Ambush, Sieges, Stratagems

Gundilas the Thracian, Roman commander, 267

Gundovald, Frankish prince, 353
  see also MHLR Vol.7

Gundulf (Indulf), Gothic general, 326, 335

Gurgenes, Gourgenes, Guaram, king of Iberia/ Georgia and then probably also of Lazica in about 526/7–540/1, 39, 49, 203, 223

Gurzil, *see* Ammon

Hadrian, Tomb of, 135–7, 327, 344

Hadrianopolis, *see* Adrianople

Hadrumentum, 90, 191–2, 196

Hagia Sophia / Hagia Sofia, in Constantinople, 75, 78, 363, 391

Hebrus River (mod. Maritza), 329

Henoticon, 1, 30, 325

Hephthalites, White Huns, 52

Heraclea, Herakleia (Perinthus), 87, 360

Heraclius, emperor (611–641), 366, 393
  see Syvänne, *MHLR Vol.7 (565–641)*

Hermichiones, Turkish tribe, 363

Hermione, 89

Hermogenes, *Mag. Off.*, 44, 54–9, 61, 63, 68, 70, 72–3

Herodian, Herodianus, inf. gen., 120, 129, 165, 176, 218, 249, 254, 262

Heron of Byzantium, military theorist, 122, 382

Heruli / Heruls, Germanic tribe, 8, 13, 23–4, 50, 57, 62, 76, 83, 99, 101, 112, 115–16, 155, 164, 167–8, 179, 184, 206, 233, 237–8, 245, 255–6, 258, 265, 271, 306, 314–15, 329–30, 340–2, 347, 349–53, 361, 377, 380, 383, 388

Hezibus, phylarch, 81

Hierapolis, 56, 59, 211–12, 233

Hieron, customs post, 112, 359

Hildericus / Hilderic / Ilderic, Vandal king, 34–5, 75, 82, 105

Himerius/Himerus the Thracian, general, 190–1